PUBLIC HEALTH CRISIS MANAGEMENT AND CRIMINAL LIABILITY OF GOVERNMENTS

Government responses to the COVID-19 pandemic differed vastly in terms of both the choice of strategies adopted (herd immunity, test-and-trace, lockdown, etc) and the quality and speed of government implementation of those strategies and associated interventions. Both factors impacted the number of infections and casualties. It is not outlandish to consider forms of criminal liability for failure of individual members of government, including specific public authorities, to act to the best of their abilities, in as timely a manner as possible, and in accordance with expert advice. This study addresses potential avenues of criminal liability for public health crisis management in the context of the COVID-19 pandemic, under national and international criminal law, especially for causing death and bodily harm.

Public Health Crisis Management and Criminal Liability of Governments

A Comparative Study of the COVID-19 Pandemic

Edited by
Michael Bohlander
Gerhard Kemp
and
Mark Webster

·HART·

OXFORD · LONDON · NEW YORK · NEW DELHI · SYDNEY

HART PUBLISHING

Bloomsbury Publishing Plc

Kemp House, Chawley Park, Cumnor Hill, Oxford, OX2 9PH, UK

1385 Broadway, New York, NY 10018, USA

29 Earlsfort Terrace, Dublin 2, Ireland

HART PUBLISHING, the Hart/Stag logo, BLOOMSBURY and the Diana logo are
trademarks of Bloomsbury Publishing Plc

First published in Great Britain 2023

A catalogue record for this book is available from the British Library.

A catalogue record for this book is available from the Library of Congress.

ISBN: HB: 978-1-50994-631-0
       ePDF: 978-1-50994-633-4
       ePub: 978-1-50994-632-7

Typeset by Compuscript Ltd, Shannon

To find out more about our authors and books visit www.hartpublishing.co.uk.
Here you will find extracts, author information, details of forthcoming events
and the option to sign up for our newsletters.

Preface

'Kill one man, and you are a murderer. Kill millions of men, and you are a conqueror.
Kill them all, and you are a God.'

Jean Edmond Cyrus Rostand (1894–1977) | Thoughts of a Biologist, 1938.

R OSTAND'S FAMOUS QUOTE describes the essence of what this book is about: the well-known double standards history has applied across the ages to the actions of ordinary people, and to those of the powerful. In the context of the COVID-19 pandemic, an infected person who spat at another with the intent of infecting them could easily face criminal prosecution, whereas those in government whose actions or more often inaction, complacency and not infrequently incompetence, caused the deaths of many people around the globe, seek to hide behind the complexities of public health crisis management to evade any form of personal responsibility. And more often than not, the legal systems of the world provide loopholes in criminal liability. The purpose of the book is to initiate a discussion with the aim of changing that state of affairs permanently. The chapter on international criminal law is evidence that there is not much of a conceptual distance to what are commonly called mass atrocities.

The development of the pandemic was, and still is, so fast that a number of otherwise relevant events happened after the manuscripts by the individual authors were finished and submitted to the editors. So there is no uniform cut-off date for all countries, other than the submission of the full manuscript to the publisher on 30 September 2022.

The study started out with a larger number of jurisdictions, including some where the spread of the pandemic and the government responses raised serious questions, an analysis of which would have been very useful. Alas, for one reason or another, some authors abandoned their contribution to the book, and a few at such a late stage that keeping within the publishing schedule did not allow for choosing a new author to take up the baton and start afresh, especially if we wanted to remain timely in our presentation. Some delay was inevitable, however, and we are grateful to all contributors for making their best efforts to deliver on time, and to Hart Publishing for their patience and generous support. Michael Bohlander is grateful for the permission to reuse material from his books *Principles of German Criminal Law* (2008) and *Principles of German Criminal Procedure* (2nd edn, 2021).

Michael Bohlander
Gerhard Kemp
Mark Webster
Durham, Nottingham and Sarajevo
September 2022

Table of Contents

List of Contributors

Suman Dash Bhattamishra (PhD) is an Assistant Professor of Law (Criminal and Gender Laws) and Chairperson, Internal Complaints Committee, at the National Law University Odisha, Cuttack.

Michael Bohlander is the Chair in Global Law and SETI Policy at Durham University. He is the International Co-Investigating Judge at the Extraordinary Chambers in the Courts of Cambodia, and a former judge at Kosovo Specialist Chambers (2017–22).

Dana Alan Curhan has focused on appellate practice since graduating from Harvard Law School in 1984. He began his career as an appellate prosecutor and later became Chief of the Appeals and Training Unit in the Bristol County District Attorney's Office in Massachusetts. Since 1989, he has practised in Boston, Massachusetts concentrating in criminal and civil appeals.

Denis De Castro Halis is an Associate Professor of the PhD and Master Programs of Law at UNESA, Rio de Janeiro (Brazil). He is an External Associate Professor of the Centre for European and Comparative Legal Studies (CECS) Faculty of Law at the University of Copenhagen, Denmark. He is a Trustee of the Asian Law & Society Association, and a Member of the International Law Committee of the Brazilian Bar Association/Rio de Janeiro.

Alejandro De Pablo (PhD) is a Criminal Law Associate Professor at Valladolid University. He is a Postdoctoral Researcher at Universidad Autónoma de Madrid.

Caroline Fournet (DEA, LLM, PhD) is a Professor of Law at the University of Exeter.

Mohammad M Hedayati-Kakhki (LLB, LLM, PhD, Bar (Iran)) is a Visiting Professor at Durham University.

Gerhard Kemp (BA LLB, LLM, LLD) is Professor of Criminal Law at UWE Bristol Law School, and Extraordinary Professor in Public Law at Stellenbosch University.

Birju Kotecha (LLB(Hons), MA, PhD, Bar (England & Wales)) is an Assistant Professor at the University of Northumbria Law School.

Andra Le Roux-Kemp (BA LLB, CML, LLD, B Mus, Hons BMus, FRSA) is an Associate Professor at the University of Lincoln.

Dennis Martinsson (LLD, LLM, LLM) is an Assistant Professor of Law at Stockholm University.

Murat Önok (Associate Professor, Dr iur) is a Faculty Member at Koç University Law School, Istanbul.

Frédéric Rolland (PhD, MPhil, MPhil) is a Senior Lecturer in Law at the University of Exeter. He is the Director of the LLB in English Law and French Law/Master 1 (Maîtrise en Droit).

Topo Santoso (SH, MH) is a Professor of Criminal Law and Head of Criminal Law Department in the Faculty of Law at the Universitas Indonesia.

Phillip Louis Weiner received a Bachelor of Arts degree from Northeastern University in 1977 and was awarded a Juris Doctor from Boston College Law School in 1980. From 1980 to 2000, he worked primarily as a prosecutor in the Commonwealth of Massachusetts. He served as an International Judge at the Court of Bosnia and Herzegovina, as an International Prosecutor at the International Criminal Tribunal for the Former Yugoslavia, and as a Legal Advisor at the Extraordinary Chambers in the Courts of Cambodia. He now works as an attorney and consultant in Massachusetts.

Thomas Christie Williams (MA, MB, BChir, MRCPCH, PhD) is a Clinical Lecturer at the University of Edinburgh.

Natalie Wortley (BA(Hons), LLM, Bar (England & Wales)) is an Associate Professor at Northumbria University.

Abbreviations

ANVISA	National agency of Brazil responsible for sanitary measures and regulation of use of drugs
BGH	German Federal Court of Justice (*Bundesgerichtshof*)
BNPB	Indonesian National Disaster Management Agency (*Badan Nasional Penanggulangan Bencana*)
BVerfG	German Federal Constitutional Court (*Bundesverfassungsgericht*)
CC	Spanish Constitutional Court
CCP	Chinese Communist Party
CEPEDISA	The Health Law Research and Studies Center of the Faculty of Public Health of the University of São Paulo
Chinese CDC	Chinese Center for Disease Control and Prevention
CMO	English Chief Medical Officer
COBRA	UK Government Civil Contingencies Committee
COVID-19	Coronavirus disease in 2019 (official WHO nomenclature)
CPI Report	Report prepared by the Pandemic Parliamentary Inquiry Commission, a committee formed by members of the Federal Parliament of Brazil
CPS	England and Wales Crown Prosecution Service
CSA	UK Government Chief Scientific Adviser
DHSC	UK Government Department of Health and Social Care
DPP	Director of Public Prosecutions (England and Wales)
GISAID	Global Initiative for Sharing All Influenza Data
GNA	Turkish Grand National Assembly
ICC	International Criminal Court
ICU	Intensive Care Unit
IHR	International Health Regulations
IVDC	Chinese National Institute of Viral Disease Control and Prevention
KPK	Indonesian Corruption Eradication Commission (*Komisi Pemberantasan Korupsi*)

KSSK	Indonesian Financial System Stability Committee (*Komite Stabilitas Sistem Keuangan*)
MERS-CoV	Middle Eastern Respiratory Syndrome Virus
MoH	Turkish Ministry of Health
mRNA vaccine	Messenger RNA vaccine
NCCC	South African National Covid Command Council
NHCC	Iranian National Headquarters to Combat Corona
NHS	National Health Service of the UK
NPA	South African National Prosecuting Authority
NPI	Non-pharmaceutical Intervention
OAB Opinion	Legal opinion by a special committee of renowned Brazilian legal experts chaired by a former judge of Brazil's Federal Supreme Court on behalf of the Brazilian Bar
PCR	Reverse Transcription Polymerase Chain Reaction (otherwise 'RT-PCR')
PHE	Public Health England
PHEIC	Public Health Emergency of International Concern (as determined by the WHO)
PPE	Personal protective equipment
RNA	Ribonucleic acid
Rt	the reproduction number of a virus
RT-PCR/PCR	Reverse Transcription Polymerase Chain Reaction
SAGE	UK Government's Scientific Advisory Group for Emergencies
SAMRC	South African Medical Research Council
SARS	severe acute respiratory syndrome
SARS-CoV-2	Severe Acute Respiratory Syndrome Coronavirus 2
SNSC	Iranian Supreme National Security Council
TRC	South African Truth and Reconciliation Commission
WHO	World Health Organization

1

Introduction

MICHAEL BOHLANDER, GERHARD KEMP AND MARK WEBSTER

O N 11 MARCH 2020, the World Health Organization (WHO) made a fateful declaration: the community transmission of the so-called 'novel coronavirus', COVID-19 ('coronavirus disease in 2019'), had reached the level of a global pandemic. Senior government officials in countries across the globe adopted different responses to this pandemic. These responses can be divided in the choice of strategies (herd immunity, test-and-trace, lockdown etc) and the question of the quality and speed of government implementation of such strategies. Both factors have in one way or another had an impact on the number of infections and casualties. Given the number of deaths and instances of serious illness, it is appropriate to consider the possibility of criminal liability for failure of individual members of government (and of corporate entities), to act to the best of their abilities, as timely as possible, and in accordance with expert advice to prevent these calamitous consequences. Because of the complexity, scale and reach of the pandemic, it is not surprising that there already exists a significant body of literature on the origins, spread and impact of COVID-19. It is hard to imagine a single aspect of human existence in virtually all corners of the world not affected by the pandemic. Apart from the medical aspects, it became clear, early on, that the pandemic would have significant, even devastating and unsettling, economic, social, political, diplomatic, security and legal consequences. These consequences would be felt not only during the height of the pandemic (2020–21) but it is indeed anticipated that individuals and societies in all regions of the world will have to deal with the impact of COVID-19 for years to come.

The focus of this book is the possible criminal liability of senior government officials, and in appropriate contexts, the possible criminal responsibility of corporate entities. The chapter on epidemiology aims to give an overview of the origins and spread of the coronavirus from 2019 onwards. The epidemiology chapter also provides a discussion of the most important scientific features of the novel coronavirus and its most important variants. The comparative (country) chapters contain a common research grid that aims to assist the reader in understanding how governments reacted to the pandemic, with an emphasis on the period immediately following the declaration by the WHO in March 2020. This period was crucial. Governments had to make decisions and had to implement policies against the backdrop of a rapidly changing epidemiological and social situation. Constitutional, political and economic factors formed part of the calculus. The comparative chapters show how, faced with a common global enemy, governments opted for very different strategies to deal with the pandemic. This was especially true in the early stages after the WHO declaration of March 2020. Later, with the availability of vaccines and ever increasing knowledge and data-sets, and with more pathways for meaningful cooperation, governments could choose different policies from a broader range of options.

The reality is that, as the coronavirus started to spread rapidly through populations in Asia, Europe, North America, Africa and other regions of the world, and as the number of deaths rose to devastating levels, governments had limited initial options. But there were, nevertheless, options – and our interest from a criminal law point of view is whether and to what extent some choices *caused more* people to die or to get seriously ill compared to other options that have mitigated the number of COVID-19 deaths and serious illness. Looking at the various comparative chapters, it is clear that certain governments were not only passive in the face of the pandemic, but even recklessly dismissive. Some tried to couch their conduct in rational terms, most notably the plan to just let the pandemic run its course with the hope that a level of so-called 'herd immunity'[1] could be achieved at some point. That point, of course, would not only be determined by science but was also in many instances a political calculation. The price of many of these strategies and inactions was (excess) death and serious illness. While the direct cause of death and serious illness was the coronavirus, governments also had to take into account the potentially calamitous impact of pandemic measures on the economy and on social cohesion. It is no use stopping death because of COVID-19 only to deal with death by hunger because of a collapsed economy. And yet, many governments, including governments in the developing world, opted to make tough calls. 'Lockdown' became a hated word, introduced by governments, some early on, others following reluctantly. Many critics regarded lockdowns as a blunt instrument, but it was informed by the simple scientific fact: coronavirus is transmitted by humans in close proximity. It was therefore crucial that governments introduced these harsh measures very early on in the pandemic in order to stop the spread of the virus. Herein lies the crux of the criminal law question: to what extent did senior government officials cause death or serious illness that would otherwise not have occurred had it not been for the officials' conduct? The conduct in question could have been a policy of action or inaction (most notably, the choice to let the virus run its course through community spread to hopefully lead to 'herd immunity'). From a criminal law perspective, then, the issue is often primarily one of causation. But the other elements of criminal liability, notably mens rea, also need to be examined. And mens rea is often difficult to establish, especially in a context of collective decision-making, or where complex scientific and policy factors weigh on the decision-maker's mind. Nevertheless, it is not unheard of that senior government officials are held criminally liable for conduct in their official capacities. The criminal law question therefore needs to be analysed in a broader constitutional and criminal justice context. This is done in the comparative chapters by way of an overview of the most pertinent constitutional and prosecutorial features relevant to the question of potential criminal liability of senior government officials for policy decisions. But more context is required to understand the state of mind of the officials that had to respond to the fast-developing pandemic.

---

[1] For a critical account of the aim to achieve 'herd immunity' in the early stages of the pandemic, see J Calvert and G Arbuthnott, *Failures of State* (London, Mudlark, 2021) 167–93.

It was noted by Richard Horton, Editor-in-Chief of the respected scientific journal, *The Lancet*, that there existed an ever-growing gap between the 'accumulating evidence of scientists and the practice of governments'.[2] According to Horton, western governments were particularly at fault for the way in which they responded to the pandemic. He identified six crucial failures that resulted in unnecessary death and serious illness, namely: a failure of technical advice, a failure of political process, a failure of political leadership, failure of preparedness,[3] failure of implementation and failure of communication.[4] Having said that, it is also clear, from the literature and from the introductory parts of the comparative chapters in this book, that governments often faced very difficult choices. Many of the measures recommended by the scientists involved a direct cost to the economy and to the public purse.[5] Indeed, by April 2020 many people, especially poor people and people in the developing world, faced starvation as a result of the disruption of supply chains and other regular economic activities, not only because of the pandemic itself, but also because of the measures that many governments implemented to stop the spread of the virus.[6]

The proposed drastic measures to respond to the pandemic involved other costs as well. These were costs that could not easily be measured in economic terms, but they were costs to civil liberties and constitutional and democratic norms.[7] States of emergency and states of disaster, whether stemming from human action or natural phenomena, almost always pose challenges to the freedoms and legalities expected in democratic societies. One common thread that we find in the comparative chapters is how governments responded to the pandemic with legislative measures which conferred increased and broad discretionary powers on the state executive. While the broader legal and constitutional implications of these measures are relevant for context, these are not the primary focus areas of the book. But the constitutional and legal context of emergency powers are directly relevant for our research question in one important respect: the executive-centred response to COVID-19 put the focus of potential criminal liability for the avoidable deaths and serious illnesses on senior government officials, especially those in the state executive. It is therefore not outlandish to consider forms of criminal liability for failure of individual members of government, including specific public authorities, to act to the best of their abilities, as timely as possible and in accordance with expert advice.

This book is meant to address potential avenues of criminal liability, especially for causing death and bodily harm. Major factors investigated in the comparative chapters are: individual and corporate liability, causation, act or omission, mens rea, as well as rules of participation and possible defences.

---

[2] R Horton, *The COVID-19 Catastrophe* (Cambridge, Polity Press, 2020) ix.

[3] Other commentators also make the point that many government responses were based on the wrong assumptions of how the pandemic would evolve and how many people would be killed. See D Mackenzie, *COVID-19 – The Pandemic that Never Should Have Happened and How to Stop the Next One* (New York, Hachette Books, 2020) 191–92.

[4] Horton, *COVID-19 Catastrophe* (n 2) 84–86.

[5] D Cowan and A Mumford (eds), *Pandemic Legalities* (Bristol, Bristol University Press, 2021) xiii; A Tooze, *Shutdown – How Covid Shook the World's Economy* (New York, Viking, 2021) 111–30.

[6] By April 2020, the World Food Programme estimated that while the amount of food available in the world was unaffected by the pandemic, the number of people facing starvation doubled because of lockdowns and other measures. See Mackenzie, *COVID-19* (n 3) 188.

[7] For a comprehensive analysis, see A Greene, *Emergency Powers in a Time of Pandemic* (Bristol, Bristol University Press, 2020).

The book covers domestic responses, but also possible liability under international criminal law for crimes against humanity. The latter category of crimes under international criminal law is adopted as a frame of analysis, rather than the crime of genocide, which requires the element of specific genocidal intent.[8] We assumed that none of the case studies would reveal anything approximating specific intent to destroy a population in whole or in part required for genocide. The systematic and quantitative aspects of crimes against humanity are therefore more appropriate elements to analyse for purposes of this book.

Apart from performing a thorough stocktaking exercise, the book is meant to serve as a benchmark for evaluating – and hopefully guiding – government conduct in the future, when, rather than if, the next pandemic will engulf the planet. We think that the experience of the COVID-19 pandemic and the sometimes disastrous and quite possibly avoidable consequences for the over 600 million people who were infected, and the almost six-and-a-half million people who had died, at the time of writing,[9] should put an end to the practice of simply resigning ourselves to accepting that there will be never be any consequences to the complacency, if not reckless insouciance or even denial, displayed by some of the world's leaders.

---

[8] For a rebuttal of the proposition that government policies (or, inaction) in the US could amount to the crime of genocide, see J Heieck, 'Trump's Coronavirus Response: Genocide by Default?' (*Opinio Juris*, 15 May 2020), http://opiniojuris.org/2020/05/15/trumps–coronavirus–response–genocide–by–default/.

[9] See, eg the World Health Organization's tracking webpage, https://covid19.who.int/.

2

The Emergence and Global Spread of SARS-CoV-2, and Clinical and Virological Features

THOMAS CHRISTIE WILLIAMS

I. TIMELINE OF THE COVID-19 PANDEMIC

ON 31 DECEMBER 2019, reports began to circulate in Chinese state[1] and international media[2] of a cluster of cases of pneumonia of unknown origin in the city of Wuhan, Hubei Province, in the People's Republic of China. The same day the Wuhan Municipal Health Commission stated on its Weibo social media account: 'The cause of the disease is not clear ... We cannot confirm it is what's being spread online, that it is SARS virus. Other severe pneumonia is more likely'.[3] An official at Wuhan Central Hospital, where local media reported some of the cases were being treated, declined to comment when contacted by Reuters.[4] A number of these news reports stated that a team of senior health experts had been dispatched to the city of Wuhan, reported by the state broadcaster CCTV to be conducting 'relevant inspection and verification work'.[5]

On the same day, the Wuhan Municipal Health Commission in Wuhan City reported a cluster of 27 pneumonia cases with a link to Wuhan's Huanan Seafood Wholesale Market,[6] which was picked up by the World Health Organization's (WHO) Country

---

[1] A report on the Chinese State Television CCTV was subsequently quoted by Radio Television Hong Kong, but this link is now no longer available at the published address. This is a recurring issue with Chinese state media statements during the initial stages of the pandemic. However, the webpage was archived by the website web.archive.org and can be accessed at web.archive.org/web/20200126025845/https://news.rthk.hk/rthk/en/component/k2/1500301-20191231.htm?spTabChangeable=0.

[2] See, eg 'Chinese officials investigate cause of pneumonia outbreak in Wuhan' (*Reuters*, 31 December 2019), www.reuters.com/article/us-china-health-pneumonia-idUSKBN1YZ0GP; M Zuo et al, 'Hong Kong takes emergency measures as mystery "pneumonia" infects dozens in China's Wuhan city' *South China Morning Post* (online, 31 December 2019), www.scmp.com/news/china/politics/article/3044050/mystery-illness-hits-chinas-wuhan-city-nearly-30-hospitalised.

[3] Cited by *Reuters*, ibid.

[4] *Reuters*, 'Chinese officials investigate' (n 2).

[5] 'China investigates SARS-like virus as dozens struck by pneumonia' (*Deutsche Welle*, 31 December 2019), www.dw.com/en/china-investigates-sars-like-virus-as-dozens-struck-by-pneumonia/a-51843861.

[6] This webpage was cited by the WHO on 5 January 2021 (www.who.int/csr/don/05-january-2020-pneumonia-of-unkown-cause-china/en/) but the link is now no longer available at the published address. The webpage was archived by the web.archive.org and can be accessed at web.archive.org/web/20200106064908/http://wjw.wuhan.gov.cn/front/web/showDetail/2019123108989.

Office in China. The Health Commission stated that of these 27 cases, seven were in a critical condition, 18 stable and two recovered. In addition, they reported that initial laboratory tests showed that the cases were viral pneumonia, with no obvious human-to-human transmission, and no medical staff infected.[7] The WHO China Country Office then notified the WHO Western Pacific Regional Office about this report.[8]

Also on the same day, the Hong Kong Health Authorities announced they were stepping up measures to increase border screening, and they put hospitals on alert.[9] Seventeen years before, in 2002, an outbreak of viral pneumonia caused by the coronavirus SARS-CoV (Severe Acute Respiratory Syndrome Coronavirus) had occurred in the province of Guangdong, bordering Hong Kong.[10] The SARS outbreak eventually led to over 8,000 cases globally and 774 deaths, 299 of these in Hong Kong.[11]

On 1 January 2020 the Chinese state-run Xinhua news agency reported that Huanan Seafood Market had been closed for cleaning and disinfection.[12] The same report stated that some individuals had disseminated 'false information on the Internet without verification, causing adverse social impact', and that public security officials had 'summoned 8 illegal personnel and dealt with them in accordance with the law'.

On 3 January the outbreak was reported by the British Broadcasting Corporation (BBC).[13] By this stage 44 cases had been confirmed, 11 of which were severe.[14] The Wuhan Municipal Health Commission reported that 121 contacts had been traced, with ongoing contact tracing still in progress. By this point Singapore had followed Hong Kong in bringing in screening processes for travellers from Wuhan. It subsequently emerged that also on 3 January the first complete genome (genetic code) of the novel beta genus coronavirus (2019–nCoVs) was identified in samples of fluid from the lungs of a patient in Wuhan by the Chinese National Institute of Viral Disease Control and Prevention (IVDC),[15] although this information was only released publicly a week later on 10 January.

On 4 January the WHO posted on Twitter that China had reported a cluster of pneumonia cases, with no deaths, in Wuhan, Hubei Province, and that investigations were underway to identify the cause of this illness.[16] On 5 January the WHO[17] reported that it

---

[7] *Deutsche Welle*, 'China investigates' (n 5).

[8] WHO, 'Timeline: WHO's Covid-19 response', www.who.int/emergencies/diseases/novel-coronavirus-2019/interactive-timeline#.

[9] M Zuo et al, 'Hong Kong takes emergency measures' (n 2).

[10] S Knobler et al, '*Learning from SARS: Preparing for the next Disease Outbreak: Workshop Summary*' (Washington, National Academies Press (US), 2004).

[11] WHO, 'SARS: How a global epidemic was stopped' (World Health Organization, 2006), https://apps.who.int/iris/bitstream/handle/10665/207501/9290612134_eng.pdf, 185.

[12] Xinhua News Agency, webpage from 1 January 2021, link no longer available.

[13] 'China pneumonia outbreak: Mystery virus probed in Wuhan' (*BBC*, 3 January 2020), www.bbc.co.uk/news/world-asia-china-50984025.

[14] Wuhan Municipal Health Commission, '武汉市卫健委关于不明原因的病毒性肺炎情况通报' (3 January 2020), original link now inactive, recovered through web.archive.org, web.archive.org/web/20200103094922/http://wjw.wuhan.gov.cn/front/web/showDetail/2020010309017.

[15] W Tan et al, 'A Novel Coronavirus Genome Identified in a Cluster of Pneumonia Cases – Wuhan, China 2019–2020' (2020) 2 *China CDC Weekly* 61.

[16] WHO (Twitter), '#China has reported to WHO a cluster of #pneumonia cases – with no deaths – in Wuhan, Hubei Province. Investigations are underway to identify the cause of this illness' (4 January 2020, 7:13pm), https://twitter.com/WHO/status/1213523866703814656?s=20.

[17] WHO, 'News: COVID-19 – China' (5 January 2020), www.who.int/csr/don/05-january-2020-pneumonia-of-unknown-cause-china/en/.

was monitoring the situation and was in close contact with national authorities in China. It announced that it did not 'recommend any specific measures for travellers' and 'advised against the application of any travel or trade restrictions on China based on the current information available on this event'.[18]

On 10 January the complete genome of the new virus was released publicly on the GISAID (Global Initiative for Sharing All Influenza Data) platform,[19] confirming its similarity to the other betacoronaviruses SARS-CoV and MERS-CoV (Middle Eastern Respiratory Syndrome Coronavirus). On 11 January the first fatal case caused by the novel coronavirus was reported.[20] On 13 January the first case outside of China was confirmed in Thailand.[21] On 14 January the WHO noted in a press briefing that, contrary to prior reports, there was now evidence for limited human-to-human transmission, mainly through family members, and that there was therefore the risk of a possible wider outbreak.[22] On 16 January cases were confirmed in Japan.[23]

On 20 January cases were confirmed in the Republic of Korea and the United States, and the first cases in healthcare workers caring for patients with the disease were confirmed in Wuhan.[24] On 20 and 21 January WHO representatives conducted a field trip to Wuhan, and on 22 January issued a statement confirming there was evidence of human-to-human transmission in Wuhan.[25] Cases were reported on 21 January in Taiwan, and on 22 January in Hong Kong and Macau.

On 22 January the WHO convened an Emergency Committee under the International Health Regulations (IHR) (2005).[26] The Committee was unable to arrive at a decision that day, but on 23 January met again and issued a statement stating that they did not believe the outbreak of coronavirus constituted a public health emergency of international concern (PHEIC).[27] By this point 584 cases had been reported to the WHO, including 17 deaths. All but nine cases, and all the deaths, were in China. The Committee stated at the meeting that on an initial estimate the reproductive number (R_0) for the novel coronavirus, *i.e.*, the number of people that an individual with the virus would infect,

---

[18] ibid.

[19] Available at www.gisaid.org.

[20] 'First death from China mystery illness outbreak' *The Guardian* (online, 11 January 2020), www.theguardian.com/world/2020/jan/11/china-mystery-illness-outbreak-causes-first-death.

[21] WHO, 'Archived: WHO Timeline – COVID-19' (27 April 2020), www.who.int/news/item/27-04-2020-who-timeline---covid-19.

[22] S Nebehay, 'WHO says new China coronavirus could spread, warns hospitals worldwide' (*Reuters*, 14 January 2020), www.reuters.com/article/us-china-health-pneumonia-who-idUSKBN1ZD16J.

[23] WHO, 'COVID-19 – Japan – (ex-China) (16 January 2020), www.who.int/emergencies/disease-outbreak-news/item/2020-DON236.

[24] '15 medical staff in Wuhan get infected with new coronavirus' *Global Times* (online, 21 January 2020), www.globaltimes.cn/content/1177519.shtml.

[25] WHO, 'Archived Timeline' (n 21).

[26] WHO, 'WHO Director-General's statement on IHR Emergency Committee on Novel Coronavirus' (22 January 2020), www.who.int/director-general/speeches/detail/who-director-general-s-statement-on-ihr-emergency-committee-on-novel-coronavirus.

[27] WHO, 'WHO Director-General's statement on the advice of the IHR Emergency Committee on Novel Coronavirus' (23 January 2020), www.who.int/director-general/speeches/detail/who-director-general-s-statement-on-the-advice-of-the-ihr-emergency-committee-on-novel-coronavirus.

was 1.4 to 2.5.[28] This estimate by the WHO put the R_0 in the range of that calculated for SARS in 2002–03, and for the 2009 H1N1 influenza pandemic.[29]

In addition to the countries listed above, on 23 January Singapore and Vietnam reported their first coronavirus cases, bringing the total number of countries reporting cases to six. Also on 23 January the local government in Wuhan announced the complete suspension of public transportation, with closure of airports, railway stations and highways in the city, to prevent further disease transmission.[30]

On 24 January the WHO reported the first evidence of human-to-human spread outside China, in Vietnam.[31] On the same day the first peer-reviewed medical reports about the initial cases of pneumonia appeared in *The Lancet* and the *New England Journal of Medicine*. The article in *The Lancet* described the clinical features of the first 41 patients infected with the 2019 novel coronavirus in Wuhan.[32] The paper reported that these patients were all admitted to a designated hospital in the city (Jin Yin-tan Hospital). Patients were admitted from 16 December 2019 to 2 January 2020. The earliest patient to develop symptoms had done so on 1 December 2019, and had no known links to the Huanan Seafood Market. The majority of the patients were found to be men (30/41, 73 per cent), with 27 (66 per cent) found to have been exposed to the Huanan Seafood Market. The most common features described at the onset of illness were fever, cough and myalgia (muscle aches) or fatigue. All patients were found to have abnormalities in imaging of their lungs, with bilateral changes suggestive of a viral (rather than bacterial) infection. A third of patients were admitted to an intensive care unit and six (15 per cent) died.

The Brief Report in the *New England Journal of Medicine* described the virological results from an epidemiologic and aetiological investigation conducted by the Chinese Center for Disease Control and Prevention (Chinese CDC), dispatched to Wuhan on 31 December 2019.[33] This investigation took samples from the lungs of four patients with pneumonia of unknown cause, and isolated the causative virus. They showed its genetic similarity to bat coronaviruses detected in bats, to MERS-CoV and SARS-CoV, and described it as a novel betacoronavirus belonging to the sarbecovirus subgenus of the Coronaviridae family, which they named 2019-nCoV (2019 novel coronavirus).

On 29 January the Peter Doherty Institute for Infection and Immunity in Melbourne announced that they had successfully grown the 2019 novel coronavirus from a patient sample,[34] an important step in allowing testing and validation of testing for the virus

---

[28] WHO, 'Statement on the first meeting of the International Health Regulations (2005) Emergency Committee regarding the outbreak of novel coronavirus (2019-nCoV)' (23 January 2020), www.who.int/news/item/23-01-2020-statement-on-the-meeting-of-the-international-health-regulations-(2005)–emergency-committee-regarding-the-outbreak-of-novel-coronavirus-(2019-ncov).

[29] 'Coronavirus: the first three months as it happened' (*Nature*, 22 April 2020), www.nature.com/articles/d41586-020-00154-w.

[30] C Wang et al, 'A Novel Coronavirus Outbreak of Global Health Concern' (2020) 395 *The Lancet* 470.

[31] WHO, 'Novel Coronavirus (2019-nCoV) Situation Report – 4) (24 January 2020), www.who.int/docs/default-source/coronaviruse/situation-reports/20200124-sitrep-4-2019-ncov.pdf?sfvrsn=9272d086_2.

[32] C Huang et al, 'Clinical Features of Patients Infected with 2019 Novel Coronavirus in Wuhan, China' (2020) 395 *The Lancet* 497.

[33] N Zhu et al, 'A Novel Coronavirus from Patients with Pneumonia in China, 2019' (2020) 382 *New England Journal of Medicine* 727.

[34] 'Doherty Institute scientists first to grow and share 2019 novel coronavirus' (*Doherty Institute*, 29 January 2020), www.doherty.edu.au/news-events/news/coronavirus#:~:text=Scientists%20from%20The%20Peter%20Doherty,to%20help%20combat%20the%20virus.

globally. On 30 January the Emergency Committee was re-convened by the WHO Director-General. After the meeting, the WHO declared the outbreak a Public Health Emergency of Public Concern.[35] By this stage in China there had been 7,711 confirmed cases, 12,167 suspected cases, 1,370 severe cases and 170 deaths. Globally, 82 cases had been detected in 18 countries, with human-to-human transmission in countries outside of China (Vietnam,[36] Japan[37] and Germany[38]). Again, at this stage the Committee did 'not recommend any travel or trade restriction based on the current information available'. Furthermore, the Committee asserted:

> Under Article 43 of the IHR, States Parties implementing additional health measures that significantly interfere with international traffic (refusal of entry or departure of international travellers, baggage, cargo, containers, conveyances, goods, and the like, or their delay, for more than 24 hours) are obliged to send to WHO the public health rationale and justification within 48 hours of their implementation. WHO will review the justification and may request countries to reconsider their measures. WHO is required to share with other States Parties the information about measures and the justification received.[39]

On 30 January the first human-to-human transmission was reported in the United States[40] and South Korea.[41] On 1 February the first death due to the virus outside mainland China was reported in the Philippines, of a Chinese male who had travelled from Wuhan,[42] and on 4 February a second death was reported in Hong Kong.[43] By 10 February China's National Health Commission had received 40,171 reports of confirmed cases, and 908 deaths,[44] surpassing the death toll from SARS in 2002–03.

By the start of February 2020, daily coronavirus case rates and deaths were being reported by the Hubei Health Commission.[45] Meanwhile, in Europe by the 7 February, 29 coronavirus cases had been confirmed, 12 of which represented locally acquired cases

---

[35] WHO, 'Statement on the second meeting of the International Health Regulations (2005) Emergency Committee regarding the outbreak of novel coronavirus (2019-nCoV)' (30 January 2020), www.who.int/news/item/30-01-2020-statement-on-the-second-meeting-of-the-international-health-regulations-(2005)–emergency-committee-regarding-the-outbreak-of-novel-coronavirus-(2019-ncov).

[36] WHO, 'Situation Report – 4' (n 31).

[37] J Kyodo, 'Japan reports first domestic transmission of coronavirus' *Japan Times* (online, 28 January 2020), www.japantimes.co.jp/news/2020/01/28/national/japan-first-domestic-transmission-coronavirus/.

[38] 'Germany confirms human transmission of coronavirus' (*Deutsche Welle*, 28 January 2020), www.dw.com/en/germany-confirms-human-transmission-of-coronavirus/a-52169007.

[39] WHO, 'Statement on the second meeting' (n 35).

[40] Centers for Disease Control and Prevention, 'CDC Confirms Person-to-Person Spread of New Coronavirus in the United States' (30 January 2020), www.cdc.gov/media/releases/2020/p0130-coronavirus-spread.html.

[41] '신종코로나 확진자 2명 늘어…6번째 환자, 국내 최초 '2차감염' (*Doctors' Times*, 30 January 2020), www.doctorstimes.com/news/articleView.html?idxno=209807.

[42] C Jiao and D Wallbank, 'Coronavirus Death in Philippines Is First Fatality Outside China' (*Bloomberg*, 2 February 2020), www.bloomberg.com/news/articles/2020-02-02/first-person-outside-of-china-dies-from-virus-in-philippines (paywall).

[43] 'Deaths in China Rise, With No Sign of Slowdown' *New York Times* (online, 4 February 2020), www.nytimes.com/2020/02/04/world/asia/coronavirus-china.html#link-658f6486.

[44] National Health Commission of the People's Republic of China, 'Feb 10: Daily briefing on novel coronavirus cases in China' (10 February 2020), http://en.nhc.gov.cn/2020-02/10/c_76383.htm.

[45] Original link no longer available, but data captured on Twitter: TC Williams (Twitter), 'sobering reading from Hubei Health Commission …' (5 February 2020, 12:18am), https://twitter.com/Williams_T_C/status/1224834615900286977.

and the remainder were imported.[46] Nineteen cases had been reported in the Americas,[47] 15 in Oceania and 31,438 in Asia, 221 of which were in 13 countries outside China.[48]

On 9 February, the largest study of patients hospitalised with coronavirus was published.[49] This study reported outcomes on 1,099 patients from 552 hospitals in 31 provinces across China. Of this cohort, 5 per cent were admitted to Intensive Care Units (ICUs), with an overall mortality of 1.36 per cent (this was likely to be a significant underestimate, as over 90 per cent of patients remained hospitalised). Also on 9 February, reports emerged of coronavirus being spread by attendees at an international conference in Singapore.[50] On 11 February, the WHO officially named the disease caused by the novel coronavirus COVID-19 (coronavirus disease in 2019).[51] The same day, the International Committee on Taxonomy of Viruses released a preprint naming the virus SARS-CoV-2 (Severe Acute Respiratory Syndrome Coronavirus 2).[52]

On 19 February the number of coronavirus cases in South Korea started to rise, with a jump of 20 cases, confirming likely community transmission.[53] Also on 19 February the first coronavirus cases were reported in Iran in the city of Qoms.[54] On 21 February it was clear that there was significant community transmission of the disease in Italy, and the first death there was reported.[55] By the 25 February, 50 deaths had been reported in Qoms, confirming significant community transmission in Iran.[56] By 27 February there was evidence of community transmission in Spain.[57]

---

[46] European Centre for Disease Prevention and Control, 'Communicable Disease Threats Report, 2–8 February 2020, week 6' (7 February 2020), www.ecdc.europa.eu/en/publications-data/communicable-disease-threats-report-2-8-february-2020-week-6.

[47] ibid.

[48] ibid, 8: 'Asia: China (31 217), Japan (86), Singapore (30), Thailand (25), Republic of Korea (24), Malaysia (14), Taiwan (16), Vietnam (12), United Arab Emirates (5), India (3), the Philippines (3), Cambodia (1), Nepal (1) and Sri Lanka (1)'.

[49] WJ Guan et al, 'Clinical Characteristics of 2019 Novel Coronavirus Infection in China' (2020) 382 (18) *New England Journal of Medicine* 1708.

[50] C Ryan, 'Virus Fallout From Singapore Meeting Spreads Across Europe' (*Bloomberg*, 9 February 2020), www.bloomberg.com/news/articles/2020-02-09/virus-fallout-from-singapore-conference-spreads-across-europe.

[51] WHO (Twitter), 'BREAKING "We now have a name for the #2019nCoV disease"' (11 February 2020, 4:09pm), www.twitter.com/WHO/status/1227248333871173632.

[52] AE Gorbalenya et al, 'Severe Acute Respiratory Syndrome-Related Coronavirus: The Species and Its Viruses – a Statement of the Coronavirus Study Group', https://www.biorxiv.org/content/10.1101/2020.02.07.937862v1.full.

[53] H Shin and S Cha, '"Like a zombie apocalypse": Residents on edge as coronavirus cases surge in South Korea' (*Reuters*, 20 February 2020), www.reuters.com/article/us-china-health-southkorea-cases/like-a-zombie-apocalypse-residents-on-edge-as-coronavirus-cases-surge-in-south-korea-idUSKBN20E04F.

[54] 'Two Iranians die after testing positive for coronavirus' (*CNBC*, 19 February 2020), www.cnbc.com/2020/02/19/two-iranians-die-after-testing-positive-for-coronavirus.html.

[55] E Anzolin and A Amante, 'First Italian dies of coronavirus as outbreak flares in north' (*Reuters*, 21 February 2020), www.reuters.com/article/us-china-health-italy/coronavirus-outbreak-grows-in-northern-italy-16-cases-reported-in-one-day-idUSKBN20F0UI.

[56] Y Fazeli, 'About 50 dead from coronavirus in Qom, Health Minister to blame: Iran MP on ILNA' (*Al Arabiya News*, 24 February 2020), english.alarabiya.net/News/middle-east/2020/02/24/Iranian-MP-50-dead-from-coronavirus-in-Qom-Health-Minister-to-blame-ILNA.

[57] O Guell and J Martin-Arroyo, 'Spain reports first locally transmitted coronavirus case' (*El País*, 27 February 2020), english.elpais.com/society/2020-02-27/spain-reports-first-locally-transmitted-coronavirus-case.html?ssm=TW_CM_EN.

On 11 March the WHO declared the COVID-19 situation a global pandemic.[58] By this time, there had been more than 118,000 cases in 114 countries, and 4,291 people had lost their lives. Subsequent developments globally are described in the sections below, and government measures to limit the spread of SARS-CoV-2 are summarised in Table 1 at the end of this chapter.

II. VIROLOGY

As noted above, the sequence for what is now called SARS-CoV-2 was first identified on 3 January 2020 by the Chinese CDC,[59] and released publicly on 10 January 2020. This confirmed that the virus was a coronavirus (named after the crown-shaped appearance on electron microscopy). The genetic evidence suggests that SARS-CoV-2 is most closely related to coronaviruses in horseshoe bats,[60] but there is still uncertainty about how the virus was transmitted to humans, and whether this occurred directly from bats or via an intermediate species. Although early data suggested that this might have occurred via a species such as pangolins,[61] recent analyses suggest that the virus is more likely to have spread directly from bats directly to humans.[62]

SARS-CoV-2 is the seventh human coronavirus to be described. SARS-CoV, which caused a global outbreak in 2002–03, and MERS-CoV (Middle Eastern Respiratory Syndrome Virus), first detected in Saudi Arabia in 2012, both cause severe disease, with an estimated mortality rate of approximately 10 per cent[63] and 30 per cent[64] respectively. The other four coronaviruses (HKU1, NL63, OC43 and 229E) cause mild disease, mainly upper and lower respiratory tract infections in children and adults, and are endemic, causing intermittent global epidemics.[65]

Early on in the pandemic, there was concern that the virus might be transmitted through 'fomites' – inanimate objects which the virus would become deposited on, and cause disease spread through individuals placing their hands on them and acquiring the virus. This led to an emphasis on hand-washing and sanitisation as a means to interrupt viral transmission. However, with time, it became clear that the airborne transmission

---

[58] WHO, 'WHO Director-General's opening remarks at the media briefing on COVID-19' (11 March 2020), www.who.int/director-general/speeches/detail/who-director-general-s-opening-remarks-at-the-media-briefing-on-covid-19---11-march-2020.

[59] China CDC (http://weekly.chinacdc.cn/en/article/ccdcw/2020/4/61).

[60] KG Andersen et al, 'The Proximal Origin of SARS-CoV-2' (2020) 26 *Nature Medicine* 450.

[61] D Fisher and D Heymann, 'Q&A: The Novel Coronavirus Outbreak Causing COVID-19' (2020) 18 *BMC Medicine* 57.

[62] OA MacLean et al, 'Natural Selection in the Evolution of SARS-CoV-2 in Bats Created a Generalist Virus and Highly Capable Human Pathogen' (2021) 19 *PLOS Biology* e3001115.

[63] E Petersen et al, 'Comparing SARS-CoV-2 with SARS-CoV and Influenza Pandemics' (2020) 20 *The Lancet Infectious Diseases* e238.

[64] AE Ahmed, 'The Predictors of 3- and 30-Day Mortality in 660 MERS-CoV Patients' (2017) 17 *BMC Infectious Diseases*.

[65] VM Corman et al, 'Hosts and Sources of Endemic Human Coronaviruses' (2018) 100 *Advances in Virus Research* 163.

was the main mode of viral spread, with proximity to index cases (the infected individual spreading disease) the main risk factor for transmission, in either droplets or smaller aerosols.[66] The virus initially infects the upper respiratory tract (nose, mouth and throat) and can then spread into the lungs (lower respiratory tract). Individuals are most infectious at the point of symptom onset, although they have also been demonstrated to be infectious prior to this (pre-symptomatic transmission); they remain most infectious for the first five days after symptom onset,[67] which develops at a median of five to six days after the initial exposure to the initial virus, and probably earlier for subsequent lineages such as Delta.[68] There remains uncertainty about the role of asymptomatic (where the individual never develops symptoms) transmission – this appears to be possible, but individuals with asymptomatic infections are likely to be less infectious than those about to develop or who have developed symptoms.[69]

The SARS-CoV-2 genome contains coding information for 26 proteins, the most significant of which is the Spike (S) protein, which allows the virus to attach to the Angiotensin Converting Enzyme 2 (ACE2) receptor on the surface of cells, and to enter them. The Spike protein has two sub-units, S1, which allows the virus to attach to cells, and S2, which allows the virus to fuse to cells and enter them. Mutations in the Spike protein have the potential to affect transmissibility of the virus, and also influence whether the virus can be neutralised by human antibodies. The first variant to be recognised as showing different transmissibility to previous strains was the D614G variant (also called the G clade or the B1 clade). Work looking at the distribution of different strains of the virus showed that viruses with this mutation appeared to be more transmissible than pre-existing lineages.[70] Protein modelling work showed that the mutation at this position in the Spike protein alters the conformation of the protein, potentially affecting its biological properties, and samples from patients showed that they had a higher viral load when infected by this lineage, offering another explanation for why this lineage appeared to be outcompeting other lineages: individuals infected with this variant carry more of the virus and are therefore more likely to spread it. Subsequent laboratory work showed that this mutation also leads to different biological properties of the virus, leading to more effective viral entry into cells.[71] Subsequent strains of SARS-CoV-2 have similarly been shown to carry mutations that lead to increased transmissibility, as discussed below.

In December 2020, reports began to circulate in England of a new variant that also appeared to be more transmissible than previous variants: the so-called Kent variant. This variant was associated with a deletion in the S protein that served as a useful way to identify cases through national PCR testing. By the end of December it became clear

---

[66] For a detailed review of transmission see EA Meyerowitz et al, 'Transmission of SARS-CoV-2: A Review of Viral, Host, and Environmental Factors' (2021) 174 *Annals of Internal Medicine* 69.

[67] For a review of clinical features and transmission see M Cevik et al, 'Virology, Transmission, and Pathogenesis of SARS-CoV-2' (2020) 371 *BMJ*.

[68] B Li et al, 'Viral Infection and Transmission in a Large, Well-Traced Outbreak Caused by the SARS-CoV-2 Delta Variant' (2022) 13 *Nature Communications* 460.

[69] P Wilmes et al, 'SARS-CoV-2 Transmission Risk from Asymptomatic Carriers: Results from a Mass Screening Programme in Luxembourg' (2021) 4 *The Lancet Regional Health – Europe* 100056.

[70] B Korber et al, 'Tracking Changes in SARS-CoV-2 Spike: Evidence That D614G Increases Infectivity of the COVID-19 Virus' (2020) 182 *Cell* 812.

[71] S Ozono et al, 'SARS-CoV-2 D614G Spike Mutation Increases Entry Efficiency with Enhanced ACE2-Binding Affinity' (2021) 12 *Nature Communications* 1.

that this variant (named B.1.1.7, VOC 202012/01 or Alpha)[72] had rapidly spread through England and become the predominant strain. Large-scale national studies from England and Denmark showed that in addition to being more transmissible, this variant was associated with a higher chance of hospitalisation[73] and mortality[74] than pre-existing strains.

The same month, reports were published showing the circulation of new variants, originally identified in South Africa (501Y.V2 or B.1.351) and Brazil (P1). A number of laboratory experiments showed that this mutation in particular is associated with reduced efficiency of antibody neutralisation in sera (blood samples) from individuals infected with previous strains of SARS-CoV-2.[75] The possibility that previous infection, or even vaccination, might not prevent infection with these new strains was confirmed in a large vaccine trial, which showed that immunisation with the Oxford/AstraZeneca vaccine, based on the original sequence of SARS-CoV-2, showed minimal protection against infection with the 501Y.V2/B.1.351 variant of the virus.[76]

In June 2021 it became clear that a new SARS-CoV-2 variant, B.1.617.2 or Delta, originally identified in Maharastra, India, was spreading rapidly throughout the United Kingdom, which had set up a national sequencing infrastructure to monitor the spread of SARS-CoV-2. Public Health England reported that this new variant was up to 60 per cent more transmissible than the pre-existing B.1.1.7/Alpha variant.[77] By August 2021 it was the dominant lineage globally, and it was clear that vaccinations were less effective in preventing the transmission of this variant than previous ones,[78] although they appeared to maintain protection against severe disease.[79]

III. CLINICAL FEATURES AND TESTING

Early clinical reports of COVID-19 reported the main features as being cough and fever.[80] However, with time it became clear that the disease could present more heterogeneously,

---

[72] Public Health England, 'Investigation of Novel SARS-COV-2 Variant of Concern 202012/01' (6 January 2021), www.gov.uk/government/publications/phe-investigation-of-novel-sars-cov-2-variant-of-concern-20201201-technical-briefing-3-6-january-2021.

[73] P Bager et al, 'Increased Risk of Hospitalisation Associated with Infection with SARS-CoV-2 Lineage B.1.1.7 in Denmark' (2021) SSRN Electronic Journal. Final publication in (2022) 22 *Lancet Infectious Diseases* 967.

[74] R Challen et al, 'Risk of Mortality in Patients Infected with SARS-CoV-2 Variant of Concern 202012/1: Matched Cohort Study' (2021) 372 *BMJ*; NG Davies et al, 'Increased Mortality in Community-Tested Cases of SARS-CoV-2 Lineage B.1.1.7' (2021) May *Nature* 270.

[75] These experiments are detailed in TC Williams and WA Burgers, 'SARS-CoV-2 Evolution and Vaccines: Cause for Concern?' (2021) 9 *The Lancet Respiratory Medicine* 333.

[76] SA Madhi et al, 'Efficacy of the ChAdOx1 NCoV-19 Covid-19 Vaccine against the B.1.351 Variant' (2021) 20 *New England Journal of Medicine* 384.

[77] Public Health England, 'SARS-CoV-2 variants of concern and variants under investigation in England Technical briefing 13' (27 May 2021) https://assets.publishing.service.gov.uk/government/uploads/system/uploads/attachment_data/file/990339/Variants_of_Concern_VOC_Technical_Briefing_13_England.pdf_VOC_Technical_Briefing_14.pdf.

[78] A Singanayagam et al, 'Community Transmission and Viral Load Kinetics of the SARS-CoV-2 Delta (B.1.617.2) Variant in Vaccinated and Unvaccinated Individuals in the UK: A Prospective, Longitudinal, Cohort Study' (2022) 2 *The Lancet Infectious Diseases* 183.

[79] JL Bernal et al, 'Effectiveness of Covid-19 Vaccines against the B.1.617.2 (Delta) Variant' (2021) 385 *New England Journal of Medicine* 585.

[80] Huang et al, 'Clinical Features' (n 32).

and include symptoms of malaise, myalgia, headache and taste and smell disturbances.[81] Following this early phase, which is likely to represent the body's immediate response to the virus itself, some individuals go on to develop more severe disease, most commonly pneumonia, which is likely to represent the fall-out from a dysregulated inflammatory response.

Active replication of the virus in the host cells is likely to cause the initial features of disease. Viral replication leads to T-cell recruitment to infected cells, and in most people clearance of infection. However, in a subset of individuals, SARS-CoV-2 infection leads to an inappropriate immune response, with the over-production of inflammatory cytokines (cell signalling molecules) that accumulate in the lungs and lead to damage. Other individuals experience shock (inability of the heart to meet the demands of the body, with low blood pressure and inadequate perfusion) and multi-organ (kidneys, liver, lungs) dysfunction and failure. In some there is an inflammatory cascade leading to leakage of the capillaries, formation of blood clots and failure of organs such as the heart or kidneys.[82]

Those who are at the highest risk of developing severe disease are older individuals, those with obesity, high blood pressure or other heart disease, diabetes or chronic lung disease such as emphysema; those with cancer also appear to be at higher risk of severe disease. These individuals are more likely to admitted to hospital, to an intensive care unit, and to require respiratory support. The male sex has also been associated with an increased risk of severe disease and higher mortality. Another risk factor associated with severe disease has been certain racial or ethnic groups, notably Black or Hispanic persons in the United States,[83] or South Asians in the United Kingdom.[84] This distribution of severe disease is likely to be related in large part to the social determinants of health – that is, non-medical factors that influence health outcomes, such as living conditions, occupation and access to healthcare.

Severe disease manifests with dyspnoea (shortness of breath), a raised respiratory rate, evidence of low oxygen saturation and evidence of infection on chest x-rays.[85] The mainstay of treatment for COVID-19 is the administration of oxygen. Oxygen can be given through a face mask, nasal cannulae (prongs), continuous positive airway pressure or invasive mechanical ventilation, breathing support provided by a mechanical ventilator. In addition to respiratory support, treatment for severe disease can include administration of intravenous fluids, the use of agents to raise blood pressure, treatment of secondary bacterial infection with antibiotics and kidney replacement therapy if there is evidence of kidney failure.

Despite a large number of randomised controlled trials, the only early treatment to show an unequivocal improvement in outcomes was the administration of the steroid dexamethasone in patients with disease severe enough to necessitate the use of oxygen.[86] The antiviral drug remdesivir was shown to possibly shorten the duration of hospital

---

[81] Cevik et al, 'Virology' (n 67).

[82] DA Berlin et al, 'Severe Covid-19' (2020) 383 *New England Journal of Medicine* 2451.

[83] JAW Gold et al, 'Race, Ethnicity, and Age Trends in Persons Who Died from COVID-19 – United States, May–August 2020' (2020) 69 *Morbidity and Mortality Weekly Report* 1517.

[84] EM Harrison et al, 'Ethnicity and Outcomes from COVID-19: The ISARIC CCP-UK Prospective Observational Cohort Study of Hospitalised Patients' (2020) SSRN Electronic Journal.

[85] Berlin et al, 'Severe Covid-19' (n 82).

[86] The RECOVERY Collaborative Group, 'Dexamethasone in Hospitalized Patients with Covid-19' (2021) 384 *New England Journal of Medicine* 693.

admission if administered early on in the disease course, but has subsequently not been shown to lead to a reduction in mortality;[87] by November 2020 advice from the WHO was not to use this in hospitalised patients.[88] Other therapies such as ivermectin, hydroxychloroquine and convalescent plasma were also shown to have no impact on disease course or mortality.[89] However, by the end of 2021, in addition to dexamethasone there were a number of treatments shown to be effective for COVID-19, including the monoclonal antibodies to SARS-CoV-2 casirivimab and imdevimab given in combination, and the IL-6 receptor blockers tocilizumab or sarilumab.[90]

The mainstay of testing early on in the pandemic was the use of Reverse Transcription Polymerase Chain Reaction (RT-PCR, often referred to simply as PCR) testing, where ribonucleic acid (RNA) from the virus is amplified from nose or throat swabs from individuals suspected of having COVID-19. A protocol was published early in the pandemic by a consortium of global laboratories and a preliminary protocol provided to the WHO on 13 January 2020.[91] This test was widely adopted in the initial stages of the outbreak, but notably not in the United States, where problems designing and implementing an effective RT-PCR test led to significant delays in testing being rolled out across the country.[92] With time it became clear that the WHO testing protocol was not particularly sensitive (able to detect all positive cases)[93] and by May 2020 there were a large number of highly sensitive commercial tests available.

A subsequent development in testing for SARS-CoV-2 was the introduction of rapid antigen lateral flow tests, which take a sample and provide a read-out of whether an individual is positive or negative for the virus in 15–30 minutes. Lateral flow testing has been performed as part of a number of different strategies to identify and contain viral infection, including focused symptomatic testing (Japan), focused asymptomatic testing (discussed in more detail below) and mass testing (China, Vietnam and Slovakia). It is now clear that lateral flow testing is most likely to detect infection in those who have the highest viral load, and therefore the most likely to be infectious.[94] Focused asymptomatic testing can take place as part of strategies including test to protect (regular testing to find cases in high risk settings), test to release (as part of quarantine of travellers), or to test large numbers of individuals in regions with high infection.[95]

---

[87] C-C Lai et al, 'Clinical Efficacy and Safety of Remdesivir in Patients with COVID-19: A Systematic Review and Network Meta-Analysis of Randomized Controlled Trials' (2021)76 *Journal of Antimicrobial Chemotherapy* 1962.

[88] WHO, 'Recommendation on use of Remdesivir' (20 November 2020), app.magicapp.org/#/guideline/nBkO1E/section/Egz0xn.

[89] C Baraniuk, 'Where Are We with Drug Treatments for Covid-19?' (2021) 373 *BMJ* (Clinical research ed.) n1109.

[90] WHO, 'Therapeutics and COVID-19: living guideline' (14 July 2022), www.who.int/publications/i/item/WHO-2019-nCoV-therapeutics-2021.3.

[91] VM Corman et al, 'Detection of 2019 Novel Coronavirus (2019–NCoV) by Real-Time RT-PCR' (2020) 25 *Eurosurveillance* 2000045.

[92] S Boburg et al, 'Inside the coronavirus testing failure: Alarm and dismay among the scientists who sought to help' *Washington Post* (online, 3 April 2020), www.washingtonpost.com/investigations/2020/04/03/coronavirus-cdc-test-kits-public-health-labs/.

[93] TC Williams et al, 'Sensitivity of RT-PCR Testing of Upper Respiratory Tract Samples for SARS-CoV-2 in Hospitalised Patients: A Retrospective Cohort Study' (2020) 5 *Wellcome Open Research* 254.

[94] T Peto et al, 'COVID-19: Rapid Antigen Detection for SARS-CoV-2 by Lateral Flow Assay: A National Systematic Evaluation of Sensitivity and Specificity for Mass-Testing' (2021) 36 *EClinicalMedicine* 100924.

[95] Different testing strategies are described in detail in A Crozier et al, 'Put to the Test: Use of Rapid Testing Technologies for Covid-19' (2021) 372 *BMJ* n208.

IV. NON-PHARMACEUTICAL INTERVENTIONS (NPIS)
TO LIMIT THE SPREAD OF SAR-COV-2

A. Evidence for the Effectiveness of Different Non-pharmaceutical Interventions Prior to the COVID-19 Pandemic

Prior to the COVID-19 pandemic, a number of governments had recommendations in place outlining possible actions to be taken in the event of a pandemic respiratory virus, mainly focusing on influenza, and in particular in response to the 2009 H1N1 influenza pandemic. In 2017 the Centers for Disease Control and Prevention in the United States issued guidelines for how to mitigate the spread of influenza in the event of a new pandemic.[96] The guidelines recommended that the following measures could be implemented to slow the spread of disease of an infectious agent:

> personal protective measures, such as home isolation of unwell individuals and quarantine of exposed individuals, a focus on hand hygiene, encouragement of respiratory etiquette and use of facemasks in community settings for unwell individuals;
>
> community measures aimed at increasing social distancing, such as school closures and dismissals, social distancing in workplaces and postponement or cancellation of mass gathering; and
>
> environmental measures such as routine cleaning of frequently touched surfaces in homes, child care facilities, schools and workplaces.

These guidelines acknowledged that the only measures for which there is firm evidence to support the recommendations were hand hygiene,[97] school closures[98] and social distancing measures,[99] but nevertheless advised that:

> Personal, community, and environmental NPIs should be 1) initiated early in a pandemic before local epidemics begin to grow exponentially, 2) targeted toward the nexus of transmission (in affected areas where the novel virus circulates), and 3) layered together to reduce community transmission to the greatest extent possible.[100]

A point of particular debate at the start of the COVID-19 pandemic was the role of facemasks in prevention, acquisition and transmission of infection. A systematic review published in 2012 found that there was no consistent evidence to support a role for

---

[96] N Qualls et al, 'Community Mitigation Guidelines to Prevent Pandemic Influenza – United States, 2017' (2017) 66 *Morbidity and Mortality Weekly Report: Recommendations and Reports I* 1.

[97] M Talaat et al, 'Effects of Hand Hygiene Campaigns on Incidence of Laboratory-Confirmed Influenza and Absenteeism in Schoolchildren, Cairo, Egypt' (2011) 17 *Emerging Infectious Diseases* 619.

[98] 'Emergency Preparedness and Response: School Dismissals to Reduce Transmission of Pandemic Influenza' (*The Community Guide*, August 2012), www.thecommunityguide.org/findings/emergency-preparedness-and-response-school-dismissals-reduce-transmission-pandemic-influenza.

[99] MA Herrera-Valdez et al, 'Multiple Outbreaks for the Same Pandemic: Local Transportation and Social Distancing Explain the Different "Waves" of A-H1N1pdm Cases Observed in México during 2009' (2011) 8 *Mathematical Biosciences and Engineering* 21.

[100] Qualls et al, 'Community Mitigation Guidelines' (n 96).

facemasks in the reduction on influenza transmission, but noted that 'eight of nine retrospective observational studies found that mask and/or respirator use was independently associated with a reduced risk of severe acute respiratory syndrome (SARS)'.[101]

B. Retrospective Evidence for the Effectiveness of NPIs Following the Emergence of SARS-CoV-2

A study published in *Nature Human Behaviour* in November 2020 analysed the effects of different non-pharmaceutical interventions on the effective reproduction number, 'Rt', of SARS-CoV-2.[102] It found that the most effective measures, ranked in descending order, were small gathering cancellations, closure of educational institutions, border restrictions, increasing availability of personal protective equipment, individual movement restrictions and national lockdown. The authors noted that it was difficult to disentangle the exact individual effect of each strategy as often these were implemented as part of a package of measures to reduce the spread of infection. This conclusion is supported by another study of the effectiveness of different NPIs in the first months of the pandemic, which found that the simultaneous implementation of two or more types of NPIs was associated with a greater decrease in the Rt.[103] A similar study looked at the effectiveness of hand-washing, mask wearing and physical distancing for the prevention of SARS-CoV-2 infection, and found evidence for a 53 per cent reduction in COVID-19 for both handwashing and mask wearing, although of the two measures only mask wearing was found to show a statistically significant reduction.[104]

Measures with uncertain effectiveness include tracing and tracking approaches. Studies have shown conflicting results for the effectiveness of these approaches, with heterogeneity in the approach taken by different countries making comparison difficult. However, a study making use of a natural experiment in England found that contact tracing appeared to be more effective than previously assumed for the prevention of COVID-19 cases and deaths.[105]

Amongst the least effective measures found in these studies were land border and airport health checks, and environmental cleaning.[106] Reasons for this include the fact that many people travelling with COVID-19 infection did not have a temperature, and the fact that SARS-CoV-2 transmission is more likely to take place via direct touch, droplets and aerosols than through viral particles adhering to environmental surfaces.

---

[101] F bin-Reza et al, 'The Use of Masks and Respirators to Prevent Transmission of Influenza: A Systematic Review of the Scientific Evidence' (2012) 6 *Influenza and Other Respiratory Viruses* 257.

[102] N Haug et al, 'Ranking the Effectiveness of Worldwide COVID-19 Government Interventions' (2020) 4 *Nature Human Behaviour* 1303.

[103] Y Bo et al, 'Effectiveness of Non-Pharmaceutical Interventions on COVID-19 Transmission in 190 Countries from 23 January to 13 April 2020' (2021) 102 *International Journal of Infectious Diseases* 247.

[104] S Talic et al, 'Effectiveness of Public Health Measures in Reducing the Incidence of Covid-19, SARS-CoV-2 Transmission, and Covid-19 Mortality: Systematic Review and Meta-Analysis' (2021) 375 *BMJ* e068302.

[105] T Fetzer and T Graeber, 'Measuring the Scientific Effectiveness of Contact Tracing: Evidence from a Natural Experiment' (2021) 118 *Proceedings of the National Academy of Sciences* e2100814118.

[106] Haug et al, 'Ranking' (n 102).

C. Travel Restrictions

Shortly following news about human-to-human spread of the virus, a number of countries took steps to limit travel with China, and international travel more generally. On 21 January 2020 a travel alert for Wuhan was issued in Taiwan,[107] and on the 26 January 2021 all travel to and from China to Taiwan was suspended. On 2 February the United States restricted travel with China and imposed a two-week home-based quarantine on those returning from Hubei Province.[108] On 3 February New Zealand followed Australia and the United States in banning travel from China. A paper published in *Proceedings of the National Academy of Sciences* on the 13 March 2020 found that 'that travel restrictions cannot be expected to fully arrest the global expansion of COVID-19, but may decrease the rate of case exportations if enacted during the early stages of the epidemic'.[109]

From the 14 March 2021, all travellers returning to Taiwan from Europe, and those who had transferred through China, Hong Kong, Macau and Dubai were obliged to quarantine at home for 14 days.[110] On 17 March the European Union restricted all non-essential travel to the EU.[111] New Zealand closed its borders to all non-residents on the 19 March 2020,[112] and Australia took similar measures on 20 March 2020.[113] As countries re-opened their borders, most implemented a period of quarantine for incoming travellers with mandatory COVID-19 testing to minimise the risk of importation of SARS-CoV-2.[114]

D. Lockdowns and Other Social Distancing Measures

As noted above, realisation within China of the seriousness of the challenges posed by the pandemic lead to a city-wide lockdown of Wuhan on 23 January 2020,[115] a lockdown

---

[107] Taiwan Centers for Disease Control, 'Taiwan timely identifies first imported case of 2019 novel coronavirus infection returning from Wuhan, China through onboard quarantine; Central Epidemic Command Center (CECC) raises travel notice level for Wuhan, China to Level 3: Warning' (21 January 2020), www.cdc.gov.tw/En/Bulletin/Detail/pVg_jRVvtHhp94C6GShRkQ?typeid=158.

[108] 'A Timeline of COVID-19 Developments in 2020' (2021) *American Journal of Managed Care*, www.ajmc.com/view/a-timeline-of-covid19-developments-in-2020.

[109] CR Wells et al, 'Impact of International Travel and Border Control Measures on the Global Spread of the Novel 2019 Coronavirus Outbreak' (2020) 117 *Proceedings of the National Academy of Sciences* 7504.

[110] 'Taiwan: Authorities implement quarantine measures for travelers from Europe and Dubai March 14 / update 9' (*Crisis 24/Garda*, 16 March 2020), www.garda.com/crisis24/news-alerts/323051/taiwan-authorities-implement-quarantine-measures-for-travelers-from-europe-and-dubai-march-14-update-9.

[111] 'Video conference of the members of the European Council' (*European Council of the European Union*, 17 March 2020), www.consilium.europa.eu/en/meetings/european-council/2020/03/17/#.

[112] J Walls, 'Coronavirus: NZ shutting borders to everyone except citizens, residents – PM Jacinda Ardern' *NZ Herald* (online, 19 March 2020), www.nzherald.co.nz/nz/news/article.cfm?c_id=1&objectid=12318284.

[113] K Burke, 'Australia closes borders to stop coronavirus' (*7 News*, 19 March 2020), https://7news.com.au/lifestyle/health-wellbeing/australia-closes-borders-to-stop-coronavirus-c-752927.

[114] E Han et al, 'Lessons Learnt from Easing COVID-19 Restrictions: An Analysis of Countries and Regions in Asia Pacific and Europe' (2020) 396 *The Lancet* 1525.

[115] Again, the original link to this report is no longer accessible, but it is reported in Wang et al, 'A Novel Coronavirus' (n 30).

which was to last 76 days. Lockdowns were subsequently extended through China, so that by 21 February 2020 an estimated 500 million people across the country[116] had been placed in so-called 'closed' or 'closed-off management'.[117] Under this approach, entry to and exit of defined geographical areas was monitored and policed by resident communities and Chinese Communist Party members, civil servants and volunteers. This strategy proved highly effective in limiting transmission of SARS-CoV-2, but at the time raised concerns about individual privacy.[118]

Faced with a global COVID-19 pandemic, other national governments implemented a variety of measures to limit the spread of SARS-CoV-2. In broad terms, in addition to travel restrictions, these included the implementation of social distancing measures, and personal protective measures. The first national lockdown outside of China started in Italy on 9 March 2020.[119] It required people to maintain at least one metre distance from one another, mandated the closure of non-essential businesses, schools and universities, restricted travel and banned public gatherings. Following this, Spain implemented a national lockdown on 14 March 2020,[120] followed by other European countries, including France on 17 March,[121] and the United Kingdom on 23 March.[122] Germany, instead of issuing a national lockdown, opted for strict social distancing measures, which were introduced on 22 March 2020.[123] Sweden elected not to introduce national lockdown measures, opting instead to implement some social distancing measures including gatherings of more than 50 people, and restricting visits to nursing homes.[124]

Another aspect of NPIs is the use of personal protective measures, including hand hygiene and wearing of facemasks. On 29 January 2020, the WHO recommended that handwashing should be performed frequently, using either alcohol-based hand-rub or soap and water. It restricted the use of facemasks to those with respiratory symptoms, their carers and those sharing a living space with them, and medical professionals.[125]

---

[116] E Feng and A Cheng, 'Restrictions And Rewards: How China Is Locking Down Half A Billion Citizens' (*NPR*, 21 February 2020), www.npr.org/sections/goatsandsoda/2020/02/21/806958341/restrictions-and-rewards-how-china-is-locking-down-half-a-billion-citizens.

[117] 'Why is China able to practice closed-off community management?' (*China Daily*, 7 April 2020), https://covid-19.chinadaily.com.cn/a/202004/07/WS5e8c1d2aa310aeaeeed507c1.html.

[118] Feng and Cheng, 'Restrictions And Rewards' (n 116).

[119] 'Coronavirus: Italy extends emergency measures nationwide' (*BBC*, 10 March 2020), www.bbc.co.uk/news/world-europe-51810673.

[120] M Hernández, 'Pedro Sánchez anuncia el estado de alarma para frenar el coronavirus 24 horas antes de aprobarlo' *El Mundo* (online, 13 March 2020), www.elmundo.es/espana/2020/03/13/5e6b844e21efa0dd258b45a5.html.

[121] A Cuthbertson, 'Coronavirus: France imposes 15-day lockdown and mobilises 100,000 police to enforce restrictions' *The Independent* (online, 16 March 2020), www.independent.co.uk/news/world/europe/coronavirus-france-lockdown-cases-update-covid-19-macron-a9405136.html.

[122] H Stewart et al, 'Boris Johnson orders UK lockdown to be enforced by police' *The Guardian* (online, 23 March 2020), www.theguardian.com/world/2020/mar/23/boris-johnson-orders-uk-lockdown-to-be-enforced-by-police.

[123] 'Coronavirus: What are the lockdown measures across Europe?' (*Deutsche Welle*, 14 April 2020), www.dw.com/en/coronavirus-what-are-the-lockdown-measures-across-europe/a-52905137.

[124] ibid.

[125] WHO, 'Advice on the use of masks in the community, during home care and in health care settings in the context of the novel coronavirus (2019-nCoV) outbreak: interim guidance' (29 January 2020), apps.who.int/iris/handle/10665/330987.

In June 2020 this advice changed to recommend the wearing of non-medical fabric masks in areas with known or suspected transmission, and that vulnerable populations including those over 60, those with respiratory symptoms, and healthcare workers should wear surgical or procedure masks.[126]

V. SUCCESSFUL EARLY RESPONSES TO THE SARS-COV-2 PANDEMIC

Taiwan and New Zealand saw notable initial success in limiting the arrival and spread of SARS-CoV-2. In the first four months of the pandemic, Taiwan documented only 28 deaths from SARS-CoV-2,[127] in stark contrast to much higher figures in other countries. Its success was attributed to the establishment of a National Health Command Centre after the SARS outbreak in 2003, and the implementation of 124 'action items' to protect public health.[128] New Zealand similarly saw a very low number of deaths due to SARS-CoV-2 (25 deaths to October 2020),[129] its success was again attributed to stringent public health interventions. However, both countries encountered difficulties in later phases of the pandemic, coinciding with the arrival of the Delta variant and relatively low vaccination coverage compared to other countries.[130]

VI. IMMUNISATION AND 'HERD IMMUNITY'

Early on in the pandemic it was recognised that ultimately the only way to limit the spread of infection would be the implementation of successful immunisation programmes. The principle of immunisation is to present a version of the pathogen to be protected against (this can be an inactivated pathogen, or one of the constituent proteins) to enter the individual's immune system. The host's adaptive (as opposed to innate) immune system will then build a response to the pathogen, so that if that individual is exposed to that pathogen in the future, circulating antibodies and T cells will prevent, ideally, against both infection and severe disease, or, as has proven to be the case for SARS-CoV-2, with

---

[126] WHO, 'Mask use in the context of COVID-19 – Interim guidance' (1 December 2020), www.who.int/publications/i/item/advice-on-the-use-of-masks-in-the-community-during-home-care-and-in-healthcare-settings-in-the-context-of-the-novel-coronavirus-(2019–ncov)-outbreak.

[127] K Everington, 'Taiwan reports 263 local COVID cases, 28 deaths' *Taiwan News* (online, 11 June 2021), www.taiwannews.com.tw/en/news/4219867.

[128] CJ Wang et al, 'Response to COVID-19 in Taiwan: Big Data Analytics, New Technology, and Proactive Testing' (2020) 323 *Journal of the American Medical Assocation* 1341.

[129] S Kung et al, 'Reduced Mortality in New Zealand during the COVID-19 Pandemic' (2021) 397 *The Lancet* 25.

[130] For Taiwan see H Davidson, 'A victim of its own success: how Taiwan failed to plan for a major Covid outbreak' *The Guardian* (online, 7 June 2021), www.theguardian.com/world/2021/jun/07/a-victim-of-its-own-success-how-taiwan-failed-to-plan-for-a-major-covid-outbreak; for New Zealand see S Ray, 'New Zealand Gives Up On "Zero Covid" Strategy Amid Persistent Delta Variant Outbreak' *Forbes Magazine* (online, 4 October 2021), www.forbes.com/sites/siladityaray/2021/10/04/new-zealand-gives-up-on-zero-covid-strategy-amid-persistent-delta-variant-outbreak/.

varying degrees of effectiveness against infection, but robustly against the risk of severe disease or death.

The way in which a successful immunisation campaign works is to create herd immunity: a threshold after which a high enough proportion of the population have been infected (and recovered, with resultant immunity to disease), that there are no longer sufficient susceptible individuals for infection to spread throughout the population. No countries explicitly took a herd immunity approach to mitigating the effects of SARS-CoV-2 infection on a national population. However, the possibility of aiming for herd immunity through natural infection was briefly aired in the United Kingdom at the start of March 2020,[131] and some have argued that Sweden, by introducing only voluntary social distancing measures, implemented a 'de-facto herd immunity approach'.[132]

Work on vaccine development began the day that the SARS-CoV-2 genome was released publicly.[133] In March 2020 Phase I trials began for the Moderna mRNA vaccine,[134] followed in April by those for another mRNA vaccine (Pfizer/BioNTech)[135] and an adenovirus vector vaccine (Oxford/AstraZeneca).[136] Messenger RNA (mRNA) vaccines work by introducing the genetic sequence for the SARS-CoV-2 Spike protein in an injection into muscle cells, which use this sequence to make copies of the Spike protein, which in turn stimulates the host's immune response. The adenovirus vector vaccines (the AstraZeneca vaccine is one of a number of different vaccines using this technology, including Russia's Sputnik vaccine) take an adenovirus virus, which would normally cause a cold-like respiratory infection, and co-opt this virus to produce copies of the Spike protein.

By the summer of 2020 the Pfizer/BioNTech, Moderna and Oxford/AstraZeneca vaccines had all entered Phase II/III trials after showing evidence of efficacy in the initial Phase I trials. The first vaccine to show efficacy against infection in a large clinical trial was Pfizer/BioNTech, which announced its results on 9 November 2020,[137] with an interim

---

[131] H Stewart and M Busby, 'Coronavirus: science chief defends UK plan from criticism' *The Guardian* (online, 13 March 2020), www.theguardian.com/world/2020/mar/13/coronavirus-science-chief-defends-uk-measures-criticism-herd-immunity.

[132] M Claeson and S Hanson, 'COVID-19 and the Swedish Enigma' (2021) 397 *The Lancet* 259.

[133] B Graham (Twitter), 'One of the main questions being asked and a reason for COVID-19 vaccine hesitancy is "how was this done so fast?" ...' (11 January 2021, 3:32pm), https://twitter.com/BarneyGrahamMD/status/1348641727113003008.

[134] U.S. Department of Health & Human Services: National Institutes of Health, 'NIH clinical trial of investigational vaccine for COVID-19 begins' (16 March 2020), www.nih.gov/news-events/news-releases/nih-clinical-trial-investigational-vaccine-covid-19-begins.

[135] 'BioNTech and Pfizer announce completion of dosing for first cohort of Phase 1/2 trial of COVID-19 vaccine candidates in Germany' (*Pfizer Press Release*, 29 April 2020), www.pfizer.com/news/press-release/press-release-detail/biontech-and-pfizer-announce-completion-dosing-first-cohort.

[136] 'Oxford COVID-19 vaccine begins human trial stage' (*Oxford University Press Release*, 23 April 2020), www.ox.ac.uk/news/2020-04-23-oxford-covid-19-vaccine-begins-human-trial-stage.

[137] 'Pfizer and BioNTech Announce Vaccine Candidate Against COVID-19 Achieved Success in First Interim Analysis from Phase 3 Study' (*Pfizer Press Release*, 9 November 2020), www.pfizer.com/news/press-release/press-release-detail/pfizer-and-biontech-announce-vaccine-candidate-against.

analysis showing an efficacy in preventing infection of 91.3 per cent. The following week, on 16 November 2020, the United States National Institutes of Health announced an efficacy of 94.5 per cent for the Moderna vaccine in preventing symptomatic infection with pre-Alpha lineages of the virus.[138] On 23 November AstraZeneca and Oxford University announced that their vaccine was 70.4 per cent effective in preventing infection, although this announcement was subsequently criticised for incorporating data on two different treatment dose regimen, and a lack of clarity on the fact that one of these regimens was in fact due to a dosing error.[139]

Accompanying, and sometimes preceding, the release of data from clinical trials was the pre-ordering of vaccines – by 30 November 2020, the United Kingdom, with a population of 66 million, had pre-ordered 357 million doses of COVID-19 vaccines;[140] Canada, with a population of 37 million, had ordered almost as many.[141]

The first country to approve the use of a coronavirus vaccine was the United Kingdom. On 2 December 2020 the Medicines and Healthcare Products Regulatory Agency approved the Pfizer/BioNTech vaccine for widespread use, and immunisation of vulnerable populations and healthcare workers commenced the following week, of 8 December 2020.[142] On 11 December 2020 the Pfizer/BioNTech vaccine was issued with an emergency use authorisation for the USA by the United States Food and Drug Administration.[143]

At some point in 2020, the Israeli Government entered into a deal with Pfizer, in which a guaranteed supply of vaccines was offered in exchange for public health data about the implementation and real world effectiveness of the vaccine.[144] This immunisation campaign was initiated on 19 December 2020, with the then Prime Minister Benjamin Netanyahu becoming the first person to receive the vaccine on live TV.[145] Immunisation in Israel proceeded rapidly, with over 90 per cent of Israelis over the age of 65 receiving a first dose by early February 2021,[146] with evidence of a protective effect of immunisation in this age group. Vaccine roll-out also proceeded rapidly in the United Kingdom and from

[138] U.S. Department of Health & Human Services: National Institutes of Health, 'Promising Interim Results from Clinical Trial of NIH-Moderna COVID-19 Vaccine' (16 November 2020), www.nih.gov/news-events/news-releases/promising-interim-results-clinical-trial-nih-moderna-covid-19-vaccine.

[139] E Mahase, 'Covid-19: UK government asks regulator to assess Oxford vaccine as questions are raised over interim data' (2020) 371 *BMJ* m4670.

[140] V Rees, 'UK secures total of 357 million doses of various COVID-19 vaccines' (*European Pharmaceutical Review*, 30 November 2020), www.europeanpharmaceuticalreview.com/news/134958/uk-secures-total-of-357-million-doses-of-various-covid-19-vaccines/.

[141] A Mullard, 'How COVID vaccines are being divvied up around the world' (*Nature*, 23 November 2020), www.nature.com/articles/d41586-020-03370-6.

[142] 'Covid-19 vaccine: First person receives Pfizer jab in UK' (*BBC*, 8 December 2020), www.bbc.co.uk/news/uk-55227325#:~:text=A%20UK%20grandmother%20has%20become,%22best%20early%20birthday%20present%22.

[143] U.S. Food & Drug Administration, 'FDA Takes Key Action in Fight Against COVID-19 By Issuing Emergency Use Authorization for First COVID-19 Vaccine' (11 December 2020), www.fda.gov/news-events/press-announcements/fda-takes-key-action-fight-against-covid-19-issuing-emergency-use-authorization-first-covid-19.

[144] 'Real-World Epidemiological Evidence Collaboration Agreement' (*Government of Israel & Pfizer*, 6 January 2020), govextra.gov.il/media/30806/11221-moh-pfizer-collaboration-agreement-redacted.pdf.

[145] 'Israeli PM Benjamin Netanyahu receives Pfizer vaccine' (*NBC*, 19 December 2020), www.nbcnews.com/video/israeli-pm-benjamin-netanyahu-receives-pfizer-vaccine-98079813595.

[146] S Mallapaty, 'Vaccines are curbing COVID: Data from Israel show drop in infections' (*Nature*, 5 February 2021), www.nature.com/articles/d41586-021-00316-4.

January 2021 in the United States, where newly elected President Joe Biden committed to 100 million vaccine doses in the first 100 days of his presidency,[147] a promise subsequently increased to 200 million.[148]

The European Union was slower to initiate vaccination, due to a delay in approving vaccines, issues in delivery of vaccines[149] and concerns from nation states initially about the effectiveness of the Oxford/AstraZeneca vaccine in older populations, and from April 2021 onwards, concerns about safety in younger people, as cases emerged of increased rates of unusual patterns of blood clots and deaths in those who had received the vaccine.[150] Later in 2021 concerns arose about the safety of mRNA vaccines, particularly cases of myocarditis (inflammation of the heart muscle) in male teenagers,[151] although the rates of these severe complications appeared to be low.

VII. CONCLUSION

SARS-CoV-2 was a novel coronavirus that first emerged in the city of Wuhan in China at the end of 2019. Media reports of clusters of cases of pneumonia in the city, associated with the Huanan Seafood Market, were first posted on 31 December 2019. The genome of the virus was released on 10 January 2020, and the first case reports in the medical literature were published on 24 January 2020. By the end of January 2020 there were cases in 18 countries globally, and the WHO declared the situation a Public Health Emergency of Public Concern. In February the disease caused by the virus was named COVID-19, and cases spread globally, with evidence for community transmission of the virus outside China. It became clear that age and pre-existing medical conditions such as heart disease and cancer put individuals at higher risk of severe disease and death. On 9 March 2020, Italy became the first country outside China to institute a national lockdown to limit the spread of the virus, and on 11 March 2020 the WHO declared the COVID-19 situation a global pandemic.[152] In subsequent months effective treatments and vaccinations for COVID-19 were developed and implemented, although the emergence of new SARS-CoV-2 variants such as Alpha and Delta challenged the success of these developments.

---

[147] B Kamisar, 'Biden chief of staff says 100 million vaccinations in 100 days is just a start' (*NBC*, 24 January 2021), www.nbcnews.com/politics/meet-the-press/ron-klain-100-million-vaccinations-100-days-just-start-n1255451.

[148] J Murphy, 'Biden pledged 200 million Covid vaccinations in 100 days. The country hit that goal with a week to spare' (*NBC*, 26 January 2021), www.nbcnews.com/politics/white-house/150-million-vaccinations-tracker-biden-goal-n1255716.

[149] S Amaro, 'Europe's stumbling vaccine rollout provides a lesson in EU politics' (*CNBC*, 2 April 2021), www.cnbc.com/2021/04/02/europe-covid-vaccine-slow-rollout-gives-lesson-in-eu-politics.html.

[150] European Medicines Agency, 'AstraZeneca's COVID-19 vaccine: EMA finds possible link to very rare cases of unusual blood clots with low blood platelets' (7 April 2021), www.ema.europa.eu/en/news/astrazenecas-covid-19-vaccine-ema-finds-possible-link-very-rare-cases-unusual-blood-clots-low-blood.

[151] Centres for Disease Control and Prevention, 'Selected Adverse Events Reported after COVID-19 Vaccination' (25 July 2022), www.cdc.gov/coronavirus/2019-ncov/vaccines/safety/adverse-events.html.

[152] WHO, 'WHO Director-General's opening remarks at the media briefing on COVID-19' (11 March 2020), www.who.int/director-general/speeches/detail/who-director-general-s-opening-remarks-at-the-media-briefing-on-covid-19---11-march-2020.

Table 1 Time-series of SARS-CoV-2 Infections and Non-pharmaceutical Interventions Introduced in the Countries Covered in this Book. Data from Covid-19 Government Response Tracker (University of Oxford)

Country	First SARS-CoV-2 case	Stay at home recommendation	Stay at home requirement	School closures	Workplace closures	International travel: arrivals banned from some regions	Ban on arrivals from all regions or total border closure	Facemasks recommended	Facemasks mandatory
Brazil	25/02/20	13/03/20	05/05/2020	NA	NA	19/03/2020	27/03/2020	02/03/2020	22/03/2020
China	01/12/19	23/01/20	01/02/2020	26/01/2020	26/01/2020	26/03/2020	NA	NA	21/01/2020
France	24/01/20	NA	17/03/2020	16/03/20	17/03/2020	17/03/2020	NA	22/01/2020	11/05/2020
Germany	27/01/20	09/03/20	22/03/2020	18/03/20	22/03/2020	16/03/2020	18/03/2020	01/04/2020	06/04/2020
India (IND)	30/01/20	26/01/20	22/03/2020	18/03/20	22/03/2020	15/03/2020	22/03/2020	02/04/2020	09/04/2020
Indonesia (IDN)	02/03/20	NA	10/04/2020	16/03/20	10/04/2020	05/02/2020	19/03/2020	05/04/2020	06/04/2020
Iran (IRN)	19/02/20	19/03/20	06/10/2020	23/02/20	26/02/2020	11/07/2020	NA	NA	05/07/2020
South Africa (ZAF)	05/03/20	NA	26/03/2020	18/03/20	26/03/2020	18/03/2020	26/03/2020	01/04/2020	01/05/2020
Spain (ESP)	31/01/20	NA	14/03/2020	14/03/20	14/03/2020	10/03/2020	17/03/2020	NA	04/05/2020
Sweden (SWE)	31/01/20	25/03/20	NA	17/03/20	16/03/2020	02/03/2020	NA	07/01/2021	17/02/2021
Turkey (TUR)	10/03/20	09/03/20	31/03/2020	16/03/20	16/03/2020	05/02/2020	27/03/2020	NA	07/06/2020
United Kingdom	31/01/20	13/03/20	23/03/2020	23/03/20	23/03/2020	24/12/2020	NA	28/04/2020	22/06/2020
USA	20/01/20	NA	15/03/2020	05/03/20	19/03/2020	02/03/2020	NA	10/03/2020	04/04/2020

3

Brazil

DENIS DE CASTRO HALIS*

I. BACKGROUND AND CONTEXTUAL INTRODUCTION

BRAZIL'S PRESIDENT IS the head of State and government. Throughout the COVID-19 pandemic, the country's elected President has been Jair Bolsonaro, whose term started on 1 January 2019 and is to end on 31 December 2022. His scientific scepticism and indifference to the massive number of deaths during the pandemic has been reported by national and foreign media outlets.[1] Besides making insensitive remarks towards the human tragedy in many instances, he has been outspoken about his lack of responsibility while continuously expressing his worries about the economic costs of policies recommended by the World Health Organization (WHO). These policies were supported and promoted by many state and municipal authorities in Brazil but challenged by the President. With record after record in number of cases and deaths, burials literally took place around the clock. In the State of São Paulo, Brazil's richest state, there were burials throughout the night and the use of excavators to dig new graves. Surprisingly enough, by 10 March 2021, Brazil was the only emerging country in the world to take a stand against India and South Africa's proposed suspension of patents on vaccines against COVID-19 before the WTO.[2]

Sources reported that in April 2021, at the peak of the pandemic in Brazil, over 4,000 deaths occurred daily in the country.[3] In early 2022, the number of confirmed cases had

* The author acknowledges and thanks UNESA – Rio de Janeiro and its Post-Graduation Program of Law (PPGD) for the partial funding of his investigations through its Scholarship Programs. The author would also like to thank Professor Hiroshi Fukurai, of the University of California – Santa Cruz, and Professor Hanne Petersen and the Faculty of Law of the University of Copenhagen for their support and intellectual exchange, who have greatly enriched my work in recent years. Finally, the author thanks the editors of this book for their very insightful and careful comments.

[1] There are many illustrations of this. On 20 April 2020, a journalist asked Bolsonaro about the growing number of deaths by COVID-19 in Brazil and his reply was: 'I'm not a gravedigger'. On 28 April 2020, when asked about the record number of deaths in the country, he replied: 'So what?' In a later video widely circulated in the social media, the President imitated a patient with lack of breath. As a last example, from 2021, he used very particular Brazilian expressions roughly translated as 'enough whining! Until when will you be crying?'. See, for all: I Soares, '"Chega de frescura e de mimimi. Vão ficar chorando até quando?", diz Bolsonaro' *Correio Braziliense* (online, 5 March 2021), www.correiobraziliense.com.br/politica/2021/03/4910286-chega-de-frescura-e-de-mimimi--vao-ficar-chorando-ate-quando--diz-bolsonaro.html/.

[2] Senado Federal, 'CPI da Pandemia' (Final Report, 26 October 2021) (CPI Report), https://legis.senado.leg.br/comissoes/comissao?codcol=2441, 19.

[3] W Cota, 'Monitoring the number of COVID-19 cases in Brazil' (*Universidade Federal de Viçosa*), https://covid19br.wcota.me/en/#footer.

surpassed 22 million, while that of deaths surpassed 620,000.[4] Even though the vaccination had severe delays and involved great controversy, it gained momentum and popular acceptance. As the vaccination process started and advanced, the number of fatalities reduced significantly. By January 2022 almost 80 per cent of the population had received at least one dose of the vaccine[5] and the number of daily deaths radically dropped to about a 100 or less in early 2022.[6]

This contribution is based on COVID-19 statistics, available on government and other organisations' platforms, and on publicised sources that include: media reports; the legal opinion by a special committee of renowned Brazilian legal experts chaired by a former judge of Brazil's Federal Supreme Court on behalf of the Brazilian Bar (OAB) (the OAB Opinion);[7] scholarly reports and articles; relevant domestic legislation[8] and applicable international law; and a report prepared by a committee formed by members of the Federal Parliament (a Parliamentary Commission of Inquiry or CPI – its acronym in Portuguese) after months of investigation into the conducts of high-profile government members, its agents and supporters, including companies.[9] This latter report is referred to throughout as the CPI Report.[10] Most of these sources, including most of the legislation, are originally written in Portuguese. The OAB Opinion and the CPI Report are no exception and their passages quoted here have been translated into English.

The sources list episodes demonstrating the actions and omissions of the Federal government, and several assert that the number of deaths by COVID-19 would have been lower had the President appropriately tackled the challenges brought by the virus. The President's behaviour and public statements led many people, political parties and organisations to file requests for his impeachment. The Federal Council of the Brazilian Bar relied on the OAB Opinion to do so. By early 2022, there were over 140 other requests for his impeachment, most of which remain to be admitted and analysed by the leaders of Brazil's Parliament.[11] Those requests attribute several criminal acts to the President.

Brazil has been among the countries most seriously hit by COVID-19. It is second in the number of deaths, only falling behind the USA.[12] More astonishing than the numbers, were the attempts of the Federal government to disguise, conceal and misinterpret COVID-19 related data. Throughout the pandemic, the government modified the methodology to obtain and present data, the time of its release, and even suspended

---

[4] H Ritchie et al, 'Brazil: Coronavirus Pandemic Country Profile' (*Our World in Data*), https://ourworldindata.org/coronavirus/country/brazil.

[5] H Ritchie et al, 'Share of people who received at least one dose of COVID-19 vaccine' (*Our World in Data*), https://ourworldindata.org/grapher/share-people-vaccinated-covid?country=~BRA.

[6] Cota, 'COVID-19' (n 3).

[7] OAB Nacional, 'Comissão Especial Para Análise E Sugestões De Medidas Ao Enfrentamento Da Pandemia Do Coronavírus', https://s.oab.org.br/arquivos/2021/04/38a7e5c2-a16f-4aa6-8965-570b8d26efd9.pdf.

[8] The links to the legislation refer to official government websites, in Portuguese.

[9] See s II.D below.

[10] CPI Report (n 2).

[11] According to *Pública*, a non-profit news agency in Brazil, as at 4 January 2022, 143 requests for the President's impeachment had been filed in one of the country's Parliament houses, 'Os Pedidos De Impeachment De Bolsonaro' (*Pública*), https://apublica.org/impeachment-bolsonaro/.

[12] WHO, 'WHO Coronavirus (COVID-19) Dashboard', https://covid19.who.int/.

online portals of information to influence the public's perception about the impact of the pandemic, while accusing most of the media of disseminating 'fake news'. When numbers first became difficult to find, media reports talked about a 'government data blackout'.[13] From that point, several non-Federal government and alternative platforms were created or became references to find the latest data. Those included the websites of organizations such as Fiocruz,[14] one of the institutes producing the vaccine in Brazil, and those belonging to media vehicles that formed a consortium to seek and gather the data directly from all individual states rather than from the Federal government. State-level governments' online portals also became references.[15]

After much criticism of and excuses from the Federal government about the 'data blackout', it launched a website to display the official COVID-19 numbers.[16] The website was in line with the President's rhetoric, often minimising the importance of the pandemic and dismissing health experts' recommendations. It starts by displaying the number of recovered patients and uses different background colours and font sizes to highlight and draw readers' attention to that number, while it minimises the numbers of confirmed cases and of deaths.

A joint academic investigation by CEPEDISA/USP and Conectas Human Rights concluded that there was abundant evidence of an institutional strategy to disseminate the COVID-19 virus in Brazil.[17] The investigation analysed all legal norms – including by-laws, executive orders and resolutions – issued by the Federal government as well as the public speeches of the President. Further, it analysed the obstructive acts of the government towards the actions of state and municipal governments addressing the pandemic according to scientific criteria. The data was collected and produced throughout 2020 and included over 3,000 Federal norms and over 4,000 State-level norms related to the pandemic. The investigation's report argues that, rather than exclusive incompetence and negligence on the part of the Federal government, the data revealed its 'clear and efficient commitment towards the wide dissemination of the virus'. It also asserts that the President's public speeches and conduct have amounted to serious propaganda against the interests of public health. It demonstrates that his speeches articulated economic, ideological and moral arguments as well as false news and inaccurate technical information, without scientific grounds, to discredit sanitary authorities and to weaken popular adherence to health recommendations, while promoting political activism public health measures to contain the pandemic.

---

[13] R Barifouse, 'Coronavírus: onde acompanhar os números da pandemia no Brasil após apagão de dados do governo' (*BBC*, 8 June 2020), https://www.bbc.com/portuguese/brasil-52974181/.

[14] Instituto de Comunicação e Informação Científica e Tecnológica em Saúde (Fiocruz), 'Monitora Covid-19', https://bigdata-covid19.icict.fiocruz.br/.

[15] Secretariat of Health of the State of São Paulo, 'SP contra o novo coronavírus', www.seade.gov.br/coronavirus/#.

[16] Ministry of Health, 'Coronavírus Brasil – Covid19 – Painel Coronavirus', https://covid.saude.gov.br/.

[17] CEPEDISA is the Health Law Research and Studies Center of the Faculty of Public Health of the University of São Paulo (USP). CEPEDISA/USP, 'Boletim Direitos na Pandemia no 10a' (São Paulo, 2021), www.conectas.org/publicacao/boletim-direitos-na-pandemia-no-10/. See also E Brum, 'Pesquisa revela que Bolsonaro executou uma "estratégia institucional de propagação do *coronavírus*"' *El País* (online, 21 January 2021), https://brasil.elpais.com/brasil/2021-01-21/pesquisa-revela-que-bolsonaro-executou-uma-estrategia-institucional-de-propagacao-do-virus.html/.

The Federal government's tragic performance has been noticed and documented in reports published internationally as well. *The Lancet*, in early 2021, stated: 'Despite the clear threat of Covid-19 to Brazilians, health experts are becoming increasingly worried about getting people to take a vaccine that President Jair Bolsonaro regularly lambasts'.[18] The article continues:

> Bolsonaro has repeatedly questioned the efficacy of COVID-19 vaccines and has said that he will refuse to be vaccinated when offered. 'If you turn into a crocodile, it's your problem', the bellicose leader told local media in December, 2020, about the side-effects of the vaccine developed by Pfizer and BioNTech, which was at the time already being administered in the USA and the UK. 'Some people say I'm giving a bad example, but to the imbeciles and idiots that say this, I tell them I've already caught the virus, I have the antibodies, so why get vaccinated?'[19]

Rapid vaccination in Brazil and in many parts of the world throughout 2021 was accompanied by a continuous and significant decrease in the number of casualties. Brazil's President, however, has maintained his sceptical position, and repeatedly said, 'we cannot force anyone to vaccinate. I didn't vaccinate'.[20] Further, in one of his speeches he declared, 'I had the best vaccine, it was the virus, without side effects'.[21]

II. CONSTITUTIONAL, LEGAL AND POLICY OVERVIEW

Brazil has been a federation since 1889, when the country became a republic with the classic three-branch separation of political power. Its current Federal Constitution dates from 1988, after the end of a 21-year military dictatorship. The 1988 Constitution continues to display its resilience despite its critics and the fact that it has been amended over 100 times. The Constitution structures and details Brazil's current model of federalism. Article 76 states that Executive Power is exercised by the President of the Republic with the assistance of the Ministers of State.[22] The Union, States and Municipalities are entities of the federal structure. The latter have been included in the federal structure, enjoying independent and coequal status, and have been granted considerable powers and resources. Municipalities' powers include the competence to decide on issues such as municipal public health, land development, environment, local taxation, industrial development and territorial management.

There are over 5,000 municipalities, 26 states and the Federal District of Brasilia (the Capital) in Brazil's federation. States have their own state constitutions, and municipalities have 'organic laws'. The decentralisation of political power and resources was aimed

---

[18] JP Daniels, 'Health Experts Slam Bolsonaro's Vaccine Comments' (2021) 397 *The Lancet* 361.

[19] ibid.

[20] For a report on one of those instances, see 'Bolsonaro diz que não tomará vacina e chama de "idiota" quem o vê como mau exemplo por não se imunizar: "Eu já tive o vírus"' (*G1 Bahia*, 17 December 2020), https://g1.globo.com/ba/bahia/noticia/2020/12/17/bolsonaro-diz-que-nao-tomara-vacina-e-chama-de-idiota-quem-o-ve-como-mau-exemplo-por-nao-se-imunizar-eu-ja-tive-o-virus.ghtml.

[21] M Schuch, 'Bolsonaro diz que já teve a "melhor vacina" contra Covid-19, o próprio vírus' *Valor Econômico* (online, 23 December 2020), https://valor.globo.com/politica/noticia/2020/12/23/bolsonaro-diz-que-ja-teve-a-melhor-vacina-contra-Covid-19-o-proprio-virus.ghtml.

[22] Constitution of the Federative Republic of Brazil, 6th edn (Brasilia: The Federal Senate, Undersecretariat of Technical Publications, 2013) (Constitution), www2.senado.leg.br/bdsf/item/id/243334.

to bring government close to the people after the 21-year period of military dictatorship. There is an underpinning aspiration of cooperation between the authorities and entities at the central, state and municipal levels. This has proven challenging during the pandemic, though, as there were severe clashes between State Governors and the President of the Republic about public policies to handle the pandemic. Due to these clashes, Brazil's Supreme Court issued a decision underscoring the joint responsibility and shared competence of the entities at the three levels to tackle the pandemic. In fact, article 23, II, of the Constitution states that: 'The Union, the states, the Federal District and the municipalities, in common, have the power: ... II – to provide for health and public assistance, for the protection and safeguard of handicapped persons'. Despite this provision, the President repeatedly misrepresents his constitutional role and that judicial decision by claiming not to have the legal competence to handle the pandemic given that the court transferred the responsibility to governors and city mayors. He contends, however, to have continuously distributed money and resources, assisting the people and regional and local authorities in all possible (but in actuality, limited) ways.

The performance of Brazil's executive branch in addressing the pandemic has been scrutinised in detail not only by judges, political parties, civil society, national and foreign media and scholars, but also by the National Congress (*i.e.*, the Federal Parliament). The Congress is divided into two chambers or houses: the Federal Senate and the Chamber of Deputies. Every and each state, irrespective of its territorial or population size, is represented in the Senate by three senators. Conversely, the Chamber of Deputies is mainly composed of elected representatives in proportion to the population of each state. The President and his Cabinet's actions, omissions and mismanagement of pandemic-related problems have led to the creation of a Parliamentary Inquiry Commission, which is a special committee formed by members of the parliament to investigate a specific matter. In April 2021, despite strong government resistance and with the Supreme Court's backing, the 'Pandemic Parliamentary Inquiry Commission' was created, with extensive powers to investigate the President and his government's actions. The work of the Commission lasted until 26 October 2021 and revealed several crimes and illegal conduct by authorities, individuals and companies in relation to the pandemic and the management of resources to tackle it.[23] The Commission's report or CPI Report is some 1,287 pages in length and offers a list of indictments to diverse prosecutorial and investigative official organs to charge, or further analyse. The CPI Report's various sections address several authorities and persons' conduct that contributed to widely disseminate the virus.

At the outset of the pandemic in Brazil, a plethora of Federal, State and Municipal legal norms was enacted, from the most general and applicable to the entire country, to the most localised and specific measures. The following norms were enacted at the Federal level either by the National Parliament or by the President.

The Parliament passed Law 13.979/20, prescribing a wide range of measures to address public health emergencies such as the restrictions of movement of people and of commercial activities and the mandatory use of face masks in public as well as private spaces accessible to the public, which were recommended by specialists as suitable measures

---

[23] For details about the Commission, see s II.D below.

connected to social distancing guidelines.[24] In brief, the law authorises and regulates compulsory measures that authorities can implement. These measures include medical and laboratory tests; restriction of movement on roads, ports and airports according to technical assessments by ANVISA, the country's national agency in charge of sanitary measures; appropriation of goods and services from natural and legal persons, in which case the subsequent payment of a fair indemnity will be guaranteed; and exceptional and temporary importation of products subjected to sanitary vigilance without ANVISA's registration, as long as these products are registered by an authorised foreign sanitary authority and provided that takes place by an act of the Ministry of Health.

To regulate further and provide specification regarding the previous law, the President issued Federal Decree 10.282/20, which lists essential public services and activities and provides exceptions to legal norms prescribing restrictive measures.[25] Additionally, the Decree creates exemptions for auxiliary and supportive activities needed for the production chain of essential public services and activities, while also prohibiting restrictions on the movement of workers who provide essential services, as well as transport cargo of any kind that may result in a shortage of supplies that are necessary to the population. The President provoked great controversy by amending this decree as well as by issuing others with the aim of expanding the items on the exemption list by classifying them as essential additional activities. Examples of these decrees are Decree 10.292/20, which included religious activities and lottery shops, and Decree 10.344/20, which included beauty salons and barbershops, sport academies of all types and industrial activities (without specification) among such essential activities. Other legal norms were enacted at the Federal level for determined time, including '*Portaria*' (a Federal Ordinance) 125/20 (about the closure of land borders)[26] and '*Portaria*' 126/20 (containing rules about international flights).[27]

At the State level of the federation, Governors enacted complementary and more stringent measures. Examples of these were Quarantine Decree 64.881/20[28] in the State of São Paulo, and Decree 46.973/20, declaring a State of Emergency in the Public Health in the State of Rio de Janeiro.[29] Some Governors called for reducing the transport and movement of people; the closure of or reduced attendance at bars, restaurants, hotels, entertainment venues, public spaces (*e.g.*, including beaches and parks); and even the regulation of flights (*e.g.*, to suspend) from other States and countries. At the municipal level, rules concerned local measures and restrictions, such as the opening and closing times of businesses, and the use of masks in public spaces as well as private spaces open to the public.

---

[24] Law no 13.979, 6 February 2020 (Presidência da República, Secretaria-Geral, Subchefia para Assuntos Jurídicos), www.planalto.gov.br/ccivil_03/_ato2019-2022/2020/Lei/L13979.htm.

[25] Decree no 10.282, 20 March 2020 (Presidência da República, Secretaria-Geral, Subchefia para Assuntos Jurídicos), www.planalto.gov.br/ccivil_03/_ato2019-2022/2020/decreto/D10282.htm.

[26] Ordinance no 125, 19 March 2020 (Imprensa Nacional), www.in.gov.br/en/web/dou/-/portaria-n-125-de-19-de-marco-de-2020-248881224.

[27] Ordinance no 126, 19 March 2020 (Imprensa Nacional), www.in.gov.br/en/web/dou/-/portaria-n-126-de-19-de-marco-de-2020-248881688.

[28] Decree no 64.881, 22 March 2020 (Assembleia Legislativa do Estado de São Paulo), www.al.sp.gov.br/repositorio/legislacao/decreto/2020/decreto-64881-22.03.2020.html.

[29] Decree no 46.973, 16 March 2020, www.fazenda.rj.gov.br/sefaz/faces/oracle/webcenter/portalapp/pages/navigation-renderer.jspx?_afrLoop=78787583440620292&datasource=UCMServer%23dDocName%3A WCC42000008239&_adf.ctrl-state=19b25jgfk3_9.

A. Overview of and Specific Constitutional and Legal Principles Regarding Criminal Liability of High-Ranking Government/Public Officials

Brazil's Constitution provides the legal grounds to determine whether government authorities have properly performed their legal duties. Its chapter on Public Administration (chapter VII within title III of the Organization of the State) provides the principles and rules concerning government officials. Article 37 announces the broad legal principles to guide officials' work: 'Governmental entities and entities owned by the Government in any of the powers of the Union, the States, the Federal District and the Municipalities shall obey the principles of lawfulness, impersonality, morality, publicity, and efficiency'. Moreover, the same article's paragraphs 3, 4 and 5 provide for officials' responsibilities when rendering public service and the liabilities concerning their unlawful behaviour. These norms include references to complaints against negligence or abuse in the exercise of an office, position or function in government services, as well as acts of administrative dishonesty that may lead to the suspension of political rights, loss of public function, prohibition on the transfer of personal property and reimbursement to the Public Treasury. Also, they do not exclude additional criminal liability of authorities and other agents acting on behalf of public authorities or the government.

The Constitution also contains other sections and provisions addressing the duties and liabilities of specific government agents and organs. Acts leading to the criminal liability of the President are in chapter II (Executive Power) of title IV (Organization of the State Powers). Articles 85 and 86 are particularly relevant. Article 85 mentions acts of the President against the Constitution, which includes seven special issues such as the existence of the Union, the free exercise of the Legislative and Judicial Powers and those constitutional powers of the Public Prosecution and of the units of the Federation; the exercise of political, individual and social rights; the internal security of the country; probity in the administration; the budgetary law; and compliance with the laws and with court decisions. Article 86 provides for charges of a different nature against the President, and their consequences, including the moment when he shall be suspended from his functions. In case of acceptance of such charges by two-thirds of the Chamber of Deputies, the President shall be submitted to trial before the Supreme Federal Court for common criminal offences or before the Federal Senate for crimes of malversation.

Federal Law 1.079/50 regulates some of the constitutional provisions regarding 'crimes of responsibility' (or 'crimes of liability') and corresponding trial procedures imputable to the President, State Ministers and other high-level Federal authorities. Crimes of responsibility by the President are acts against the Federal Constitution and notably against the exercise of people's political, individual and social rights. Crimes of responsibility by Ministers of State are found in article 13, and can be performed or ordered by them, and 'acts provided for in this law that the Ministers sign with the President of the Republic or practice themselves by order of the latter'. They can also be charged under such crimes if they fail to appear without justification before the Chamber of Deputies or the Federal Senate and their committees when summoned, and if they fail to provide, in writing, within 30 days and without good reason any of the Chambers of the National Congress the information requested, or if they give it falsely.

Chapter 3 of Law 1.079/50 sets out those authorities' conduct that violates the free exercise of people's political, individual and social rights. Article 7 provides specific protection for social rights, including health and medical care, which are foreseen in the Constitution. The Constitution's article 6 expressly provides protection of 'education, health, food, work, housing, transport, leisure, safety, social security, maternity and childhood protection, and assistance to the destitute'. The COVID-19 pandemic highlighted officials' responsibilities in relation to public health. Moreover, the Constitution's article 23, II, prescribes the authorities' shared competence concerning people's health and medical assistance. Further, the section about Health – within the chapter about Social Welfare – contains articles. 196 and 197, which determine the overall responsibility of the State concerning those issues.[30]

B. Scope of Responsibility and Area of Tolerated Risk

The main government authorities in Brazil are the President of the Republic and the Ministers appointed by the President. The OAB Opinion and several reports have mapped many instances when the President, his Ministers and other government officials acted contrary to the advice of their own medical and policy experts. Brazil's law tolerates and allows that people take certain risks when conducting their affairs. Driving a vehicle, for instance, is risky conduct, as it may bring death and injuries or damages to third parties, but the law allows people to drive in accordance with relevant regulations. To establish if a conduct harmful to others will have criminal relevance and will lead to criminal liability, it is necessary to evaluate the intention behind the agent's conduct and if the corresponding result should be imputed to him in accordance with criteria that includes three important issues: (1) the conduct created an impermissible (non-tolerated) risk; (2) the risk materialises in a concrete result; (3) the result was within the scope of the legal description of a crime. A non-tolerated (impermissible) risk can be ruled out when the conduct under analysis reduces the risk or does not create any legally relevant risk; when it does not increase the risk; or when the direct damages are outside the sphere of protection of the legal norm.

The legal experts' opinions and reports represent investigations into the measures, taken or ignored, to counter the pandemic, that were carried out by members of the government and its agents which somehow created or increased risks that are legally impermissible. The CPI Report asserts that the government structure, with specialised bodies and required scientific expertise, facilitates and demands the calculation of risk.[31] It also underscores that the legislation arising from the pandemic directly requires risk calculation (article 5 of Law 14.124/21) and concludes that the Federal government created a situation of impermissible risk, reprehensible by any cost-benefit calculation, exposing lives to concrete danger while not taking effective measures to minimise the results produced.

---

[30] Constitution, art 196 ('Health is a right of all and a duty of the State and shall be guaranteed by means of social and economic policies aimed at reducing the risk of illness and other hazards and at the universal and equal access to actions and services for its promotion, protection and recovery'), art 197 ('Health actions and services are of public importance, and it is incumbent upon the Government to provide, in accordance with the law, for their regulation, supervision and control, and they shall be carried out directly or by third parties and also by individuals or private legal entities').

[31] CPI Report (n 2) 1031.

C. Impact of Immunities

The CPI Report cites and then dismisses a legal opinion from prominent legal scholars in Brazil who attempt to exempt the President from any criminal responsibility related to common crimes, crimes of responsibility, and crimes against humanity.[32] Those scholars focus on two issues. First, the Supreme Court decided that States and Municipalities are directly in charge of the fight against the pandemic. Second, the much criticised and controversial manifestations of the President are protected by the constitutional principle of freedom of expression.

Article 23, II of the Constitution establishes joint responsibility of *all the entities* within the Federation for health and public assistance. Further, the CPI Report counter-argues that the manifestations of the President were not merely opinions without consequences, but represent an institutional decision to follow an illegal path favouring the widespread contamination of the population to achieve herd immunity at the lowest possible cost. Moreover, that decision was planned and caused many deaths of people whose lives he had the legal duty to protect. Moreover, unlike ordinary citizens, he cannot repeatedly externalise frivolous opinions without factual or scientific grounds that, through the media, reach large audiences – as the constitutional leader of the country, his opinions influence the conduct of many people. The report concludes:

> The President's 'opinion' is fruit of a complex decision-making process involving a parallel cabinet to the Ministry of Health and a public policy that, embracing all the items of the negationist agenda, without the support of the WHO and the scientific community, aggravated the result of the pandemic.[33]

D. Prosecutorial Matters

Brazil's National Congress can create Parliamentary Commissions of Inquiry (or 'CPI' in Portuguese) – committees created for a determined period and with the formal aim to investigate authorities' conduct. The 'Pandemic Parliamentary Inquiry Commission' was formed in April 2021 to investigate the conduct and responses of the President and other high-level agents of the Federal government concerning the COVID-19 pandemic. Its creation faced strong resistance from the Federal government and its supporters in the Congress, but opposition lawmakers requested the Supreme Court to create the Commission. One of the judges of the Court then ordered the Federal Senate's President to install that Commission of Inquiry.

The Pandemic Inquiry Commission exercised its extensive investigative powers and increased its relevance and visibility throughout 2021. CPIs hold investigative powers like those of judicial authorities, including to summon and interrogate witnesses and suspects. They do not, however, have the power to criminally charge those suspects based on the results of their investigations. The formation and competences of such Commissions are broadly defined in paragraph 3 of article 58 of the Constitution. Their conclusions may

[32] ibid.
[33] ibid, 1032–33.

be forwarded to the Public Prosecution Office to determine the civil or criminal liability of the offenders.

The Commission's work revealed several instances of government omission, irregularities and corruption. It provoked reactions towards the government, highlighted the importance of Brazil's public and universal health system and evaluated the government's performance of its constitutional duties. In November 2021, the Commission released its final report, with serious accusations towards government authorities and agents, alongside individuals and companies who played a role in how the pandemic developed in Brazil.

Both the CPI Report and OAB Opinion underscore the role of the General-Procurator of the Republic, who is the head of the Federal Public Prosecutors Office (or Procuratorate) and represent the Public Prosecutors at the Federal Supreme Court, which is the highest Constitutional Court, and at the Superior Court of Justice, which is the highest Court regarding non-constitutional law matters. He also receives *notitiae criminis* against high-level government agents. The OAB Opinion contains strong language concerning the view that he did not appropriately perform his duties, asserting his 'patent immobility even after numerous criminal representations have been offered regarding the very serious facts narrated'.[34]

The Supreme Court is the judicial organ acting as a court of first instance to rule on the charges involving the President and other high-level authorities. Article 102 of the Constitution states that the Court's role is to safeguard the Constitution, and provides for its competence to institute legal proceedings and to try common criminal offences in the first instance, allegedly commit by the following authorities: the President and Vice-President; the members of the National Congress; the Court's own judges; and the Attorney-General of the Republic. In addition, it has the competence to institute legal proceedings and to try, in the first instance, common criminal offences and crimes of malversation allegedly committed by the Ministers of State and the Commanders of the Navy, the Army and the Air Force, among others. Another high federal court, The Superior Court of Justice, has competence to rule on criminal charges involving other high-level authorities. Article 105 of the Constitution provides its competence to institute legal proceedings and to try, in the first instance, common crimes allegedly committed by the Governors of the states and of the Federal District, among others.

Further, the Federal Public Prosecutor's Office is competent to act in the first instance of Federal Justice, in accordance with the Constitution's article 109. With regard to the context of this chapter, federal judges have competence to rule on cases regarding human rights violations. The CPI Report alone has attributed legal responsibility to almost 80 individuals in relation to several crimes urging – among others – the General-Procurator of the Republic, the Federal Public Prosecutor's Office, Public Prosecutors' Offices at the State level, the Federal Public Defender's Office, the General Counsel of the Federal Senate, the Procuratorate of the Republic in the Federal District, the Federal Police and Secretaries for Police at the State Level to charge or further investigate those individuals and their activities related to the pandemic.

---

[34] OAB Opinion (n 7) 23.

Both the CPI report and OAB Opinion (inter alia) asserted the competence of the Prosecutor of the International Criminal Court in relation to crimes against humanity, due to the inertia of Brazilian authorities to act.[35] Both documents underscore that as a result of that inertia, due to unwillingness or inability to conduct criminal investigations the International Criminal Court enjoys jurisdiction to act in accordance with article 17, a and b, of the Rome Statute.[36]

III. CAUSATION

A. Causation (General Principles)

Brazil's law categorises conduct as crime both regarding actions and omissions. In the latter case, there is a generic duty of protection. Besides these two types of conduct, the law also prescribes another, under the category of 'relevant criminal omission', as provided in article 13, paragraph 2, of the Penal Code:[37]

> Article 13. The result, on which the existence of the crime depends, is only attributable to the person who caused it. Cause is the action or omission without which the result would not have occurred.
>
> §2 – The omission is criminally relevant when the person who omits should and could act to avoid the result. The duty to act is the responsibility of the person who: a) has by law an obligation of care, protection or surveillance; b) otherwise, assumed the responsibility for preventing the result; c) with their previous behaviour, created the risk of the result occurring.

In cases where the law specifies an action and it is not performed by the individual, even though they could and should act to avoid the result, there is a special duty of protection. The person occupies, thus, the position of 'guarantor' because they have the legal obligation of care, protection, or surveillance; they have assumed the responsibility for preventing the outcome; or they have created the risk of the outcome occurring.

As demonstrated in Section II above, the Constitution and ordinary law contain provisions on the legal duties that must be observed by the President of the Republic and other authorities. To support its conclusions against the President and other agents, the OAB Opinion[38] states that the Brazilian Penal Code adopts the formal legal duty theory, explaining it as the duty to act to avoid the result, and that it derives exclusively from the law, from the assumption of responsibility (or liability) and from dangerous precedent conduct, which constitute the formal sources of the guarantor's position as such. It contends that, 'The president not only failed to comply with his duty to ensure public health, but he also systematically tried to prevent adequate measures to combat Covid-19 being taken'.[39]

---

[35] See also ch 16, 'COVID-19 and Crimes Against Humanity'.

[36] CPI Report (n 2); OAB Opinion (n 7) 22–23; Rome Statute of the International Criminal Court, art 17. See also ch 16, 'COVID-19 and Crimes Against Humanity'.

[37] Decree no 2.848, 7 December 1940 (Brasil, Presidência da República, Casa Civil, Subchefia para Assuntos Jurídicos, Código Penal), www.planalto.gov.br/ccivil_03/decreto-lei/del2848compilado.htm.

[38] OAB Opinion (n 7) 2.

[39] ibid.

Among the arguments to support the view of the President's criminal omission (*i.e.*, a non-action or negation of a particular act that was required and expected), the OAB Opinion cites an estimate by scientist Pedro Hallal, published in *The Lancet* in March 2021, according to which around 180,000 people died as a direct consequence of the Federal government's omission at a point at which Brazil recorded 262,000 deaths.[40]

To sustain that the President also has liability via commission, the Opinion states:

> [T]he attack of the President of the Republic on this fundamental social right took place in a double dimension: not only by no longer caring for public health, but also by creating a series of embarrassments and obstacles to its realization.[41]

The Opinion then offers examples of conduct, which took place when the President vetoed legal initiatives passed by the Parliament aimed at fighting the pandemic and by filing lawsuits before the Supreme Court alleging the unconstitutionality of actions by state Governors to fight the pandemic:

> On 07.02.2020, the President of the Republic vetoed twenty-five provisions of Law 14.019/20, regarding the mandatory use of masks in commercial and industrial establishments, religious temples, schools and other closed places where there can be agglomeration. And more recently, through ADI 6764/DF [a lawsuit aimed at forcing the Supreme Court to exercise its power of judicial review based on alleged violations of the Constitution], tried to prevent Governors from complying with their duty to enact restrictive measures necessary to coping with the new coronavirus pandemic (SARS-CoV2).[42]

Brazilian law follows the theory of *conditio sine qua non* (*i.e.*, a theory of equivalence of antecedents or conditions). In principle, everything that contributes to the result, be it condition or a contributing cause, is cause. Hence, to find out if a given fact is a cause of a given result, it is enough to mentally suppress it from the causal line. If one realises that the result would not have occurred, that fact is to be considered the cause. The analysis of culpability, in which intent or fault is considered, is used to limit an apparent infinite causal chain. Regarding the role of intent and fault considerations, article 18 of the Penal Code states that crimes are wilful (with intent or intentional) when the agent wanted the result or assumed the risk of producing it and, on the other hand, provides for crimes by fault, when the agent caused the result by imprudence, negligence or malpractice.

Starting with fault, the provision addresses cases in which an agent may have criminal liability despite a purpose that might be lawful, if they do not undertake what is called an objective duty of care, or because of a behaviour driven by recklessness, negligence or malpractice, causing a harmful outcome, which was predictable (but not accepted) and that could have been avoided.

Regarding wilful crime or crimes with intention: the provision connects the volitional (will) and intellectual elements (conscience or knowledge) directed to the criminal behaviour. Brazil's Penal Code embraces the theories of will and assent to the intent. The first reflects the effective intention of the agent to commit the crime, as typified by the

---

[40] ibid, 14.
[41] ibid, 19.
[42] ibid.

legislation. This is called a direct intent (*dolo direto*). The second addresses the situations in which the agent foresees the result provided for in the penal type, even if not wishing to do so, and proceeds with the conduct, therefore assuming the risk of producing it. In such cases, agents commit crimes with the so-called 'indirect intent' (*dolo eventual*). The CPI Report[43] explores those two facets of intention within Brazilian doctrine, underscoring the discussion about volitive and cognitive approaches. It states that the Penal Code adopts the consent theory, which interprets 'wanting the result' in both a psychological sense (*i.e.*, desiring, accepting, approving, consenting), or in a normative sense ('wanting' in the sense of not being able to claim to be exempt from responsibility).[44] It sustains that the intention is in the degree of knowledge of the risk and that the competent authority to decide the legal meaning of danger is not the agent, but the law. Most importantly and to frame the conduct of the President not merely as negligent, it affirms that:

> [T]he imputation by way of intention then becomes legitimate when the agent's behaviour to avoid the result was so weak that not even the high probability of the result could assert itself to pull him out of inertia or deflect him from his plan of action.[45]

Regarding the argument about the relevance of the law in establishing the risk or danger of the result that it wishes to avoid, the provisions of Law 1.079/50 become an important source of legal duties, as it defines the crimes of responsibility of the President. These are criminal conducts against the Federal Constitution, and especially against the exercise of political, individual and social rights (article 4, item 3). More specifically, the Law's article 7, item 9, defines as a crime of responsibility conduct against the free exercise of political, individual, and social rights that 'patently violate any individual right or guarantee … as well as social rights'. The right to health is included in the Constitution (chapter about Social Rights, title II about Fundamental Rights and Guarantees) of the Constitution. Indeed, article 6 expressly mentions health among other social rights (education, food, work, housing, transport, leisure, security, social security, maternity and childhood protection and assistance to the destitute). Moreover, article 23, item II, of the Constitution is the source of the President's duty to ensure public health.[46] Since the President represents the 'Union' and exercises the Federal Executive Power within the Federation, he has both the duty to ensure public health, through the implementation of social and economic policies, and the duty to avoid situations that can endanger the lives and physical integrity of individuals.

The OAB Opinion concludes that the President violated those constitutional duties and, as a result, 'blatantly defiled' that fundamental social right to health.[47] As evidence of the importance that the Constitution attributes to public health and to the duty of the Federal government to safeguard it, the Opinion evokes the Constitution's article 34:

> The Union shall not intervene in the states or in the Federal District, except … VII – to ensure compliance with the following constitutional principles: … e) the application of the minimum

---

[43] CPI Report (n 2) 1028 ff.
[44] ibid, 1029.
[45] ibid, 1030.
[46] See s II above.
[47] OAB Opinion (n 7) 17.

required amount of the revenues resulting from state taxes, including revenues originating from transfers to the maintenance and development of education and to health actions and public services.[48]

Hence, the Opinion sustains a 'systematic and deliberate violation' of the duties of the President and his Health Minister first for the lack of implementation and, second, for not timeously implementing the social and economic policies that could have reduced the progressive risks of the coronavirus.[49] It supports its conclusion by evoking three important examples that became well-known to the public.

The first, 'one of the most eloquent examples of the omission of President of the Republic', concerns the government's lack of interest towards the vaccine produced by the pharmaceutical company Pfizer.[50] It was found that Pfizer had offered the vaccine to the President, the Vice-President and three State Ministers, more than once, and that it received no answer whatsoever. The lack of reply led the company to try to negotiate directly with State Governors. Invoking transcripts from a letter from the CEO of Pfizer to those authorities, the Opinion concludes that the national authorities, including the President, were fully aware of the very serious consequences that the delay in immunisation could generate, having, therefore, at best, assumed the risk of producing a very high number of deaths and personal injuries.[51]

The Opinion's second example of criminal omission by the President and other government agents refers to the situation involving another vaccine, the CoronaVac, developed by Sinovac Biotech, a Chinese pharmaceutical company. In October 2020, Eduardo Pazuello, then Minister of Health, communicated with a renowned research and drug producer institute located in the State of São Paulo, the Butantan Institute, expressing the Federal government's intention to purchase the CoronaVac vaccine. The Institute was far ahead of the Ministry of Health and, by the order of the Governor of São Paulo, had already entered agreements with Sinovac to first purchase and then locally produce CoronaVac. The purchase of 46 million doses of that vaccine had already been announced.

One day after the announcement, however, the President of the Republic disavowed his own Minister and suspended that purchase. The President announced through a social network that, 'The Brazilian people will not be anyone's guinea pig. … My decision is not to purchase the aforementioned vaccine'.[52] On the same day, the executive secretary of the Ministry of Health publicly stated 'there is no intention to purchase the vaccine' and the President himself publicly confirmed his decision not to buy the vaccine claiming the numbers showed that the pandemic was fading. At the time, the pandemic had already claimed about 154,000 lives, and there was a daily average of almost 700 deaths.[53] In 2021, the Director of Butantan Institute revealed that he had offered the vaccines to the Health Ministry since July 2020, but the offers were refused. Had the offers been accepted, the vaccines could have been delivered by November 2020.

---

[48] ibid.
[49] ibid, 3.
[50] ibid.
[51] ibid, 7.
[52] ibid, 8.
[53] ibid.

The OAB Opinion contends that the two examples – related to the acquisition of Pfizer and CoronaVac vaccines – illustrate deliberate omissions to delay the immunisation of the population, with tragic consequences. The Opinion advances a third example, which goes beyond the mere omission of legally required acts. It refers to the resistance of the President to operationalise measures, prescribed in Law 13.979/20, to address public health emergencies, which include medical tests, restriction of movement and commercial activities. Those measures foreseen in the law were aimed to prevent the spread of the COVID-19 in line with epidemic experts and sanitary authorities, both national and international, and to preserve lives and the physical integrity of people. The OAB Opinion states that the President filed a lawsuit before the Supreme Court (ADI 6.764/DF), in which he challenged the constitutionality of those measures, to try to prevent Governors from fulfilling their duty to order restrictive measures that were then needed. This attempt, further, ignored that Court's previous decision (in ADI 6,341/DF) that the Union, the States, the Federal District and the Municipalities have concurrent competence to manage the current health crisis caused by COVID-19.[54] Moreover, 'had he fulfilled his constitutional duty, numerous deaths and bodily injuries caused by Covid-19 would have been avoided with "probability close to certainty"'.[55]

Criteria adopted by German and Italian doctrines and case law that are well known in Brazil were invoked to support the OAB Opinion's claim that crimes may be imputed to subjects in cases of omission or improper omissions when the damage would have been avoided through the required conduct with 'probability close to certainty'.[56] German case law starts from the consideration that an omission causes a result when this would have been avoided through the required action 'with probability close to certainty'. The same criterion is predominant in Italian case law in crimes committed by omission or improper omissions when the result can be imputed to a plaintiff when the performance of the due conduct would have probably been avoided. The performance of the proper conduct of the President and his team would have avoided the tragic results 'with a probability close to certainty'.[57]

The OAB Opinion concludes:

[T]he omissions and actions of the President of the Republic throughout the pandemic of the new coronavirus (SARS-CoV2) are perfectly subsumable to the type prescribed in Art. 7, item 9 of Law 1.079/50, representing a frontal attack to one of the nuclei of the Citizen Constitution, that is, the right to health and, ultimately, life itself.[58]

B. Causation and 'Thin Skull' Scenarios

The fact that part of the population – such as the elderly or people with chronic diseases – is particularly vulnerable to COVID-19 does not exclude the criminal liability of authorities. As discussed in the previous section, article 13 of the Penal Code states that

[54] ibid, 10.
[55] ibid.
[56] ibid, 11–13.
[57] ibid.
[58] ibid, 20.

'the action or omission without which the result would not have occurred is considered a cause'. This provision must be interpreted to include as a cause all actions that may in any way interfere with the causal course. This is argued by the CPI Report, which continues: 'the action or omission is considered the cause without which the result would not have happened, as it did', and concludes 'the agent that interferes in the causal course must also answer for the crime, even if, without his collaboration, the result was inevitable'.[59] Moreover, paragraph 1 of article 13 also illuminates the matter providing for the supervenience of independent causes (*actus novus interveniens*): 'The supervenience of a relatively independent cause excludes imputation when it produced the result by itself; the previous facts, however, are imputed to those who practiced them'.

Hence, even if many deaths or other harms occurred to people who were in some way vulnerable due to pre-existing conditions, or even if the cause of the pandemic was natural and, thus, would occur and impact the lives of populations worldwide, authorities may still be criminally charge if their actions or omissions interfered in some way in the propagation of the virus and the harmful results following. The CPI Report and OAB Opinion (inter alia) demonstrate how the delay in the purchase of vaccines, the lack of preventive campaigns, the emphasis on treatments without proven efficacy, the unnecessary and frivolous controversies concerning the use of masks and social distancing and isolation have all interfered in the causal course of the pandemic, causing it to have far worse results than those likely had the pandemic been managed differently.

C. Restricting Causality: Policy and Doctrinal Issues

These issues are covered in Sections III.A and III.B above.

IV. THE STRUCTURE OF HOMICIDE OFFENCES AND ASSAULT/AGGRAVATED ASSAULT/SERIOUS BODILY HARM OFFENCES

The OAB Opinion alleges several crimes were committed by the President and his officials. It divides and addresses those crimes in two parts: crimes at the national level and crimes at the international level. Among the first, there are (1) crimes of murder and bodily harm by indirect fault and (2) crimes of responsibility. At the international level, there is a crime against humanity (article 7 of the Rome Statute), subject to denunciation before the International Criminal Court.

The CPI Report goes further and identifies the following 21 crimes (here accompanied by the relevant articles of the Penal Code or other special laws).[60] They are:

1) Attempted murder (article 121 combined with article 14). The Report does not mention murder here, but only attempted murder. Immediately after the list of crimes, however, it starts by detailing the crime of murder; 2) Danger to the life or health of others (article 132). The report does not list the crime of bodily harm and its modalities (of a very serious nature, article 129,

---

[59] CPI Report (n 2) 1042.
[60] ibid, 996.

paragraph 2, and followed by death, article 129, paragraph 3); 3) Epidemic (article 267); 4) Violation of preventive sanitary measure (article 268); 5) Omission of notification of illness (article 269); 6) Quackery (*charlatanismo*) (article 283); 7) Incitement to crime (article 286); 8) Forgery of private documents (article 298); 9) Ideological falsehood (article 299); 10) Use of false documents (article 304), 11) Irregular use of public funds or revenue (article 315); 12) Passive corruption (article 317); 13) Malfeasance (*prevaricação*) (article 319); 14) Public administration lobbying (*advocacia administrativa*) (article 321); 15) Usurpation of public functions (article 328); 16) Influence peddling (article 332); 17) Active corruption (article 333); 18) Fraud in public bidding or contract (article 337-L); 19) Procedural fraud (article 347).

The crime against humanity was also identified (Decree 4,388/02, Rome Statute of the ICC, article 7, 1, k) as well as the crime of criminal organisation, as provided in Law 12,850/13, article 2.

This section offers a brief overview of the most important and relevant crimes imputed to Brazilian authorities in accordance with the sources used in this investigation.

A. Murder and Manslaughter (Culpable Homicide)[61]

In principle, homicide or murder is a crime of commission, but it can also be the result of omission in cases in which the agent is a guarantor but remains inert and with the will to achieve the resulting death. The crime can occur due to intention as well as fault.

It is possible to argue that relevant authorities have committed the crime of homicide when addressing the challenges of the pandemic. The OAB Opinion asserts that if the President had fulfilled his constitutional duty to protect public health, thousands of lives would have been saved and his improper omission amounts to the crime of homicide. Also, he is to answer for the bodily harm of people who would not have been affected if effective measures had been implemented.[62] Further, 'Even if it were not possible to scientifically prove that thousands of deaths and bodily injuries could have been avoided with "probability close to certainty", ... part of the modern doctrine considers sufficient, for purposes of imputation, that the performance of the due actions would at least have diminished the risk of producing such results'.[63]

Hence, for the attribution of the result, it is only necessary to evaluate whether those authorities had the possibility of acting differently. If they had such possibility and did not act upon it, they can be charged with homicide and other crimes. It is not necessary to prove that the performance of the action would have avoided thousands of deaths with probability close to certainty.[64] The President's indifference to the seriousness of the situation, coupled with the possibility of acting differently (guided by numerous recommendations by experts and daily alerts on the pandemic's development) supports the argument that he acted at best with possible or indirect intent (*dolo eventual*). As explained in Section III above, '*dolo eventual*' is a sort of indirect culpability in which the

---

[61] In Brazil's Penal Code, murder and what other jurisdictions call manslaughter are strongly connected and must be understood and considered in relation to one another.
[62] OAB Opinion (n 7) 15.
[63] ibid.
[64] ibid, 16.

agent can and foresees the unlawful result of his conduct and, even if they do not desire it, they assume the risk of producing it. The OAB Opinion cites Claus Roxin, whose ideas are very influential in Brazil, to state that 'indifference is a sure sign that the agent resigned himself to the result and, therefore, acted intentionally'.[65]

Article 121 of the Penal Code defines homicide (to kill someone) and provides for its different modalities and sanctions. Manslaughter occurs when the homicide is involuntary.

B. Offences Related to Actions that Cause Serious Bodily Harm (Assault; Grievous Assault; Assault with Intent to Cause Serious Bodily Harm)

This crime and its modalities are regulated in article 129 of the Penal Code, as follows. Offending the bodily integrity or health of others is the definition of 'bodily harm', which can become 'serious bodily harm' that is further divided into two categories related to the results produced. First, in case of inability to perform usual occupations for more than 30 days; a danger to life; a permanent weakness of a limb, sense or function; or birth acceleration, the penalty is imprisonment from one to five years. Second, in case of permanent incapacity to work; incurable disease, loss or destruction of the limb, sense or function; permanent deformity; or abortion, the penalty is imprisonment from two to eight years. In addition to these, there is the type of 'bodily injury followed by death', when 'death results and the circumstances show that the agent did not want the result, nor did he take the risk of producing it' (from four to 12 years); and the 'culpable bodily harm', when the injury is caused by fault (from two months to one year).

C. Danger to the Life or Health of Others

Article 132 of the Penal Code foresees this crime, which involves the conduct of putting the life or health of someone at direct, imminent and actual risk (or danger). The crime is said to take place regardless of the realisation of the risk created, by simply performing the act of exposure mentioned. The CPI Report states that a requirement here is that the potential victims must be a certain and determined person. The prescribed penalty is detention, from three months to one year, if the fact does not constitute a more serious crime.

D. Offences Regarding Unborn Foetuses; Interrupting the Course of a (Viable) Pregnancy

No officials in Brazil have been charged with such offence and no significant discussion, either academic, political or legal have been carried out to that effect.

---

[65] ibid.

E. Failure to Render Assistance

Other criminal charges have absorbed this issue and no officials in Brazil have been charged with such an offence.

F. Crime of Epidemic

This crime is prescribed in the Penal Code's chapter about 'Crimes Against Public Health'. Article 267 and article 13 of the Penal Code (prescribing criminally relevant omissions) are commonly connected to indict the President, some of his Ministers and other high-level officials by contending that their behaviour (both actions and omissions) caused an epidemic.[66] Article 267 prescribes the criminal conduct, which can occur either with intention or fault (*e.g.*, negligence):[67] 'To cause an epidemic, through the propagation of pathogenic germs'. The sanction is imprisonment, and it ranges from 10 to 15 years, unless death results (when the penalty applied is double). Also, in the case of fault, the penalty is detention, from one to two years, or, if death results, two to four years.

Moreover, in light of article 1, I, of the Law on Heinous Crimes – Law 8072/90 – the described acts are considered heinous crimes when they are practiced with intention and result in death.[68] The CPI Report concludes that the President 'acted with indirect intent [*dolo eventual*], insofar as he assumed the risk of the deaths of thousands of Brazilians by refusing or delaying the purchase of vaccines that were insistently offered' and, thus, he acted intentionally, 'either in relation to the typical conduct of an epidemic, or in relation to the result of death, which aggravates the crime of art. 267 of the Penal Code'.[69]

Throughout its pages, the CPI Report asserts that the President and other agents' behaviour altered and aggravated the course of events of the pandemic leading to the large dissemination of the virus, which is also a form of causation.

G. Crimes against Humanity[70]

Crimes against Humanity are provided for in the Rome Statute of the International Criminal Court (ICC), which has become domestic law in Brazil through Legislative Decree No. 112/2002 and Decree No. 4,388/2002. Article 7 of the Rome Statute prescribes what criminal conduct constitutes crimes against humanity, which are 'committed as part of a widespread or systematic attack directed against any civilian population, with knowledge of the attack'. Among the conduct more closely related to the accusations against Brazilian authorities, there are: murder, persecution against any identifiable group or collectivity on political, racial, national, ethnic, cultural or religious grounds,

---

[66] CPI Report (n 2) 1038.
[67] See s III.A above.
[68] CPI Report (n 2) 1000.
[69] ibid, 1041–42.
[70] See also ch 16, 'COVID-19 and Crimes Against Humanity'.

and other inhumane acts of a similar character intentionally causing great suffering, or serious injury to body or to mental or physical health.

The CPI Report underscores the role of the President as the ultimate authority, with the highest responsibility, for acts and omissions that harmed the entire population and specially the first nations (*i.e.*, native peoples) of Brazil with the aim of destroying that part of the country's population.[71] The Report accuses the President, some Ministers, and others in light of various modalities of crimes against humanity but it has taken a step back, however, from a common accusation of genocide against the President. Such accusations have not only become usual, with the President constantly being called a genocider,[72] but have also been formalised by one organisation of the indigenous movement of the country (The Articulation of Indigenous Peoples of Brazil). This organisation denounced the President in a filing to the ICC, for crimes against humanity (article 7, b, h and k, Rome Statute) and genocide (article 6, b and c of the Rome Statute) for causing severe physical and mental damage and deliberately inflicting conditions aimed at the destruction of indigenous peoples.[73]

That organisation's 86–page supporting document[74] presents a timeline of Bolsonaro's attacks against native or indigenous peoples (through administrative acts and norms, speeches, meetings and projects), describes the consequences of the destruction of public infrastructure to guarantee indigenous and socio-environmental rights (including the impact of the COVID-19 pandemic on indigenous peoples), and offers an account about the invasions, deforestation and mining in indigenous lands as well as on the dissemination of the COVID-19 pandemic among indigenous peoples.

V. DEFENCES, JUSTIFICATIONS AND EXCUSES

In the case of Brazil's Federal authorities acting in line with the President's statements, justifications were constantly changing and were not legally grounded. The OAB Opinion concludes: 'Through systematic actions and omissions, the Bolsonaro government ended up having the pandemic under its control, under its dominion, using it deliberately as an instrument of attack (biological weapon) and submission of the entire population'.[75] All sources used demonstrate that high-level Federal government authorities and allies used the pandemic to gain political legitimacy through the creation of controversies not backed by scientific data while infringing their constitutional duty to public health: 'the President not only did not fulfil his duty to take care of public health, but also systematically tried to prevent appropriate measures to combat Covid-19'.[76]

[71] CPI Report (n 2) 1101–08.

[72] T Phillips, 'Bolsonaro's "genocidal" Covid response has led to Brazilian catastrophe, Dilma Rousseff says' *The Guardian* (online, 10 April 2021), www.theguardian.com/world/2021/apr/10/brazil-bolsonaro-dilma-rousseff-coronavirus-crisis.

[73] 'Unprecedented: APIB denounces Bolsonaro before the ICC, in The Hague, for indigenous genocide' (*The Articulation of Indigenous Peoples from Brazil*, 9 August 2021), https://apiboficial.org/2021/08/09/unprecedented-apib-denounces-bolsonaro-before-the-icc-in-the-hague-for-indigenous-genocide/?lang=en.

[74] ibid.

[75] OAB Opinion (n 7) 22.

[76] ibid, 21.

In excerpts from the CPI Report, there is an attempt to entertain defences that could serve in favour of the authorities' decisions. They do not stand, though, as seen in the case of the continuous encouragement by the President for doctors and population to adopt drugs not only ineffective but also that harmed people. Chloroquine was among those drugs. The Report sustains that the use of chloroquine for COVID-19 was not endorsed by the National Agency in charge of regulating the use of drugs (ANVISA) and the order to produce the drug was illegal and led to the President and the Minister of Health's conduct falling under article 315 of the Penal Code, which criminalises irregular use of public money.[77] However, the Report also admits that at the pandemic's early stage, a possible legal excuse would likely exist, as the authorities could claim to be in search for a cure and this would overlap with compliance with the regulations related to the use of public resources. Again, the Report dismisses such hypothetical and acceptable legal excuses by stating that: 'It turns out that this was not an isolated act though. Even after demonstrated that chloroquine was ineffective in the fight against Covid-19, the President of the Republic and the then Minister of Health, Eduardo Pazuello continued to use public resources in the production and purchase of the said medicine'.[78]

VI. CORPORATE CRIMINAL LIABILITY

A. Overview of Corporate Criminal Liability

As a rule, Brazilian law does not provide for the criminal liability of legal entities. Under the current Brazilian legal system, legal entities are criminally liable only for environmental crimes as seen in article 225, paragraph 3, of the Constitution: 'Procedures and activities considered as harmful to the environment shall subject the offenders, be they individuals or legal entities, to penal and administrative sanctions, without prejudice to the obligation to repair the damages caused'. The Constitution's article 173, paragraph 5, is another provision that, in theory, could support the criminal liability of companies:

> The law shall, without prejudice to the individual liability of the managing officers of a legal entity, establish the liability of the latter, subjecting it to punishments compatible with its nature, for acts performed against the economic and financial order and against the citizens' monies.

This provision remains unregulated, however. Hence, there is no possibility for companies to be criminally charged for crimes against life, public health and so forth. Despite clearly underscoring many illegalities committed by companies' legal representatives, and for the profit and benefit of companies, the CPI Report only attributes criminal liability to individuals (*i.e.* owners, administrators and staff) and not to the corporate entities themselves.

---

[77] CPI Report (n 2) 1074.
[78] ibid.

VII. FORMS OF PARTICIPATION

As a general rule on forms of participation, article 29 of the Penal Code provides:

> Whoever, in any way, contributes to the crime is subject to the penalties assigned to it, in the measure of its culpability. The potential sanctions may vary, as follows: If the participation is of minor importance, the penalty may be reduced from one sixth to one third; ... If any of the competitors wanted to participate in a less serious crime, the penalty for this will be applied; this penalty will be increased by up to half, in the event that the most serious outcome was foreseeable.

Article 76 of the Federal Constitution provides that 'the Executive Power is exercised by the President of the Republic, aided by the Ministers of State'. This provision attaches accountability to the President's Ministers, and, in fact, most potential indictments raised in the sources go beyond the President himself. Eventual criminal liability of Ministers cannot be excluded with the justification that they were merely following orders.

Further, several authorities' public conduct, or their conduct directed to the general public, have been seen as inciting crimes. Article 287 of the Penal Code provides for the crime of apology of crime or criminal (*apologia*): 'To publicly make an apology for a criminal fact or the author of a crime: Penalty – detention, from three to six months, or fine'.

In committing several of the crimes listed in this investigation, authorities and others have collaborated with each other, leading to the application of article 288 of the Penal Code, about criminal association, when three or more people act together for the specific purpose of committing crimes. Law 12,850/13 defines and regulates cases of criminal organisation. Article 1, paragraph 1 offers an initial definition:

> A criminal organization is considered to be the association of 4 (four) or more people structurally organized and characterized by the division of tasks, even if informally, with the objective of obtaining, directly or indirectly, an advantage of any nature, through the practice of criminal offenses whose maximum sentences exceed 4 (four) years, or which are transnational in nature.

Article 2 deals with 'Promoting, constituting, financing or integrating, personally or through an intermediary, a criminal organization'. The penalties are imprisonment, from three to eight years, and fine, without prejudice to the penalties corresponding to other criminal offences committed.

VIII. ATTEMPT

The rule concerning the attempt of crimes is found in article 14, II, of the Penal Code: 'the crime is said: attempted, when, initiated the execution is not consummated by circumstances beyond the agent's will'. The general rule is provided in the sole paragraph of the same article, which provides that the attempt is punishable with the penalty corresponding to the consummated crime, reduced by one- to two-thirds.

With regard to the crimes of responsibility, committed by high-level authorities and regulated by Law 1.079/50,[79] articles 2 and 3 provide that even when simply attempted, the

---

[79] See s II.A above.

authorities are subject to relevant sanctions (*e.g.*, penalty of loss of office, disqualification from exercising any public function). Further, article 3 provides that: 'The imposition of the penalty referred to in the previous article does not exclude the process and trial of the accused for a common crime, in ordinary justice, under the terms of the criminal procedure laws'.

IX. SANCTIONS, SENTENCING, PUNISHMENT, REPARATIONS AND/OR RESTORATIVE JUSTICE

A. General Sentencing Framework for the Crimes under Discussion

Most of the sentencing-related issues of the crimes here discussed have been addressed in the previous sections. The so-called 'crimes of responsibility' foreseen in Law 1.079/50 contain specific sanctions that are arguably more political than criminal. Article 2 of the Law mentions the penalty of loss of office, with disqualification, for up to five years, to exercise any public function, imposed by the Federal Senate in proceedings against the President of the Republic or Ministers of State, among other authorities.

B. Sanctions Specifically for Senior Government/Public Officials

In some of the crimes, the penalty is aggravated if the agent is a public servant. Illustrative of this are the crimes related to criminal organisations (Law 12.850/13) in which the participation of such a servant benefits the commission of crimes by the organisation. In this case, the penalty is increased by one-sixth to two-thirds (article 2, paragraph 4, II). Moreover, paragraphs 5 and 6 address the specific sanctions to public servants:

§ 5 If there are sufficient indications that the public official is part of a criminal organization, the judge may determine his precautionary removal from the position, job or function, without prejudice to remuneration, when the measure is necessary for the investigation or procedural instruction.

§ 6 The conviction with final and unappealable result will result in the public official losing his or her position, function, job or elective mandate and being prohibited from exercising a public function or position for a period of eight (8) years following the completion of the sentence.

4

England

NATALIE WORTLEY AND BIRJU KOTECHA

I. BACKGROUND AND CONTEXTUAL INTRODUCTION

UNDER THE UK's constitutional framework, the UK Parliament (Westminster) exercises control over the criminal justice system in England and Wales, whereas legislative authority and oversight of the criminal justice systems of Scotland and Northern Ireland is devolved to the Scottish Parliament and the Northern Ireland Assembly, respectively. Healthcare is also a devolved responsibility and measures implemented in Scotland, Northern Ireland and Wales diverged from those in England throughout the Covid-19 pandemic. This chapter discusses the criminal law of England and Wales but focusses on potential liability arising from decisions affecting England. Readers should therefore be alert to the context in which the terms 'the UK' and 'England and Wales' are used.

By the time the first UK case of Covid-19 was reported on 30 January 2020, the Government's Scientific Advisory Group for Emergencies (SAGE) had advised that Covid-19 was 'now being sustained by human-to-human transmission'.[1] Richard Horton, editor of medical journal *The Lancet*, argues that at this point there was 'a duty to immediately put the NHS and British public on high alert'.[2] Instead, the UK's four Chief Medical Officers recommended increasing the UK risk level to 'moderate', adding that although it was likely there would be 'individual cases', the National Health Service (NHS) could 'manage these in a way that protects the public and provides high quality care'.[3]

On 3 February, the Scientific Pandemic Influenza Group on Modelling (SPI-M) expressed concerns that outbreaks might not be capable of containment by isolation and contact-tracing alone.[4] Later that month, SAGE concluded that four non-pharmaceutical interventions – university and school closures, home isolation, household quarantine and social distancing – could 'slow but not halt' the spread of the virus and would 'require

---

[1] SAGE, 'SAGE 2 minutes: Coronavirus (COVID-19) Response' (28 January 2020), www.gov.uk/government/publications/sage-minutes-coronavirus-covid-19-response-28-january-2020.

[2] R Horton, 'COVID-19 and the NHS – "a National Scandal"' (2020) *The Lancet* 1022.

[3] Department of Health and Social Care, 'Statement from the 4 UK Chief Medical Officers on novel coronavirus' (30 January 2020), www.gov.uk/government/news/statement-from-the-four-uk-chief-medical-officers-on-novel-coronavirus.

[4] SPI-M, Operational Sub-group, 'Consensus Statement on 2019 Novel Coronavirus' (SPI-M-O, 3 February 2020).

implementation for a significant duration in order to be effective'.[5] On 3 March, UK Prime Minister Boris Johnson launched an 'action plan' including phased actions to contain, delay and mitigate any outbreak.[6] The contain phase, initiated that day, was supposed to detect early cases and follow up close contacts to 'prevent the disease taking hold in this country for as long as reasonably possible.'[7] The plan anticipated that the majority of those displaying symptoms would have 'mild-to-moderate, but self-limiting illness – similar to seasonal flu'.[8] Concerns over the likening of Covid-19 to seasonal flu were amplified in the coming weeks by comments suggesting that the government might 'allow the virus to move through the population' in pursuance of a 'herd immunity' strategy.[9]

On 16 March, Imperial College London published a report suggesting the Government's 'mitigation strategy' was unworkable and, even if all patients were treated, there would be around 250,000 deaths in the UK.[10] It appears that government officials had been aware of these figures from 3 March. Although the Prime Minister accepted (on 14 March) that a lockdown was necessary, the first national lockdown was not announced until 23 March,[11] accompanied by regulations and guidance imposing severe restrictions on freedom of movement and association.[12] The Government, particularly the Prime Minister, received trenchant criticism regarding both the time taken to formulate policy to tackle Covid-19 risks and the initial decision to pursue a contain and delay strategy despite projected death tolls.[13] Retrospective modelling has suggested that 14,000 people in the UK were infected on 14 March, rising to 1.5 million by 23 March.[14]

Easing of lockdown rules commenced in mid-May and most remaining restrictions were lifted on 4 July 2020. A series of 'local lockdowns' followed in an effort to control spikes in infection numbers. Further national restrictions were announced in September 2020, including the 'rule of six',[15] followed by a return to working from home. In October, the Prime Minister announced a three-tier system of local restrictions, which failed to contain the spread of the virus.

---

[5] SAGE, 'Tenth SAGE meeting on Wuhan Coronvirus (Covid-19)' (25 February 2020), www.gov.uk/government/publications/sage-minutes-coronavirus-covid-19-response-25-february-2020.

[6] Department of Health and Social Care, 'Coronavirus Action Plan: A Guide to What You Can Expect Across the UK' (3 March 2020), www.gov.uk/government/publications/coronavirus-action-plan/coronavirus-action-plan-a-guide-to-what-you-can-expect-across-the-uk.

[7] ibid.

[8] ibid.

[9] 'Boris Johnson on Priti Patel, Coronavirus and Changing Nappies' *This Morning* (5 March 2020), www.youtube.com/watch?v=vOHiaPwtGl4. Herd immunity is the point at which a population is protected either by vaccine or after natural infection (and no vaccines were available at this time). See also A Forrest, 'Coronavirus: Internal Emails Reveal Herd Immunity Messaging Chaos in Government' *The Independent* (London, 23 September 2020).

[10] NM Ferguson et al, 'Report 9: Impact of Non-pharmaceutical Interventions (NPIs) to Reduce COVID-19 Mortality and Healthcare Demand' (Imperial College London, 16 March 2020), www.imperial.ac.uk/mrc-global-infectious-disease-analysis/covid-19/report-9-impact-of-npis-on-covid-19/.

[11] Prime Minister's Office, 'Prime Minister's Statement on Coronavirus (COVID-19)' (23 March 2020), www.gov.uk/government/speeches/pm-address-to-the-nation-on-coronavirus-23-march-2020.

[12] Baroness Hale of Richmond, 'The Pandemic and the Constitution' in J Brennan et al (eds), *Essays from the Pandemic* (London, LAG, 2020) 4.

[13] ibid 16.

[14] J Calvert et al, '22 Days of Dither and Delay on Coronavirus that Cost Thousands of British Lives' *The Times* (London, 23 May 2020).

[15] Cabinet Office, 'Coronavirus (COVID-19): What has Changed?' (9 September 2020), www.gov.uk/government/news/coronavirus-covid-19-what-has-changed-9-september.

A second national lockdown commenced on 5 November, under which the rules were slightly more lenient, allowing people to meet outdoors with one other person from outside their 'support bubble'. December 2020 saw the reintroduction of local tiers. A fourth tier entailing similar restrictions to the second national lockdown failed to prevent the spread of new variants. Schools reopened in England in January 2021 but, after just one day, the country was placed under a third national lockdown, with the UK death toll crossing 100,000 on 13 January 2021.[16]

A phased exit from lockdown from 8 March 2021 followed a 'roadmap' designed to 'gradually and safely' ease restrictions and reopen the economy.[17] The UK's vaccination programme, which commenced on 8 December 2020 and was widely regarded as successful, enabled the lifting of most remaining Covid-19 restrictions on 19 July 2021. However, concerns were raised that 'exponential growth will probably continue until millions more people are infected, leaving hundreds of thousands of people with long-term illness and disability'.[18] As of 10 September 2021, the UK had recorded a total of 7,165,200 confirmed cases of Covid-19 and 134,166 deaths, with 270,285 new cases and 922 deaths in the preceding week.[19]

It has been alleged that lack of preparedness and shortages of personal protective equipment (PPE) contributed to the death toll. At an early stage, frontline NHS staff pleaded with the Prime Minister to intervene to ensure they had adequate PPE.[20] The Government has also faced criticism of its approach to 'test and trace' and procurement decisions.[21] And in addition to criticisms of incumbent officials, it has been argued that previous administrations should bear their share of the blame for systemic failings. Following cuts to funding for pandemic planning, Public Health England (PHE) declared in 2016 that 'the UK's preparedness and response, in terms of its plans, policies and capability, is currently not sufficient to cope with the extreme demands of a severe pandemic'.[22] A recent report concluded that the Government had failed to learn key lessons from PHE's testing of the likely response to a serious influenza outbreak, particularly as regards social care capacity.[23] Holding past and present governments to account is complicated, however, by the UK's constitutional framework.

---

[16] C Barr et al, 'UK Coronavirus Deaths Pass 100,000 after 1,564 Reported in One Day' *The Guardian* (London, 13 January 2021).

[17] Cabinet Office, 'COVID-19 Response – Spring 2021 (Roadmap)' (22 February 2021), www.gov.uk/government/publications/covid-19-response-spring-2021/covid-19-response-spring-2021.

[18] D Gurdasani et al, 'Mass Infection is not an Option: We Must do More to Protect our Young' (2021) 398 *The Lancet* 297.

[19] Johns Hopkins University & Medicine: Coronavirus Resource Centre, 'United Kingdom: Overview', coronavirus.jhu.edu/region/united-kingdom.

[20] R Parmar et al, 'Coronavirus Letter to the Editor: Without Protection, NHS Staff are Cannon Fodder' *The Sunday Times* (London, 22 March 2020); see also UK Parliament, 'Question for Department of Health and Social Care' (13 July 2021), questions-statements.parliament.uk/written-questions/detail/2021-06-29/24136/#.

[21] National Audit Office, 'Investigation into Government Procurement During the COVID-19 Pandemic' (HC 959, 26 November 2020), www.nao.org.uk/report/government-procurement-during-the-covid-19-pandemic/; House of Commons Public Accounts Committee, 'COVID-19: Test, Track and Trace (Part 1)' (HC 932, 10 March 2021), https://committees.parliament.uk/publications/4976/documents/50058/default/.

[22] Public Health England, 'Exercise Cygnus Report: Tier One Command Post Exercise – Pandemic Influenza – 18 to 20 October 2016' (13 July 2017), https://assets.publishing.service.gov.uk/government/uploads/system/uploads/attachment_data/file/927770/exercise-cygnus-report.pdf.

[23] N Davies et al, 'How Fit were Public Services for Coronavirus?' (Institute for Government and The Chartered Institute of Public Finance and Accounting, August 2020), www.instituteforgovernment.org.uk/sites/default/files/publications/how-fit-public-services-coronavirus.pdf.

II. CONSTITUTIONAL, LEGAL AND POLICY OVERVIEW

Under the United Kingdom's uncodified Constitution, the activities of the three branches of State – the executive, legislature and judiciary – are shaped by a combination of legislation, convention and historical principles.[24] Executive power is concentrated in the hands of the UK's Central Government, which is responsible for the proposal of policy and the day-to-day administration of collective services in England, such as education, social welfare and, of course, responses to public health crises.[25]

Westminster holds the executive to account by way of debates, ministerial questions and, in particular, 'Select Committees', which can direct ministers to give oral evidence and issue recommendations.[26] Parliament also exercises supervisory control by authorising the executive's enforcement of law. And yet, the executive sits in Parliament and represents the governing political party with the majority of seats in the House of Commons. Hence, by convention, the executive can enact laws in Parliament when it can be assured, as is often the case, that the governing party will vote as instructed by the Cabinet.[27]

Outside Parliament, the judiciary can review the legality of executive policies and decisions based on principles of administrative law and under the Human Rights Act 1998. During the pandemic several unsuccessful judicial review proceedings sought to challenge the validity of lockdown.[28] Even where a challenge is successful, the judiciary is unable to declare domestic legislation 'unconstitutional', unlike in the United States.[29] In recent times, this has not inured the UK Supreme Court from allegations that it has exceeded its jurisdiction by declaring unlawful 'political' activities which are properly within the exclusive domain of the sovereign and democratically elected Parliament.[30]

Returning to Covid-19 policy and the imposition of lockdown, the legal basis of the Prime Minister's instruction to 'stay at home' was secondary legislation in the form of regulations passed under the Public Health (Control of Disease) Act 1984 (the 1984 Act).[31] On 26 March 2020, the Secretary of State for Health and Social Care introduced those regulations which confirmed that, during the 'emergency period', business premises, as well as places of worship, were to close, public gatherings of more than two people were prohibited and, most notoriously, 'no person may leave the place where

---

[24] See J Jowell and D Oliver, *The Changing Constitution* 7th edn (Oxford, Oxford University Press, 2011).

[25] The Government is also responsible for all non-devolved matters across the UK such as national security and foreign affairs. See generally, R Rhodes, 'From Prime Ministerial Power to Core Executive' in R Rhodes and P Dunleavy (eds), *Prime Minister, Cabinet and Core Executive* (London, Palgrave Macmillan, 1995) 12.

[26] See, eg House of Commons Health and Social Care and Science and Technology Committees, 'Coronavirus: Lessons Learned to Date' (HC 92, 12 October 2021), https://committees.parliament.uk/publications/7496/documents/78687/default/.

[27] See generally A Le Seur, *The Nature, Powers and Accountability of Central Government* (Oxford, Oxford University Press, 2009).

[28] *R (Dolan) v Secretary of State for Health and Social Care* [2020] EWCA Civ 1605, [2021] 1 WLR 2326.

[29] See generally, J Jowell, 'Beyond the Rule of Law: Towards Constitutional Judicial Review' (2000) PL 671.

[30] J Sumption, *Trials of the State: Law and the Decline of Politics* (London, Profile Books, 2019). See generally 'Independent Review of Administrative Law Report' (CP 407, March 2021), https://assets.publishing.service.gov.uk/government/uploads/system/uploads/attachment_data/file/970797/IRAL-report.pdf.

[31] Much early attention was given to the Coronavirus Act 2020, a bespoke piece of legislation which, after a fast-tracked passage through Parliament, received Royal Assent on the 25 March 2020. There was, however, no specific lockdown power in this Act.

they are living without reasonable excuse'.[32] These regulations, and related governmental guidance, were updated at various stages. Notably, the regulations could remain in force for whatever period the Government decided, although in some cases regulations were accompanied by a sunset clause.[33] The reliance on these regulations, including their enactment under an 'urgent' power conferred on ministers under the 1984 Act, has been subject to considerable criticism not least because they were passed without parliamentary scrutiny or approval.[34]

There were several government officials exercising executive power who were chiefly responsible for the policies that became regulations. Leading the Government was the Prime Minister, and whilst their official status is *'primus inter pares'*, *i.e.*, first among equals – meaning that he or she is of equivalent rank to other ministers – the Prime Minister enjoys a set of additional powers over the allocation of ministerial functions, appointments, and the overall direction of government policy, as well as enjoying a public profile on the national and international stage.[35] Chief among their ordinary governmental duties is chairing the Cabinet which takes collective decisions on government strategy, policy and national security.[36] The Cabinet is comprised mainly of Secretaries of State who exercise responsibility for their departments, such as Education, Justice, and Health and Social Care. At times of emergency, the Prime Minister usually chairs the Civil Contingencies Committee (COBRA)[37] which is convened to take urgent decisions and to co-ordinate responses that require multiple agencies to act.

In addition to the Prime Minister, frequently appearing in press conferences to explain scientific data and answer questions were the Chief Medical Officer (CMO), Professor Chris Whitty, and the Chief Scientific Adviser (CSA), Sir Patrick Vallance. The CMO acts as an interface between the medical profession and the Government and is the principal medical adviser to the Secretary of State for Health and, when necessary, the Prime Minister. The CMO recommends policy changes and has a crucial role during public health emergencies. The CSA is the head of the Government's Science and Engineering Profession and provides advice to the Prime Minister and other Cabinet members on science and technology policy and the use of scientific evidence across government.

The Department of Health and Social Care (DHSC) acts as the 'guardians of the health and care framework including whether the legislative, financial, administrative and policy frameworks are fit for purpose and work together'.[38] It is ultimately responsible in emergency situations where the public and Parliament expect it to resolve crucial and complex issues.[39] In May 2020, the DHSC established NHS Test and Trace, with the aim of breaking chains of transmission and identifying those people potentially carrying the

---

[32] The Health Protection (Coronavirus, Restrictions) (England) Regulations 2020, SI 2020/350, regs 4–8.

[33] ie a clause confirming they would expire at a specified future date (if not already revoked): House of Lords Select Committee on the Constitution, 'Covid-19 and the Use and Scrutiny of Emergency Powers' (HL Paper 15, 2021) 17–18.

[34] ibid 15–16.

[35] See A Le Seur, 'The Nature, Powers and Accountability of Central Government' in D Feldman (ed), *English Public Law* (Oxford, Oxford University Press, 2009) para 3.09.

[36] ibid, paras 3.12–3.14. See also *The Cabinet Manual* 1st edn (London, 2011).

[37] C Haddon, 'Political Decision-Making in a Crisis' (2010) 16 *British Academy Review* 9.

[38] DHSC, 'About us', www.gov.uk/government/organisations/department-of-health-and-social-care/about.

[39] ibid.

virus in order to instruct them to isolate from others.[40] The executive chair of NHS Test and Trace, Baroness Dido Harding, initially reported directly to the Prime Minister but, in December 2020, began reporting to the Secretary of State for Health who retained ministerial accountability for the programme.[41] The NHS Test and Trace programme, including its Chair, received severe criticism for its very costly failure to deliver on its central promise to avoid a further lockdown and its inability to demonstrate a measurable impact on mitigating the progress of the pandemic.[42]

The DHSC exercises operational and financial oversight over various executive non-departmental agencies that fulfil crucial health and care functions. NHS England is responsible for the budget and delivery of commissioned services across the NHS; the Care Quality Commission is the independent regulator of health and adult social care in England; and, before being replaced by the UK Health Security Agency in October 2021, PHE had a role in protecting the nation from biohazards and responding to emergencies. These agencies are run by executive boards comprised of senior executives alongside non-executive directors.

Government ministers are bound by the constitutional convention of 'individual ministerial responsibility'. They are responsible for their departments, including the conduct of the civil service and their advisers,[43] but 'advisers advise, ministers decide'.[44] In this light, the extent to which the CMO and the CSA were themselves individually *culpable* for their role in the Government's response to the pandemic has been a recurring point of debate.[45] Likewise, the extent to which the Government was, as it frequently declared, always 'following the scientific advice' obscured the assessment of responsibility for decisions, particularly the timing in implementing lockdowns.[46]

Individual ministerial responsibility has been described as 'malleable and precarious in practice, depending … upon intangible understandings and traditions, and upon political circumstances'.[47] In recent years, and precipitated by a suite of modern public management reforms,[48] ministers have often sought to resist responsibility for *operational* failings. Instead, ministers, at times, have sought to maintain a distinction between policy responsibility (*i.e.*, the frameworks, plans and strategies within which executive agencies work) and operational responsibility (*i.e.*, the day-to-day implementation and execution of policies). Whilst ministers are still accountable to Parliament (and thus the public) for operational matters, those holding (greater) responsibility for operations are executives, *i.e.*, those in charge. Leaving aside other constitutional concerns, the inextricable working relationship between ministers and such executives, particularly during times of national emergency, renders the division between policy and operation rather artificial.[49]

---

[40] See eg 'Covid-19: NHS Test and Trace Made No Difference to the Pandemic, Says Report' (2021) *BMJ* 372.
[41] Public Accounts Committee, 'Test, Track and Trace' (n 21) 9.
[42] ibid.
[43] This convention is often accompanied by 'collective Cabinet responsibility' ie decisions made by Cabinet must be publicly supported irrespective of whether individual ministers express dissent in private.
[44] 'Even in a Pandemic, Politicians Must Decide' *Financial Times* (London, 1 May 2020).
[45] ibid.
[46] C Rovelli, 'Politics Should Listen to Science, not Hide Behind it' (2021) 20 *Nature Materials* 272.
[47] C Turpin, cited in Jowell and Oliver (n 24) 201.
[48] For a recent discussion, see V Lapuente and S Van de Walle, 'The Effects of New Public Management on the Quality of Public Services' (2020) 33 *Governance* 461.
[49] G Drewry, 'The Executive: Towards Accountable Government and Effective Governance?' in Jowell and Oliver (n 24) 200–05.

A. Overview of and Specific Constitutional and Legal Principles Regarding Criminal Liability of High-Ranking Government/Public Officials

In the absence of a codified Constitution, there are no express rules exempting high-ranking government officials from criminal liability. By convention in the United Kingdom, the starting point is the rule of law. For AV Dicey, writing in 1885, 'every man, whatever be his rank or condition, is subject to the ordinary law of the realm and amenable to the jurisdiction of the ordinary tribunals'.[50] Equality before the law is a cornerstone of the rule of law in the UK.[51] The constitutional status of the rule of law has two effects: (1) government officials do not enjoy immunity from criminal liability; and (2) the criminal liability of government officials is governed by ordinary criminal procedure relying on the independent exercise of prosecutorial discretion (see below Section II.D).[52]

B. Scope of Responsibility and Area of Tolerated Risk

Hence, for the purposes of potential criminal liability of a minister or government official, the Constitution makes no distinctions between ministerial *official* conduct in the discharge of ministerial responsibilities, and *non-official* conduct outside the scope of ministerial responsibilities. Of course, conduct outside of the scope of the ministerial role, *i.e.* acts in a private capacity, would be subject to possible criminal investigation and sanction. In this case, a minister may be criminally responsible as other private citizens and there is precedent for ministers being subject to police investigations.[53]

Nonetheless, for official conduct, the picture is more uncertain. First, it is important not to forget that ministers are *legally* responsible for political actions, *e.g.*, decisions, policies and strategies and, under judicial review proceedings, can be held to have acted unlawfully.[54] However, leaving aside the barriers outlined below, decisions made in the course of official ministerial functions are likely to attract de facto immunity. In other words, prosecuting authorities would tend to afford elected ministers (rather than non-elected public agency officials) deference due to the democratic legitimacy that serving ministers enjoy, as well as to acknowledge that such prosecutions would likely not be in the public interest given the availability of non-criminal sanctions such as intense media scrutiny, being required to resign, or losing their mandate at the next election.

---

[50] AV Dicey, *An Introduction to the Study of the Law of the Constitution* (JWF Allison ed, first published 1885, Oxford, Oxford University Press, 2013) 193.

[51] T Bingham, *The Rule of Law* (London, Penguin Books, 2010) 55–59.

[52] See European Commission for Democracy Through Law, 'Report on the Relationship Between Political and Criminal Ministerial Responsibility' (Study No 682/2012, 11 March 2013), www.venice.coe.int/webforms/documents/default.aspx?pdffile=CDL-AD(2013)001-e.

[53] 'MPs' Expenses: Tony McNulty May Face Police Investigation Over Claims' *The Guardian* (online, 8 May 2009); D King, 'Alex Salmond Claimed £116k Expenses for just Six Westminster Visits' *Daily Record* (Glasgow, 27 March 2008).

[54] eg to have breached natural justice requirements or to have breached duties under the Human Rights Act 1998. See eg R *(Good Law Project and others) v Secretary of State for Health and Social Care* [2021] EWHC 346.

C. Impact of Immunities

For government ministers there is no immunity from criminal jurisdiction for official conduct in the course of their ministerial responsibilities. The only available form of immunity derives from ministers being elected to sit in Parliament, and when engaging in legislative activities such as introducing and debating Bills.[55] In a very limited sense, then, parliamentarians enjoy qualified immunity or 'privilege'. This privilege enables members to undertake parliamentary duties without fear or favour and free from external interference, and the privilege accords respect to the traditional right of both the House of Commons and House of Lords to regulate their own affairs.[56]

D. Prosecutorial Matters

In England and Wales, the majority of criminal prosecutions are brought by the Crown Prosecution Service (CPS), which is an independent State agency headed by the Director of Public Prosecutions (DPP) responsible for instigating and overseeing the prosecution of offences.[57] Several other public agencies retain statutory powers to prosecute and individuals may bring private prosecutions.[58] Private prosecutions for certain offences require the consent of the Attorney-General or the DPP. Of the offences considered below, only a prosecution for corporate manslaughter requires the DPP's agreement.[59]

CPS prosecutors must follow the Code for Crown Prosecutors and must first consider whether there is sufficient reliable, credible and admissible evidence to provide a 'realistic prospect of conviction'.[60] If this 'evidential test' is satisfied, the next question is whether a prosecution is required in the public interest.[61] Factors to be considered at the second stage include the seriousness of the offence, culpability of the alleged offender and harm caused to the victim(s).[62]

The DPP has the power to take over and conduct prosecutions instigated by another organisation or individual, and may take over proceedings to discontinue them.[63] In deciding whether to take over a prosecution, the DPP will have regard to the seriousness of the offence and whether the case is of a type that would typically be investigated by the police and prosecuted by the CPS. The offences considered in this chapter are likely to fall into this category. In addition to the barriers outlined above and below, it is therefore unlikely that a private prosecution could either be brought or sustained.

---

[55] Lord Burnett of Maldon, 'Parliamentary Privilege – Liberty and Due Limitation' (21st Commonwealth Law Conference, 9 April 2019).

[56] See House of Lords, House of Commons, Joint Committee on Parliamentary Privilege, 'Parliamentary Privilege' (HC 100, 2013).

[57] Prosecution of Offences Act 1985 (POA 1985) s 3.

[58] ibid s 6(1).

[59] Corporate Manslaughter and Corporate Homicide Act 2007 (CMCHA 2007) s 17(a).

[60] Director of Public Prosecutions, *Code for Crown Prosecutors* (2018) paras 4.6–4.8.

[61] ibid paras 4.9–4.13.

[62] ibid para 4.14.

[63] POA 1985 s 6(2).

III. CAUSATION

A. Causation (General Principles)

Where causation is disputed, the prosecution must make the jury sure the defendant (D) caused the relevant consequence. Causation is approached in two stages. First, D must be a factual cause of the prohibited result such that, 'but for' D's act or omission, the result would not have occurred.[64] The second question is whether D's conduct made a 'significant contribution' to the Victim's (V's) death.[65] A contribution is significant if it is 'more than minimal';[66] it 'need not be the sole cause, or even the main cause'.[67]

Although there is no general duty to act in English criminal law[68] many offences may be committed by omission, including murder, most forms of manslaughter and offences involving causing or inflicting grievous bodily harm.[69] Omissions liability is contingent upon a pre-existing duty to act.[70] Four main categories of duty have been identified at common law: duty arising out of a relationship;[71] contractual duty;[72] duty arising from assumption of responsibility;[73] and duty arising from the creation of a dangerous situation.[74] Case law exploring the existence and scope of the latter three categories, which are of particular relevance to this chapter, frequently involves consideration of whether D was under a duty to preserve V's life.[75]

The extent to which the scope of a contractual duty depends upon the terms of the applicable contract is unclear.[76] Indeed, contractual duty is sometimes framed as a subcategory of a more general duty arising from the voluntary assumption of care for another, which is a similarly nebulous concept.[77] The common law neither delineates the circumstances in which a person will be deemed to have assumed a legal duty to care for another, nor the steps they must take to discharge such a duty.[78] Indeed, in a number of cases the appellate courts have upheld convictions for manslaughter by omission without articulating the basis upon which a duty was owed.[79]

Where D's conduct creates a dangerous situation which risks harm to V or to her property, D is under a duty to take reasonable steps to address the peril she has created.[80]

---

[64] See *R v White* [1910] 2 KB 124 (CCA).
[65] *R v Pagett* (1983) 76 Cr App R 279 (CA) 288.
[66] *R v Hughes* [2013] UKSC 56, [2013] 1 WLR 2461 [22].
[67] *Pagett* (n 65).
[68] *R v Khan & Khan* [1998] EWCA Crim 971, [1998] Crim LR 830.
[69] *R v Gibbins & Proctor* (1918) 13 Cr App R 134, (CA).
[70] *Khan & Khan* (n 68).
[71] *Gibbins & Proctor* (n 69); *R v Smith* [1979] Crim LR 251 (CCt); *R v Hood* [2003] EWCA Crim 2772.
[72] *R v Pittwood* (1902) 19 TLR 37 (Assizes); *R v Adomako* [1995] 1 AC 171 (HL).
[73] *R v Nicholls* (1874) 13 Cox CC 75; *R v Instan* [1893] 1 QB 450 (CCR); *Gibbins & Proctor* (n 69); *R v Broadhurst* [2019] EWCA Crim 2026.
[74] *R v Miller* [1983] 2 AC 161 (HL); *R v Evans* [2009] EWCA Crim 650, [2009] 1 WLR 1999.
[75] *Khan & Khan* (n 68).
[76] *R v Dytham* [1979] QB 922 (CA).
[77] *R v Stone & Dobinson* [1977] QB 354 (CA).
[78] See A Ashworth, 'The Scope of Criminal Liability for Omissions' (1989) 105 *LQR* 424.
[79] For example, *Stone & Dobinson* (n 77); *R v Ruffell* [2003] EWCA Crim 122.
[80] *R v Miller* (n 74). See M Bohlander, *Principles of German Law* (London, Hart, 2009).

Unlike voluntarily assumed duties, this principle of supervening fault applies because D is 'causally responsible' for the original event 'and so ought to bear the duty to take action to minimise further harm', even where the initial conduct was faultless or accidental.[81]

In the context of Covid-19 it would be necessary to identify the precise omission relied upon to found criminal charges. Who failed to act, when and how? What was the basis of their duty of care and what actions could have discharged that duty? It might be argued that members of the Government owe a duty of care to all British citizens arising out of their office. This duty could be framed as: (1) a contractual duty, since ministers are paid officials; (2) an assumed duty, since they assumed responsibility for tackling Covid-19; or (3) a duty arising from the creation of a dangerous situation based upon early policy decisions that allowed the virus to spread. However, while it has been suggested that the Government failed to take the virus sufficiently seriously in early 2020, a general attitude of complacency is not something to which the criminal law's duty situations are likely to attach.

If a duty of care could be established, failures or delays in tackling Covid-19 could conceivably constitute a breach of that duty. For example, there is evidence that deaths would have been 50 per cent lower if the first lockdown had been introduced one week earlier.[82] Similarly, delaying the second lockdown until November 2020 deviated from scientific advice: 'a circuit-breaker in September and an earlier, more stringent lockdown, would likely have reduced deaths'.[83] However, even if decision-making delays could be regarded as a breach of duty, it would be difficult to prove to the criminal standard that an omission to lock down sooner was a 'but for' cause and/or made a more than minimal contribution to the death of a specific individual(s). In the case of *Broughton*, the Court of Appeal held that where liability rested on D's failure to summon medical assistance, D could only be a substantial cause of death if the prosecution could prove to the criminal standard that V would have lived if medical attention had been provided.[84] If the ratio of *Broughton* were to be applied to the failure to lockdown sooner, the prosecution would have to prove that each alleged victim would otherwise have lived. A general claim that locking down earlier could have prevented 21,000 first wave deaths[85] lacks the degree of specificity and detail that a criminal court would require.[86]

B. Causation and 'Thin Skull' Scenarios

Criminal defendants 'must take their victims as they find them';[87] it is 'perfectly immaterial' that V was already in poor health before D's act or omission because, 'if [D] was

---

[81] A Ashworth, *Positive Obligations in Criminal Law* (London, Hart, 2013) 53.

[82] Science and Technology Committee, 'Oral Evidence: UK Science, Research and Technology Capability and Influence in Global Disease Outbreaks' (HC 136, 2020) Q883.

[83] Health and Social Care and Science and Technology Committees, 'Lessons Learned' (n 26) 137.

[84] *R v Broughton* [2020] EWCA Crim 1093, [2021] 1 WLR 543.

[85] ED Knock et al, 'Report 41: The 2020 SARS-CoV-2 Epidemic in England: Key Epidemiological Drivers and Impact of Interventions' (Imperial College London, 22 December 2020) 10.

[86] A Norrie, 'Legal and Social Murder: What's the Difference?' (2018) *Crim LR* 531.

[87] *R v Blaue* [1975] WLR 1411 (CA).

so unfortunate as to accelerate her death, he must answer for it'.[88] The presence of comorbidities is associated with increased risk/severity of Covid-19 infections. Legal causation will be established if D's act or omission resulted in Covid-19 infection, which was an 'operating and substantial cause' of death.[89] This might sometimes be difficult to evidence given apparent inconsistencies in approaches to recording Covid-19 as the cause of death, particularly in the early stages of the pandemic when access to testing was scarce.[90]

Causation may also be established where, for example, V died as a result of being unable to undergo an operation due to injuries inflicted by D.[91] There is uncertainty as to how many 'non-Covid-19 deaths' have been indirectly caused by the virus. In June 2020, the Office for National Statistics posited that excess deaths not involving coronavirus may be attributable to pressure on the healthcare system resulting from Covid-19 and/ or delays by individuals in accessing healthcare due to fearing exposure to the virus or being reluctant to burden the NHS.[92] Again, difficulties would be likely to arise in identifying a specific defendant(s) and victim(s), as well as evidencing factual and legal causation.

C. Restricting Causality: Policy and Doctrinal Issues

It is usually assumed that an unforeseeable natural event will break the chain of causation between D's actions and V's death.[93] This rule would not obstruct liability in the scenarios posited above for two reasons. First, Covid-19 is a precursor to the conduct potentially giving rise to liability and not a supervening event. Second, Covid-19 was not unforeseeable, as evidenced by the existence of the UK Government's Pandemic Preparedness Strategy.[94]

Similarly, a free, deliberate and informed act by a capacitous adult will break the causal chain.[95] However, recent case law indicates that, where V is vulnerable, a different perspective on individual autonomy and voluntariness may be warranted.[96] If the appellate courts were willing to develop this somewhat paternalistic approach, causation might be easier to satisfy in the context of particularly vulnerable sets of Covid-19 victims, *e.g.*, the elderly in care homes, or those with comorbidities.

---

[88] *R v Martin* (1832) 5 C & P 128.

[89] *R v Smith* [1959] 2 QB 35 (CMAC).

[90] See eg D Oliver, 'Mistruths and Misunderstandings about Covid-19 Death Numbers' (2021) 8279 *BMJ* 352.

[91] *R v McKechnie* (1992) 4 Cr App R 51 (CA).

[92] Office for National Statistics, 'Analysis of Death Registrations not Involving Coronavirus (COVID-19), England and Wales: 28 December 2019 to 1 May 2020' (ONS, 5 June 2020).

[93] RM Perkins, 'The Law of Homicide' (1946) 36 *J Crim L & Criminology* 393.

[94] DHSC, 'UK Influenza Pandemic Preparedness Strategy 2011' (10 November 2011), www.gov.uk/government/publications/responding-to-a-uk-flu-pandemic.

[95] *R v Kennedy* [2007] UKHL 38, [2008] 1 AC 269.

[96] *R v Rebelo* [2021] EWCA Crim 306, [2021] 4 WLR 52; *R v Field* [2021] [EWCA Crim 380, [2021] 1 WLR 3543.

IV. THE STRUCTURE OF HOMICIDE OFFENCES AND ASSAULT/AGGRAVATED ASSAULT/SERIOUS BODILY HARM OFFENCES

A. Murder/Intentional Homicide

The common law offence of murder is a crime 'whose central definition connects it with the core ideal at the heart of the view that life is sacrosanct'.[97] The 'separate status of the crime of murder', along with the 'uniqueness' of the mandatory life sentence that follows upon conviction, 'reflect[s] the "sanctity of life" ideal'.[98] It is, then, highly problematic that a conviction of murder does not depend upon proof of either direct intention or foresight of death as a consequence of one's actions. Rather, murder is committed when D unlawfully kills V, intending either to kill V or to cause V serious bodily harm.[99]

Murder is distinguished from manslaughter by the requirement of express malice (intention to kill) or implied malice (intention to cause serious bodily harm).[100] Direct intention is present if the prohibited result was D's aim or purpose; would D regard his action as a failure if he did not achieve the result?[101] Whatever level of responsibility government ministers, officials or corporations may bear for Covid-19 related deaths, it cannot plausibly be contended that anyone directly intended death or serious harm. Oblique (or indirect) intent is a rule of evidence rather than a rule of law.[102] In the context of murder, a jury may find intent if satisfied that death or serious harm was a virtually certain consequence of D's actions and that D had appreciated such was the case.[103] If it is right that 'tens of thousands died who didn't need to die' as a result of government decisions and delays,[104] the question would be whether officials who were in a position to act differently (or earlier) realised that death(s) were virtually certain to occur as a result of their (in)actions.

In May 2021, former adviser Dominic Cummings told the BBC that the Prime Minister initially refused to impose a second lockdown in the autumn of 2020 because those dying from Covid-19 were 'essentially all over 80'.[105] Cummings' allegations to a parliamentary committee chimed with contemporaneous statements suggesting that the Prime Minister was pursuing a herd immunity strategy by deliberately deciding to allow people to become infected, knowing that some would die as a result. This appears to be capable of satisfying the threshold for oblique intent. However, even if charges could be brought on the basis that a particular individual(s) omitted to act in the knowledge that preventable deaths would result, it would be for the jury to decide whether to infer that D

---

[97] Law Commission, 'A New Homicide Act for England and Wales?' (Law Com CP No 177, 2005) para 2.30.

[98] ibid.

[99] Sir Edward Coke (Chief Justice), *Institutes of the Law of England, Pt III* (Clarke, 1797) Ch 7, 47.

[100] *R v Moloney* [1985] AC 906 (HL).

[101] RA Duff, Intention, *Agency and Criminal Liability: Philosophy of Action and the Criminal Law* (New Jersey, Wiley-Blackwell, 1990).

[102] *R v Matthews* [2003] EWCA Crin 192, [2003] 2 Cr App R 30.

[103] *R v Woollin* [1999] 1 AC 82 (HL).

[104] Health and Social Care Committee and Science and Technology Committee, 'Oral evidence: Coronavirus: Lessons Learnt' (HC 95, 2021) Q1133 (evidence of Dominic Cummings, former Chief Adviser to the Prime Minister).

[105] 'Covid: Boris Johnson Resisted Autumn Lockdown as Only Over-80s Dying – Dominic Cummings' *BBC News* (20 July 2021), www.bbc.co.uk/news/uk-politics-57854811.

intended death or serious harm. Because there is no rule of law that foresight of a virtually certain consequence *is* intention, the jury retains some 'moral elbow-room within which to decide whether the defendant's indifference to the death of the victim was so callous that she deserves to be labelled as a murderer'.[106] The courts have not sought to circumscribe factors a jury may consider in making this evaluative decision.[107] When considering murder liability arising from Covid-19 deaths it would therefore be open to individual jurors to bring their own moral, ethical and political values to bear in deciding the question of intent.

B. Culpable Homicide/Manslaughter

The 'catch-all' category of involuntary manslaughter encompasses homicide offences that do not require proof of intention to kill or cause serious harm,[108] of which there are three forms at common law.[109] The breadth of these offences and their blurred boundaries have attracted criticism,[110] but their continued existence contributes towards fulfilment of the State's duty to ensure that effective criminal law measures are in place to protect the lives of its citizens from threats by the State or third parties.[111]

All three non-statutory forms of involuntary manslaughter require proof that D caused the death of a human being. Constructive manslaughter is made out where D intentionally commits an unlawful and dangerous act, which causes V's death.[112] It is necessary to identify a specific, criminally unlawful act upon which to base liability for this form of manslaughter.[113] Criticisms of ministers and officials' handling of Covid-19 more commonly relate to failures or delays in acting. Accordingly, the remainder of this section will focus on gross negligence manslaughter and reckless manslaughter, both of which may be committed by omission.

Gross negligence manslaughter liability arises where death was caused by the grossly negligent breach of a duty of care, when it was reasonably foreseeable that the breach would give rise to a serious and obvious risk of death.[114] A duty is breached if D fails to exercise a fair and reasonable standard of care and competence.[115] The breach must give rise to a serious and obvious risk of death to V, or to a class of people to which V belongs.[116] Risk is assessed objectively and prospectively, based on the information available to D at the time of the breach.[117] The circumstances of the breach must have been

---

[106] J Horder, 'Intention in the Criminal Law – A Rejoinder' (1995) 58 *MLR* 678, 687.

[107] V Tadros, 'The Homicide Ladder' (2006) 69 *MLR* 601, 605.

[108] Law Commission, 'Murder Manslaughter and Infanticide' (Law Com No 304, 2006) para 2.9.

[109] Constructive manslaughter, gross negligence manslaughter and reckless manslaughter.

[110] See *Andrews v DPP* [1937] AC 576 (HL) 581 (Lord Atkin); Law Commission, 'Murder, Manslaughter and Infanticide' (n 108) para 2.9.

[111] European Convention on Human Rights, art 2; *Osman v UK* (2000) 29 EHRR 245 para 115.

[112] *Attorney-General's Reference (No. 3 of 1994)* [1998] AC 245 (HL) 274 (Lord Hope).

[113] *R v Franklin* (1883) 15 Cox CC 163; *R v Kennedy (No 2)* [2007] UKHL 38, [2008] 1 AC 269 [7].

[114] *Adomako* (n 72); *R v Misra* [2004] EWCA Crim 2375, [2005] 1 Cr App R 21; *R v Rose* [2017] EWCA Crim 1168, [2018] QB 328.

[115] *R v Bateman* (1927) 19 Cr App R 8 (CCA).

[116] *R v Kuddus* [2019] EWCA Crim 837, [2019] 1 WLR 5199.

[117] *Rose* (n 114) para 77.

'truly exceptionally bad and so reprehensible as to justify the conclusion that it amounted to gross negligence and required criminal sanction'.[118]

If it were possible to identify precise acts or omissions that caused specific victims to contract Covid-19 from which they died, then given the state of knowledge from at least March 2020, it seems likely jurors would conclude there was a serious and obvious risk of death. A jury would then need to determine whether the failures were so bad that they ought to attract a criminal sanction and the label 'manslaughter'. This is an objective test, and 'indifference to an obvious risk of injury to health' may suffice.[119]

Determining whether conduct was grossly negligent invites the jury to make a value judgement.[120] As the relevant CPS guidance notes, 'a course of conduct by an individual', 'a series of serious breaches' and 'ignoring warnings' all mean 'the test of grossness is more likely to be met'.[121] All of the circumstances in which D was working will be relevant but, where death is a result of (in)action by several people, their conduct cannot be aggregated when considering whether an individual's negligence was so bad as to amount to a criminal act.[122]

The final form of common law involuntary manslaughter is reckless manslaughter, which is generally understood to apply where D kills with awareness of a risk of death or serious harm.[123] Stark contends that reckless manslaughter charges are rare because most situations in which it might apply are adequately captured by the better established offences of either constructive manslaughter or gross negligence manslaughter.[124] Where advertent risk-taking is alleged but there is doubt as to whether a jury would view D's act or omission as deserving of criminal punishment, reckless manslaughter may be a more appropriate charge because its model of culpability more clearly links D's risk-taking with her blameworthiness.[125]

C. Offences Related to Actions that Cause Serious Bodily Harm (Assault; Grievous Assault; Assault with Intent to Cause Serious Bodily Harm)

Non-fatal offences against the person form a loose hierarchy, according to the severity of injury and the intention/foresight of the perpetrator. At the top of the hierarchy is the offence of causing grievous bodily harm (or wounding) with intent contrary to section 18 of the Offences Against the Person Act 1861 (OAPA 1861), which carries a maximum sentence of life imprisonment. Both factual and legal causation must be proved (see Section III.A, above) and the offence encompasses harm caused by omission and/or

---

[118] ibid.

[119] *R v Stone* [1977] QB 354 (CA) 363; *Attorney-General's Reference (No.2 of 1999)* [2000] QB 796 (CA) 809.

[120] A Lodge, 'Gross Negligence Manslaughter on the Cusp: the Unprincipled Privileging of Harm over Culpability' (2017) 81 *Journal of Criminal Law* 125.

[121] Crown Prosecution Service, 'Gross Negligence Manslaughter – Legal Guidance' (CPS, 14 March 2019), www.cps.gov.uk/legal-guidance/gross-negligence-manslaughter.

[122] ibid.

[123] *R v Lidar* (unreported, 11 November 1999) (CA).

[124] F Stark, 'Reckless Manslaughter' [2017] *Crim LR* 763, 768–69.

[125] ibid, 779–80; JC Smith, 'R v DPP ex p Jones – Case Comment – Prosecution: Director of Public Prosecutions – Decision Not to Prosecute' [2000] *Crim LR* 858.

indirectly,[126] including via the transmission of a virus.[127] Grievous bodily harm (GBH) means really serious harm,[128] which includes psychiatric harm (although not 'psychological disturbance').[129] Whether harm is serious is determined objectively and not from V's standpoint,[130] although the effect on the particular victim may be taken into account.[131] Accordingly, viral symptoms that might not be serious for a healthy adult may be so regarded if V was physically vulnerable.[132] Infection with Covid-19 may therefore result in GBH, depending upon the nature and degree of symptoms and the infected person's characteristics, including their age. The symptoms of 'long Covid' might also constitute GBH, particularly given their indefinite prognosis and the lack of an effective cure.[133] If harm suffered by any individual were not deemed to be sufficiently serious, liability for assault occasioning actual bodily harm would be an available alternative.[134]

Liability under section 18 OAPA 1861 also requires proof of ulterior intent which, for our purposes, means intent to do GBH; no lesser mens rea will suffice.[135] As with the mental element of murder, a jury may find intent if satisfied that a defendant foresaw GBH as a virtually certain consequence of their actions. On this basis, those responsible for decisions to delay lockdown and to pursue a herd immunity strategy, for example, could theoretically be said to have intended GBH. The less serious offence of maliciously inflicting GBH contrary to section 20 OAPA 1861 merely requires proof that D foresaw that her conduct might result in some harm, and this reduced level of culpability is reflected in a lower maximum sentence of five years' imprisonment. For the reasons discussed above, it is hardly controversial to suggest that decision-makers foresaw, at the very least, that some harm might result from their acts and omissions in tackling Covid-19. In autumn of 2020, the impact of delaying the first lockdown on Covid-19 infection rates was known, yet the idea of a 'circuit-breaker' was rejected and the second lockdown was delayed, resulting in the virus spreading. However, any attempt to prosecute for non-fatal offences would likely be thwarted by the impracticality of proving to the criminal standard that a specific individual(s) would not have contracted the virus if different decisions had been taken.

D. Offences Regarding Unborn Foetuses; Interrupting the Course of a (Viable) Pregnancy

An unborn foetus is not regarded as a human being for the purposes of the law of homicide. Separate statutory offences of child destruction and attempting to procure a miscarriage may be applicable, subject to the Abortion Act 1967. The former offence

---

126 *DPP v K* [1990] 1 WLR 1067 (QBD).
127 *R v Golding* [2014] EWCA Crim 889, [2014] Crim LR 686.
128 *DPP v Smith* [1961] AC 290 (HL); *R v Janjua* [1999] 1 Cr App R 91 (CA).
129 *Golding* (n 127).
130 *R v Brown (Damien)* [1998] Crim LR 485 (CA).
131 *R v Bollom* [2004] EWCA Crim 2846, [2004] 2 Cr App R 6.
132 ibid.
133 *Golding* (n 127) [62].
134 OAPA 1861, s 47.
135 *R v Taylor* [2009] EWCA Crim 544.

criminalises the intentional killing of any child that is capable of being born alive. The latter offence encompasses attempting to procure a miscarriage at any stage from conception until the child's birth. Liability for both offences depends upon proof of intent to destroy the foetus, so it is difficult to imagine that destruction via the mother's infection with Covid-19 could fall within their scope.

E. Failure to Render Assistance

There is no distinct offence of failing to render assistance in England and Wales but the majority of offences discussed in this chapter may be committed by omission provided D was under a duty to act. In addition, the offence of misconduct in public office may be committed where an office holder acts (or fails to act) in a manner that constitutes a breach of the duties of that office.[136]

Misconduct in public office is a common law offence and is comprised of four elements. The first is that the defendant is a public officer. The second is wilful neglect in the performance of a duty, or wilful misconduct which, third, is of such a degree so as to amount to an abuse of the public's trust in the officer. Finally, the public officer must not have a reasonable excuse or justification for the conduct.[137]

Government officials are, of course, public officers, but they would be unlikely to be liable for misconduct arising from management of the pandemic response.[138] *Wilful* neglect requires proof that the official deliberately did something which was wrong, knowing it to be wrong or with reckless indifference as to whether it is wrong or not.[139] Alleged incompetence does not meet the required threshold. In respect of Covid-19 decision making, although there were strong objective indications of risk, *e.g.*, the lives that would be lost as a result of failing to impose lockdown earlier than eventually implemented, particularly in respect of the second and third lockdowns, it is unlikely that any official exhibited the required degree of deliberate or reckless wrongdoing because decisions were both morally and politically contestable. Against the backdrop of intense public debate, it could not be said that decision-makers *knowingly* took the wrong decisions given that the boundaries between 'right' and 'wrong' were often blurred and determining the 'right' approach was subject to a wide range of opinion, including from SAGE.

With respect to an abuse of the public's trust, the threshold is high, such that the misconduct injures the public interest so as to call for condemnation and punishment.[140] The misconduct must be an affront to the public conscience.[141] Ultimately this test is subjective and, to a degree, influenced by the consequences of the conduct and the motive from which it proceeded, 'whether from a dishonest, oppressive or corrupt motive ... or from mistake or error.'[142] Whether government officials 'abused' public trust remains

---

[136] *Dytham* (n 76).
[137] *Attorney-General's Reference (No 3 of 2003)* [2004] EWCA Crim 868.
[138] *R v Friar* 1 Chit. Rep (1819) (KB) 702; *R v Cosford* [2013] EWCA Crim 466.
[139] ibid.
[140] *Dytham* (n 76).
[141] *A-G's Ref (No 3 of 2003)* (n 137).
[142] *R v Borron* [1820] 3 B & Ald 432, 434.

open to question, especially as public narratives have since cast key decisions as poor, sometimes incompetent, mistaken, and taken under insurmountable pressure in response to an emergency during which, particularly in the early days, information was imperfect and limited. Equally, errors such as the timing of lockdown decisions are viewed as being motivated by benevolent reasons, *e.g.*, keeping children in school, preserving mental health and avoiding more damage to people's livelihoods. It is in that sense that the Government has drawn retrospective sympathy in some quarters, especially taking into account the successful distribution of vaccinations.[143]

Finally, and in light of the above, it is very likely there would be a reasonable excuse or justification in response to any alleged misconduct. There is evidence that official decisions and policies were based on fine, complex discretionary judgments which were informed by a wide range of stakeholders and influenced by imperfect scientific opinion.[144] The fact that these decisions and policies, at a later time, proved to be errors would not mean they amounted to misconduct at the time they were made. Indeed, it is in the nature of government policy-making that errors can occur and, when they do, they result in an opportunity to heed lessons, however stark.[145]

V. DEFENCES, JUSTIFICATIONS AND EXCUSES

A. Necessity

It has been alleged on a number of occasions that the Prime Minister prioritised saving the economy over saving lives when formulating his Covid-19 strategy.[146] Leaving aside the argument that presenting these alternatives as a binary choice is a false premise, it is necessary to consider whether avoiding lockdown on the basis that the resultant economic damage will also cost lives engages the doctrine of necessity.[147]

Concerns have long been expressed about the uncertain theoretical basis, scope and form of the doctrine of necessity in England and Wales.[148] While the notorious case of *Dudley v Stephens*[149] is often said to hold that necessity can never be a defence to murder, it may be permissible to take a human life in certain circumstances.[150] The Court of Appeal has suggested that the doctrine of necessity will apply provided: (1) D's act was

---

[143] Opinion poll data on Government support relative to opposition.

[144] See generally House of Commons Health and Social Care and Science and Technology Committees, 'Coronavirus: Lessons Learned to Date' (n 26).

[145] ibid.

[146] See, eg Health and Social Care Committee and Science and Technology Committee, 'Lessons Learnt' (n 104) Q1092; D Parsley, 'Boris Johnson "Privately Accepts" up to 50,000 Annual Covid Deaths as an Acceptable Level' *inews* (27 August 2021), inews.co.uk/news/boris-johnson-privately-accepts-up-to-50000-annual-covid-deaths-as-an-acceptable-level-1170069.

[147] K Proctor, 'Saving Lives or UK Economy from Covid a "False Choice", MPs Warn' *The Guardian* (London 26 August 2020).

[148] See B Kotecha, 'Necessity as a Defence to Murder: an Anglo-Canadian Perspective' (2014) 78 *Journal of Criminal Law* 341.

[149] *Dudley v Stephens* (1884) 14 QBD 273.

[150] See M Bohlander, 'Of Shipwrecked Sailors, Unborn Children, Conjoined Twins and Hijacked Airplanes – Taking Human Life and the Defence of Necessity' (2006) 70 *Journal of Criminal Law* 147.

necessary to avoid inevitable and irreparable evil; (2) no more was done than reasonably necessary for the purpose to be achieved; and (3) the evil inflicted was not disproportionate to the evil avoided.[151] More recently, however, the appellate courts have made clear that they are not prepared to clearly define the boundaries of a necessity defence in the 'complex and controversial field' of voluntary euthanasia.[152] It therefore seems highly unlikely that the criminal courts would be willing to fashion a defence of necessity capable of applying in the context of complex and controversial decisions taken in the course of responding to an unprecedented pandemic.

VI. CORPORATE CRIMINAL LIABILITY

A. Overview of Corporate Criminal Liability

A corporation cannot be liable for murder but may be liable for manslaughter and/or non-fatal offences against the person.[153] Corporate liability requires proof that an individual with sufficient seniority to be regarded as the 'directing mind and will' of the company acted (or failed to act) with mens rea.[154] The Corporate Manslaughter and Corporate Homicide Act 2007 (CMCHA 2007) was introduced to address the particular problems inherent in satisfying this 'identification principle' in homicide cases.

Section 1 of the CMCHA 2007 provides that an 'organisation' (O) will be liable for manslaughter if the way in which its activities are managed caused V's death and amounted to a gross breach of a relevant duty of care owed by O to V. 'Organisations' are defined widely to include specified government departments, including the DHSC, the Home Office and the Cabinet Office.[155] In deciding whether there has been a 'gross breach' of duty, the jury may consider the extent to which attitudes, policies, systems or accepted practices encouraged any failure to comply with health and safety legislation.

In July 2020 the House of Commons' Public Accounts Committee found that the fragmented nature of the adult social care system led by the DHSC contributed to inadequate provision of Personal Protective Equipment for staff,[156] and deaths of health care workers from Covid-19 have been 'linked to' occupational exposure.[157] The policy of releasing hospital patients into the adult care system is also thought to have seeded outbreaks of Covid-19 in care homes, leading to deaths. Proving that a governmental organisation caused the death of a specific individual is likely to be problematic for the reasons discussed at Section III.A, above, although recent case law may presage a more protective

---

[151] *Re A (Conjoined Twins: Medical Treatment) (No.1)* [2001] Fam 147.

[152] *R (Nicklinson) v Ministry of Justice* [2013] EWCA Civ 961 [56].

[153] Criminal Justice Act 1925, s 33(3); *P & O European Ferries (Dover) Ltd* (1991) 93 Cr App R 72 (CCC).

[154] *Tesco Supermarkets Ltd v Nattrass* [1972] AC 153 (HL); *Meridian Global Funds Management Asia ltd v Securities Commission* [1995] 2 AC 500 (PC); *Attorney-General's Reference (No 2 of 1999)* [2000] QB 796 (CA).

[155] CMCHA 2007, sch 1.

[156] House of Commons Public Accounts Committee, 'Readying the NHS and Social Care for the COVID-19 Peak' (HC 405, 29 July 2020). https://committees.parliament.uk/publications/2179/documents/20139/default/.

[157] National Audit Office, 'The Supply of PPE during the COVID-19 Pandemic' (HC 961, 25 November 2020), www.nao.org.uk/wp-content/uploads/2020/11/The-supply-of-personal-protective-equipment-PPE-during-the-COVID-19-pandemic.pdf.

attitude towards vulnerable victims (see Section III.C, above). This might effectively lower the causal threshold given that hospitals, and not patients, had the primary care responsibility of weighing up clinical risks involved in placing residents in care homes. In addition, the CMCHA 2007 contains a number of broad exemptions from liability relating to public policy decisions, the exercise of public functions and conduct in response to emergency circumstances.[158]

Conduct by public sector agencies and private companies relating to Covid-19 may fall within the scope of the CMCHA 2017 or the OAPA 1861. For example, failure to plan properly and assess the risk to staff required to physically attend their workplace may breach the basic duty owed by employers towards their employees.[159] Again, it is likely to be difficult to prove that harm or death from Covid-19 infection was the result of an employee contracting the virus in the workplace. While prosecutions for health and safety offences could potentially be brought in appropriate circumstances, there is unlikely to be sufficient evidence to provide a realistic prospect of conviction for offences of either corporate manslaughter or causing/inflicting grievous bodily harm upon individuals.

B. Accessory or Perpetrator

The term 'person' includes both corporations and unincorporated bodies, so either may be liable for statutory offences as principal. Secondary liability is itself a statutory offence, so an organisation that aids or abets a statutory offence may be liable as an accessory, subject to the requirement to prove that someone with sufficient seniority in the company both intended to assist and had knowledge of the substantive offence.

VII. FORMS OF PARTICIPATION

The liability of the perpetrator of a criminal offence depends upon proof that they performed the actus reus of the offence with the required mens rea. Alternatively, a person may be liable as a secondary party (or 'accessory') if she aided, abetted, counselled or procured the offence.[160] An accessory may be tried and punished in the same way as a principal offender, but the liability of the accessory depends upon proof that the principal committed the offence or, at least, the actus reus of that offence. For the reasons discussed hitherto, difficulties in establishing causation are likely to impede the prosecution of any individual or corporation as principals for any offences arising out of the national response to Covid-19.

Conspiracy is essentially now a statutory offence involving the making of an agreement to commit a crime, regardless of whether that agreement is put into effect.[161] D and at least one other person must agree that a course of conduct shall be pursued which, if

---

[158] See CMCHA 2007, s 3 and s 6.

[159] Health and Safety at Work Act 1974, s 2.

[160] Ordinary principles of secondary liability are also now applicable where one party commits an offence in the course of a 'joint criminal venture': *R v Jogee* [2016] UKSC 8, [2017] AC 387.

[161] Criminal Law Act 1977, s 1.

the agreement is carried out in accordance with their intentions, will necessarily result in the commission of an offence by one of the parties. There is a need to identify the nature of the agreement with a degree of precision.[162] Even if it could be established that ministers, MPs or advisers agreed upon a particular policy knowing that it would result in the deaths of citizens, it is submitted this would not be evidence of conspiracy to murder; an agreement to delay lockdown, for example, is not an agreement to cause death.[163]

VIII. ATTEMPT

An attempt occurs when D does an act that is more than merely preparatory to the commission of an indictable offence[164] with intent to commit that offence.[165] Where D embarked upon the substantive crime of murder with intent to kill but it cannot be established that her actions in fact contributed to V's death, D may be liable for attempted murder.[166] Liability requires proof of a positive act, so omissions or delays by public officials in relation to Covid-19 would not be covered. While some corporations have committed positive acts that may be regarded as reprehensible, such as supplying unusable masks,[167] in practice, it would be impossible to attribute any specific death(s) to such acts and it would likely also be difficult to establish any intention to kill.[168]

IX. SANCTIONS, SENTENCING, PUNISHMENT, REPARATIONS AND/OR RESTORATIVE JUSTICE

A. General Sentencing Framework for the Crimes under Discussion

Courts must have regard to the following non-hierarchical purposes of sentencing: punishment; crime reduction; reform and rehabilitation; public protection; and reparation.[169] Guidelines issued by the Sentencing Council are designed to promote consistency and may be general (such as the guideline on reduction in sentence for a guilty plea) or offence-specific (such as the gross negligence manslaughter guideline). Offence-specific guidelines require judges to consider the offender's culpability and the harm caused by the offence in order to identify a sentencing category. Each category has a suggested starting point and a category range within which the judge should normally sentence the offender.

---

[162] P Jarvis and M Bisgrove, 'The Use and Abuse of Conspiracy' (2014) *Crim LR* 261.

[163] D Ormerod and K Laird, *Smith, Hogan & Ormerod's Criminal Law* 16th edn (Oxford, Oxford University Press, 2021) 456.

[164] An indictable offence is one that either may or must be tried by a judge and jury in the Crown Court (ie generally those offences that are more serious).

[165] Criminal Attempts Act 1981, s 1.

[166] See, eg *R v White* (n 64).

[167] K Rawlinson, 'Labour Calls for Inquiry into Purchase of 50m Unusable Face Masks' *The Guardian* (London, 6 August 2020).

[168] While murder may be satisfied by an attempt to kill or cause serious harm, only an intention to kill will suffice for attempted murder: *R v Whybrow* (1951) 35 Cr App R 141 (CCA).

[169] Sentencing Act 2020, s 57.

The mandatory sentence for murder is life imprisonment, although the court will usually set a minimum term after which the offender may be considered for release on licence. Parliament has laid down various starting points for judges to apply when fixing the minimum term, the lowest of which is 15 years for a murder with no aggravating features. A 'whole life order' may be appropriate if the seriousness of the offence is exceptionally high, such as the murder of two or more persons with a substantial degree of premeditation, or a murder done to advance a political, religious, racial or ideological cause.[170]

Life imprisonment is available for all forms of manslaughter except corporate manslaughter, but the relevant guidelines identify ranges of fixed term sentences. The harm caused by manslaughter 'will inevitably be of the utmost seriousness'[171] and the focus of any plea in mitigation will be the offender's culpability. For gross negligence manslaughter, the lowest starting point is two years' imprisonment for cases involving a momentary lapse in an offender's otherwise satisfactory standard of care, with a category range of one to four years' custody. At the opposite end of the scale, an offender whose negligence was of an extreme character and involved continued or repeated conduct in the face of obvious suffering may face a starting point of 12 years' imprisonment and would be appropriately sentenced within a range of 10 to 18 years.

The maximum sentence for causing grievous bodily harm with intent is life imprisonment but the usual sentencing range is two to 16 years' imprisonment for an offence involving a single victim. The lesser offence of maliciously inflicting grievous bodily harm has a maximum sentence of five years' custody. In all cases, the existence of multiple victims will result in either an uplift to the sentence for the main offence and concurrent sentences for the remainder, or consecutive sentences, depending on the circumstances.[172]

B. Sanctions Specifically for Senior Government/Public Officials

The convention of individual ministerial responsibility shapes the various 'political' ways in which a minister is held responsible for official acts, omissions and departmental failures, and that is irrespective of whether there are objective grounds for critique.[173] Ministerial responsibility takes the shape of being *held to account*, *i.e.*, to publicly inform, explain, justify and if needed demonstrate change to various audiences and stakeholders.[174] This may take the form of answering to Parliament, being interviewed by the media, being subject to detailed scrutiny via a formalised Select Committee, and otherwise called to give evidence to independent public inquiries (such as the one

---

[170] ibid, sch 21.

[171] Sentencing Council, 'Guideline: Gross Negligence Manslaughter' (1 November 2018), www.sentencingcouncil. org.uk/offences/crown-court/item/gross-negligence-manslaughter/.

[172] Sentencing Council, 'Guideline: Totality' (11 June 2012), www.sentencingcouncil.org.uk/overarching-guides/ crown-court/item/totality/.

[173] European Commission for Democracy Through Law, 'Report on the Relationship Between Political and Criminal Ministerial Responsibility' (n 52).

[174] Institute For Government, 'Accountability in Modern Government: What are the Issues?' (23 April 2018), www.instituteforgovernment.org.uk/publications/accountability-modern-government-issues.

that is being planned for the pandemic due to commence work in 2022).[175] Although not without exception, the ultimate censure for a minister is to be asked to tender their resignation.[176] Leaving aside the option of the Prime Minister dismissing a minister from post, the prospect of resignation depends on the individual minister's political ability to resist responsibility for the failings.[177]

C. Corporations and Sentencing

Where an organisation is successfully prosecuted (as opposed to an individual within the organisation), the only available sanctions are fines and ancillary orders. There is usually no limit to the amount of any fine, but guidelines lay down starting points based on the seriousness of the offence and the organisation's annual turnover. Factors increasing seriousness (and therefore increasing the level of fine) include cost-cutting at the expense of safety, whereas a sentence may be mitigated if death(s) were contributed to by external events beyond the organisation's control.[178] The court may additionally impose ancillary orders including: a publicity order, whose object is deterrence and punishment; a remedial order, requiring the organisation to remedy any specific failings involved in the offence; and/or the payment of compensation where this is not being dealt with separately in the civil courts.[179]

---

[175] See The Inquiries Act 2005.

[176] Often, individuals are asked to tender their resignation to avoid the public embarrassment of a minister being dismissed.

[177] See, eg 'Foreign Secretary Dominic Raab Rejects Calls to Quit over Afghan Interpreters' *BBC News* (19 August 2021), www.bbc.co.uk/news/uk-58265160.

[178] Sentencing Council, 'Guideline: Corporate Manslaughter' (1 February 2016), www.sentencingcouncil.org.uk/offences/crown-court/item/corporate-manslaughter/.

[179] CMCHA 2007, ss 9–10.

5

France

CAROLINE FOURNET AND FRÉDÉRIC ROLLAND

I. BACKGROUND AND CONTEXTUAL INTRODUCTION

'IN RECENT WEEKS, our country has been facing the spread of a virus, Covid-19, which has affected several thousand of our compatriots'.[1] It is with these words that French President Emmanuel Macron opened his first televised allocution in relation to the Covid-19 pandemic on Thursday 12 March 2020. In his first allocution – the first of many[2] – related to the pandemic, the French President of the Republic, while announcing a series of measures to combat the spread of the virus, unequivocally affirmed that health was the absolute priority and renewed his faith in science as the guiding principle in the management of the crisis.[3] Since then, the statistics related to the virus confirmed the warning the President of the Republic gave in March 2020 that the pandemic was only starting. As per 24 April 2022, the numbers speak for themselves: 26,802,654 confirmed cases and 145,060 deaths (116,345 in hospital and 28,715 in EHPAD retirement homes).[4] In the course of these two years, various coercive measures and policies have been adopted by the French executive to fight the virus, among which lockdowns, closures, curfew, travel restrictions, obligation to wear masks in public spaces, obligation to hold a sanitary pass and, for some professions, obligation to be vaccinated.

To adopt these measures, the state of health emergency was declared by the Prime Minister's decree of 16 March 2020 and was translated into the law with the adoption by Parliament of law n° 2020-290 on 23 March 2020.[5] Crucially, with this law, the French

---

[1] Elysée, 'Adresse aux Français' (12 March 2020), www.elysee.fr/emmanuel-macron/2020/03/12/adresse-aux-francais. Translation by the authors, the original version reads: 'Depuis quelques semaines, notre pays fait face à la propagation d'un virus, le Covid-19, qui a touché plusieurs milliers de nos compatriotes'.

[2] From March 2020 to November 2021, President Macron gave nine such allocutions.

[3] Elysée, 'Adresse aux Français' (12 March 2020), www.elysee.fr/emmanuel-macron/2020/03/12/adresse-aux-francais: 'the absolute priority for our Nation will be our health. I will not compromise on anything. A principle guides us to define our actions, it has been guiding us since the beginning to anticipate this crisis and for several weeks to manage it; it must continue to do so: it is faith in science'. Translation by the authors, the original version reads: 'la priorité absolue pour notre Nation sera notre santé. Je ne transigerai sur rien. Un principe nous guide pour définir nos actions, il nous guide depuis le début pour anticiper cette crise puis pour la gérer depuis plusieurs semaines et il doit continuer de le faire: c'est la confiance dans la science'.

[4] See B Deshayes, 'Chiffres du Covid en France: une "forte hausse" des décès rapportée' (*L'Internaute*, 8 July 2022), www.linternaute.com/actualite/guide-vie-quotidienne/2489651-chiffres-covid-cas-morts-le-bilan-du-coronavirus-en-france. The research for this contribution stopped on 19 June 2022, the date of the outcome of the French legislative election.

[5] Loi n° 2020-290 du 23 mars 2020 d'urgence pour faire face à l'épidémie de covid-19, *Journal Officiel de la République Française* n° 0072 (24 March 2020).

Parliament agreed to temporarily delegate its legislative competence to the government; a delegation which allows massive recourse to the *ordonnance* procedure[6] and gives the government a considerable margin of action,[7] as evidenced by the different phases and the various legal increments via which the state of health emergency has been implemented. Although by nature provisional and temporary, this emergency mechanism was regularly extended to adapt to the sanitary evolution, on the basis of a report by the Health Minister advised by a committee of scientific experts. The legislative mechanism in force allows, nationally the Prime Minister and the Health Minister and locally the public authorities, to take any general and individual police measures that are legally motivated by the prevention of health risks linked to the Covid-19 pandemic and proportionate to these risks.

Brunet usefully depicts the timeframe in which these different measures were brought in, recalling that '[t]he Prime Minister's Decree 2020-260 of 16 March 2020 ... introduced a general lockdown of the population from 17 to 31 March 2020'.[8] The lockdown

> was extended to 15 April 2020, then 11 May, the date on which a progressive ending of the lockdown began according to sectors activity ... and regions .... However, in view of the resumption of the active circulation of the virus after the summer and the 'second wave' of the epidemic, the state-of-emergency regime was once again activated for one month, starting on 17 October 2020. It allowed the introduction of a night curfew policy over a large part of the country. It was not, however, enough to stop the epidemic and a new national lockdown was decreed from 30 October ... It was to last until 15 December, the date on which a night curfew has been re-imposed.[9]

The lockdown was lifted on 20 June 2021. On 11 November 2021, a law was enacted to fix the end of the state of health emergency to 31 July 2022.[10] During this transition period, the Prime Minister may still limit travels and access to public transports and to certain places, and may also restrict the rights to assemble or demonstrate in public spaces.[11]

Even if unprecedented, the state of health emergency[12] is not a legal oddity and is legally rooted in the theory of exceptional circumstances, which results from the

---

[6] ibid arts 13 and 38. Functioning as a provisional law enacted by the government pending its ratification by Parliament, an *ordonnance* stands as a statutory instrument issued by the Council of Ministers in an area of primary legislation falling under the remit of Parliament. Failing ratification by Parliament, the 'ordonnance' remains an executive regulation.

[7] This margin of action is abundantly commented upon and often heavily criticised. See, eg 'La fin de la République?' (*Academia*, 23 March 2020), https://academia.hypotheses.org/21454.

[8] S Brunet, 'The Hyper-Executive State of Emergency in France' in MC Kettemann and K Lachmayer (eds), *Pandemocracy in Europe: Power, Parliaments and People in Times of COVID-19* (Oxford, Hart Publishing, 2022) 202.

[9] ibid 203.

[10] The first law of 31 May 2021 fixed the end of the state of health emergency to 30 September 2021, postponed by a law of 5 August 2021 to 15 November 2021. See Direction de l'information légale et administrative, 'Régime de sortie de crise sanitaire: jusqu'à quand ?' (*Service Public*, 5 July 2022), www.service-public.fr/particuliers/actualites/A14937#:~:text=La%20loi%20portant%20diverses%20dispositions,de%20recourir%20au%20passe%20sanitaire.

[11] Loi n° 2021-1465 du 10 novembre 2021 portant diverses dispositions de vigilance sanitaire, *Journal Officiel de la République Française* n° 0263 (11 November 2021).

[12] Note that the French Constitution, in art 36, only envisages the state of siege rather than the state of emergency.

jurisprudence de principe of the Conseil d'État.[13] Thus, even if the state of health emergency undeniably establishes an exceptional regime which strengthens the powers of the government while infringing on the rights and freedoms of citizens, it remains a lawful governmental action of legislative origin. This however does not mean that these measures cannot be contested. To the contrary, they can be legally challenged via two procedures before the Conseil d'État to obtain their annulment: the *recours pour excès de pouvoir* (recourse for excess of power) and the *référés administratifs* (administrative summary procedure). In addition, the legal arrangements specific to the state of health emergency may be subject to judicial review before the Conseil constitutionnel.[14]

It is worthwhile reminding here that, in the context of these procedures, what is at stake is not the restrictions to individual freedoms and civil liberties per se. In their great majority, these are not absolute and can be lawfully curtailed 'in the interests of public safety, for the protection of public order, health or morals, or for the protection of the rights and freedoms of others', to use the language of the European Convention on Human Rights. Rather, what can be judicially challenged is the proportionality of the measures adopted to the targeted goal.[15] In the context of the Covid-19 pandemic, the official objectives of the French executive – President of the Republic as head of state, Prime Minister as head of government, and government – have always been to protect the health of individuals and to stop the spread of the virus *'quoiqu'il en coûte'* ('whatever the cost'). In so doing, the French executive has resorted to a series of coercive measures, all legally framed, to try and achieve a balance between its official objectives and the preservation of as many individual and collective freedoms as possible.

Following the twentieth century's positivist conception of the law, contemporary democracies are based on a system of legal norms formulated by legally competent public authorities which dismiss morality, revelation and the inner nature of things as sources of law. According to legal positivism, the refutation of the coercive value of moral obligations or natural law means that the predictability of legal rules, binding on citizens and enforceable by public powers, is ultimately constituted in relation to the highest rules of the legal order enacted by legally habilitated public authorities. From the legal positivism perspective, the mandatory character of legal rules derives exclusively from the validation of the legal system by itself at the highest normative echelon; the key aspect being that – notwithstanding the fact that social morality and political ideology in the adoption and implementation of legal rules permeate intrinsically any legal system in relation to its historical background – the legal order itself is indifferent to the moral and ideological content of the legal rules it generates, provided that these rules are enacted via the appropriate procedures within the officially authorised system of production of legal norms.[16]

---

[13] See CE 28/06/1918 *Heyriès*, Rec. 651; CE 28/02/1919 *Dames Dol et Laurent*, Rec. 208; CE 2/03/1962 *Rubin de Servens et autres*, Rec. 143; CE ass 19/10/1962 *Canal, Robin et Godot*, Rec. 552.

[14] See Constitution of the French Republic of 4 October 1958 (Constitution), art 61-1.

[15] C Le Bri, 'La sauvegarde des libertés en temps de « guerre » contre le coronavirus' *The Conversation* (online, 27 March 2020) theconversation.com/la-sauvegarde-des-libertes-en-temps-de-guerre-contre-le-coronavirus-134913.

[16] ibid.

Parliamentary France of the fifth Republic is no exception to this positivist and liberal postulation embodied in its written and codified Constitution. Hence, an academic assessment of the political and legal treatment of the Covid-19 pandemic which ultimately lies in a potent mix of history, science, politics and personalities, needs to focus on the mechanisms of the Constitution and the content of the law, indifferent to any moral judgement, so as to differentiate clearly what falls within the legal competence and coercive action of the political authorities from what refers to individual moral choices devoid of any direct legal consequences. Captive of the historical, constitutional and political forces of the time in which it operates, the management of the Covid-19 pandemic under the fifth Republic parliamentary regime cannot be separate, both in terms of political declarations and legal procedures and instruments, from the idea that constitutional arrangements, politics and history are determining aspects of behaviour for both the political actors and the citizens.

For all that, since the adoption of the law of 23 March 2020 establishing the state of health emergency, the French population has been confronted with a vast and miscellaneous amount of public announcements, political decisions and legal provisions and, problematically, with a discourse on the part of the executive that is at times inconsistent, unclear and contradictory. The presidential allocutions have invariably been followed by uncertainties and hesitations and have revealed a rather concerning degree of superficiality in the decision-making process. The mask is perhaps one of the most telling illustrations of such confusion, starting with what turned out to be a blatant lie from the then Health Minister Agnès Buzin that any purchase of masks was not necessary since France had a stock of tens of millions of them,[17] to the affirmation by the then government's spokesperson Sibeth Ndiaye that masks were not only not required but in fact potentially counter-productive,[18] to the obligation to wear masks in public spaces and the imposition of a fine in case of breach,[19] all this over a relatively short time span of less than three months. In a similar vein, the French executive has at times showed little cohesion, with for instance the Education Minister affirming that schools will not be closed before being expressly contradicted the very next day by the President of the Republic.[20] Supporters of the President of the Republic and of the government have justified their actions and contradictions by invoking the unprecedented nature of the situation; their detractors have criticised their amateurism and incompetence. Some have even lodged complaints with the specific jurisdiction that is the Cour de justice de la République to seek the

---

[17] Editorial, 'Contre le coronavirus, Agnès Buzyn juge "inutile" l'achat de masques' *Huffington Post* (online, 27 January 2020), www.huffingtonpost.fr/entry/contre-le-coronavirus-agnes-buzyn-deconseille-lachat-de-masques_fr_5e2e163ec5b6d6767fd6c826.

[18] O Faye, 'Port du masque: le gouvernement amorce un virage à 180 degrés' *Le Monde* (online, 6 April 2020), www.lemonde.fr/politique/article/2020/04/06/port-du-masque-l-executif-amorce-un-virage-a-180-degres_6035698_823448.html.

[19] See, eg Décret n° 2020-860 du 10 juillet 2020 prescrivant les mesures générales nécessaires pour faire face à l'épidémie de covid-19 dans les territoires sortis de l'état d'urgence sanitaire et dans ceux où il a été prorogé, *Journal Officiel de la République Française* n° n° 0170 du 11 juillet 2020.

[20] See C Pol, 'Coronavirus: quand Blanquer soutenait que le gouvernement n'avait «jamais envisagé la fermeture totale» des écoles' (*Libération*, 13 March 2020), www.liberation.fr/politiques/2020/03/13/coronavirus-quand-blanquer-soutenait-que-le-gouvernement-n-avait-jamais-envisage-la-fermeture-totale_1781540/.

establishment of the criminal liability of the Prime Minister and of the government.[21] The question whether the criminal liability of the French executive for its management of the Covid-19 can be engaged is precisely what this contribution seeks to address. The answer primarily lies not in criminal law but rather in constitutional law which regulates not only the roles and functions of the executive but also its criminal liability regime. The scientific analysis of the political discourse and the law deployed by the French executive during the Covid-19 crisis thus imperatively requires both an accurate understanding of the distribution of powers according to the text of the Constitution, *i.e.* the political *regime*, and a sheer appreciation of the idiosyncratic political interpretation of the political regime by the public authorities and its subsequent constitutional conventions, *i.e.* the political *system*.

The presidential allocutions to the French Nation featuring a deciding head of state is perfectly in line with the preponderant role of the President of the Republic as envisaged by the Constitution of the fifth Republic.[22] In the constitutionally established two-headed executive power required in any parliamentary regime, the specificity of the French rationalised and presidentialised parliamentarism usually gives the perception that the President of the fifth Republic decides while the Prime Minister implements.[23] Yet, and perhaps paradoxically, the former is very much shielded from responsibility while the members of government – including the Prime Minister – are the ones exposed when it comes to criminal liability. It is thus in the light of the Constitution that this chapter will explore the potential criminal liability of the President of the Republic, of the Prime Minister and of the government. In so doing, the question of the criminal qualification of the acts of the French executive will be addressed, with a reflection on the key issue of causation and an analysis of both the material and mental elements of the possible criminal charges.

II. CONSTITUTIONAL, LEGAL AND POLICY OVERVIEW

The political regime set up in the French Constitution is a parliamentary regime, the crucial characteristic of which is to constitutionally organise the superiority of the executive power and, within the executive power, the formal and legal superiority of the President of the Republic over the Prime Minister and the government.

---

[21] See, eg J Tilouine, 'Covid-19: la Cour de justice de la République rejette une série de près de 20 000 plaintes contre le gouvernement' *Le Monde* (online, 24 January 2022), www.lemonde.fr/societe/article/2022/01/24/covid-19-la-cour-de-justice-de-la-republique-rejette-une-serie-de-pres-de-20-000-plaintes-contre-le-gouvernement_6110806_3224.html.

[22] See Constitution, www.assemblee-nationale.fr/connaissance/constitution.asp. All English translations of the Constitution are taken from the translation available at: www.conseil-constitutionnel.fr/sites/default/files/as/root/bank_mm/anglais/constiution_anglais_oct2009.pdf.

[23] On the classification principles related to the fifth Republic and their challenges, see M-A Cohendet, 'La classification des régimes politiques, un outil pertinent dans une conception instrumentale du droit constitutionnel' in D de Béchillon, V Champeil-Desplats, P Brunet and E Millard (eds), *L'architecture du droit – Mélanges Michel Troper* (Paris, Economica, 2006) 299; E Georgitsi, 'La Spécificité de la Vème République et les classifications: une opposition fausse' (2010) 83 *Revue Française de Droit Constitutionnel* 543.

A. Overview of and Specific Constitutional and Legal Principles Regarding Criminal Liability of High-Ranking Government/Public Officials

By virtue of article 5 of the Constitution, the President of the Republic is a constitutional arbiter,[24] holder of supreme powers, who remains politically unaccountable before Parliament. Put differently, the President of the Republic holds the very substance of State power. As the guardian of the Constitution, he or she is its political interpreter. This presidential interpretative function finds a double legitimacy: first, in the fact that this presidential role as political interpreter of the Constitution is implicitly acknowledged in article 5 itself; second, save for the application of article 68 on the impeachment of the President of the Republic,[25] in the absence of political control over the exercise by the President of the Republic of his or her political interpretation of the Constitution. Apart from the Conseil constitutionnel's exclusive attribution powers,[26] no other public authority has the power to politically control the conformity of the political interpretation of the Constitution by the President of the Republic.

The supreme presidential arbitral position is reinforced by article 19 of the Constitution which confers on the President of the Republic personal and exclusive constitutional powers, that is, powers exempt from ministerial countersignature.[27] As a corollary to article 5, article 19 establishes the President of the Republic's exclusive legal means by which he or she can carry out his or her arbitration without any legal mechanism of political accountability. By inscribing the legal supremacy of the President of the Republic in the Constitution, article 19 implodes the classic parliamentary logic of balance based on an association between political power and political accountability.

Nevertheless, the established constitutional superiority of the President of the Republic is fortified by an undeniable political legitimacy. Indeed, this leading legal pre-eminence of the President of the Republic within the Constitution finds itself democratically reinforced with the constitutional revision of 6 November 1962, which established his or her election by direct universal suffrage. This revision undeniably consolidated the institutional and legal prevalence of the President of the Republic, giving him or her a democratic political legitimacy rigorously similar to that of the Assemblée Nationale (lower house of Parliament). Strengthened by this political legitimacy, the President of the Republic as supreme political arbiter of the Constitution becomes a very active and prominent political actor; a function aptly embodied by President Macron in the management of the Covid-19 pandemic. Yet, the President of the Republic remains politically unaccountable before Parliament, contrary to the rest of the executive.

The French government derives its political legitimacy from its parliamentary majority. If the President of the Republic is somehow limited by this democratic necessity, he remains the one who has the discretion to appoint the Prime Minister.[28] As with the presidential functions, the French Constitution regulates the role and functions of the

---

[24] M-A Cohendet, 'L'Arbitrage du Président de la République' (2009) 52 *Archives de philosophie du droit* 15.
[25] See below s II.B.
[26] See arts 58–60 of the Constitution on the powers of the Conseil constitutionnel with respect to elections and referendums.
[27] This is a new feature of the 1958 Constitution and of the fifth Republic: in the preceding regimes of the third and fourth Republics, Parliament very much dominated the situation.
[28] See Constitution, art 8.

government as well as the main legal competences of the Prime Minister in its articles 20 and 21. The numerical disparity in the Constitution between the articles devoted to the President of the Republic and those specifically concerning the government and the Prime Minister is rather telling: while the function of head of government is necessarily and clearly established, this is done rather succinctly. This absence of detailed analysis within the Constitution implicitly but distinctly informs the institutional inferiority of the Prime Minister vis-à-vis the President of the Republic.

This constitutional inferiority notwithstanding, the Prime Minister still holds constitutionally important powers: as clearly stipulated in article 21, he or she directs the action of the government. According to parliamentary principles, with governmental power comes political accountability; article 20 could not be clearer, the government 'Shall be accountable to Parliament in accordance with the terms and procedures set out in articles 49 and 50'.[29]

Yet, the specificity of the French fifth Republic's presidentialised parliamentarism means that the practical extent of prime ministerial executive powers is understood primarily in relation to presidential political activity and activism, *i.e.* it is directly linked to the political system within which the executive authorities operate. Indeed, the collegial powers of government, the individual powers of ministers and the personal powers of the Prime Minister can always be potentially limited by the constitutionally recognised legal powers of the President of the Republic. In turn, the activation of presidential powers and the subsequent genesis of governmental decisions thus depend on the alternative influence exerted by the political system in place, whether the system is one of *présidentialisme* – as it has been consistently the case during the pandemic – or one of *cohabitation*.

As it appears obvious that during the pandemic crisis the control of the political discourse and the executive decisions in health matters belong to the President of the Republic, it is crucial to realise that the critical assessment of presidential actions proceeds not only from the original constitutional conformation specific to the rationalised parliamentarism of the fifth Republic, but also derives from its systemic configuration which, on an electoral basis, is conventionally specific to it. This preliminary point is fundamental to distinguish between the political authorship of an executive decision and the political accountability it generates.[30] Indeed, the originality of the fifth Republic stems fundamentally from the consubstantial relationship between the political regime, *i.e.* the text of the Constitution, and the political interpretation of the political regime by political actors, *i.e.* the political systems. What motivates the occurrence of *présidentialisme* or *cohabitation* as political systems is solely the choice of the voters; the text of the Constitution remaining unchanged. Consequently, from a political majority and partisan viewpoint, it is always necessary to measure the political scope of presidential power and the political space reserved for the Prime Minister and the government in the light of the

---

[29] 'Le Gouvernement ... est responsable devant le Parlement dans les conditions et suivant les procédures prévues aux articles 49 et 50', Constitution, art 20. Arts 49 and 50 deal with the different procedures of political accountability, as the embodiment of the *parlementarisme rationalisé* specific to the Constitution of the fifth Republic.

[30] See T Mulier, 'La crise du Covid 19, reflet des anomalies du fonctionnement de la Vème République' (*JP Blog*, 11 June 2020), blog.juspoliticum.com/2020/06/11/la-crise-du-covid-19-reflet-des-anomalies-du-fonctionnement-de-la-ve-republique-par-thibaud-mulier.

political system that results from the consecutive presidential and legislative elections; results which can either coincide (*présidentialisme*) or not (*cohabitation*).[31]

Within the framework of *présidentialisme*, there is a stratification of the executive functions in favour of the President of the Republic and thus a legal and political subordination of the Prime Minister to the point that the President of the Republic becomes undoubtedly, although in practice only, the head of government. He or she imposes his or her policies on the Prime Minister who must apply them; the margin of action of the government thus finds itself considerably reduced. In practice, the ministerial counter-signature of all presidential acts thus becomes an administrative formality: rather than manifesting a resolutely voluntary process of conjunction of the executive wills, it merely endorses the President of the Republic's decisions. The political power of the President of the Republic in *présidentialisme* is not only constitutionally apparent via the discretionary use of his or her own powers under article 19 but also conventionally evident via the merely formal nature of the affixing of the ministerial countersignature on presidential acts. For all that, and this is key in the context of the present contribution, the Prime Minister, institutionally inferior and politically subordinated under the *système présidentialiste*, legally assumes political accountability for presidential decisions and is conventionally 'dismissible' at any time by the President of the Republic.[32] Interestingly, the President of the Republic and the Prime Minister may have different political affiliations leading to *cohabitation*, an admittedly tense situation. To mitigate the risk of such *cohabitation* – which has occurred on three occasions prior to 2000 – via a harmonisation of the electoral calendar starting with the presidential election,[33] the constitutional law of 2 October 2000 established the presidential five-year term with the clear intention of favouring *présidentialisme* over *cohabitation*.[34]

Had the pandemic occurred at a time of *cohabitation*, the Prime Minister, as head of government, would have been the deciding power of the executive branch – although he or she would have clearly remained under the supervision of the President of the Republic who not only presides over the council of Ministers but also, by virtue of constitutional custom, sets its agenda, regardless of the political system.[35] In a certain sense,

---

[31] See generally F Hamon and M Troper, *Droit Constitutionnel* 42nd edn (Paris, LGDJ collection Manuels, 2021–22). On the distinction between 'régime politique' and 'système politique' in French Constitutional Law, see generally M-A Cohendet, *Droit constitutionnel* 4th edn (Paris, LGDJ-Lextenso, coll. Cours, 2019).

[32] Under art 8 of the Constitution, the termination of the Prime Minister's function legally results from a voluntary and autonomous resignation of the government presented to the President of the Republic by the Prime Minister. In a system of *cohabitation*, the Prime Minister becomes de facto irremovable and regains the political and legal powers attached to his or her office: he or she governs in both law and in practice, which is nothing but his or her role in both parliamentary and constitutional terms.

[33] The constitutional reform establishing the presidential five-year term effectively aims to make the presidential and legislative elections coincide, starting chronologically with the elections of the President of the Republic, thus reducing the political probability of a situation of *cohabitation* without however eliminating its electoral possibility. A *cohabitation* thus remains constitutionally and politically possible, insofar as it is decided democratically by the people on the basis of elections. While not establishing a *cohabitation*, the mixed outcome of the 2022 legislative election failed to give President Macron a full majority.

[34] It should also be noted that the President of the Republic, by application of art 12 of the Constitution, can always dissolve Parliament, thus triggering legislative elections. This is one of his or her personal and exclusive prerogatives under art 19 of the Constitution.

[35] Constitution, art 9. See M-A Cohendet, 'Commentaire des articles 9 et 21 de la Constitution' in F Luchaire, G Conac and X Prétot (eds), *La Constitution de la Vème République* (Paris, Economica, 2009) 370–87 and 604–35.

and notwithstanding the political implications and complications that a *cohabitation* might generate, this system would potentially have been more in line with the applicable political accountability and criminal liability regimes of the French executive. As detailed below, since the Prime Minister and the government are the ones who bear accountability for the acts of the executive, this accountability might be more legitimately grounded in a *cohabitation* system where the Prime Minister is also the one at the origin of the executive actions.

What remains speculative is how decisive would the supervision of the President of the Republic have been in relation to the management of a national health emergency, such as the Covid-19 pandemic, by a government of *cohabitation*. Everything would have depended on the intensity of the political control the President of the Republic, as both supreme political arbiter and leader of the parliamentary opposition, would have aimed to exercise over the actions of a politically hostile government in a context of extreme crisis. In such a case, the President of the Republic would undoubtedly have to ensure a perilous but potentially politically profitable balance for him or her; on the one hand by knowing how to take advantage of his or her political unaccountability in relation to a largely autonomous government action (since, politically, it would not have been his or hers) and, on the other hand, by organising a first rank personal political visibility as guardian of the Constitution and arbiter of the regular functioning of public powers. By leaving entirely to a *cohabitation* government the political accountability of a health crisis policy from which he or she is strictly speaking politically detached, the President of the Republic would perhaps have found all his or her future political and electoral interests in magnifying his or her arbitration position and the pre-eminence of his or her constitutional status as the keystone of the institutions by performing calibrated and possibly spectacular political interventions. Consequently, from a methodological point of view, this contribution would have approached from a slightly different angle the institutional positioning and political latitude that the head of state would have given himself or herself in his or her assessment of the management of a severe health crisis by a government acting under a system of *cohabitation* – taking for granted that the visibility of the President of the Republic remains intrinsically part of his or her constitutional function in all political systems.

While it is obvious that during the pandemic the command of the political narrative and of the executive decisions in health matters belongs to the President of the Republic, the particularities of the French political regime – especially when functioning in a *système présidentialiste*[36] – mean that he or she is very much protected from criminal responsibility while the Prime Minister and the ministers, who merely implement the presidential decisions, are the ones likely to be held criminally responsible.

B. Scope of Responsibility and Area of Tolerated Risk

The criminal liability of the President of the fifth Republic could be triggered in two distinct scenarios envisaged by articles 67 and 68 of the Constitution which establish the current general liability regime applicable to the sitting President of the Republic.

[36] Due to the coincidental outcomes of the 2017 presidential and legislative elections.

Article 67 is unequivocal: 'The President of the Republic shall incur no liability by reason of acts carried out in his official capacity, subject to the provisions of Articles 53-2 and 68 hereof'.[37] In other words, the President of the Republic cannot be held criminally liable for the acts committed in the exercise of his or her functions. This principle knows of only two exceptions, as enshrined in articles 53-2 and 68 respectively.[38]

Since the constitutional reform of 23 February 2007,[39] under article 68, the criminal responsibility of the head of state can be activated in case of 'a breach of his duties patently incompatible with his continuing in office'.[40] What exactly can qualify as a breach of duties patently incompatible with presidential functions remains cryptic and, since this procedure has never been used in the fifth Republic, attempting to determine its concrete meaning would be speculative.[41] Yet, this is a key issue in the context of the present contribution as the question necessarily arises whether a criminal offence would characterise such a breach and expose the President of the Republic to removal from office. As will be discussed later, if they were to be criminally qualified, the acts of the executive – including those of the President of the Republic – would most likely fall under the category of involuntary offences against the physical integrity of the person. Would the decisions undertaken by President Macron in the management of the Covid-19 crisis qualify as such offences? In turn, would such offences constitute breaches patently incompatible with his continuing in office? A positive answer to these questions would be absolutely required to trigger the removal from office procedure and engage the criminal liability of the President of the Republic. And even then, a criminal prosecution would most likely collide with the immunity of jurisdiction attached to the acts of the President of the Republic in the exercise of his or her functions, under which the management of the sanitary crisis undoubtedly falls.

Placed in a radically opposite position to that of the President of the Republic whose criminal liability may only be engaged in very restricted circumstances and whose official acts remain immune from jurisdiction,[42] the Prime Minister and the government can be held criminally liable for acts performed in the exercise of their functions, even if these acts were decided by the President of the Republic under the present systemic configuration specific to *présidentialisme*. Historically, the scope of criminal responsibility when it comes to members of the government was at the heart of a health scandal that made headline news, namely, the case known as the infected blood case (*affaire du sang contaminé*). The facts date back to 1985 when HIV-infected blood was used for transfusing haemophiliac patients; a use which was known and authorised at the highest governmental level. Faced with the immunity enjoyed by members of government at the

---

[37] The original version reads: 'Le Président de la République n'est pas responsable des actes accomplis en cette qualité, sous réserve des dispositions des articles 53-2 et 68'.

[38] Art 53-2 will be addressed in s II.C.

[39] Loi constitutionnelle n° 2007-238 du 23 février 2007 portant modification du titre IX de la Constitution, *Journal Officiel de la République Française* n° n° 0047 du 24 février 2007.

[40] The original version reads: 'manquement à ses devoirs manifestement incompatible avec l'exercice de son mandat'.

[41] This new concept (of a breach 'patently incompatible …') replaced the former notion of high treason (*haute trahison*), for which former head of state Maréchal Philippe Pétain (tried for the crime against internal security and intelligence with the enemy) was convicted on 15 August 1945.

[42] See below s II.C.

time, President François Mitterrand criticised the impossibility to hold them liable.[43] It is thus this health crisis that led to a constitutional reform, the establishment of the Cour de justice de la République and the specification that it could operate retroactively.[44] With this reform, then Prime Minister Laurent Fabius, Social Affairs Minister Georgina Dufoix and Health Minister Edmond Hervé were all made to answer a charge of manslaughter. In its judgment of 9 March 1999, the Cour de justice de la République found Fabius and Dufoix not guilty. Hervé was convicted but the finding of guilt was not accompanied with a sentence.[45] While this was the first case before this court, it is possible that its outcome fuelled ongoing contestation of this institution, heavily criticised for being inherently political.[46]

C. Impact of Immunities

The members of the French government do not enjoy immunity from prosecution. By contrast, the criminal liability regime of the President of the fifth Republic is a protective regime essentially akin to a privilege of jurisdiction in the name of the principles of the separation of powers and of the continuity of the State. In other words, the absence of criminal responsibility of the President of the Republic must be understood principally as a circumscribed jurisdictional criminal immunity, since it is limited to the duration of the presidential mandate. To be sure, the scope of this criminal immunity has been specified by the Conseil constitutionnel in its decision of 22 January 1999, in which it recalled that:

> By Article 68 of the Constitution, the President of the Republic may not be held liable for acts performed in the exercise of his duties except in the case of high treason; moreover, during his term of office he may be indicted only in the High Court of Justice by the procedure determined by that Article.[47]

Put differently, the acts performed in the exercise of the presidential functions are immune from criminal jurisdiction, even after the President of the Republic ceases to be in office. For acts performed in a private capacity, the criminal immunity of the President of the Republic, conceived as an absence of criminal responsibility before the ordinary judge during the exercise of his or her functions, is therefore explicitly legally temporary; the prescription of public action being suspended only for the duration of the presidential mandate. This is thus very likely a closed avenue for any complaint linked to the acts of the President of the Republic related to the Covid-19 pandemic since these acts were performed in an official and public capacity.

---

[43] President François Mitterrand declared that 'ministers should be held accountable for their acts' ('les ministres doivent rendre compte de leurs actes'). 'Entretien à l'Elysée avec François Mitterrand' (*Archives Vidéo INA*, 9 November 1992), www.youtube.com/watch?v=akTvsKGNhus.

[44] Constitution, art 68-3.

[45] Arrêt du 9 mars 1999, Cour de justice de la République, N° affaire: 99-001, www.courdecassation.fr/files/files/D%C3%A9cisions_CJR/Arret_du_9_mars_1999.pdf.

[46] See below s II.D.

[47] Conseil constitutionnel, Decision no. 98-408 DC of 22 January 1999, Treaty laying down the Statute of the International Criminal Court, www.conseil-constitutionnel.fr/en/decision/1999/98408DC.htm.

The only exception to this immunity, expressly mentioned in article 67, features in article 53-2 of the Constitution, which recognises the jurisdiction of the International Criminal Court and which, by accepting the conditions of the Rome Statute, simultaneously accepts the lifting of head of state immunity in cases of genocide, crimes against humanity, war crimes and aggression.[48] Going into the detail of each of these offences would fall outside the scope of this analysis. Suffice here to note that the management of the Covid-19 pandemic by President Macron obviously falls short of meeting any of the definitional elements of these crimes. While allegations of war crimes or aggression would be fundamentally erroneous since the definitional elements of the crimes – a conflict situation for the former and an aggressive act towards another state for the latter – would not be met, accusations of crimes against humanity or genocide would be equally mistaken. Even worse, they would trivialise the meaning of these atrocities and make a sordid mockery of both the crimes and their victims. Even if the Covid-19 pandemic has generated deaths *en masse*, this does not mean that a crime against humanity or genocide has been perpetrated; calling upon international criminal law in the French context would fundamentally distort its very substance.

Ultimately, both French constitutional criminal law and international criminal law are ill-adapted to the current situation: while the former is overly politicised, the latter is conceptually ill-suited. This means that the possible routes via which the criminal liability of the sitting President of the fifth Republic could be envisaged are actually not available when it comes to his management of the Covid-19 pandemic. He is not only constitutionally unaccountable politically but is also de facto shielded from any form of criminal liability.

D. Prosecutorial Matters

If the President of the Republic faces prosecution for 'a breach of his duties patently incompatible with his continuing in office',[49] he or she is answerable to Parliament constituted as a Haute Cour (High Court).[50] As clarified by the Conseil constitutionnel, the Haute Cour does *not* constitute a jurisdiction – it is not a criminal court or tribunal – but rather a parliamentary assembly.[51]

By contrast, the current criminal liability regime of ministers stems from the constitutional law of 27 July 1993 and the adoption of articles 68-1, 68-2 and 68-3 in the Constitution. These dispositions established the Cour de justice de la République

---

[48] See the Rome Statute of the International Criminal Court (Rome Statute) (Rome, 17 July 1998).

[49] Original version reads: 'manquement à ses devoirs manifestement incompatible avec l'exercice de son mandat'.

[50] The High Court combines members of the National Assembly and of the Senate. It entered into force with the adoption of the organic law of 24 November 2014. See Loi organique n° 2014–1392 du 24 novembre 2014 portant application de l'article 68 de la Constitution, *Journal Officiel de la République Française* n°0272 du 25 novembre 2014.

[51] See Conseil constitutionnel, Décision n° 2014-703 DC du 19 novembre 2014, Loi organique portant application de l'article 68 de la Constitution, www.conseil-constitutionnel.fr/decision/2014/2014703DC.htm.

precisely to exercise jurisdiction over ministers and settle disputes that may arise in relation to the exercise of their functions. As per article 68-2:

> The Court of Justice of the Republic shall consist of fifteen members: twelve Members of Parliament, elected in equal number from among their ranks by the National Assembly and the Senate after each general or partial renewal by election of these Houses, and three judges of the Cour de cassation, one of whom shall preside over the Court of Justice of the Republic.[52]

With this mixed composition, the Constitution expressly opts for a combination of political and ordinary justice. Interestingly for the purposes of the present contribution, the enactment of this constitutional law was directly linked to the previously mentioned infected blood case (*affaire du sang contaminé*). Since its inception, this court has been expressly denounced on the grounds that it continues to embody a form of political justice within which the partisan political logic in the minds of members of Parliament judging their peers risks taking precedence over the objective assessment of a criminal offence. In 2018, a reform aiming at the suppression of the Cour de justice de la République and its replacement with the already existing Cour d'appel de Paris – *i.e.* an ordinary jurisdiction – was initiated. If this reform were to materialise, members of the executive would still not be treated as purely ordinary litigants: to avoid any abusive judicial interference with the ministerial function, a Commission des Requêtes would, as is currently the case, carry out a filtering.[53]

Until then, the Cour de justice de la République remains the judicial formation competent to adjudicate complaints relating to the management of the Covid-19 pandemic by the government. To that effect, article 68-2 specifies that:

> Any person claiming to be a victim of a serious crime or other major offence committed by a member of the Government in the holding of his office may lodge a complaint with a petitions committee.[54]

And indeed, a number of complaints have been lodged in relation to the governmental management of the Covid-19 pandemic.[55] The investigation of complaints is carried out by a complaints commission, which 'shall order the case to be either closed or forwarded to the Chief Public Prosecutor at the Cour de cassation for referral to the Court of Justice of the Republic'.[56]

Ultimately, the proceedings before the Cour de justice de la République, if they do occur, risk being politically tainted and, under the current criminal liability regime of the

---

[52] The original version reads: 'La Cour de justice de la République comprend quinze juges: douze parlementaires élus, en leur sein et en nombre égal, par l'Assemblée nationale et par le Sénat après chaque renouvellement général ou partiel de ces assemblées et trois magistrats du siège à la Cour de cassation, dont l'un préside la Cour de justice de la République'.

[53] See Projet de loi constitutionnelle pour un renouveau de la vie démocratique, introduced and then suspended in 2018, www.vie-publique.fr/loi/273301-reforme-constitutionnelle-2019-pour-un-renouveau-de-la-vie-democratique.

[54] The original version reads: 'Toute personne qui se prétend lésée par un crime ou un délit commis par un membre du Gouvernement dans l'exercice de ses fonctions peut porter plainte auprès d'une commission des requêtes'.

[55] By 5 July 2021, over 160 such complaints had been lodged in relation to the Covid-19 pandemic. See 'Cour de justice de la République: quelle est cette juridiction, seule habilitée à juger les ministres en exercice?' (*le dauphiné*, 5 July 2021), www.ledauphine.com/faits-divers-justice/2021/07/05/cour-de-justice-de-la-republique-quelle-est-cette-juridiction-seule-habilitee-a-juger-les-ministres-en-exercice.

[56] Constitution, art 68-2.

Prime Minister and members of government, such criminal proceedings – not to mention conviction – might prove volatile. Even if not, the fact is that while the criminal liability of the Prime Minister and of the relevant members of government is engaged and recognised, the President of the Republic will remain shielded from criminal prosecution. Throughout the Covid-19 crisis, the successive Prime Ministers, Edouard Philippe and Jean Castex, and Health Ministers, Agnès Buzyn and Olivier Véran, have undoubtedly been visible with regular interventions on television – at one point the Health Minister was intervening on a daily basis to convey the contamination figures and death rate – yet, President Macron is the one deciding the policies to be adopted and the measures to be taken. Even if exposed and visible in the media, the Prime Minister and the Health Minister merely specify or clarify the presidential decisions, which are sometimes in direct contradiction with what they themselves had previously enounced. Thus, although they are active executants with a relatively limited scope of manoeuvre – the presidential decisions always taking precedence, their only option being resignation – they will be the ones against whom charges are brought if criminal prosecutions are initiated.[57]

III. CAUSATION

A. Causation (General Principles)

The causal link between the offender's behaviour and the wrong caused, *i.e.* causation (*lien de causalité*), needs to be established to determine criminal liability.[58] Since a law of 10 July 2000, a distinction was made in French criminal law between direct and indirect causation.[59] Direct causation can be defined as the most proximate cause, and generally stems from a physical contact between the offender and the victim. It is thus unlikely that direct causation could be established in trying to link the decisions of the French executive with the harm caused by the pandemic. By contrast, and by virtue of article 121-3 of the French Code Pénal, indirect causation would be more plausible. Indirect causation exists when:

> Natural persons who have not directly contributed to causing the damage, but who have created or contributed to create the situation which allowed the damage to happen who failed to take steps enabling it to be avoided, are criminally liable where it is shown that they have broken a duty of care or precaution laid down by statute or regulation in a manifestly deliberate manner, or have committed a specified piece of misconduct which exposed another person to a particularly serious risk of which they must have been aware.[60]

---

[57] For an opinion against the criminal prosecution of the French executive for the management of the Covid-19 crisis, see O Beaud, 'Mal gouverner est-il un crime? Réflexions critiques sur les perquisitions effectuées dans le cadre de l'enquête judiciaire relative aux ministres impliqués dans la gestion de l'épidémie du Coronavirus' (*Blog de Jus Politicum*, 21 October 2020), blog.juspoliticum.com/2020/10/21/mal-gouverner-est-il-un-crime-reflexions-critiques-sur-les-perquisitions-effectuees-dans-le-cadre-de-lenquete-judiciaire-relative-aux-ministres-impliques-dans-la-gestion-de-lepidem/. See also Brunet, 'The Hyper-Executive State' (n 8) 210.

[58] On the attribution of responsibility in French criminal law, see generally F Rousseau, *L'imputation dans la responsabilité pénale* (Paris, Dalloz, 2009).

[59] See Loi n° 2000-647 du 10 juillet 2000 tendant à préciser la définition des délits non intentionnels, *Journal Officiel de la République Française* n°159 (11 July 2000).

[60] All English translations of the French Code pénal are taken from the translation available at: www.legislationline.org/download/id/3316/file/France_Criminal%20Code%20updated%20on%2012-10-2005.pdf.

Interestingly, the scope of this disposition was specified – and admittedly narrowed – by a law of 11 May 2020 which extended the state of health emergency and added article L. 3136-2 to the Code of Public Health according to which:

> Article 121-3 is applicable by taking into consideration the competences, power and means that were at the disposal of the author of the acts in the crisis situation that justified the state of health emergency as well as the nature of his or her missions or functions, notably as local authority or employer.[61]

In establishing causation, Rousseau notes that the French 'criminal jurisprudence is not insensitive to the theory of adequate causation',[62] according to which it is the most likely cause that will be retained, notably – although not exclusively – in cases of manslaughter and involuntary offences.[63] He illustrates this argument by reference to two cases in which the victim died in the aftermath of an accident provoked by the defendant which however *should not* have caused the death of the victim and in which the defendant was thus discharged of manslaughter.[64] For Rousseau, resort to adequate causation seems to be a means for the court to establish causation with certainty rather than to distinguish between direct and indirect causation.[65] Whether the decisions – or lack of – on the part of the French executive can be considered as the most probable cause of the harm linked to the Covid-19 pandemic is the exact question the below sections on criminal offences will explore.

B. Causation and 'Thin Skull' Scenarios

Under French criminal law, causation need not be exclusive:

> Even if causation is shared by several participants (coactivity), linked to other events (intervention of a third party …), or in connection with a wrongdoing attributable to the victim, the defendant remains entirely responsible, save in the case of force majeure.[66]

The original version reads: 'les personnes physiques qui n'ont pas causé directement le dommage, mais qui ont créé ou contribué à créer la situation qui a permis la réalisation du dommage ou qui n'ont pas pris les mesures permettant de l'éviter, sont responsables pénalement s'il est établi qu'elles ont, soit violé de façon manifestement délibérée une obligation particulière de prudence ou de sécurité prévue par la loi ou le règlement, soit commis une faute caractérisée et qui exposait autrui à un risque d'une particulière gravité qu'elles ne pouvaient ignorer.'

[61] Translation by the authors. The original version reads: 'L'article 121-3 du code pénal est applicable en tenant compte des compétences, du pouvoir et des moyens dont disposait l'auteur des faits dans la situation de crise ayant justifié l'état d'urgence sanitaire, ainsi que de la nature de ses missions ou de ses fonctions, notamment en tant qu'autorité locale ou employeur'.

[62] See Rousseau, *L'imputation* (n 58) 85. Translation by the authors. The original version reads: 'la jurisprudence pénale n'est pas insensible à la théorie de la causalité adéquate'.

[63] See Rousseau, *L'imputation* (n 58) 86.

[64] Such was the outcome in a case where a motorist had slightly wounded a cyclist who later died of a heart attack while trying to follow the vehicle, as well as in a case where the motorist had wounded a pedestrian who later died of a nosocomial infection caught in hospital. See Crim. 25 April 1967, *Bull. crim.* 1967, n°119 and Crim. 5 October 2004, *Bull. crim.* 2004, n°230, cited in Rousseau, *L'imputation* (2009) 85.

[65] Rousseau, *L'imputation* (n 58) 85.

[66] Y Mayaud, *Droit pénal général* 7th edn (Paris, Presses Universitaires de France, 2021) 360. Translation by the authors. The original version reads: 'En droit pénal, [la causalité] serait-elle commune à plusieurs participants (coactivité), associée à d'autres événements (fait d'un tiers …), voire en rapport avec une faute imputable à la victime elle-même, la responsabilité reste totale pour le prévenu, réserve faite de la force majeure'.

Practically speaking, this means that if the actions of the defendant contributed to the wrong caused, the defendant may be held criminally liable: their actions do not need to be the sole and exclusive cause of the harm suffered. With respect to the harm suffered as a result of the alleged ill-management of the Covid-19 pandemic by the French executive, this ill-management – while it still needs to be demonstrated – need not be the exclusive cause of the harm for the members of the French government to be held criminally liable. Yet, as mentioned, first, the ill-management must be proven and second, it must be established as one of the causes of the harm suffered.

C. Restricting Causality: Policy and Doctrinal Issues

French criminal law operates a distinction between direct and indirect causation. As Mayaud explains, 'a mere misconduct is sufficient when the harm is direct, while a deliberate or characterised wrongdoing is required when the harm is indirect'.[67] In this instance, direct causation seems to be excluded since there has been no physical contact between the potential offenders – members of the French executive – and the victims who suffered or died from Covid-19. Yet, the theory of indirect causation would still allow for the recognition of their criminal liability if it is shown that they have committed a wrongdoing, for instance by creating, or contributing to create, a situation which allowed the suffering or death of individuals from Covid-19 or that they failed to take the necessary steps to avoid such suffering and death. It would also be necessary to demonstrate that they broke a duty of care or precaution as enshrined in the law in a manifestly deliberate manner or that they have committed a certain misconduct which exposed individuals to serious health risks of which they must have been aware. It is thus in the light of indirect causation that the different available criminal offences need to be approached.

IV. THE STRUCTURE OF HOMICIDE OFFENCES AND ASSAULT/AGGRAVATED ASSAULT/SERIOUS BODILY HARM OFFENCES

This section will review and consider the possible criminal charges that the successive Prime Ministers and ministers – and, as mentioned earlier, the President of the Republic if such charges qualify as breaches incompatible with his presidential duties – could potentially be facing. Although speculative since the complaints lodged against the Prime Minister and ministers are not readily available, this analysis generates key reflections on the criminal liability of the French executive.

---

[67] See Mayaud, *Droit pénal général* (n 66) 361. Translation by the authors. The original version reads: 'une simple faute suffit lorsque le dommage est direct, alors qu'une faute délibérée ou caractérisée est exigée en cas de dommage indirect'.

A. Murder/Intentional Homicide

The French Penal Code defines murder in a fairly swift manner as: 'The wilful causing of the death of another person'.[68] When 'committed with premeditation', the French Penal Code specifies that murder is assassination.[69] Using any of these two offences to qualify the behaviour of the French executive in its management of the Covid-19 pandemic would be preposterous and defamatory. There is indeed no evidence at all that any members of the French executive wilfully caused the death of any person from Covid-19.

Under article 221-5 of the French Penal Code: 'Making an attack against the life of another person by the use or administration of substances liable to cause death constitutes poisoning'.[70] Interestingly, it was this charge that the defendants initially had to face in the previously mentioned *affaire du sang contaminé*; a charge that was subsequently dropped following the Cour de cassation's finding that 'the mental element of the crime of poisoning includes not only the intent to administer a deadly substance but also the intent to kill'.[71] Practically speaking, this means that it is only if the anti-Covid 19 vaccine was qualified as a deadly substance, if the members of the executive knew of this lethal character, and if they had the intent to kill that the vaccination campaign they orchestrated could be characterised as poisoning. Unless falling for the various conspiracy theories, this hypothesis seems whimsical and highly improbable. Applied to the management of the Covid-19 pandemic, it is here also highly unlikely that such a charge would be applicable due to an impossibility to establish either the intent to administer a deadly substance or the intent to kill on the part of the French executive.

B. Culpable Homicide/Manslaughter

In its article 221-6, the French Penal Code defines manslaughter as: 'Causing the death of another person by clumsiness, rashness, inattention, negligence or breach of an obligation of safety or prudence imposed by statute or regulations'.[72]

It is conceivable that certain complaints will invoke the clumsiness and/or negligence of the successive Prime Ministers and Health Ministers, and will underpin their claims with evidence of their ill-preparation, for instance when it came to the poorly managed

---

[68] French Penal Code, art 221-1. The original version reads: 'Le fait de donner volontairement la mort à autrui constitue un meurtre'.

[69] French Penal Code, art 221-3.

[70] The original version reads: 'Le fait d'attenter à la vie d'autrui par l'emploi ou l'administration de substances de nature à entraîner la mort constitue un empoisonnement'.

[71] Cass. Crim., 2 July 1998, n° 98-80.529, available at: www.legifrance.gouv.fr/juri/id/JURITEXT000007069037/. Translation by the authors. The original version reads: 'l'élément intentionnel du crime d'empoisonnement suppose non seulement l'intention d'administrer une substance mortifère, mais l'intention de tuer'. See also: Cass. crim., 18 juin 2003, n° 02-85.199, *Procureur général près la cour d'appel de Paris et autres*, www.legifrance.gouv.fr/juri/id/JURITEXT000007069442/. See generally Mayaud, *Droit pénal général* (n 66) 305–06.

[72] The original version reads: 'Le fait de causer … par maladresse, imprudence, inattention, négligence ou manquement à une obligation de prudence ou de sécurité imposée par la loi ou le règlement, la mort d'autrui constitue un homicide involontaire'.

supply of masks. This was not the sole example of ill-management. In the course of the pandemic, the French executive also decided to reduce the number of hospital beds, thereby increasing the pressure on hospitals and generating delays in the treatment of other diseases, including potentially lethal ones.[73] Showing a clear lack of discernment and insight, the French executive also failed to anticipate the disastrous consequences of the lockdown on the increase of domestic violence.[74]

While one can only acknowledge that, with the Covid-19 pandemic, political decisions are taken in a context of sanitary and scientific uncertainty, it seems clear that caution is required. Yet, the decisions and actions of the executive reveal a high degree of political carelessness. Whether this lack of prudence was prompted by the circumstances, encouraged by media pressure and/or aggravated by the exponential use of social media or stemmed for a combination of these and other factors is open to interpretation. What is more certain is that when the health and life of individuals are endangered by a political lack of vigilance, this failure can become criminal. If the causal link can be established, the offence defined in article 221-6 of the French Penal Code – in terms of both its material and moral dimensions – could be established.

C. Offences Related to Actions that Cause Serious Bodily Harm (Assault; Grievous Assault; Assault with Intent to Cause Serious Bodily Harm)

Article 222-7 of the French Penal Code criminalises 'acts of violence causing an unintended death'.[75] Article 222-8 specifically envisages the scenario in which these acts are perpetrated 'against a person whose particular vulnerability, due to age, sickness or infirmity, to a physical or psychological disability or to pregnancy, is apparent or known to the perpetrator'.[76] Deprived of the obligation to prove the intent to cause death, this qualification could at first glance appear more appropriate if the actions of the French executive were to be prosecuted – although proving the violence might be close to impossible.

Still, acts of violence that cause bodily harm are criminalised and differentiated by the impact of the outcome on the health of the victim. Article 222-9 of the French Penal Code punishes '[a]cts of violence causing mutilation or permanent disability'[77] while article 222-11 punishes '[a]cts of violence causing a total incapacity to work for more than eight days'.[78] Both dispositions also envisage the specific case of persons of 'particular vulnerability'.[79] In this respect, it is worth noting that article 222-13 punishes '[a]cts of violence causing an incapacity to work of eight days or less or causing no incapacity

---

[73] See, eg 'Olivier Véran tente d'expliquer la fermeture de plus de 5 700 lits à l'hôpital' *Le Monde* (online, 27 October 2021), www.lemonde.fr/societe/article/2021/10/27/difficultes-a-recruter-absenteisme-et-demissions-a-l-origine-de-la-fermeture-des-lits-dans-les-hopitaux-selon-olivier-veran_6100123_3224.html.

[74] See A Taub, 'A New Covid-19 Crisis: Domestic Abuse Rises Worldwide' *The New York Times* (online, 14 April 2020), www.nytimes.com/2020/04/06/world/coronavirus-domestic-violence.html.

[75] The original version reads: 'Les violences ayant entraîné la mort sans intention de la donner'.

[76] The original version reads: 'Sur une personne dont la particulière vulnérabilité, due à son âge, à une maladie, à une infirmité, à une déficience physique ou psychique ou à un état de grossesse, est apparente ou connue de son auteur'.

[77] The original version reads: 'Les violences ayant entraîné une mutilation ou une infirmité permanente'.

[78] The original version reads: 'Les violences ayant entraîné une incapacité totale de travail pendant plus de huit jours'.

[79] See French Penal Code, arts 222-10 (2) and 222-12 (2).

to work'[80] when committed against particularly vulnerable persons. Here also however, these different acts of violence punishable under French criminal law might be inadequate qualifications since it is hard to conceive how violence on the part of the French executive could be established.

In any event, at the time of writing, it appears that it is another criminal charge that has been brought against one member of the government. Former Health Minister Agnès Buzyn was indeed charged by the Cour de justice de la République in September 2021[81] under article 223-1 of the French Penal Code that criminalises the act of endangering the lives of others. Explicitly requiring a manifest and deliberate violation of an obligation of safety and prudence, this offence is defined as:

> The direct exposure of another person to an immediate risk of death or injury likely to cause mutilation or permanent disability by the *manifestly deliberate violation of a specific obligation of safety or prudence* imposed by any statute or regulation.[82]

Three elements are thus cumulatively required for this offence to be established: a 'violation of a specific obligation of safety or prudence' imposed by law; a causal link between this violation and the 'direct exposure of another person to an immediate risk of death or injury likely to cause mutilation or permanent disability'; and the manifestly deliberate character of this violation.[83] According to the case law, a manifestly deliberate violation may be characterised by an 'accumulation of reckless behaviour that may be simultaneous or successive'.[84] Yet, it is precisely this last element of 'manifestly deliberate' that may prove problematic before the Court. Political missteps and mistakes might reflect 'clumsiness, rashness, inattention, negligence or breach of an obligation of safety or prudence', as per article 221-6, rather than a manifest and deliberate violation of such obligation. Charging Buzyn – or other members of the government – with endangering the lives of others might thus be a step too far.

D. Offences Regarding Unborn Foetuses; Interrupting the Course of a (Viable) Pregnancy

The French Penal Code contains a series of dispositions devoted to the protection of the embryo[85] as well as two articles criminalising respectively '[t]he termination of a

---

[80] The original version reads: 'Les violences ayant entraîné une incapacité de travail inférieure ou égale à huit jours ou n'ayant entraîné aucune incapacité de travail'.

[81] See 'France's former health minister charged over handling of Covid crisis' *The Guardian* (online, 10 September 2021), www.theguardian.com/world/2021/sep/10/frances-former-health-minister-charged-over-handling-of-covid-crisis.

[82] Emphasis added. The original version reads: 'Le fait d'exposer directement autrui à un risque immédiat de mort ou de blessures de nature à entraîner une mutilation ou une infirmité permanente par la violation manifestement délibérée d'une obligation particulière de prudence ou de sécurité imposée par la loi ou le règlement'.

[83] See P-H Bovis, 'Mise en danger de la vie d'autrui' (*Village de la Justice*, 6 April 2020), www.village-justice. com/articles/mise-danger-vie-autrui,34539.html.

[84] Vigo Avocats, 'Flash info: les infractions de mise en danger délibérée de la vie d'autrui et de blessures ou homicide involontaires: éléments constitutifs' (30 March 2020), vigo-avocats.com/legal-news/flash-info-les-infractions-de-mise-en-danger-deliberee-de-la-vie-dautrui-et-de-blessures-ou-homicide-involontaires-elements-constitutifs/#_ftn6. In terms of case law they refer to: Crim. 5 janv. 2005, *Gérard X. et a.*, n° 04-82.738 and Crim. 29 juin 2010, n° 09-81.861.

[85] See arts 511–15 to 6511-25-1.

pregnancy without the consent of the person concerned'[86] and the attempt to terminate a pregnancy without the consent of the person concerned.[87] These offences require an intent to harm the embryo and/or terminate the pregnancy.

The most likely hypothesis in which this characterisation could be envisaged would be the previously dismissed poisoning scenario related to the vaccination campaign.[88] Another hypothesis would be the murder scenario, which as already explained would be equally inapplicable, even if article 221-4 (3) of the French Penal Code specifically provides for a higher sentencing in cases of murder committed 'against a person whose particular vulnerability, due to age, sickness or infirmity, or to any physical or psychological disability or to *pregnancy*, is apparent or known to the perpetrator'.[89]

Interestingly, this 'particular vulnerability' is also recognised in the case of 'acts of violence causing an unintended death',[90] which do not require proof of the intent to cause death and which could thus potentially provide for a judicial avenue if it is established that the acts of the French executive caused the interruption of the pregnancies.

Another – and admittedly more reasonable – argument could be based on the failures of the hospital system to fully comply with its duty of care, in all of its aspects. Yet, establishing causation between these alleged failures and the behaviour of the French executive would prove arduous, unless it is established that such failures stem directly from the above-mentioned executive decision to reduce hospital beds. As a result, it is highly unlikely that the French executive could be prosecuted for offences regarding unborn foetuses and interruptions of pregnancies.

E. Failure to Render Assistance

Under Article 223-6 of the French Penal Code: 'Anyone who, being able to prevent by immediate action a felony or a misdemeanour against the bodily integrity of a person, without risk to himself or to third parties, wilfully abstains from doing so' and 'anyone who wilfully fails to offer assistance to a person in danger which he could himself provide without risk to himself or to third parties, or by initiating rescue operations'[91] may be charged with failure to offer assistance to a person in danger.

Against the French executive, the plaintiffs could argue that the hesitations in decision-making triggered delays, which in turn endangered the health and life of the

---

[86] Art 223-10. The original version reads: 'L'interruption de la grossesse sans le consentement de l'intéressée'.

[87] Art 223-11.

[88] See above s IV.A.

[89] Emphasis added. The original version reads: 'Sur une personne dont la particulière vulnérabilité, due à son âge, à une maladie, à une infirmité, à une déficience physique ou psychique ou à un état de grossesse, est apparente ou connue de son auteur'.

[90] See art 222-8.

[91] The original version reads: 'Quiconque pouvant empêcher par son action immédiate, sans risque pour lui ou pour les tiers, soit un crime, soit un délit contre l'intégrité corporelle de la personne s'abstient volontairement de le faire … quiconque s'abstient volontairement de porter à une personne en péril l'assistance que, sans risque pour lui ou pour les tiers, il pouvait lui prêter soit par son action personnelle, soit en provoquant un secours'.

population. However, unlike with the qualification of manslaughter, they would here need to prove a failure to act; failure which could constitute indirect causation. In the context of the management of the Covid-19 pandemic by the government, the tergiversations and delayed actions coupled with a certain form of voluntary refusals to take action (for example when it came to the government's initial refusal to re-stock masks)[92] could coincide with the qualification of failure to offer assistance to a person in danger. This conclusion is however speculative as existing relevant case law – dealing with individual acts rather than with governmental ones – would not extend to this particular context.

The plaintiffs could also rely on another criminal qualification, that of abstaining from combatting a natural disaster which, as per article 223-7 of the French Penal Code, is characterised when a person 'voluntarily abstains from taking or initiating measures, which involve no risk to himself or to third parties, to combat a natural disaster likely to endanger the safety of others'.[93]

With this qualification, the plaintiffs would first need to establish that the Covid-19 is a natural disaster. This might seem fairly straightforward but could open a debate within the courtroom as to the origins of the pandemic, requiring the hearing of scientific experts who might not agree and who might be unable to effectively guide the judges in their determination. The plaintiffs would here also need to demonstrate that the successive Prime Ministers and Health Ministers '*voluntarily* abstained from taking or initiating measures'. This voluntariness would characterise indirect causation, as in the above-mentioned example of the explicit refusal to re-stock masks.

V. DEFENCES, JUSTIFICATIONS AND EXCUSES

French criminal law knows of four '*faits justificatifs généraux*': the order of the law, the command of lawful authority, self-defence and necessity.[94]

A. The Order of the Law

Under French criminal law, the order of the law relieves a person from criminal liability when that person 'performs an act prescribed or authorised by legislative or regulatory provisions'.[95] This justification would not be available to the members of the French executive since they are the ones who initiated the impugned legislation and practice.

---

[92] See 'Contre le coronavirus, Agnès Buzyn juge "inutile" l'achat de masques' *Huffington Post* (online, 27 January 2020), www.huffingtonpost.fr/entry/contre-le-coronavirus-agnes-buzyn-deconseille-lachat-de-masques_fr_5e2e163ec5b6d6767fd6c826.

[93] The original version reads: 'Quiconque s'abstient volontairement de prendre ou de provoquer les mesures permettant, sans risque pour lui ou pour les tiers, de combattre un sinistre de nature à créer un danger pour la sécurité des personnes'.

[94] See Mayaud, *Droit pénal général* (n 66) 518.

[95] French Penal Code, art 122-4. The original version reads: 'N'est pas pénalement responsable la personne qui accomplit un acte prescrit ou autorisé par des dispositions législatives ou réglementaires'.

B. The Command of Lawful Authority

In the same vein, the command of lawful authority can be validly invoked when the person 'performs an action commanded by a lawful authority, unless the action is manifestly unlawful'.[96] Just like the order of the law, this justification is inapplicable in the case at hand since the members of the French executive are the lawful authority.

C. Self-Defence

The third objective justification under French criminal law is self-defence, envisaged in article 122-5 of the French Penal Code as:

> A person is not criminally liable if, confronted with an unjustified attack upon himself or upon another, he performs at that moment an action compelled by the necessity of self-defence or the defence of another person, except where the means of defence used are not proportionate to the seriousness of the attack.

> A person is not criminally liable if, to interrupt the commission of a felony or a misdemeanour against property, he performs an act of defence other than wilful murder, where the act is strictly necessary for the intended objective the means used are proportionate to the gravity of the offence.[97]

Article 122-6 specifies that:

> A person is presumed to have acted in a state of self-defence if he performs an action:

> i)   to repulse at night an entry to an inhabited place committed by breaking in, violence or deception;

> ii) to defend himself against the perpetrators of theft or pillage carried out with violence.[98]

As per these definitions, the only way the executive could claim they acted in self-defence would be for them to demonstrate that Covid-19 was an unjustified attack to which they responded, which seems a rather stretched line of argumentation.

---

[96] French Penal Code, art 122-4. The original version reads: 'N'est pas pénalement responsable la personne qui accomplit un acte commandé par l'autorité légitime, sauf si cet acte est manifestement illégal'.

[97] French Penal Code, art 122-5. The original version reads: 'N'est pas pénalement responsable la personne qui, devant une atteinte injustifiée envers elle-même ou autrui, accomplit, dans le même temps, un acte commandé par la nécessité de la légitime défense d'elle-même ou d'autrui, sauf s'il y a disproportion entre les moyens de défense employés et la gravité de l'atteinte.

N'est pas pénalement responsable la personne qui, pour interrompre l'exécution d'un crime ou d'un délit contre un bien, accomplit un acte de défense, autre qu'un homicide volontaire, lorsque cet acte est strictement nécessaire au but poursuivi dès lors que les moyens employés sont proportionnés à la gravité de l'infraction'.

[98] French Penal Code, art 122-6. The original version reads: 'Est présumé avoir agi en état de légitime défense celui qui accomplit l'acte:

1° Pour repousser, de nuit, l'entrée par effraction, violence ou ruse dans un lieu habité;

2° Pour se défendre contre les auteurs de vols ou de pillages exécutés avec violence'.

D. Necessity

The fourth and last objective justification is necessity, which relieves a person of criminal liability when that person

> if confronted with a present or imminent danger to himself, another person or property, ... performs an act necessary to ensure the safety of the person or property, except where the means used are disproportionate to the seriousness of the threat.[99]

This objective justification could potentially be validly invoked by the French executive.

While trying to preserve economic interests as far as it was feasible to do so, to avoid 'greater evil' of economic disaster, hunger and hardship, the French executive – under the direction of the President of the Republic – had one objective: to stop the spread of the virus '*quoiqu'il en coûte*' ('whatever the cost'). This probably explains why, so far, no member of the French government has claimed necessity when facing accusations of ill-management of the pandemic. Rather, faced with these accusations and potential criminal charges, the successive Prime Ministers and members of the government have so far claimed that they have consistently acted in good faith and recalled that their decisions had been taken in accordance with scientific advice.[100] The two successive Health Ministers themselves are physicians and thus scientifically trained and knowledgeable. Their scientific background could thus be invoked as a shield from criminal responsibility. It could however backfire in the sense that, as physicians, they should have exercised their duty of care, as discussed above, with particularly acute diligence.

VI. CORPORATE CRIMINAL LIABILITY

A. Overview of Corporate Criminal Liability

Article 121-2 of the French Penal Code is unequivocal: 'Legal persons, *with the exception of the State*, are criminally liable for the offences committed on their account by their organs or representatives'.[101] Yet, 'local public authorities and their associations incur criminal liability only for offences committed in the course of their activities which may

---

[99] French Penal Code, art 122-7. The original version reads: 'N'est pas pénalement responsable la personne qui, face à un danger actuel ou imminent qui menace elle- même, autrui ou un bien, accomplit un acte nécessaire à la sauvegarde de la personne ou du bien, sauf s'il y a une disproportion entre les moyens employés et la gravité de la menace'.

[100] For instance, before the Senate's investigative commission on 23 September 2020, Sibeth Ndiaye – former spokesperson of the government – reaffirmed that she never lied in relation to the masks stock and policies. See G Jacquot, '"À aucun moment, on ne m'a demandé de mentir sur ce qu'était la situation des masques", déclare Sibeth Ndiaye' (*Public Sénat*, 23 September 2020), www.publicsenat.fr/article/parlementaire/a-aucun-moment-on-ne-m-a-demande-de-mentir-sur-ce-qu-etait-la-situation-des.

[101] Emphasis added. The original version reads: 'Les personnes morales, à l'exclusion de l'Etat, sont responsables pénalement'.

be exercised through public service delegation conventions'.[102] Ultimately, '[t]he criminal liability of legal persons does not exclude that of any natural persons who are perpetrators or accomplices to the same act'.[103]

Under French criminal law therefore, and with the exception of the State, 'Legal persons may incur criminal liability' for all the offences listed in the French Penal Code, including wilful injury to life,[104] and could thus be found responsible for murder, assassination, poisoning, or manslaughter. In the context of the Covid-19 pandemic, it is difficult to identify legal persons that could reasonably be prosecuted for criminal wrongdoings although, as previously mentioned, hospitals could see their criminal responsibility engaged for alleged failures to fulfil their duty of care. Other concerned legal persons could be pharmaceutical companies for possible side effects of the anti-Covid-19 vaccine(s), or the media for alleged misinformation.

B. Perpetrator or Accessory

Insofar as the State is immune from criminal prosecution, it cannot be the perpetrator or the accomplice of a crime. Where this question could however arise is with respect to the criminal responsibility of other legal persons, such as those identified in the previous section. If criminal prosecutions were to be engaged against them, their exact role would depend on the particular factual circumstances of each case. This assessment would rely on the dispositions of the French Penal Code which explicitly differentiates between perpetrator and accomplice.

On the one hand it defines the perpetrator as 'the person who: 1° commits the criminally prohibited act; 2° attempts to commit a felony or, in the cases provided for by Statute, a misdemeanour'.[105] On the other hand, the accomplice to a felony or a misdemeanour is

> the person who knowingly, by aiding and abetting, facilitates its preparation or commission
>
> or
>
> any person who, by means of a gift, promise, threat, order, or an abuse of authority or powers, provokes the commission of an offence or gives instructions to commit it, is also an accomplice.[106]

---

[102] French Penal Code, art 121-2. The original version reads: 'les collectivités territoriales et leurs groupements ne sont responsables pénalement que des infractions commises dans l'exercice d'activités susceptibles de faire l'objet de conventions de délégation de service public'.

[103] French Penal Code, art 121-2. The original version reads: 'La responsabilité pénale des personnes morales n'exclut pas celle des personnes physiques auteurs ou complices des mêmes faits'.

[104] French Penal Code, art 221-5-2. The original version reads: 'Les personnes morales déclarées responsables pénalement, dans les conditions prévues par l'article 121-2, des infractions définies à la présente section'.

[105] French Penal Code, art 121-4. The original version reads: 'Est auteur de l'infraction la personne qui: 1° Commet les faits incriminés; 2° Tente de commettre un crime ou, dans les cas prévus par la loi, un délit'.

[106] French Penal Code, art 121-7. The original version reads: 'Est complice d'un crime ou d'un délit la personne qui sciemment, par aide ou assistance, en a facilité la préparation ou la consommation.
Est également complice la personne qui par don, promesse, menace, ordre, abus d'autorité ou de pouvoir aura provoqué à une infraction ou donné des instructions pour la commettre'.

Under French criminal law, a distinction is thus drawn between acts with 'tend to prepare, facilitate and realise the offence' and acts 'which, by the simultaneity of action and reciprocate assistance, constitute the perpetration' of the offence, whose authors thus qualify more as co-authors than as accomplices.[107]

VII. FORMS OF PARTICIPATION

The French Penal Code punishes both the author of the crime or of the attempt to commit the crime and the accomplice. Complicity itself is divided into two forms of participation: aiding and abetting as well as provoking or instructing. Under article 121-7, the aider and abetter who 'facilitates [the] preparation or commission of the offence' is criminally liable,[108] as is someone who 'by means of a gift, promise, threat, order, or an abuse of authority or powers, provokes the commission of an offence or gives instructions to commit it'.[109] Rousseau notes that this disposition 'solely requires an intentional participation of the accomplice, without mentioning any association with the perpetrator'.[110]

This is however not to say that French criminal law does not encompass the *entente criminelle* understood as:

A criminal association consist[ing] of any group formed or any conspiracy established with a view to the preparation, marked by one or more material actions, of one or more felonies, or of one or more misdemeanours punished by at least five years' imprisonment.[111]

As we have previously established, the State cannot be held criminally liable, be it as an author, a co-author, an accomplice or a member of a criminal association while the participation of other legal persons would need to be judicially assessed. In theory, and contrastingly, individual members of the French executive could see their criminal liability engaged for their management of the Covid-19 pandemic either on their own or as part of an association. Regardless of the form of participation, if it was established that a criminal offence was indeed perpetrated, it would be for the Haute Cour (for the President of the Republic), the Cour de justice de la République (for the Prime Minister and the members of the government) or ordinary courts (for legal persons or other natural persons) to qualify the mode of perpetration.

---

[107] See Crim., 17 December 1859, D.P. 1860.1.196. Translation by the authors. Cited in Mayaud, *Droit pénal général* (2021) 483: 'Dans les actes de complicité, il faut distinguer ceux qui, extrinsèques à l'acte, tendent à en préparer, faciliter et réaliser la consommation, de ceux qui, par la simultanéité d'action et l'assistance réciproque, en constituent la perpétration même; il suit que les individus coupables de ces derniers actes sont bien moins des complices que des coauteurs de l'infraction'.

[108] French Penal Code, art 121-7(1).

[109] French Penal Code, art 121-7(2).

[110] Rousseau, *L'imputation* (n 58) 258. Translation by the authors. The original version reads: 'l'article 121-7 exige seulement une participation intentionnelle du complice, sans évoquer une quelconque entente avec l'auteur'.

[111] French Penal Code, art 450-1. The original version reads: 'Constitue une association de malfaiteurs tout groupement formé ou entente établie en vue de la préparation, caractérisée par un ou plusieurs faits matériels, d'un ou plusieurs crimes ou d'un ou plusieurs délits punis d'au moins cinq ans d'emprisonnement'.

VIII. ATTEMPT

As per the above, the person who attempts to commit the crime will be considered as the author of the crime. Article 121-5 of the French Penal Code clarifies that 'an attempt is committed where, being demonstrated by a beginning of execution, it was suspended or failed to achieve the desired effect solely through circumstances independent of the perpetrator's will'.[112]

In the context of the management of the Covid-19 pandemic, this attempt scenario is difficult to envisage: what would this 'desired effect' be? Since it cannot be reasonably conceived as the death of hundreds of thousands of people, it follows that the qualification of attempt seems irrelevant to the case at hand.

IX. SANCTIONS, SENTENCING, PUNISHMENT, REPARATIONS AND/OR RESTORATIVE JUSTICE

A. General Sentencing Framework for the Crimes under Discussion

Murder is punished with thirty years' imprisonment[113] while assassination is punished by a criminal imprisonment for life.[114] Also punished by criminal imprisonment for life are:

> Murder which precedes, accompanies or follows another felony;[115]
>
> Murder which is intended either to prepare or to facilitate a misdemeanour, or to assist an escape or to ensure the impunity of the misdemeanant or an accomplice to a misdemeanour;[116]
>
> [Murder committed] against a person whose particular vulnerability, due to age, sickness or infirmity, or to any physical or psychological disability or to pregnancy, is apparent or known to the perpetrator.[117]

Poisoning, which also necessitates an intent to kill, is 'punished by thirty years' criminal imprisonment. It is punished by criminal imprisonment for life where it is committed in any of the circumstances provided for by articles 221-2, 221-3 and 221-4',[118] that is to say when poisoning is a means to commit murder.

---

[112] The original version reads: 'La tentative est constituée dès lors que, manifestée par un commencement d'exécution, elle n'a été suspendue ou n'a manqué son effet qu'en raison de circonstances indépendantes de la volonté de son auteur'.

[113] French Penal Code, art 222-1.

[114] French Penal Code, Art 221-3. The original version reads: 'Le meurtre commis avec préméditation ou guet-apens constitue un assassinat. Il est puni de la réclusion criminelle à perpétuité'.

[115] French Penal Code, Art 221-2. The original version reads: 'Le meurtre qui précède, accompagne ou suit un autre crime est puni de la réclusion criminelle à perpétuité'.

[116] French Penal Code, Art 221-2. The original version reads: 'Le meurtre qui a pour objet soit de préparer ou de faciliter un délit, soit de favoriser la fuite ou d'assurer l'impunité de l'auteur ou du complice d'un délit est puni de la réclusion criminelle à perpétuité'.

[117] French Penal Code, Art 221-4 (3). The original version reads: 'Sur une personne dont la particulière vulnérabilité, due à son âge, à une maladie, à une infirmité, à une déficience physique ou psychique ou à un état de grossesse, est apparente ou connue de son auteur'.

[118] French Penal Code, Art 221-5. The original version reads: 'L'empoisonnement est puni de trente ans de réclusion criminelle. Il est puni de la réclusion criminelle à perpétuité lorsqu'il est commis dans l'une des circonstances prévues aux articles 221-2, 221-3 et 221-4'.

The French Penal Code provides for less severe sentences when it comes to non-intentional offences. Manslaughter entails a prison sentence of three or five years and a fine of €45,000 or €75,000, depending on whether the violation of the obligation of safety or prudence was deliberate or not.[119] Acts of violence causing an unintended death are punished by a prison sentence of 15 years,[120] although this sentence may increase to 20 years of imprisonment if the acts were committed 'against a person whose particular vulnerability, due to age, sickness or infirmity, to a physical or psychological disability or to pregnancy, is apparent or known to the perpetrator'.[121] Acts of violence causing mutilation or permanent disability are punished by 10 years' imprisonment and a fine of €150,000[122] and this sentence may increase to 15 years' imprisonment when committed against particularly vulnerable persons.[123] Acts of violence causing a total incapacity to work for more than eight days are punished by three years' imprisonment and a fine of €45,000;[124] a sentence which might be increased to five years' imprisonment and a fine of €75,000 when committed against particularly vulnerable persons.[125] Finally, acts of violence causing an incapacity to work of eight days or less or causing no incapacity to work are punished by three years' imprisonment and a fine of €45,000 when committed against particularly vulnerable persons.[126]

The act of endangering the lives of others is punished by one year's imprisonment and a fine of €15,000.[127]

All the above-listed offences may also incur a whole series of complementary penalties.[128]

With respect to illegal interruptions of pregnancies, both the termination of a pregnancy without the consent of the person concerned and the attempt to forcefully terminate the pregnancy are punished by five years' imprisonment and a fine of €75,000.[129]

Failure to act is also punishable. As per article 223-6 of the French Penal Code, failure to offer assistance to a person in danger is punished by five years' imprisonment and a fine of €75,000. The same penalties apply to anyone who wilfully fails to offer assistance.[130]

---

[119] See French Penal Code, art 221-6.

[120] See French Penal Code, art 222-7.

[121] French Penal Code, art 222-8 (2). The original version reads: 'Sur une personne dont la particulière vulnérabilité, due à son âge, à une maladie, à une infirmité, à une déficience physique ou psychique ou à un état de grossesse, est apparente ou connue de son auteur'.

[122] French Penal Code, art 222-9. The original version reads: 'Les violences ayant entraîné une mutilation ou une infirmité permanente sont punies de dix ans d'emprisonnement et de 150 000 euros d'amende'.

[123] French Penal Code, art 222-10 (2).

[124] French Penal Code, art 222-11. The original version reads: 'Les violences ayant entraîné une incapacité totale de travail pendant plus de huit jours'.

[125] French Penal Code, art 222-12 (2).

[126] French Penal Code, art 222-13. The original version reads: 'Les violences ayant entraîné une incapacité de travail inférieure ou égale à huit jours ou n'ayant entraîné aucune incapacité de travail'.

[127] French Penal Code, art 223-1. The original version reads: 'puni d'un an d'emprisonnement et de 15 000 euros d'amende'.

[128] See French Penal Code, arts 221-8 to 221-11-1.

[129] See French Penal Code, arts 223-10 and 223-11. The original versions read: 'L'interruption de la grossesse sans le consentement de l'intéressée est punie de cinq ans d'emprisonnement et de 75 000 euros d'amende' and 'La tentative du délit prévu à l'article 223-10 est punie des mêmes peines'.

[130] The original version reads: 'Quiconque pouvant empêcher par son action immédiate, sans risque pour lui ou pour les tiers, soit un crime, soit un délit contre l'intégrité corporelle de la personne s'abstient volontairement de le faire est puni de cinq ans d'emprisonnement et de 75 000 euros d'amende.

The penalties are increased to seven years of imprisonment and a fine of €100,000 when the endangered person is a minor of 15 years old.[131] As per article 223-7 of the French Penal Code, abstaining from combatting a natural disaster is punished by two years' imprisonment and a fine of €30,000.[132]

Different forms of participation may also have an influence on sentencing, although – as previously noted – the person who attempts to commit an offence will be considered as the perpetrator and will thus incur the exact same penalties. With respect to criminal associations, the French Penal Code specifies that:

> Where the offences contemplated are felonies or misdemeanours punished by ten years' imprisonment, the participation in a criminal association is punished by ten years' imprisonment and a fine of €150,000. Where the offences contemplated are misdemeanours punished by at least five years' imprisonment, the participation in a criminal association is punished by five years' imprisonment and a fine of €75,000.[133]

Complementary sentences are also provided for,[134] including for legal persons.[135]

Defined as 'one which allows a victim as well as an offender to be actively involved in the resolution of the difficulties resulting from the offence and more particularly in the reparation of any caused harm',[136] a measure of restorative justice necessarily implies an acute exploration of the causes and consequences of the offence and of the ways to address them. In the context of the pandemic, restorative justice would be multidimensional and require an extensive self-reflection on the part of those whose criminal responsibility could be engaged.

B. Sanctions Specifically for Senior Government/Public Officials

Since the start of the Covid-19 pandemic, President Macron has fully endorsed the role of the President of the Republic as conceived in the Constitution of the fifth Republic.

Sera puni des mêmes peines quiconque s'abstient volontairement de porter à une personne en péril l'assistance que, sans risque pour lui ou pour les tiers, il pouvait lui prêter soit par son action personnelle, soit en provoquant un secours'.

[131] French Penal Code, art 223-6.

[132] The original version reads: 'Quiconque s'abstient volontairement de prendre ou de provoquer les mesures permettant, sans risque pour lui ou pour les tiers, de combattre un sinistre de nature à créer un danger pour la sécurité des personnes est puni de deux ans d'emprisonnement et de 30 000 euros d'amende'.

[133] French Penal Code, art 450-1. The original version reads: 'Lorsque les infractions préparées sont des crimes ou des délits punis de dix ans d'emprisonnement, la participation à une association de malfaiteurs est punie de dix ans d'emprisonnement et de 150 000 euros d'amende.
Lorsque les infractions préparées sont des délits punis d'au moins cinq ans d'emprisonnement, la participation à une association de malfaiteurs est punie de cinq ans d'emprisonnement et de 75 000 euros d'amende'.

[134] See French Penal Code, arts 450-3 and 450-5.

[135] See French Penal Code, arts 450-4 and 450-5.

[136] French Code of Criminal Procedure, art 10-1. See generally R Cario and B Sayous, 'Restorative Justice in France: Some Reflections on its Current Development by the French Institute for Restorative Justice' (2018) 1 *The International Journal of Restorative Justice* 122. Translation by the authors. The original version reads: 'Constitue une mesure de justice restaurative toute mesure permettant à une victime ainsi qu'à l'auteur d'une infraction de participer activement à la résolution des difficultés résultant de l'infraction, et notamment à la réparation des préjudices de toute nature résultant de sa commission'.

Although he does act in consultation with scientific committees, the Prime Minister and the government, he is undoubtedly the main decision-maker. Yet, as this contribution has shown, as President of the Republic, he bears no political accountability before Parliament and is essentially immune from criminal jurisdiction for the acts performed as part of his presidential management of the health crisis generated by Covid-19, except in the highly unlikely situation of removal from office activated in case of 'a breach of his duties patently incompatible with his continuing in office'.[137]

This is not to say that the French executive is fully shielded from criminal liability. The Prime Minister and the ministers are not only politically accountable to Parliament, they could also be held criminally responsible for their actions while in office even if they merely implement the decisions of the President of the Republic. As mentioned, a substantial number of complaints have already been lodged with the Cour de justice de la République to establish the criminal liability of the successive Prime Ministers and Health Ministers in their management of the pandemic. Whether these will be successful cannot be speculated upon at this stage. What is certain however is that the determination of criminal responsibility, if any, must be deprived of all partisan considerations; a neutrality which will admittedly be difficult to reach since all the decisions that have been taken to deal with the Covid-19 pandemic have been taken by the executive power, through the person of the President of the Republic, and have thus been highly political.

Since President Macron promulgated the law of 23 March 2020 establishing the state of health emergency, the French public has been confronted with numerous public announcements and a substantial number of political decisions accompanied by legal provisions, all of which oscillate between the governmental imposition of strict prohibitions and behavioural rules *and* the personal exercise of free will. These political interventions and public actions on the part of the executive present an interesting combination of opposites gradually blurring the differentiation between legal requirements and moral responsibilities. The political treatment of the Covid-19 pandemic in France exposes a fluctuating mix of legal obligations and moral obligations purposely insisting on the responsibility of the individual in the respect of confinement measures.[138] The striking moralisation of the political discourse and its legal implications with emphasis deliberately put on personal conscience and responsibility, which is admittedly not specific to France, generates a new kind of ambiguity in modern democratic societies. Interestingly for the purposes of this contribution, the moralisation of the political discourse necessarily implies a responsibilisation of the individual and the concomitant de-responsibilisation of the political actors initiating the discourse, *i.e.* the President of the Republic, the Prime Minister and the government.

This contribution aimed at showing the real difficulties encountered when trying to determine in the French legal framework, both under constitutional law and criminal law, the moment when defective decision-making and political negligence on the part of the executive will call upon not only their political accountability, but also their criminal

---

[137] See Constitution, art 68. The original version reads: 'manquement à ses devoirs manifestement incompatible avec l'exercice de son mandat'.

[138] M Febvre-Issaly, 'Droit, Morale et Epidémie' (*Revue Esprit*, April 2020), esprit.presse.fr/actualites/matthieu-febvre-issaly/droit-morale-et-epidemie-42688.

responsibility. The issue of the legitimacy of the French constitutional orchestration of the criminal liability regime of the executive power and of the wide functional protection granted to the President of the Republic is at the core of the – currently suspended – reform project of 2018 that contemplates replacing the Cour de justice de la République with the Cour d'appel de Paris.[139] Whether this reform will materialise remains to be seen.

C. Corporations and Sentencing

Under article 121-6 of the French Penal Code: 'The accomplice to the offence, in the meaning of article 121-7, is punishable as *a* perpetrator'.[140] Mayaud emphasises the importance of the term '*a* perpetrator' rather than '*the* perpetrator' as it simplified sentencing and allowed for its adaptability to the criminal responsibility of legal persons which cannot necessarily be subjected to the same type of punishment than natural persons.[141] Articles 131-37 to 131-49 of the French Penal Code list the different penalties that may be imposed to legal persons.

As per article 131-37: 'Penalties for felonies and misdemeanours incurred by legal persons are: 1° a fine; 2° in the cases set out by law, the penalties enumerated under Article 131-39 [and] Article 131-39-2'.[142] Article 131-39 provides for:

> Dissolution ...; prohibition to exercise, directly or indirectly one or more social or professional activity, either permanently or for a maximum period of five years; placement under judicial supervision for a maximum period of five years; permanent closure or closure for up to five years of the establishment, or one or more of the establishments, of the enterprise that was used to commit the offences in question; disqualification from public tenders, either permanently or for a maximum period of five years; prohibition, either permanently or for a maximum period of five years, to make a public appeal for funds; prohibition to draw cheques, except those allowing the withdrawal of funds by the drawer from the drawee or certified cheques, and the prohibition to use payment cards, for a maximum period of five years; confiscation of the thing which was used or intended for the commission of the offence, or of the thing which is the product of it; posting a public notice of the decision or disseminating the decision in the written press or using any form of communication to the public by electronic means.[143]

---

[139] See Projet de loi constitutionnelle pour un renouveau de la vie démocratique, introduced and then suspended in 2018, www.vie-publique.fr/loi/273301-reforme-constitutionnelle-2019-pour-un-renouveau-de-la-vie-democratique.

[140] Emphasis added. The original version reads: 'Sera puni comme auteur le complice de l'infraction, au sens de l'article 121-7'.

[141] See Mayaud, *Droit pénal général* (n 66) 503.

[142] The original version reads: 'Les peines criminelles ou correctionnelles encourues par les personnes morales sont: 1° L'amende; 2° Dans les cas prévus par la loi, les peines énumérées à l'article 131-39 et la peine prévue à l'article 131-39-2'.

[143] French Penal Code, art 131-39. The original version reads: '1° La dissolution ...; 2° L'interdiction, à titre définitif ou pour une durée de cinq ans au plus, d'exercer directement ou indirectement une ou plusieurs activités professionnelles ou sociales; 3° Le placement, pour une durée de cinq ans au plus, sous surveillance judiciaire; 4° La fermeture définitive ou pour une durée de cinq ans au plus des établissements ou de l'un ou de plusieurs des établissements de l'entreprise ayant servi à commettre les faits incriminés; 5° L'exclusion des marchés publics à titre définitif ou pour une durée de cinq ans au plus; 6° L'interdiction, à titre définitif ou pour une durée de cinq ans au plus, de procéder à une offre au public de titres financiers ou de faire admettre ses titres

This is in addition to an obligation to be subjected to a compliance programme.[144] Interestingly dissolution and placement under judicial supervision 'do not apply to those public bodies which may incur criminal liability. Nor do they apply to political parties or associations'.[145]

Article 131-38 specifies that:

> The maximum amount of a fine applicable to legal persons is five times that which is applicable to natural persons by the law sanctioning the offence. Where this is an offence for which no provision is made for a fine to be paid by natural persons, the fine incurred by legal persons is €1,000,000.[146]

As per article 131-40:

> The penalties incurred by legal persons for petty offences are: 1° a fine; 2° the penalties entailing forfeiture or restriction of rights set out under article 131-42. These penalties do not preclude the imposition of one or more of the additional penalties set out under article 131-43.[147]

Under article 131-41: 'The maximum amount of a fine applicable to legal persons is five times that which is applicable to natural persons by the regulation sanctioning the offence'.[148]

As previously stressed, for the purposes of French criminal law, the State is not a legal person. Yet, this does not amount to a full immunity of its representatives – President of the Republic, Prime Minister and members of the government. In the present context of moralisation of the political discourse and penalisation of individual conscience, it seems both logically inevitable and ultimately democratic that the only sanction President Macron could have faced was electoral. This is by no means a new type of political test in

---

financiers aux négociations sur un marché réglementé; 7° L'interdiction, pour une durée de cinq ans au plus, d'émettre des chèques autres que ceux qui permettent le retrait de fonds par le tireur auprès du tiré ou ceux qui sont certifiés ou d'utiliser des cartes de paiement; 8° La peine de confiscation, dans les conditions et selon les modalités prévues à l'article 131-21; 9° L'affichage de la décision prononcée ou la diffusion de celle-ci soit par la presse écrite, soit par tout moyen de communication au public par voie électronique; 10° La confiscation de l'animal ayant été utilisé pour commettre l'infraction ou à l'encontre duquel l'infraction a été commise; 11° L'interdiction, à titre définitif ou pour une durée de cinq ans au plus, de détenir un animal; 12° L'interdiction, pour une durée de cinq ans au plus de percevoir toute aide publique attribuée par l'Etat, les collectivités territoriales, leurs établissements ou leurs groupements ainsi que toute aide financière versée par une personne privée chargée d'une mission de service public. La peine complémentaire de confiscation est également encourue de plein droit pour les crimes et pour les délits punis d'une peine d'emprisonnement d'une durée supérieure à un an, à l'exception des délits de presse.'

[144] French Penal Code, art 131-39-2.

[145] French Penal Code, art 131-39. The original version reads: 'Les peines définies aux 1° et 3° ci-dessus ne sont pas applicables aux personnes morales de droit public dont la responsabilité pénale est susceptible d'être engagée. Elles ne sont pas non plus applicables aux partis ou groupements politiques'.

[146] The original version reads: 'Le taux maximum de l'amende applicable aux personnes morales est égal au quintuple de celui prévu pour les personnes physiques par la loi qui réprime l'infraction.
Lorsqu'il s'agit d'un crime pour lequel aucune peine d'amende n'est prévue à l'encontre des personnes physiques, l'amende encourue par les personnes morales est de 1 000 000 euros'.

[147] The original version reads: 'Les peines contraventionnelles encourues par les personnes morales sont:
1° L'amende; 2° Les peines privatives ou restrictives de droits prévues à l'article 131-42; 3° La peine de sanction-réparation prévue par l'article 131-44-1. Ces peines ne sont pas exclusives d'une ou de plusieurs des peines complémentaires prévues à l'article 131-43'.

[148] The original version reads: 'Le taux maximum de l'amende applicable aux personnes morales est égal au quintuple de celui prévu pour les personnes physiques par le règlement qui réprime l'infraction'.

the fifth Republic; it is however one that is eminently open to interpretation notably when it comes to evaluating the political strength of the electoral victory. While French voters ultimately enjoy a key sanctioning power, it paradoxically proves impossible to ascertain whether the executive power, represented by President Macron, leading in practice the government and acting in the political context of *présidentialisme*, is perceived – or not – as either *coupable et/ou responsable*.[149] The result of the 2022 presidential election only provides lines of thought as to whether, in the light of a fierce and vocal opposition manifested by the mixed outcome of the consecutive legislative election, President Macron's electoral victory was or not a *vote-sanction* reflecting the personal expectations and political assertions of citizens in the wake of the pandemic and of the '*quoiqu'il en coûte*' policy.[150]

---

[149] In the course of the proceedings related to the infected blood case, which triggered a radical change in the criminal liability regime of ministers – including the Prime Minister – then Social Affairs minister Georgina Dufoix, who was facing charges of manslaughter, (in)famously said she was 'responsible but not guilty'. We thought it apt to here paraphrase this sentence – yet this is of course not to say that we are equating the two cases.

[150] D Roman, '"Ils ne mourraient pas tous, mais tous étaient frappés" Le coronavirus, révélateur des ambiguïtés de l'appréhension juridique de la vulnérabilité' (2020) chronique n°15 *Revue des droits et libertés fondamentaux*, www.revuedlf.com/droit-administratif/ils-ne-mouraient-pas-tous-mais-tous-etaient-frappes-le-coronavirus-revelateur-des-ambiguites-de-lapprehension-juridique-de-la-vulnerabilite.

6

Germany

MICHAEL BOHLANDER

I. BACKGROUND AND CONTEXTUAL INTRODUCTION[1]

A. Development of the Pandemic

THE FIRST CASE of an infection was registered on 27 January 2020; containment of this and a few others was at first successful. However, during the Carnival season in February 2020, new infections arose and in the following weeks the virus spread across Germany, reaching the first nationwide peak of more than 6,000 new cases per day on 16 March 2020 during the first wave, with the exception of numbers in older age groups which continued to rise until the end of March. The daily infection rate began to drop from the middle of April 2020, creating the impression that this was an effect of the contact restrictions which had been introduced in the meantime (see under Section I.B below). From mid-June 2020 and especially from October 2020 onwards, the numbers rose again in the second wave which reached its peak in December 2020, with a daily rate of 28,000 on 14 December 2020. The nationwide seven-day incidence or case rate (average number of new infections per 100,000 inhabitants over seven days) rose to a peak of 197.6 on Christmas Eve. On 15 January 2021, two million people had been infected. Shortly before and during the ensuing lockdown, numbers receded again, with the incidence rate dropping to 60.4 on 14 February 2021. After this, based on the more contagious Alpha-variant, the third wave began. From December 2020, new variants including the British B.1.1.7 also began to appear in Germany and influence the rise of infections, especially from February 2021. In the following weeks, the incidence rate was typically above 100 and on 12 April 2021, three million had been infected. At the end of April, the third wave incidence rate peaked at 174.8, with the maximum for daily infections at 23,400 registered on 19 April 2021. Cases began to drop again after that, with all member states registering an incidence rate below 50 on 30 May 2021, dropping further to 5.2 in July 2021. Then the more aggressive Delta-variant became prevalent and case numbers rose. On 5 September 2021, more than four million had been infected. The incidence rate had been briefly regressing again to 64.4 on 27 September 2021 but

---

[1] Wikipedia entries are not (yet) usually accepted as academic sources. However, the entry (in German) at https://de.wikipedia.org/wiki/COVID-19-Pandemie_in_Deutschland is an excellent, extensive and continually updated compendium of the development and hence has been used here as the main repository of information from which this section is drawn. The English language entry is not of the same detail and quality, see https://en.wikipedia.org/wiki/COVID-19_pandemic_in_Germany.

with the emerging fourth wave it crossed the threshold of 100 on 23 October 2021, reaching 400 on 24 November 2021. On 25 November 2021, the total number of 100,000 deaths was breached and the daily infections had risen to 75,000. The incidence rate remained above 200 until the end of the year. With the advance of the Omicron variant, it rose to 300 on 6 January 2022 and to the highest peak of 500 since the beginning of the pandemic on 16 January 2022, which was, however, already doubled on 27 January 2022 when it exceeded 1,000, with more than 200,000 new infections per day registered for the first time.[2]

B. Reaction of the Federal and State Governments[3]

On 25 March 2020, the Federal Parliament declared an epidemic situation of nationwide concern under the Act on Preventing and Combatting Infectious Diseases in Humans (*Gesetz zur Verhütung und Bekämpfung von Infektionskrankheiten beim Menschen [Infektionsschutzgesetz]* – IfSG), a finding which remained in force until 25 November 2021. On 27 March 2020, the first related legislation entered into force, to be followed by three others until 23 April 2021, when the *Bundesnotbremse* (federal pandemic emergency brake) legislation was passed. Since the middle of March 2020, the governments of the member states and of the Federation have introduced a number of far-reaching – but often not properly coordinated – restrictions for public life, some of which were temporarily lifted at the beginning of May 2020. However, due to rising positive test figures, the measures were tightened again significantly from October and November 2020, leading to the lockdown from mid-December 2020. The population had been asked to support the effort by complying with distancing, hygiene and mask regulations etc, including airing rooms regularly and using the Corona Warn(ing) App. Table 1 gives an overview of the measures taken in chronological order until January 2022.

Table 1 Chronological sequence of measures taken by the government(s)

Date	Measure
31/01/2020	Duty of notification about positive tests
08/03/2020	Recommendation to cancel events with more than 1,000 participants
17/03/2020	First lockdown: entry ban for people from third countries, global travel warning for German residents, restriction of non-essential travel to other EU countries, closure of a large number of shops
22/03/2020	Social contact restrictions (personal distance of 1.5 m; cap on numbers meeting in- and outside, closure of restaurants etc)
10/04/2020	14-day home quarantine for people returning from abroad

(continued)

---

[2] See 'COVID-19-Pandemie in Deutschland – Chronik der Ausbreitung' (*Wikipedia*), https://de.wikipedia.org/wiki/COVID-19-Pandemie_in_Deutschland#Chronik_der_Ausbreitung, from which this summary is taken.

[3] This table and the summary are taken from 'COVID-19-Pandemie in Deutschland – Reaktionen und Maßnahmen der Politik – Bundesweite Infektionsschutzmaßnahmen' (*Wikipedia*), https://de.wikipedia.org/wiki/COVID-19-Pandemie_in_Deutschland#Bundesweite_Infektionsschutzma%C3%9Fnahmen.

Table 1 *(Continued)*

Date	Measure
15/04/2020	Contact restrictions at least until 3 May 2020, opening schools gradually from 4 May, opening of shops with a size of under 800 m² not before 20 April, no major events until 31 August, urgent recommendation to wear masks
29/04/2020	Compulsory masks on public transport and in shops
06/05/2020	Easing of restrictions for shops and outdoor sports, visits to hospitals, care homes and disabled facilities; minimum distance to remain. Contact restrictions extended to 5 June 2020 but members of two households may meet. The states may decide on further easing up to 50 new infections per 100,000 per week. Emergency cover in schools and kindergartens extended.
14/10/2020	Establishing the 'Hotspot Strategy': contact restrictions based on incidence rate by county
28/10 and 25/11/2020	'Lockdown light': renewed nationwide restrictions of public life and social contacts
13/12/2020, 11/ and 25/01/2021	'Hard Lockdown' with nationwide restrictions
23/04–30/06/2021	'*Bundesnotbremse*' (Federal Pandemic Emergency Brake): contact restrictions everywhere automatically from an incidence rate of 100
10/08/2021	3G (*getestet, geimpft, genesen* – tested, vaccinated, recovered) access rules in many places. Temporary end of free citizens' tests.
18 and 25/11/2021	Amendment of the IfSG; declaration of epidemic situation of national concern lifted.
02 and 21/12/2021	2G (*geimpft, genesen* – vaccinated or recovered) access rules in many public places; new restrictions also for those who are vaccinated or who have recovered
07/01/2022	2G access rules in gastronomy sector; shortened quarantine

II. CONSTITUTIONAL, LEGAL AND POLICY OVERVIEW

Responsibility for public health management is split according to the different levels of constitutional hierarchy. Germany is a Federation of 16 member states. The relationship between the legislature, government and judiciary of the member states (*Land/Länder*) and those of the Federation (*Bund*) is regulated in the Federal Constitution, or Basic Law (*Grundgesetz – GG*). Each *Land* has its own constitution, but the lowest rank of federal law breaks even a state constitution (article 31 GG).[4] Legislative and executive competences are shared between the states and the Federation depending on the substance matter.

---

[4] For the details and other collision norms see P Huber, 'Commentary on Article 31' in M Sachs (ed), *Grundgesetz, Kommentar* 9th edn (Munich, CH Beck, 2021), marginal numbers (mn) 10–14 (hereafter 'Sachs-contributor' by article and mn).

The default rule is that states have jurisdiction unless the GG assigns it to the Federation (article 70 GG). The GG grants either exclusive or concurrent jurisdiction to the Federation. Under the former, the states can legislate only if a federal law authorises them to do so (article 71 GG), under the latter the above default rule applies until and unless the Federation exercises its power to legislate; in some cases the Federation has legislative competence if the uniformity of conditions across the Federation so demands, and finally the states may deviate from federal laws in certain areas (article 72 GG). Foreign affairs, for example, which includes EU membership issues, are in principle a federal matter (article 32, 73(1) No 1 GG), as are matters of immigration, air and (partly) rail travel (article 73(1) Nos 3, 6 and 6a GG).

Matters of disease control fall under the general heading of prevention of danger to the public order (*Gefahrenabwehr*) such as, for example, preventive policing – as opposed to criminal investigation – and as such are a matter for the individual states.[5] The Federation, however, has concurrent competence to deal with measures against diseases which are contagious or otherwise pose a public risk, and the law of medicines and other medical products, under article 74(1) No 19 GG. The law in the context of the Covid-19 pandemic had been progressively regulated by amendments of the IfSG.[6] After a number of successful judicial review challenges as well as a period of laborious joint state-Federation crisis management with a multitude of different approaches in individual states, the overall control of the executive management, and especially for the regulation of the trigger criteria for specific protective measures, was shifted to the Federal Ministry of Health in April 2021 (*Bundesnotbremse*).[7] This general transfer of power to the federal level, however, expired on 30 June 2021.

The Federal Constitutional Court (*Bundesverfassungsgericht* – BVerfG) in its decisions on the so-called *Bundesnotbremse I*, on contact restrictions and curfews, and *Bundesnotbremse II* on school closures of 19 November 2021,[8] made it clear that this federal competence based on prevention of and protection against infectious diseases is a *lex specialis* that, once exercised, trumps any competence that states might otherwise have. On 16 December 2021, the Court also decided that the legislature at federal level had a duty to regulate, by proper act of parliament, the treatment of persons with disabilities in triage situations, to ensure that the disability was not a near-automatic trigger of being removed from the list of persons eligible for scarce intensive care resources; not having done so until that date violated the specific non-discrimination clause for persons with disabilities in article 3(3) 2nd sentence GG. The only criterion that mattered, according to the Court, was the chance of recovering from the *current* illness; any considerations related to a generally reduced life expectancy due to the disability were irrelevant. Within that framework, however, the government and parliament had a wide discretion as to which criteria to choose.[9]

---

[5] Sachs-Degenhart (n 4) art 74, mn 83.

[6] R Esser and M Tsambikakis, *Pandemiestrafrecht* (Munich, CH Beck, 2020) (hereafter 'PandStR'), 4–6.

[7] The exact sequence of the amendments of all sections of the IfSG, especially ss 28(a)–(c), can be traced on the website www.buzer.de/gesetz/2148 (in German).

[8] BVerfG, Decision of 19 November 2021, docket no 1 BvR 781/21 et al '*Bundesnotbremse I*', www.bverfg.de/e/rs20211119_1bvr078121.html (hereafter: *Bundesnotbremse I*); and Decision of 19 November 2021, docket no 1 BvR 971/21 '*Bundesnotbremse II*', www.bverfg.de/e/rs20211119_1bvr097121.html (hereafter: *Bundesnotbremse II*).

[9] BVerfG, Decision of 16 December 2021, docket no 1 BvR 1541/20 '*Triage*', www.bverfg.de/e/rs20211216_1bvr154120.html. See on the prior discussion PandStR (n 6) 51–75.

A. Overview of and Specific Constitutional and Legal Principles Regarding Criminal Liability of High-Ranking Government/Public Officials

There are no separate rules governing the criminal liability of high-ranking officials; they fall under the general criminal law, as set out below.

B. Scope of Responsibility and Area of Tolerated Risk

The question of tolerated risk relates mainly to liability for negligent behaviour, because under German law a risk knowingly taken is very quickly classified as intentional conduct under *dolus eventualis* or conditional intent. Once intent is shown, different liability rules apply. The line to advertent negligence is thin. Conditional intent is more than mere recklessness under English law – which as such is not a legal category in German law – and defined by the majority view as the offender realising the danger that a certain result will materialise and accepting the result; he does not necessarily have to approve of it morally.[10] Negligence is the violation of a duty of diligence, when the offender either could have foreseen the risk (simple negligence), or realised the danger but hoped it would not materialise (advertent negligence).[11] As a general principle, any degree of negligence can be the basis of liability for a negligent offence, yet the legislator has increasingly displayed a tendency to restrict these offences to cases of gross negligence (*Leichtfertigkeit*).[12] The category of the result-qualified offences (*erfolgsqualifizierte Delikte*) plays a special part in the scenario of negligence liability, with § 18 StGB requiring at least negligence with regard to the extended result. Negligence offences can be committed by omission, if all other criteria for that form of liability are fulfilled. The general structure of negligence offences is divided into an objective part in the actus reus and a subjective part. It requires a breach of a duty of diligence on the objective level[13] and causation of the result by that breach. For positive acts in the context of dangerous activities, the situations giving rise to such a duty are endless. For omission offences, they are less abundant, and would be primarily listed under the general heading of a duty to act.

The actus reus standard for deciding whether due diligence was violated is similar to that under civil law. It is, according to the prevailing view, an objective one, which means any special skills or defects that D may have will not normally enter into the evaluation.[14] However, this does not mean that certain generalised categories of abilities and skills expected of certain classes and groups of persons will not play a role.[15] There may be general requirements over and above that asked of the average person, such as for the members of a certain trade, profession or public service. However, these must be

---

[10] PandStR (n 6) 44; T Fischer, *Strafgesetzbuch* 67th edn (Munich, CH Beck, 2020) § 15 mn 11–16.

[11] Fischer (n 10) § 15 mn 9, 19–22.

[12] F Schuster in A Schönke, H Schröder et al, *Strafgesetzbuch: Kommentar* 30th edn (Munich, CH Beck, 2019) (hereafter 'Sch/Sch-contributor') § 15, mn 105–08.

[13] ibid § 15, mn 116.

[14] See the discussion at Sch/Sch-Sternberg-Lieben/Schuster (n 12) § 15, mn 116–19. Note, however, that within the examination of guilt, personal abilities can play a role.

[15] Sch/Sch-Sternberg-Lieben/Schuster (n 12) § 15, mn 134, 141.

distinguished from the individual special abilities of persons working within one of those categories.

Negligence can be summed up in the concepts of foreseeability and avoidability.[16] If D cannot foresee that his actions might cause harm, or even if he foresees it, cannot avoid causing that harm, then it would be unfair to hold him liable for the consequences of his actions. However, there are activities which contain both foreseeable and avoidable risks of a potentially disastrous magnitude, which are nevertheless legal, such as, for example, the operation of a chemical factory[17] or the production of cars. Yet society accepts these activities as socially adequate risks, because it is more beneficial to run these risks and try to contain them than not to have their benefits and have no risks. The measure for deciding whether a certain result was foreseeable is the ex ante standard from the point of view of the offender at the time the harmful conduct occurred. A common thread that runs through these cases is that foreseeability is more likely to be accepted if and when the harm is caused by a factor which is under the control of the offender, rather than that of the victim or under nobody's control.

However, the BVerfG, in its *Bundesnotbremse I* and *II* decisions of 19 November 2021,[18] gave the government a wide margin of discretion about the choice of the appropriate measures to be taken in the fight against the pandemic, as long as they were a reasonable inference from the available scientific evidence and expert opinion. It was also very clear in its view that the longer the pandemic lasted and the more solidified the expert evidence became, the more that margin of appreciation would shrink. On that basis, the approach of the federal government to the necessary severity of restrictions was deemed constitutional. This case law has been heavily criticised as giving *carte blanche* to the executive and relinquishing any control of the legislature who passed the underlying act worthy of the name.[19] While the BVerfG was primarily concerned with the constitutionality of what some have called excessively heavy-handed measures unnecessarily restricting the fundamental freedoms under the Basic Law, its decision could arguably also be invoked to inform the interpretation of the due diligence criterion in difficult scenarios of precautionary and prognostic decisions based on a rapidly changing situation, which require fast decision-making in a public emergency context. However, the Court's triage decision of 16 December 2021 mentioned above made it clear that certain decisions had to be taken by the government immediately as a matter of principle, but that within that general duty, there was an equally wide discretion. Each case will therefore ultimately turn on the scientific advice of the day and the degree to which the government followed, or deviated from, it for purely political reasons: the more it did the latter, the greater the likelihood that a finding of negligence could be made. Equally, if there is reasonable doubt about whether the government could have avoided the consequences even if it had followed scientific advice at the time, a finding of negligence would be unlikely.

---

[16] ibid § 15, mn 124–25.

[17] Examples by Sch/Sch-Sternberg-Lieben/Schuster, § 15, mn 127.

[18] *Bundesnotbremse I*; *Bundesnotbremse II* (n 8).

[19] O Lepsius, *Nach BVerfG zur Bundesnotbremse: Zerstörerisches Potential für den Verfassungsstaat* (*Legal Tribune Online*, 3 December 2021), www.lto.de/recht/hintergruende/h/bverfg-1bvr78121-1bvr97121-corona-bundes-notbremse-massnahmen-kontakt-ausgang-schule-kinder-grundrechte-kommentar-verfassung-rechtstaat/.

C. Impact of Immunities

There are no immunities under German law for federal government officials, unless they are also members of the Federal Parliament (*Bundestag*), when article 46 GG applies:

1) At no time may a Member be subjected to court proceedings or disciplinary action or otherwise called to account outside the Bundestag for a vote cast or a remark made by him in the Bundestag or in any of its committees. This provision shall not apply to defamatory insults.

2) A Member may not be called to account or arrested for a punishable offence without permission of the Bundestag unless he is apprehended while committing the offence or in the course of the following day.

3) ...

4) Any criminal proceedings ... against a Member and any detention or other restriction of the freedom of his person shall be suspended at the demand of the Bundestag.[20]

Similar rules apply under the state constitutions.[21] The Federal President, who does not partake in day-to-day government activity, enjoys a separate position as he can only be prosecuted in ordinary criminal proceedings if the Bundestag lifts the immunity under article 60(4) GG; the indemnity rule of Art 46(1) GG does, however, not apply.[22] For the impeachment procedure of the Federal President under article 61 GG, see below at Section IX.B.

D. Prosecutorial Matters

Under the principles of mandatory and discretionary prosecution (*Legalitätsprinzip* and *Opportunitätsprinzip*), the investigation and prosecution of all crimes are in the hands of the Public Prosecution Service, the *Staatsanwaltschaft* (and its support service, the police), which alone has the power to investigate and prosecute regardless of the identity of the offender or the wishes of the victim. There are a few exceptions that mainly deal with minor offences, where the victim must either formally request prosecution, the so-called *Antragsdelikte*;[23] or where the victim may prosecute the offence herself (§ 374 StPO[24] – *Privatklage*);[25] or where certain persons, such as civil service superiors and line

---

[20] Official translation by the Federal Ministry of Justice, online at www.gesetze-im-internet.de/englisch_gg/englisch_gg.html#p0229.

[21] For details, see Sachs-Magiera (n 4) art 46, mn 1–26.

[22] Sachs-Nierhaus/Brinktrine (n 4) art 60, mn 17–18.

[23] For example, minor cases of trespass, insults, etc. See T Fischer in *Karlsruher Kommentar zur Strafprozessordnung* 8th edn (Munich, CH Beck, 2019) (hereafter: 'KK-contributor'), Einleitung, mn 7, for further examples.

[24] StPO is the abbreviation for *Strafprozessordnung* (Code of Criminal Procedure).

[25] The prosecution may, however, at any stage of the proceedings join the private prosecutor or take over the case completely (§ 377). If they do take it over, which they normally will only do if it is in the public interest (see § 376), the proceedings change their nature and transmogrify into normal proceedings as if upon indictment, with the consequence that the private prosecutor is no longer a party to them unless he joins the prosecution as a *Nebenkläger* under §§ 395–402. This also means that the prosecution and the court can discontinue the proceedings under §§ 153 ff without the consent of the prior private prosecutor or the *Nebenkläger*; the *Nebenkläger* must, however, be heard before a discontinuance is issued, which is why a court intending to discontinue the proceedings under §§ 153(2), 153(a)(2), 153b(2) and 154(2) must first decide whether a person

managers, political organs, foreign States, etc have the discretion to request prosecution or not (so-called *Ermächtigungsdelikte*).[26]

The monopoly given to the prosecution requires a corrective mechanism to ensure that no arbitrary choices are made. This is found in § 152(2) StPO, which requires the prosecution in principle to investigate, prosecute and indict any offence for which sufficient evidence exists. German doctrine therefore takes the opposite approach from that of England and Wales, famously expressed in 1951 by the former Attorney-General Shawcross, who stated that '[i]t has never been the rule in this country – I hope it never will be – that suspected criminal offences must automatically be the subject of prosecution'.[27] However, as with so many things doctrinal, theory and practice are two different things. The basic rule in Germany has been watered down considerably by the introduction of §§ 153 ff StPO, which allow the prosecution and the courts to discontinue proceedings for minor offences with a minimum sentence under one year if in their discretion it is opportune to stop the case (*Opportunitätsprinzip*) because the guilt of the offender is of a minor nature and/or may be sufficiently sanctioned by way of a conditional discontinuance. It is clear from the statistics that in practice the *Legalitätsprinzip* has already de facto been replaced as the guiding principle. It now merely means that the prosecution has to start an investigation if sufficient facts warrant it, but that a formal prosecution by indictment or a written summary order, the *Strafbefehl*, occurs in less than a quarter of all cases.[28]

In the context of misconduct of senior members of government, a conditional discontinuance was controversially applied to former Chancellor Helmut Kohl in 2001, who was given a fine of then 300,000 DM for not disclosing the names of donors who had given millions of DM to his party. Kohl was under law considered innocent despite having admitted wrongdoing, because no material judicial finding of guilt is involved in that procedure.[29] Whether any judge would be prepared to sign such an order of discontinuance in the case of thousands of unnecessary deaths is open to question. This procedure would, however, in any event not be available if the charge was murder, which is a felony with a minimum sentence above one year.

III. CAUSATION

A. Causation (General Principles)

i. Handlung and Unterlassen – *Act and Omission*

German law has realised that the mere physical concept of causation would lead to an excessive scope of liability. This has led to the development of *legal concepts of causation*

---

is allowed to join the prosecution, and hear that person before ordering the discontinuance; Meyer-Goßner/Schmitt, *Strafprozessordnung* 63rd edn (Munich, CH Beck, 2020), (hereafter: 'MGS') § 396, mn 18.

[26] For examples, see KK-Fischer (n 23) Einleitung, mn 7.

[27] HC Debs, vol 483, 29 January 1951.

[28] More detail in M Bohlander, *Principles of German Criminal Procedure* 2nd edn (Oxford, Bloomsbury, 2021) 25–27.

[29] See for a contemporary report 'Mit Beugehaft zum Reden zwingen?' (*Spiegel Politik*, 2 March 2021), www.spiegel.de/politik/deutschland/kohl-verfahren-eingestellt-mit-beugehaft-zum-reden-zwingen-a-120495.html.

or conceptual restrictions on the *ascription of legal responsibility* for physically causal acts. The base line[30] is the formula of the *conditio sine qua non*, or the 'but for' test: fact F is considered to be causal for result R, if R would not have occurred but for F. However, this formula is at the same time too wide and too narrow. In its strict application, it would catch any positive act but it would not cover omissions liability where there is no F, but rather the absence of F. Its operation in its exact form is also dependent on the actual scientific knowledge about cause and effect, which sometimes may not exist, as can be exemplified by the *Thalidomide* (*Contergan* in Germany) litigation in the last century[31] and more recent case law focusing on product liability.[32] Finally, it allows for the inclusion of hypothetical causes: if D1's bullet had not hit and killed V, the shot fired by D2 would have done so a second later. It would appear absurd to say that D1 did not cause V's death because D2 would have killed him anyway.[33] This shows the second ground rule which causation theory in a moral and legal context should adhere to: what matters is what happened, not what could or would have happened hypothetically.[34] Whether society and its laws should hold D responsible for a result caused unlawfully if the same thing would have happened if D had acted with all due diligence is another matter. In the context of omissions liability, the formula does not work at all; causation there is by definition hypothetical and adheres to the following rule of thumb: D's omission of F will be considered causal to result R if the occurrence of F cannot be imagined without R being extinguished with a probability bordering on certainty.[35] Another feature, according to the German majority view, is that all relevant causes are equal in causal value (*Äquivalenztheorie*).[36] This means that a certain fact among several need not be the sole or even main cause of a result.[37]

German law operates on the general idea that a crime requires a positive act and that by doing nothing you do not normally violate any legal commands. Omissions are thus only criminally relevant if the law expressly provides for an offence based on inactivity (genuine omission offences – *echte Unterlassungsdelikte*), or if the offender is under a duty to act and prevent the occurrence of an event that forms part of an offence normally committed by positive acts and the omission equals commission by a positive act in seriousness (derivative omission offences – *unechte Unterlassungsdelikte*; see § 13(1) StGB).[38] § 13(2) StGB provides for a facultative reduction in sentence for this second category. Genuine omission offences present no great conceptual challenge. A prime example is § 323c StGB, the offence of omitting to effect an easy rescue or rendering assistance (*unterlassene Hilfeleistung*), which applies to anyone. The central feature of the second category is the requirement of a duty to act, which in German law is split up into two

---

[30] See Sch/Sch-Bosch (n 12) Vor §§ 13 ff, mn 71–102 for an overview of the arguments and different approaches.
[31] See Sch/Sch-Bosch (n 12) Vor §§ 13 ff, mn 74.
[32] See BGHSt 37, 106 ('Leather spray case') and BGHSt 41, 206 ('Wood impregnation case'). BGHSt (*Amtliche Sammlung der Entscheidungen des Bundesgerichtofes in Strafsachen*) is the the official series of criminal case law reports of the *Bundesgerichtshof* (BGH), the Federal Court of Justice.
[33] See BGHSt 2, 24.
[34] *cf* BGHSt 10, 370; 13, 14.
[35] See the discussion at Sch/Sch-Bosch (n 12) § 13, mn 61 with further references to case law and commentary.
[36] Sch/Sch-Bosch (n 12) Vor §§ 13 ff, mn 76.
[37] BGHSt 39, 137.
[38] StGB is the abbreviation for *Strafgesetzbuch* (Criminal Code).

sub-concepts, the duty of care (*Garantenstellung*) and the scope of the duty to act in the strict sense (*Garantenpflicht*)[39] in the specific circumstances, meaning that although there may be a legal basis for D's duty of *care* towards V, that duty of care may not entail D's duty to *act* with regard to all dangers to or circumstances of V. For example, although the fact that D as V's employer took her into his home may create a duty of care towards her, that duty does not require D to prevent V from having an illegal abortion.[40] So although D may have a duty of care towards V, it is always necessary to determine the exact scope of the action that D is required to take. The two main[41] categories of duties of care relevant for our purposes are as follows:

duties based on specific legislation when that legislation does not provide for genuine omissions liability already; and

duties based on the creation of dangerous situations.

ii. Duty Based on Legislation

The *BGH* held, in the context of the criminal responsibility of the members of the former GDR government for border killings, that even norms of constitutional law can in exceptional cases create a duty of care towards the citizens of a country.[42] However, the general duty of care owed by a government to its citizens, if applied to the present (or previous West German) government, does apparently not suffice to establish a duty that entails criminal liability or even state liability, such as, for example, when a prisoner on furlough commits a murder, if there was no indication that he posed a danger in that respect.[43] As discussed below, the question is whether the handling of the pandemic is in essence a case of omissions liability at all.

iii. Duty Based on Creation of Dangerous Situations

German law[44] recognises a duty, arising out of prior conduct which created a source of risk or danger, to take all necessary steps in order to prevent the risk from materialising. The risk-causing conduct may in turn have been an omission in violation of a duty to act.[45] The exact conditions regarding the nature and qualities of the dangerous conduct are unclear, but it would appear that the prevailing view does not tend to require any fault on the part of D. However, his or her conduct must have been dangerous as such in relation to the legal interest threatened as a result of his or her actions, and it must have been in breach of a duty itself, meaning that behaviour which is legal cannot normally give rise

---

[39] The *Garantenpflicht*, ie the duty to act as such is not an element of the *Tatbestand*, but of the second tier of the tripartite structure, the general unlawfulness criterion, or *Rechtswidrigkeit* (BGHSt 16, 148). This may have an impact on the question of mistake.

[40] See OLG Schleswig, 'Beihilfe durch Unterlassung' (1954) *Neue Juristische Wochenschrift* 285.

[41] For an overview of the ramifications, see Sch/Sch-Bosch (n 12) § 13, mn 17 ff.

[42] BGHSt 48, 77 at 84.

[43] Fischer (n 10) § 13 mn 19–35, see also ECtHR, *Mastromatteo v Italy*, Judgment of 24 October 2002, Application No 37703/97.

[44] For an overview of categories and examples from the case law, see Sch/Sch-Bosch (n 12) § 13, mn 32–42.

[45] *Entscheidungen des Reichsgerichts in Strafsachen* (RGSt) 68, 104.

to omissions liability. Exceptions to this are the cases where the legal reasons for creating a certain source of danger cease to apply after a while: in that case, D is required to eliminate the danger source as soon as the reasons for its creation have ceased. Government incompetence leading to dangerous situations could thus be seen as creating a duty to act.

B. Causation and 'Thin Skull' Scenarios

German legal commentators and the courts have tried to address the conundrum of causation and ascription of responsibility through various theories and models; some still retain the normative ascription criteria within their concept of causation (for example, the *Adäquanztheorie* – theory of adequate causation); others have externalised them into theories of legal and moral ascription of blameworthiness to a factually causal behaviour, the term mostly used nowadays for this kind of approach being *objektive Zurechnung*, or objective attribution. The courts do formally still adhere to the *Äquivalenztheorie*, but have admitted a number of normative correctives within that framework which in substance means that they are moving towards a form of *Adäquanztheorie*, which is the prevailing approach in civil law,[46] or a version of objective attribution. However, the results are by and large very similar.

i. Contributory Acts of the Victim

D cannot in principle evade liability by arguing that V's own circumstances or actions contributed to the result in its actual form (but see the next heading). The same applies if V's physical or mental constitution is special or even abnormal ('thin skull rule'). Fortuity of consequence has no room in negating causation.[47]

ii. Free, Deliberate and Informed Third-Party Interventions

The rule is that as long as the conduct of D is still operating as a cause of the intervener's acts, even if these are made intentionally and on a free, deliberate and informed basis, there will be no *novus actus* breaking the chain. Only if D's acts have no more influence on the result will there be a lack of causality. The general rule is that the less D's acts continue to operate on the final result, the less likely they are to be considered as causal. Whether a person may be considered to be causing another's death if he assisted the 'victim' in her free and deliberate self-administering of drugs that had a lethal effect has been contentious for some time. Under German law, the person providing the tools for the other's own actions is not liable.[48] As long as D merely assists V, who is responsible and fully *compos mentis*, in her free, deliberate and informed decision to endanger herself, he cannot be seen to be causal of or as being a party to her self-endangerment. The line into causality and criminal liability as a principal perpetrator is crossed once it is D who

---

[46] *Amtliche Sammlung der Entscheidungen des Bundesgerichtshofs in Zivilsachen* (Official Law Reports of the Federal Court of Justice in Civil Matters) (BGHZ) 37, 19; BGH NJW 2002, 2233.

[47] Sch/Sch-Bosch (n 12) Vor §§ 13 ff, mn 76.

[48] See the case of BGHSt 32, 262 which is almost identical on the facts to *Kennedy*.

is in control of the situation because V may be ill, mentally unstable, a minor, etc, or if D has superior knowledge of the danger that V is putting herself in. Cases of consensual endangerment of V by *direct* action of D, *i.e.*, D injects V himself, are excluded from the exception and can only be tackled under the heading of consent as a defence, which will often be lacking.[49]

In the context of the Covid scenario, an obvious problem under this heading are the so-called 'anti-vaxxers' or vaccine refusers:[50] as soon as an effective vaccine is available to everyone or to members of certain societal groups, their refusal to be vaccinated (or for that matter, to wear masks or the decision to have contact with infected persons) acts as a free, deliberate and informed decision covered by the fundamental freedoms of the GG to endanger themselves and hence erases any legal causal link with the acts of the government.[51] It is questionable whether one could view the fact that many of the vaccine refusers subscribe to wild and obviously unfounded conspiracy theories peddled by social media influencers, even if they are or pose as medical experts, as sufficient to call them mentally unstable, rather than poorly informed or manipulated. This evaluation may change if there is a general legal obligation to be vaccinated and the government does not sufficiently enforce it: are fines and other sanctions for non-compliance enough if they do not actually impress the refusers, or is the state under a duty to vaccinate them by force and becoming liable if it does not do so?

iii. Alternative and Cumulative Causes

These scenarios occur, for example, when there are several offenders acting separately and not as joint principals, etc. Alternative causation covers those cases where two or more causes, each of which would have been sufficient to cause the result, impact at the same time: D1 and D2 each independently administer a lethal dose of poison to V, V dies of the simultaneous effect of both poisons. D1 and D2 are both guilty of murder. If, however, it cannot be established whether one of them did not take effect before the other, both D1 and D2 are each only guilty of attempted murder[52] (based on *in dubio pro reo*, because each cause could be seen as breaking the chain started by the other). Alternative causality may also apply if D initiated two causes, each of which in itself could have caused the result alone; this can be important with respect to the *mens rea* with which the causes were set.[53] If, in the above example of D1 and D2 using poison on V, the lethal result was only reached by the *combined* effect, we speak of *cumulative* causality. In this context, both are still causal. The question of whether V's death could be fully attributed to both D1 and D2 as in the case of alternative causality is much more difficult. The tendency appears to be not to do so and, depending on the *mens rea*

---

[49] See on this the discussion and further references at Sch/Sch-Bosch (n 12) Vor §§ 13 ff, mn 101–101d.

[50] On the demographic distribution of Covid-19 vaccination refusers in Europe see the study by the Max-Planck-Institute for Social Law and Social Policy: M Bergmann et al, *Determinants of SARS-CoV-2 vaccinations in the 50+ population* (Max Planck Institute for Social Law and Social Policy/Munich Center for the Economics of Aging, July 2021), www.mpisoc.mpg.de/fileadmin/user_upload/MEA_DP_07-2021.pdf.

[51] See PandStR (n 6) 42.

[52] Sch/Sch-Bosch (n 12) Vor §§ 13, ff, mn 82; BGH NJW 1966, 1823.

[53] BGHSt 39, 195.

of D1 and D2, convict of attempted murder and/or causing grievous bodily harm or administering noxious substances.[54]

The issues of alternative and/or cumulative causation are also highly relevant for the criminal liability of members of decision-making committees, such as boards of directors, councils of ministers etc. Unless it can be proved that they acted intentionally as joint principals, which is hardly ever likely, the court will be faced with the dilemma that each one of those who voted for the activity that gave rise to the damaging result could argue that their vote did not make a difference if the sum of the other votes already passed the required majority, and was thus not causal. The case where D's vote, possibly a casting vote, was necessary to pass the threshold is incomparably easier to solve. However, even in the first scenario, the prevailing view seems to be to hold all those who voted affirmatively as causal for the result.[55]

iv. Risk Diminishment

D should not normally be held liable if what she tried to do was to minimise a risk for V. Such cases occur when D1 comes to the rescue of V and deflects a knife stab aimed by D2 at V's heart into her arm. Although D1 is physically causing a wounding of her arm, it makes no sense to ascribe the result to him as he averted a more serious harm.[56] Government incompetence, but with honest intention, in carrying out badly planned or executed protective measures resulting in harm to a multitude of persons may in theory be caught by this exception, depending on the degree and causes of its incompetence.

v. Lawful Alternative Behaviour

German law recognises a category of cases where there is no functional causal relationship between the *violation of a legal duty* and the actual result, although on a purely physical level D caused it, as shown by the leading case:[57] D, the driver of a lorry, ran over and killed V, a drunken cyclist, when overtaking him. D did not maintain the necessary and prescribed distance between the lorry and V. However, it could not be excluded that V would have collided with the lorry even if D had abided by the rules. There was thus no connection between his violation of the law and V's death. This has led to the generally recognised exception of lawful alternative behaviour, or *rechtmäßiges Alternativverhalten*. If the government had caused the same results even by acting lawfully, *i.e.*, in accordance with prevailing scientific advice, causality will be lacking.

vi. Overall Consequences for Government Action

Causation by the government will be a major issue for all offences related to causing bodily harm or death, mainly because of difficulties of proof and not only for doctrinal reasons. In cases on an individual level, *i.e.*, one person accused of infecting another,

---

[54] See Sch/Sch-Bosch (n 12) Vor §§ 13 ff, mn 83.
[55] BGHSt 37, 107. See also BGHSt 48, 95 regarding recalls of defective products and omissions liability.
[56] Sch/Sch-Bosch (n 12) Vor §§ 13 ff, mn 94.
[57] BGHSt 11, 1.

the likelihood of causation is inversely proportionate to the rise/state of the overall level of infected people within a certain population. However, if the responsibility of the government for provision of essential public protection on the macro-level is examined, such as procuring a sufficient supply of masks, personal protective clothing and indeed, vaccines, the matter quickly becomes one of statistics along a spectrum of options. Relying on achieving the necessary herd immunity by simply letting everyone be infected, 'let[ting] the bodies pile high'[58] or letting the 'virus rip',[59] as allegedly seems to have been a policy considered by some[60] in the early days of the UK's response – and to all intents and purposes again during the Omicron variant wave in late 2021/ early 2022 – or by the PM after the first serious lockdown, inevitably involves the virtually certain foresight of a virtually certain larger number of unnecessary deaths compared to a more cautious approach – without doubt enough for both causation based on the statistics of excess mortality while such a policy was in operation and at least conditional intent to cause an uncontrollable number of unnecessary deaths (the exact number and the identity of each unnecessary victim being irrelevant for either).[61] Equally, the 'collateral damage' of persons dying or suffering irreversible damage to their health because planned surgeries are cancelled in order to have sufficient capacity to deal with Covid patients or merely strengthen the vaccination campaign needs to be borne in mind: these results are also caused by Covid-related government policy. The collateral cases might even be proved by tracking the relationship of cancelled surgeries to the number of deaths or cases of serious illness caused by non-treatment of the condition for which the surgery was planned. If the government was incompetent in its protective efforts or prioritised political considerations of any sort over the protection of lives – which as the BVerfG reaffirmed in the *Bundesnotbremse* and *Triage* decisions mentioned above is the highest good – it will depend on the individual circumstances, *i.e.*, whether the incompetence was so gross as to still allow a judgment of conditional intent, or at the very least gross or simple negligence.[62] In the latter case, what was said

---

[58] As Prime Minister Boris Johnson was reported to have said in early 2021; see 'Covid: Boris Johnson's "bodies pile high" comments prompt criticism' (*BBC*, 26 April 2021), www.bbc.com/news/uk-politics-56890714; J Elgot and R Booth, 'Pressure mounts on Johnson over alleged "let the bodies pile high" remarks' *The Guardian* (online, 26 April 2021), www.theguardian.com/politics/2021/apr/26/pressure-mounts-on-boris-johnson-over-alleged-let-the-bodies-pile-high-remarks; 'UK PM's former adviser confirms Johnson said "let the bodies pile high" (*Reuters*, 26 May 2021), www.reuters.com/world/uk/uk-pms-former-adviser-confirms-johnson-said-let-bodies-pile-high-2021-05-26/.

[59] T Gillespie, 'COVID-19: Dominic Cummings claims ministers backed COVID "herd immunity" and lockdowns could have been avoided' (*Sky News*, 23 May 2021), https://news.sky.com/story/covid-19-dominic-cummings-claims-ministers-backed-covid-herd-immunity-and-lockdowns-could-have-been-avoided-12314246.

[60] See S Kermani, 'Coronavirus: Whitty and Vallance faced "herd immunity" backlash, emails show' (*BBC*, 23 September 2020), www.bbc.com/news/uk-politics-54252272.

[61] I note that my colleague Natalie Wortley in the England chapter rightly refers to the discretion of the jury in finding or declining to find *Woollin* oblique intent to kill even in such a scenario. That approach is, in my respectful view, a typically English procedural safety valve to a problem of substantive law, based on the judge/jury role distinction and considerations of justice in the individual case, or 'warm confusion', as Mirjan Damaska would have put it; it is difficult to imagine such considerations succeeding in a German judge-only environment of 'cool consistency'; see his *The Faces of Justice and State Authority: A Comparative Approach to the Legal Process* (New Haven, Yale University Press, 1986) 28.

[62] German law professor Volker Erb published a paper on 26 January 2021 in which he asserted that the German government might be liable for negligent homicide or negligent bodily harm by omission under §§ 13, 222, 229 StGB for not procuring vaccines efficiently enough or allowing them to be distributed in the EU rather than keeping them for the German population; see V Erb, 'Strafbarkeit des Unterlassens einer maximalen Beschleunigung der COVID-19-Impfungen in Deutschland durch die Bundesregierung', https://erb.jura.

above regarding the margin of discretion given to the government by the BVerfG, may come to have a larger effect.

On 18 February 2021, the Scientific Research Service (*Wissenschaftliche Dienste*) of the Federal Parliament provided a report to the Government which claimed that no omissions liability existed because there was no official duty to act and any attempt at establishing one based on the oath of office or the fundamental freedoms under the GG would run afoul of the fair labelling/certainty of law requirement of article 103(2) GG.[63] Volker Erb critiqued the report, which he called 'superficial', with formidable arguments[64] but was at the end of the day forced to concede that based on this report the members of the government could probably claim an unavoidable mistake of law under § 17 StGB and thus escape criminal liability. After the *Bundesnotbremse* decisions of the BVerfG cited above, which also dealt with the question of whether the summary fine provisions in the IfSG were precise enough (it found they were)[65] it is more than questionable whether the reference to article 103(2) GG would hold water in a criminal court. In any event, the first question to be asked is whether the emphasis really lies on an omission or whether we do not actually have a positive act, *i.e.*, the government's actions in the procurement or distribution of protective materials and vaccines: in that case, duties of care and duties to act are irrelevant. The report of the *Wissenschaftliche Dienste* left this matter open, referring to the circumstances of the individual case, and rather blithely stated that the emphasis was on omissions liability.[66]

IV. THE STRUCTURE OF HOMICIDE OFFENCES AND ASSAULT/AGGRAVATED ASSAULT/SERIOUS BODILY HARM OFFENCES[67]

A. Murder/Intentional Homicide

The intentional homicide offences relevant for our purposes are §§ 211 on aggravated murder and 212 on 'plain vanilla' murder; the latter reads as follows:

§ 212 Murder

1) Whosoever kills a person without being a murderer under § 211 shall be convicted of murder and be liable to imprisonment of not less than five years.
2) In especially serious cases the penalty shall be imprisonment for life.

The aggravated form of § 211 StGB will not apply in the pandemic scenario, and § 212 will be the only relevant intentional homicide offence. Killing means causing death.

---

uni-mainz.de/files/2021/03/Gutachten-Coronaimpfstoff.pdf. This caused quite a controversy at the time, see his 10 February 2021 ('Offener Brief an Herrn Kollegen Markus Ogorek') reply to a critic at https://crb.jura. uni-mainz.de/files/2021/02/Coronaimpfstoff-Replik-Ogorek-.pdf. He consolidated his views in the article 'Die Vernachlässigung strafrechtlicher Wertungen in der Bekämpfung der Corona-Pandemie' (2021) *Zeitschrift für Internationale Strafrechtsdogmatik* 95, www.zis-online.com/dat/artikel/2022_1_1471.pdf.

[63] 'Report of the Wissenschaftliche Dienste des Deutschen Bundestags', WD 7–3000 – 012/21, www.bundestag. de/resource/blob/829898/542c143a0152558970c821201b06999c/WD-7-012-21-pdf-data.pdf.

[64] Erb, 'Die Vernachlässigung' (n 62) 102–05.

[65] *Bundesnotbremse I* (n 8) paras 152–65.

[66] 'Report of the Wissenschaftliche Dienste' (n 63) 7–8.

[67] For an overview of the law of homicide see K Ambos and S Bock, 'Germany' in A Reed, M Bohlander et al (eds), *Homicide in Criminal Law – A Research Companion* (London and New York, Routledge, 2019) 245–63.

The homicide offences (negligent and intentional) only apply to persons who have been born.[68] A person is considered to be born once the dilating pains begin. If the birth is effected by Caesarian section, the equivalent point in time is the opening of the uterus. Whether the child has the capacity to survive in the longer term is irrelevant as long as she is alive at the moment of the offence and lives independently of the mother.[69] For the purposes of the law, brain death is the relevant point when life ends, yet its exact definition is anything but clear,[70] including what evidence is required to establish brain death.[71] The mens rea for murder is intent, including *dolus eventualis*, as to the lethal result – German law does not recognise constructive GBH murder as in English law. The courts have traditionally been reluctant to infer conditional intent to kill from risky and dangerous behaviour alone and referred to the individual circumstances of the case.[72] Regarding Covid, and in the absence of any settled case law so far, the view in the literature seems to be to restrict the inference to victims who are especially vulnerable, or members of certain risk groups.[73] Care home residents are an obvious category which played a large role early on in the pandemic in many countries and, given what was said above regarding the macro-level of causation (and intent), might make a suitable case for querying such an intent.

i. Negligent Homicide Offences

German law under § 222 StGB also knows of a form of negligent homicide that does neither require gross negligence nor a specific duty of care:

> § 222 Negligent homicide
>
> Whosoever through negligence causes the death of a person shall be liable to imprisonment of not more than five years or a fine.

There are many other homicide offences in other sections of the StGB in the form of result-qualified offences, *i.e.*, offence combinations where a basic offence has a further, extended consequence that is not an element of that basic offence as, for example, § 227 on bodily harm causing death where D causes death by committing a non-homicide basic offence. In these cases, it is a question of the link between basic offence and aggravated result under § 18 whether D will be held liable for the result.

Result-qualified offences require, on the actus reus side, that the extended result must have been immediately, or directly (*unmittelbar*), caused by the commission of the basic offence. (One should bear in mind that even if the result-qualified offence option cannot be used for lack of that link, in many instances there may be a subsidiary liability based on a direct negligence offence, but with a lesser sentencing frame.) An intermediary cause

---

[68] It can be difficult to determine the nature of acts committed in the pre-natal stage, the effects of which manifest themselves in death only after V's birth. See Sch/Sch-Eser and Sternberg-Lieben (n 12) Vor §§ 211 ff, mn 15.

[69] BGHSt 10, 292; 31, 348; 32, 194; OLG Karlsruhe, 'Strafbarkeit bei geburtshilflichen Maßnahmen' (1985) *Neue Zeitschrift für Strafrecht* 315. See generally on the constitutional issues surrounding sanctity of life, BVerfGE 39, 1; 88, 203.

[70] See Sch/Sch-Eser and Sternberg-Lieben (n 12) Vor §§ 211 ff, mn 19–20.

[71] Sch/Sch-Eser and Sternberg-Lieben (n 12) Vor §§ 211 ff, mn 19a.

[72] Recently especially in the context of illegal street racing or dangerous driving. See M Bohlander, 'Case Note: Murder by Dangerous Driving: Decision of the BGH of 16 January 2019, Case No 4 StR 345/18; Judgment of the LG Hamburg of 19 February 2018, Case No 621 Ks 12/17' (2019) *The Journal of Criminal Law* 191.

[73] PandStR (n 6) 48.

may lead to extinction of liability, even if it is set by the victim. However, there is no real bright line in the case law that would assist in determining when such an intervening event would break the link. The nature of the necessary link is thus best deduced from the specific danger created by the basic offence; the BGH is, however, certainly right in taking a restrictive approach in general.

§ 18 StGB on the standard of negligence provides:

§ 18 More severe penalty based on specific results of offence

If the law imposes a more severe penalty based on a specific result of an offence, the offender or the participant is only liable to the more severe penalty in the event of being charged with at least negligence with respect to that result.

Since the 6th Criminal Law Reform Act of 1998, result-qualified offences under § 18 require *at least* negligence with regard to the extended result – which somewhat counterintuitively now includes intent, with consequences with regard to multiple charges/convictions[74] – but as said above, the legislator has increasingly restricted the mens rea required for the extended result to gross negligence (*Leichtfertigkeit*). Any liability for a more serious result than that intended has to be based on negligence and foresight of *that* result, not just of any harm. As the offender is normally already acting in violation of a duty of diligence by committing the basic offence, all that is usually needed for the serious result is the foreseeability of the extended result. The standard for foreseeability, according to the decision, is as follows: could the offender at the relevant time with his abilities and knowledge foresee death as a potential *result* of his or her actions? It is not necessary that he has foresight of all the details of the causal chain. The courts, however, allow for an exclusion of liability if the lethal danger was so far outside what could normally be expected that it can no longer be attributed to the offender. The offender must have had cause to exercise his or her diligence according to *his* abilities.[75]

B. Culpable Homicide/Manslaughter

German law does not recognise other types of homicide offences, in particular those of constructive liability such as unlawful act manslaughter in English law.

C. Offences Related to Actions that Cause Serious Bodily Harm (Assault; Grievous Assault; Assault with Intent to Cause Serious Bodily Harm)

German law uses the concepts of physical attack or damage to health as the basic alternatives for the overarching term of causing bodily harm in non-lethal offences against the person, set out in § 223 StGB:

§ 223 Causing Bodily harm

1) Whosoever physically assaults or damages the health of another person shall be liable to imprisonment for a term not exceeding five years or a fine.
2) The attempt is punishable.

[74] Fischer (n 10) § 18 mn 3; § 227 mn 12.
[75] Fischer (n 10) § 227, mn 7a.

A mere infection can constitute bodily harm in the form of damage to health, regardless of whether the person develops symptoms. It needs to cross a seriousness threshold, which is, however, clearly the case with a serious disease such as Covid-19.[76]

This basic offence requires intent, including *dolus eventualis*, but there is also a simple negligence offence in § 229 StGB. § 223 is aggravated by a number of qualifications, in our context § 224 and § 226 StGB.

§ 224 Causing bodily harm by dangerous means

1)   Whosoever causes bodily harm

   1.   by administering poison or other noxious substances,
   2.   using a weapon or other dangerous instrument;
   3.   by acting by stealth;
   4.   acting jointly with another; or
   5.   by using methods which pose a danger to life;

   shall be liable to imprisonment for a term from six months to 10 years, in less serious cases imprisonment for a term of from three months and five years.

2)   The attempt is punishable.

§ 224 requires intent for all elements, conditional intent is enough.[77] Of the alternatives, § 224(1) No 1 2nd Alternative (noxious substance) and No 1 5th Alternative (methods which pose a danger to life) are in principle applicable to infections; again, a certain concrete risk based on the viral effects in each case is required, which should be the case in more serious Covid infections.[78] In HIV cases, for example, the BGH considers the offender's knowledge that any unprotected intercourse, regardless of statistic likelihood, could be the one leading to the partner's infection as sufficient for the mens rea regarding danger to life.[79]

§226 Grievous bodily harm

1)   If the bodily harm results in the victim

   1.   losing their sight in one eye or both eyes, hearing, speech or ability to procreate,
   2.   losing, or losing permanently the ability to use, an important body part,
   3.   being permanently and seriously disfigured or contracting a lingering illness, becoming paralysed, or mentally ill or disabled,

   the penalty shall be imprisonment for a term from one to 10 years.

2)   If the offender intentionally or knowingly causes one of the results indicated in subsection (1), the penalty shall imprisonment for a term of not less than three years.

§ 226, as can be seen from its sub-section (2), in its basic version is a result-qualified offence in connection with § 18 StGB.[80] Intent for, or knowledge of, the serious consequences is regulated expressly in § 226(2) and triggers a higher minimum and maximum

---

[76] PandStR (n 6) 39–40.
[77] Fischer (n 10) § 224, mn 32.
[78] PandStR (n 6) 43–44.
[79] Fischer (n 10) § 224, mn 32.
[80] Fischer (n 10) § 226, mn 2.

sentence, *i.e.*, three to 15 years. The alternative 'lingering illness' in § 226(1) No 3 would seem to be applicable to a Covid infection, especially in the light of the so-called 'long Covid' effect.[81]

§ 227 Infliction of bodily harm causing death

1) If the offender causes the death of the victim by inflicting bodily harm (sections 223 to 226a), causes the victim's death, the penalty shall be imprisonment of not less than three years.
2) In less serious cases, the penalty shall imprisonment from one year to 10 years.

This is also a result-qualified offence;[82] intent – including *dolus eventualis* – to cause death will, of course, also trigger § 212 StGB directly; however, as discussed above, since the 6th Criminal Law Reform Act of 1998, § 18 StGB now reads 'at least' by negligence and thus includes intentional causation of the extended result. As a rule, when it comes to multiple convictions for the same acts, the direct intentional offence will take precedence over the result-qualified offence and the conviction be based only on the former, but there are scenarios imaginable where both of them can be the basis for the conviction.[83]

D. Offences Regarding Unborn Foetuses; Interrupting the Course of a (Viable) Pregnancy

Abortion is regulated in an intricate system of provisions. It is addressed to the woman and to the doctor who performs the abortion, with the woman receiving special treatment because of her circumstances.[84] The basic offence is found in § 218:

§218 Abortion

1) Whosoever terminates a pregnancy shall be liable to imprisonment of not more than three years or a fine. Acts the effects of which occur before the conclusion of the nidation shall not be deemed to be an abortion within the meaning of this law.
2) In especially serious cases the penalty shall be imprisonment from six months to five years. An especially serious case typically occurs if the offender

    1. acts against the will of the pregnant woman; or
    2. through gross negligence causes a risk of death or serious injury to the pregnant woman.

For the purposes of this chapter, abortion under German law will be largely irrelevant, because it requires knowledge of the pregnancy and intent to terminate it and that may be difficult to establish for a pandemic-related scenario, even for the alternative of *dolus eventualis*.

---

[81] PandStR (n 6) 46.
[82] Fischer (n 10) § 227 mn 2.
[83] See Fischer (n 10) § 227, mn 12 for the details.
[84] For an overview of the development and the problems of the individual provisions, see Sch/Sch-Eser/Weißer (n 12) Vor §§ 218–19b.

E. Failure to Render Assistance

The specific offence of neglecting to effect an easy rescue/render assistance under § 323c StGB was mentioned above.

> §323c Failure to render assistance; obstruction of persons rendering assistance
>
> 1)   Whoever does not render assistance in the case of an accident or a common danger or emergency although it is necessary and can reasonably be expected under the circumstances, in particular if it is possible without substantial danger to that person and without breaching other important duties, incurs a penalty of imprisonment for a term not exceeding one year or a fine.
> 2)   Whoever obstructs a person who is rendering or wishes to render assistance to another person in such a situation incurs the same penalty.

§ 323c does not require any specific duty of care. Covid should qualify for either a common danger or common emergency. As a fall-back offence, § 323 c will be displaced by more specific offences.

V. DEFENCES, JUSTIFICATIONS AND EXCUSES

A. Necessity

The defence that comes to mind in this context is necessity, *i.e.*, the lesser evil defence, which in principle is recognised as a justificatory defence in § 34 StGB and some provisions in the Civil Code.[85] The argument is made that in order to keep the economy running and to protect people's livelihood, some concessions need to be made vis-à-vis the degree of protective measures to control the spread of the virus and thus save lives and protect the health of millions of people. Governments like to speak of a 'balanced approach' which in other words means nothing else but that a certain number of deaths and non-lethal infections are factored in. Especially in the context of the less aggressive Omicron variant, this argument became more prominent – but its force was, of course, immediately diminished by the danger caused to staffing levels in essential services.

It is already questionable whether the economic argument could wash with regard to accepting millions of potentially serious infections, even if transitory and non-lethal, but based on the BVerfG's above-mentioned *Triage* decision which ranked human life as the highest good, and its previous ruling on the Air Traffic Security Act 2005 (which would have allowed the shooting down of a passenger plane in a 9/11 scenario) where the Court stated that human lives may not be set off against each other numerically,[86] it would seem even more questionable that mere economic concerns could override the protection of a vast number of lives, especially in a developing pandemic.

---

[85] See for an overview of the law of necessity K Ambos and S Bock, 'Germany', in A Reed, M Bohlander et al (eds), *General Defences in Criminal Law* (London and New York, Routledge, 2014) 233–35.

[86] See on this decision and for a critique M Bohlander, 'In Extremis – Hijacked Airplanes, "Collateral Damage" and the Limits of Criminal Law' (2006) *Criminal Law Review* 579; M Bohlander, 'Of Shipwrecked Sailors, Unborn Children, Conjoined Twins and Hijacked Airplanes – Taking Human Life and the Defence of Necessity' (2006) *Journal of Criminal Law* 147.

VI. CORPORATE CRIMINAL LIABILITY

German criminal law does not (yet) subscribe to the idea of corporate criminal liability proper. § 14 StGB makes provision for the liability of certain officers of companies, corporations, etc. Otherwise only natural persons over 14 years of age (§ 19 StGB) can commit criminal offences. It is generally thought that because of the stress on personal blameworthiness as the basis of liability, substantive criminalisation in the sense of direct criminal responsibility does not make sense vis-à-vis legal entities that cannot act for themselves, but are represented by human beings.

VII. FORMS OF PARTICIPATION

German law recognises liability for being involved in the criminal activity of others, such as co-perpetration, aiding and abetting, incitement and conspiracy-like scenarios.[87] These either require a common (criminal) purpose or the knowledge of somebody else's criminal acts which the offender is meant to intentionally procure or support. Given the description of the German political environment under section 1 above, it is very unlikely that there was a common purpose between ministers at the federal and state level, because they had been constantly quarrelling over jurisdiction and the proper way of addressing the risks of Covid. Some states were more, others less cautious, and the constantly changing variety of measures taken across the different states – which made travelling across state lines a game of roulette, as the author can confirm from personal experience – suggests that there were no sinister agreements or intentional support of another's criminal activity, but at worst sheer incompetence and personal grandstanding in the competition for the most statesman-like posture, which in many cases may have been enough for gross negligence, and in a very few, depending on the circumstances, possibly also conditional intent. This may best be caught under the concept of independent multiple principals (*Nebentäterschaft*), which is not a form of participation at all.[88] It serves little purpose therefore to dwell in more detail on forms of participation in this context.

VIII. ATTEMPT

Attempts are punishable for all intentional offences which either carry a minimum sentence of one year (*Verbrechen* – felonies), but for misdemeanours (*Vergehen*) only if the law expressly so provides. Attempts can be committed by omission. Negligent offences can, of course, conceptually not be attempted. The law on attempted result-qualified offences is complex and in parts still controversial. Two scenarios are more or less accepted: D attempts the intentional basic offence but the attempt already causes the

---

[87] For an overview, see K Ambos and S Bock, 'Germany' in A Reed and M Bohlander (eds), *Participation in Crime – Domestic and Comparative Perspectives* (Farnham, Ashgate, 2011) 323–40.

[88] See M Bohlander, *Principles of German Criminal Law* (Oxford, Hart, 2009) 160–61.

serious extended result, or he attempts the basic offence with *intent* to cause the extended result.[89] The offender needs to cross a certain threshold, *i.e.*, do something more than merely preparatory.[90] Conditional intent is generally sufficient, unless a specific offence requires direct intent for certain elements. The attempt may be punished less severely than the complete offence (§ 23 StGB). In the cases of intentional offences, and absent of proof of causation, liability for attempt may, however, remain, as conditional intent is sufficient for attempts under German law.[91]

If we were to assume the government's actions were positive acts, the arguments of the *Wissenschaftliche Dienste* about the absence of a duty to act[92] as a bar to attempt liability would be irrelevant. If one were minded to attest even conditional intent to the members of government – both at federal and at state level – in charge of protecting the public health, lack of proof of actual causation of bodily harm or death would thus not prevent liability for attempt.

IX. SANCTIONS, SENTENCING, PUNISHMENT, REPARATIONS AND/OR RESTORATIVE JUSTICE

A. General Sentencing Framework for the Crimes under Discussion

The sentencing scale for the diverse offences listed above depends on the sentencing frame provided in each provision and ranges from a mere fine to 15 years' fixed term imprisonment, or discretionary life imprisonment under § 212(2) StGB. The basic sentencing criteria are set out in § 46 StGB, which includes a reference to forms of restorative justice such as victim-offender mediation and restitution:

§ 46 General principles

1) The offender's guilt provides the basis on which the penalty is fixed. The effects which the penalty can be expected to have on the offender's future life in society are to be taken into account.

2) When fixing the penalty the court weighs the circumstances which speak in favour of and those which speak against the offender. The following, in particular, may be taken into consideration:

   – the offender's motives and objectives, in particular including racist, xenophobic or other motives evidencing contempt for humanity,

   – the attitude reflected in the offence and the degree of force of will involved in its commission,

   – the degree of the breach of the offender's duties,

   – the modus operandi and the consequences caused by the offence to the extent that the offender is to blame for them,

   – the offender's prior history, personal and financial circumstances, and

---

[89] Fischer (n 10) § 22 mn 37–37b.
[90] On the details see Bohlander, *Principles of German Criminal Law* (n 88) 141–44.
[91] Fischer (n 10) § 22, mn 31a.
[92] 'Report of the Wissenschaftliche Dienste' (n 63) 13.

– the offender's conduct in the period following the offence, in particular efforts to make restitution for the harm caused as well as efforts at reconciliation with the victim.

3) No consideration may be given to circumstances which are already statutory elements of the offence.

The details of sentencing practice are too many to be explained here and reference is made to the author's book on Principles of German Criminal Procedure.[93] Being in a high hierarchical position of power and responsibility and neglecting one's duties with numerous negative consequences will usually be an aggravating circumstance.

B. Sanctions Specifically for Senior Government/Public Officials

Being a senior official and violating official duties when causing death or bodily harm will on the one hand usually result in a harsher sentence. On the other hand, § 45 StGB provides for the loss of the ability to hold public office, to vote or be elected in public elections, once the offender is sentenced to imprisonment of not less than one year. This sanction is feared by all public officials, especially civil servants, who will lose their tenure and with it their accrued privileged state pension entitlements, according to the federal and state laws on the civil service, for example § 41(2) *Bundesbeamtengesetz* (Federal Civil Service Act). There are otherwise no sanctions on the constitutional level, such as impeachment etc, except for the Federal President, who may be indicted before the BVerfG for violation of the GG or a federal act of parliament (article 61 GG). However, since the President does not participate in the day-to-day running of government, the relevance of this procedure is minimal for our purposes – an example might be the refusal to certify an act of parliament under article 82 GG and thus delay or block measures needed to combat the pandemic. There is no such procedure for the Chancellor or the ministers; the former may have to face a vote of no confidence in parliament and the latter may be dismissed at the pleasure of the Chancellor in any event.

C. Corporations and Sentencing

See above under section 6 on corporate liability in general. Certain criminal sanctions such as forfeiture of property, etc and of *instrumenta sceleris* can be taken against legal persons. There is also the possibility of fining them for *Ordnungswidrigkeiten* (summary offences) under § 30 OWiG, but that is not a criminal sanction.

---

[93] Bohlander, *Principles of German Criminal Procedure* (n 28) 175–221.

7

India

SUMAN DASH BHATTAMISHRA

I. BACKGROUND AND CONTEXTUAL INTRODUCTION

ON 30 JANUARY 2020, India reported its first case of Covid-19, coincidentally the same day it was declared a pandemic by the World Health Organization.[1] India's first case was that of a medical student who had returned from Wuhan to his hometown in Thrissur – a district in the southern state of Kerala.[2] Within hours of his return, hundreds of Indian citizens were airlifted from China in special flights.[3] By March, India's first Covid-19 fatality was reported, as a 76-year-old man succumbed to the disease.[4] While numbers were sharply rising all over the country, all of a sudden, the Central Government imposed a nationwide lockdown for 21 days on the 24 March.[5] Four days later, there was complete or partial lockdown all over the country, following the Government's announcement that it was mandatory to prevent the virus from spreading. As businesses, universities and offices were shut down, the Indian economy came to a grinding halt. Due to the lockdown, which came without adequate notice, public transport was suspended abruptly and state boundaries were sealed. With factories and industries closing down, people working as labour force were laid off and within days, the country witnessed thousands of migrant labour on the streets, many of them walking hundreds of kilometres to reach their native places. During this time, the Central Government also announced that a special Covid-19 Task Force had been created to deal with the public health emergency arising from the spread of the novel coronavirus.

---

[1] A De, 'Coronavirus India timeline: Tracking crucial moments of Covid-19 pandemic in the country' *The Indian Express* (online, 1 October 2020), https://indianexpress.com/article/india/coronavirus-covid-19-pandemic-india-timeline-6596832/.

[2] BS Perappadan, 'India's first coronavirus infection confirmed in Kerala' *The Hindu* (online, 30 January 2020), www.thehindu.com/news/national/indias-first-coronavirus-infection-confirmed-in-kerala/article61638034.ece.

[3] 'Special Air India Flight with stranded Indians from virus hit Wuhan to leave for home on Saturday' *The Economic Times* (online, 31 January 2020), https://economictimes.indiatimes.com/industry/transportation/airlines/-aviation/special-air-india-flight-with-stranded-indians-from-virus-hit-wuhan-to-leave-for-home-on-saturday/articleshow/73811871.cms.

[4] N Dwarakanath, 'First Coronavirus Death in India: 76 year old who died in Karnataka had Covid 19, says State Government' (*India Today*, 12 March 2020), www.indiatoday.in/india/story/first-coronavirus-death-in-india-karnataka-man-1654953-2020-03-12.

[5] EPW Engage, 'Covid 19: Examining the impact of Lockdown in India after One Year' (*Economic and Political Weekly Engage*, 24 March 2021), www.epw.in/engage/article/covid-19-examining-impact-lockdown-india-after-one?0=ip_login_no_cache%3De5b3af1c62d1902ec47cf4fd322a32e3.

By the end of March and the beginning of April, there were about 10,000 positive cases and over 100 deaths, thus leading the Central Government to extend the lockdown to 3 May.[6] Amid a shortage of testing kits and essential supplies such as N95 Masks and personal protective equipment (PPE) suits, the number of people affected by Covid-19 continued to rise. In June 2020, the Central Government announced the guidelines for 'Unlock 1.0' and states were allowed to remove or impose a lockdown after assessing the nature and extent of Covid-19 infections and fatalities in their respective territories.

While quick containment measures and a strict lockdown during the first wave enabled India to keep Covid-19 related deaths and infections in check, the second wave of Covid-19 was visibly catastrophic. In many Indian states, it peaked in April 2021. Election campaigns by political parties involving large crowds of people,[7] religious congregations such as the Kumbh Mela,[8] the opening up of recreation centres like shopping malls and cinema halls, along with a premature loosening of the Covid-19 protocols marked the beginning of this wave. These were permitted despite the warning issued by the Indian Council of Medical Research (ICMR) about the inevitability and lethality of an impending second wave of Covid-19 that India was inching closer to.[9] Slack implementation of Covid-19-appropriate behaviour and a complete lack of preparedness of the Centre (*i.e.*, the Central Government) as well as the States to meet the unfolding disaster, resulted in tragic deaths and incredibly high rates of infections during this period.

As Covid-19 triggers respiratory ailments, this phase was also marked by a huge demand for oxygen that quickly resulted in an acute shortage, as many states failed to procure it. News channels and print media reported that affected people across many Indian states died of asphyxiation during this phase, as hospitals packed with seriously ill Covid-19 patients experienced short supplies of oxygen. Rates of vaccination were also low and several vaccination centres were closed down due to a shortage of vaccines. Therefore, it will not be an exaggeration to state that the second wave was marked by acute mismanagement by the Central and State Governments and the open infraction of Covid-19 protocols during mass religious, political and social gatherings.

However, on 20 July 2021, the Home Minister in a statement on the floor of the Parliament, declared that there had been no deaths due to shortage of oxygen, as reported by a number of states. The Home Minister's statements were met with fierce criticism and the states responded by saying that they would furnish the required data to prove the contrary. The Delhi, Allahabad and Karnataka High Courts, taking note of deaths in hospitals due to a shortage of oxygen, asked the Centre to ensure the equitable

---

[6] Press Bureau of India, 'Lockdown Measures for containment of COVID-19 pandemic in the country to continue to remain in force up to May 3, 2020' (Ministry of Home Affairs, 14 April 2020), https://pib.gov.in/PressReleasePage.aspx?PRID=1614481.

[7] S Kumar, 'Second Wave of COVID-19: Emergency Situation in India' (2021) 28 *Journal of Travel Medicine*, taab082, https://doi.org/10.1093/jtm/taab082.

[8] G Pandey, 'India Covid: Kumbh Mela pilgrims turn into super-spreaders' (*BBC*, 10 May 2021), www.bbc.com/news/world-asia-india-57005563.

[9] N Bhowmick, 'How India's second wave became the worst COVID-19 surge in the world' (*National Geographic*, 24 April 2021), www.nationalgeographic.com/science/article/how-indias-second-wave-became-the-worst-covid-19-surge-in-the-world.

distribution and supply of oxygen to all states.[10] In May, the Supreme Court of India also issued guidelines to the Centre, as well as the states, for distributing oxygen equitably.[11]

II. CONSTITUTIONAL, LEGAL AND POLICY OVERVIEW

The Indian Constitution prescribes a partly federal structure of governance, with the Union Executive at the top, followed by the State Executives of the different states, which wield exclusive executive powers within the territories of the respective states. Local self-governments or '*Panchayats*' form the third rung of the governance structure. While the Members of the State Executive are called Members of Legislative Assemblies (MLAs), members of the Union Executive are called Members of Parliament.

In India, the obligation of the State to protect the health of its citizens stems from the Indian Constitution (Constitution). The Executive is duty-bound to protect the fundamental rights of its citizens that are listed in Part III of the Constitution. These rights are considered to be elemental and enforceable in a court of law by writs, in case of violation. In Part IV, the directive principles of state policy are enlisted in the form of directives for the State. Although non-enforceable, their implementation by the government is expected and encouraged. Although the right to health is not recognised directly as a fundamental right, the Supreme Court of India, through several judgments, has made it clear that the right to health is an integral part of the right to life guaranteed under article 21 of the Constitution and the State has a positive obligation to extend it to citizens. In *Paschim Banga Khet Mazdoor Samity v Union of India*,[12] the Supreme Court observed that in a welfare state, extending medical facilities to people is an essential part of the obligations undertaken by the federal as well as state governments. In *Vincent Panikurlangara v Union of India and ors*,[13] the Supreme Court, while pointing out the significance of the right to health, had observed that maintenance and improvement of public health is indispensable, as it is essential to the very physical existence of society and, therefore, the obligations of the state with respect to this must always rank very high.

Emphasising the significance of safeguarding public health, Indian Courts, from time to time, have called upon governments to implement public health schemes properly so that their benefits reach intended beneficiaries.[14] In 2016, the Supreme Court of India also held that it is the obligation of the Union as well as the States to ensure effective implementation of schemes announced by the Government, and the Union Government's role cannot be confined to mere announcement of such schemes. Keeping these factors in mind, it goes without saying that members of the government and other public servants who were allotted with duties to shape policies and strategies to protect the health of people have a constitutional mandate to implement such policies in good faith.

---

[10] 'No deaths due to Oxygen Shortage: Opposition accuses Centre of insensitivity as BJP defends govt's response' *The Times of India* (online, 21 July 2021), https://timesofindia.indiatimes.com/india/no-deaths-due-to-oxygen-shortage-opposition-accuse-centre-of-insensitivity-as-bjp-defends-govts-response/articleshow/84618280.cms.

[11] *In Re: Distribution of Essential Supplies and Services during Pandemic* [2021] SC, [2021] LL 228 (SC).

[12] *Union of India v Iqbal Singh Cheema* [1995] SC, [1996] AIR 426 (SC).

[13] *Vincent Panikurlangara v Union of India* [1987] SC, [1987] AIR 990 (SC).

[14] *Laxmi Mandal v Deen Dayal Harinagar Hospital* [2010] Del HC, [2010] 172 DLT 9 (Del HC).

A. Overview of and Specific Constitutional and Legal Principles Regarding Criminal Liability of High-Ranking Government/Public Officials

In India, public health emergencies are jointly dealt with by the Central as well as the State Governments. Under article 246, the Constitution authorises the Central as well as State Governments to frame laws and policies in the interests of public health. Under List 1 of the 7th Schedule of the Constitution, the Central Government is empowered to make laws in matters concerning port and seamen's quarantine, marine hospitals, as well as interstate migration and quarantine. Simultaneously, List 2 of the same schedule allows State Governments to make laws concerning public health and sanitation, hospitals and dispensaries. The Concurrent List, that is, List 3 of the 7th Schedule allows both the Central as well as the State Governments to make laws regarding prevention or transmission of infectious and contagious diseases. So, the Constitution envisions a shared responsibility of the Centre and States in matters of public health emergencies, such as Covid-19.

While India lacks a comprehensive public health legislative framework, currently two specific pieces of legislation are being invoked for enacting and implementing rules, regulations and policies to contain the spread of Covid-19: the Epidemic Diseases Act, 1897 (the EDA) and the Disaster Management Act, 2005 (the DMA).

The EDA is an archaic, yet important piece of legislation devised by the Central Government to deal with epidemic diseases. It empowers the Centre as well as States to take various measures to prevent the spread or outbreak of epidemic diseases. For example, under the Act, the Centre may make laws for detention and inspection of individuals suspected to be infected with a deadly disease. Likewise, it also allows States to make temporary regulations to deal with a dangerous epidemic disease to prevent its spread. Under section 2, States have the power to make regulations for people travelling by railway (or otherwise) and to segregate them in 'hospitals or other temporary accommodations', if there is suspicion that such people are inflicted with the disease. Previously, the legislation was invoked by various Indian States to counter diseases such as Swine flu, Cholera, Malaria, etc.[15] In March 2020, when the number of people affected by Covid-19 rose to 60, the Ministry of Health and Family Welfare (MoHFW) advised all State and Union territories to invoke section 2 of the EDA. It was predicted that by invoking the EDA, states would be in a position to enforce all advisories issued from time to time by the Centre. As Covid-19 was found among people with a history of travel to other countries, it was assessed that the provisions of the EDA to test and quarantine people with a travel history was a necessary step in preventing the disease and this is one of the many wide powers conferred by the EDA on the State Governments.[16] Several Indian states have invoked powers under the EDA since then.[17]

---

[15] 'Explained: Govt invokes Epidemic Diseases Act, 1897 to fight Coronavirus, what is it?' *The Indian Express* (online, 12 March 2020), https://indianexpress.com/article/explained/explained-what-is-the-epidemic-act-of-1897-govt-has-invoked-to-fight-coronavirus-6309925/.

[16] 'What is 1897 Epidemic Act that Centre wants states to invoke to tackle coronavirus' *Hindustan Times* (online, 12 March 2020), www.hindustantimes.com/india-news/what-is-1897-epidemic-act-which-government-proposes-to-invoke-to-tackle-coronavirus/story-A063TFrMf8bDobyG0kB0qL.html.

[17] Kumar, 'Second Wave' (n 7).

The second piece of legislation which has been invoked by the Indian Government is, as mentioned before, the DMA. Under this Act, a disaster is defined as any catastrophe, calamity, mishap or grave occurrence in any area, arising from natural or man-made causes, or by accident or negligence, which results in substantial loss of human life or suffering, or damage to or destruction of property, or degradation of the environment.[18] Under the Act, authorities have been created at three distinct levels to tackle disasters: National, State and District levels.[19] As Covid-19 broke out in India, the Centre declared the situation as a 'notified disaster' and invoked the powers conferred under the DMA. Broadly, the powers include constitution of special committees to draw up a National Plan for coping with the disaster, creating necessary sub-committees, laying down guidelines, policies, and issuing orders for dealing with the disaster.[20] Under the Act, government officers found to be acting in contravention with its provisions would be deemed to be guilty unless they are able to show that the acts took place without their knowledge or that they took appropriate measures to prevent them.[21]

B. Scope of Responsibility and Area of Tolerated Risk

In order to decide the extent of liability of the members of various task forces, elected representatives and other officials of the government, it is important to ascertain the statutory and constitutional responsibility of such members towards members of the public, that they serve by virtue of their office. Previously, in India, Members of Parliament and Legislative Assemblies have sought immunity from criminal proceedings on the ground that they do not qualify as 'public servants' within the meaning of section 21 of the Indian Penal Code, which lists various categories of persons who qualify as public servants and against whom criminal proceedings may be initiated for dereliction of duties, while in office. So, under section 21, commissioned officers of the Army, Air Force or Navy, Judges, Members of Panchayat, Government officers legally bound to enforce the law, revenue officers, etc qualify as public servants. The section does not explicitly mention that members of the Parliament or Legislative Assemblies qualify as public servants. For a long time in India, this has been the ground on which criminal proceedings have not been initiated against ministers. However, pursuant to decisions of the Supreme Court in *PV Narasimha Rao*, *M Karunanidhi* and *Jayalalitha*, the law is clearly settled that they qualify as public servants.[22]

This is by virtue of the fact that they discharge public duties and receive remuneration from the Government of India.[23] Likewise, members of statutory bodies such as National, State and District Disaster Management Authorities or constitutional bodies

---

[18] Disaster Management Act 2005 (DMA 2005), s 2(d).
[19] ibid, ss 3, 14, 25.
[20] Ministry of Home Affairs, 'Guidelines for effective control of COVID-19' (Order No. 40-3/2020-DM-I(A), 23 March 2020).
[21] DMA 2005, s 55.
[22] *P.V. Narasimha Rao v State* (CBI/SPE) [1998] SC, [1998] 4 SCC 626 (SC); *M Karunanidhi v Union of India* [1979] SC, [1979] 3 SCC 431 (SC).
[23] ibid.

such as the Election Commission also qualify as public servants for being in service of the Government and can, therefore, be subject to the provisions of the Indian Penal Code.[24]

C. Impact of Immunities

Under the Constitution, Members of the Parliament and State Legislative Assemblies enjoy certain powers and privileges by virtue of their office. Articles 105 and 194 clearly spell out that ministers cannot be made liable for anything said or any vote made in the Parliament/State Legislature or any Committee thereof.[25] However, such immunity does not extend to criminal prosecutions in case of individual or group culpability.[26] This position is further strengthened by the Supreme Court's stance that ministers are 'public servants' and can therefore, be prosecuted for offences mentioned in the Indian Penal Code. Civil servants, on the other hand, do not enjoy any of these privileges.

While ministers cannot be prosecuted for anything said by them on the floor of the Parliament, the immunity is not extended to their conduct outside the House.[27] Further, a minister cannot be arrested in civil cases when the Parliament/State Legislature is in session, or 40 days before and after a session.[28] This rule is not applicable in criminal matters.[29]

Parliamentary Privileges under the Constitution are based on the idea that in the absence of certain immunities, democracy would be throttled in the absence of free speech and expression by elected representatives. However, these privileges must be read together with the idea of ministerial responsibility, which the Constitution spells out through the principle of individual and collective responsibility of the Council of Ministers.[30] But this responsibility, while being political, is not legal, with the latter form of accountability being that of the Union of India.[31] Therefore, ministers cannot be made individually liable for an error of judgment or for pursuing a wrong policy.[32] But they may certainly be made accountable for flouting existing laws and policies in the same way as other public servants.

Considering that the EDA is in operation during the pandemic, it is necessary also to examine liabilities under the Act. Section 3 provides that anyone who violates an order or regulation that has been made under the EDA shall be punished under section 188 of the Indian Penal Code – thus making such person liable for a punishment of up to one month of imprisonment or a fine, or both.[33] At the same time, however, section 4 provides that no suit or legal proceeding can lie against any person or authority for anything either done or intended to be done, in good faith, under this Act.[34] This section, therefore, gives

---

[24] Indian Penal Code 1860 (IPC 1860), ss 21(11), (12).
[25] The Constitution of India 1950 (COI 1950), art 105, 194.
[26] UR Rai, *Constitutional Law – I Structure* (Lucknow, Eastern Book Company, 2016) 220.
[27] ibid 128.
[28] Code of Civil Procedure 1908 (CPC 1908), s 135.
[29] Rai, *Constitutional Law* (n 26) 128.
[30] COI 1950, art 74.
[31] MP Singh, *VN Shukla's Constitution of India* 7th edn (Lucknow, Eastern Book Company, 2013) 428.
[32] ibid 429.
[33] IPC 1980, s 188.
[34] Epidemic Diseases Act 1897 (EDA 1897), s 4.

a wide range of powers as well as immunity to authorities at all levels for implementing the laws made in exercise of the powers conferred under the Act – provided the element of good faith is established.

D. Prosecutorial Matters

With an aim to protect ministers from frivolous prosecutions, the Code of Criminal Procedure also provides that a criminal case cannot be instituted against a minister without the sanction of the Government.[35] This presents a tricky situation considering that the arrest of a minister who is a member of the ruling party may not be sanctioned by the government at all. In 2013, a five-judge Bench of the Supreme Court, while deciding a case for arresting ministers, passed a decision to the effect that when the government does not sanction such arrest, the Governor, who is the Executive Head of a State, may sanction it.[36] This case involved the question of arresting two members of the Council of Ministers in the state of Madhya Pradesh who were allegedly complicit in a case of illegal land acquisition.[37] Recently, the Supreme Court also held that no criminal proceedings can be initiated against public servants (such as bureaucrats and other government officers) without the sanction of a competent authority.[38] So, while theoretically a case may be instituted by any member of the public against ministers, it is necessary that the Government or an Executive Head sanctions the prosecution. In the case of other high-ranking officials, a competent authority must sanction it. However, such sanction is necessary only when the alleged criminal conduct directly relates to discharge of official duties.[39] In cases like these, a competent authority is one that has the capacity to remove the public servant from office.[40]

III. CAUSATION

A. Causation (General Principles)

In the Indian Penal Code (Code), a person is said to have caused an effect when he (includes he/she/they) causes it by means whereby he intended to cause it or by means, which, at the time of employing, he knew or had reason to believe to be likely to cause the said effect.[41] The section makes it clear that a person may be made liable for such effects which he may or may not have intended if such effects were the probable consequences of the means

---

[35] Criminal Procedure Code 1973 (CrPC 1973), s 197.

[36] *State of Madya Pradesh v Yashwant Trimbak* [1996] SC, [1996] AIR 765(SC).

[37] 'SC: Governor can sanction minister's prosecution' *Business Standard* (online, 3 February 2013), www.business-standard.com/article/economy-policy/sc-governor-can-sanction-minister-s-prosecution-104110601102_1.html.

[38] 'CBI can prosecute senior bureaucrats without govt sanction: Supreme Court' *The Economic Times* (online, 7 May 2014), https://economictimes.indiatimes.com/news/politics-and-nation/cbi-can-prosecute-senior-bureaucrats-without-govt-sanction-supreme-court/articleshow/34743276.cms.

[39] *Samsher Singh v State of Punjab* [1974] SC, [1974] AIR 2192 (SC).

[40] *R.S. Antulay v Ramdas Sriniwas Nayak* [1984] SC, [1984] AIR 718(SC).

[41] IPC 1860, s 39.

used by him. In such cases, the intention is inferred from what a person does or omits to do.[42] Section 32 of the Code clarifies that an act may be either in the form of commission or by omission. However, for omissions to qualify as culpable conduct, it is necessary that they should be illegal, as a person cannot be punished for the consequences of such actions unless he/she had a legal obligation to act.[43] The term illegal has been defined in the section 43 of the Code to include everything which (1) amounts to an offence; (2) is prohibited by law; or (3) furnishes ground for civil action. The section also clarifies that a person is said to be legally bound to do everything that is illegal in him to omit.[44]

Therefore, the range of what may count as a source of legal duties is very wide under section 43. For the first parameter under the section, an act or omission may qualify as an offence if it is punishable under the Code or any special or local law which is in force, for the time being.[45] Likewise, the term 'prohibited by law' is very wide and may include all laws in force in the territory of India. This also signifies that an injurious act done intentionally may not be illegal if it is permitted in law. For example, an executioner causing the death of a convict may do so intentionally but his conduct is not illegal as it is backed by the force of law. The third parameter in section 43 covers such acts and omissions which furnish ground for civil action, *e.g.*, a breach of contract.[46] Therefore, such failure to act on the part of a person who is obligated by the law to act in a prescribed manner amounts to an illegal omission under section 43 and can qualify as an actus reus. For example, a public servant who omits to perform the duties vested in him by virtue of his/her office is said to have done an 'illegal omission' within the meaning of section 43.

B. Causation and 'Thin Skull' Scenarios

For criminal liability to attach to an individual, a causal relationship must be established between the act in question and its consequence. Indian law is clear on the point that for establishing culpability, it is necessary that the consequence must be the direct effect of the act in question, *i.e.*, it should be *causa causans*. In other words, it should immediately precede the consequence and should not be intercepted by other factors or conditions that might break the chain of causation. However, the question of causation becomes complex when there are several acts that might be linked with the consequence and it is not possible to identify directness of the act and consequence. In such cases, Indian courts have opined that the primary cause must not be too remote in relation to the consequence.[47]

Causation, if minimal, does not absolve one from criminal liability under the Code. For example, if the victim sustained injuries and could have been saved by the intervention of a doctor but died because she could not be taken to one on time that does not absolve the perpetrator from criminal liability. This is because the intervention of the doctor

---

[42] KA Pandey, *BM Gandhi's Indian Penal Code* 4th edn (Lucknow, Eastern Book Company, 2018) 65.
[43] RC Nigam, *Law of Crimes in India* (New Delhi, Asia Publishing House, 1965) 43.
[44] IPC 1860, s 43.
[45] ibid.
[46] *Emperor v Ganpat Subrao Kashyapi* [1934] Bom HC, [1934] 36 BOMLR 373 (Bom HC).
[47] *Moti Singh v State of Uttar Pradesh* [1964] SC, [1964] AIR 900 (SC).

(or the lack thereof) could have played only a minor role in the victim's death.[48] Likewise, reasonable foresight is an important factor in determining causation. The principle is built into various provisions of the Code dealing with acts that are 'imminently dangerous' or 'sufficient in the ordinary course of nature' to cause the death of the victim.[49] It is also important to note that contributory negligence of the victim does not negate causation in Indian criminal law. Complications in causation may also arise due to unexpected interventions. Indian courts have clarified that a person may not be exonerated from criminal liability just because there were unexpected interventions, but they may be taken into consideration to mitigate the gravity or degree of culpability, in some cases.[50]

Indian courts have held that for consequences which are unforeseeable, unpredictable or not entirely attributable to the perpetrator because of remote connection with the act, the perpetrator cannot be held accountable.[51]

C. Restricting Causality: Policy and Doctrinal Issues

As is evident from the above discussion, Indian courts have emphasised the existence of causation for attaching criminal liability. Remoteness of causal connection between the act and its consequence may, depending on the case, negate culpability, as far as the Code is concerned.[52]

IV. THE STRUCTURE OF HOMICIDE OFFENCES AND ASSAULT/AGGRAVATED ASSAULT/SERIOUS BODILY HARM OFFENCES

The law of homicide is dealt with in three sections of the Code: sections 299, 300 and 304-A. While section 299 defines culpable homicide, section 300 deals with the offence of murder and section 304-A covers deaths by rash or negligent acts. In India, corporations cannot commit the offence of homicide as they are not capable of possessing intention and, therefore, only natural persons can cause this category of offences. The three sections vary from each other in their constituent elements as set out below.

A. Murder/Intentional Homicide

Section 300 outlines the offence amounting to murder and states that a person may be said to have committed the offence amounting to murder if he (1) causes the death of the victim with the intention of causing such death; (2) intentionally causes bodily injury which the offender knows to be likely to cause the death of the victim; (3) intentionally causes bodily injury and such bodily injury is sufficient in the ordinary course of nature

---

[48] IPC 1860, s 299.
[49] IPC 1860, ss 300(3), (4).
[50] KL Vibhute, *PSA Pillai's Criminal Law* 14th edn (Gurgaon, LexisNexis, 2019) 32.
[51] *Joginder Singh v State of Punjab* [1979] SC, [1979] AIR 1876 (SC).
[52] ibid.

to cause death; or (4) knows that an act is imminently dangerous and does it knowing that it will in all probability cause death, or such bodily injury as is likely to cause death and he commits such act without any excuse for incurring the risk of causing death or such injury as aforesaid.[53]

While the first clause requires a certainty of the consequence of death, in the second clause, intention to cause bodily injury is coupled with the component of special knowledge. The clause is applicable in cases where the accused has an intention to cause an injuring *knowing* that such injury is likely to cause the death of the victim. The knowledge is subjective and it needs to be proven by the prosecution beyond reasonable doubt that the accused had such knowledge while causing the intended injury. The third clause retains the factor of intention with respect to bodily injury (which occurs in the second clause) but states that an act is also murder if such intended injury is sufficient in the ordinary course of nature to lead to death. The form of knowledge captured here is objective unlike the one required in the preceding clause. The fourth clause deals with the mental state of recklessness, a term which does not occur in the Code but which signifies the absence of due care and attention and the purposeful disregard to the consequences of one's actions, even though they are reasonably foreseeable.[54] For example, when a person shoots indiscriminately in the middle of a crowded street and causes the death of the victim, he will be liable for murder as shooting in a crowded area is an imminently dangerous act that can lead to someone's death and such consequence is reasonably foreseeable.[55] In such cases, the perpetrator is made liable for consequences of his reckless actions even though it may be argued that he did not *intend* such consequences.

If the fourth clause of section 300 were applied in the context of various deaths resulting from Covid-19, it could be argued that individual criminal responsibility may arise from the actions of various elected representatives for organising and actively encouraging people to participate in events that necessitated huge congregations, *e.g.*, rallies by political parties for campaigning, and holding religious festivals such as the Kumbh Mela (right before the second wave) and Tableeghi Jamat (during the first wave). During a pandemic as deadly as Covid-19, such acts are imminently dangerous and ultimately ushered in a fatal second wave of Covid-19 in India. Liability may also arise for constitutional bodies such as the Election Commission of India for their failure to prevent and punish individuals blatantly violating the Covid-19 protocols at the time of campaigning, thereby ushering in the catastrophe that was unleashed by the second wave. The Madras High Court, while reprimanding the Election Commission orally, stated that it should be held responsible for the deaths of thousands of Indians as it failed to issue Covid-19-appropriate guidelines to political parties for campaigning during elections.[56] However, later, the Supreme Court cautioned that courts must refrain from making such serious allegations against constitutional bodies.[57]

---

[53] IPC 1860, s 300.

[54] Rai, *Constitutional Law* (n 26) 583.

[55] IPC 1860, s 300 (4), Illustration (d).

[56] 'Madras High Court blames EC for Covid spread, says officials ought to be booked for Murder' *The Economic Times* (online, 26 April 2021), https://economictimes.indiatimes.com/news/politics-and-nation/election-commission-responsible-for-covid-19-surge-madras-high-court/articleshow/82256082.cms?from=mdr.

[57] 'High Courts should avoid unnecessary, off-the-cuff remarks: Supreme Court' *The Hindu* (online, 30 April 2021), www.thehindu.com/news/national/high-courts-should-avoid-unnecessary-off-the-cuff-remarks-supreme-court/article34451147.ece.

Section 300 goes on to state five exceptions, which if applicable, reduce the degree of culpability from murder to that of culpable homicide not amounting to murder. The exceptions are acts resulting from grave and sudden provocation, a sudden fight, where there is consent of the victim, acts resulting from exceeding the right to private defence, and acts of public servants which are done in good faith and without any ill-will to the victim for the purpose of meeting the ends of public justice.[58] Free consent of the victim, that is devoid of factors such as misconception of facts, undue influence or coercion, is a crucial factor in mitigating the guilt of the perpetrator and reducing its degree to that of culpable homicide not amounting to murder. Therefore, if citizens voluntarily participated in the political rallies organised by political parties all over India or in religious congregations and thereby violated the Covid-19 protocols, the exception may be invoked to reduce the culpability to culpable homicide not amounting to murder.

B. Culpable Homicide/Manslaughter

The offence of culpable homicide is defined in section 299 of the Code. This section varies from section 300 in terms of the degree of mens rea and Indian Courts have clearly emphasised that the difference between the two offences is not of kind, but only of degrees.[59] The section provides that a person may be guilty of culpable homicide if he does an act with the intention of causing death or with the intention of causing bodily injury that is likely to cause death or with the knowledge that he is likely by such act to cause death. Intention and knowledge of likelihood of a consequence are important forms of mens rea captured in section 299. The third clause in section 299 refers to the existence of actual knowledge on the part of the perpetrator that such actions are likely to lead to death.[60]

In May 2021 it was reported that as thousands of people came together to participate in political rallies for the assembly elections in West Bengal, the State witnessed a sharp rise in the number of Covid-19 infections.[61] A similar rise was noticed in four other States – Assam, Kerala, Puducherry and Tamil Nadu.[62] In West Bengal, during this time the State recorded the highest single-day spikes in cases.[63] These rallies continued for over a month in States across India where assembly elections were due.[64] The Times of India, a leading national daily, called the event India's Covid-19 'tsunami' and stated that these packed rallies and political congregations, along with low vaccination rates, made way for the 'perfect storm' that ravaged India a month later.[65]

[58] IPC 1860, s 300, Exceptions 1–5.
[59] Rai, *Constitutional Law* (n 26) 592.
[60] ibid 574.
[61] P Mondal, 'Bengal elections 2021: Rallies lead to sharp rise in COVID 19 cases' *The New Indian Express* (online, 2 May 2021), www.newindianexpress.com/nation/2021/may/02/bengal-elections-2021-rallies-lead-to-sharp-rise-in-covid-19-cases-2297353.html.
[62] J Mullick, 'Polls and Covid 19: 5 regions, 5 big spikes' *The Hindustan Times* (online, 3 May 2021), www.hindustantimes.com/elections/polls-and-covid-19-5-regions-5-big-spikes-101619989743716.html.
[63] *Business Standard* (n 37).
[64] 'India's Covid Tsunami: Did election rallies lead to perfect storm?' *The Times of India* (online, 28 April 2021), https://timesofindia.indiatimes.com/india/indias-covid-tsunami-did-election-rallies-lead-to-perfect-storm/articleshow/82290041.cms.
[65] ibid.

In August 2021, Kerala, one of the smallest states in India, contributed to around 70 per cent of India's infections.[66] The low rate of vaccinations across the country including this southern coastal state, along with community-based local festivities added to the rapid rise in Kerala's cases at a time when the curve was showing signs of flattening in several states across the country. As India awaited a third wave, virologist Gagandeep Kang opined that the low rate of vaccinations combined with low seroprevalence should have been reason enough for all Indian states including Kerala to not open-up.[67] At this time, although virologists expressed concern at the chances of spreading infection, in several cities across the country, recreation centres such as shopping malls and places of worship opened up for people and some states also opened up schools in a staggered manner for vaccinated students and teachers only.[68]

In the Code, a perpetrator may be guilty of culpable homicide if he/she accelerates the process of death. In situations where the perpetrator is unaware of underlying ailments of the victim, he may be made liable for the consequences of his specific actions. Two important factors may be taken into consideration while determining the guilt of the perpetrator: first, was the consequence within reasonable foresight of the perpetrator, or should it have been within reasonable foresight of the perpetrator, and second, was the perpetrator actually aware of the victim's underlying conditions. The latter reflects the mens rea of special knowledge which is captured in the second clause of section 300.[69]

Keeping these factors in mind, it may be argued that the conduct of public servants reveals the knowledge of likelihood of the consequence of causing death of people or at least that of accelerating such death as required under section 299.

C. Death by Negligence

Section 304-A of the Code provides for death by negligence. This section was inserted following an amendment of the Code in 1870. It covers rash and negligent conduct that causes the death of a victim but which cannot be brought within the purview of section 299.

In this offence, for the perpetrator to be guilty of causing death of the victim, it is necessary that death must be a direct consequence of the former's actions. In *Re Jayraman*,[70] the Madras High Court, while elucidating the concept of direct consequence, stated that a difficulty arises when there are several recognisable contributory causes which make it very difficult to determine whether the effect was directly linked to one of the multiple causes.

[66] 'India Reports Surge with 46 K New Coronavirus Cases, Kerala accounts for nearly 70 % of Caseload' *ABP Live* (online, 28 August 2021), https://news.abplive.com/news/india/corona-cases-august-28-india-reports-over-46k-new-coronavirus-cases-as-kerala-contributes-around-70-to-the-caseload-1478852.

[67] S Mordani, 'Third wave will be a "hill" if second was a steep mountain: Virologist Gagandeep Kang' *India Today* (online, 2 August 2021), www.indiatoday.in/coronavirus-outbreak/story/third-wave-covid-india-kerala-model-onam-virologist-gagandeep-kang-1835930–2021-08-02?utm_source=taboola&utm_medium=recirculation.

[68] J Beaubien, 'Kids and Superspreaders are Driving COVID-19 Cases in India, Huge Study Finds' (*NPR*, 1 October 2020), www.npr.org/sections/goatsandsoda/2020/10/01/919237103/kids-and-superspreaders-are-driving-covid-19-cases-in-india-huge-study-finds.

[69] *State of Andhra Pradesh v Rayavarapu Punnayya* [1976] SC; [1977] AIR 45 (SC).

[70] *In Re: Jayaraman v Unknown*, 1967 CriLJ 776.

Between April and May 2021, India reported several deaths due to a short supply of oxygen in hospitals across several states, amid exponentially rising cases in the country following political rallies, strikes and religious congregations. The government of the western State of Rajasthan reported 6,500 deaths due to shortage of oxygen. While citizens blamed both the State and Central Governments, many State Governments blamed the Central Government for the absence of a strategy for production and distribution of oxygen, despite having absolute authority to do so under the DMA. There were allegations that the Covid-19 Task Force which was created at the central level to coordinate with States and provide requisite support during the Covid-19 crisis failed to meet even once in February and March 2021, right before the number of cases shot up across the country.[71] Apart from the fact that there was a shortage of oxygen in the country, there was also a lack of transportation facilities such as cryogenic tankers – as a result, oxygen could not be taken from a state that had excess of it to another that was in dire need of it.[72]

In many cases, however, states acted too late in ordering oxygen plants and communicating their oxygen requirements to the Centre. For example, according to reports, the State of Madhya Pradesh waited for positive cases to rise tenfold before placing an order for 13 of its districts.[73] As images of citizens across all age groups gasping for breath outside and inside hospitals, and crematoriums filled with funeral pyres circulated in media, questions of accountability were being raised by various Indian courts. While the Allahabad High Court stated that the deaths of citizens due to a shortage of oxygen was a criminal act, not short of genocide,[74] the Delhi High Court asked the Centre to provide oxygen to Delhi and account for the lack of it in the State.[75] The decision of the Allahabad High Court was passed in response to a public interest litigation which pointed towards the complete irresponsibility of bureaucrats in supplying liquid oxygen to hospitals, which lead to deaths of several patients in the districts of Lucknow and Meerut.[76] The Supreme Court of India, taking note of at least 12 confirmed deaths in a hospital at Delhi due to the shortage of oxygen, directed the Centre to rectify distribution of oxygen to the State within a period of two days.[77]

[71] V Krishnan, 'India's Covid Taskforce did not meet in February, March despite surge, say members' (*The Caravan*, 22 April 2021), https://caravanmagazine.in/health/india-covid-19-taskforce-did-not-meet-february-march-despite-surge-say-members.

[72] A Rehman, 'Covid deaths due to oxygen shortage no less than genocide: Allahabad High Court' *The Indian Express* (online, 5 May 2021), < https://indianexpress.com/article/india/covid-deaths-due-to-oxygen-shortage-no-less-than-genocide-allahabad-high-court-7302269/.

[73] V Lalwani, 'Last ditch efforts by MP to install oxygen plants shows even states failed to prepare for pandemic' (*Scroll.in*, 23 April 2021), https://scroll.in/article/993013/last-ditch-effort-by-mp-to-install-oxygen-plants-shows-even-states-failed-to-prepare-for-pandemic.

[74] 'No deaths due to Oxygen Shortage: Opposition accuses Centre of insensitivity as BJP defends govt's response' *The Times of India* (online, 21 July 2021), https://timesofindia.indiatimes.com/india/no-deaths-due-to-oxygen-shortage-opposition-accuse-centre-of-insensitivity-as-bjp-defends-govts-response/articleshow/84618280.cms.

[75] R Banka, 'You may be blind, but we are not: HC slams Centre over deaths due to scant oxygen supply in Delhi' *Hindustan Times* (online, 4 May 2021), www.hindustantimes.com/cities/delhi-news/you-may-be-blind-but-we-are-not-hc-slams-centre-over-deaths-due-to-scant-oxygen-supply-in-delhi-101620117558840.html.

[76] 'Death of Covid Patients Due to No Supply of Oxygen "Not Less Than Genocide": UP Court' (*NDTV*, 5 May 2021), www.ndtv.com/india-news/death-of-covid-patients-due-to-no-supply-of-oxygen-not-less-than-genocide-allahabad-high-court-2428100.

[77] P Gaur, 'Supreme Court directs Centre to rectify Delhi oxygen shortage issue in 2 days' (*Mint*, 2 May 2021), www.livemint.com/news/india/supreme-court-directs-centre-to-rectify-delhi-oxygen-shortage-issue-in-2-days-11619976507657.html.

While news and print agencies consistently reported that a number of Indians lost their lives due to the acute shortage of oxygen, the Health Ministry released an official statement on the floor of the Parliament that no deaths had occurred in India which could be attributed to such a shortage of oxygen. Few states joined the Union Health Ministry in echoing that statement while at the same time, several states strongly objected to it.[78]

Whether such omissions on the part of members of the Task Force would amount to rash and negligent acts or not would depend on the factor of 'reasonable foresight'. Was the shortage of oxygen reasonably foreseeable? Considering the fact that Covid-19 is a respiratory illness that spreads fast when there are crowds (political rallies, etc) and keeping in mind the fact that the primary job of the Task Force is to be updated about all data, facts and developments in the area of Covid-19 and to shape strategies to counter the disease, it may be argued that the event was foreseeable. The question that remains to be examined next is whether such deaths may be said to be the direct or proximate cause of the deaths of patients. If there is no other reason for the death to have occurred except a shortage of oxygen, then it may be said to be a direct consequence and the elements of section 304-A may be arguably satisfied.

D. Offences Related to Actions that Cause Serious Bodily Harm (Assault; Grievous Assault; Assault with Intent to Cause Serious Bodily Harm)

Sections 336, 337 and 338 deal with acts causing hurt or grievous hurt by endangering life or personal safety of others.[79] Section 336 may be applied when an individual does any rash or negligent act that endangers human life. Sections 337 and 338 deal with situations where an act results in simple or grievous hurt and is done in a rash or negligent manner, such rashness and negligence being of such a degree that human life or personal safety is endangered. These sections have rash and negligent acts as their fulcrum and committing such acts that affect personal safety or human life are punishable under the Code. One may argue that intentionally instigating people to violate the Covid-19 protocols by organising huge political gatherings may constitute the offences under these sections.

E. Offences Regarding Unborn Foetuses; Interrupting the Course of a (Viable) Pregnancy

Voluntarily causing miscarriage is punishable under section 312 of the Code, and under section 314, if death is caused by an act done with the intention of causing miscarriage, the person shall be punished with imprisonment that may extend to 10 years. However, for these offences to be complete, it is necessary that they were committed voluntarily and not accidentally.

---

[78] 'States join Centre in saying no one died due to oxygen shortage: Who said what' *India Today* (online, 21 July 2021), www.indiatoday.in/coronavirus-outbreak/story/states-join-centre-in-saying-no-one-died-due-to-oxygen-shortage-who-said-what-1830965-2021-07-21.

[79] IPC 1860, ss 336, 337, 338.

V. DEFENCES, JUSTIFICATIONS AND EXCUSES

In chapter IV, the Code makes a list of General Exceptions that can excuse culpable conduct under certain circumstances. Sections 76–106 enlist various grounds for exempting individuals from criminal liability. While some of these exceptions such as mistake of fact and accident are excusable in nature, others, such as those capturing the right to private defence are justifiable. Excusable defences are based on the idea that the accused was either physically incapable of generating mens rea (*e.g.*, infancy, insanity) or could not have had mens rea because of the circumstances under which the act took place (*e.g.*, accident). On the other hand, justifiable defences are those where the accused ends up committing an offence but the commission of such crime is said to be justified because it could not have been avoided (*e.g.*, private defence). The burden to prove the applicability of a general exception lies on the accused.[80] However, unlike the prosecution, the accused may discharge such burden by showing a preponderance of probabilities.[81]

A. Necessity

The defence of necessity is covered by section 81 of the Code. The defence may be used against liability arising from offences by showing that the act in question was done for the purpose of avoiding a greater harm and in good faith, without criminal intent.[82] However, while private defence may seem to coincide with necessity, the latter is not a defence to a charge of murder in Indian law.[83]

When the nationwide lockdown was announced during the first phase of Covid-19, people suffering from serious diseases suffered even more and many lost their lives as medicines could not reach them on time due to the disruption of public transportation, including flights and railways.[84] Policy-makers may argue that it was necessary to impose the lockdown due to the novelty of the coronavirus and the spread of the disease in a country as huge as India. The argument in this case would be that in order to avoid the greater risk that is, the spread of the novel coronavirus, the lesser risk, that is, the disruption of essential services, had to be taken. Likewise, despite the fact that certain virologists advised against the unlocking of the country due to low vaccination rates, it may be argued by State as well as Central Governments that complete lockdown of the economy for a protracted period could have caused irreparable damage, as people were losing their livelihoods.[85] However, good faith (defined in section 52 as the presence of due care and attention), needs to be shown to successfully plead this defence.[86]

---

[80] *State of Madhya Pradesh v Ahmadullah* [1961] SC, [1961] AIR 998 (SC).
[81] *VD Jhangan v State of Uttar Pradesh* [1966] SC, [1966] AIR 1762 (SC).
[82] Vibhute, *Criminal Law* (n 50) 91.
[83] ibid 91; GL Williams, *Textbook of Criminal Law* (Delhi, Universal Publishing, 1999) 604.
[84] A Ghosh, '70 % of India's Cancer patients couldn't access care during lockdown, experts say' *The Print* (online, 27 November 2020), https://theprint.in/health/70-of-indias-cancer-patients-couldnt-access-care-during-lockdown-experts-say/552529/.
[85] M Chaudhary et al, 'Effect of COVID-19 on Economy in India: Some Reflections for Policy and Programme' (2020) 22 *Journal of Health Management* 169; 'World's biggest lockdown may have cost Rs 7-8lakh crore to Indian economy' *The Economics Times* (online, 13 April 2020), https://economictimes.indiatimes.com/news/economy/finance/worlds-biggest-lockdown-may-have-cost-rs-7-8-lakh-crore-to-indian-economy/articleshow/75123004.cms?from=mdr.
[86] IPC 1860, ss 52, 80.

In certain cases, stakeholders may also argue that they did something because of a mistake of fact. Like the defence of necessity, an important constituent of this defence is also good faith. For example, in certain cases of deaths due to the shortage of oxygen, the Central Government may argue that due to a delay in the dissemination of information by various states, the former did not have any idea of a requirement for oxygen in those states and hence, they could not have reasonably foreseen the disastrous consequences that the event led to.

However, it would be difficult to successfully make these defences in situations where elected representatives permitted and actively hosted religious congregations. For example, when the Delhi Government permitted the organisation of the Tablighi Jamaat, was a huge religious congregation, Covid-19 had already been declared as a pandemic.[87] In West Bengal, celebrations such as the Bengali New Year took place despite the fact that all State Governments were advised against organising such events.[88] Likewise, in Uttar Pradesh, just before the second wave of Covid-19 swept in, the Kumbh Mela, which is one of the largest religious congregations in India, was organised in flagrant violation of the Covid-19 protocols.[89]

VI. CORPORATE CRIMINAL LIABILITY

A. Overview of Corporate Criminal Liability

As a general rule, in India, corporations cannot be liable either as accessories or perpetrators for offences such as homicide or grievous hurt as they cannot be said to possess an intention.[90] From time to time, the Supreme Court has held that while the mens rea of the persons running a corporation may be attributed to it and liability fixed on that basis, such a corporation cannot be prosecuted for offences that are punishable with imprisonment only or with a mandatory imprisonment along with fine.[91] In 2005, the Supreme Court emphasised that a corporation is a person and can be prosecuted for offences that carry a mandatory fine along with a term of imprisonment. However, the actual punishment to be imposed has to be that of fine only.[92]

---

[87] S Yamunan, 'Tablighi Jamaat: How did the government fail to detect a coronavirus infection hotspot' (*Scroll*.in, 1 April 2020), https://scroll.in/article/957891/tablighi-jamaat-how-did-the-government-fail-to-detect-a-coronavirus-infection-hotspot.

[88] 'Mamata Banerjee's Plans to Relax Conoravirus Lockdown For Bengali New Year Could Spell Disaster' (*Swarajya*, 26 March 2020), https://swarajyamag.com/news-brief/mamata-banerjees-plans-to-relax-coronavirus-lockdown-for-bengali-new-year-could-spell-disaster.

[89] 'Kumbh Mela Ends, 70 lakh participated in "scaled down" event held amid Covid Surge' *India Today* (online, 1 May 2021), https://www.indiatoday.in/india/story/kumbh-mela-ends-70-lakh-participated-scaled-down-covid-surge-1796833-2021-05-01.

[90] The Law Commission of India, 'The Trial and Punishment of Social and Economic Offences' (47th Report, 28 February 1972).

[91] *The Assistant Commissioner, Assessment-II, Bangalore v M/s/ Velliappa Textiles Ltd* [2003] SC, [2004] AIR 86 [SC].

[92] *Standard Chartered Bank v Directorate of Enforcement* [2005] SC, [2005] AIR 2622 (SC).

B. Accessory or Perpetrator

Statutory liability under special legislation may be fixed on directors of various companies and corporations.[93] These statutes create a presumption of guilt as far as the accused is concerned and the burden lies on individual members of the administration and management to show that offences were committed without their knowledge or that they exercised due diligence to prevent them.[94]

The most controversial incident of corporate criminal liability during Covid-19 has to be that of the corporation Patanjali, which produces, markets and advertises fast moving consumer goods. In June 2020, Patanjali marketed a drug named Coronil which was largely advertised as an anti-Covid-19 drug – leading people to falsely believe that the drug would prevent and cure Covid-19. The drug was not tried clinically and was not approved by any competent drug control authority in India.[95] While the corporation was quickly asked to withdraw its false advertisement and cases were filed against its board of directors, the criminal liability of its Board members cannot be ruled out for misbranding drugs under the Drugs and Cosmetics Act, 1940.[96] Not only that, the directors of the company could be said to be guilty of violating explicit government orders under the DMA, which prohibits spreading false information during a pandemic.[97]

VII. FORMS OF PARTICIPATION

The Code makes provisions for principal and accessorial liability in case of group offences.[98] Individuals may be liable as co-perpetrators if they commit an act in furtherance of a common intention.[99] Further, they may incur liabilities for inchoate offences such as abetment and attempt.[100] The Code also distinguishes between common intention and same or similar intention. In case of the former, a prior meeting of minds is necessary and it means that the perpetrators would be jointly liable for the commission of a crime.[101] In case of similar intention, however, the liability is several and therefore, each perpetrator would be liable only to the extent of his participation in the crime.[102]

---

[93] *SMS Pharmaceuticals Ltd v Neeta Bhalla* [2005] SC.

[94] Vibhute, *Criminal Law* (n 50) 56.

[95] 'Patanjali told to stop promoting "covid drug" before it's tested by government' (*Business Insider India*, 23 June 2020), www.businessinsider.in/india/news/patanjali-told-to-stop-promoting-coronil-before-its-tested-by-government/articleshow/76532454.cms.

[96] Drugs And Cosmetics Act 1940 (DACA 1940), s 33E.

[97] The Law Commission of India, 47th Report (n 89).

[98] IPC 1860, ss 34, 124A.

[99] ibid.

[100] IPC 1860, c V.

[101] *Suresh v State of Uttar Pradesh* [2001] SC.

[102] DMA 2005, s 55.

A. Joint Criminal Enterprise

While the Code makes a clear distinction between principal and accessorial liability, it does not expressly distinguish between principal offenders of the first and second degrees in a joint criminal enterprise.[103] Section 34 of the Code spells out the components of common intention according to which, individuals in a group may be jointly liable for the commission of an offence if a set of conditions is satisfied. The conditions are as follows: first, a criminal act must have been done by all persons in that group; second, such act must be done in furtherance of a common intention; and third, each person participated in some manner in the commission of that offence.[104] Section 33 clarifies that an act includes an omission. Thus, in matters concerning common intention, the extent of participation or the nature of the act does not have any impact in the determination of liability, if the existence of the common intention is proven. This position has been settled in *Barendra Kumar Ghosh v King Emperor*[105] where the Supreme Court held that individuals may be made liable for the whole act and not just their separate acts, if such acts are united by their common intention.[106] In cases where common intention is absent, section 38 of the Code makes it clear that persons participating in a criminal act may be liable for different offences, based on the extent of their participation.[107]

Incidents of leaders of political parties encouraging and organising large-scale congregations that continued for over a month for electoral canvassing, such as those in the States of Kerala and West Bengal, as well as the Union Territory of Puducherry arguably involved prior planning and active inter-institutional concert. This is because organising such events requires strategic mobilisation of people from amongst the public and the political parties. Considering the nature of these rallies and the significance of containing Covid-19, certain States such as Odisha refrained from organising physical gatherings during local elections and openly declared so, dissuading voters and party workers from assembling in large numbers.

Data revealed that in five states that were facing elections, there was a rapid spike in Covid-19 cases during and after the weeks following the election campaigns and this was despite the fact that in all these states, rates of infection were actually declining before the gatherings took place.[108] Media reports revealed images of unmasked people with absolute disregard for social distancing norms. It may be argued that while leaders of political parties had the duty to ensure that political congregations were organised responsibly in strict adherence to the Covid-19 protocols, the Election Commission also had a duty to promptly enforce Covid-19-appropriate political canvassing. Likewise, bureaucrats were responsible for shaping policies and enforcing Covid-19-appropriate behaviour in strict adherence to the EDA and DMA. In fact, in January 2022, after being severely criticised by the public, media and courts for their inaction in 2021, the Election

---

[103] Vibhute, *Criminal Law* (n 50) 200.
[104] ibid 56.
[105] *Barendra Kumar Ghose v King Emperor* [1925] PC, [1925] AIR 1 (PC).
[106] ibid.
[107] *Suresh v State of Uttar Pradesh* [2001] SC.
[108] D Basu, 'Did political rallies contribute to an increase in Covid 19 cases in India? (*The Wire*, 2 May 2021), https://thewire.in/politics/election-rally-covid-19-case-spike.

Commission banned political rallies and roadshows in five election-bound Indian states until 15 January 2022.[109] The Election Commission had also issued orders to State Chief Secretaries in May 2021 asking them to file First Information Reports (FIRs) and suspend Station House Officers of respective police stations where people were found to be celebrating election victories after elections.[110] However, the order was passed too late, with the country already reeling under the pressure of a deadly second wave following the election period. It therefore does not absolve the members of the Commission of their responsibility.

Their reticence in restraining errant leaders and party workers amounts to a clear illegal omission. Considering that their passivity spanned throughout the period of the campaign in April 2021, one may theoretically argue that they may be held jointly liable for causing grievous hurt to people who may have been hospitalised for more than 21 days because of Covid-19 infections that they contracted either by participating in the political gatherings or because a person who participated in such gatherings communicated the disease to them. However, establishing beyond reasonable doubt that the disease was contracted by either of the above factors would be crucial for a conviction. So, factors such as necessity of contact with the infected person, proof that the infection was caused because of the election campaign and other factors would have to be proved by the prosecution. However, extending the same arguments to fix joint responsibility for culpable homicide or murder or causing death by negligence would not be possible as these mandate the presence of a clear intention to cause death or in the case of the latter, negligence that directly resulted in the death of the concerned individual without any intervening factors. In the complex matrix of volition, existence of co-morbidities, optional non-adherence to the Covid-19 protocols and the right to political participation in a democracy, it would be difficult to establish the required mens rea.

B. Abetment

The Code defines various aspects of abetment in two separate sections. Under section 107, a person is said to abet the doing of a thing by instigation or engaging in a conspiracy or intentionally aiding the commission of an offence by an act or illegal omission.[111] Section 108 clarifies that for a person to be an abettor, the thing abetted must be an offence, whether or not such offence is committed.[112] Abetment is an inchoate offence under the Code and liability may be invoked even if the person who was abetted is incapable of committing the offence or happens to be an innocent agency.[113]

---

[109] 'Election commission bans political rallies, roadshows till Jan 15 amidst a fresh surge in COVID-19 cases: Details' (*OpIndia*, 8 January 2022), www.opindia.com/2022/01/election-commission-bans-political-rallies-roadshows-till-jan-15-amidst-fresh-surge-in-covid-19-cases-details/.

[110] A Chauhan, 'UP: ECI suspends SHO, seeks written clarification from officials on political gathering of Samajwadi Party' *The Times of India* (online, 15 January 2022), https://timesofindia.indiatimes.com/city/lucknow/up-eci-suspends-sho-seeks-written-clarification-from-officials-on-political-gathering-of-samajwadi-party/articleshow/88905269.cms.

[111] IPC 1860, s 107.

[112] IPC 1860, s 108.

[113] ibid.

C. Instigation

The term instigation used in section 107 of the Code connotes incitement, provocation or persuasion.[114] Instigation may be as much by conduct as by words.[115] An active suggestion, stimulation, suggestion or insinuation may also amount to instigation.[116] Approval that is active is also sufficient to meet the requirements of section 107 for the purpose of abetting an offence.[117] For instance, the action of political and religious leaders encouraging massive social gatherings for religious and cultural events such as traditional New Year celebrations[118] may arguably satisfy the requirements of abetment under the section. In a chain of events leading to hospitalisation or the deaths of participants, omissions of bureaucrats and political and religious leaders calling for large-scale congregations may qualify as abetment of grievous hurt or death by negligence.

D. Conspiracy

Abetment by conspiracy under the Code involves an abetment to commit an offence in pursuance of a conspiracy. In order to prove abetment by conspiracy, the prosecutor must show that the abettor instigated the doing of a thing or agreed with one or more persons to do something illegal or intentionally aided the doing of that thing.[119] However, the prosecutor need not show that the abettor was aware of every single detail of the plan.[120] For instance, as detailed earlier, inaction of senior bureaucrats despite an open violation of the Covid-19 protocols by elected representatives during election rallies, may be indicative of a tacit, if not explicit, agreement to ignore the spread of the novel coronavirus. It may be argued that wilful blindness towards the impact of such action despite the awareness that it would be deadly, is what such bureaucrats chose to agree upon.

VIII. ATTEMPT

The Code does not define the term 'attempt'. However, the Supreme Court has remarked that in the absence of any definition, the term must be taken in its ordinary sense.[121] A reading of the judgment reveals that the accused must have mens rea to commit the offence in question and such mens rea must have translated into an act as a step forward in the commission of the offence.[122] However, such step towards the commission of the offence must be interrupted for reasons beyond the control of the accused.[123] If these conditions are satisfied, the accused may be said to have attempted the commission of an offence.

---

[114] IPC 1860, s 107.
[115] ibid.
[116] ibid.
[117] ibid.
[118] *State v Amanatullah And Another*, (2020) Case No 39/2019 DLCT 12-0002472-019.
[119] Vibhute, *Criminal Law* (n 50) 205; *Saju v State of Kerala* [2001] SC, [2001] AIR 175 (SC).
[120] IPC 1860, s 108 exp 5.
[121] *Koppula Venkat Rao v State of Andhra Pradesh* [2004] SC, [2004] AIR 1874 (SC); Vibhute, *Criminal Law* (n 50) 185.
[122] *Amit Kapoor v Ramesh Chander* [2012] SC.
[123] *Mahendra Singh v State of Madya Pradesh* [1995] SC, [1995] Supp(3) SCC 731 (SC).

The Supreme Court has also held that in matters concerning physical injuries, it is not necessary for the prosecution to show that the accused must have committed the penultimate act.[124] It is sufficient to show the presence of an intention along with some overt act done with the purpose of executing it.[125] Thus, for example, abysmally low vaccination rates, a crumbling healthcare system, high rates of mortality all over the world and the nascent, highly contagious stage of the pandemic in the early months of 2021 were visibly potent factors to predict that encouraging a breach of the Covid-19 protocols would lead to serious injury to the people's health. While it may be far-fetched to argue that people in charge of shaping and implementing public health policies intended to cause the death of individuals or attempted to do so, it is not implausible to imagine recklessness on their part. An awareness of the nature and consequences of their actions may be reasonably presumed considering their positions of responsibility in structures of governance and their legal duties by virtue of their public offices.

For example, members of the Election Commission and bureaucrats in the police services were blamed by the Allahabad High Court for their failure to ensure that elections and campaigning took place in compliance with the Covid-19 protocols.[126] Considering that their omissions were illegal (as they had a legal duty which they failed to discharge), they may be said to have abetted various offences.

IX. SANCTIONS, SENTENCING, PUNISHMENT, REPARATIONS AND/OR RESTORATIVE JUSTICE

A. General Sentencing Framework for the Crimes under Discussion

The Code does not prescribe any specific or special punishment for high-ranking leaders or government officials. It also does not make a provision for fixing higher penalties for persons occupying public offices or serving the Government, except in a few cases such as offences that amount to custodial rape.[127]

B. Sanctions Specifically for Senior Government/Public Officials

Sentences prescribed in the Code for each of the offences discussed above are distinct. For example, the highest punishment which can be awarded for culpable homicide amounting to murder is the death penalty. For culpable homicide not amounting to murder, the punishment prescribed is life imprisonment. For causing death by negligence however, the punishment is only two years. In case of group offences, if the liability is joint, each member of the group would receive the same sentence.[128]

---

[124] *State of Maharashtra v Balarama Bama Patil* [1983] SC, [1983] 2 SCC 28 (SC).
[125] ibid.
[126] A Pandey, 'Election Commission, Government "Failed to Fathom Disastrous Consequences" of Polls: UP Court' (*NDTV*, 12 May,2021), www.ndtv.com/india-news/coronavirus-allahabad-high-court-says-election-commission-courts-government-failed-to-fathom-disastrous-consequences-of-polls-2439862.
[127] Criminal Law (Amendment) Act 1983, Act X of 1983.
[128] *Ramesh Singh @ Photti v State of Andhra Pradesh* 2004 (11) SCC 305.

Persons found to be guilty of abetting various offences are graded in different categories. For instance, punishments for abettors who intended to commit an offence different from the one actually committed by the principal offender are determined by the act committed by the latter.[129] But if there is difference between the intention of the abettor and principal offender in the doing of an act, the liability of the abettor has to be determined by referring to the intention of the former.[130]

As far as the law of attempt in the Code is concerned, section 511 provides that the punishment for offences punishable with death or imprisonment for life shall be punished to a term that may extend to one half of life-imprisonment or to a term that may extend to one half of the longest term of imprisonment provided for that offence. This rule would be applicable in cases where the Code does not prescribe the punishment explicitly for attempting to commit a certain offence.[131] For example, the Code provides that the punishment for attempting to commit culpable homicide may extend to seven years of simple or rigorous imprisonment.[132] Section 511 would not apply in such cases.

Considering that the Code is based on a retributive model, it contains no substantial provisions relating to reparations or restorative justice in cognisable offences.

---

[129] IPC 1860, s 111.
[130] IPC 1860, s 110.
[131] IPC 1860, s 511.
[132] IPC 1860, s 308.

8

Indonesia

TOPO SANTOSO*

I. BACKGROUND AND CONTEXTUAL INTRODUCTION

O N 28 JANUARY 2020, the Head of Indonesia's National Disaster Management Agency (*Badan Nasional Penanggulangan Bencana* – BNPB) declared 'a certain state of emergency' for an outbreak of a disease caused by the novel coronavirus in Indonesia. The emergency status was to be effective from 28 January 2020 to 28 February 2020, and was later extended by BNPB. On 2 March 2020, the announcement was made of the first case of Covid-19 in Indonesia, with two people testing positive.[1] Just over a week later, on 11 March 2020, the first death from Covid-19 was announced in Indonesia. On 31 March 2020, Presidential Decree No 11 of 2020 on the Stipulation of the Covid-19 Public Health Emergency was issued. On 7 April 2020, the first round of social restrictions began, with the Minister of Health permitting the implementation of Large-Scale Social Restrictions (*Pembatasan Sosial Berskala Besar* – PSBB) in the Special Capital Region of Jakarta. Four days later, on 11 April 2020, large-scale social restrictions also began to be implemented in several other regions. On 13 April 2020, Presidential Decree No 12 of 2020 was issued regarding the Stipulation of Non-Natural Disasters of the Spreading Coronavirus Disease 2019 as a National Disaster.[2]

The first peak of Covid-19 cases in Indonesia occurred on 16 January 2021, with 14,541 positive cases. The second peak of Covid-19 cases in Indonesia occurred on 15 July 2021, with 56,757 positive cases, after which the number of daily cases continued to decline, reaching as few as just several hundred cases per day between November 2021 and January 2022. By early February 2022, positive case numbers began increasing once more, reaching 64,718 cases on 16 February. By 7 March 2022, a total of 6,028,413 people had been infected with Covid-19 in Indonesia. There remained 78,302 active

* My gratitude goes to Djarot Dimas Achmad Andaru (djarot.dimas@ui.ac.id), a lecturer at the Faculty of Law, Universitas Indonesia, who assisted in writing this article.

[1] On 2 March 2020, for the first time, the Government of Indonesia announced two positive cases of Covid-19 patients in Indonesia. However, University of Indonesia Epidemiologist Pandu Riono said the SARS-CoV-2 type of coronavirus as the cause of Covid-19 had entered Indonesia in early January 2020. E Pranita, 'Diumumkan Awal Maret, Ahli: Virus Corona Masuk Indonesia dari Januari' (*Kompas*, 11 May 2020), www.kompas.com/sains/read/2020/05/11/130600623/diumumkan-awal-maret-ahli--virus-corona-masuk-indonesia-dari-januari?page=all.

[2] BNPB and Universitas Indonesia, *Pengalaman Indonesia dalam Menangani Wabah Covid-19* [*Indonesian Experience in Handling Covid-19 Pandemy*] (Jakarta, BNPB dan Universitas Indonesia, 2020) 67–68.

cases, while 5,794,602 people had recovered, and 155,509 had died. Overall, 92,817,150 suspected Covid-19 specimens had been examined and a total of 61,010,519 people had been examined. In terms of vaccination, 197,216,895 people had received their first vaccination and 160,935,915 their second vaccination.[3]

Indonesia saw its highest number of Covid-19 deaths recorded on 27 July 2021, with 2,069 deaths across the country. During July and August 2021, Indonesia had one of the highest Covid-19 death rates in the world, with persistently high rates of 1,000 to 2,000 deaths recorded per day. However, many different parties have raised key questions about the pandemic, including over the total number of deaths and even asking whether the government holds legal responsibility for Covid-19 deaths.

The Citizens' Coalition for the Right to Health (*Koalisi Warga untuk Hak atas Kesehatan*)[4] expressed serious concerns to President Joko Widodo and two ministers, the Minister of Health, Budi Gunadi Sadikin, and the Minister of Trade, Muhammad Lutfi. First, the Coalition highlighted the increased prices of oxygen cylinders and the uncontrolled filling of oxygen cylinders amid the surge in the number of coronavirus cases. The Coalition argued that the government should provide oxygen cylinders as a main requirement for responding to respiratory diseases. In this context, failure to do so can be fatal in some circumstances, including patients dying while waiting for hospital beds to become available as well as deaths resulting from a lack of oxygen despite being in the hospital. In addition, the government is considered to have failed to control the price of key medical equipment, including oxygen cylinders. Second, the Coalition highlighted that hospital capacity was inadequate, forcing Covid-19 patients to undergo self-isolation at home, which the Coalition claimed was inappropriate for Covid-19 patients with comorbidities, saying these patients must be treated in hospitals.[5] Third, the Coalition highlighted that Covid-19 patients with comorbidities who self-isolate without equipment are at higher risk of death than those in hospital. *LaporCovid* data shows that as at 18 July 2020, at least 675 Covid-19 patients had died while undergoing self-isolation at home. Fourth, the Coalition reported that they received complaints from relatives of Covid-19 patients who died while searching for available hospital beds. The Coalition also received reports that Covid-19 patients died in wheelchairs while queuing for rooms at hospitals while their oxygen saturation levels dropped. The letter was signed on 25 July 2021, by 107 community organisations, including the Indonesian Legal Aid Organisation (YLBHI), Indonesia Corruption Watch (ICW), Legal Aid (LBH), KontraS, Greenpeace Indonesia, the All-Indonesian Student Executive Body (*Badan Eksekutif Mahasiswa* – BEM) Alliance and many more.[6]

---

[3] Government of Indonesia, 'Distribution Map', https://covid19.go.id/peta-sebaran.

[4] The Citizens Coalition for the Right to Health consists of 107 community organisations such as YLBHI, ICW, LBH, KontraS, Greenpeace Indonesia, the All-Indonesian Student Executive Body (*Badan Eksekutif Mahasiswa* – BEM) Alliance and many more.

[5] Based on the Ministry of Health Decree No HK.01.07/MENKES/4641/2021, concerning Guidelines for Implementation of Examination, Tracing, Quarantine, and Isolation to Accelerate Prevention and Control of Coronavirus Disease 2019 (Covid-19).

[6] T Detikcom, 'YLBHI dkk Somasi Jokowi-Menkes soal Kelangkaan Oksigen' (*Detik News*, 27 Juli 2021), https://news.detik.com/berita/d-5658315/ylbhi-dkk-somasi-jokowi-menkes-soal-kelangkaan-oksigen. *LaporCovid-19* reported that until 7 August 2021, 3,018 Covid-19 patients died while undergoing self-isolation at home and outside the hospitals. 'Total Kematian Isolasi Mandiri dan Di Luar Rumah Sakit' (*LaporCovid-19*), https://laporcovid19.org/data/kematian-isoman.

Criticism has also been directed at authorities in relation to the total number of deaths. Legal expert and former Minister of Justice, Yusril Ihza Mahendra, requested that the National Human Rights Commission (*Komnas HAM*) conduct a study on the issue, with the Indonesian Doctors Association's (*Ikatan Dokter Indonesia* – IDI) input, to investigate whether the negligence and/or incorrect state policies that resulted in mass deaths can be qualified as genocide.[7]

II. CONSTITUTIONAL, LEGAL AND POLICY OVERVIEW

Indonesia is a unitary state in the form of a republic.[8] The Constitution of the Unitary State of the Republic of Indonesia is the 1945 Constitution, which has been amended four times: in October 1999, August 2000, November 2001 and August 2002. Indonesia adheres to a presidential system of government in which the executive body is led by a president who is concurrently head of state and head of government.

Criminal law in Indonesia does not differ significantly from Dutch criminal law. During the Dutch colonial period, Indonesia was known as the Dutch East Indies (Nederlands-Indië) and used criminal law originating from the *Wetboek van Strafrecht voor Nederlands Indie* 1915. In 1946, following the declaration of Indonesia's independence, the Criminal Code was stipulated to be the Indonesian Criminal Code. This law is a copy of the *Wetboek Van Strafrecht* 1881 from the Netherlands, with some adaptations to the conditions of Indonesia at the time.

Indonesia's judiciary consists of the Supreme Court and its subordinate judicial bodies: the General Court, Military Court, Religious Court, State Administrative Court and a Constitutional Court.[9] The Supreme Court has the authority to examine regulations made by the executive branch of state if they conflict with the law.[10] The Constitutional Court has the authority to constitutionally review laws that may conflict with the Constitution, resolve disputes between government agencies, dissolve political parties and resolve electoral disputes.[11]

A. Overview of and Specific Constitutional and Legal Principles Regarding Criminal Liability of High-Ranking Government/Public Officials

Indonesia does not have a provision in its Constitution that stipulates the possibility of the president and/or vice president being criminally responsible for their actions. However, if the president and/or vice president act against the law or commit certain

---

[7] J Akmal, 'Prof. Yusril: Komnas HAM Perlu Mengkaji, Apakah Kematian Tenaga Medis Bisa Dikategorikan Genosida?' (*RMOL.ID*, 2 August 2021), https://politik.rmol.id/read/2021/08/02/498896/prof-yusril-komnas-ham-perlu-mengkaji-apakah-kematian-tenaga-medis-bisa-dikategorikan-genosida.

[8] 1945 Constitution of the Republic of Indonesia (*Undang-Undang Dasar Negara Republik Indonesia Tahun 1945*) (1945 Constitution), art 1.

[9] 1945 Constitution, c IX.

[10] 1945 Constitution, art 24A.

[11] 1945 Constitution, art 24C.

criminal offences, this may result in dismissal. This is regulated in the 1945 Constitution, with article 7A stating that:

> The President and/or the Vice President may be dismissed during their term of office by the People's Consultative Assembly at the suggestion of the House of Representatives, if they are proven to have violated the law in the form of treason against the state, corruption, bribery, other serious crimes, or disgraceful acts or if it is proven that they no longer meet the requirements as President and/or Vice President.[12]

The proposal to dismiss the president and/or vice president may be submitted by the House of Representatives to the People's Consultative Assembly only by first submitting a request to the Constitutional Court to examine, try and decide in the House of Representatives that the president and/or vice president have violated the law in the form of treason against the state, corruption, bribery, other serious crimes, or disgraceful acts, and/or if the House of Representatives are of the opinion that the president and/or vice president no longer meet the requirements as president and/or vice president.[13] The submission of a request from the House of Representatives to the Constitutional Court can only be made with the support of at least two-thirds of the total members of the People's Representative Council who are present in a plenary session attended by at least two-thirds of the total members of the People's Representative Council.[14] The Constitutional Court is obliged to examine, hear and decide the House of Representatives' opinion in the fairest way possible no later than 90 days after the request of the House of Representatives is received by the Constitutional Court.[15]

Article 7A and Article 7B of the 1945 Constitution state that the dismissal of the president must begin with political judgments and decisions in the House of Representatives (impeachment), then proceed to legal examinations and decisions by the Constitutional Court (*privilegiatum* forum), before returning to the impeachment procedure (the House of Representatives forwards to the People's Consultative Assembly) to decide, politically, whether the decision of the Constitutional Court needs to be followed by the dismissal of the president and/or vice president.[16]

From the description above, it is clear that the legal process if the president and/or vice president of Indonesia commits a serious crime is regulated through the impeachment process. But what about outside impeachment? If the president and/or vice president commits a serious crime, can they be tried in a criminal court instead of through the parliament and Constitutional Court? The 1945 Constitution only regulates in general terms, specifically in Chapter XA on Human Rights, article 28D(1), which states: 'Everyone has the right to recognition, guarantees, protection, and fair legal certainty and equal treatment before the law'.[17]

Thus, normatively, a president and/or vice president who commits a crime can be legally processed by law enforcement authorities, such as the police, prosecutors or the Corruption Eradication Commission (*Komisi Pemberantasan Korupsi* – KPK).

---

[12] 1945 Constitution, art 7A (3rd Amendment to the 1945 Constitution).

[13] 1945 Constitution, art 7B(1) (3rd Amendment to the 1945 Constitution).

[14] 1945 Constitution, art 7B(3) (3rd Amendment to the 1945 Constitution).

[15] 1945 Constitution, art 7B(4) (3rd Amendment to the 1945 Constitution).

[16] M Mahfud, *Perdebatan Hukum Tata Negara Pasca Amandemen Konstitusi* (Jakarta, Rajawali Press, 2010) 143.

[17] 1945 Constitution, art 28D(1) (2nd Amendment to the Constitution).

However, this is all but unimaginable in Indonesia and a complete criminal prosecution has never happened. On 31 March 2000, the prosecutor's office named former dictator Suharto as a suspect in the alleged corruption of seven charitable foundations. In August 2000, the case entered the trial stage, yet efforts were unsuccessful, and on 11 May 2006, the prosecutor's office chose to issue a decision to terminate the prosecution, stating the case was closed for the sake of law due to Suharto's permanent health problems making it impossible for the trial to proceed.[18]

In Indonesia, it is more likely that a president and/or vice president suspected of committing serious crimes will be processed first through impeachment. If the president and/or vice president has been dismissed, then the criminal case could be criminally processed through the criminal justice system.

B. Scope of Responsibility and Area of Tolerated Risk

According to the 1945 Constitution, article 28H(1),[19] (2),[20] (3)[21] and article 34 (2),[22] (3)[23] and (4),[24] the government's responsibilities in handling a pandemic include fulfilling the rights of every citizen to the same health services, providing health care facilities and providing proper public services.

Law No 36 of 2009 concerning Health implies that every individual, family and community has the right to obtain protection for their health, and the state is responsible for regulating the fulfilment of the right to a healthy life for its population, including for the poor and underprivileged. In efforts to realise these rights, the government must provide equitable, fair and affordable health services for all levels of society. For this reason, the government needs to make efforts to ensure equal access for all residents to obtain health services. Regarding health services, article 34(3) of the 1945 Constitution mandates that 'the State is responsible for the provision of appropriate health care facilities and public service facilities'.[25] The term 'appropriate' can be interpreted to mean that the state is not only responsible for simply providing health facilities, but also health facilities with certain standards that are considered appropriate. The improvement of the quality and standard of proper health facilities is regulated by provisions in Law No 44 of 2009 concerning Hospitals.

---

[18] A Saputra, 'Ini Fakta Keputusan Hukum ke Soeharto di Kasus Korupsi' (*Detik News*, 29 November 2018), https://news.detik.com/berita/d-4322272/ini-fakta-keputusan-hukum-ke-soeharto-di-kasus-korupsi.

[19] 1945 Constitution, article 28H(1): 'everyone has the right to live in *physical and spiritual prosperity, to have a place to live, and to have a good and healthy environment and have the right to health services*' (emphasis added).

[20] 1945 Constitution, art 28H(2): 'everyone has the right to get special facilities *and treatment to get the same opportunities and benefits to achieve equality* and justice' (emphasis added).

[21] 1945 Constitution, art 28H(3): 'everyone *has the right to social security that allows his development fully as* a dignified human being' (emphasis added).

[22] 1945 Constitution, art 34(2): 'the state develops *a social security system for all people and empowers the weak and incapable in accordance with human dignity*' (emphasis added).

[23] 1945 Constitution, art 34 (3): 'the State is responsible for the *provision of appropriate health care facilities and public service facilities*' (emphasis added).

[24] 1945 Constitution, art 34 (4): 'further provisions *regarding the implementation of this article are regulated in law*' (emphasis added).

[25] 1945 Constitution, art 34(3) (4th Amendment to the 1945 Constitution).

C. Impact of Immunities

There is no provision regarding immunity for Indonesian government officials suspected of committing crimes, including crimes against life. The only provision regarding immunity is not in relation to crimes that result in death but is rather related to financial irregularities in overcoming the Covid-19 pandemic. Article 27 (2) of Government Regulation in Lieu of Law (PERPPU) No 1 of 2020 concerning Financial Policy and Financial System Stability for Handling the 2019 Coronavirus Disease (Covid-19) Pandemic and/or in Facing Threats That Endanger the National Economy and/or Financial System Stability states that:

> KSSK members,[26] KSSK Secretary, KSSK secretariat members, and officials or employees of the Ministry of Finance, Bank Indonesia, the Financial Services Authority, as well as the Deposit Insurance Corporation, and other officials, related to the implementation of this Government Regulation in Lieu of Law, cannot be charged both civilly and criminally if in carrying out the task it is based on good faith and following the provisions of the legislation.

The immunity article as contained in article 27(2) of Government Regulation in Lieu of Law No 1 of 2020 is also stated in several other laws.[27] Nevertheless, there is a regulation regarding the elimination of criminal offences in the Indonesian Criminal Code (KUHP), which we can equate to legal immunity, as legal immunity is essentially a legal status or condition that makes a person unable to be legally processed or prosecuted by the authorised law enforcer. Article 50 of the Criminal Code regulates the matter of legal immunity and stipulates that a person who commits an act (which can be criminalised) cannot be punished if they carried out the provisions of the law.

Article 50 provides that immunity can apply in respect of a person who carries out statutory regulations, including acts ordered by law and acts carried out because of the authority granted by a law.[28] Another article in the Criminal Code that can be used as a basis for immunity is article 51, which stipulates that a person cannot be convicted for committing an act based on a valid (or believed to be valid) order from an official authorised to give the order.

D. Prosecutorial Matters

The prosecution against a perpetrator of a crime is submitted by the Public Prosecutor to a competent District Court with a request to be examined and decided by a panel of judges through a court session. The prosecution process refers to the provisions in the Criminal Procedure Code and Law No 11 of 2021 concerning the Attorney's Office of the Republic of Indonesia.

---

[26] Footnote added by author: *Komite Stabilitas Sistem Keuangan* [Financial System Stability Committee].

[27] See, eg Law No 23 of 1999 concerning Bank Indonesia (BI) for the Board of Governors and Bank Indonesia officials, art 45; Law No 37 of 2008 concerning the Ombudsman of the Republic of Indonesia (ORI), art 10, which states the same for ORI Commissioners. Meanwhile for members of the DPR-RI, the right to immunity is found the 1945 Constitution, art 20A(3), and is further regulated in Law No 17 of 2014 concerning the MPR, DPR, DPD, and DPRD.

[28] R Soesilo, *Kitab Undang-undang Hukum Pidana (KUHP) Serta Komentar-Komentarnya Lengkap Pasal Demi Pasal* (Bogor, Politeia, 1988) 66.

Article 30 (1) of Law No 16 of 2004 *juncto* Law No 11 of 2021 states that:

> In the field of crime, the attorney's office has the following duties and authorities: a. carries out prosecutions; b. executes judges' decisions and court decisions that have permanent legal force; c. supervises the implementation of conditional criminal decisions, supervisory criminal decisions, and parole decisions; d. conducts investigations into certain criminal offences based on the law; and e. completes certain case files and for that purpose can carry out additional examinations before being submitted to the court which in its implementation is coordinated with investigators.

Thus, in the Indonesian legal system, only prosecutors can carry out criminal prosecutions for all types of criminal offences. Even in the context of criminal offences of corruption, although the Corruption Eradication Commission (KPK) has the power to prosecute corruption crimes, in practice, prosecution is actually carried out by prosecutors assigned to the KPK. Even for human rights crimes, although the investigator is the National Human Rights Commission (Komnas HAM), it is the prosecutor who carries out prosecutions.

III. CAUSATION

The issue of causality is a problem that is discussed in the literature and court decisions. The Criminal Code itself does not regulate causality at all. Its use refers to the doctrine/opinion of legal experts and jurisprudence. The discussion of causality here will include the definition of criminal offences, elements of criminal offences and the crimes that need the principle of causality. Criminal offences that need the use of the principle of causality in criminal law in Indonesia are material offences (criminal offences that have an element of effect, and its relationship to the act that causes them), impure omission acts (criminal offences committed with passive actions) which have an element of consequence and are related to the cause, and qualified offences (offences with an additional element, namely the occurrence of certain consequences that aggravate the crime). Also discussed here are causality and causality theories known in Indonesia.

A. Causation (General Principles)

Essentially every criminal act must consist of elements that originate from the act, including behaviour and the consequences of that behaviour. In addition to (1) behaviour and consequences, for the existence of a criminal act it is usually necessary to have (2) matters which are divided into two groups, namely those concerning the person who commits the offence and those outside the perpetrator.[29] Criminal acts can also involve (3) additional circumstances that aggravate the crime; (4) objective unlawful elements; and/or (5) subjective unlawful elements.[30]

---

[29] Moeljatno, *Asas-Asas Hukum Pidana* (Jakarta, Rineka Cipta, 1993) 58.
[30] ibid 63.

According to Bemmelen, in several articles of the Indonesian Criminal Code, it can be concluded that behaviour can be punished depending on the occurrence of a certain result. Homicide, for example, can only be punished if someone by their behaviour takes another person's life intentionally (article 287 of the Dutch Criminal Code/article 338 of the Indonesian Criminal Code). Likewise, causing a fire can only be punished as a very dangerous crime if it is feared that the fire endangered the lives of other people or goods (article 157(1) and (2) of the Dutch Criminal Code/article 187(3) of the Indonesian Criminal Code). In this event, the formulation of the offence – in which the occurrence of a certain effect is part of the offence – is called the formulation of the material offence. The word 'cause' is formulated, for example, in article 296 of the Dutch Criminal Code/article 347 of the Indonesian Criminal Code, which regulates intentionally causing the miscarriage or death of a foetus. There are also consequences that form the basis of aggravating circumstances, for example, aggravated battery that causes serious injuries or death (article 351(2) and (3) of the Criminal Code). In this context, this criminal offence is referred to as a qualified offence, in which the addition of certain elements causes the criminal sanction to become more severe.[31] Indonesian criminal law experts, AZ Abidin and Andi Hamzah, also identify other offences in this category, namely culpable offences, such as the death of another person due to negligence (article 359 of the Criminal Code) and causing serious injury (article 360 of the Criminal Code).[32]

In the event that an offence falls into the type of material offence and the qualified offence is as exemplified above, we must ask questions as to what is meant by 'cause', 'effect' and 'danger'. Danger will occur if a cause will result in a certain effect. In daily life, we frequently meet this problem of cause and effect. In an event, a symptom is caused not by one factor alone, but by several factors that must be united. In legal studies, especially criminal law, we go further, namely looking for human behaviour that causes something to happen or becomes the cause. It is very possible that the effect is the result of a certain link; therefore, if one of the links is human behaviour, it is necessary to find out which behaviour is the cause. Behaviour that occurred long before the result can still be considered as an important cause in criminal law.[33]

In addition to material offences and qualified offences that have an element of consequence, there are also offences that require the principle of causality, referred to as offences of omission. This offence occurs if the law does not want an effect (which result can be caused by neglect) that is carried out by not doing something. Examples of pure omission offences are articles 164, 224, 522 and 511 of the Criminal Code, while examples of impure omission offences are people violating the prohibition against homicide (article 338 of the Criminal Code) by starving a person to death or article 194 of the Criminal Code by not sounding a train's whistle.[34]

In a homicide offence, criminal law provides legal sanctions for crimes that result in the death of a person. However, criminal law does not specify which specific death-causing

---

[31] JM van Bemmelen, *Hukum Pidana 1, Hukum Pidana Material Bagian Umum* (Bandung, Binacipta, 1987) 153.

[32] AZ Abidin and Andi Hamzah, *Pengantar dalam Hukum Pidana Indonesia* (Jakarta, Yarsif Watampone, 2010) 212.

[33] van Bemmelen, *Hukum Pidana 1* (n 31) 154–55.

[34] Abidin dan Andi Hamzah, *Pengantar* (n 32) 129.

actions are prohibited. Criminal law generally punishes someone who commits an act that results in death, yet can also punish someone who fails to prevent an act that results in another's death.[35]

Some homicides require proof that the perpetrator's actions caused the death of the victim. Proving that a death has occurred is not difficult, but the situation becomes complicated when the homicide involves the issue of causality. In such a case, the attorney as the public prosecutor must be able to prove that the defendant's actions caused the death of the victim. In Indonesian legal tradition, to prove the death of a person, a forensic examination is usually carried out to conclude the cause of death, such as battery, poison or another cause.[36]

The doctrine of causality has a very decisive meaning when ascertaining who can be considered to be the perpetrator of a homicide. The perpetrator can only be deemed to have committed the criminal act of murder if their actions or behaviour can be seen as the cause of the consequences. That is, in the form of the loss of another person's life.[37]

Regarding deaths correlated with the omission of policies, decisions, and/or actions, for example oxygen scarcity, medicine shortage and unavailability of hospital rooms, it is an interesting situation if the deaths are associated with responsible bodies not meeting their supposed obligations. In Indonesia, this issue has arisen during the Covid-19 pandemic, but there has been little discussion of what caused the situation and who is responsible. For example, can we hold responsible hospital management, officials in charge of medical devices, trade officials, district/city health officials, provincial or national health officials (*e.g.*, the relevant director or director-general) or even the health minister? Questions from the public and the legal community do not lead to these discussions, nor do they question whether any corporations were involved and should be held responsible. There is also no discussion of whether there is a reason for the elimination of criminal offence (*e.g.*, emergency) so that the unlawful element of the negligence that occurred is no longer relevant. This is not a legal issue in Indonesia, especially when so many deaths are correlated with Covid-19. Thus, upon careful examination of the situation, it would appear that there is an element of negligence that has caused death. This could therefore be considered an offence of omission.

In general, the *omission* is defined as the failure to act by a person who has a legal obligation to prevent the occurrence of a crime or harm to others but does not do so. Thus, he can be punishable as a person who caused a crime.[38] In line with this, Indonesian criminal law expert Satochid Kartanegara states that if a person does not act while he has an obligation to do so, then such a situation is considered a cause rather than an effect.[39]

---

[35] A Leavens, 'A Causation Approach to Criminal Omissions' (1998) *California Law Review* 1. In the family common law, legal obligations or legal duties have several types, namely: duty based on relationship, duty arising from contract, duty of landowner and duty to control others (this obligation is based on civil law principles) and duty arising from creation of peril. If a person commits an act of negligence that endangers another person, then he has a legal obligation to help or save that person.

[36] A Sofian, *Ajaran Kausalitas Hukum Pidana, Edisi Kedua* (Jakarta, Kencana, 2020) 239–47.

[37] ibid.

[38] Leavens, 'Causation Approach' (n 5).

[39] S Kartanegara, *Hukum Pidana Kumpulan Kuliah Prof Satochid Kartanegara dan Pendapat-Pendapat Para Ahli Hukum Terkemuka, Bagian Satu* (Jakarta, Balai Lektur Mahasiswa, n.d.) 240.

Meanwhile, according to Schaffmeister et al, the crime of impure omission (*omissio per commissionem*) means causing consequences due to negligence. The crime of impure omission has a limited scope, requiring the perpetrator to have had the obligation to act.[40]

The concept of legal obligations can be criticised because the criteria for legal obligations are not clear regarding which omissions that cause harm can be subject to criminal liability. Some scholars state that legal obligations are obligations arising from one's job or position from the law, while others argue that legal obligations arise not only from the provisions of workers and the law but also from decisions that must be considered by everyone in social life.[41]

B. Causation and 'Thin Skull' Scenarios

In both the literature and the practice of criminal law in Indonesia, the difference between factual causation and legal causation is not often discussed.[42] In Indonesian criminal law, the principle of causality is used in cases of material offences, qualified offences due to its consequences, and impure omission crimes. Meanwhile, for offences which formulate the conduct, rather than the consequences (*formeel delicti*), causality is not applied.[43]

A material offence is considered a crime if it has caused a prohibited act. In other words, if it has caused consequences as specified in one of the articles of the Criminal Code, as criminal liability relies on the occurrence of prohibited consequences. In this case, the act becomes united with the result: the offence becomes an integral part of the consequences. However, if the prohibited consequences do not occur, it cannot be said that a crime has occurred. This shows that the criminal element of legal acts depends on whether the act has a prohibited effect or not.[44]

Indonesian courts do not use the doctrine *novus actus interveniens* in assessing whether there are factors that can break the chain of causality.[45]

C. Restricting Causality: Policy and Doctrinal Issues

The Indonesian Criminal Code (KUHP) does not include instructions on how to determine the cause of a crime. For example, in article 338 of the Criminal Code the crime of homicide is said to have been committed fully (*voltooid*) if the prohibited result has occurred, that is, the loss of another person's life. There are several theories related to the principle of causality. The first is the theory of *conditio sine qua non* of Von Buri (1973), but because Von Buri's theory is considered too broad to be used in criminal law,

---

[40] D Schafmeister et al, *Hukum Pidana* (JE Sahetapy and Agustinus Pohan eds, Bandung, Citra Aditya Bakti, 2007) 33.

[41] ibid 240–41.

[42] Sofian, *Ajaran Kausalitas* (n 36) 167–204.

[43] EY Kanter and SR Sianturi, *Asas-Asas Hukum Pidana di Indonesia* 3rd edn (Jakarta, Storia Grafika, 2018) 125.

[44] ibid 103.

[45] Sofian, *Ajaran Kausalitas* (n 36) 227.

several experts limit Von Buri's theory, including Traeger. Other theories of causality are the individualising theories of Birkmeyer, Karl Binding, and Kohler. In addition, there are generalising theories, including the subjective adequacy theory from Von Kries, and the objective adequacy theory from Rumelin. In addition to individualising and generalising theories, there are also relevance theories, for example from Langemeijer and Mezger.[46]

The Indonesian Criminal Code does not explicitly refer to any of these theories. This can be concluded from the history of the formation of the Criminal Code as well as from the articles in the Criminal Code itself.[47] According to Remmelink, the principle of relevance is the closest to the basis for understanding causality in both the Indonesian and Dutch Criminal Codes. Yet, in contrast to Remmelink, according to Wirjono Prodjodikoro, the Indonesian Criminal Code does not adhere to a certain theory of causality. Thus, prosecutors and judges are free to choose between those known causality theories.[48]

IV. THE STRUCTURE OF HOMICIDE OFFENCES AND ASSAULT/AGGRAVATED ASSAULT/SERIOUS BODILY HARM OFFENCES

In Indonesia, loss of life (death) is regulated both in the Criminal Code and outside the Criminal Code. In the Criminal Code, loss of life is regulated in the Chapter on Homicide and several other chapters (*e.g.*, Chapter on Battery, Chapter on Negligence causing death, Chapter on Crimes of Larceny, etc). Meanwhile outside the Criminal Code, the loss of life is regulated, among others, in the Law on Human Rights (UU No 39 of 1999), the Law on Combating Terrorism (UU No 15 of 2003 as amended by Law No 5 of 2018), the Health Law (UU No 36 of 2009) and the Road Traffic Law (Law No 22 of 2009). Within the Criminal Code, the chapter that specifically regulates Crimes against Human Life uses the Dutch title of *Misdrijven tegen het Leven Gericht*. This chapter consists of eight criminal offences.[49]

A. Murder/Intentional Homicide

Article 338 of the Criminal Code states that 'Anyone who deliberately takes another person's life is sanctioned due to homicide with a maximum imprisonment of 15 years'.[50] From the above formulation, there are two important elements: the subjective element, namely deliberately, and the objective element, namely taking the life of another.

---

[46] ibid 105–18.

[47] Kartanegara, 'Hukum Pidana Kumpulan Kuliah' (n 39) 200.

[48] W Prodjodikoro, *Asas-asas Hukum Pidana di Indonesia* (Bandung, Eresco, 1969) 48.

[49] (1) Manslaughter (*doodslag*), regulated in Aart 338; (2) Capital Murder, regulated in art 339; (3) Premeditated Murder (*Moord*), regulated in art 340; (4) Infanticide (*Kinder Doodslag*), regulated in art 341; (5) Premeditated Infanticide (*Kindermoord*), regulated in art 342; (6) Murder at the request of the victim, regulated in art 244; (7) Persuading/Aiding Suicide, regulated in art 345; and (8) Abortion, regulated in arts 346–49.

[50] Moeljatno, *Kitab Undang-Undang Hukum Pidana* (Jakarta, Bumi Aksara, 2007) 122–23.

Article 340 of the Criminal Code provides that 'Anyone who deliberately and with a premeditated plan takes another person's life, is sanctioned, for premeditated murder [*moord*], with the death penalty or imprisonment for life or for a certain time, maximum twenty years'.[51] From this formulation, it can be seen that the murder as referred to in article 340 of the Criminal Code has important elements. The subjective element is intentional, in the form of a premeditated plan, while the objective element is taking the life of another. The most important of the elements above that distinguishes article 340 from article 338 is the 'premeditated plan'.

B. Culpable Homicide/Manslaughter

In the context of deaths related to Covid-19 in Indonesia, it is too far to link this with criminal offences such as manslaughter (article 338 of the Criminal Code), premeditated murder (article 340 of the Criminal Code) or gross violations of human rights, such as genocide. This is because these crimes require the element of intentionality. The closest possible crime is criminally negligent homicide, which is applicable when 'negligence causes the death of another person' (article 359 of the Criminal Code). From the word 'negligent', it is clear that for these crimes, the law does not require the existence of an element of *opzet* (intent) from the perpetrator, but only requires the presence of an element of *culpa* or an element of negligence from the perpetrator. This means that in order to fulfil this crime, the perpetrator must have neglected something, resulting in the occurrence of a prohibited or unwanted consequence in the form of the loss of another person's life.

In cases of death due to the unavailability or delay of oxygen as described above, if it can be proven that a certain individual has been negligent, then this provision could be used, especially if the person does not have a reason for eliminating the crime, such as an emergency situation (article 48 of the Criminal Code).

C. Offences Related to Actions that Cause Serious Bodily Harm (Assault; Grievous Assault; Assault with Intent to Cause Serious Bodily Harm)

Additionally, there is Chapter XX of the Criminal Code on Battery. Battery resulting in death is regulated in several articles: battery resulting in death is regulated in article 351(3); battery with a plan to cause death is regulated in article 353(3); aggravated battery resulting in death is regulated in article 354(2); and aggravated battery with a plan to cause death is regulated in article 355 (2). In the Criminal Code, the elements of the battery are not defined. We have to look at jurisprudence, where battery is defined as intentionally causing suffering, pain or injury. This includes intentionally damaging people's health.[52]

---

[51] ibid 122–23.
[52] Soesilo, *Kitab Undang-undang Hukum Pidana* (n 28) 245.

D. Offences Regarding Unborn Foetuses; Interrupting the Course of a (Viable) Pregnancy

Abortion is regulated in articles 346–49 of the Criminal Code. This provision applies to a woman who aborts or terminates her own pregnancy, or to another person who performs such actions on a pregnant woman. The severity of the punishment for another person who acts to abort or kill a foetus is determined by the presence or absence of consent from the woman to have an abortion, whether their action caused the death of the woman and whether the perpetrator is a health worker. The prohibition on abortion is also regulated in articles 75–76 and article 194 of Law No 36 Year 2009 concerning Health. Exceptions for abortion are only permitted in the case of an indication of a medical emergency or if a pregnancy occurred as the result of a rape, resulting in psychological trauma.

E. Failure to Render Assistance

For provisions outside the Criminal Code, there are several other laws that regulate homicide, such as the Traffic Law, Terrorism Law, Aviation Law, Trafficking in Persons Law and others. However, in this case we will only examine Law No 36 of 2009 on Health (Health Law). There are several criminal provisions in the Health Law, including those with elements of homicide.

Article 190 reads as follows:

> (1) Leaders of health service facilities and/or health workers who practice or work in health care facilities who intentionally do not provide first aid to patients who are in an emergency condition as referred to in Article 32 paragraph (2) or Article 85 paragraph (2) shall be sentenced to a maximum imprisonment of 2 (two) years and a maximum fine of Rp200,000,000.00 (two hundred million Rupiah). (2) In the event that the act as referred to in paragraph (1) results in disability or death, the head of the health service facility and/or health worker shall be sentenced to a maximum imprisonment of 10 (ten) years and a maximum fine of Rp1,000,000,000.00 (one billion Rupiah).

V. DEFENCES, JUSTIFICATIONS AND EXCUSES

In Indonesian criminal law, the basis for elimination of crimes can be distinguished between the bases contained in the Criminal Code and those regulated elsewhere. Bases for elimination of crime in the Criminal Code are contained in articles 44, 48, 49, 50 and 51 (in Book 1 of the Criminal Code), as well as various articles in Book 2 of the Criminal Code. These bases can be broadly divided into two types: the general elimination basis (applies to all criminal offences), regulated in articles 44, 48, 49, 50 and 51 of the Criminal Code, and the specific elimination basis (only applicable to certain criminal offences), regulated separately in various articles such as article 221 and article 310 of the Criminal Code. The basis for elimination of crimes outside the Criminal Code include the existence of a permit or other form of approval; no negligence found (*afwazigheid van alle schuld*); no unlawful element in the material sense; official rights; and several others.[53]

A. Necessity

The basis for elimination of crimes in the Criminal Code can also be distinguished between justifying reasons and forgiving reasons. The justifying reasons are contained in article 48 of the Criminal Code in the form of an Emergency,[54] article 49(1) on Forced Self-Defense,[55] article 50 on Executing Law Orders[56] and article 51(1) on Carrying Out An Authorized Official's Orders.[57] Meanwhile, the forgiving reasons are contained in article 44 on Inability to Liability,[58] article 48 on Coercive Power,[59] article 49(2) on Excessive Self-Defense[60] and article 51(2) on Carrying Out An Unauthorized Official's Orders in the good faith belief that the order was issued by the proper authority.[61]

In an emergency, there are three possible scenarios. First, there is a conflict between two interests, for example, the interests of human life. The perpetrator must choose which interests he will protect and which he will sacrifice. If he sacrifices any of those interests, then he is not punished because he did so in an emergency. Second, there is a conflict between two legal obligations, for example, the perpetrator must be in two district courts as a witness at the same time. If he appears in one district court and thus does not appear as a witness in another district court, then he cannot be punished for his absence because it is an emergency. Third, there is a conflict between legal interests on the one hand and legal obligations on the other, for example, he must come as an expert in a district court yet at the same time, he must help save someone's life. If he does not appear in the district court as an expert, then he cannot be punished.[62]

---

[53] EOS Hiariej, *Prinsip-Prinsip Hukum Pidana* revised edn (Yogyakarta, Cahaya Atma Pustaka, 2016) 283–88.

[54] Criminal Code, art 48: 'Not punishable shall be the person who commits an act to which he is compelled by coercive power'.

[55] Criminal Code, art 49: '(1) Not punishable shall be the person who commits an act necessitated by the defense of his own or another one's body, chastity or property against direct or immediate threatening unlawful assault'.

[56] Criminal Code, art 50: 'Not punishable shall be the person who commits an act for the execution of a statutory provision'.

[57] Criminal Code, art 51: '(1) Not punishable shall be the person who commits an act for the execution of an official order issued by the competent authority'.

[58] Criminal Code, art 44: '(1) Not punishable shall be the person who commits an act for which by reason of the defective development or disorder of his mental capacities, he is not liable. (2) If it is evident that he is not liable for the committed act by reason of the defective development or sickly disorder of his mental capacities, the judge may give an order that he is placed in a lunatic asylum during a probation time not exceeding the term of one year. (3) The provision in the foregoing paragraph shall only apply to the Supreme Court, the High Court and the District Court'.

[59] Criminal Code, art 48: 'Not punishable shall be the person who commits an act to which he is compelled by coercive power'.

[60] Criminal Code, art 49: '(2) Not punishable shall be the excessive self-defense, if it has been the immediate result of a severe emotion caused by the assault'.

[61] Criminal Code, art 51(2): '(2) An official order issued illegitimately shall not exempt the punishment, unless it was considered in good faith by the subordinate to be issued legitimately and its execution lied within the limit of his subordination'.

[62] See Hiariej, *Prinsip-Prinsip* (n 53) 270. See also Prodjodikoro, *Asas-asas* (n 48) 90–91.

In the theoretical context, this emergency is included in the justification, thereby eliminating the unlawful element of an offence. Emergencies are included in the provisions of article 48 of the Criminal Code and thus are part of an *overmacht* or coercive power, it is necessary to explain the difference between an emergency and a coercive power (which is a forgiving reason). Specifically, article 48 of the Criminal Code mentions coercive power in a broad sense, which includes coercive power in a narrow sense (*overmacht*) and emergency situations (*noodtoestand*). According to Van Bemmelen and Van Hattum, in the narrow sense of coercive power, the perpetrator does or does not act due to psychological pressure from other people. For the perpetrator, there is no free determination of the will. He is driven by such a strong external psychological compulsion that he does things he really does not want to do. Meanwhile, in an emergency, the perpetrator is in a dangerous situation that forces or encourages the perpetrator to violate the law.[63]

VI. CORPORATE CRIMINAL LIABILITY

The Indonesian Criminal Code does not recognise corporations as the subject of criminal offences. In several crimes outside the Criminal Code, corporations are indeed the subject of criminal offences, including in relation to narcotics, terrorism, corruption, money laundering and environmental offences. None of these, however, are relevant to the Covid-19 context.

A. Overview of Corporate Criminal Liability

With regard to public corporations, several laws regulate that public corporations are criminally responsible, including Law No 15 of 2003 concerning Stipulation of Government Regulation in Lieu of Law No 1 of 2002 concerning Eradication of Criminal Offences of Terrorism into Law (Terrorism Law). Article 1(2) of the Terrorism Law defines 'person' as an 'Individual, group of people, whether civilian, military or police, who are individually or corporately responsible'. Thus, in this case, the police and military – which are state defence institutions as corporations – can be criminally responsible for violating the provisions of this law.

Regarding who can be prosecuted and convicted when a corporation is carried out by or on behalf of a corporation, several laws elaborate that prosecution and punishment of criminal offences committed by a corporation can be carried out against corporations and/or management. For example, article 20(1) of the Law on the Eradication of Criminal Offences of Corruption explains, 'In the event that a criminal act of corruption is committed by or on behalf of a corporation, the prosecution and imposition of criminal offences can be carried out against the corporation and or its management'.

---

[63] JM Van Bemmelen and WFC Van Hattum, *Hand En Leerboek Van Het Nederlands Strafrecht* (Arnheim, S.Gouda Quint – D. Brouwer En Zoon, 1953) 351.

B. Accessory or Perpetrator

In 2014, the Attorney General's Office issued Regulation of the Attorney General of the Republic of Indonesia (PERJA) No PER-028/A/JA/10/2014 concerning Guidelines for Handling Criminal Cases with Legal Subjects of Corporations. This PERJA provides criteria that are quite clear in the elaboration of which actions corporations can be charged with criminal responsibility for. The PERJA also does not strictly adopt one type of corporate criminal liability doctrine.

In addition to the above PERJA, the Supreme Court also issued a relevant regulation in 2016, Supreme Court Regulation (PERMA) No 13 of 2016 concerning Procedures for Handling Corporation Criminal Cases. In article 3 of this PERMA, it is explained that a criminal act is committed by a corporation if it is committed by a person based on an employment relationship, or based on another relationship, either individually or jointly acting for and on behalf of the corporation inside and outside the corporate environment.

Most laws and regulations use indirect criminal liability in the form of *vicarious criminal liability* and *identification doctrine*. Meanwhile, these PERJA and PERMA also adhere to direct liability in which the discovery of corporate actions and negligence is based on more concrete criteria than the way the corporation is managed.

VII. FORMS OF PARTICIPATION

According to Van Hamel, the doctrine on *deelneming* as a general doctrine is basically a doctrine of liability and the division of liabilities, namely in the case where a criminal act according to the formulation of the law can actually be carried out by one person alone, but in reality, it has been carried out by two or more people in an integrated collaboration, both intellectually and materially.[64]

Article 55(1) of the Criminal Code provides:

> Sentenced as perpetrators of criminal offences [are]: 1. person who commits, who orders to commit or participates in doing an offence; 2. people who by gift, promise, abuse of power or influence, violence, threat or fraud or by providing opportunities, means or information, intentionally persuade others to commit an offence.

Article 55(2) of the Criminal Code provides that: 'Against the persuader, only offences that are intentionally persuaded are taken into account, along with their consequences'. Article 56 of the Criminal Code provides that: 'Sentenced as complicit to crimes [are]: 1. those who intentionally provide assistance when the crime is committed; 2. those who intentionally provide opportunities, means, or information to commit crimes'.

The maximum criminal sanction is against the perpetrator as mentioned at article 55, while for people who assist a criminal offence (article 56) the criminal sanction is reduced by one-third, or if sanctioned with a death sentence/life imprisonment sentence, the criminal sanction is a maximum of 15 years. Therefore, in terms of complicity, according to Satochid Kartanegara, the Criminal Code provides details between: (1) the perpetrator

---

[64] PAF Lamintang dan Fransiscus Theojunior Lamintang, *Dasar-Dasar Hukum Pidana di Indonesia* (Jakarta, Sinar Grafika, 2019) 605.

(*dader*) and (2) assisting to commit (*medeplichtige*). Participants in line with article 55 of the Criminal Code shall be punishable as Perpetrators, while those in line with article 56 are punishable as Assistants of committing a crime.[65]

VIII. ATTEMPT

In the Indonesian legal system, it is generally determined that an attempt to commit a serious offence is punishable by law (article 53 of the Criminal Code), while an attempt to commit a minor offence is not punishable by law (article 54 of the Criminal Code). However, there is an exception from article 53 of the Criminal Code, whereby a criminal offence is not punishable if in an article it is expressly stated that the attempt of the offence is not punishable.

There remains the possibility of punishment for attempts of criminal offences of negligence, so it is not only a deliberate attempt at committing an offence (*dolus*) that is punishable. Although intention is an element of the attempt as regulated in article 53 of the Criminal Code, it does not have to be an element of the crime, as stated by Dutch criminal law expert, HB Vos, as quoted by Kanter and Sianturi.[66]

The provisions regarding attempted offences in the Indonesian Criminal Code are regulated in article 53 of the Criminal Code in which it is stated that:

> Attempts to commit a crime can be punishable if the intention to commit the offence is real, with the beginning of the implementation and the offence is not completed only because of things that do not depend on his own will.[67]

This provision formulates the conditions under which an attempted offence may be punishable: (1) there is an intention to commit a crime; (2) the commencement of implementation; and (3) the offence is not completed only because of things that do not depend on his own will. If all these conditions are met, the attempt is punishable. On the other hand, if one of the conditions is not met, the attempt is not punishable.

Sentencing for attempted offences is generally different from sentences for completed offences. The maximum principal sentence imposed for the crime is reduced by one third in the event of attempt.[68] If the crime is punishable by death or life imprisonment, the maximum sentence for attempt is 15 years.[69] For example, for a manslaughter offence (article 338 of the Criminal Code), for which the penalty is imprisonment of a maximum of 15 years, an attempt is punishable by 10 years of imprisonment. Meanwhile, for premeditated murder (article 340 of the Criminal Code), for which the penalty is the death penalty, life imprisonment or a maximum sentence of 20 years, an attempt may be sentenced to a maximum of 20 years.

The provisions in article 53 of the Criminal Code apply to all criminal offences both within the Criminal Code and outside the Criminal Code, unless the provisions in the law

---

[65] Kartanegara (n 39) 2. See also B Nawawi Arief, *Sari Kuliah Hukum Pidana II* (Semarang, Faculty of Law, Diponegoro University, 1993) 29.

[66] Kanter and Sianturi, *Asas-Asas* (n 43) 315–16.

[67] Criminal Code, art 53(1).

[68] Criminal Code, art 53(2).

[69] Criminal Code, art 53(3).

outside the Criminal Code regulate differently. For example, the trial of a crime under the Emergency Law No 7 of 1955 concerning the Investigation and Prosecution of Economic Crimes, the maximum penalty of which is not reduced by one-third.

IX. SANCTIONS, SENTENCING, PUNISHMENT, REPARATIONS AND/OR RESTORATIVE JUSTICE

A. General Sentencing Framework for the Crimes under Discussion

Sanctions for a criminal act are determined by the article regulating it, both in the Criminal Code and other laws that contain criminal provisions. The types of criminal sanctions applied in Indonesia refer to the following provisions:

Article 10 of the Criminal Code contains types of crimes, namely:

basic punishments:

capital punishment
imprisonment
light imprisonment
fine
undisclosed penitentiary (*pidana tutupan*)

additional punishments:

deprivation of certain rights
forfeiture of specific property
publication of judicial verdict.

There are several criminal offences in the Criminal Code that are punishable by capital punishment or the death penalty. These are spread across several chapters in the Criminal Code. Death penalty sanctions always offer an alternative: 'sanctioned with a death sentence or life imprisonment or a temporary imprisonment of twenty years'.

Article 12 of the Criminal Code stipulates that imprisonment can be of two kinds: (1) life imprisonment or (2) temporary imprisonment. Temporary imprisonment is a minimum of one day and a maximum of 15 years. Imprisonment can be up to a maximum of 20 years[70] in the event that: (1) there is an alternative, namely the death penalty or life imprisonment or 20 years; (2) the addition of punishment due to a combination of criminal offence; (3) an increase in sentence due to a concurrence or repetition of the crime; and (4) due to the provisions of aggravation basis in article 52 of the Criminal Code. The draft of the New Penal Code (RKUHP) lists two new types of punishment: supervision and community restitution/service.

With regard to homicide and serious bodily injury, the punishment shall be: (1) for homicide,[71] a maximum of 15 years in prison; and (2) for serious bodily injury,[72]

---

[70] The length of imprisonment may not exceed 20 years. See Criminal Code, art 12(4).
[71] Criminal Code, art 338.
[72] Criminal Code, art 354(1).

a maximum of eight years in prison; if the injury resulted in death,[73] the punishment is maximum imprisonment of 15 years.

Many regulations regarding imprisonment are regulated in Law No 12 of 1995 concerning Corrections. This law has provided the philosophy of reintegration. The goals that are expected to be achieved from reintegration are: to be aware of mistakes, to improve themselves, and not to repeat criminal acts so that they can be accepted again by the community, can play an active role in development, and can live naturally as good and responsible citizens.

The draft of the New Penal Code has set forth the objectives of punishment in article 51, namely: preventing criminal acts from being committed by enforcing legal norms, protection of the community, socialise the convicts by conducting reintegration in order that they become good people, resolve conflicts, restore balance and bring a sense of security and peace in society; and others.

In Indonesia, the concept of restorative justice has begun to be recognised, but has not yet been included in the Criminal Code and Criminal Procedure Code. However, specifically for the juvenile justice system, regulated in Law No 11 of 2012 concerning the Juvenile Criminal Justice System, a restorative justice approach must be implemented, for example through diversion. For other criminal offences, not limited to juvenile perpetrators, especially those that are not too severe (*e.g.*, imprisonment of less than under five years), restorative justice can be implemented on the basis of a Memorandum of Understanding among the Chief Justice of the Supreme Court, the Minister of Law and Human Rights, the Attorney General, and the Chief of the Indonesian National Police, regulations of the Supreme Court, regulations of the Chief of the Indonesian National Police and regulations of the Attorney General.

B. Sanctions Specifically for Senior Government/Public Officials

In Indonesia, criminal law and its sanctions apply, generally speaking, to everyone. Thus, there is no distinction for senior government officials. This is confirmed in article 28D(1) of the 1945 Constitution which states that: 'Everyone has the right to recognition, guarantees, protection, and fair legal certainty and equal treatment before the law'. In addition, Article 28I(1) states:

> The right to life, the right not to be tortured, the right to freedom of thought and conscience, the right to religion, the right not to be enslaved, the right to be recognized as a person before the law, and the right not to be prosecuted for retroactive legal framework is a human right that cannot be reduced under any circumstances.

However, in Indonesia there are also *delicta propia*, offences that can only be carried out by certain people. These people include officials, captains, military members, mothers and doctors, among others. The offences covered include office crimes, shipping crimes, crimes by members of the military, crimes committed by mothers, false information provided by doctors and crimes committed by captains.

---

[73] Criminal Code, art 354 (2).

C. Corporations and Sentencing

In addition to referring to article 10 of the Criminal Code, there are also other sanctions that can be applied against corporations. These sanctions are spread out in various laws, with the classification of sanctions as follows:

Payment of compensation;

implementation of obligations that have been neglected. Companies that are proven to damage the environment are usually subject to sanctions in the form of repairing the damaged environment;

funding for job training;

repairs due to criminal acts;

confiscation of goods or profits obtained from criminal acts. This legal rule has been regulated, among others, in Law No. 4 of 2009 concerning Mineral and Coal Mining;

fulfilment of customary obligations. Customary courts are still recognized, among others, in Law No. 21 of 2001 concerning Special Autonomy for Papua Province, and Law No. 6 of 2014 concerning Villages;

revocation of certain permits. In Law No. 28 of 2002 concerning Buildings, the revocation of building construction permits is included as an administrative sanction;

permanent prohibition to perform certain actions;

court announcements. Article 43 of the Criminal Code adds that if a judge orders a decision to be announced based on the provisions of the Criminal Code or other laws, it must determine how to carry out the order at the expense of the convict;

closure of all or part of the place of business and/or corporate activity;

freeze all or part of the business activities of the corporation; and

dissolution of the corporation.[74]

---

[74] M Yasin, 'Berhati-Hatilah!!! Ada 12 Jenis Pidana Tambahan yang Dapat Dikenakan Terhadap Korporasi' (*Hukum Online*, 18 March 2019), www.hukumonline.com/berita/a/berhati-hatilah-ada-12-jenis-pidana-tambahan-yang-dapat-dikenakan-terhadap-korporasi-lt5c8efc3f93414.

9

Iran

MOHAMMAD M HEDAYATI-KAKHKI

I. BACKGROUND AND CONTEXTUAL INTRODUCTION

IRAN OFFICIALLY REPORTED its first confirmed cases of coronavirus on 19 February 2020, in the religious city of Qom.[1] However, sources suggest that the outbreak actually started weeks previously, and that the official delay in acknowledging the spread of the virus within the country proved damaging in terms of providing a prompt public health response.[2] Whilst the government implemented various Covid-19 policies, including social distancing rules to limit transmission, in the early days of the outbreak the celebration of a number of national and religious events, such as the *Nowruz* holidays,[3] resulted in an increase in the number of afflicted persons.

The Iranian government's response to the pandemic included attempts to mitigate and manage the public health crisis without sacrificing the key ideological foundations on which the regime has been built. Since the 1979 revolution and commencement of the Iranian Islamic Republic, the government has strongly encouraged the concepts of self-reliance, resistance to 'the West' and solidarity as key elements of the state's ideology. These principles echoed throughout the early days of the Covid-19 pandemic, in which various government spokespersons made public allegations of a 'Western conspiracy' behind the spread of the virus in the country (including claims of targeted biological warfare), and also later, when vaccines were developed. The lack of clarity from official sources, particularly in the early days of the pandemic, was largely the result of political in-fighting, factionalism and competition between the various civilian, military and clerical powers which constitute the organs of government in Iran, resulting in the issuing of contradictory statements by government officials from different factions.[4]

---

[1] A Vahdat, 'Iran Reports Its First 2 Cases of the New Coronavirus' *Times of Israel* (online, 19 February 2020), www.timesofisrael.com/iran-reports-its-first-2-cases-of-the-new-coronavirus/.

[2] J Palik, 'Iran and COVID-19: Timing Matters', *MidEast Policy Brief No. 5* (Peace Research Institute Oslo, May 2020).

[3] The Iranian New Year, which is celebrated from 20 March each year, is a time when people visit extended family and often travel around the country.

[4] G Esfandiari, 'Khamenei's Ban on Western Vaccines Blasted as a "Politicization" of Iranians' Well-Being' (*Radio Free Europe*, 12 January 2021), www.rferl.org/a/iran-bans-western-coronavirus-vaccines/31043739.html.

Initially, the Iranian government's response to the pandemic was limited to the closure of all educational establishments (*i.e.*, nurseries, schools and universities), which proved to have little effect on the spread of the virus throughout Iranian society.

The Iranian economy was in trouble prior to the pandemic as a result of US-led economic sanctions and widespread corruption of officials, a situation which has only been exacerbated by the effects of the virus; allegations surfaced that imported medicines to treat Covid-19 (purchased with state-subsidised currencies) were being sold to desperate people for obscene prices on the black market. Moreover, Iran's medical industry had already been experiencing issues for a number of years in terms of acquiring medical supplies and equipment from abroad, in addition to the difficulties in accessing international financial instruments as a result of the impact of sanctions. Whilst international sanctions were not meant to directly affect the availability of medical treatments and supplies, the level of concern of financial institutions regarding the risks of trade with Iran has resulted in impacts in the medical sector, which severely hampered the Iranian government's ability to respond quickly and effectively to a novel viral outbreak.

In the first 12 months following the outbreak in Qom, more than one million Iranians lost their jobs, worsening the unemployment crisis. Moreover, the government prohibition on obtaining US- and UK-produced vaccines, absence of transparency and poor management added to the difficulties experienced by the Iranian people in terms of fighting the effects of the pandemic. Many reports suggest that the numbers of deaths/infections as well as job losses were massively under-reported in order to prevent panic across Iranian society. The government tried to stimulate domestic Covid-19 vaccine production, but the infrastructure was unable to cope and the proposed schedule for delivery was not met; furthermore, the efficacy of the domestic vaccine does not appear to be comparable with mainstream pharmaceutical company-produced vaccines. Nevertheless, the vaccination rate by March 2022 was reportedly around 57 per cent of the population (fully vaccinated), with an estimated 7.1 million cases and over 140,000 fatalities reported since the start of the outbreak.[5]

The government established a National Emergency Task Force for Fighting Coronavirus, chaired by the country's president, which acted as a central organiser bringing together ministers and their departments to propose solutions to the various crises the country faced as a result of the pandemic. The Task Force was established pursuant to the law on the Management of National Crisis (2008), which considers such circumstances as an emergency situation and empowers the government to take such measures as it deems necessary to resolve the crisis.[6]

However, the government's efforts faced widespread criticism, particularly from independent lawyers and civil rights activists, who blamed the speed and effectiveness of the government's response for the lives lost throughout the pandemic. Their attempt to file a judicial complaint against the perceived mismanagement of the pandemic was met with arrests of participants attending a preliminary meeting amongst themselves on the

---

[5] H Ritchie et al, 'Iran: Coronavirus Pandemic Country Profile' (*Our World in Data*), https://ourworldindata. org/coronavirus/country/iran.

[6] J Calabrese, 'Iran's Covid-19 Pandemic Response: Mission Critical' (*MEI@75*, 17 August 2021), www.mei. edu/publications/irans-covid-19-pandemic-response-mission-critical.

subject, in order to prevent the filing taking place, with the group accused of an 'intention' to bring action against officials.[7] Ultimately, they faced charges of 'acting against national security' and forming a 'hostile group aiming to harm the country's security and make propaganda against the state'.[8]

II. CONSTITUTIONAL, LEGAL AND POLICY OVERVIEW

Islam is the main source of the law in Iran, and the Constitution requires that all laws and regulations are in accordance with Islamic *Shari'a*.[9] Article 94 of the Constitution mandates that the Guardian Council[10] must approve all legislation passed by parliament (the *Majlis*), by reviewing proposals to ensure their compatibility with Islamic criteria (as well as the Constitution).

The Constitution also provides for universal access to basic healthcare services under article 29, requiring the government to ensure that everyone is provided with medical treatment, particularly in case of accident or emergency, whether via medical insurance or state funding. The latter is drawn from national income and public contributions, with the aim that no Iranian citizen will be left without necessary medical intervention.

There are additional provisions of the Constitution that can be considered relevant to the government's responsibility towards the public in the context of the Covid-19 pandemic, including the provision of basic needs such as housing, clothing, food and education (articles 3, 21, 30 and 43), particularly in view of the large numbers rendered unemployed and without income as a result of the outbreak.

Iran is also a signatory of the International Covenant on Economic, Social and Cultural Rights 1966. Article 12 provides that the States parties recognise the right of everyone to the enjoyment of the 'highest attainable standard of physical and mental health'. It mandates the State to take steps to 'achieve the full realisation of this right' including by way of 'the prevention, treatment and control of epidemic, endemic, occupational and other diseases' and 'the creation of conditions which would assure to all medical service and medical attention in the event of sickness'.

The World Health Organization (WHO)'s International Health Regulations have also been integrated into Iranian domestic law following signature of the instrument (2005) and ratification in domestic law in 2007.[11] According to these Regulations, State parties

---

[7] M Sinaiee, 'Six Arrested For 'Intention' To Sue Iran Officials Over Mismanaging Covid' (*Iran International*, 15 August 2021), https://old.iranintl.com/en/iran/six-arrested-intention-sue-iran-officials-over-mismanaging-covid.

[8] 'Iran: Rights lawyers on trial for lawsuit against Supreme Leader over vaccine ban' (*IAPL Monitoring Committee on Attacks on Lawyers*, 16 April 2022), https://defendlawyers.wordpress.com/2022/04/18/iran-rights-lawyers-on-trial-for-lawsuit-against-supreme-leader-over-vaccine-ban.

[9] The Constitution of the Islamic Republic of Iran (Constitution), art 4.

[10] According to the Constitution, the Guardian Council has three principal responsibilities: a veto over parliamentary legislation; supervision of elections; and approval and disqualification of candidates applying to run in local, parliamentary, presidential, and Assembly of Experts elections. The Guardian Council has 12 members, six of whom are experts on Islamic law and the remainder of whom hold expertise in constitutional law. For further information see 'The Guardian Council' (*Iran Data Portal*), https://irandataportal.syr.edu/the-guardian-council.

[11] WHO, 'International Health Regulations – Treaty Registration No. 44861', https://treaties.un.org/Pages/showActionDetails.aspx?objid=08000002801dceba&clang=_en.

must provide a prevent/treat/control approach to disease outbreaks in order to protect public health.[12]

Iran ultimately considered the Covid-19 pandemic a state of national emergency following protracted internal government debate over the definition and examples of a 'national emergency' and whether or not Covid-19 fell within the definition at law. The matter was referred to the Supreme National Security Council (SNSC)[13] which decided to establish the National Headquarters to Combat Corona (NHCC) in response;[14] with the NHCC benefiting from the same degree of authority in respect of their orders as the SNSC. It should be noted that all decisions of the SNSC are subject to the approval of the Supreme Leader.

The Iranian Constitution limits the scope and duration of emergency restrictions. Article 79 specifies that:

> The proclamation of martial law is forbidden. In case of war or emergency conditions akin to war, the government has the right to impose temporarily certain necessary restrictions, with the agreement of the Islamic Consultative Assembly. In no case can such restrictions last for more than thirty days; if the need for them persists beyond this limit, the government must obtain new authorization for them from the Assembly.

To comply with the provisions of the above-mentioned article in the context of the Covid-19 pandemic, an emergency bill (triple urgency) was put to parliament proposing a month-long national lockdown to reduce the spread of the virus; however, this was firmly rejected when put to the vote in April 2020.[15]

Furthermore, article 176 of the Constitution is also relevant to the government's response to Covid-19, as it allocates responsibilities to the Supreme Council for National Security including the determination of defence and national security policies within the general policy framework supplied by the president and co-ordinating activities in relation to politics, intelligence, social, cultural and economic areas. The Council also encourages the exploitation of domestic resources in response to internal or external threats (*e.g.*, creation and distribution of a domestic vaccine).

Regarding the general legal framework in operation in Iran, a 1941 Act entitled the Prevention of Sexually-Transmitted Diseases and Epidemics (PSTDE)[16] mandates government responsibility for provision of treatment (where available) as well as imposition of plans and appropriate measures to combat any outbreak of disease amongst the population.

---

[12] R Habibi et al, 'The Stellenbosch Consensus on Legal National Responses to Public Health Risks' (2020) *International Organizations Law Review* 1, https://brill.com/view/journals/iolr/aop/article-10.1163-15723747-2020023/article-10.1163-15723747-2020023.xml?language=en.

[13] SNSC members consist of the following government officials: the heads of the three branches of the government; planning and budget affairs chief; Head of the Supreme Council of the Armed Forces; Supreme Leader's representatives (2); Minister of Foreign Affairs; Minister of the Interior; the Intelligence Minister; commanders of the Armed Forces and the Islamic Revolution's Guards Corps.

[14] M Tofighi Darian, 'Iran's Covid-19 Response: Who Calls the Shots?' (*Verfassungsblog on Matters Constitutional*, 12 March 2021), https://verfassungsblog.de/irans-covid-19-response-who-calls-the-shots/.

[15] S Alasti, 'The Iranian Legal Response to Covid-19: A Constitutional Analysis of Coronavirus Lockdown' (*Verfassungsblog on Matters Constitutional*, 24 April 2020), https://verfassungsblog.de/the-iranian-legal-response-to-covid-19-a-constitutional-analysis-of-coronavirus-lockdown/.

[16] MA Byouki, 'An International and National Evaluation of Child Abuse in Iran and Germany' (*University of Frieburg/Max Planck Gesellschaft*, July 2015), https://freidok.uni-freiburg.de/fedora/objects/freidok:10358/datastreams/FILE1/content.

The Iranian government has been notable for its fluctuating policy approach to the Covid-19 pandemic, gradually increasing measures as the death toll increased, demonstrating the urgency of the unfolding situation. Whilst initially reluctant to introduce national measures to control the transmission of the disease, educational lockdowns were first introduced, followed by lockdowns across other areas such as shopping centres, markets, shrines, etc, as well as a wider ban on travel. The government made attempts to support the most vulnerable members of society, offering small payments to those most affected/impoverished by the effects of societal restrictions, following an emergency loan application to the International Monetary Fund for $5 billion. Ultimately, the Iranian government lifted societal restrictions, arguing that it had no option but to keep the economy going by opening up society again.

The criminal justice system was also targeted for policy changes as a result of the pandemic, with the judiciary instructed to reduce the numbers of individuals being sent to prison and mass temporary releases of 'low risk' prisoners in order to reduce the overcrowding in the country's prisons which was seen as a potential transmission issue. Reports emerged of a discriminatory policy when determining which prisoners were eligible for temporary release, with political and religious prisoners being largely ignored. As a result of this policy, there were a number of prison riots and escapes, with those involved subject to inhumane and degrading treatment (sometimes resulting in death) once control was re-established.

The Iranian government became increasingly careful with respect to controlling information surrounding the effects and impact of the outbreak, often maintaining a public perception of its unparalleled successes fighting the Covid-19 pandemic. Relevant government departments rallied together to 'prevent the spread of false information'. For example, the Cyber Police announcement that action was being taken against those considered to be 'spreading photos and videos containing false information about coronavirus'; however, in practice, it would appear that those critical of the government handling of the situation were targeted for arrest and detention, with over 3,600 people arrested for 'spreading rumours' about the pandemic/mismanagement of the outbreak by officials.[17]

A. Overview of and Specific Constitutional and Legal Principles Regarding Criminal Liability of High-Ranking Government/Public Officials

The Iranian Constitution accepts the responsibility of government officials[18] for acts conducted during their terms of office; however, there is little in terms of clear and concise express provisions to this effect. Article 173 provides that 'in order to investigate the complaints, grievances, and objections of the people with respect to government officials, organs and statutes, a court will be established to be known as the Court of Administrative

---

[17] 'Iran Says 3,600 Arrested For Spreading Coronavirus-Related Rumors' (*Radio Free Europe*, 29 April 2020), www.rferl.org/a/iran-says-3600-arrested-for-spreading-coronavirus-related-rumors/30583656.html.

[18] National Management of Administration Services Code, art 7, defines a government official as a person who has been employed by any of the government's organs, whether on a permanent, temporary or contract for service basis.

Justice' (*Divan-e Edalat-e Edari*). This court was created following the implementation of the Law on Organisation and Procedure of the Court of Administrative Justice
(as amended in 2013).[19] This judicial body is responsible for investigating and hearing
complaints against government officials as well as government policy. If a complaint is
found to have merit, the decision/policy will be effectively cancelled and returned to the
relevant department should further action be required. This court is limited in respect of
the remedies it is able to offer to complainants, and cannot impose any criminal liability
on the offending decision/policy-maker; rather if in the court's view criminal conduct has
taken place the matter will be referred to the appropriate judicial body, namely the Special
Government Employees Court who deal with criminal offences committed by government
officials. The type of offences considered by this 'special court' are divided into financial
(*i.e.*, bribery and corruption) and non-financial (everything else). Therefore, in theory,
any grievances surrounding the government handling of the pandemic (particularly
policy decisions) would fall under the latter category and the relevant decision-makers
may be tried within the Special Government Employees Court in relation to the harm
their actions have caused to victims. However, it is worth mentioning in this context that
the jurisdiction of the Court of Administrative justice does not extend to challenges on
decisions of the SNSC (per article 12 of the Law on Organization and Procedure of the
Court of Administrative Justice), and it has even been suggested that parliament lacks the
power to amend or overrule the SNSC. Clearly, this places the SNSC in a privileged position, with few (if any) available routes for a legal challenge or to ensure accountability for
the detrimental outcomes of SNSC decisions.[20]

There are various pieces of secondary legislation which are also applicable to cases
involving allegations of criminal liability for high-ranking government officials. They are
mainly discussed within chapter 10 of the Islamic Penal Code (IPC) (*offences of government officials and agents*). Article 570 provides that 'any official and/or agent associated
with State organisations and institutions, who unlawfully strips members of the public of
their personal freedom or deprives them from their rights provided in the Constitution,
shall be sentenced to imprisonment from two months to three years', in addition to
dismissal from the service and prohibition of employment in state offices for one to five
years. A recent and relevant example of the application of article 570, is that its breach is
used as the justification for a complaint made by over 50 lawyers in a letter to Iran's chief
justice, Gholamhossein Mohseni Ajeeh, demanding the release of their colleagues who
had intended to take legal action against the government for their mismanagement of the
pandemic, by quoting article 9 of the Constitution and article 570 of the IPC.[21]

Article 571 of the IPC mandates that State employees who abuse the powers conveyed
by the Constitution by knowingly creating/disseminating a forged Ministerial Order will
face three to ten years in prison. Furthermore, article 576 provides that any State official abusing their authority, or refusing to obey orders/statutes/judicial decisions, shall be
suspended from the civil service for a period of one to five years.

---

[19] Available at Civil Court website, https://divan-edalat.ir/translate.
[20] Tofighi Darian, 'Iran's Covid-19 Response' (n 14).
[21] 'Protests against the arrest of lawyers and activists' (*The News Glory*, 19 August 2021), https://thenews-
glory.com/protests-against-the-arrest-of-lawyers-and-activists-they-tried-to-sue-khamenei.

Additionally, article 597 of the IPC is of particular relevance to the situation of those lawyers and activists incarcerated for criticising the government and making a complaint regarding their handling of the pandemic. The article provides that:

[A]ny judicial authority to whom a complaint or petition is referred according to the law, but fails to accept or deal with the case, or postpones the issuance of the verdict against the law, or acts contrary to the explicit provision of law, on the first occasion shall be sentenced to six months to one year imprisonment and on the second occurrence will be permanently dismissed from judicial office and in any case shall be also sentenced to compensation of damages.[22]

There is also the possibility of disciplinary action being brought against a State official who may have acted beyond their authority/the law and/or in dereliction of duty; however, as this is not a criminal process (in the majority of cases) and results only in disciplinary action (*e.g.*, dismissal) it has not been considered in detail here. The victim may be able to bring a personal civil claim for damages against the individual concerned if the official's actions have resulted in a measurable loss. This situation should be contrasted with those in which, for example, a military official causes death or injury whereby criminal liability arises not only personally, but also vicariously (*e.g.*, payment of *diya*, *i.e.*, blood money, by the government for injuries sustained).

Whilst Iran has a number of laws that may be used to establish criminal liability for acts or omissions of government officials in relation to the Covid-19 pandemic, the theoretical existence of legislation on the statute book must be distinguished from what actually occurs in practice in a country in which criticism of the government is met with a firm hand and public information is highly controlled under the guise of protecting national security, as well as a lack of independence and impartiality in a judiciary which promotes those willing to toe the regime's line. Thus, the likelihood of relevant domestic or international laws being successfully enforced against high-ranking officials within the Iranian State is low to non-existent, due to the fact the judiciary shares the same core values and objectives as the executive and other State organs.

B. Scope of Responsibility and Area of Tolerated Risk

Generally, criminal responsibility under Iranian law is personal, per article 141 of the IPC, and can only be established where the accused is 'sane, has reached puberty, and is free at the time of the commission of the offence' (with some exceptions) according to article 140 of the same Code. Moreover, an individual can only be held criminally responsible for the acts of another if they are deemed responsible by law and/or if they are 'at fault regarding the outcome of the conduct of another' (per article 142).[23]

The scope of responsibility decreases with the seniority in position of the individuals concerned, particularly insofar as they continue to occupy their position (or one of a

---

[22] 'Islamic Penal Code of the Islamic Republic of Iran – Book V (English translation)' (*Iran Human Rights Documentation Centre*, 15 July 2013), https://iranhrdc.org/islamic-penal-code-of-the-islamic-republic-of-iran-book-five/.

[23] 'Islamic Penal Code of the Islamic Republic of Iran – Books I & II (English translation)' (*Iran Human Rights Documentation Centre*, 4 April 2014), https://iranhrdc.org/english-translation-of-books-i-ii-of-the-new-islamic-penal-code/#25.

similar level). The likelihood of lower-level officials being 'held accountable' for mismanagement during the pandemic (*i.e.*, scapegoated for the failures of their commanders) is
far greater than for those actually issuing the orders from the top, as a result of the government's hesitancy to publicly admit senior officials are incompetent, particularly those
who have obtained their positions by virtue of their conservative religious backgrounds.

Furthermore, the scope of liability may be limited for junior personnel following the
orders of superiors, where their mistake in believing that the order was lawful is 'acceptable'. Article 159 of the IPC provides that:

> [W]hen an offence is committed in compliance with an unlawful order of an official authority,
> both the commanding official and the offender shall be sentenced to the punishment provided
> by law. However, the offender who has committed the act in reliance on an acceptable mistake
> and on the assumption that the order was lawful, shall not be punished.[24]

It can be safely concluded that if the harm resulting from the Covid-19 pandemic was
caused by the unlawful decisions/actions of senior officials, those who were more junior
and tasked with implementing policies may enjoy a reduced scope of responsibility
in any resulting court action, often limited to the payment of financial compensation
(*diya*).

The scope of criminal responsibility is also limited under article 158 of the IPC, which
provides that conduct considered at law to be an offence will not be punished if the
conduct is mandated or permitted by law; or the conduct is necessary for the enforcement
of a more important law; or if the conduct occurs on the lawful order of a competent
authority and the order is not against *Shari'a*. Article 158 is likely to be an important
defence argument for any Iranian official accused of causing harm to the population as a
result of their actions/inaction in relation to the pandemic.

The IPC also confirms that government officials will face liability under Iranian law
for offences committed outside of Iran's territorial jurisdiction in relation to their office
and duties (article 6). Therefore, it is also possible that Iranian officials stationed abroad
could be held criminally liable within the Iranian courts for any unlawful acts/decisions
made in response to the Covid-19 pandemic in their official capacity.[25]

C. Impact of Immunities

There are few, if any, provisions clearly granting immunity to Iranian State officials for
actions taken as part of their duties, as the Constitution specifies that everyone is equal
in the eyes of the law (even the Supreme Leader). In practice, however, key officials are
highly unlikely to face any consequences for decisions made, even if threats of taking

---

[24] ibid.
[25] As an example, if the Ambassador were to require all staff to attend the office and work as normal, despite
working from home and social distancing policies being in effect, and harm was caused as a result of this decision, the Ambassador may face prosecution on return to Iran, despite the existence of diplomatic immunity
from prosecution by the host state. This is due to the fact that this article grants extraterritorial jurisdiction to
the Iranian criminal justice system to enable the prosecution of Iranian officials residing abroad for offences
they have committed under Iranian law, regardless of the location of the act.

action against them are voiced. It should be highlighted that these comments are limited to the context of Covid-19: financial crimes by senior State officials are often dealt with far more harshly following a change in government (and/or Ministers/senior judiciary) on the basis of damage to public confidence and perception, but in reality, signifying a new power dynamic and settling of political scores between factions.[26]

It is also relevant to mention article 103 of the Constitution, which is the closest provision to an immunity for State officials contained within the law, albeit under Western interpretations it is framed more along the lines of a defence of superior orders. Under this article, regional/provincial officials 'must abide by all decisions taken by the councils within their jurisdiction'; therefore, it can be argued that any criminal liability arising out of the actions they have taken (in accordance with the relevant councils) should be re-allocated to the official(s) that made the initial decision/order to take that action.

D. Prosecutorial Matters

Any affected party may instigate a criminal case against a State official, whether individually or in a group, and the judiciary is duty-bound to hear such complaints. Article 156 of the Constitution provides that 'the judiciary is an independent power, the protector of the rights of the individual and society, responsible for the implementation of justice'. It falls within the remit of the judiciary to investigate and pass judgment on grievances/complaints/disputes, violations of rights, etc, as well as to restore/maintain public rights, justice and freedom and to ensure the proper enforcement of the law/judgments. The body responsible for the investigation of alleged offences is known as the Public and Revolutionary Prosecutor's Office (*dadsar-ye 'omumi va enqelab*). Other law enforcement agencies support the work of the Prosecutor's office by taking orders and providing reports to this judicial body, which will then determine whether there is sufficient evidence to proceed with a prosecution. Complaints may be filed directly by affected citizens, or referred by a government official/agency if they have specific concerns.

The Prosecutor enjoys a broad discretion in determining whether or not formal charges should be brought against a State official, following the initial investigative process. Should the Prosecutor elect not to bring charges, their decision is subject to appeal in the criminal court if the affected party chooses to challenge it.

Aggrieved parties who have a complaint regarding the workings of the judiciary, State officials and/or the government can submit this in writing to parliament, who must then investigate and reply under the provisions of article 90 of the Constitution. Should the matter be considered to be one of public interest (such as a national pandemic), the response of the parliament must be made public also.

---

[26] For example, following the replacement of President Rouhani by President Raiesi, some of Rouhani's senior officials/advisors were prosecuted for various offences, including financial crimes and national security offences (on the basis of breach of confidentiality). See, eg 'Arrest of Vice-President's Brother in Iran Seen as a Political Move' (*Iran International*, 28 January 2021), https://old.iranintl.com/en/iran/arrest-vice-presidents-brother-iran-seen-political-move.

III. CAUSATION

A. Causation (General Principles)

Under Islamic principles of law, as applied in Iran, a duty of care is owed by State officials to the country's citizens. The principle of *tasbib* dictates that any causation of injury, directly or indirectly to an individual by a State official, will result in compensation (*diya*) being payable for the harm. Liability rests with both the State official personally, as well as the government for directing the actions of the State official (whether through orders or policy-making). Failure to act in accordance with the statutory duty of care will be examined further within the section on omissions liability.[27]

The IPC specifically defines causation, in line with the generally accepted 'but for' test, within article 506, which states that:

> [C]ausation of a crime consists of when a person causes death or injury to another without directly committing the crime, in a way that the crime would not have occurred without his/her actions, such as when a person digs a well into which another falls and gets injured.[28]

Therefore, this article may apply to the circumstances of the Covid-19 pandemic, in respect of the actions/omissions of decision/policy-makers causing harm to others indirectly. However, article 536 may also be applicable in such circumstances as it provides for liability in the case of State officials carrying out unauthorised actions resulting in harm to others; in such cases the official would be held personally liable for their unlawful act(s), having been the direct cause of the harm.

Under Iranian law, both the omission and commission of acts resulting in harm to others may result in criminal liability for the perpetrator, including State officials, per article 2 of the IPC. For an omission to attract liability, the official in question must be under a duty to act and the failure to do so must have resulted in harm (for example, under article 606 of the IPC a special omissions offence is provided for in which certain officials with a duty to report specified crimes and transgressions will be guilty of an offence if they fail to do so).

Under Iranian criminal law, any act or omission is generally assessed and judged based on the intention of the doer, a concept known as *niyya* or *amd* within *Shari'a*. Unintentional acts resulting in harm, such as those arising from mistake, negligence, recklessness or omission will also be punished if it is established that the perpetrator is at fault for the harm resulting from their act.[29]

Criminal liability for State officials cannot be established unless the individual is under a legal duty to act in a certain manner. When considering the harm caused by the Covid-19 pandemic, it is therefore necessary for there to be a positive duty to act which has been breached in order for liability to rest with the decision-maker/government employee tasked with implementing the relevant decisions. State officials must act

---

[27] PR Powers, 'Offending Heaven and Earth: Sin and Expiation in Islamic Homicide Law' (2007) 14 *Islamic Law and Society* 42.

[28] Deliberate acts of self-harm on the part of the victim are considered to break the chain of causation.

[29] F Ahadi, 'Re-visiting the Concept of *Mens Rea*: Challenging the Common Approaches Employed under Islamic Jurisprudence and Statute Law' (2016) 9 *Journal of Politics and Law* 1.

within the boundaries imposed by the law; exceeding the scope of such defined duties, causing harm, will result in criminal responsibility (an example of which can be found in article 157 of the IPC).[30]

There are various pieces of legislation (primary and secondary) within Iran creating legal duties on State officials with regards to matters of public health and prevention of the transmission of communicable diseases. As the Iranian legal system is based on statute, the main source of legal duties for State officials are the relevant provisions of legislation, with limited operation of judicial precedent to support interpretation.[31] To prevent duplication within this section, the reader is referred to Sections II and II.A above in which the most relevant provisions of law have already been discussed.

Failure to act may result in criminal responsibility for State officials, providing that the duty to act is clearly defined and specified within legislation and there is a sufficient causal link between the failure and the resultant harm to others. Generally speaking, Iranian law considers a large victim pool as an indication of a relatively serious crime; therefore, it is likely that a higher-than-normal mortality rate as a result of the pandemic, if it can be shown evidentially/causally, would result in liability for the actors responsible for the relevant decision-making which led to the detrimental outcome. It is the responsibility of the Public Prosecutor to initiate investigation in such circumstances, although as previously noted this may be triggered by an affected private complainant or a government official/department.

Iranian law considers a failure to act/intervene in circumstances in which the official had the ability and opportunity to do so the 'negation of a particular act' rather than an action in and of themselves. For instance, as the government has a duty to protect public health and prevent the wide scale transmission of disease throughout the community, but has failed to do so effectively, this would be considered as an omission, leading to criminal liability for those responsible.

If the consequences of an act or omission can be reasonably causally linked to resultant harm to others (*tasbib* principle) then the State official will be held criminally responsible. To clarify, if the harm would not have resulted but for the act or omission, and it is a substantial contributing cause to the harm suffered, then the official will be liable. If, however, the harm is considered too remote (by the standards of a reasonable person) then liability will be avoided.

B. Causation and 'Thin Skull' Scenarios

Under Iranian law the principle of taking one's victim as one finds them similarly applies,[32] and therefore State officials may be held criminally liable for the increased level

---

[30] According to this article 'any resistance against the police and other law enforcement officials whilst performing their duties shall not be considered a defence unless the officials have exceeded the scope of their duties and there is a legitimate fear that their actions may cause death or injury or violation of bodily integrity'.

[31] To clarify, whilst Iranian law is statute-based, judges have scope to exercise discretion and use previous case law from the General Assembly of the Supreme Court to assist with the interpretation of statute and/or Islamic law principles in cases with similar facts/circumstances.

[32] H Aghababaei and A Nazari, 'The General Aspects of Killing in Iran's Criminal Law: From Legal Changes to Legal-Judicial Challenges' (2021) 9 *Journal of Criminal Law Research* 187.

of harm to those suffering from health conditions which made them more vulnerable to serious illness and/or death as a result of infection with Covid-19. The fact that State officials will not have been aware of individual citizen's specific circumstances/vulnerabilities does not negate the harmful effects of their actions/omissions on this sector of the population; it is reasonable to assume that the elderly and those with comorbidities/underlying health issues would be at greater risk of serious medical complications and thus required greater protection from infection. Therefore, the chain of causation will not be broken in the case of the most vulnerable, who suffered the most harm, and State officials will be forced to 'take their victims as they found them' and may be held criminally responsible for their acts/omissions which led to said harm. This should be distinguished from circumstances in which the acts or omissions of the victim, or a third party, may have significantly contributed to the harmful outcome experienced which would break the chain of causation (*novus actus interveniens*).

In this regard article 537 of the Penal Code should be considered, as it provides for cases in which the victim may have contributed to the ultimate outcome of their situation, mandating that where the crime is exclusively attributed to the deliberate act or the fault of the victim, no liability shall be engaged; however, in cases where the perpetration of the principal crime is attributed to the deliberate act or fault of the perpetrator, but its consequences were attributed to the deliberate act or fault of the victim, the perpetrator shall not be liable for the harmful consequences the victim brought upon himself. A possible example of this 'contributory negligence' concept in the context of the pandemic and the level of responsibility attributable to State officials may include elderly/vulnerable individuals who were advised by the government to self-isolate for their own protection, but instead continued to mix with others as normal and became seriously ill or died from the disease. Likewise, those refusing Covid-19 vaccination may find themselves in a similar position should they fall seriously ill.

As an example of this principle being enshrined within the codified law of Iran, paragraph (c) of article 290 provides that if the perpetrator does not have the intention to kill and his act would not usually result in severe harm against ordinary people, it is not intentional murder. However, if the victim suffers from any condition (*e.g.*, elderly, ill-health, etc), and the perpetrator is either aware of or should reasonably know of the victim's condition/vulnerabilities, then the crime will be categorised as first-degree murder (intentional).[33] It can be inferred from this article that State officials have a duty to take into consideration the potential harm to vulnerable members of the community during an outbreak of a novel viral disease.

The chain of causation will not be broken by comorbidities if it can be established that the underlying illness resulting in death was aggravated by exposure to Covid-19 and/or that the failure of the Iranian government to promptly take measures to protect the vulnerable resulted in serious harm to this group. Generally speaking, liability for State officials in this regard will be removed by the introduction of an *actus novus interveniens*, if the intervening act can be proven to break the chain of causation and render too remote the link between the State officials' acts/omissions and the harm suffered as a result.

---

[33] A Zanganeh and M Nozari Ferdowsiehm, 'A Jurisprudential Analysis of Paragraphs B and C of Article 290 of Islamic Penal Code' (2020) 10 *Journal of Advanced Pharmacy Education & Research* 147.

The principle of *tasbib* is clear in that indirect causes of harm must be reasonably established, and not too distant from a causation perspective.

C. Restricting Causality: Policy and Doctrinal Issues

Beyond the concept of *actus novus interveniens* and the principle of *tasbib*, there is little limitation to causality within the Iranian criminal justice system.

IV. THE STRUCTURE OF HOMICIDE OFFENCES AND ASSAULT/AGGRAVATED ASSAULT/SERIOUS BODILY HARM OFFENCES

A. Murder/Intentional Homicide

The *Shari'a* principles underpinning the Iranian Islamic Republic consider that human life is the most valuable gift from Allah.[34] The right to life is considered by the Qur'an to be sacrosanct and it is consequently deeply entrenched in the codified legal system of Iran. Any unlawful interference with this right will constitute *qatl* (homicide) and is deemed to be a severe breach of the law. Islam considers the unlawful killing of another as tantamount to the '[killing] of all people'.[35] Iranian law sets out strong substantive protection of the right to life and clear procedural guidelines as to how a defendant ought to be treated.[36]

Murder occurs when a living individual is killed, either intentionally or by a perpetrator who is reckless as to the potential consequences of their actions. An exception may occur in the case of pregnant women who suffer harm to their unborn foetuses, in that Iranian law recognises that a foetus of 16 weeks or over gestation is a living being for the purposes of homicide law, and any harm to such foetus resulting in death would be prosecuted accordingly.

The offender may be a natural person or legal person, depending on the circumstances of the case. Government organs/bodies are considered legal persons for the purposes of criminal law in Iran; however, the penalties imposed against such organisations are substantially different to natural persons. This is due to the fact that the punishment for murder is twofold, including the *qisas* and *diya* elements (*i.e.*, the retributive sentence (talionic principle) and financial compensation), and a non-natural person cannot be subjected to *qisas*, but those responsible for the harm (within the relevant government body) can be compelled to pay compensation (blood money) in addition to being sentenced to a term of imprisonment for the public interest element of the punishment.

Iranian law considers that the victim should be a natural living person after birth; however, one notable exception to this rule is the position of the unborn foetus, which is considered to be 'alive' and to have a soul from the point of four months into the

---

[34] SS Shah, 'Homicide in Islam: Major Legal Themes' (1999) 14 *Arab Law Quarterly* 159.
[35] Qur'an, 5:32.
[36] M Hedayati-Kakhki, 'Islamic Law' in A Reed and M Bohlander (eds), *Homicide in Criminal Law – A Research Companion* (London, Routledge, 2018) 326.

pregnancy.[37] Consequently, any act or omission which results in the death of a foetus of four months or more will be considered as murder (intentional or otherwise).[38]

In order for a homicide offence to be established under Iranian law, the perpetrator must have caused harm resulting in death to a living victim through their act or omission. The level of culpability may be influenced by whether or not the requisite intent has been formed, and/or whether the perpetrator was reckless as to the likely or unlikely consequences of their actions; however, liability will usually be ascribable to the perpetrator in the case of harm caused by an act or omission.

All other elements of causation discussed above are applicable to cases of homicide; there is a need for a causal link between the act or omission and the harmful consequences.

The foundation of 'intent' in Iranian law is embodied in the *Shari'a* principle of *al-umur bi maqasidiha*, i.e., the individual must be judged according to the intentions and purpose behind their action. Therefore, when establishing criminal liability for State officials the intent (or lack thereof) plays a significant role, particularly in cases where their actions or omissions have resulted in death and/or serious bodily harm: As discussed above, punishment would be via *qisas* or *diya* depending on the circumstances, *i.e.*, level of intent.

Generally speaking, the offence of murder requires an intention to kill on the part of the defendant, if it is to qualify as intentional homicide (first degree murder). Some jurists believe that this can only be demonstrated by the use of a fatal weapon; however, others go further and suggest that such an intention could even be present where the defendant hits another with his hands or gives a false testimony against a defendant in a murder trial. Whilst the latter interpretation provides a broader scope of intent, this category is unlikely to be applicable to State officials in the context of the Covid-19 pandemic as it is highly improbable that officials deliberately set out to create policy, make decisions and fail to act with the intent of killing numerous members of the civilian population.

However, there are two further categories of murder, 'quasi-intentional' and 'accidental', in which the offender does not require a pure intent to kill, but rather the consequence of his act/omission is the death of the victim. These categories employ a slightly different interpretation of the intent of the perpetrator, for example, the mental state required for the offence of accidental murder is a genuine and honest intention to perform a lawful act.[39]

As noted above, murder offences are divided into the intentional, the quasi-intentional and the accidental, per article 289 of the IPC. Intentional killing is discussed within article 290 of the same Code which further subdivides the offence into four categories. The first category is the perpetrator who intends to kill without regard to whether or not their act/omission typically results in the death of the victim. The second set of circumstances are where the perpetrator does not intend to kill yet acts in a manner that is likely

---

[37] K Aramesh, 'A Closer Look at the Abortion Debate in Iran' (2009) 9 *American Journal of Bioethics* 57.

[38] Abortion is illegal in Iran (as it is considered to be the murder of a foetus); however, in very special circumstances (such as the foetus suffering from abnormalities that will prevent it being viable at birth) abortion may be authorised, but only up until four months.

[39] E Ghodsi, 'Murder in the Criminal Law of Iran and Islam' (2004) 68 *The Journal of Criminal Law* 160.

to result in serious injury or death to another (and is aware of the potential lethal nature of their actions).[40] The third example includes the perpetrator who does not intend to kill and commits an act which would not usually result in death but inadvertently kills the victim due to their particular vulnerabilities. The final category is where the perpetrator intends to kill but does not target a specific victim (*e.g.*, indiscriminate terrorist attack).

As discussed above, the codified provisions of Iranian law in relation to omissions are also relevant. Article 295 of the IPC provides that 'if the law places a specific duty on someone and they fail to perform that duty (that they were competent to perform) thereby causing the death of another, they will be held liable for murder'.[41] From the examples provided (as a note to the article), and of particular relevance in the context of the Covid-19 pandemic, if a doctor or nurse (who have a legal duty to care for patients) fails in that duty they will be liable for murder.

Article 291 of the Code covers the circumstances of quasi-intentional homicide, which is defined as circumstances in which the perpetrator intends to carry out the act, but does not intend the results of carrying out said act to be the death of another. An example of circumstances which may be considered quasi-intentional homicide is where an individual intends to take their car out for a drive but does not intend to run over and kill a pedestrian whilst driving.[42]

Article 292 of the IPC provides for mistaken homicide, with examples provided including killing someone whilst sleepwalking or insane, as well as a hunter intending to shoot a deer but accidentally killing a nearby human being.

The acts/omissions of State officials in relation to the Covid-19 pandemic in Iran are likely to fall within the boundaries of intentional homicide (*i.e.*, not intended but occurred due to individual vulnerabilities) or quasi-intentional homicide (*i.e.*, intended an act/omission but did not intend/foresee the consequences of said act/omission being the deaths of others). Therefore, it is likely that government officials could theoretically be held responsible at law for the harms caused to the populace by inaction and/ or mismanagement during the pandemic; however, the practical considerations (*e.g.*, the arrest of those intending to bring such a claim) may well detract from this theoretical position in respect of obtaining effective and tangible accountability from those in positions of responsibility.

B. Culpable Homicide/Manslaughter

Iranian law does not distinguish between murder and manslaughter, as noted above there are simply different categories of murder relevant to the level of intent of the perpetrator. However, article 616 of the IPC mandates that:

> [I]f manslaughter is committed as a result of negligence or recklessness of the offender or caused by an act for which the offender lacks the required skills, or because of disregard for

---

[40] This scenario may be considered similar to that espoused in England and Wales in the case of *R v Woollin* [1999] AC 82.

[41] M Hedayati-Kakhki, 'Islamic Law' in A Reed and M Bohlander (eds), *Participation in Crime: Domestic and Comparative Perspectives* (Abingdon, Routledge, 2013) 354–55.

[42] See further Hedayati-Kakhki, 'Islamic law' (n 36) 345.

the regulations, the offender shall be sentenced to one to three years' imprisonment and also payment of *diya* in cases in which the *uliya-ye dam* [owners of blood money] apply for, unless it is a case of absolute negligence.[43]

C. Offences Related to Actions that Cause Serious Bodily Harm (Assault; Grievous Assault; Assault with Intent to Cause Serious Bodily Harm)

Offences relating to bodily harm involve the same principles as discussed above in relation to homicide (*tasbib*, etc) as they are similarly derived from *Shari'a* sources. The punishment is usually payment of *diya* in addition to any public interest element of the punishment (usually term of imprisonment of up to three years), although *qisas* may be applied at the victim's request. Therefore, State officials may find themselves liable under article 614 of the IPC for serious injuries (falling short of death) to the population as a result of Covid-19 infection during the pandemic.[44]

D. Offences Regarding Unborn Foetuses; Interrupting the Course of a (Viable) Pregnancy

Iranian law prohibits abortion, unless medical necessity requires the procedure to be carried out to save the mother's life (article 623 of the IPC).[45] As discussed above, any act or omission that results in the death of a foetus of four months or more will result in criminal liability as if the foetus was born/a living natural person. Prior to this gestation age, harm to the foetus remains illegal, but does not fall within the scope of homicide as the foetus is not considered a living person at law.[46]

E. Failure to Render Assistance

There is no general duty to render aid and no specific offence of failing to render assistance under Iranian law. Criminal liability will only be established in cases where the codified legislation provides for a specific duty to act (see above); if the law is silent on the matter, then no criminal responsibility will be attached to the failure to assist.

---

[43] 'Islamic Penal Code of the Islamic Republic of Iran – Book V' (n 22).

[44] Art 614 provides that 'Anyone who commits an assault and battery against someone else that results in damaging or breaking or disabling a victim's limb or causes him a permanent illness or defect or loss of a sense or ability or loss of mind, in cases where *qisas* is not possible, if his act disrupts public order and the safety of the society or it is thought that it emboldens the offender or others [to commit assault again], he shall be sentenced to two to five years' imprisonment; and if the victim applies for it, shall be sentenced to *diya* as well. Note – If the injury does not result in the abovementioned defects, and the means of committing the assault is a gun or knife or the like, the offender shall be sentenced to three months to one year of imprisonment.'

[45] According to art 623, 'Anyone who causes the miscarriage of a pregnant woman by giving her drugs or other means shall be sentenced to six months to one year of imprisonment, and if knowingly and deliberately guides a pregnant woman to use drugs or other means to abort her baby shall be sentenced to three to six months' imprisonment, unless it is proved that it was necessary to save the mother's life; in any case the *diya* shall be paid according to the relevant provisions'.

[46] RJ Simon, *Abortion: Statutes, Policies, and Public Attitudes the World Over* (Westport, Praeger, 2007) 25–26.

V. DEFENCES, JUSTIFICATIONS AND EXCUSES

Common defences applied to other categories of crime may also be employed in defence of homicide/serious bodily harm charges (perpetrator is a minor, insane, acted in self-defence etc). Additionally, article 158 of the IPC may be of significance in the context of State officials' responsibility for the handling of the Covid-19 pandemic, as it clarifies that conduct ordinarily considered by law as an offence will not be punished where legislation mandates or permits said conduct, or it is necessary for the enforcement of a more important law, or it is committed on the lawful order of a competent authority in compliance with *Shari'a* principles). This article therefore provides an overarching set of defined parameters for dealing with conflicting domestic legislation.

A. Necessity

Iranian law recognises that criminal responsibility may be excluded by the necessity of the conduct to save the life or property of another in circumstances of 'grave and imminent danger', including disease outbreaks. Under article 152 of the IPC, the offender shall not be punished in such circumstances providing the conduct is proportional to the danger, necessary to counter the risks, and they did not create the dangerous situation intentionally. According to an explanatory note, individuals with a duty to act under the law cannot refuse to perform said duty(ies) on the basis of this article, meaning that it will not provide a defence in the case that the duty-bound individual failed to act to avert danger. The law does not distinguish between State officials and civilians; therefore, in the context of the state of national emergency caused by the Covid-19 pandemic, this article will apply to government officials with a legal duty to act (*e.g.*, the Ministry of Health) providing that their conduct is necessary and proportionate.[47]

VI. CORPORATE CRIMINAL LIABILITY

Iranian law provides for the criminal responsibility of legal persons; however, the circumstances in which a prosecution may be brought are somewhat limited and the sentencing options are different to those imposed on a natural person (*e.g.*, limited to payment of *diya*, dissolution of the legal person, confiscation of property, ban on activities for up to five years, etc; per article 20 of the IPC).[48]

---

[47] M Abedi and M Arefi Rad, 'Legal Analysis of the Exemption of Iranian Red Crescent Relief Workers from Compensation for Traffic Accident Injuries' (2021) 13 *Journal of Rescue and Relief* 177.

[48] Art 20 provides that 'If a legal person is held responsible under article 143 of this law, considering the severity of the crime and its harmful consequences, it shall be sentenced to one or two of the following, although this shall not prevent punishing the natural person: (a) Dissolution of the legal person; (b) Confiscation of all properties; (c) Ban from one or more social or professional activity (activities) permanently or for up to five years; (d) Ban from public invitation to increase the capital for legal persons permanently or for up to five years; (e) Ban from drawing some commercial bills for up to five years; (f) Fine; (g) Publication of the convicting judgment in the media. Note- The punishment provided in this article shall not be applied on governmental bodies or public or non-governmental entities that implement the state administration'.

A. Overview of Corporate Criminal Liability

Article 143 of the IPC provides, in respect of criminal responsibility, that:

> [T]he natural person shall bear responsibility by default and the legal person shall only bear criminal responsibility if the legal representative of the legal person commits a crime under its name or in line with its interests. Criminal responsibility of legal persons shall not prevent the responsibility of natural persons who commit an offence.

Therefore, regardless of any organisational liability amongst government departments, it can be said that Iranian law exhibits a preference for accountability to rest with a natural person (as far as possible) for criminal acts and the harms stemming therefrom.

B. Accessory or Perpetrator

Regarding the issue of whether or not a governmental body can be held responsible as an accessory or perpetrator of a crime, the law makes an important exception (in the note to article 20), stating that 'the punishment provided in this article shall not be applied on governmental bodies or public or non-governmental entities that implement the state administration'. Therefore, despite corporate criminal liability existing within Iranian criminal law as a concept, the scope of such liability will not extend to organs of the State and this article cannot be used to hold such bodies to criminal accountability for the outcomes relating to their decisions/actions/inaction during the Covid-19 pandemic.

VII. FORMS OF PARTICIPATION

Islamic law considers, in the circumstances of multiple individuals being responsible for a crime, that each perpetrator must bear his own burden and be held accountable for his own actions. This is supported by the following verse of the *Qur'an*: 'And no bearer of burdens shall bear another's burden, and if one heavily laden calls another to (bear) his load, nothing of it will be lifted even though he be near of kin' [Surah 35:18]. The scope of participation in a crime under Iranian law is defined within article 125 of the IPC, which provides:

> Any person who associates with other person(s) in the operational stage of an offence, and where the offence is attributed to their collective conduct, whether or not the conduct of each one would be sufficient for committing the offence, and whether the result of their conduct is equal or different, shall be regarded as an accomplice to the offences and his/her punishment shall be as though one person has individually committed the offence. In the case of unintentional offences if the offence is committed as a result of wrongdoing of two or more people, the wrongdoers shall be regarded as accomplices to the offences and the punishment for each offender shall be as though one person has individually committed the offence.

The law considers accomplices fall within the unified perpetrator theory, meaning that all of the perpetrators bear criminal responsibility for the act/its consequences regardless of whether or not only one of the group actually committed it.

Relevant to this issue as well as causation, article 214 dictates that where injuries are inflicted by multiple assailants on the same person, with a lethal result attributable to all those injuries separately, then the assailants will be joint principals (thus primarily guilty of murder). Furthermore, article 215 sets out the position where an assailant would be guilty of being an accessory instead; the difference between the two appears to be the extent of the causal link between the injury inflicted by that person and the lethal outcome for the victim. Article 125 therefore provides for a general accomplice liability offence, whereas articles 214 and 215 are specific to physical injury to the victim.

Article 526 clarifies the causal connection between the victim's injuries and the actions of the perpetrators. It states that:

> [W]here two or more perpetrators, some of them directly, some by causality contribute to occurrence of a crime, the perpetrator to whom the crime is attributed shall be liable, and where the crime is attributable to all perpetrators, they will be liable equally, save where the impact of the action of perpetrators differ, in which case each perpetrator shall be liable to the extent of contribution of his action. Where the direct perpetrator of a crime lacked free will or was ignorant, undiscerning minor, insane or the like, only the direct perpetrator or the cause shall be liable.

Also of relevance is article 533, which provides for equal liability in cases:

> [W]here two or more persons cause perpetration of a crime of infliction of damage upon another by collaboration in such manner that the crime or damage could be attributed to both or all of them, they shall be equally liable.

Iran's approach to accomplice liability is covered by articles 42 and 43. Article 42 mandates that:

> [A]any person who knowingly and intentionally associates with other(s) in an offence punishable according to *Ta'zir*[49] or deterrent punishments, and the offence is committed by their collective actions, whether the action of each one would be sufficient for committing the offence, whether the result of their actions are equal or not, is regarded as an accomplice to the offences. His/her punishment will be as though that of the person who had committed the offence.

Article 43 dictates the types of actions that can lead to accomplice liability, such as inciting, encouraging, plotting, tricking or deceiving into criminal offences; or otherwise facilitating the offence. It specifies further that the court will punish the accomplice according to their circumstances and means and previous records.

Additionally, chapter 3 of the IPC deals with accessories to an offence in a more general manner. Article 126 initially defines accessories as:

> (a) Anyone, who encourages or threatens or suborns or incites someone else to commit an offence, or through a plot, deception, or abuse of power causes an offence to be committed; or (b) Anyone who makes or provides the means for commission of an offence, or shows the offender the way to commit an offence; or (c) Anyone who facilitates the commission of an offence.

Article 127 details the prescribed punishments for accessories to an offence.

Therefore, taking into consideration the provisions of law applicable to accomplice liability, discussed above, it can be concluded that the level of ascribed liability is likely to vary depending on the particular circumstances of any given case, but all offenders risk punishment based on their level of involvement in the offence, with the accessories

---

[49] Iranian law categorises punishment of offenders into four types: *hadd*, *qisas*, *diyat* and *taz'ir*. The latter involves punishment at the presiding judge's discretion, ranging from lashes to fines, to imprisonment and exile.

facing a reduced sentence in comparison to the principal offender unless, for example, their conduct falls within the parameters of article 215 where they would be considered equally criminally responsible.

VIII. ATTEMPT

Iranian law punishes those who intend to commit a crime but whose acts are frustrated due to factors beyond their control (article 122 of the IPC).[50] The law clarifies (per article 123) that a

> mere intention to commit an offence or any operation or measures that are only the preparation of an offence and have no direct connection to commission of the offence, shall not be considered as an attempt to commit an offence and shall not be punishable in this respect.[51]

If the perpetrator attempts an offence but then 'gives up' voluntarily, they will only be punished for any actions they have taken up until that point which are considered to be offences (per article 124). Otherwise, the fact that the requisite intent has been formed to commit the illegal act will render any efforts taken in pursuit of that goal punishable, even if a third party prevents the completion of the crime. It is worth mentioning that an attempt to commit a crime under Iranian law is not an offence unless an attempt at that type of crime is defined within the law and corresponding punishment provided for in the statute books. In other circumstances if the preliminary steps of an offence involve the commission of other crimes (*e.g.*, a thief breaks a window with the intent of theft but is interrupted and flees they will be convicted of breaking and entering as well as criminal damage, rather than theft). In the context of the Covid-19 pandemic, it is difficult to speculate on circumstances in which attempt may be relevant to the actions of State officials.

IX. SANCTIONS, SENTENCING, PUNISHMENT, REPARATIONS AND/OR RESTORATIVE JUSTICE

A. General Sentencing Framework for the Crimes under Discussion

Punishments for homicide and serious bodily harm offences are specified within the IPC. For example, article 381 provides for the punishment of death (*qisas*) in cases of intentional murder (defined at article 290). The article further specifies that the 'guardian of blood' (*Walial-dam*/victim's family) have the right to request *qisas* punishment of the offender. The enforcement of a *qisas* punishment in murder cases must be approved by the Head of Judiciary or other authorities. Criminal liability for the executioner is avoided via article 418 which allows the killing of the person sentenced to *qisas*, so long as the victim's heir requests such action and the appropriate judicial authorisation is in place.[52]

---

[50] 'Islamic Penal Code of the Islamic Republic of Iran – Books I & II' (n 23).
[51] ibid.
[52] MA Byouki, 'Qisās (retaliation) for Children in Iran: a Socio-Criminological Approach' (*University of Freiburg*, 2015), https://freidok.uni-freiburg.de/dnb/download/10359.

If the heirs waive the right to *qisas* the offender will instead be sentenced to payment of *diya* (compensation/blood money) and 10 years' imprisonment.

Qisas is considered retribution in kind, and is one of the punishments for causing injury intentionally. Articles 396–416 of the IPC regulate the imposition of *qisas*, *i.e.*, the carrying out of the same injuries to the perpetrator, and article 386 provides for *qisas* on request of the victim or their guardian in cases of intentional bodily injury, which constitutes any damage less than murder and includes penalties such as amputation of body parts, blinding, removal of teeth, etc.[53]

In cases of unintentional killing or causing bodily harm, the appropriate punishment is the payment of *diya*; the amount and conditions of the payment of *diya* are provided for within articles 448–727 of the IPC.

In terms of the imposition of the sentence for an attempt to commit a crime, article 122 of the IPC specifies the sentences to be imposed as follows:

(a) In the cases of offences for which their punishments under law are deprivation of life, life imprisonment, or ta'zir imprisonment of the first to third degree, [they shall be sentenced] to a ta'zir imprisonment of the fourth degree; (b) In the cases of offences for which their punishments under law are amputation of limbs or a ta'zir imprisonment of the fourth degree, [they shall be sentenced] to a ta'zir imprisonment of the fifth degree; (c) In the cases of offences for which their punishments under law are a *hadd* flogging or a ta'zir imprisonment of the fifth degree, [they shall be sentenced] to a ta'zir imprisonment or flogging or fine of the sixth degree.[54]

B. Sanctions Specifically for Senior Government/Public Officials

The punishments for offences relevant to State accountability for the harms caused by mishandling the Covid-19 pandemic, as well as the applicable sentencing frameworks, are governed by the sentencing provisions identified above. State officials should, theoretically, face the same punishment as an ordinary citizen for the consequences of their actions/decisions in office.

C. Corporations and Sentencing

The sentencing of non-natural persons has been discussed above and is not replicated here. However, it should be noted that a corporate offender will face increased fines in comparison to a natural person (two to four times the amount provided for at law, per article 21 of the IPC). Moreover, article 22 of the same Code considers that dissolution of the legal person and confiscation of property is appropriate in circumstances where the corporation has been established to commit unlawful acts, or has moved away from lawful goals towards committing crime.[55]

---

[53] 'Flawed Reforms: Iran's New Code of Criminal Procedure' (*Amnesty International*, 2016), www.amnestyusa. org/files/flawed_reforms_-_irans_new_code_of_criminal_procedure.pdf.

[54] This is an English translation of art 122. See 'Islamic Penal Code of the Islamic Republic of Iran – Books I & II' (n 23).

[55] 'Islamic Penal Code of the Islamic Republic of Iran – Books I & II' (n 23).

10

People's Republic of China

ANDRA LE ROUX-KEMP

I. BACKGROUND AND CONTEXTUAL INTRODUCTION

IT IS GENERALLY accepted that the *fons et origo* of the ongoing Covid-19 pandemic is Wuhan city, Hubei province China, where, in early December 2019, a cluster of patients presented with symptoms of an atypical pneumonia.[1] At first, the local hospital reported these cases to the Wuhan Municipal Health Department as unexplained pneumonia, and the official response and advice was that 'the disease was preventable and controllable, and there was no need to panic'.[2] On 31 December 2019, however, with hospitals continuing to receive more patients with unknown pneumonia-like symptoms, the Chinese National Health Commission officially reported to the World Health Organization (WHO) the possibility of a new virus with symptoms of pneumonia, but of unknown etymology.[3] This virus was later identified as a novel coronavirus – SARS-CoV-2 (Severe Acute Respiratory Syndrome Coronavirus 2) – and the disease it caused was formally named Covid-19.[4]

The Chinese government's initial response to the outbreak of Covid-19 was pragmatic and localised.[5] On 1 January 2020, Wuhan's Huanan Seafood Wholesale Market was

---

[1] C Huang et al, 'Clinical Features of Patients Infected with 2019 Novel Coronavirus in Wuhan, China' (2020) 395 *The Lancet* 497; X Yu and N Li, 'Understanding the Beginning of a Pandemic: China's Response to the Emergence of COVID-19' (2021) 14 *Journal of Infection and Public Health* 347, 348.

[2] Yu and Li, 'Understanding the Beginning of a Pandemic' (n 1) 348.

[3] Compared to the 2002–03 outbreak of severe acute respiratory syndrome (SARS), during which the Chinese government reported that outbreak to the WHO after 300 confirmed cases and five deaths, the official notification to the WHO of what is now known as the Covid-19 outbreak followed after only 27 cases and zero deaths. Generally, the Chinese government seems to have improved its epidemic response capacity. World Health Organization, 'Pneumonia of Unknown Cause' (5 January 2020), www.who.int/emergencies/disease-outbreak-news/item/2020-DON229. J DeLisle and S Kui, 'Lessons from China's Response to Covid-19: Shortcomings, Successes, and Prospects for Reform in China's Regulatory State' (2020) 16 *University of Pennsylvania Asian Law Review* 66, 70–71. For an appraisal of the Chinese government's response to the outbreak of Covid-19 compared to that of SARS, see J Li, 'Appraisal of China's Response to the Outbreak of Covid-19 in Comparison with SARS' (2021) 9 *Frontiers in Public Health* 1; Z Wu and J McGoogan 'Characteristics of and Important Lessons from the Coronavirus Disease 2019 (COVID-19) Outbreak in China' (2020) 323 *JAMA* 1239.

[4] Z Allam, 'Chapter 1: The First 50 Days of Covid-19: A Detailed Chronological Timeline and Extensive Review of Literature Documenting the Pandemic' in Z Allam, *Surveying the Covid-19 Pandemic and its Implications: Urban Health, Data Technology and Political Economy* (London, Elsevier, 2020) 2.

[5] Yu and Li, 'Understanding the Beginning of a Pandemic' (n 1) 348.

indefinitely closed after an investigation by the Wuhan Center of Disease Control and Prevention and based on the known associated link between the sale of endangered species for human consumption and the outbreak of zoonotic infectious diseases.[6] In addition to the environmental sanitation and disinfection of this wet market, the sale of live animals from wet markets, online markets and other similar markets were banned as a precautionary measure,[7] and the Chinese government also pursued various public awareness campaigns emphasising hygiene and sanitation, especially amongst farmers.[8] Regrettably, and characteristic of the Chinese administrative state, efforts were also made to suppress or control the flow of information about the outbreak of this then, yet unknown disease. The Public Security Bureau, for example, arrested and imprisoned individuals accused of spreading rumours about the virus and instilling fear and panic of another SARS-type outbreak.[9] Noteworthy was the arrest and detention of doctor Li Wenliang (who subsequently died of Covid-19 on 7 February 2020), along with seven other individuals on 6 January 2020, for whistleblowing on the coronavirus situation in China.[10] That control over information about the virus and its suspected outbreak was a key priority for the Chinese government from early on, is also evident from the closing down for 'rectification' of the laboratory at the Shanghai Public Health Clinical Centre, presumably for its role in releasing the genome sequence of the coronavirus before Chinese officials could publish theirs.[11]

The virus continued to spread rapidly throughout the entire territory of China, and ultimately also beyond,[12] and with 7,711 confirmed and 12,167 suspected cases of Covid-19 in China, and 83 confirmed cases in 18 countries globally, the WHO declared on 30 January 2020, the outbreak of Covid-19 a Public Health Emergency of International Concern (PHEIC).[13] This declaration prompted various containment measures including border restrictions, nationwide lockdowns and banning of transportation in or out of different states, provinces and even countries.[14] Similar containment and public health measures were also adopted in China from 20 January 2020, when the Chinese National Health Commission announced Covid-19 a 'Class B infectious disease' requiring a 'Class A-level public health emergency response', which included compiling and keeping data on Covid-19 infections and related deaths.[15] Class B infectious diseases, according to the 1989

---

[6] ibid; Allam, 'Chapter 1: The First 50 Days of Covid-19' (n 4) 3.

[7] This was followed on 26 January 2020 with a nationwide ban on trading wildlife in China. Allam, 'Chapter 1: The First 50 Days of Covid-19' (n 4) 3 and 13.

[8] Allam, 'Chapter 1: The First 50 Days of Covid-19' (n 4) 3.

[9] ibid 3 and 14.

[10] ibid 18.

[11] ibid 4.

[12] Z Allam, 'Chapter 2: The Second 50 Days of Covid-19: A Detailed Chronological Timeline and Extensive Review of Literature Documenting the Pandemic' in Z Allam, *Surveying the Covid-19 Pandemic and its Implications: Urban Health, Data Technology and Political Economy* (London, Elsevier, 2020) 1–39.

[13] World Health Organization, 'WHO Director-General's Statement on IHR Emergency Committee on Novel Coronavirus (2019-nCoV)' (30 January 2020), www.who.int/director-general/speeches/detail/who-director-general-s-statement-on-ihr-emergency-committee-on-novel-coronavirus-(2019-ncov) and www.who.int/news/item/30-01-2020-statement-on-the-second-meeting-of-the-international-health-regulations-(2005)-emergency-committee-regarding-the-outbreak-of-novel-coronavirus-(2019-ncov).

[14] Allam, 'Chapter 2: The Second 50 Days of Covid-19' (n 12) 9.

[15] Announcement by the National Health Commission of the People's Republic of China, 2020 No.1 (中华人民共和国国家卫生健康委员会公告, 2020 年第 1 号) (20 January 2020), https://perma.cc/N9YT-LE8M.

Law on the Prevention and Treatment of Communicable Diseases (中华人民共和国传染病防治法),[16] include severe acute respiratory syndrome (SARS), measles, influenza type A virus (H1N1) and dengue fever, amongst others, while there are only two Class A infectious diseases; the plague and cholera.[17] President Xi Jinping also made a public announcement on the same day, 'declaring that all Chinese Communist Party committees and governments at all levels should take effective measures to address the virus'.[18] With this announcement, Covid-19 became a top national public health priority and all provinces were placed on high alert to implement the most stringent public health emergency responses.[19] Thus, despite different local Covid-19 epidemiological conditions, all the provincial-level governments introduced various public health measures to prevent and contain the spread of the disease,[20] including compulsory mask wearing and advising residents to open windows for ventilation; to maintain indoor circulation and to avoid closed, non-ventilated and crowded places; public events were cancelled;[21] stay-at-home orders issued;[22] and large-scale testing and contact tracing implemented.[23] In terms of containment measures, 14 cities in Hubei Province, including Wuhan city with its approximately 11 million residents,[24] were placed in lockdown by 23 January 2020, with no inbound or outbound travel allowed until further notice, and movement within the cities, although allowed, severely restricted.[25] These were the first known, large-scale

---

[16] Law of the People's Republic of China on Prevention and Treatment of Communicable Diseases (中华人民共和国传 染病防治法) promulgated by the Standing Committee of the National People's Congress on 21 February 1989, revised 29 June 2013, effective 29 June 2013, www.mee.gov.cn/ywgz/fgbz/fl/202002/t20200201_761166.shtml.

[17] Article 3 of the Law of the People's Republic of China on Prevention and Treatment of Communicable Diseases (n 16). X Yu and N Li, 'How did Chinese Government Implement Unconventional Measures Against Covid-19 Pneumonia' (2020) 13 *Risk Management and Healthcare Policy* 491, 492.

[18] DeLisle and Kui, 'Lessons from China's Response to Covid-19' (n 3) 75. Zhou Chuqing (周楚卿), Xi Jinping Dui Xinxing Guanzhuang Bingdu Ganran de Feiyan Yiqing Zuochu Zhongyao Zhishi; Qiangdiao Yaoba Renmin Qunzhong Shengming Anquan He Shenti Jiankang Fangzai Diyiwei; Jianjue Ezhi Yiqing Manyan Shitou; Li Keqiang Zuochu Pishi (习近平对新型冠状病毒感染的肺炎 疫情作出重要指示 强调要把人民群众生命安全和身体健康放在第一位 坚决 遏制疫情蔓延势头 李克强作出批示 [Xi Jinping Issues an Important Instruction on Novel Coronavirus Infectious Pneumonia Epidemic; Emphasis on the People's Lives and Health in the First Place; Resolutely Contain the Epidemic Spread; Li Keqiang Issues Instructions], XINHUA (20 January 2020, 7:27 PM), https://perma.cc/EJP9-SUJS.

[19] Yu and Li, 'Understanding the Beginning of a Pandemic' (n 1) 349; J Liu, 'Health Security and Public Health Emergency Management in China' in Chi Zhang (ed), *Human Security in China – A Post-pandemic State* (London, Palgrave Macmillan, 2022) 175, 188.

[20] F Peng et al, 'Management and Treatment of Covid-19: The Chinese Experience' (2020) 36 *Canadian Journal of Cardiology* 915, 917; Y Zhang et al, 'Chinese Provincial Government Responses to Covid-19' (Working paper BSG-WP-2021/041, June 2021), www.bsg.ox.ac.uk/sites/default/files/2021-06/BSG-WP-2021-041.pdf, 22.

[21] S Chen et al, 'Covid-19 Control in China During Mass Population Movements at New Year' (2020) 395 *The Lancet* 764.

[22] ibid.

[23] ibid; Zhang et al, 'Chinese Provincial Government Responses to Covid-19' (n 20) 4–5.

[24] This lockdown of Wuhan city was only lifted on 8 April 2020. See Wuhan Municipality Novel Coronavirus Infection Pneumonia Epidemic Prevention and Control Command Center, Wuhan Shi Xinxing Guanzhuang Bingdu Ganran de Feiyan Yiqing Fangkong Zhihui Bu Tonggao (Di 1 Hao) (武汉市新型冠状病毒感染的肺炎疫情防控指挥部通告 (第 1 号)) [Notice from the Municipal Novel Coronavirus Infection Pneumonia Epidemic Prevention and Control Command Center (No. 1)], State Council of the PRC (23 January 2020), www.gov.cn/xinwen/2020-01/23/content_5471751.htm. Allam, 'Chapter 2: The Second 50 Days of Covid-19' (n 12) 51.

[25] Some sources reference sixteen cities having been placed in lockdown. Allam, 'Chapter 2: The Second 50 Days of Covid-19' (n 12) 10. Wu and McGoogan, 'Characteristics of and Important Lessons from the Coronavirus Disease' (n 3); DeLisle and Kui, 'Lessons from China's Response to Covid-19' (n 3) 75–76.

local lockdowns for containing the spread of Covid-19, with approximately 41 million people affected for an indefinite period of time.[26] With the impending annual Lunar New Year migration, the Chinese government also extended the Lunar New Year Holiday in some provinces in order for the duration of the holiday to be sufficiently long to fully cover the suspected incubation period of Covid-19.[27] Medical resources were also reallo-cated to address the increasingly critical situation of medical supply shortages which were exacerbated by the fact that most manufacturers and distributors were closed due to the Lunar New Year holidays.[28] To relieve the burden on the healthcare system, some public places such as conference centres and stadiums were converted into Fangcang (方舱医院) shelter hospitals for patients with mild to moderate symptoms, and on 24 January 2020 construction commenced to build two temporary hospitals in less than a fortnight.[29]

Despite these concerted efforts, confirmed Covid-19 cases and Covid-19 related deaths in China continued to rise, and by the end of February 2020, China had reported 72,528 confirmed cases and 1,870 deaths, but with the real number of cases and deaths esti-mated to be much higher, due to the general insufficient testing capacity for Covid-19 which existed at that time and the inherent difficulties in identifying and counting mild and asymptomatic cases.[30] Since February 2020, the Chinese government has adopted a stringent nationwide approach to Covid-19, which has been described as consisting of 'whole offensive and whole defensive tactics'.[31] In terms of 'offensive tactics', the Chinese National Health Commission introduced a hierarchical diagnosis and treat-ment programme for Covid-19, with exclusively designated hospitals and health facilities for this purpose.[32] The Chinese National Health Commission and Chinese Centre for Disease Control and Prevention also compiled the Covid-19 Prevention and Control Plan and the Covid-19 Diagnosis and Treatment Plan to guide the diagnosis and treatment of Covid-19 patients.[33] In terms of medical resources the government accelerated the produc-tion and procurement of medical equipment,[34] and also deployed several technical routes in the research, development, distribution and administering of Covid-19 vaccines.[35] The 'defensive tactics' include detailed, mandatory guidance for the effective implementation

---

[26] By 30 January 2020 it was estimated that approximately 60 million of the Chinese population were under lockdown in different cities. Allam, 'Chapter 2: The Second 50 Days of Covid-19' (n 12) 10 and 14.

[27] Chen et al, 'Covid-19 Control in China During Mass Population Movements at New Year' (n 21).

[28] S Sun et al, 'COVID-19 and Healthcare System in China: Challenges and Progression for a Sustainable Future' (2021) 17 *Globalisation and Health* 1, 3.

[29] Sun et al, 'COVID-19 and Healthcare System in China' (n 28) 4; Allam, 'Chapter 2: The Second 50 Days of Covid-19' (n 12) 11 and 14.

[30] Wu and McGoogan, 'Characteristics of and Important Lessons from the Coronavirus Disease' (n 3); S Neuman, 'China Raises Wuhan Death Stats by Half to Account for Reporting Delays and Omissions' *NPR* (online, 17 April 2020), www.npr.org/sections/coronavirus-live-updates/2020/04/17/836700806/china-raises-wuhan-death-stats-by-half-to-account-for-reporting-delays-and-omiss; Allam, 'Chapter 2: The Second 50 Days of Covid-19' (n 12) 54.

[31] Yu and Li, 'Understanding the Beginning of a Pandemic' (n 1) 350.

[32] ibid; Yu and Li, 'How did Chinese Government Implement Unconventional Measures Against Covid-19 Pneumonia' (n 17) 494.

[33] Yu and Li, 'Understanding the Beginning of a Pandemic' (n 1) 350.

[34] ibid; Yu and Li 'How did Chinese Government Implement Unconventional Measures Against Covid-19 Pneumonia' (n 17) 494.

[35] See Z Huang et al, 'Review on Drug Regulatory Science Promoting Covid-19 Vaccine Development in China' (2022) 10 *Engineering* 127, https://pubmed.ncbi.nlm.nih.gov/35096437/.

of all the typical containment and public health measures for the prevention and control of Covid-19, including detailed mandatory guidance on testing and mask-wearing, and extended areas being placed under lockdown, or made subject to travel restrictions, quarantine or isolation requirements and other conditions.[36]

By 11 March 2020, when the WHO declared Covid-19 a pandemic due to its alarming level of spread and severity,[37] the epicentre of the pandemic had seemingly shifted away from China to Europe, and subsequently also to the rest of the world.[38] By 29 February 2020, the confirmed cases outside China for the first time since the outbreak of Covid-19, surpassed those reported in China,[39] and by February 2022, there were 120,611 confirmed cases and 4,849 Covid-19 deaths. A pragmatic and localised approach is still the order of the day, with provincial, municipal and local governments authorised to adjust their emergency response levels according to the number of local confirmed cases in their area.[40]

II. CONSTITUTIONAL, LEGAL AND POLICY OVERVIEW

The Chinese Communist Party (CCP) has ruled the country since its founding in 1949, and although the Constitution of The People's Republic of China (中华人民共和国宪法)[41] is rather vague about who wields supreme political power, the CPP 'is unequivocally in charge at all levels, and the state merely executes party directives'.[42] A defining feature of the Chinese communist system is therefore its party-state structure, whereby the institutions of the governing political party and the state are intimately intertwined, and the top officials of the governing political party also concurrently hold the most important positions in the government.[43] With the party embedded at every level of government from the centre in Beijing to the grassroots of rural China,[44] it is crucial to understand 'where true power lies, how decisions are made, what role top leaders and key institutions play, and what interaction one can expect between them'.[45]

In terms of health, articles 21 and 45 of the Constitution place a general duty on the state to provide the necessary financing, infrastructure, resources and services, for the advancement, maintenance and provision of the people's health.[46] Up until

---

[36] Allam, 'Chapter 2: The Second 50 Days of Covid-19' (n 12) 21; Zhang et al, 'Chinese Provincial Government Responses to Covid-19' (n 20) 5.

[37] World Health Organization, 'WHO Director-General's Opening Remarks at the Media Briefing on COVID-19' (11 March 2020), www.who.int/director-general/speeches/detail/who-director-general-s-opening-remarks-at-the-media-briefing-on-covid-19---11-march-2020.

[38] Allam, 'Chapter 2: The Second 50 Days of Covid-19' (n 12) 9, 24 and 43.

[39] ibid 24–25.

[40] Peng et al, 'Management and Treatment of Covid-19' (n 20) 927.

[41] Constitution of the People's Republic of China (中华人民共和国宪法) (last amended on 14 March 2004), www.npc.gov.cn/zgrdw/englishnpc/Constitution/2007-11/15/content_1372963.htm.

[42] C Li, *Chinese Politics in the Xi Jinping Era: Reassessing Collective Leadership* (Washington DC, Brookings Institution Press, 2016) 45.

[43] ibid 44–45.

[44] K Lieberthal *Governing China: From Revolution Through Reform* 2nd edn (New York, W.W. Norton & Company Inc., 2004) 77; Li, *Chinese Politics in the Xi Jinping Era* (n 42) 45.

[45] Li, *Chinese Politics in the Xi Jinping Era* (n 42) 67.

[46] See also arts 36 and 42, where reference is made to health in terms of the exercise of other rights and the obligation of the government to provide for and/or safeguard these (and other) rights.

28 December 2019, when the Law of the People's Republic of China on Basic Healthcare and Health Promotion (中华人民共和国基本医疗卫生与健康促进法) was promulgated, there was no comprehensive health law giving effect to these constitutional aspirations with regard to health.[47] And while the Basic Healthcare and Health Promotion Law, which came into effect on 1 June 2020, has been described as a 'de facto constitutional charter for public health, guiding health policy and development in the next decade and beyond', it is generally also accepted that 'the law is unlikely to revolutionise public health in China overnight'.[48] This is mostly due to the wording of many of the law's provisions remaining ambiguous and abstract, rather than providing concrete, practical, and enforceable rules.[49]

The Basic Healthcare and Health Promotion Law, for the first time in Chinese constitutional and legal history, introduced a right to health in article 4: 'The state and society respect and protect citizens' right to health', and defines this right as a concrete entitlement in article 5: 'Citizens shall, in accordance with applicable laws, have the right to receive basic medical and healthcare services from the state and society'. Article 6 places an obligation on every level of government to 'place people's health at the strategic position of priority development', article 15 entitles every citizen access to basic medical and healthcare services free of charge, and article 16 places an obligation on every level of government to, inter alia, improve the level of disease prevention and control. Articles 19 to 21 focus specifically on public health emergencies and infectious disease, mandating the state to establish and improve a health emergency response system, an infectious diseases prevention and control system, as well as an effective vaccination system. However, and as already indicated above, the provisions of this law, although symbolically bold, will ultimately be dependent on the enactment, implementation and enforcement of laws and regulations that give effect to and make operational and enforceable the various rights and obligations it introduced.[50] In fact, '[t]here is little hope for the law to take full effect without momentous modifications in the broader Chinese legal and political systems'.[51] A particular practical difficulty in this regard is the decentralised nature of the Chinese administrative state including its health system, which is an inevitable consequence of China's vast territory, large population, and regional diversity.

The Chinese health system is generally regarded as a 'comparatively weak actor' in China's complex bureaucratic politics, and has been the subject of major and ongoing reforms since its establishment in 1949.[52] Since 2018, the apex health administrative bodies are the National Health Commission of the People's Republic of China

---

[47] The Law of the People's Republic of China on Basic Healthcare and Health Promotion (中华人民共和国基本医疗卫生与健康促进法) adopted by the Standing Committee of the National People's Congress on 28 December 2019, www.npc.gov.cn/englishnpc/c23934/202012/0e545b3ed6544a4fa93a1bb2feb13b3a.shtml. World Health Organization, *People's Republic of China Health System Review* (Geneva, WHO, 2015) 18; E Ip, 'China's New Public Health Constitution: A Cause for Hope?' (2020) 5 *The Lancet* E190.

[48] Ip, 'China's New Public Health Constitution: A Cause for Hope?' (n 47).

[49] ibid.

[50] ibid.

[51] ibid; DeLisle and Kui, 'Lessons from China's Response to Covid-19' (n 3) 69.

[52] World Health Organization, *People's Republic of China Health System Review* (n 47) 16 and 22; Y Wang et al, 'Assessing the Design of China's Complex Health System – Concerns on Equity and Efficiency' (2020) 1 *Health Policy* 1, 2; Q Meng et al, 'What Can We Learn from China's Health System Reform?' (2019) 365 *The British Medical Journal* 1, 1.

(中华人民共和国国家卫生健康委员会)[53] and the National Healthcare Security Administration (国家医疗保障局).[54] The National Health Commission is responsible for implementing and enforcing health policy and laws, while the National Healthcare Security Administration is responsible for the administration and financing of the public health system and medical service delivery.[55] Both the National Health Commission and the National Healthcare Security Administration are part of the State Council (国务院), which can be described as China's Cabinet and constitutes a complex bureaucracy of commissions, central government agencies and ministries.[56] The State Council answers to the National People's Congress (全国人民代表大会) which is the highest organ of state, and as China's legislature, is empowered to, inter alia, enact laws, ratify treaties and amend the Constitution.[57]

This organisational structure and operational features of the central health governance system are replicated across a four-level territorial hierarchy, from the centre in Beijing to all the urban and rural areas of the country, such as its provinces (省),[58] prefectures or municipalities (市), the counties or districts (县) and the townships and villages in rural areas.[59] At the lowest township level, however, there is no independent health commission or security administration; the community or township medical centres are generally under the administration and direction of the county health authorities.[60] While the policies and directives of the central government must be implemented and executed at all levels of this decentralised health hierarchy, the lower levels of government – based on their status in the hierarchy and in terms of the principles and directions established by the central government – also have considerable powers to formulate and implement provincial or local health policies, plans and decisions.[61] This is also recognised in the Basic Healthcare and Health Promotion Law, which provides as follows in article 108: 'A province, autonomous region, municipality, or city with districts and autonomous prefecture may, in light of its actual situation, formulate detailed measures for the development of local medical and healthcare undertakings'. Provincial governments thus play an important role, and are said to operate at a level equal to that of central government ministries in the State Council. The rational for this is 'to allow each province a higher level of discretion within their own jurisdictions when implementing centrally designed policies so that these can be tailored to local health needs and reflect local fiscal capacity'.[62] All these state or government institutions are furthermore intimately

---

[53] The Chinese National Health Commission was previously known as the National Health and Family Planning Commission, and until 2013, as the Ministry of Health. World Health Organization, *People's Republic of China Health System Review* (n 47) 16 and 27.

[54] Wang et al, 'Assessing the Design of China's Complex Health System' (n 52) 2–3.

[55] ibid 2–3.

[56] Lieberthal, *Governing China: From Revolution Through Reform* (n 44) 177. Li, *Chinese Politics in the Xi Jinping Era* (n 42) 65.

[57] Lieberthal, *Governing China: From Revolution Through Reform* (n 44) 176. Li, *Chinese Politics in the Xi Jinping Era* (n 42) 63–64; World Health Organization, *People's Republic of China Health System Review* (n 47) 19.

[58] There are also four municipalities with provincial status: Beijing, Shanghai, Chongqing and Tianjin.

[59] Lieberthal, *Governing China: From Revolution Through Reform* (n 44) 172.

[60] World Health Organization, *People's Republic of China Health System Review* (n 47) 26; Wang et al, 'Assessing the Design of China's Complex Health System' (n 52) 2.

[61] World Health Organization, *People's Republic of China Health System Review* (n 47) 16 and 19.

[62] Wang et al, 'Assessing the Design of China's Complex Health System' (n 52) 6.

intertwined with the institutions of the governing political party, and according to the Chinese party-state governance structure, 'the party structure always exercises ultimate authority over its government counterpart'.[63]

The relevant legislative framework for public health emergencies and infectious diseases, and to which the new Basic Healthcare and Health Promotion Law also applies, was fundamentally revised subsequent to the outbreak of SARS in 2002,[64] and consists of various laws and regulations[65] for the prevention, containment and treatment of infectious diseases, as well as for preventing the spread of infectious diseases into or out of the country. The most important of these include the 1989 Law on the Prevention and Treatment of Communicable Diseases; the 2007 Emergency Response Law (中华人民共和国突发事件应对法);[66] the 1987 Frontier Health and Quarantine Law of the People's Republic of China (中华人民共和国国境卫生检疫法) which focusses on preventing infectious diseases from spreading into or out of the country;[67] and an infectious disease outbreak Direct Reporting System to the China Centre for Disease Control and Prevention, adopted in 2004.[68] This Direct Reporting System is the world's largest internet-based communicable disease reporting system,[69] and requires all the epidemic prevention stations at all the different administrative or territorial levels of government, as well as private health facilities, to directly report infectious diseases as prescribed by law (*i.e.*, notifiable diseases) to the national level.[70]

The Law on the Prevention and Treatment of Communicable Diseases follows a 'top-down' management system and assigns responsibility to the various levels of government, 'for directing the work of prevention of infectious diseases, issuing timely early warnings concerning outbreaks and possible epidemics of infectious diseases, and receiving reports

---

[63] Lieberthal, *Governing China: From Revolution Through Reform* (n 44) 79–81 and 172–73; DeLisle and Kui, 'Lessons from China's Response to Covid-19' (n 3) 108.

[64] Li et al, 'Appraisal of China's Response to the Outbreak of Covid-19 in Comparison with SARS' (n 3); J Bouey, 'Strengthening China's Public Health Response System: From SARS to COVID-19' (2020) 110 *AJPH* 939–40; Y Cao, 'Status and Challenges of Public Health Emergency Management in China related to Covid-19' (2020) 8 *Frontiers in Public Health* 1–6.

[65] For example, the National General Emergency Plan for Public Emergencies, the Regulations on handling Public Health Emergencies, and the Reporting Regulations for Public Health Emergencies and Communicable Disease Surveillance. Lieberthal, *Governing China: From Revolution Through Reform* (n 44) 177. Li, *Chinese Politics in the Xi Jinping Era* (n 42) 65; Liu, 'Health Security and Public Health Emergency Management in China' (n 19) 182.

[66] The Emergency Response Law of the People's Republic of China (中华人民共和国突发事件应对法) promulgated by the Standing Committee of the National People's Congress on 30 August 2007, effective 1 November 2007, www.gov.cn/flfg/2007-08/30/content_732593.htm.

[67] The Frontier Health and Quarantine Law of the People's Republic of China (中华人民共和国国境卫生检疫法) enacted in 1987 and amended in 2007, www.mca.gov.cn/article/zt_gjaqr2021/flfg/202104/20210400033208.shtml.

[68] See the Chinese Center for Disease Control and Prevention, www.chinacdc.cn/en/aboutus/orc_9349/. DeLisle and Kui, 'Lessons from China's Response to Covid-19' (n 3) 70.

[69] Li et al, 'Appraisal of China's Response to the Outbreak of Covid-19 in Comparison with SARS' (n 3) 7; World Health Organization (WHO), *People's Republic of China Health System Review* (n 47) 132.

[70] See also the Report of the State Council on Work on Control and Prevention of Infectious Diseases and Implementation of the Law on Control and Prevention of Infectious Diseases, issued by the National People's Congress on 28 August 2013, https://perma.cc/P77Z-XKT4; World Health Organization, *People's Republic of China Health System Review* (n 47) 132; L Wang et al, 'The Development and Reform of Public Health in China from 1949 to 2019' (2019) 15 *Globalisation and Health* 1, 6; World Health Organization, *People's Republic of China Health System Review* (n 47) 132.

of epidemics'.[71] The provisions of this law empower the various levels of government to mobilise people and resources to address an epidemic and to oversee specialised disease control and prevention institutions at the same level,[72] and also give the various levels of government the authority to

> address infectious disease outbreaks in their [respective] jurisdictions by imposing isolation or quarantine measures (which must be reported to the next-higher-level government), ordering shutdowns of economic and social activities and other emergency measures (with approval from the next-higher-level government), suspending transporting (in order to check the spread of an outbreak), and declaring an 'epidemic area' – thereby authorising an area-wide imposition of the above-described restrictions (again, with the approval of the next-higher-level government).[73]

The Emergency Response Law, in turn, focusses principally on establishing a 'bottom-up' emergency management system that fosters unified leadership, comprehensive coordination, categorised management, graded responsibility and territorial management.[74] This law specifically provides for declaring an emergency based on four levels of severity, and also assigns primary responsibility and sets out the concomitant roles and powers of government institutions and officials at each level of government, and for each of these four levels of emergency severity.[75] Both the Law on the Prevention and Treatment of Communicable Diseases and the Emergency Response Law, as well as the regulations promulgated thereto, include provisions detailing the duties, responsibilities and powers of the National Health Commission and the Chinese Centre of Disease Control, at state level, and also across the territorial levels of government.[76] To this end, Centres for Disease Control, at the state, provincial, prefecture and county level were also introduced in 2006,[77] and in terms of this nationwide network, all provinces (municipalities reporting directly to the government and autonomous regions), prefectures,[78] counties and townships set up their own epidemic prevention stations, each responsible for disease control and surveillance, health inspection, health promotion and scientific research and training in their territory.[79]

---

[71] DeLisle and Kui, 'Lessons from China's Response to Covid-19' (n 3) 80; Liu, 'Health Security and Public Health Emergency Management in China' (n 19) 182.

[72] DeLisle and Kui, 'Lessons from China's Response to Covid-19' (n 3) 80.

[73] ibid.

[74] Li et al, 'Appraisal of China's Response to the Outbreak of Covid-19 in Comparison with SARS' (n 3) 7; Liu, 'Health Security and Public Health Emergency Management in China' (n 19) 182.

[75] See also the Regulations on Responses to Public Health Emergencies (突发公共卫生事件应急条例) promulgated by the State Council on 7 May 2003, revised 8 January 2011, effective 8 January 2011, and the Measures for the Administration of Information Reporting on Monitoring Public Health Emergencies and Epidemics of Infectious Diseases (突发公共卫生事件与 传染病疫情监测信息报告管理办法) promulgated by the Standing Committee of the National People's Congress on 7 November 2003, revised 26 August 2006, effective 26 August 2006. Li et al, 'Appraisal of China's Response to the Outbreak of Covid-19 in Comparison with SARS' (n 3) 2; DeLisle and Kui, 'Lessons from China's Response to Covid-19' (n 3) 79.

[76] DeLisle and Kui, 'Lessons from China's Response to Covid-19' (n 3) 81.

[77] Li et al, 'Appraisal of China's Response to the Outbreak of Covid-19 in Comparison with SARS' (n 3) 7; Sun et al, 'COVID-19 and Healthcare System in China' (n 28) 1.

[78] Prefectures are administrative subdivisions of provincial-level divisions.

[79] Wang et al, 'The Development and Reform of Public Health in China' (n 70) 4.

These distinctive features of the Chinese administrative state not only give context to China's handling of the Covid-19 outbreak and pandemic, but also inform any possible criminal liability government officials may face for their actions or inactions in this regard.[80]

A. Overview of and Specific Constitutional and Legal Principles Regarding Criminal Liability of High-Ranking Government/Public Officials

There are no specific constitutional provisions providing for the liability – criminal or otherwise – of government officials for their actions or inactions in the context of public health emergencies. Government officials are, however, generally subject to the provisions of the criminal law, and may also bear civil liability for official actions that cause damage or injury to the person or property of others. Articles 330 to 337 of the 1979 Criminal Law of the People's Republic of China (中华人民共和国刑法),[81] make specific provision for crimes against public health. Relevant to the discussion here is article 330(5) which criminalises the refusal to implement preventive and control measures proposed by the people's government or the relevant disease prevention and control institution in accordance with the Law on the Prevention and Control of Communicable Diseases. Convicted officials shall be sentenced to fixed-term imprisonment of not more than three years or criminal detention, and if the consequences are serious, to three years but no more than seven years' imprisonment. According to article 332 of the Criminal Law, a violation of the provisions of frontier health and quarantine, causing the spread of a quarantine infectious disease or the serious risk of such spread, is punishable with fixed-term imprisonment of not more than three years or criminal detention and/or a fine. When a health unit or similar institution commit such a crime, it shall be fined and the persons in charge and/or directly responsible for the illegal conduct and consequences shall be punished with fixed-term imprisonment of not more than three years or criminal detention and/or a fine.[82]

Provision is also made for the legal liability of government and medical officials in the legislative framework for public health emergencies and infectious diseases. Articles 65 to 76 of the Law on the Prevention and Treatment of Communicable Diseases stipulate that administrative sanctions may be imposed on a government official or medical personnel if an action or inaction leads to the spread of infectious disease or another serious consequence, and, if a crime is thereby constituted, criminal responsibility may be investigated. A people's government official at a higher level than the government level and/or medical institution in question, may also order corrections, give a warning and/or report a notice of criticism against the government level or medical institution in question. Conduct that may attract legal liability includes concealing or falsely reporting or delaying the report of an epidemic situation of infectious diseases, or failing to organise

---

[80] DeLisle and Kui, 'Lessons from China's Response to Covid-19' (n 3) 68–69.
[81] The Criminal Law of the People's Republic of China (中华人民共和国刑法) enacted in 1979, major revisions in 1997, and most recently amended in 2020, www.lawinfochina.com/display.aspx?id=34470&lib=law.
[82] ibid.

treatment and take timely preventive and control measures etc.[83] Provision is also made for the demotion, dismissal or removal from office those government officials or medical personnel who had failed to execute their duties and responsibilities in terms of the provisions of the act. Medical personnel and institutions may also have their practice certificate, permit or licence, as the case may be, revoked. Article 77 of the Law on the Prevention and Treatment of Communicable Diseases furthermore states that institutions or individuals who have violated the provisions of this law, and whose conduct has led to the spread and epidemic of infectious diseases which caused damage to the person and property of others, shall bear civil liability according to law. Similar provisions can also be found in articles 63 to 68 of the Emergency Response Law, articles 20 to 23 of the Frontier Health and Quarantine Law of the People's Republic of China, as well as in articles 98 to 106 of the newly enacted Basic Healthcare and Health Promotion Law.

In addition to the general criminal and legal liability discussed above, government officials' dereliction of positive duties as functionaries of the state, and specifically during public health emergencies, may also incur criminal liability. See the discussion at Section IV.E below.

B. Scope of Responsibility and Area of Tolerated Risk

The distinctive features of the Chinese administrative state as described above, specifically the party-state structure and the decentralised territorial system of governance, impact fundamentally on government officials' scope of responsibility and area of tolerated risk.[84] This is largely due to the bureaucratic challenges this system of government presents, as well as the fluidity of party and state at all levels of government.

> In times of normal politics, the party-state-society triangle is conductive to crises; but in times of crises, it enables the central government to respond to the crisis efficiently. The party-state-society triangular dictates that state cadres are accountable only to their superior, rather than the public. As the local authority has little motivation to consider public accountability and transparency, over time, the societal system accumulates risks and thereby becomes susceptible to crises of human security, such as outbreaks of infectious diseases. However, the central government is able to respond to crises efficiently, because its monopoly on the state cadre evaluation and the society's freedom of expression allowed it to whip cadres, with reward and punishment, into large, campaign-style mobilisation against public health crises, attribute wrongdoings to local cadres, and manage resources in unnegotiable terms.[85]

In the context of public health emergencies specifically, government officials and even provincial authorities are therefore generally unwilling to release or report information about possible disease outbreaks, because they regard it as politically sensitive and

---

[83] See also Andrew Silver, 'Covid-19: Why China is Sticking to "Zero Tolerance" Public Health Measures' (2021) 375 *The British Medical Journal* 1.

[84] C Zhang, 'Introduction' in C Zhang (ed), *Human Security in China – A Post-pandemic State* (London, Palgrave Macmillan, 2022) 14.

[85] Hai Guo, 'Human Security and the Party-State-Society Triangle: Rethinking the CCP's Legitimacy Management in COVID-19' in Chi Zhang (ed), *Human Security in China – A Post-pandemic State* (London, Palgrave Macmillan, 2022) 50.

believe that 'releasing sensitive health statistics may spark civil unrest or have a negative impact on foreign investment or tourism, all of which reduce a local official's prospects for promotion within the party or civil service'.[86] In China, the government's interest in collective stability and individuals' interests in their own upward career path and position in the party, often dictate how responsibility is exercised and accountability is assigned.[87]

C. Impact of Immunities

Article 4 of the Criminal Law emphasises that everyone is equal before the law, and that no person has any privileges that would allow them to transgress the law.[88] Article 6 further provides that the criminal law applies to all who commit crimes within the territory of China, except as specifically stipulated by law,[89] and provision is also made in article 7 for extra-territorial jurisdiction over government officials and military personnel who commit the crimes specified in the law outside the territory of China. Yet, certain high-ranking government officials enjoy qualified immunity, in that they may not be arrested or prosecuted without the consent of a designated government official or institution.[90] For example, article 74 of the Chinese Constitution provides that no deputy (or member) of the National People's Congress may be arrested or prosecuted without the consent of the Presidium of the current session of the National People's Congress or, when the National People's Congress is not in session, without the consent of the Standing Committee.[91] In terms of party governance, there is also an unspoken norm, since the end of the cultural revolution, of 'Politburo Standing Committee Criminal Immunity' (刑不上 常委), that shield both incumbent and retired Politburo Standing Committee members – including the General Secretary of the Chinese Communist Party who is the highest-ranking official and a standing member and head of the Politburo Standing Committee and President of the People's Republic of China[92] – from criminal investigation and prosecution.[93]

The Central Commission for Disciplinary Inspection of the CCP (中国共产党中央纪律检查委员会) is responsible for the internal discipline of CCP members and answers to the Politburo.[94] Although lower in the hierarchy of the CCP than the Central

---

[86] Liu, 'China's Public Health-care System' (n 64) 533.

[87] See generally Guo, 'Human Security and the Party-State-Society Triangle' (n 85).

[88] See also Article 5 of the Constitution of the People's Republic of China (n 41), which provides no organisation or individual is privileged to be beyond the Constitution or other laws, and Article 33 which states that all citizens are equal before the law.

[89] See also art 16(6) of the Criminal Procedure Law of the People's Republic of China (中华人民共和国刑事诉讼法) adopted on 1 July 1979, with major revisions incorporated on 17 March 1006 and most recently amended on 26 October 2018, www.chinalawtranslate.com/en/criminal-procedure-law-2018/.

[90] See also art 19 of the Criminal Procedure Law of the People's Republic of China (n 89).

[91] Art 75 also provides that deputies to the National People's Congress may not be held legally liable for their speeches or votes at its meetings.

[92] Lieberthal, *Governing China: From Revolution Through Reform* (n 44) 175.

[93] J Che et al, 'The King can do no wrong: On the Criminal Immunity of Leaders' (2019) 170 *Journal of Public Economics* 15, 15; E Smith, 'On the Informal Rules of the Chinese Communist Party' (2021) 248 *The China Quarterly* 141.

[94] Lieberthal, *Governing China: From Revolution Through Reform* (n 44) 177; H Chan and J Gao 'Old wine in new bottles: A county-level case study of anti-corruption reform in the People's Republic of China' (2008) 49 *Crime Law Soc Change* 97.

Committee, the Central Commission for Disciplinary Inspection plays an important role as an anticorruption body; 'monitoring and investigating party officials for abuse of power, corruption, and other wrongdoings – and disciplining them, if necessary'.[95] In recent years, however, and under President Xi Jinping's unprecedented campaign against corruption in leadership, the Central Commission for Disciplinary Inspection has become 'enormously powerful' and the most powerful discipline inspection commission in CCP history.[96] Since 2012, the Central Commission for Disciplinary Inspection has also increasingly referred party members/government officials for criminal prosecution.[97]

D. Prosecutorial Matters

The Supreme People's Procuratorate (最高人民检察院), is the highest prosecutorial organ,[98] and together with the people's procuratorates at the various territorial levels of government, as well as the military procuratorates and other special people's procuratorates, are the state organs responsible for initiating public prosecutions.[99] Part 2 and specifically Article 176 of the 1979 Criminal Procedure Law of the People's Republic of China (中华人民共和国刑事诉讼法), places a duty on people's procuratorates to initiate a prosecution upon discovering – through various sources including reports from victim(s) – clear facts and credible and sufficient evidence of a crime or a criminal suspect within their jurisdiction.[100] A criminal prosecution is not pursued where there are no facts showing the suspects' crime, or under certain circumstances, such as where the statute of limitations on the crime has already passed, or other statutes provide for immunity from criminal prosecution.[101] In reviewing cases for prosecution, the People's Procuratorate must determine:

(1) Whether the facts and circumstances of the crime are clear, whether the evidence is reliable and sufficient, whether the class of crime and the charges are correct;
(2) Whether or not there is any omitted criminal conduct or persons who should be prosecuted for criminal responsibility;
(3) Whether or not it is a case that should not be pursued for criminal responsibility;
(4) Whether there are any attached civil suits;
(5) Whether investigative activities were lawful.[102]

---

[95] Li, *Chinese Politics in the Xi Jinping Era* (n 42) 48.

[96] ibid; G Yong, 'The Evolvement of the Chinese Communist Party Discipline Inspection Commission in the Reform Era' (2012) 12 *China Review* 1.

[97] See, eg S Ma, 'The Dual Nature of Anti-Corruption Agencies in China' (2008) 49 *Crime Law Soc Change* 153 and Che et al, 'The King can do no Wrong' (n 93); J DeLisle, 'Law in the China Model 2.0: Legality, Developmentalism and Leninism under Xi Jinping' (2017) 26 *Journal of Contemporary China* 68.

[98] Art 126 of the Constitution of the People's Republic of China (n 48).

[99] Arts 129 and 130 of the Constitution of the People's Republic of China (n 48); Arts 3, 6 and 8 of the Criminal Procedure Law of the People's Republic of China (n 89).

[100] Arts 109–14 and 169–82 of the Criminal Procedure Law of the People's Republic of China (n 89).

[101] Arts 16 and 177 of the Criminal Procedure Law of the People's Republic of China (n 89).

[102] Art 171 of the Criminal Procedure Law of the People's Republic of China (n 89); Y Mou, *The Construction of Guilt in China – An Empirical Account of Routine Chinese Injustice* (Oxford, Hart/Bloomsbury Publishing, 2020) chs 4 and 5.

Article 131 of the Chinese Constitution provides that the people's procuratorates exercise prosecutorial power independently, in accordance with the provisions of law, and are not subject to interference by any administrative organ, public organisation or individual. However, the Supreme People's Procuratorate is not a truly independent body, and is subject to the authority and supervision of the National People's Congress and its Standing Committee, who also elects, and has the power to remove from office, the Procurator-General as well as the President of the Supreme People's Court.[103] The same also applies to local people's congresses at or above the county level, and with regard to presidents of people's courts and chief procurators of people's procuratorates at the corresponding level.[104] The party-state structure described earlier, therefore also applies to the People's Procuratorate, which has been described as a 'political institution and a legal institution with strong political orientation, [and] whose cardinal principle is the Party's absolute leadership and centralised authority'.[105] Prosecutorial discretion in China therefore 'does not neatly follow the binary sense of being within or outside of what is permitted by the law. Hidden rules are given priority over formal laws. The prosecution criteria are not always applied equally to all suspects'.[106]

Provision is also made for private prosecutions and these must be lodged by the aggrieved or interested parties directly with the relevant people's courts, usually that is with the people's court at the site of the crime.[107]

III. CAUSATION

A. Causation (General Principles)

In China, a crime is conduct (an act or omission) that endangers or causes harm to society.[108] Such conduct must not only be punishable by law,[109] but must be in violation of Chinese laws, including violations of relevant resolutions, decisions, orders, instructions and policies issued by the various organs of state.[110] For criminal liability to be established, the following four elements must be satisfied: there must be a criminal subject – either a

---

[103] Arts 62(7)–(8), 63(4)–(5), 67(6) and (12) and 133 of the Constitution of the People's Republic of China (n 48). Art 3 provides that 'All administrative, judicial and procuratorial organs of the State are created by the people's congresses to which they are responsible and by which they are supervised'.

[104] Arts 101, 104 and 133 of the Constitution of the People's Republic of China (n 48).

[105] Mou, *The Construction of Guilt in China* (n 102) 125.

[106] ibid 167.

[107] Arts 19, 25, 46, 51, 114, 180 and 210–13 of the Criminal Procedure Law of the People's Republic of China (n 89).

[108] JA Cohen, *The Criminal Process in the People's Republic of China 1949–1963: An Introduction* (Cambridge, Harvard University Press, 1968) 328; Criminal Research Group, Law Institute, Chinese Academy of Social Sciences 'Lecture III: The Concept of Crime and Its Characteristics in China's Criminal Law' (1980) 13(2) *Chinese Law and Government* 21, 23–25; W Luo, 'China' in KJ Heller and MD Dubber (eds), *The Handbook of Comparative Criminal Law* (Stanford, Stanford University Press, 2011) 147; Arts 13016 of the Criminal Law of the People's Republic of China (n 81).

[109] J Chen, *Criminal Law and Criminal Procedure Law in the People's Republic of China: Commentary and Legislation* (Leiden, Martinus Nijhoff Publishers, 2013) 27–28; J Chen, *Chinese Law: Context and Transformation* (Leiden, Martinus Nijhoff Publishers, 2008) 280.

[110] Luo, 'China' (n 108) 146; Cohen, *The Criminal Process in the People's Republic of China* (n 108) 329.

natural or legal person – with the necessary capacity to assume criminal responsibility (犯罪主体); there must be a violation of Chinese laws, widely construed (犯罪客体); the criminal conduct must cause harm or pose a social danger (犯罪客观方面); and the criminal subject must have had the necessary *mens rea* (犯罪主观方面).[111]

The social danger posed or harm caused by the criminal conduct is the most essential characteristic of crime in Chinese criminal law, and is also referred to as the objective aspect of crime (犯罪客观方面).[112] Prior to the adoption of the 1979 Criminal Law, the determination

> of fault and causation required a thorough reporting of the relevant circumstances of the crime, an explanation of the apparent motivations of the individuals involved, a complete examination and assessment of all physical injuries and any weapons used, and a clear delineation of the relative status of victims, perpetrators, and other principals.[113]

Under the current provisions of the Criminal Law, the primary objective is still to determine the seriousness of the conduct committed in order to determine the most appropriate punishment, and article 5 directly links the degree of a defendant's alleged offence in terms of its (potential) societal harm and the corresponding punishment, to that defendant's intent.[114] The degree of social danger or harm caused by the alleged criminal conduct is therefore determined by all the objective and subjective circumstances and considerations of the conduct, and what differentiates a non-crime from a crime is a matter of substance rather than form,[115] in that a person who had caused a harmful consequence will not be charged with a crime if that person did not also intend to cause that harmful consequence or was not negligent in causing it.[116] The Criminal Law does not specifically prescribe general rules on causation, but some of its provisions use words and phrases related to causation to describe the relationship between criminal conduct and the social danger posed or harm caused, such as 'causing' (引起), 'leading to' (指使), 'resulting in' (造成) and 'as a result' (因而发生).[117]

Generally, the Chinese government's response to Covid-19 has been much quicker and more comprehensive than its response to SARS.[118] The question *when* exactly Chinese government officials should have reported and taken more concerted action against Covid-19 remains vexed, and it will be difficult to make the case that the response

---

[111] A le Roux-Kemp 'China' in A Reed and M Bohlander (eds.), *Substantive Issues in Criminal Law – Fault – A Research Companion* (Abingdon, Routledge/Taylor and Francis, 2022); Luo, 'China' (n 108) 146–48.

[112] Cohen, *The Criminal Process in the People's Republic of China 1949–1963* (n 108) 328; Criminal Research Group, Law Institute 'Lecture III' (n 108) 23–25.

[113] T Buoye, 'Filial Felons – Leniency and Legal Reasoning in Qing China' in RE Hegel and K Carlitz (eds), *Writing and Law in Late Imperial China* (Washington DC, Washington Press, 2007) 112; D Bodde and C Morris, *Law in Imperial China Exemplified by 190 Ch'ing Dynasty Cases* (Cambridge, Harvard University Press, 1967) 30.

[114] Art 5 can be described as a proportionality principle whereby the degree of punishment must be commensurate with the crime committed and the criminal responsibility born by the offender. C Bricker and M Vitiello, 'Chinese Homicide Law, Irrationality and Incremental Change' (2015) 27 *Temple International and Comparative Law Journal* 43, 44 and 49; I Dobinson, 'The Criminal Law of the People's Republic of China (1997): Real Change or Rhetoric?' (2002) 11 *Pacific Rim Law and Policy Journal* 1, 30–32.

[115] Cohen, *The Criminal Process in the People's Republic of China 1949–1963* (n 108) 332.

[116] Luo, 'China' (n 108) 148.

[117] ibid 153.

[118] Li, 'Appraisal of China's Response to the Outbreak of Covid-19' (n 3) 7.

of government officials in the early outbreak of the disease caused the death of those who subsequently contracted and died from Covid-19.[119] However, and as is evident from the discussion in Sections II.A above and IV.E below, government officials may face legal liability for their actions or inactions having caused the spread and pandemic of Covid-19.

B. Causation and 'Thin Skull' Scenarios

According to article 16 of the Criminal Law, even though conduct results in harmful consequences, if it does not result from intent or negligence, but rather stems from unavoidable or unforeseeable circumstances, it does not constitute a crime. Thus, while a causal link between the conduct and the harmful consequence is generally required, unavoidable or unforeseeable events will break this causal link.[120] The concept of 'unavoidable circumstances' is similar to force majeure, and refers to those instances 'where the occurrence of the harmful consequences was beyond the control of the person involved, no matter how hard that person tried to avoid those circumstances'.[121] Unforeseeable circumstances, in turn, refers to situations where the person not only failed to foresee that their conduct would result in harmful consequences, but where the person was also unable to foresee those consequences at the time of the conduct.[122]

C. Restricting Causality: Policy and Doctrinal Issues

The objective aspect of crime (犯罪客观方面), that is the social danger posed or harm caused by the criminal conduct, has always been the most essential characteristic of an offence and the determination of criminal responsibility in China, to the extent that conduct in which there is an absence of any harm caused generally does not constitute a crime.[123] However, recent amendments to the Chinese Criminal Law, specifically the eighth amendment of 2011, reflect a preventive turn in Chinese criminal justice, with the *actus reus* or criminal conduct becoming less important, and risk control and risk liability – as opposed to harm liability – featuring increasingly in the enactment of various crimes of endangerment.[124] These crimes of endangerment are furthermore focussed on general public well-being, such as road and drug safety and environmental protection, as well as public health, as is also evident with the recent enactment of the Law on Basic Healthcare and Health Promotion. It is suggested that this preventive turn in Chinese

---

[119] DeLisle and Kui, 'Lessons from China's Response to Covid-19' (n 3) 70–71.
[120] Luo, 'China' (n 108) 147.
[121] ibid 149.
[122] ibid.
[123] Cohen, *The Criminal Process in the People's Republic of China 1949–1963* (n 108) 328; Criminal Research Group, Law Institute 'Lecture III' (n 108) 23–25. G MacCormack, 'Issues of Causation in Homicide Decisions of the Qing Board of Punishments from the Eighteenth and Nineteenth Centuries' (2010) 73 *Bulletin of SOAS* 285–319.
[124] See generally Y Ji, *The Making of Chinese Criminal Law – The Preventive Shift in the Context of the Eighth Amendment* (Abingdon, Routledge/Taylor Francis Group, 2021).

criminal justice will continue, and that the focus will continue to shift from punishment of harms to risk prevention, which is particularly important in the context of public health emergencies.[125]

IV. THE STRUCTURE OF HOMICIDE OFFENCES AND ASSAULT/AGGRAVATED ASSAULT/SERIOUS BODILY HARM OFFENCES

A. Murder/Intentional Homicide

Articles 232 and 233 of the Criminal Law respectively provide for the crime of murder or intentional homicide (杀人) and manslaughter (or voluntary manslaughter). For murder – the intentional killing of another person – a defendant shall be sentenced to death, life imprisonment, or fixed-term imprisonment of not less than 10 years. Article 14 of the Criminal Law defines an intentional crime and makes provision for both direct and indirect intent; if the defendant expected the consequences of their conduct and foresaw it as inevitable, the defendant's intent was direct, but if the defendant foresaw the consequences only as a possible consequence of the criminal act, the intent was indirect.[126] Although there is no Chinese term for manslaughter specifically, article 232 makes provision for murder where 'the circumstances are minor', and the defendant may be sentenced to fixed-term imprisonment of not less than three years but not more than 10 years may be imposed. Such minor circumstances include 'righteous and indignant killing ..., heat-of-passion killing, assisted suicides, contract killings, suffocating newborn babies ..., and excessive self-defense'.[127]

B. Culpable Homicide/Manslaughter

Article 233 of the Criminal Law provides for the crime of negligent homicide or involuntary manslaughter (过失杀人), *i.e.*, where there is no intention to kill or cause serious injury. 'Although the Criminal Code does not further divide the category of negligent homicides, Chinese criminal law theory recognises two kinds of negligent homicides: those caused by carelessness and those caused by overconfident negligence'.[128] This is evident from article 15 of the Criminal Law, which defines a negligent crime in terms of the foreseeability of socially dangerous or harmful consequence of conduct, and distinguishes between a defendant who was either careless of his legal duty in this regard, or believed that the dangerous consequences could be avoided.[129] A defendant convicted of negligent homicide shall be sentenced to fixed-term imprisonment of not less than three

---

[125] ibid 2.
[126] L Tao, 'Criminal Law of Communist China' (1966) 52 *Cornell Law Review* 43, 61.
[127] Luo, 'China' (n 108) 165; Bricker and Vitiello, 'Chinese Homicide Law, Irrationality and Incremental Change' (n 114) 49–50.
[128] Luo, 'China' (n 108) 165.
[129] Tao, 'Criminal Law of Communist China' (n 126) 59–60.

years and not more than seven years, and if the circumstances are minor, to fixed-term imprisonment of not more than three years. If the unintentional conduct amounts to gross negligence, however, 'as to amount to willful or depraved indifference to human life', the defendant may be charged with murder rather than negligent homicide.[130] This may be the case where a defendant foresees the possibility (rather than the inevitability) of the occurrence of the criminal consequences, but recklessly assumes that the consequences can be avoided.[131]

C. Offences Related to Actions that Cause Serious Bodily Harm (Assault; Grievous Assault; Assault with Intent to Cause Serious Bodily Harm)

Article 234 of the Criminal Law deals with the intentional injury of the body of another person (assault), for which a defendant shall be sentenced to fixed-term imprisonment of not more than three years, criminal detention or public surveillance. Where serious injury is caused, the defendant shall be sentenced to fixed-term imprisonment of not less than three years but not more than 10 years, and where the conduct causing the serious injury was particularly cruel or caused the death or serious disability of another person, the defendant shall be sentenced to fixed-term imprisonment of not less than 10 years, or life imprisonment or the death penalty will be imposed. Article 234 of the Criminal Law therefore allows prosecutors to charge defendants who otherwise satisfy article 232's elements, with a lesser offence.[132]

D. Offences Regarding Unborn Foetuses; Interrupting the Course of a (Viable) Pregnancy

Since 1979, China has adopted various family planning policies, such as the one-child policy, to control population growth.[133] A rather liberal approach has also been applied with regard to abortion and the termination of pregnancy for family planning or secondary contraception.[134]

> In Chinese thinking, primacy is given to the fact that the birth fundamentally affects the family and the state, and whether it fundamentally affects the person is a less important consideration ... Yet, the fact that the Chinese are not 'pro-choice' does not at all imply that

---

[130] Luo, 'China' (n 108) 166.

[131] ME Badar, *The Concept of Mens Rea in International Criminal Law: The Case for a Unified Approach* (Oxford, Hart Publishing, 2013) 186; HM Wang, 'Chinese and American Criminal Law: Some Comparisons' (1956) 46 *Journal of Criminal Law and Criminology* 796, 818–19, 824.

[132] Bricker and Vitiello, 'Chinese Homicide Law, Irrationality and Incremental Change' (n 114) 51–54.

[133] E Hemminki et al, 'Illegal Births and Legal Abortions – The Case of China' (2005) 2 *Reproductive Health* 1; W Cao, 'The Regulatory Model of Abortion in China through a Feminist Lens' (2013) 29 *Asian Women* 27, 30.

[134] Hemminki et al, 'Illegal Births and Legal Abortions – The Case of China' (n 133) 2; SM Rigdon, 'Abortion Law and Practice in China: An Overview with Comparisons to the United States' (1996) 42 *Social Medicine* 543; J-B Nie, 'Chinese Moral Perspectives on Abortion and Foetal Life: An Historical Account' (2002) 3 *New Zealand Bioethics Journal* 15; Cao, 'The Regulatory Model of Abortion in China' (n 133) 31.

they are 'pro-life'. Both the family and the state understand a birth in purely instrumental terms, as it affects the welfare of the family unit or of the polity. The idea of valuing an unborn life in and of itself, without regard for its social significance, is alien and irrelevant in Chinese social thinking.[135]

Abortion in China is regulated by the 1995 Law on Maternal and Infant Health (中华人民共和国母婴保健法)[136] and the 2002 Law on Population and Family Planning (中华人民共和国人口与计划生育法),[137] read together with the state's population policy.[138] In terms of this legislative framework, there is no set time limit for an abortion to be performed lawfully, there are no penalties for having or performing an abortion at any stage of a pregnancy, and only since 2021 are there prescribed or set statutory grounds for an abortion to be carried out.[139] These are provided for in article 18 of the Law on Maternal and Infant Health, which stipulates that a woman may obtain an abortion if the foetus suffers from serious hereditary diseases, the foetus has serious defects, or due to serious diseases, the continuation of the pregnancy may endanger the life or safety of the pregnant woman or otherwise seriously endanger the health of the woman. The only other legal requirement is that an abortion can only be lawfully performed by registered doctors of gynaecology and obstetrics in public medical institutions or authorised private medical sector units.[140] Likewise, abortion pills may only be prescribed by and used under the supervision of a registered or an associate registered physician in approved healthcare institutions.[141]

E. Failure to Render Assistance

In addition to the general criminal and legal liability of government officials and medical personnel discussed above at Section II.A, government officials' dereliction of their positive duties as functionaries of the state, and specifically during public health emergencies, may also incur criminal liability. For example, article 397 of the Criminal Law states that any functionary of a state organ that abuses their power or neglects their duty, and whose conduct results in loss of public property and/or infringe on the interests of the state and the people, shall be sentenced to fixed-term imprisonment of not more than three years or criminal detention and if the circumstances are especially serious, to fixed-term

---

[135] SH Potter and JM Potter, *China's Peasants: The Anthropology of a Revolution* (New York, Cambridge University Press, 1990) 231.

[136] Law on Maternal and Infant Health (中华人民共和国母婴保健法) adopted on 27 October 1994, amended on 27 August 2009 and 4 November 2017, www.npc.gov.cn/zgrdw/englishnpc/Law/2007-12/12/content_1383796. htm.

[137] Law on Population and Family Planning (中华人民共和国人口与计划生育法) adopted on 29 December 2001, amended on 27 December 2015 and 20 August 2021, https://zh.wikisource.org/wiki/中华人民共和国人口与计划生育法.

[138] Cao, 'The Regulatory Model of Abortion in China' (n 133) 30.

[139] The only exception hereto is a termination of pregnancy for non-medical sex-selection of a foetus, which is illegal. See art 39 of the Law on Population and Family Planning (n 137). Cao, 'The Regulatory Model of Abortion in China' (n 133) 30–31; Rigdon, 'Abortion Law and Practice in China' (n 134) 545.

[140] Art 336 of the Criminal Law of the People's Republic of China (n 81). See also Arts 35 and 36 of the Law on Maternal and Infant Health (n 136).

[141] Cao, 'The Regulatory Model of Abortion in China' (n 134) 32.

imprisonment of not less than three years but not more than seven years. Article 409 of the Criminal Law prescribes fixed-term imprisonment of not more than three years or criminal detention for functionaries of the administrative department of public health engaged in the prevention and treatment of infectious diseases, who are 'seriously irresponsible' and whose conduct results in the spread or epidemic of infectious diseases. If the circumstances are particularly serious, such functionaries shall be sentenced to fixed-term imprisonment of not more than three years or criminal detention.

Although it is generally accepted that much of the Chinese government officials' initial behaviour during this current and ongoing Covid-19 pandemic 'flouted, or at best skirted, a variety of legal requirements'[142] as set out in the public health framework discussed in Section II above, it must also be considered that all of these government officials find themselves 'in an environment of ambiguity born of legal and policy mandates, from multiple sources, that sometimes do not clearly delineate functions and responsibilities',[143] and are furthermore entangled in the *tiao-tiao/kuai-kuai* (条条/块块) of Chinese governance. The pattern of dual rule or *tiao-tiao/kuai-kuai* refers to government officials at the subnational level having to simultaneously answer to two masters:

> 'vertically' to their superiors in a functionally defined, hierarchical bureaucratic structure that reaches up to a ministry in charge of the same field, or a similar central government entity, in Beijing (for which the metaphor is *tiao* – a long, narrow piece); and 'horizontally' to the general-purpose government at the official's own level – provincial, municipal, or still-lower (for which the analogy *kuai* – a lump or block).[144]

When faced with the uncertainty of a possible outbreak of a communicable disease, therefore, government officials are often conflicted in raising alarm immaturely and possibly also unnecessarily, which may attract career-damaging criticism for overreacting, or leaving matters for too late, when the outbreak has become unmanageable and even graver consequences, both in terms of career (and party) aspirations as well as possible criminal liability, may follow.[145] This certainly proved true in the case of Covid-19, when President Xi Jinping, in early February 2020, gave a speech to the Politburo Standing Committee, pointing to shortcomings by local party, government and public health officials in the initial handling of the outbreak in Wuhan, resulting in the dismissal of the party chiefs in Wuhan and Hubei, as well as hundreds of lower-level officials in those jurisdictions and in other Covid-19-hit areas.[146]

---

[142] DeLisle and Kui, 'Lessons from China's Response to Covid-19' (n 3) 88–89.

[143] ibid 102.

[144] DeLisle and Kui, 'Lessons from China's Response to Covid-19' (n 3) 77–78. Liu, 'Health Security and Public Health Emergency Management in China' (n 19). See generally P Schroeder, 'Territorial Actors as Competitors for Power: The Case of Hubei and Wuhan', in Kenneth G Lieberthal and D Lampton (eds), *Bureaucracy, Politics, and Decision Making in Post-Mao China* (Berkeley, University of California Press, 1992) 283–307; K Lieberthal and M Oksenberg, *Policy Making in China: Leaders, Structures, and Processes* (Princeton, Princeton University Press, 1988); A Mertha, 'China's "Soft" Centralisation: Shifting Tiao/Kuai Authority Relations' (2005) 184 *China Quarterly* 791–810.

[145] DeLisle and Kui, 'Lessons from China's Response to Covid-19' (n 3) 83.

[146] Subsequent to the outbreak of SARS in 2002, more than 1,000 government officials, including China's Minister of Health and the mayor of Beijing, were dismissed or penalised for their slow response. DeLisle and Kui, 'Lessons from China's Response to Covid-19' (n 3) 92. Bouey, 'Strengthening China's Public Health Response System' (n 64) 939–40.

V. DEFENCES, JUSTIFICATIONS AND EXCUSES

A. Necessity

China's Criminal Law does not make specific provision for defences and justifications, but some of the Articles in Chapter I entitled 'Crime and Criminal Liabilities' and Chapter II entitled 'Crimes', also deal with possible defences. Article 21 provides for the defence of necessity, or averting imminent harms, and states that no criminal liability shall follow from the conduct of a defendant aimed at protecting the state, public interest, the person, property and other rights of themselves or others from emerging danger.[147] If, however, this conduct for emergency avoidance exceeds the necessary limits and causes undue damage, the defendant shall bear criminal responsibility but the punishment shall be mitigated or exempted. A defendant invoking the necessity defence must satisfy the following four requirements:

1. The protected interest must be threatened by imminent peril. The peril must be real and not simply possible. Therefore, the necessity defense should not be applied to perils that may not happen.
2. The protected interests must be legitimate. To prevent people who hold special positions or are engaged in important professions from putting themselves in situations in which they need to act to avert imminent harm to their personal interests, the Criminal Code provides [in article 21] that such people cannot use necessity as a defense.
3. The action must be the only way to avoid the imminent harm.
4. The action that averts the imminent harm must be appropriate. This means that the damaged interests must be smaller than the protected interest.[148]

Curiously, China's current 'Zero-Covid' strategy or 'whole offensive and whole defensive tactics'[149] as described in Section I above, is generally posited by the Chinese government as absolutely necessary for protecting lives and alleviating the burden on the public healthcare system. Yet, the long-term impact of such strict measures, particularly on society's normal order, including the economy, employment and mental health, place into question the proportionality and reasonableness of such strict measures.

VI. CORPORATE CRIMINAL LIABILITY

A. Overview of Corporate Criminal Liability

When the Criminal Law was first enacted, it did not expressly provide for, nor absolutely exclude, the criminal responsibility of a legal person.[150] The prevailing criminal law theory of that time, however, did not lend much support for corporate criminal liability.[151]

---

[147] Luo, 'China' (n 108) 155.
[148] ibid.
[149] Yu and Li, 'Understanding the Beginning of a Pandemic' (n 1) 350.
[150] Chen, *Criminal Law and Criminal Procedure Law in the People's Republic of China* (n 109) 20.
[151] ibid 21.

With the emergence of economic crimes, however, and especially after China's opening up from approximately 1978 onwards, the legal recognition of corporate criminal liability became a necessity.[152] With the 1997 amendments, provision was consequently made for corporate criminal liability (or unit crimes 单位饭醉, because not all 'units' that can be held criminally liable are corporations) in articles 30 and 31 of the Criminal Law, and companies, enterprises, institutions, state organs or organisations, can now be held liable for acts endangering society when prescribed by law, and will be liable to a fine.[153] Units can only be held criminally liable if it can be proved that

> the crime was committed in the name of the unit (in other words, the criminal acts were decided or carried out by the unit's governing body, leaders, or authorised personnel) or that the illegal gains resulting from the criminal acts were obtained by the unit.[154]

Incorporated public entities, such as companies, will usually be prosecuted as a criminal syndicate and the persons responsible for the company and/or the illegal conduct will be prosecuted for having committed a joint intentional crime.[155]

B. Accessory or Perpetrator

According to article 31 of the Criminal Law, persons directly in charge of or responsible for such companies, enterprises, institutions, state organs or organisations, as the case may be, and which have been found guilty of having committed a crime, may also be prosecuted and held liable in their personal capacity and be punished accordingly.

VII. FORMS OF PARTICIPATION

According to article 25 of the Criminal Law, a joint crime refers to a joint intentional crime committed by two or more defendants. It is furthermore provided that if two or more defendants commit a joint negligent crime, they shall not be punished as a joint crime if they are convicted, but shall rather be punished separately, each according to their own conduct and the crimes they have committed. The differing roles played by different participants to a joint crime therefore has more influence on sentencing than crime labelling.[156] The focus of article 26 of the Criminal Law is on principal offenders in a joint enterprise, which is defined as a relatively fixed criminal organisation composed of more than three persons who jointly commit a crime. Principal offenders of such a joint enterprise constitute a broad category of offenders, and who either organise or lead the joint enterprise or play a major role in the joint crimes, and shall therefore be

---

[152] ibid 21–25.
[153] Chen, *Criminal Law and Criminal Procedure Law in the People's Republic of China* (n 109) 25; Luo, 'China' (n 108) 152.
[154] Luo, 'China' (n 108) 152.
[155] ibid.
[156] B Wang, 'Complicity Liability: English and Chinese Approaches Compared' (2021) 8 *Journal of International and Comparative Law* 175, 178.

punished for all the crimes committed by the joint enterprise.[157] Accomplices, who play a secondary or supplementary role in the joint enterprise, shall, according to article 27, be given lighter or mitigated punishment or be exempted from punishment. Whether an offender is therefore charged as a principal offender or an accomplice will ultimately depend on their specific role in and contribution to the commission of the offence.[158] For example, an 'instigated' offender who had prepared, attempted, or committed the instigated crime, may be held liable and be punished either as the principal offender or as an accomplice.[159] Article 28 provides that defendants who were coerced to participate in a crime shall be mitigated or exempted from punishment according to the specific facts and circumstances of the case. Finally, article 29 of the Criminal Law provides that whoever instigated another to commit a crime, shall be punished in accordance with their role in the joint crime, and whoever instigated a person under the age of 18 to commit a crime, shall be given a heavier punishment. If the defendant, having been instigated, did not commit the crime, that defendant may be given a lighter or mitigated punishment.

The actus reus of complicity crimes in Chinese law includes organising or leading the commission of the target offence, instigation and facilitation, and the mens rea for complicity in Chinese law requires a common intention or common purpose – all the parties should therefore 'have realised that they are acting together, pursuing the same criminal goal'.[160] Despite this common purpose also including subjective recklessness in Chinese law – that is where all the parties foresaw the possibility of the prohibited harm but were indifferent as to its occurrence[161] – it will remain difficult to prove, under Chinese law, complicit liability for Covid-19 related deaths.

VIII. ATTEMPT

The Criminal Law provides for three types of inchoate crimes: in article 22, provision is made for preparation to commit a crime, and refers to defendants who, for the purpose of committing a crime, prepared tools or created conditions in order to commit a crime. Luo explains that preparing tools to commit a crime includes making and acquiring tools, while creating conditions for committing a crime includes:

(1) surveying crime scenes,
(2) planning,
(3) removing obstacles that hinder the commission of a crime,
(4) stalking or approaching victims,
(5) being on the way to commit a crime or luring a victim to a crime scene,
(6) conspiring with others to commit a crime, or
(7) planning to escape after committing a crime or covering up criminal activity.[162]

---

[157] ibid 179.
[158] ibid 181–82.
[159] ibid 182.
[160] ibid 181 and 183–84.
[161] ibid 183.
[162] Luo, 'China' (n 108) 150.

Such defendants shall be given a lighter or mitigated punishment, or may be exempted from punishment depending on the circumstances of the case.[163] Attempt is provided for in article 23, and refers to defendants who attempted to commit a crime, but failed in its execution for reasons other than the will of that defendant. In practice, two possibilities exist: attempt to commit a crime but the conduct is not completed for reasons beyond the control of the defendant, and attempt to commit a crime and while the conduct is completed, the harmful consequences do not transpire for reasons beyond the control of the defendant.[164] Such defendants shall be given a lighter or mitigated punishment (compared to those defendants who had succeeded in the execution of a crime).[165] And article 24 provides for incomplete crimes, specifically where a defendant was in the process of committing a crime, but voluntarily abandoned its execution or effectively prevented its occurrence. If no damage or harm was caused by the incomplete crime, such a defendant shall be exempted from punishment, but if damage or harm was caused, the punishment shall be mitigated.

IX. SANCTIONS, SENTENCING, PUNISHMENT, REPARATIONS AND/OR RESTORATIVE JUSTICE

A. General Sentencing Framework for the Crimes under Discussion

According to article 3 of the Criminal Law, all criminal conduct (an act or omission) is explicitly stipulated in law, together with the prescribed criminal penalties that apply. The degree of punishment is furthermore commensurate with the crime committed and the criminal responsibility of the defendant.[166] See the discussion at Section IV above.

B. Sanctions Specifically for Senior Government/Public Officials

See the discussion at Sections II.A and IV.E above.

C. Corporations and Sentencing

See the discussion at Section VI above.

---

[163] Art 22 of the Criminal Law of the People's Republic of China (n 81).
[164] Luo, 'China' (n 108) 150.
[165] Art 23 of the Criminal Law of the People's Republic of China (n 81).
[166] Art 5 of the Criminal Law of the People's Republic of China (n 108); Luo, 'China' (n 108) 145–46.

11

South Africa

GERHARD KEMP

I. BACKGROUND AND CONTEXTUAL INTRODUCTION

FOLLOWING THE WORLD Health Organization's (WHO) pandemic declaration of 11 March 2020,[1] the South African government declared a national state of disaster, on 15 March 2020. This was done in terms of the Disaster Management Act,[2] which defines a 'disaster' as:

[A] progressive or sudden, widespread or localized, national or human-caused occurrence which causes (i) death, injury or disease (ii) damage to property or the environment; or (iii) disruption of life or a community; is of a magnitude that exceeds the ability of those affected by the disaster to cope with its effects using their own resources.[3]

At the time of this declaration, South Africa was not yet a Covid 'hotspot'. The country would later attain the unfortunate status of not only being a Covid hotspot, but would indeed also lend its name to one of the Covid-19 variants. The B.1.351 ('Beta') variant of the coronavirus was identified after a significant rise in cases in the Eastern Cape metropolitan area of Nelson Mandela Bay. The Beta lineage was sequenced on 15 October 2020. The Beta variant became known as the 'South Africa variant' and was found to be 50 per cent more transmissible or 20 per cent more effective in evading the immune response, compared to the previous variants. It was later also found that some of the first Covid-19 vaccines were less effective against the Beta/South Africa variant, compared to the effectiveness against other variants.[4] The identification of the Beta variant in October 2020 sealed South Africa's status as a Covid hotspot, and by December 2020, 56,000 excess natural deaths were recorded in the country (or, approximately 950 per million population).[5] By September 2021, the number of excess deaths recorded since the onset of the pandemic in South Africa jumped to more than 250,000, and this was even before

---

[1] WHO, 'Director-General's opening remarks at the media briefing on COVID-19' (11 March 2020), www.who.int/director-general/speeches/detail/who-director-general-s-opening-remarks-at-the-media-briefing-on-covid-19---11-march-2020.

[2] Disaster Management Act 57 of 2002 (Disaster Management Act).

[3] Disaster Management Act, s 1.

[4] M Le Page and AM Conlon, 'Beta covid-19 variant (B.1.351)' (*New Scientist*, 8 September 2021), www.newscientist.com/definition/south-african-covid-19-variant/.

[5] H Tegally et al, 'Emergence and rapid spread of a new severe acute respiratory syndrome-related coronavirus 2 (SARS-CoV-2) lineage with multiple spike mutations in South Africa' (2020) *medRxiv* [preprint 21 December 2020], www.medrxiv.org/content/10.1101/2020.12.21.20248640v1.full.pdf.

the identification of the B.1.1.529 ('Omicron') variant of the coronavirus in Southern Africa in November 2021,[6] which also coincided with a sharp rise of Covid-19 cases in the Gauteng province of South Africa.[7]

Not all of the reported excess deaths were Covid-related, but modelling by the University of Cape Town and the South African Medical Research Council (SAMRC) indicate that between 85 per cent and 95 per cent of excess natural deaths in South Africa in the period 2020–21 were related to Covid-19.[8] An in-depth and comprehensive analysis of all the deaths in South Africa during 2020–21 may yet reveal something different, but the SAMRC and scientists at the various medical schools have gained significant experience in modelling and estimates of the causes of excess natural deaths during South Africa's HIV/AIDS epidemic, and it can therefore be assumed that their estimate that Covid-19 was the major contributor to excess natural deaths will be confirmed in years to come. The data that the SAMRC and other scientists rely on come from the Department of Home Affairs, which classifies deaths by natural or unnatural causes. The latter category refers to deaths from suicides, accidents and homicides. Natural causes, then, would be medical causes of death.[9]

Regarding the more than 250,000 excess natural causes deaths between May 2020 and September 2021, a few observations:

About 75 per cent of deaths were of people over the age of 60.

While the impact was felt most severely in the older population, co-factors such as diabetes, hypertension and obesity contributed to Covid-19 related mortality in the younger population.

Scientific modelling suggests that there is a significant undercount of Covid-19 deaths in South Africa (this is based on an analysis of the number of excess deaths estimated compared to the official reporting by the National Department of Health). The Department has released daily numbers of people known to have died from Covid-19.[10] However, these numbers were largely based on deaths in health facilities, thus not taking into account the many deaths in rural areas, private dwellings and places other than government facilities.[11]

It is clear, therefore, that things took a significant turn for the worse since the national disaster declaration in March 2020, when there were only 116 confirmed cases of Covid-19 in South Africa; and most of these cases were individuals with a recent history of international travel (there were a small number of cases that could not be linked to international travel).[12]

[6] E Callaway, 'Heavily mutated Omicron variant puts scientists on alert' (*Nature*, 25 November 2021), www.nature.com/articles/d41586-021-03552-w.

[7] 'Tshwane District Omicron Variant Patient Profile – Early Features' (*South African Medical Research Council*, 23 December 2021), www.samrc.ac.za/news/tshwane-district-omicron-variant-patient-profile-early-features.

[8] For analysis of the weekly death reports, see 'Report on Weekly Deaths in South Africa' (*South African Medical Research Council*, updated weekly), www.samrc.ac.za/reports/report-weekly-deaths-south-africa.

[9] T Moultrie, 'Unpacking South Africa's excess deaths. What is known and where the gaps are' (*The Conversation*, 17 September 2021), https://theconversation.com/unpacking-south-africas-excess-deaths-what-is-known-and-where-the-gaps-are-167920.

[10] Department of Health, 'COVID-19' (updated daily), www.health.gov.za/covid19/.

[11] Moultrie, 'Unpacking South Africa's excess deaths' (n 9).

[12] Department of Health, 'Latest confirmed cases of COVID-19' (18 March 2020), https://sacoronavirus.co.za/2020/03/18/latest-confirmed-cases-of-covid-19-18th-march-2020/.

Despite the relatively low number of confirmed cases of Covid-19 in March 2020, the government of President Cyril Ramaphosa opted for one of the harshest responses to the pandemic, an almost total shutdown of South Africa's economy. Commentators noted that Ramaphosa (and the South African government) were keen to adopt a science-based policy, thus following the same approach adopted by countries like Chile, Germany and France.[13] By taking this route, the government of Ramaphosa clearly differentiated itself from several governments which in March 2020 were still for the most part either very slow to act or in outright denial.[14] But the South African government was not motivated by a superficial or rhetorical adherence to a 'follow-the-science' narrative. The country has had a recent and tragic history of dealing with the HIV/AIDS epidemic,[15] and the spectre of an uncontrolled Covid-19 pandemic engulfing South Africa's already crippled public health facilities, was simply an unbearable prospect. President Ramaphosa justified the harsh lockdown measures that were put in place since March 2020, as follows:

> The national lockdown succeeded in delaying the spread of the virus by more than two months, preventing a sudden and uncontrolled increase in infections in late March. Had South Africans not acted together to prevent this outcome, our health system would have been overwhelmed in every province. This would have resulted in a dramatic loss of life.[16]

The strategy was thus to delay the spread of the virus and to give the healthcare providers (especially in the public sector and in the impoverished and densely populated townships of metropolitan areas) a window to prepare for the expected increase in cases, and to give government an opportunity to build temporary hospitals. There were no easy or good choices; indeed, the choice in the early part of the Covid-19 pandemic as it played out in South Africa, was between a hard lockdown (that would delay the spread of the virus but which would disproportionately affect the poorest and economically most vulnerable part of the population), and the lifting of the lockdown (which would undoubtedly have resulted in an accelerated spread of the virus through the South African population).[17] The government of President Ramaphosa opted for an extension of the lockdown measures.

The declaration of the national state of disaster, in terms of the Disaster Management Act, provided the government with the statutory tools to implement various measures aimed at the management of the Covid-19 pandemic in South Africa. The Act defines 'disaster management' as 'a continuous and integrated multi-sectoral, multi-disciplinary process of planning and implementation of measures aimed at [addressing a disaster]'.[18] To this end, the relevant government minister (in this instance, the Minister of

---

[13] A Tooze, *Shutdown – How Covid Shook the World's Economy* (Dublin, Allen Lane, 2021) 12.

[14] For an account of one such 'populist', or, at best, dithering approach, see J Calvert and G Arbuthnott, *Failures of State – The Inside Story of Britain's Battle with Coronavirus* (London, Mudlark, 2021); see also Chapter 4, 'England'.

[15] As recently as 2019 South Africa has been described as being the 'epicenter of the HIV pandemic as the largest AIDS epidemic in the word'. S Allinder and J Fleischman, 'The World's Largest HIV Epidemic in Crisis: HIV in South Africa' (*Center for Strategic & International Studies*, 2 April 2019), www.csis.org/analysis/worlds-largest-hiv-epidemic-crisis-hiv-south-africa.

[16] M Dayimani, 'Covid-19 lockdown prevented dramatic loss of life, Ramaphosa says as cases pass 500,000' (*News24*, 2 August 2020), www.news24.com/news24/SouthAfrica/News/covid-19-lockdown-prevented-dramatic-loss-of-life-ramaphosa-says-as-cases-pass-500-000-20200802?isapp=true.

[17] C Staunton et al, 'Between a Rock and a Hard Place: COVID-19 and South Africa's Response' (2020) 7 *Journal of Law and the Biosciences* 1.

[18] Disaster Management Act, s 1.

Cooperative Government), 'may make regulations or issue directions or authorize the issue of directions'.[19] The aims, scope and reach of the regulations are informed by South Africa's risk-adjusted strategy for social, cultural, sport and economic activities.[20] There are five risk levels, with the fifth level being associated with high virus spread and low levels of health system readiness. Alert Level 1, at the other end of the spectrum, is associated with low virus spread and high health system readiness.[21] Even though South Africa's Covid-19 cases were relatively low in March 2020 and at the time of President Ramaphosa's announcement that the country was in a national state of disaster, the first lockdown, announced on 27 March 2020, was based on a risk-adjusted assessment at Alert Level 5. The government was clearly very concerned about the spread of the virus and the level of readiness of the health systems to cope with an anticipated wave of Covid-19 cases.

Level 5 restrictions (the 'hard' lockdown) included the prohibition of individuals from leaving their places of residence (certain emergency and essential exceptions applied), prohibition of retail stores from selling non-essential goods, and the closure of most workplaces.[22] International and domestic travel restrictions applied. On 31 March 2020, Level 5 regulations were published, prohibiting all international and domestic passenger flights. Evacuation flights for South African nationals abroad were authorised.[23] Under Level 5 restrictions, no foreign nationals from high-risk countries were allowed to disembark, and crew from high-risk countries were subject to medical screening and had to quarantine for up to 21 days. South African citizens and permanent residents were advised to refrain from all use of air travel, but they were allowed to disembark. Detailed rules applicable to rail, road and maritime travel were also published. Limited international travel was allowed under Alert Levels 1 to 4, but various rules regarding testing, quarantine and isolation applied. Under Alert Level 1, and as from 30 December 2021, international travel to and from South Africa is generally allowed, but a traveller must provide a valid certificate with a negative Covid-19 test outcome. In case of a positive test, the traveller is required to isolate (at their own cost) for 10 days.[24]

Alert Level 5 lasted from 27 March to 30 April 2020. The alert levels were gradually relaxed. Alert Level 1 was announced on 21 September 2020. At the time of writing, South Africa was still at Alert Level 1, but with ever more relaxing rules. For instance, the rules under Alert Level 1 announced on 31 January 2022 provide that those who test positive for coronavirus with no symptoms do not have to isolate; if someone tests positive with symptoms, the isolation period has been reduced from 10 to seven days;

---

[19] Disaster Management Act, s 27(2).

[20] South African Government, 'Regulations and Guidelines – Coronavirus COVID-19' (updated regularly), www.gov.za/covid-19/resources/regulations-and-guidelines-coronavirus-covid-19.

[21] Department of Health, 'COVID-19 Risk Adjusted Strategy' (updated 28 June 2021), https://sacoronavirus. co.za/covid-19-risk-adjusted-strategy/.

[22] ibid Level 5 Regulations.

[23] Regulations issued under the Disaster Management Act, published in Government Gazette 438, 31 March 2020.

[24] For a summary of the travel restrictions and regulations pertaining to the various Alert Levels, see South African Government, 'Travel – Coronavirus COVID-19' (updated regularly), www.gov.za/covid-19/ individuals-and-households/travel-coronavirus-covid-19#5.

and persons who have been in contact with Covid positive individuals no longer have to isolate unless they develop symptoms.[25] It should be noted that by early 2022, and despite South Africa's status as a 'Covid hotspot country',[26] an improvement in the Covid situation was reported.[27] There has also been a relaxing of the Alert Level restrictions, which is not only the result of the various preventative measures imposed by Government, but also because of the (initially rather slow) rollout[28] of Covid-19 vaccines.[29]

A key feature of South Africa's initial lockdown measures is that they did not only entail increased regulation of daily life for most people, but included the criminalisation of conduct that were deemed to be in violation of the stringent lockdown measures. For instance, individuals who left their places of residence for reasons other than to receive urgent medical care, or to purchase essential goods or services, or to attend funerals, were not only in violation of government regulations, but were indeed susceptible to criminal prosecution. Upon conviction, such individuals would be liable to pay a fine or to imprisonment of up to six months, or both.[30] Criminalisation as a strategy to curb the spread of Covid-19 went beyond regulatory offences; notable in this regard is the offence of intentional exposure of another person to Covid-19, in terms of which the accused may be prosecuted for existing common law crimes like murder, attempted murder and assault.[31] These measures also have implications for corporations and other corporate entities (see Section VI below).

II. CONSTITUTIONAL, LEGAL AND POLICY OVERVIEW

South Africa is a constitutional democracy founded on, amongst others, a multi-party system of democratic government, 'to ensure accountability, responsiveness and openness'.[32] An important aspect of accountability is that government is generally required to explain its laws, policies and actions if so demanded, either through the political processes or, where appropriate, the courts.[33] In particular, members of Cabinet

---

[25] South African Government, 'Cabinet approves changes to adjusted Alert Level 1 Covid-19 Regulations' (1 February 2022), www.gov.za/speeches/cabinet-approves-changes-adjusted-alert-level-1-covid-19-regulations-1-feb-2022–0000.

[26] Largely as a result of the detection of first the Beta, and thereafter the Omicron variants of the coronavirus. See Moultrie, 'Unpacking South Africa's excess deaths' (n 9), regarding excess natural causes deaths between May 2020 and September 2021, discussed above.

[27] 'Latest Confirmed Cases of Covid-19 in South Africa' (*National Institute for Communicable Diseases*, 4 February 2022), www.nicd.ac.za/latest-confirmed-cases-of-covid-19-in-south-africa-4-february-2022/.

[28] The first Covid-19 vaccines arrived in South Africa on 16 February 2021. The initial rollout was aimed at health workers (as part of the Sisonke Programme). See further 'Sisonke Study', http://sisonkestudy.samrc.ac.za/indexsisonke.html#[object%20Object].

[29] For daily and cumulative data, see Department of Health, 'Latest Vaccine Statistics', https://sacoronavirus.co.za/latest-vaccine-statistics/.

[30] Level 5 Regulations, reg 11; Level 4 Regulations, regs 14, 31.

[31] Level 4 Regulations, reg 14(3) (29 April 2020).

[32] The Constitution of the Republic of South Africa, 1996 (Constitution), s 1.

[33] *University of the Western Cape v Member of the Executive Committee for Health and Social Services* 1998 (3) SA 124 (C).

are accountable collectively and individually to Parliament.[34] The Constitution further provides that public administration:

> [M]ust be governed by the democratic values and principles enshrined in the Constitution, including people's needs must be responded to, and the public must be encouraged to participate in policy-making. Transparency must be fostered by providing the public with timely, accessible and accurate information.[35]

An important check on power and an element of accountability is the principle of separation of powers. Although it is not explicitly referenced in the Constitution, the text and structure of the Constitution as a whole clearly provide for separation of powers. It provides for legislative authority (vesting at the national level in Parliament and at the provincial level in the provincial legislatures),[36] judicial authority in the courts[37] and the executive authority of the Republic in the President and at the provincial level in the premiers.[38]

It falls beyond the scope of this chapter to consider all the theories concerning the appropriate division of labour and power between the three spheres and as demanded by the Constitution. Suffice to note that the lines are by no means absolute. An evolving constitutional jurisprudence suggests significant scope for a judicial role in what would be regarded as 'policy areas'. An example of this is the Constitutional Court's intervention in the early 2000s, in the midst of the HIV/AIDS epidemic in South Africa, when the court ordered the Government to extend availability of the anti-retroviral drug Nevirapine to hospitals and clinics, to provide counsellors and to take reasonable measures to extend the testing and counselling facilities throughout the public health sector.[39] Nevirapine was offered to the Government for free for a period of five years, and yet, the Government was only willing to introduce it in certain pilot sites, thus denying mothers nationwide the crucial treatment. The order by the Constitutional Court was more than just a constitutional review of existing legislation or government policy; in a sense this was policy-making by the highest court in the land and an encroachment on the traditional domain of the Executive. But it was found to be justifiable action by the Constitutional Court, because the Executive was not performing their constitutional obligations diligently and without delay.[40]

While the government of President Thabo Mbeki in the early 2000s was accused of abdicating its role in the fight against HIV/AIDS, the government of Cyril Ramaphosa took centre stage in response to the unfolding Covid-19 pandemic. Apart from the legislative powers granted to relevant government ministers (notably under the Disaster Management Act), the national and operational strategy to combat the pandemic was directed by the National Covid Command Council (NCCC). The NCCC was created

---

[34] Constitution, s 92(2). For an overview of the composition and powers of the Executive, and of relevant governing principles and constitutional accountability, see H Klug, *The Constitution of South Africa* (Oxford, Hart, 2010) 187–222.

[35] Constitution, ss 195(1)(e)–(g).

[36] Constitution, s 43.

[37] Constitution, s 165.

[38] Constitution, ss 85, 125.

[39] *Minister of Health v Treatment Action Campaign (2)* 2002 (5) SA 721 (CC).

[40] I Currie and J de Waal, *The Bill of Rights Handbook* 6th edn (Cape Town, Juta, 2013) 22.

on 15 March 2020, initially as a cabinet committee that consisted of the President and 19 ministers. On 20 March 2020 the NCCC was expanded to include the entire cabinet. In this sense the entire Executive authority of South Africa became consumed by efforts to curb the spread of the coronavirus.[41] The creation of the NCCC, a structure not provided for in the Constitution, was not uncontroversial. A constitutional challenge of the NCCC directions and regulations was however largely rejected by the Supreme Court of Appeal.[42]

With the focus on the Executive's reaction to the Covid-19 pandemic, some think-tanks and civil society organisations became increasingly concerned that the legislative authority (Parliament) was not active enough – not only in terms of oversight, but also in terms of lack of Covid-19 specific legislation. The question of whether there is a constitutional duty on Parliament to consider Covid-19 specific legislation, came before the high court in Pretoria. The court however rejected the application by a prominent civil society organisation to force Parliament to consider such legislation. The court was of the view that existing legislation (notably the Disaster Management Act) provides for a legislative framework that grounds the Government's response to the Covid-19 pandemic. The constitutional standard is that the state must fulfil its constitutional obligations to protect, fulfil, respect and promote human rights. When Parliament adopted the Disaster Management Act, it also delegated regulation-making powers in terms of that Act to the Executive, a fact that was not challenged by the civil society applicant. The court further noted that the Disaster Management Act provides for a detailed and sophisticated structure to deal with and manage disasters. This structure includes government and executive agencies such as the Inter-Governmental Committee on Disaster Management, a National Disaster Management Advisory Forum, a National Disaster Management Framework and a National Disaster Management Centre. The court rejected the argument that there was a need for specific Covid-19 legislation because the Disaster Management Act already provided the short- and longer-term tools for the Executive to respond to the pandemic.[43]

As noted, the South African Government's response to the pandemic, and particularly the ministerial regulations issued in terms of the Disaster Management Act, were generally considered to be drastic and far-reaching; these included the initial shutdown of South Africa's economy as an immediate measure to delay the spread of the coronavirus. Unsurprisingly, private individuals, families and the business community in general found these measures to be uncomfortable, disruptive and even destructive of their sources of income. A collective of individuals, non-governmental organisations and business associations challenged the constitutionality of various regulations promulgated under the Disaster Management Act. They were initially successful, with the High Court in Pretoria declaring almost all of the regulations to be unconstitutional and invalid. The Government took the matter on appeal. The Supreme Court of Appeal upheld the appeal. Indeed, the Court was quite scathing and noted that the original

---

[41] South African Government, 'President Cyril Ramaphosa meets with political parties to combat Coronavirus COVID-19' (18 March 2020), www.gov.za/speeches/president-cyril-ramaphosa-meets-political-parties-combat-coronavirus-covid-19-18-mar-18-mar.

[42] *Duwayne Esau and Others v Minister of Cooperative Governance and Traditional Affairs* [2021] ZASCA 9 (28 January 2021), www.saflii.org/za/cases/ZASCA/2021/9.html.

[43] *Helen Suzman Foundation v Speaker of the National Assembly* [2020] ZAGPPHC 574 (5 October 2020), www.saflii.org/za/cases/ZAGPPHC/2020/574.html.

application to declare the regulations unconstitutional and invalid had an underlying theme of 'Covid-19 denialism'.[44] The Supreme Court of Appeal was specific in its rejection of the unscientific basis of the applicants' case, and noted that the Government, in contrast to the applicants, 'took advice from medical and scientific experts on the ministerial task team which had been established locally to advise government on its response to the pandemic'.[45] Regarding the impact of the strict Covid-19 regulations, the Supreme Court of Appeal noted that a 'generalised disquiet that the regulations constrain liberty, lack coherence or may have been less restrictively formulated does not suffice to secure a declaration of invalidity'.[46] By upholding the appeal, the Supreme Court of Appeal put down clear markers regarding the role and responsibility of the Executive which is governed by laws such as the Disaster Management Act in its fight against the Covid-19 pandemic. Constitutional and legal challenges to the Government's response would have to satisfy a rather high bar showing irrationality on the side of the Government and individual members of the Executive. Vague, denialist and essentially unscientific attacks on Government policies would certainly not prove executive irrationality.

A. Overview of and Specific Constitutional and Legal Principles Regarding Criminal Liability of High-Ranking Government/Public Officials

South African constitutional and criminal law do not provide for a discrete dispensation for high-ranking government officials. In principle, all persons are equal before the law and there is nothing in the Constitution, in substantive criminal law, or in criminal procedure that would bar a criminal investigation and prosecution of senior government officials, including members of cabinet and the President (see also Section II.C below). In recent history, there have been criminal investigations and prosecutions of a Deputy President (for rape), a Commissioner of Police (for corruption) and a Director-General of the National Intelligence Agency (for fraud).[47] It should be noted that the rape case against (then) Deputy President Zuma was concluded after his suspension from office. He was acquitted on the rape charge[48] and would later become leader of the governing African National Congress and President of the Republic. It was during his time in office that South Africa faced one of its most serious post-apartheid political and constitutional crises. The matter concerned the reinstatement of corruption charges against (then) President Zuma and others allegedly involved in weapons procurement. The saga has a long and complicated history that will not be discussed here, suffice to note the decision by the Supreme Court of Appeal that the earlier discontinuation of criminal charges against Zuma were irrational, thus confirming an order by a lower court that the discontinuation of the criminal charges should be set aside. The practical consequence of the court decision was that charges of racketeering, corruption, money laundering

---

[44] *Minister of Cooperative Governance and Traditional Affairs v De Beer and another* [2021] ZASCA 95 (1 July 2021), www.saflii.org/za/cases/ZASCA/2021/95.html, para 16.
[45] ibid para 20.
[46] ibid para 116.
[47] Klug, *Constitution* (n 34) 220.
[48] *S v Zuma* (8 May 2006) WLD, www.saflii.org/za/cases/ZAGPHC/2006/45.pdf.

and fraud could be reinstated against the sitting president.[49] Jacob Zuma subsequently resigned from office.[50]

B. Scope of Responsibility and Area of Tolerated Risk

There are constitutional and political expectations concerning good governance, and executive and administrative behaviour that deviate from these expectations are generally subject to political and constitutional remedies (notably in parliament through the people's representatives, oversight by constitutional structures, remedies imposed by the courts). Executive and administrative misconduct that amounts to criminal conduct are subject to the criminal laws of the land and there is no separate dispensation for senior government officials (elected or appointed). It is assumed that the prosecution authority will exercise the prosecutorial discretion with due regard to the complexities of policy matters. There are checks on the potential abuse of the criminal process for political purposes (see also Section II.D below), and policy decisions that were made and executed in good faith (even if the results are less than desirable) should generally fall outside the domain of criminal sanction.

C. Impact of Immunities

It is clear from the discussion under Section II.A above that there are no special immunities applicable to the category of high-level government officials (elected or appointed) relevant for this book. Before the entry into force of the Constitution, 1996, the President had certain powers under the Indemnity Act, 1990, the Indemnity Amendment Act, 1992 and the Further Indemnity Act, 1992, in terms of which the President could grant to any person or category of persons either temporary amnesty or immunity or conditional or unconditional permanent indemnity. All of these statutes were repealed by the Promotion of National Unity and Reconciliation Act, 1995. This statute established South Africa's Truth and Reconciliation Commission (TRC) that dealt with gross human rights violations committed during the apartheid period. The work of the TRC ended in 2009.[51] It is politically, constitutionally and legally inconceivable that any of South Africa's transitional justice mechanisms would be revived to deal with potential criminal matters related to government conduct during the Covid-19 pandemic, especially if any such conduct would potentially amount to gross human rights violations and serious crimes like murder and culpable homicide. It should for purposes of this chapter thus be assumed that no immunities will apply and any government official, including the President, could in principle be held criminally liable for Covid-19 related decisions and conduct.

---

[49] *Zuma v Democratic Alliance and Others* [2017] ZASCA 146, www.saflii.org/za/cases/ZASCA/2017/146.html.

[50] 'South Africa's Jacob Zuma resigns after pressure from party' (*BBC*, 15 February 2018), www.bbc.co.uk/news/world-africa-43066443.

[51] For a discussion, see JJ Joubert et al, *Criminal Procedure Handbook* 13th edn (Cape Town, Juta, 2020) 550–51.

D. Prosecutorial Matters

South Africa has one, national prosecution service, the National Prosecuting Authority (NPA), headed by the National Director of Public Prosecutions.[52] There is, strictly speaking, not a total state monopoly on criminal prosecutions, because the law provides for the possibility of private prosecutions in certain circumstances and subject to certain conditions.[53] Private prosecutions can be described as complementary, available only if the state (the NPA) is unwilling to prosecute a prima facie case and if the prospective private prosecutor can show a substantial and peculiar interest in the matter.[54] Private prosecutions on this basis are only available to natural persons (as opposed to juristic persons). Juristic persons (like corporations) can only institute private prosecutions if it is specifically provided for in legislation.[55]

The independence of the NPA is constitutionally guaranteed. While the principle of prosecutorial discretion is a central feature of South Africa's criminal justice system, the exercise of this discretion must always be in terms of the law, in good faith and in the interest of justice. This is especially crucial in the context of high-profile prosecutions involving powerful persons in the public and private sectors. In one such case involving a senior politician, the court noted the following:

> The Constitution guarantees the professional independence of the National Director of Public Prosecutions and every professional member of his staff, with the obvious aim of ensuring their freedom from interference in their functions by the powerful, the well-connected, the rich and the peddlers of political influence.[56]

As the initial discontinuation of the corruption case against former President Zuma has shown, the NPA has not always adhered to the constitutional ideal (see Section II.A above). This has led some commentators to call for the creation of a special branch of the NPA specifically tasked with the prosecution of high-profile or politically sensitive cases.[57] Whether such an innovation may yield the desired results is open for debate. At any rate, as things stand, the current legal framework governing the NPA does not provide for a branch specifically responsible for the prosecution of senior politicians or government officials.

It is important to note that there is no compulsory prosecution in South Africa. In terms of the principle of prosecutorial discretion, there is only a duty to prosecute so-called prima facie cases and if there are no compelling reasons for a refusal to prosecute. A case

---

[52] Constitution, s 179. The National Prosecuting Authority Act 32 of 1998 was passed to give effect to s 179 of the Constitution. The prosecution of children and the legal consequences of diversion are dealt with in the Child Justice Act, 2008. Child justice is not relevant for this chapter and will not be further discussed here.

[53] Criminal Procedure Act, 1977, s 7.

[54] *Phillips v Botha* 1999 (1) SACR 1 (SCA); *Singh v Minister of Justice and Constitutional Development* 2009 (1) SACR 87 (N).

[55] *National Society for the Prevention of Cruelty to Animals v Minister of Justice and Constitutional Development* [2016] ZACC 46 (8 December 2016), www.saflii.org/za/cases/ZACC/2016/46.html.

[56] *S v Yengeni* 2006 (1) SACR 405 (T), para 51.

[57] J Omar, 'How South Africa can stop political interference in who gets prosecuted' (*The Conversation*, 26 June 2017), https://theconversation.com/how-south-africa-can-stop-political-interference-in-who-gets-prosecuted-79442.

will be regarded as prima facie prosecutable when it has reached a certain evidentiary strength. This is, the

> allegations, as supported by statements and real and documentary evidence available to the prosecution, are of such a nature that if proved in a court of law by the prosecution on the basis of admissible evidence, the court should convict.[58]

The NPA's discretion not to prosecute a prima facie case is, of course, open to manipulation and abuse. The NPA can refuse to prosecute even prima facie cases, but this should be done as exceptions, rather than the rule. Factors typically impacting the NPA's decision whether to prosecute prima facie cases include the relative triviality of the offence, the advanced age or very young age of the perpetrator, where a plea agreement was concluded between the prosecutor and the perpetrator and the antiquated nature of the offence.[59]

The NPA's Prosecution Policy – a guiding document issued in terms of the National Prosecuting Authority Act, 1998 – provides for the possibility of a refusal to prosecute a prima facie case where such a refusal would be in the 'public interest'. The Prosecution Policy provides as follows:

> There is no rule in law which states that all the provable cases brought to the attention of the Prosecuting Authority must be prosecuted. On the contrary, any such rule would be too harsh and impose an impossible burden on the prosecutor and on a society interested in the fair administration of justice.

The Prosecution Policy describes several factors that are considered relevant for purposes of determining whether a prosecution or a refusal to prosecute will be in the 'public interest':

The nature and seriousness of the offence:

- The seriousness of the offence, taking into account the effect of the crime on the victim, the manner in which it was committed, the motivation for the act and the relationship between the accused and the victim.
- The nature of the offence, its prevalence and recurrence, and its effect on public order and morale.
- The economic impact of the offence on the community, its threat to people or damage to public property, and its effect on the peace of mind and sense of security of the public.
- The likely outcome in the event of a conviction, having regard to sentencing options available to the court.

The interests of the victim and the broader community:

- The attitude of the victim of the offence towards a prosecution and the potential effects of discontinuing it. Care should be taken when considering this factor, since public interest may demand that certain crimes should be prosecuted – regardless of a complainant's wish not to proceed.
- The need for individual and general deterrence, and the necessity of maintaining public confidence in the criminal justice system.

---

[58] Joubert et al, *Criminal Procedure* (n 51) 76.
[59] ibid 77.

- Prosecution priorities as determined from time to time, the likely length and expense of a trial and whether or not a prosecution would be deemed counter-productive.

The circumstances of the offender:

- The previous convictions of the accused, his or her criminal history, background, culpability and personal circumstances, as well as other mitigating or aggravating factors.
- Whether the accused has admitted guilt, shown repentance, made restitution or expressed a willingness to co-operate with the authorities in the investigation or prosecution of others. (In this regard the degree of culpability of the accused and the extent to which reliable evidence from the said accused is considered necessary to secure a conviction against others, will be crucial.)
- Whether the objectives of criminal justice would be better served by implementing non-criminal alternatives to prosecution, particularly in the case of juvenile offenders and less serious matters.
- Whether there has been an unreasonably long delay between the date when the crime was committed, the date on which the prosecution was instituted and the trial date, taking into account the complexity of the offence and the role of the accused in the delay.[60]

Prosecutorial decisions involving senior political and government officials will by their nature always be difficult, despite the constitutional, legal and policy principles and guidelines described here. The corruption case of former president Zuma put these principles to the test, and was it not for principled court decisions the matter would probably have turned out quite differently – and for the worse. An admission by the NPA in 2019 of political interference regarding decisions not to prosecute apartheid-era crimes despite clear directions by the Truth and Reconciliation Commission underscored the vulnerability of the principle of prosecutorial independence. It was again left to the courts to provide principled guidance for the NPA.[61] Any decision to prosecute senior government officials for Covid-19 related crimes discussed in this chapter would, yet again, put the NPA's independence to the test.

III. CAUSATION

A. Causation (General Principles)

The usual test for factual causation (that is, whether the accused's conduct was the actual or scientific cause of the unlawful consequence) is the *conditio sine qua non* ('but for') test. In the case of a commission (a positive act), the act will be regarded as the cause of a consequence 'if the act cannot be notionally eliminated from the sequence of events, without the consequence also disappearing'.[62] In the case of omission, the court will hypothetically insert the required conduct and if the unlawful consequence no longer

---

[60] Prosecution Policy para 4(c), reproduced in Joubert et al, *Criminal Procedure* (n 51) 77–78.
[61] *Rodrigues v National Director of Public Prosecutions* [2021] ZASCA 87 (21 June 2021), www.saflii.org.za/za/cases/ZASCA/2021/87.html.
[62] J Burchell, *Principles of Criminal Law* 5th edn (Cape Town, Juta, 2016) 98.

appears reasonably likely, it will be an indication of factual causation.[63] The *conditio sine qua non* test works relatively well in simple or less complex scenarios, but it can produce inconclusive and even bizarre results in complex scenarios where multiple potential perpetrators and variables are at play.[64] The *conditio sine qua non* test for factual causation is therefore helpful, but only up to a point. It is left to the courts to apply further causality principles to determine legal causation. This is to say, even a scientific, factual determination that someone (either alone, or with others) had caused something or had contributed to a factual outcome, does not mean that person should be held liable for the consequence(s) in question. The courts have adopted two approaches to determine legal causation. The individualisation approach requires the court to identify the single act (commission or omission) that can be regarded as the most important, direct or proximate cause of the unlawful outcome. The obvious flaw in this approach is the assumption that outcomes can only have one cause; indeed, it boils down to an artificial ranking exercise. The second approach, known as the adequate cause approach or generalisation approach, is based on the richness and nuances of human experience. This approach asks the question: what is the ordinary human expectation or experience of the relationship between certain types of events and certain types of consequences?[65] While the adequate cause approach may be regarded as more realistic and more sophisticated compared to the individualisation approach, there is one more problem to take note of: the impact of an intervening act (*novus actus interveniens*) on the final outcome of the causality enquiry (see Section III.B below).

B. Causation and 'Thin Skull' Scenarios

The Supreme Court of Appeal defined a *novus actus interveniens* as 'an event which is, in the context of the act that was committed, abnormal and completely independent of the acts of the accused'.[66] Evidently, if the intervening event or occurrence was planned, intended or foreseen by the accused, it will not be accepted by the courts as a true *novus actus interveniens*.[67] It is clear, then, that the accused will not be able to hide behind an ostensible intervening event that was a calculated part of the chain of causation which the accused started, and if the eventuality was foreseen by the accused as a possibility and which they desire to employ to obtain the object.[68]

A medical intervention on behalf of the victim, and the inherent risks associated therewith, is not a *novus actus interveniens*. The courts are even willing to accept that medical negligence in the context of a treatment of a victim of crime is not necessarily

---

[63] *S v Van As* 1967 (4) SA 594 (A); G Kemp et al, *Criminal Law in South Africa* 4th edn (Cape Town, Oxford University Press, 2022) 82.

[64] For a critical assessment of the *conditio sine qua non* test for causation, see: CR Snyman, *Criminal Law* (Durban, LexisNexis, 2014) 82.

[65] ibid; Kemp et al, *Criminal Law* (n 63) 85; *R v Loubser* 1953 (2) PH H190 (WPD); *S v Daniels* 1983 (3) SA 275 (A).

[66] *S v Lungile* 1999 (2) SACR 597 (SCA), para 30.

[67] PQR Boberg, *The Law of Delict Volume I: Aquilian Liability* (Cape Town, Juta, 1984) 440.

[68] The Supreme Court of Appeal, in *Ex parte Die Minister van Justisie: In re S v Grotjohn* 1970 (2) SA 355 (A), 364B–C.

a *novus actus interveniens*, provided certain conditions are met, including the relative seriousness of the medical negligence.[69]

In crimes like murder and assault a crucial question is whether the act or actions of the perpetrator caused the death or injury of the victim. A problem in this context is that an act that may cause superficial injury to one person may, due to underlying health issues, cause more significant or even fatal injury to another person. This problem is sometimes referred to as 'thin skull' or 'eggshell skull' scenarios. The general proposition in South African criminal law is that the perpetrator 'must take his victim as he finds him'. Thus, a perpetrator who attacks someone with underlying health problems (for instance, a weak heart) with the intent to only cause minor injury, and where the victim dies because of a heart attack caused by shock for being assaulted, the answer as to causation will be that the underlying health issue is not a *novus actus interveniens*. Causation will thus be established. This is not to say that the perpetrator in this scenario will be guilty of murder, as the other elements of murder (notably *mens rea*) need to be established as well. But a conviction of at least culpable homicide in a scenario such as this is a distinct possibility. From a causation point of view, it is clear that underlying health issues must be taken into account when evaluating the causation question. The courts don't view a pre-existing condition as an intervening act or event.[70]

Apart from underlying health issues (the 'thin skull' scenarios), another issue to consider is the victim's own conduct as a possible intervening act that may impact on the causation question. A rather radical view in this regard holds that any voluntary intervening human conduct must logically and as a matter of principle qualify as a *novus actus interveniens*.[71] According to this view, a victim of an assault who subsequently refused medical treatment will have to live with the consequences and the perpetrator of the initial assault will not be responsible for any deterioration in the victim's health; the victim's own, voluntary refusal to submit to medical treatment will thus constitute a *novus actus interveniens*. South African courts don't always follow this approach, and have settled on a more nuanced (and equitable) view of the impact of a victim's own voluntary conduct. This approach puts the emphasis on the duty of the accused not to have caused the risk in the first place. If it can truly be established that the victim's objectively unreasonable conduct (for instance, the refusal to follow medical advice or treatment)[72] constituted a 'conscious act of another volition', and not merely a response to the situation created by the accused, then the victim's conduct will be regarded as a *novus actus interveniens*.[73]

C. Restricting Causality: Policy and Doctrinal Issues

The discussions under Sections III.A and III.B above make clear that the courts in South Africa have developed principles to restrict or qualify factual causation. The rules pertaining to legal causation, including the principles governing the impact of a *novus actus*

---

[69] *S v Counter* 2000 (2) SACR 241 (T).
[70] *R v Makali* 1950 (1) SA 340 (N).
[71] HLA Hart and T Honoré, *Causation in the Law* (Oxford, Clarendon Press, 1959) 69.
[72] *S v Mokgethi* 1990 (1) SA 32 (A).
[73] *R v De Bruyn* 1953 (4) SA 206 (SWA), 215E.

interveniens on causation, must be viewed holistically, and various policy and normative issues are considered.

IV. THE STRUCTURE OF HOMICIDE OFFENCES AND ASSAULT/AGGRAVATED ASSAULT/SERIOUS BODILY HARM OFFENCES

A. Murder/Intentional Homicide

The common law crime of murder is defined as 'the intentional unlawful killing of another human being'.[74] There are no degrees or special categories of murder (for material purposes), however sentencing law and practice distinguish between certain categories of murder (see also Section IX.A below). In principle, the crime of infanticide (the intentional killing of a newborn child), exists as a separate crime (with its roots in the Roman-Dutch notion of *crimen expositionis infantis*, or the abandoning of a newborn child with the expectation that the child would die). In practice, and given the similar elements, infanticide is simply prosecuted as the crime of murder.[75]

For the crime of murder, the accused must cause the death of another living human being. It is therefore crucial to determine whether the victim was alive at the time of the conduct in question. A living human being is defined as someone who 'has been born alive and who is still alive when the fatal conduct occurs'.[76] The perpetrator is usually a human being, but general principles on corporate criminal liability allow for the prosecution of juristic persons for crimes like murder and attempted murder (see also Section VI.B below).

To prove murder, it must be shown that the killing was unlawful. Only the generally recognised defences (such as self-defence) can render an intentional killing lawful. 'Mercy killings', including assisted suicide and active euthanasia are still unlawful in South Africa.[77] However, passive assisted suicide is viewed differently, with the courts evaluating the lawfulness on a case-by-case basis.[78]

Fault in the form of intent (*dolus*) is required for the crime of murder. Intent is often determined by drawing inferences from the circumstances of the killing.[79] No special form of intent is required. *Dolus eventualis* will also suffice, but this form of intent is not without conceptual complexity and controversy. Although South African criminal law does not recognise 'recklessness' as a distinct form of fault, intent in the form of *dolus eventualis* is often described with reference to an element of recklessness. There is, however, more to *dolus eventualis* than mere reckless behaviour. For the crime of murder, the alleged perpetrator must have subjectively foreseen the possibility of causing the death of the victim, that is, the killing of the deceased or someone in the same position,

---

[74] *S v Ntuli* 1975 (1) SA 429 (A); Burchell, *Principles* (n 62) 577; Kemp et al, *Criminal Law* (n 63) 323. See also G Kemp, 'South Africa', in A Reed and M Bohlander (eds), *Homicide in Criminal Law* (London, Routledge, 2019) 195–215.

[75] Kemp et al, *Criminal Law* (n 63) 325.

[76] Burchell, *Principles* (n 62) 580; Criminal Procedure Act, 1977, s 239(1).

[77] *Minister of Justice v Estate Stransham-Ford* 2017 (3) SA 152 (SCA).

[78] *Minister of Justice v Estate Stransham-Ford*, paras 55–56.

[79] *S v Van Aardt* 2009 (1) SACR 648 (SCA).

class or category and in substantially the same manner as the deceased was in fact killed. This cognitive part is not the end of the *dolus eventualis* analysis. It must also be shown that the alleged perpetrator had accepted the foreseen possibility into the bargain. This is known as the conative part of the analysis.[80]

For a murder charge, negligence, even gross negligence, or recklessness (short of *dolus eventualis*) will not suffice. Constructive liability (where no fault is required for the result) is not recognised in South African homicide law. The Supreme Court of Appeal furthermore abolished the doctrine of *versari in re illicita* (which forms the basis for the English felony-murder rule) in 1965, reasoning that this 'primitive relic from canon law' has no place in South African criminal law; indeed, the principled position, according to the court, is that an accused cannot be punished without fault, or, *actus non facit reum nisi mens sit rea*.[81]

B. Culpable Homicide/Manslaughter

Culpable homicide is the unlawful, negligent causing of the death of another human being.[82] The essential difference between the crimes of murder and culpable homicide resides in the fault element. Negligence is usually described with reference to the objective standard of the 'reasonable person'. An accused person who acted in a certain way, but who ought to have acted differently (that is, different from what society expects from a reasonable person under the circumstances), can be said to have acted negligently.[83] The different fault requirements constitute, in theory at least, a clear border between the two homicide offences, murder and culpable homicide. In practice, the line is sometimes a bit blurry. For instance, reckless behaviour, constituting the first leg of the test for fault in the form of *dolus eventualis*, can come very close to gross negligence, thus making a determination of whether murder or culpable homicide is at stake, quite difficult. Courts don't always get this right, and the precise difference between negligence, gross negligence, conscious negligence ('*luxuria*') and *dolus eventualis* is not always clear or beyond dispute.[84]

C. Offences Related to Actions that Cause Serious Bodily Harm (Assault; Grievous Assault; Assault with Intent to Cause Serious Bodily Harm)

(Common) assault and assault with intent to do grievous bodily harm are crimes at common law. Common assault is the unlawful and intentional application of force to the complainant, or inspiring a belief of imminent use of force against the complainant.[85]

---

[80] Kemp et al, *Criminal Law* (n 63) 227; *S v Ndlanzi* 2014 (2) SACR 256 (SCA).

[81] *S v Bernardus* 1965 (3) SA 287 (A) at 296E–F.

[82] *S v Burger* 1975 (4) SA 877 (A); Burchell, *Principles* (n 62) 584; Kemp et al, *Criminal Law* (n 63) 328.

[83] J Neethling et al, *Law of Delict* 2nd edn (Durban, Butterworths, 1994) 124–26.

[84] See, eg the controversial judgment by the Supreme Court of Appeal in *S v Humphreys* 2013 (2) SACR 1 (SCA). For a critical assessment, see P Carstens, 'Revisiting the relationship between *dolus eventualis* and *luxuria* in context of vehicular collisions causing the death of fellow passengers and/or pedestrians' (2013) 26 *South African Journal of Criminal Justice* 67, https://repository.up.ac.za/bitstream/handle/2263/37009/Carstens_Revisiting_2013.pdf?sequence=2.

[85] Kemp et al, *Criminal Law* (n 63) 334.

Assault with the intention to do grievous bodily harm is the application of force to the complainant with the intention to cause serious bodily harm. There is not an exhaustive list[86] of what type of injuries would qualify as 'serious bodily harm'. Rather, a material test is applied, and the high court has held on occasion that 'it is clear that there must be an intent to do more than inflict the casual and comparatively insignificant and superficial injuries which would ordinarily follow upon assault'. Indeed, there 'must be an intent to injure and to injure in a serious respect'.[87]

D. Offences Regarding Unborn Foetuses; Interrupting the Course of a (Viable) Pregnancy

Women's reproductive rights have seen dramatic changes in post-apartheid South Africa. While abortion was historically largely criminalised under both common law and statutory law, the Choice on Termination of Pregnancy Act, 1996, introduced a progressive and largely decriminalised statutory framework for the regulation of abortion. In essence, termination of pregnancy is a matter of choice, involving the pregnant woman and her medical practitioner. A termination of a pregnancy is the medical or surgical separation and expulsion of the contents of the pregnant uterus.[88] Three different stages of the pregnancy are relevant.

First 12 weeks: the pregnancy can be terminated by a medical practitioner or registered nurse at the request of the pregnant mother.

Weeks 13 to and including the twentieth week: termination of pregnancy is conditional on certain therapeutic, eugenic and humanitarian considerations. The termination must be performed by a medical practitioner.

After the twentieth week: a medical practitioner can only terminate the pregnancy after consultation with other medical experts and when the pregnant person's life is in danger or because the prognosis for the foetus is that it may suffer from 'severe malformation'.

There is no general crime of abortion in South Africa, so the statutory offences concerning the unlawful termination of pregnancy are provided for in the Choice on Termination of Pregnancy Act and relate to the unlawful termination of pregnancies. For instance, a nurse (who is not a registered medical practitioner) who intentionally and unlawfully performs an abortion in the fourteenth week of pregnancy commits a criminal offence. If, however, the nurse in this scenario genuinely believed that the foetus was no longer alive, the fault element will be missing and there will be no criminal liability.[89]

Causing the destruction of a living and viable foetus in situations other than the framework provided for in the Choice on Termination of Pregnancy Act, can constitute

---

[86] The Transkei Penal Code (repealed in 1951) provided a list of injuries that included: emasculation, permanent loss of sight or hearing, privation of any member or joint, loss of the use of a limb or organ, disfiguration of the head or face and fracture or dislocation of a bone.

[87] *S v Mbelu* 1966 (1) PH H176 (N), 178. This approach was confirmed in later cases, see for instance: *S v Dipholo* 1983 (4) SA 757 (T), 760.

[88] Choice on Termination of Pregnancy Act 92 of 1996, s 1.

[89] Kemp et al, *Criminal Law* (n 63) 333.

a crime, but it will be a crime against the life and/or bodily integrity of the pregnant woman (murder, attempted murder, culpable homicide, assault, assault with intent to cause grievous bodily harm). The offence will not be against the foetus. Some commentators argue for the introduction of a statutory offence of feticide in South Africa, but it is left to Parliament to consider this proposal.[90] The courts have thus far declined to develop the common law crimes of murder, attempted murder and culpable homicide to include the intentional or negligent destruction of a living and viable foetus.[91]

Preliminary studies show that pregnant women with Covid-19 are at higher risk of severe disease (compared to women of the same age who are not pregnant). However, the same studies show that the coronavirus rarely crosses from mother to foetus. There is a low risk of damage to the placenta, which can cause injury to the foetus. It appears therefore that Covid-19 is not a big risk from a termination of pregnancy point of view. There is, however, a clear risk for the health of pregnant women.[92]

E. Failure to Render Assistance

While several European penal codes criminalise the failure to render reasonable aid or assistance in cases of danger or peril, South African criminal law, like many comparable Anglo-American jurisdictions, does not provide for a general duty to assist. Unless there exists an explicit statutory duty, the only other basis for a duty to render assistance will be founded on general principles, namely, the legal convictions of the community. South African courts have historically been reluctant to create new legal duties, however, private law (the law of delict) has seen recent developments in this regard, with constitutional theory of state responsibilities vis-à-vis the people it serves influencing the creation of new duties, especially in the area of policing and the duty of the state to provide safe environments.[93] Given the South African Government's firm and early reaction concerning the spread of the coronavirus (see Section I above), it will be hard to imagine what more the Executive could have done to fulfil the basic constitutional responsibility to protect South Africa's population and public healthcare in particular.

V. DEFENCES, JUSTIFICATIONS AND EXCUSES

A. Necessity

The defence of necessity (or compulsion) is applicable in situations where a person faces a choice between two evils and must decide whether they would break the law, or whether

---

[90] GA du Plessis, 'Feticide: Creating a Statutory Crime in South Africa' (2013) *Stellenbosch Law Review* 73.

[91] *S v Mshumpa* 2008 (1) SACR 126. A pregnant woman was seriously assaulted. She was in the 38th week of her pregnancy and medical evidence indicated that the foetus was healthy and viable. The foetus died as a result of the assault on the mother. The judge in this case declined to develop the common law of murder to include the killing of a viable foetus, even if the assault occurred very close to the date of the expected live birth.

[92] N Subbaraman, 'Pregnancy and COVID: what the data say' (*Nature*, 9 March 2021), www.nature.com/articles/d41586-021-00578-y.

[93] For a discussion, see Burchell, *Principles* (n 62) 78–81.

they would suffer the consequences of the alternative.[94] The alternative in this scenario can be the result of human or non-human agency. The latter can come in different forms, including natural disasters or other calamities (such as pandemics). For the defence to be considered, the accused must commit some or other prima facie unlawful positive act (in the case of a prima facie unlawful omission the defence will be known as 'impossibility'). But this act (or omission) must be committed with reference to a threat, danger, disaster or other calamity that satisfies certain requirements, namely:

A legally protected interest must be in danger (this includes life, bodily integrity, and property).

The danger must have commenced or be imminent.

The danger must not have arisen through the accused's own fault (but this requirement is not expressed in absolutist terms).

The accused's response to the perceived threat, emergency or calamity must satisfy two basic requirements:

the response must be reasonable (in essence: the accused must only do what was necessary to avert or mitigate the emergency or calamity and the harm done must in principle not exceed the harm avoided); and

the response must be necessary (there must be a sense that the greater harm would necessarily have followed was it not for the opted response).

Necessity and impossibility are general defences to all crimes, including the homicide offences of murder and culpable homicide. Some commentators question the constitutionality of these defences (at least in their current conceptualisation and application), given the protection of fundamental rights such as the right to life and equality. Indeed, a successful defence of necessity on a charge of murder may suggest that the law regards one life to be more worthy of protection than others.[95] This debate will not be settled here and for present purposes it is assumed that the courts will continue to follow the basic principles as described above.

Consideration of the defence of necessity to the crimes discussed in this chapter is made redundant because of the submission that South Africa's President, the national Executive and other senior government officials' conduct pertaining to the crucial first months of the Covid-19 pandemic do not constitute a basis for the crimes of murder, culpable homicide, assault, assault with intent to cause grievous bodily harm or any of the crimes related to the unlawful termination of pregnancy. The Government of President Ramaphosa faced a difficult choice, but as Adam Tooze noted, 'South Africa was one of the countries with the most reason to fear the pandemic'.[96] This is because of South Africa's large urban population and the country's recent experience of the HIV/AIDS epidemic. Faced with the choice between economic hardship caused by a hard lockdown, or widespread death caused by a fast-spreading coronavirus, the Government opted for a hard lockdown, thus sending the economy into an 8 per cent contraction in 2020.

---

[94] For an overview, see Kemp et al, *Criminal Law* (n 63) 113–19.
[95] ibid 116.
[96] Tooze, *Shutdown* (n 13) 166.

As indicated in Section I above, there were still thousands of excess deaths as a result of Covid-19, but the government did what they reasonably could to avoid more deaths and severe illness, and there certainly was no intent (direct or otherwise) to cause deaths.

VI. CORPORATE CRIMINAL LIABILITY

A. Overview of Corporate Criminal Liability

Juristic persons (such as corporations) can be held criminally liable under South African law. The matter was historically dealt with in terms of common law principles, mainly under influence of English law. At present, corporate criminal liability is dealt with in terms of statutory law.[97] The statutory concept of corporate criminal liability is based on the theory that the directors, members and employees of a corporate entity, when acting in official capacity, are in fact acting as organs of the corporation. The corporation therefore 'acts' and 'thinks' via its human organs. This is not the same as vicarious liability. The statutory concept of corporate criminal liability (closer to the 'identification' or 'directing mind' theories)[98] means that the corporate entity is deemed to have fault because of the notion of corporate *mens rea*, formed in the mind of the corporation (usually via the directors or other senior employees).[99] And, just like human accused persons, corporations are also entitled to fair trial rights.[100] This construction of corporate criminal liability means that corporations can, in theory, be liable for any criminal offence.

For purposes of the focus of this book, it is important to note that corporate criminal liability is governed by general principles and South African criminal law does not provide for discrete corporate homicide offences.[101] The application of the general principles will determine whether the corporation is guilty of the relevant common law or statutory crimes. Historically, corporations have been prosecuted for crimes ranging from theft[102] to culpable homicide[103] to various regulatory offences.

B. Accessory or Perpetrator

It is clear from the discussion under Section VI.A that corporations can be held criminally liable as perpetrators. In the context of criminal liability for death or illness caused by exposure to Covid-19, an application of the general principles of corporate criminal

---

[97] Criminal Procedure Act, 1977, s 332; Kemp et al, *Criminal Law* (n 63) 263.

[98] D Ormerod and K Laird, *Smith, Hogan & Ormerod's Criminal Law* 16th edn (Oxford, Oxford University Press, 2021) 263–65.

[99] Criminal Procedure Act, 1977, s 332(2).

[100] *S v SA Metal & Machinery Co (Pty) Ltd* 2010 (2) SACR 413 (SCA).

[101] For a proposed statutory framework for a discrete statutory crime of corporate homicide, see D Farisani, 'A comparative study of corporate criminal liability – Advancing an argument for the reform of corporate criminal liability in South Africa, by introducing a new offence of corporate homicide' (Unpublished Doctoral Thesis, University of Kwazulu-Natal, 2014), https://researchspace.ukzn.ac.za/bitstream/handle/10413/13913/Farisani_Dorothy_Mmakgwale_2014.pdf?sequence=1&isAllowed=y.

[102] *R v Markins Motors (Pty) Ltd* 1959 (3) SA 508 (AD).

[103] *R v Bennett & Co (Pty) Ltd* 1941 TPD 194.

liability should be able to hold corporations to account for crimes like murder, culpable homicide and assault. The more likely scenario is that corporations might face criminal prosecutions for regulatory offences that govern industry. For instance, businesses (and individual business owners) may face criminal liability under the Occupational Health and Safety Act, 1993, for exposing employees, business partners or members of the public to Covid-19. Furthermore, the Disaster Management Act, 2002, read with the relevant Covid-19 regulations published in April 2020,[104] create a framework for criminal liability of senior management or senior corporate representatives of corporations that expose staff or members of the public to Covid-19. While the focus of these measures is the liability of management, an application of the general principles on corporate criminal liability, as discussed under Section VI.A, could also lead to criminal liability of the corporate entity itself, and not only the human beings that are employed in senior management.

VII. FORMS OF PARTICIPATION

South African criminal law distinguishes between three broad categories of participants in crime, namely: perpetrators, accomplices and accessories after the fact.

Perpetrators, in essence, are those who commit the crime, that is, those who complete all the elements of the crime as defined by law. Perpetrators can commit the crime personally, or can get an agent to commit the crime. Two or more perpetrators can also act in concert and associate together to commit a crime. In the latter instance the participants who act with a common purpose will be regarded as co-perpetrators. The common purpose can be determined with reference to a common plan, a conspiracy or because of active association.[105]

An accomplice is not a perpetrator or co-perpetrator, but associates him/herself with the commission of the crime. This association comes in the form of assistance. There must be a causal connection between the accomplice's assistance and the commission of the crime by the perpetrator. Accomplice liability is thus accessorial in nature.[106]

An accessory after the fact is a participant in crime who intentionally associates him/herself with the crime, but only after its commission is complete (for example by assisting the perpetrator to conceal or dispose of evidence).[107]

Both incitement to commit a crime and criminal conspiracies are criminalised in South African criminal law as incomplete crimes. Incitement, in essence, is to unlawfully communicate to another with the intention of influencing the target audience to commit a crime.[108] Conspiracy to commit a crime is when two or more persons agree to commit a crime, or agree to assist in the commission of a crime.[109]

---

[104] Level 4 Regulations, reg 14 (29 April 2020), issued under the Disaster Management Act, www.gov.za/sites/default/files/gcis_document/202004/43258rg11098gon480s.pdf. See also comments by Z Mohamed, 'Covid-19 Business Criminal Law and Other Issues in South Africa' (*CMS*, 8 June 2021), https://cms.law/en/int/expert-guides/cms-expert-guide-to-covid-19-corporate-crime-regulatory-issues/south-africa.

[105] *S v Thebus* 2003 (2) SACR 319 (CC); Kemp et al, *Criminal Law* (n 63) 283–95.

[106] *S v Williams* 1980 (1) SA 60 (A); see also Burchell, *Principles* (n 62) 505.

[107] Kemp et al, *Criminal Law* (n 63) 300.

[108] *S v Nkosiyana* 1966 (4) SA 655 (A); Riotous Assemblies Act 17 of 1956, s 18(2)(b).

[109] *S v Agliotti* 2011 (2) SACR 437 (GSJ); Riotous Assemblies Act 17 of 1956, s 18(2)(a).

There existed no plan or conspiracy amongst senior government officials in South Africa to cause death or serious illness due to the coronavirus. As noted under Section V.A above, the plan was to *curb* the spread of coronavirus through drastic measures, including a hard economic lockdown.

VIII. ATTEMPT

In principle, an attempt to commit any of the remaining common law crimes (like murder) is punishable as a discrete common law crime, whereas attempts to commit statutory crimes are criminalised as statutory attempts under a law of general application.[110] The general principles on attempts distinguish between completed attempts (the perpetrator has done everything they set out to do but failed to achieve the end result) and incomplete attempts (the perpetrator set out to do the crime but is interrupted by some external agency). The lines can get blurry, but the principle is that mere acts of preparation are normally not punishable; there needs to be a step or actions indicating that the perpetrator has commenced the consummation of the crime.[111] There are no indications that senior government officials individually or collectively attempted to kill fellow human beings or to cause severe illness due to the spread of coronavirus (see also background discussion in Section I, above).

IX. SANCTIONS, SENTENCING, PUNISHMENT, REPARATIONS AND/OR RESTORATIVE JUSTICE

A. General Sentencing Framework for the Crimes under Discussion

South African criminal law is uncodified, and so is sentencing law. The courts have a general sentence discretion (which must be exercised according to general principles, reasonably and judicially),[112] but some statutes provide for minimum or maximum[113] sentences, which obviously qualify or limit the general sentencing discretion. Common law crimes like assault and culpable homicide are still sentenced according to general principles as developed by the courts (lower courts are limited in terms of sentencing jurisdiction; high courts may in principle impose any sentence according to the general principles), but the crime of murder is subject to a minimum sentences framework that was introduced in 1997.[114] The rules on minimum sentences are complex and a detailed discussion falls beyond the scope of this chapter, suffice to note that discretionary minimum sentences apply to the crime of murder, with life imprisonment applicable to

---

[110] Riotous Assemblies Act 17 of 1956, s 18(1).

[111] Kemp et al, *Criminal Law* (n 63) 305.

[112] *S v Pieters* 1987 (3) SA 717 (A); *S v Zinn* 1969 (2) SA 537 (A).

[113] Statutes that provide for statutory offences usually provide for penalty clauses. The specific parameters of the penalty will be determined by statutory interpretation.

[114] Criminal Law Amendment Act 105 of 1997, s 51; Criminal Law (Sentencing) Amendment Act 38 of 2007; *S v Malgas* 2001 (1) SACR 469 (SCA); *S v Dodo* 2001 (1) SACR 594 (CC).

planned or premeditated murder,[115] murder committed by a group of persons executing a common purpose or conspiracy, and in murder cases where the victim was killed for body parts. For other murder cases a different discretionary regime is applicable,[116] with sentences varying from not less than 15 years' imprisonment for a first offender, not less than 20 years for a second offender, and not less than 25 years for a third or subsequent offender.

B. Sanctions Specifically for Senior Government/Public Officials

There is no criminal sentence regime specifically for senior government officials. As discussed under Sections II.A, II.C and II.D, above, senior government officials suspected of criminal conduct are prosecuted, and upon conviction, sanctioned in terms of the criminal laws that apply to everyone.

Apart from possible criminal liability and criminal sanctions, senior government officials are also accountable to the constitutional structures created for democratic and transparent governance. It falls beyond the scope of this chapter to discuss all these measures, suffice to note the importance of Parliament and the committee system, as well as the independent institutions created in terms of chapter 9 of the Constitution, namely: the Public Protector, South African Human Rights Commission, the Commission for the Promotion and Protection of the Rights of Cultural, Religious and Linguistic Communities, the Commission for Gender Equality, the Auditor General and the Electoral Commission.[117]

C. Corporations and Sentencing

It was noted under Section VI above that juristic persons (such as corporations) can be held criminally liable for virtually any crime. It is obvious, however, that juristic persons cannot be sentenced in the same way as human beings. Fines (in terms of the general sentencing discretion of the courts) as well as specific statutory (criminal and regulatory) sanctions are applicable to juristic persons.[118]

---

[115] *S v PM* 2014 (2) SACR 481 (GP).

[116] Criminal Law Amendment Act 105 of 1997, s 51(2).

[117] For a discussion, see Klug, *Constitution* (n 34) 212–16.

[118] Examples of criminal sanctions for corporations can be found in: the Compensation for Occupational Injuries and Diseases Act 130 of 1993, the Companies Act 71 of 2008 and the Financial Intelligence Centre Act 38 of 2001.

12

Spain

ALEJANDRO DE PABLO[1]

I. BACKGROUND AND CONTEXTUAL INTRODUCTION

T HE COVID-19 PANDEMIC has severely affected Spain since its outbreak at the end of February 2020. Since then and after five waves, the official figures speak of 106,341 deaths and 12,326,264 registered cases of infection, as of 27 May 2022.[2] Spain is therefore in eleventh position among the most affected countries by deaths.

On 14 March 2020, amidst painful and worrying data on infection rates and deaths, the Council of Ministers discussed and approved Royal Decree 463/2020 declaring a State of Alarm. Subsequently, the Congress of Deputies agreed six extensions, each of 15 days: on 27 March, 11 April, 25 April, 9 May, 23 May and 6 June.

On 21 June 2020, the State of Alarm ended and a complex process of relaxing the restrictions began, coinciding with the arrival of summer. Greater flexibility was, however, an error that came with a high price tag: both the infection rates and the deaths noticeably increased throughout July and August. It was the second wave of the pandemic. The situation was so critical when the school year and daily work routines began after summer, in September and in October, that a new State of Alarm (although less severe than the earlier ones) was declared on 25 October, which was extended up until 9 November. This last extension, nevertheless, was very controversial and was challenged before the Constitutional Court. The third wave took place after the Christmas holidays of 2020, the worst since the start of the pandemic, both in terms of infection rates and deaths; the fourth wave fell around the Easter holidays (March and April 2021). Finally, the most recent wave, the fifth, continued throughout the months of June, July and August 2021.

[1] This research was completed within the framework of the Investigation Project "Criminal Law addressing health crisis", financed by the Department of Innovation, Universities, Science and Digital Society of the Government of Valencia (GV/2021/103), directed by Professor León Alapont (University of Valencia).

[2] It is possible that these figures are slightly above those from the Ministry of Health, because 'both the National Institute of Statistics (*Instituto Nacional de Estadística*) (INE) and the Daily Mortality Monitoring System (*Sistema de Monitorización de la Mortalidad Diaria*) (MoMo) have estimated that, in general, there were between 43,000 and 44,600 more deaths than were estimated during the first wave in Spain. Among them, around 28,000 corresponded to the official figure for deaths due to Coronavirus from the Ministry of Health'. The data and graphs presented in this paper were drawn from the information that Europa Press presented on the basis of official data from the competent Ministries, see 'La evolución del coronavirus en España, en gráficos' (*EP Data*), www.epdata.es/datos/coronavirus-china-datos-graficos/498.

Each successive wave coincided with both holiday periods and the loosening of restrictive measures approved by public authorities to stimulate tourism and economic activity. The high infection rates within Spain were reflected by the 14-day accumulated incidence rate: between 22 August 2020 and November 2021, Spain was always situated in a high-risk incidence zone (incidence rate over 150 cases for every 100,000 inhabitants) and extreme risk (over 250 cases), with moments of great concern, such as the peak of the fourth wave (900 cases every day) or the peak of the fifth wave, with 700 cases per 100,000 inhabitants.

In economic terms, a conjunction of very negative circumstances (lockdown, the absolute collapse of tourism, entertainment and cultural sectors, together with the closure of firms and a general lack of confidence) meant that in the second quarter of 2020, in full lockdown, Spanish GDP shrunk 21.6 per cent with regard to the same quarter in 2019, representing the sharpest fall in GDP, even more acute than the one registered during the Spanish Civil War, 1936–39. Economic recovery, through the reactivation of the main sectors and the injection of European funding meant that growth of 19.7 per cent GDP was reached in the second quarter of 2021.

Finally, in February 2021 Spain saw the worst unemployment data of the pandemic: over four million people without employment, according to data from the State Public Employment Service, and therefore dependent on the Ministry of Work and Social Economy.[3] Since then, the data have obviously improved, descending to 3.3 million people. Macroeconomic projections for the Spanish economy provided by international organisations (International Monetary Fund, World Bank and the European Commission)[4] are positive, as Spain will continue creating employment and increasing its GDP above most other European Union member states (by approximately 6 per cent throughout 2021 and 2022, as against the projected European average of 4.5 per cent over that same period).

II. CONSTITUTIONAL, LEGAL AND POLICY OVERVIEW

On 14 March 2020, the Government approved Royal Decree 463/2020 declaring the State of Alarm for the management of the health crisis caused by Covid-19, due to reasons of extraordinary and urgent need.[5] Nevertheless, before even the Royal Decree and before the World Health Organization had declared the international emergency due to the pandemic, the Government had adopted some measures: the establishment of a coordinating committee in liaison with the autonomous communities, preparation of rapid-response plans, activation of a supervisory network for periodically informing international organisations. The adoption of a Royal Decree implied the severest and the most extensive restrictions of fundamental rights in the democratic history of Spain

---

[3] Servicio Público de Empleo Estatal, 'Resumen Datos Estadísticos', www.sepe.es/HomeSepe/que-es-el-sepe/estadisticas/datos-avance/paro.html.

[4] European Commission, 'Economic forecast for Spain', https://ec.europa.eu/info/business-economy-euro/economic-performance-and-forecasts/economic-performance-country/spain/economic-forecast-spain_es.

[5] Decreto Real 463/2020, por el que se declara el estado de alarma para la gestión de la situación de crisis sanitaria ocasionada por el COVID-19, www.boe.es/buscar/doc.php?id=BOE-A-2020-3692.

(not even matched by the curfew decreed on the night of 23 February 1981 in the wake of the failed *coup d'état*). The Government asserted that article 4b of Organic Law 4/1981 of 1 June 1981 on the state of alarm, exception and siege authorised it to declare the state of alarm when confronting health crises that implied serious upheaval to normal life.

The core content of the Royal Decree on the state of alarm is formed of what is colloquially called 'lockdown'. Article 7 of the Royal Decree imposed broad limitations on freedom of circulation: people could only circulate on public roadways to carry out the following activities:

> a) Purchase of food, pharmaceutical products and primary needs; b) Assistance at health centers, services and health establishments; c) Travel to the place of work to complete labor, professional duties; d) Return to the normal place of residence; e) Assistance and care of older people, younger people, employees, people with disability and especially vulnerable people; f) Travel to financial entities and insurance companies; g) Due to *force majeure* or overriding need; h) Any other activity of a similar nature that will have to be done individually, except when accompanying people with disability or for any justified reason.

Together with that restriction, others were within the field of education and training (moving all educational levels to online sessions) (article 9), as well as in commercial fields, cultural equipment establishments and recreational activities, catering and restauration (article 10).

The lockdown measures were completed with the imposition of frontier controls by the Police. On 16 March 2020, the Ministry for Home Affairs issued an order which absolutely restricted travel to Spain by any means except for the following people: (1) Spanish citizens and residents of Spain (who wished to return home to spend the subsequent weeks of lockdown there); (2) cross-border workers; (3) and other people with documented accreditation of reasons relating to *force majeure* or a situation of need. There were also other movement restrictions between the Spanish Regions. In this sense, it is important to remember that Spain is a decentralised unitary state. Beneath the Central Government and the General Administration of State, a second tier of public policies are set out at a territorial level: the Autonomous Communities or Regions. Throughout 2021 it was forbidden to travel, except for reasons related to work or health, between different Regions.

The Royal Decree of March 2020 established no specific system of fines for public infringements of the lockdown restrictions and other obligations. As Amoedo-Souto said, the Royal Decree 'turns its back on a specific sanctioning regime'[6] and refers to the ordinary juridical system of fines: 'will be fined in accordance with the provisions of the Law' (article 20). And, on this point, Organic Law 4/2015 on the Protection of Public Security has been the principal sanctioning instrument, which authorises law enforcement bodies to impose fines in a wide range of circumstances, including under the generic 'heading' of disobedience. Thus, the application of sanctions has been linked to the idea of authority and the duty of obedience.[7] This way of proceeding is very problematic,

---

[6] C-A Amoedo-Souto, 'Vigilar y castigar el confinamiento forzoso. Problemas de la potestad sancionadora al servicio del estado de alarma sanitaria' (2020) 86–87 *El Cronista del estado social y democrático de Derecho* 66, 70–73, 77.

[7] G Quineto Olivares, 'Los poderes públicos y la pandemia: cuestiones penales y sancionadoras' (2020) 28 *Teorder* 61.

given that there is no scaling of the most and the least serious obligations foreseen in the Royal Decree. On that basis, the security forces, if disobeyed when reminding members of the public about the lockdown, had broad powers to impose fines on the grounds of disobedience, with little regard for the principles of taxativity and proportionality.

At a higher level of sanctions, failure to observe the lockdown restrictions imposed by article 7 of the Royal Decree could have implied criminal liability. As Bardavío affirmed, the offence of serious disobedience (article 556 Penal Code – *active non-serious resistance and serious passive resistance*) could even have led to custodial detention[8] where law enforcement officers had made a prior request or given an order to an individual who had immediately refused to follow it (*i.e.*, refusal to go home).

On 28 April 2020, the Spanish political party, VOX, challenged the constitutionality of the core set of restrictions on rights and freedoms approved by the Government through the state of alarm. In essence, the appeal hinged on one idea: the Royal Decree had broadly restricted various constitutional rights (above all, freedom of circulation and residency as guaranteed by article 17). Rather than having produced a restriction or limitation of rights, the Royal Decree had suspended all rights for all practical purposes. Against that reality, VOX alleged that the State of Alarm in no way authorised the suspension of constitutional rights of the first title of the Spanish Constitution (SC): article 55.1 SC only permits the suspension of fundamental rights under the states of exception and siege, but not the state of alarm; in addition, article 11 of Organic Law 4/1981 of 1 June 1981 on the state of alarm, exception and siege merely contemplates the possibility of 'limiting free circulation' in situations of a state of alarm, disregarding any mention of its suspension.

In a complex and tense discussion (six votes in favour and five against), the Constitutional Court (CC) concluded by declaring as unconstitutional some central aspects of the Royal Decree, striking a political and juridical blow to the Government during the first and worst months of the pandemic.[9] The majority of the CC understood that the restriction on the liberty of circulation had gone beyond a simple limitation of fundamental rights. The CC stated that the Royal Decree authorised the possibility of circulating 'not as a rule, but as an exception' and that this exception was conditioned by the purpose of the circulation (only possible to carry out certain activities) and by the ('individual') circumstances. And the key here is that: 'a restriction of this right that is, at the same time, general with regard to those affected, and highly intense with regard to its content' goes beyond what is permitted in article 55 SC and the Organic Law on the state of alarm, exception and siege. The CC therefore concluded that the freedom of circulation of Spanish citizens had been violated. According to the CC, the Government should have declared the state of exception through which fundamental rights may be suspended.

---

[8] See C Bardavío Antón, 'Imputación de resultados lesivos y muerte por contagio de covid-19: ¿modificación de la tolerancia del riesgo?' (2020) 144 *La Ley Penal* 4 ff. There have been criminal convictions within this field: Court of First Instance and Instruction no 3 of Gandía, Judgment 75/2020, of 25 March 2020; Court of First Instance and Instruction no 3 of Las Palmas de Gran Canaria, Judgment of 26 March 2020.

[9] Constitutional Court Judgment 110/2021, of 13 May 2020, www.boe.es/buscar/doc.php?id=BOE-A-2021-10023.

VOX not only instituted proceedings against the Royal Decree on the grounds of unconstitutionality, but it also presented a criminal suit against the Government of Spain because of its management of the pandemic. Various associations of lawyers, police, doctors, nurses and, once again, the political party VOX, submitted challenges before the Criminal Chamber of the Supreme Court, accusing the Government and the Ministries of having been party to crimes of, inter alia, negligent manslaughter and negligent bodily harm, committed by omission.[10] The claimants alleged that the Government had failed in its duty to provide due care as the guarantor of public life and the health of Spanish citizens (whence the imprudence), for not having adopted adequate measures (whence the omission) either before the outbreak of the pandemic or during the worst months of the first lockdown, to control the pandemic, to neutralise the focus of danger and to avoid thousands of deaths and injuries (whence the manslaughter and injuries).

These claims were examined by the Public Prosecutor before the Supreme Court, who in an extensive text of over 300 pages dated September 2020 (to which we will refer in this work as the 'Writ of the Public Prosecutor'),[11] requested the dismissal of the case, without admitting any legal action due to a lack of criminal evidence. In a Writ of 18 December 2020, the Criminal Chamber of the Supreme Court acknowledged the report from the Prosecutor's Office and agreed, without accepting any criminal case because: the High Court understood that it was not possible to affirm that deaths and injuries caused by Covid-19 were a consequence of the omissions of public authorities. The 'relation of causality cannot be constructed in diffuse generic terms'; on the contrary, it is necessary to perform an individual analysis that scientifically demonstrates that the infection had its immediate origin in the omissive behaviour of the public authorities. The Supreme Court affirmed that the 'actual state of the medicine cannot let us affirm that causal link between the omission of the Government and the place or the time of an infection, and, above all, to do so in a way that excludes other alternative explanations'.[12] For that reason it referred the cases to specific courts so that they might examine, one by one, the facts that had been reported and analyse whether it might be necessary to seek further criminal evidences.

A. Overview of and Specific Constitutional and Legal Principles Regarding Criminal Liability of High-Ranking Government/Public Officials

The 'competent authority' during the state of alarm was the Government. Under the higher direction of the Presidency of the Government, 'competent delegated authorities' were appointed, in their respective areas of responsibility: the Minister of Defense, the Minister for Home Affairs, the Minister of Transport, Mobility and Urban Agenda and the Minister of Health (article 4).

---

[10] As well as many other offences that we will not examine here, for example administrative prevarication, criminal offences against workers' rights, failure in the duty to provide assistance.

[11] Prosecutor's Office before the Supreme Court, 'Writ of a stay on the special case brought against the Government due to the pandemic', September 2020, https://static.ecestaticos.com/file/064/5b6/65d/0645b665d2 c7a6675ce61d9875b185c1.pdf.

[12] Writ of Supreme Court 11985/2020, Legal Ground no 7.1.2, p 26.

In accordance with article 71 SC, during their term of office, Members of Congress and Senators shall likewise enjoy freedom from arrest and may be arrested only in the event of *flagrante delicto*. They may be neither indicted without prior authorization of their respective legislative House. In criminal proceedings brought against Members of Congress and Senators, the competent court shall be the Criminal Section of the Supreme Court. Article 102 SC, in turn, provides that 'The President and other members of the Government shall be held criminally liable, should the occasion arise, before the Criminal Section of the Supreme Court'.

The joint reading of both implies that the President of the Government and his Ministers (whether or not Deputies) are subject to criminal liability for acts carried out during the exercise of their functions and that criminal liability will be judged before the Supreme Court. The President of the Government and his Ministers will enjoy immunity, a procedural privilege unlike total criminal inviolability (such as the inviolability of the King, according to article 56.3 SC). Parliamentary immunity is a prerogative of the legislative Chambers (not a personal privilege of the Deputies and the Senators), as established by the Constitutional Court, which protects the parliamentarians, so that no cases are brought against them for political ends, inter-party wrangling, which might otherwise affect the normal functioning of the Spanish Parliament.[13] When a case is brought before the Supreme Court against a Minister, a Deputy or a Senator, this organ must first petition the relevant chamber (Congress or Senate), in order to investigate and to judge the matter. It must do so to bypass the procedural barrier of parliamentary immunity: in formal terms, the Chamber receives the 'petition' (to investigate and to judge a parliamentarian). Subsequently, the Chamber (Congress or Senate) has to vote on the decision to withdraw immunity, so that the parliamentarian or senator can stand trial, or has to reject (with reasoned arguments) the petition from the Supreme Court.

B. Scope of Responsibility and Area of Tolerated Risk

Spanish case law and criminal doctrine draw no distinction between different tolerable levels of care or risk in relation to the people that exercise an activity (the subjective viewpoint, one might say), but they do in accordance with the social activity that is at stake (objective viewpoint). In modern society, the permitted level of risk is decided by the utility associated with the activity: the greater the utility, the higher the level of risk that we find acceptable. Therefore, in relation to the question of the possible responsibility of public authorities because of their behaviour in the management of the pandemic, we will ascribe quite a high level of tolerable risk to public authorities as a starting point for discussion and, where necessary, for imputing certain criminal responsibilities, because the decisions of these authorities affect the fields of medicine and public health care that are of great social utility.

Unlike activities such as driving vehicles, the manufacture of dangerous substances, and industrial activities, which are not only affected by criminal norms (above all, administrative law) that regulate the permitted level of tolerable risk, medical and health care

---

[13] Constitutional Court Judgments 90/1985 of 22 July 1985; 206/1992 of 27 November 1992.

lack legal norms on the regulation of risk. It would be impossible to condense scientific advances, which are incessant and very numerous, into legal norms. As the Supreme Court maintained in its Judgment of 3 February 1997, 'guilt or negligence as a result of death or injury within the field of health care presents certain peculiarities ... as the delivery of medical or health care already takes place in dangerous situations',[14] hence the heightened level of tolerable risk. In this context, all that is needed is that the authorities take public-health-related decisions assessing the consensus of specialists and the scientific community. In cases of injury and death caused by Covid-19, the point to be assessed should be whether the public health authorities took risky decisions (authorisation of certain social activities faced with the outbreak of the pandemic, and the imposition of confinement at home, afterwards) based on medical *lex artis* and on the state of scientific knowledge at that time. During the pandemic, the public authorities had no legally guaranteed general duty in criminal law to hold certain medical or health-related knowledge. Instead, their duty of care consisted in taking informed decisions relating to the consensus on scientific knowledge and experience and the available scientific evidence at those critical moments.[15] These points form the thresholds that determine the risk tolerance levels of the public authorities in their decision-making.

C. Impact of Immunities

In cases where a petition is accepted, the investigation and judgment of the criminal case will be the responsibility of the Criminal Section of the Supreme Court. The procedure represents an exception in the Spanish legal system: the matter will not correspond to one court or another according to the place of the possible offence or the type of offence in question. The Supreme Court will assume responsibility based on the individual under investigation. It is a privileged jurisdiction, known in Spain as '*aforamiento*' (parliamentary immunity) that implies being tried exclusively before the Supreme Court. The constitutional provision of article 102 is developed in the Organic Law on Judicial Power (1985), whose article 57.1.2° lays down that 'The Criminal Section of the Supreme Court shall hear: 2.°. The examination and trying of proceedings brought against the President of the Government, ..., Members of the Government, Deputies and Senators ...' (among others).[16]

At this second level, we find similar dispositions on parliamentary immunity in case of eventual crimes. It is commonplace to read in the Autonomous Statutes (basic norms of each Region) that the members of the regional legislative assemblies may not be detained due to alleged criminal acts committed within the Region except in the case of flagrante

---

[14] Supreme Court Judgment 171/1997 of 3 February 1997.

[15] BJ Feijoó-Sánchez, *Homicidio y lesiones imprudentes. Requisitos y límites materiales* (Santiago, Ediciones Olejnik, Chile, 2021) 139–42 and 147–49.

[16] This normative framework explains why the cases to which we will refer later on regarding deaths and injury caused as a consequence of the management of Covid-19 by the Government have been submitted to the Supreme Court, which is the competent judicial organ to judge these suits against the President of the Government and his Ministers.

delicto; and in that case, it is the High Court of Justice of each Region that will decide upon accusation, preventive custody, indictment and trial.

D. Prosecutorial Matters

Cases against serving members of government can be initiated by several procedural parties, following the provisions of the Criminal Procedural Act:

According to article 101, 'Criminal proceedings are public. All Spanish citizens may exercise it in accordance with the requirements of the Law'. It means that anyone who is considered a direct victim of a crime can initiate a criminal case.

Additionally, 'Criminal proceedings may also be initiated by associations of victims and by legal persons who the law recognizes as having legitimacy to defend victims' rights'. These associations would act using de *'actio popularis'*, as recognised in article 270: 'All Spanish citizens, whether or not they are aggrieved by the crime, may file a complaint, exercising the *"actio popularis"* provided for in article 101 of this Law'.

Finally, the Criminal Procedural Act authorizes the intervention of the Public Prosecution. According to article 105, 'the civil servants at the Public Prosecution Service will be under the obligation, in accordance with the provisions of the Law, to initiate all criminal proceedings that they consider appropriate, whether or not there is a private prosecutor in the cases, except for those which the Criminal Code reserves exclusively for private lawsuits' (*e.g.*, cases of defamation).

III. CAUSATION

A. Causation (General Principles)

The first problematic question debated by scholars in relation to the pandemic has been whether the tally of deaths and injuries was a consequence of the omission of health care and supervisory measures that the Government of Spain should have applied, as the ultimate guarantor of the protection of public health. This question leads us to study two central matters of Criminal Law: (1) the relation of causality between an action (or an omission) and a result (natural causality) (Sections III.A and III.B); (2) once that causal link is confirmed, the prohibited result must be imputed to the action (or omission) (juridical causality) (Section III.C). Altogether, we are discussing the theory of objective imputation. This theory is applied to criminal results, such as manslaugher and injuries. Nevertheless, these crimes could have been committed by omission, possibility recognised under article 10 of the Spanish Criminal Code. The mechanism for the imputation of crime by omission is explained in article 11:

> Criminal offences that consist of the production of a result shall only be construed to have been committed by omission when not avoiding the result thereof, by infringing a special legal duty of the offender, is equivalent, pursuant to the sense of the wording of the Law, to its causation. To such end, a deed shall be equivalent to an omission: a) If there is a specific legal or

contractual obligation to act; b) If the party in omission has created an occasion wherein the right protected by law is at risk, by means of a preceding deed or omission.

We must now combine the theory of objective imputation, applicable to crimes of result, with the elements of commission by omission. The Supreme Court has pointed to the requirements to connect the prohibited results to an omission:[17]

(1)   A result foreseen by a norm has occured and it is described in active terms by the Law.

(2)   An action has been omitted and it has a relation of hypothetical causality with the avoidance of that result. Article 11 therefore states 'not avoiding the result thereof ... is equivalent to its causation'.

(3)   The party in omission is classed as the author of the active crime in question (manslaughter or bodily harm), especially if facing a special crime (that can only be committed by specific individuals invested with certain powers, e.g., civil servants, doctors, public authorities). In other words, the role of a guarantor is needed.

(4)   The party in omission would have had capacity to perform the action voluntarily that could have avoided or frustrated the result.

(5)   Omission implies the infringement of a legal duty to act, because of a specific legal or contractual obligation to act or because the party in omission has created an occasion wherein a right protected by law is at risk, as a consequence of a preceding deed or omission. The position of guarantor of the party in omission arises from these sources of the legal duty to act, which can be defined as 'the relation existing between an individual and a legal asset, by virtue of which the former assumes responsibility for the indemnity of the legal asset'.[18]

Some of the requirements mentioned above are decisive in the doctrinal debate surrounding Covid-19 cases. First, the position of guarantor of the Government in the Covid-19 crisis has its sources, in relation to a legal duty to act, in the Royal Decree declaring the state of alarm. Thus, up until the entry into force of the Royal Decree, the Government neither occupied the position of guarantor, nor did it have 'competencies of an executive nature to implement the opportune measures to curtail the pandemic and to protect the life and the integritiy of the possible victims'.[19] Infection levels before that date, as a consequence of participation at crowded events (demonstrations on 8 March and political rallies) were steps towards danger, a consequence of freedom of action and within the 'socially acceptable'.[20] Nevertheless, before even the Royal Decree and before the World Health Organization had declared the international emergency due to the pandemic, the Government had adopted some measures.[21] After the Royal Decree, the Government applied a wide range of measures (lockdown, purchase of sanitary materials, extraordinary contracts for medical staff, as well as very abundant norms in the form of royal decrees of urgent necessity) aimed as far as possible at tackling the health crisis. One can neither talk of omission of due action nor failure in its duty to act: the public authorities

---

[17] Supreme Court Judgments 320/2005 of 10 March 2005; 37/2006 of 25 January 2006; 213/2007 of 15 March 2010; 234/2010; 64/2012 of 27 January 2012; 325/2013 of 2 April 2013; 25/2015 of 3 February 2015.

[18] Supreme Court Judgment 682/2017 of 18 October 2017.

[19] Prosecutor's Office, 'Writ' (n 11), pp 45, 81, 151, 264 and 283.

[20] I Navas Mondaca, 'COVID-19 e imputación objetiva de su contagio' (*Criminal Justice Network*, 9 June 2020), www.criminaljusticenetwork.eu/es/post/covid-19-e-imputacion-objetiva-de-su-contagio.

[21] See s II above.

did take action, they fulfilled their obligation and mitigated the perverse effects of the pandemic as reasonably as possible.

Second, it is important to affirm in relation to Covid-19 cases that the doctrine on causality and crimes of omission states that punishable omission must be equivalent in valuative terms to the action that produces the result. The debate at this point consists of whether the omission of stronger measures by the public authorities could have avoided deaths and injuries or whether that omission was not the cause of the results, because either no further actions could be taken or there were other causes. Omission is reproachable 'because it neither controls nor prevents a pre-existing danger or because it increases a pre-existing one'.[22] It is not enough to point out that the individual with responsibility in the position of the guarantor (here, public authorities) has omitted some behaviour, but it must be a significant omission and of such a broad scope that the results of death and injury have, valuatively, been the consequence of one action (that would have avoided the results). But in Covid-19 cases, it is really unknown, with the state of modern-day science, what more the Government could have done in the month of March to control the risk of viral infection, in a chaotic global context. The Government did what it could and what it had to do, which is why in its role as guarantor it fulfilled its duty to act.

B. Causation and 'Thin Skull' Scenarios

Having affirmed the relation of causality between an action or omission and the result, it is necessary to be more precise, given that there are on occasion relations of apparent causality that are broken because the causal nexus is missing. This question is a decisive one in the cases arising from Covid-19, as it could be debated whether the failure to adopt earlier and subsequent measures at the outbreak of the pandemic caused deaths, injuries and abortions, or, whether there were, on the contrary, other concurrent causes or risks (such as previous illnesses or the precarious state of health of some victims) which broke the relation of causality.

We consider that, in this case, any such causality cannot be verified. As the Procedural Decision of the Supreme Court warned, the 'relation of causality cannot be constructed in diffuse generic terms'.[23] A broad and vague connection is not enough between the omission and the result (*i.e.*, 'all deaths are the responsibility of the Government that never acted'). It is necessary to perform an individual analysis that scientifically demonstrates that the infection had its immediate origin in the omissive behaviour of the public authorities. In other words, it must be proven that, had the omitted action been executed, harmful and mortal results could have been avoided, but there is no such evidence. The Supreme Court affirmed that the 'current state of medicine cannot let us affirm that causal link between the omission of the Government and the place or the time of an infection, and, above all, cannot do so in a way that excludes other alternative explanations'.[24]

---

[22] Supreme Court Judgment 1058/2010 of 13 December 2010.
[23] Supreme Court, 'Writ' (n 12), Legal Ground no 7.1.1, p 32.
[24] ibid p 33.

This element of 'other alternative explanations' forces us to discard the causal nexus between the supposed negligent omission of the Government and the lethal results, and likewise, for a second reason. Unfortunately, many injuries and deaths caused at the time of Covid-19 affected people of advanced age, with other previous illnesses (comorbidities) or younger people also affected by previous complaints. Following Gimbernat, 'the unfavorable physical predisposition of the victim' can function by breaking the causal nexus'.[25] The final demise produced by aggravation of previous illnesses and because of weaker health among older people 'cannot be imputed to the public authority that omitted the due actions, as the resulting final outcome was unforeseeable and inevitable in accordance with the state of modern science'.[26]

In those tragic moments, it is unknown what other 'alternative lawful behaviour' the public authorities could have instituted to reduce the deaths and bodily harms, such that if another prudent and foreseeable behaviour of the authorities had led to the same saddening results; then the result cannot be imputed to omission on the part of the authorities. The Supreme Court pointed out that the unlawfulness disappears if the causal result due to an act or a negligent omission would likewise have been produced despite having lent greater attention. Acquittal must follow, provided at all times that there is no likelihood of borderline doubt over the certainty that the result could have been avoided through proper behaviour.[27] Another alternative lawful behaviour of the public authorities, with the knowledge that was held at the time, could also have produced the damaging result, as the possibility of saving life and health with that alternative behaviour was proven to be null[28] or very slim.

It may be said, in view of all the above, that the deaths were in the end the consequence of an 'irregular causal process' and the 'result of a fortuitous case' not imputable to the public authorities.[29]

C. Restricting Causality: Policy and Doctrinal Issues

Finally, having noted the relation of causality between omission and the result, the theory of objective imputation, completely dominant in Spanish case law and doctrine, enters

---

[25] E Gimbernat Ordeig, *Cursos causales irregulares e imputación objetiva* (Montevideo, BdeF Editores, 2011) 92 ff.

[26] ibid.

[27] Supreme Court Judgment 4541/1990 of 12 June 1990.

[28] E Díaz-Aranda, 'Imputación normativa del resultado a la conducta', in E Díaz-Aranda and M Cancio Meliá (eds), *Imputación normativa del resultado a la conducta* (Buenos Aires, Rubinzal-Culzoni Editores, 2004) 95.

[29] E Gimbernat Ordeig, *Cursos causales irregulares e imputación objetiva* (Montevideo, BdeF Editores, 2011) 92 ff. See also E Ariza Ugalde, 'Responsabilidad penal y COVID-19' (*Hay Derecho*, 24 June 2020), www.hayderecho.com/2020/06/24/responsabilidad-penal-y-covid-19/. Further, the Public Prosecutor's Office, 'Writ' (n 11), pp 47, 85, 154, 267 and 288 and the Supreme Court, 'Writ' (n 12), Legal Ground no 7, pp 24 and 25 presented the pandemic as an extraordinary, unforeseeable event that surpassed any expectations or any prudent previsions of the authorities. In a case like this one, a generic imputation of the deaths and the injuries to the actions or omissions of the public authorities solely because of the position or office that they hold, could imply the establishment of a regime of strict liability (alongside the concrete intervention of the

into play. This theory adds a series of requirements so that natural causality between omission and result is also converted into legal causality. In other words, objective imputation is an additional requirement, the last one, which delimits a broad group of cases in which natural causality is attributed to those in which an acceptable relation of causality has also in legal terms been noted. The Criminal Chamber of the Supreme Court has repeatedly affirmed that:

> [T]he verification of natural causality will be a minimum, but not a sufficient limit for the attribution of the result. In accordance with these assumptions, once the necessary natural causality is confirmed, the imputation of the result also requires verification of the following: 1°. If the action of the author has created a juridically disapproved danger of producing the result. 2°. If the result produced by such an action is the emergence of the same (juridically disapproved) danger created by the action. In case either one of both conditional assumptions complementary to natural causality are missing, the prohibition of the conduct will be annulled and, in consequence, so too its relevance to criminal law.[30]

In the Spanish criminal doctrine the theory of objective imputation is widely employed, especially using the model that Roxin advanced.[31] Thus, the theory of objective imputation has been the norm in Spain, for decades, thanks to the outstanding scientific works of Gimbernat Ordeig[32] and Martínez Escamilla, among others. Objective imputation for the latter is the 'creation of a legally relevant risk and its realization in a legally defined result, within the zone of protection of the norm'.[33] Muñoz Conde maintained that:

> A result can only be attributed to an individual when: a) the (active or passive) behaviour of the individual is the cause of the result; and b) when the result can be objectively imputed to the individual behaviour. If the following three requirements arise concurrently, then there are grounds for objective imputation: 1. The behaviour has to create or to increase a risk beyond a permitted level (juridically relevant); ... 2. The result that is produced must make a substantive contribution to the risk that is created or increased by the author through such behaviour (risk ratio) ... 3. Finally, the result that is produced must be included within the scope of the protection of the norm.[34]

---

accused), completely contrary to the principle of culpability of criminal law in a social and democratic State under the rule of law.

[30] Supreme Courts Judgments 470/2005 of 14 April 2005; 936/2006 of 10 October 2006; 1026/2007 of 10 December 2007, among others.

[31] C Roxin, *Derecho Penal. Parte general. Tomo I. Fundamentos. La estructura de la Teoría del Delito* 2nd edn (Madrid, Civitas, 2006) 362 ff.

[32] With numerous leading doctrinal works: E Gimbernat Ordeig, 'La causalidad en el Derecho Penal' (1962) 15 *Anuario de Derecho Penal y Ciencias Penales* 543; E Gimbernat Ordeig, 'Causalidad, omission e imprudencia' (1994) 47 *Anuario de derecho penal y ciencias penales* 5; E Gimbernat Ordeig, *Delitos cualificados por el resultado y causalidad* (Madrid, Centro Ramón Areces, 1990).

[33] M Martínez Escamilla, *La imputación objetiva del resultado* (Madrid, Edersa, 1992) 39–47; see also Feijoó-Sánchez, *Homicidio y lesiones imprudentes* (n 15) 25.

[34] F Muñoz Conde, *Derecho Penal, Parte General* (Valencia, Tirant lo Blanch, 2019) 215–17. See also S Mir Puig, *Derecho Penal, Parte General* 10th edn (Barcelona, Rapporteur, 2015) 259–64. For a panoramic vision of the reception and the extension of the theory of objective imputation in Spain, see E Anarte Borrallo, *Causalidad e imputación objetiva. Estructura, relaciones y perspectivas* (Huelva, Publicaciones Universidad de Huelva, 2002) 157 ff.

IV. THE STRUCTURE OF HOMICIDE OFFENCES AND ASSAULT/AGGRAVATED ASSAULT/SERIOUS BODILY HARM OFFENCES

A. Murder/Intentional Homicide

The crime of intentional homicide is foreseen in article 138.1 Criminal Code: 'Whoever kills another shall be convicted of manslaughter, punishable with a prison sentence of ten to fifteen years'. The main questions surronding this crime are the following:

Legal object: the right to independent human life.

Subjects: it is a common crime, which can be perpetrated by any physical person on any victim. The commission of this crime by legal persons is not foreseen.

The material object is the human body. Temporally, this legal good starts at birth, once the complete detachment from the mother's womb has taken place (article 30 Civil Code) and ends with death (cerebral failure, cardiorrespiratory blockage, etc).

Constitutive elements: homicide can be perpetrated by any means (except the forms that turn the homicide into murder); and we could say there are three forms of mens rea applicable to homicide (in Spanish the term '*dolo*' is used):

mens rea of the first degree (the subject knows what he is doing and desires the results; according to the Model Penal Code it is therefore a purposeful act);

mens rea of the second degree or of necessary consequences (the subject knows what he is doing and is aware of the results that will ensue, although some of them are not desired; according to Model Penal Code, the subject acts knowingly);

reckless mens rea: the most complex category to describe and the one that may be of greatest utility for our analysis of the cases linked to Covid-19:

> The active subject conjectures that the result is probable and although not wishing to produce the result directly, continues with the prohibited behaviour, accepting or assuming the eventual death of the victim ... In other words, it is thought that a person is acting with intention who, knowing that he is creating a specific and unlawful danger, nevertheless acts and continues with the same behaviour. This action subjects the victim to highly relevant risks that the author has no certainty of being able to control or to neutralize; [but it is not necessary] that the author directly pursues the causation of the resulting homicide.[35]

Degrees of homicide:

aggravated homicide is punishable to a higher degree, according to article 138.2, when: (1) the victim is under 16 years of age, or is an especially vulnerable individual due to his age, illness or disability; (2) the deed takes place following a criminal offence against sexual freedom committed by the perpetrator against the victim; (3) the deed is committed by an individual belonging to a criminal group or organisation; (4) the deed accurs as a consequence of assaults on the authority;

we should refer to the homicide as a 'murder' when one or more of the circumstances foreseen in article 139 concurs: '1. With premeditation; 2. For a price, reward or

---

[35] Supreme Courts Judgments 166/2017 of 14 March 2017; 44/2019 of 1 February 2019.

promise; 3. With wanton cruelty, deliberately and inhumanely increasing the victim's suffering; 4. To facilitate the perpetration of another criminal offence or to prevent discovery'; and

there is also a crime of murder, punishable with permanent, reviewable imprisonment (introduced into the 2015 Criminal Code reform) when any of the following circumstances concur (article 140): (1) the victim is under 16 years of age, or is an especially vulnerable individual due to his age, illness or disability; (2) the deed takes place following a criminal offence against sexual freedom committed by the perpetrator against the victim; (3) the deed is committed by an individual belonging to a criminal group or organisation.

B. Culpable Homicide/Manslaughter

Negligent homicide can also be committed and is punished according to article 142 under the modalities of gross negligence and less serious negligence. In both cases, the legal right, material object and objective constitutive elements are the same for intentional homicide. The difference is only the subjective side of the crime:

(1)   whoever causes the death of another due to gross negligence shall be convicted of manslaughter and punished with a prison sentence of one to four years (article 142.1);

(2)   whoever causes the death of another due to less serious negligence shall be punished with a fine of three to eighteen months (article 142.2); and

(3)   there is no criminal liability below the level of negligent homicide (and, in general, for any crimes involving negligence). In Spain there is no strict liability (the old model of *'versari in res illicita'*). According to article 5: 'No punishment shall be imposed in the absence of either mens rea or negligence'.

Both the doctrine and Spanish jurisprudence coincide in affirming that there are two defining elements in imprudent crimes: the duty of care for the individual and the likelihood of the harmful effects finally taking place; notwithstanding the application of the theory of objective imputation to crimes of negligence.[36] There is no imprudence if the active individual has acted as may be expected in accordance with the duty of care, without infringing it, nor showing negligent attitudes, and if the real (and not the desired) result were impossible to foresee or could only have been predicted with difficulty. These two matters have reciprocal connections with and impact on the pandemic: in our opinion, there was no negligent crime in the actions of the public authorities.

The Supreme Court has stated that to determine the seriousness of negligence (serious or less serious) and, therefore, the level where a slight infringement of the duty of care is not even punishable imprudence, depends on 'the circumstances of each specific case'. As criteria that should be considered:

> The greater or lesser intensity or importance of infringing the duty of care and the foreseeability of the result. This foreseeability is an inherent element in the same concept of the duty

---

[36] Supreme Court Judgment 802/2017 of 11 December 2017.

of care, as it is the only foreseeable result that can serve to affirm that somebody has omitted the duty of care.[37]

If we descend to another level, the duty of care is defined in the doctrine as prudent and advisable behaviour, in the light of the circumstances known at the time and that is adopted in accordance with technical rules of experience-based science. Corcoy Bidasolo described it as 'that which at one place and one time is considered socially adequate' and that has technical rules to guide it; these rules 'express prohibitions and orientations for the cases in which the general experience of life demonstrates a high probability that an action will provoke certain results'. In short, 'the duty of care is founded on its foreseeableness', which is in turn founded on experience.[38]

Imprudence plays a decisive role in the cases arising from the public authorities and their management of the pandemic. As Quintero Olivares said in a very illustrative and accurate manner, the technical rules:

> Have as their function and end-purpose to avoid the production of results such as those that have been produced, because experience teaches us that is what can happen if those rules are not respected or, summed up in a few words, *because experience tells us so*. If without experience, only with difficulty may it be said that the result that could have happened was foreseeable.[39]

The Covid-19 health crisis represents a unique event, never before witnessed, of the number of people affected and the deadliness of the virus.[40] When the explosion of the pandemic took place (even now, some months on), the state of the science held no better solution than lockdown, the minimisation of personal contacts to reduce infection, so that hospitals could confront the avalanche of patients (and despite everything, hospitals collapsed). Thus, scientific knowledge then (as now) and the rules of experience recommended the lockdown measures that were adopted – as prudent behaviour, within the duty of care. For all these reasons, we may say there was no infraction of the duty of care nor was there imprudent behaviour.

Could action have been taken sooner to prevent the contacts and displacements? Of course: one can always act sooner. Ex post everything appears possible and even easy. But two points must be remembered: (1) the form of organising our style of life in a free society; and, (2) the scientific knowledge available to us:

on the one hand, 'the only form of staying ahead of those risks and extraordinary causal chains of events would be to stop them in advance at the cost of an "unsupportable limitation on freedom of action"';[41] and

---

[37] Supreme Court Judgments 598/2013 of 28 June 2013; 802/2017 of 11 December 2017.

[38] See especially M Corcoy Bidasolo, *El delito imprudente. Criterios de imputación del resultado* (Barcelona, PPU, 1989) 216–23. See eg M Martínez Escamilla, *La imputación* (n 33) 323–25; JA Choclán Montalvo, *Deber de cuidado y delito imprudente* (Barcelona, Bosch, 1998) 91–98.

[39] G Quintero Olivares, 'Los poderes públicos y la pandemia: cuestiones penales y sancionadoras' (2020) 28 *Teorder* 65.

[40] Against, Bardavío Antón, 'Imputación' (n 8) 11–12.

[41] See especially W Frisch, *La imputación objetiva. Desarrollo, fundamentos y cuestiones abiertas* (Barcelona, Atelier, 2015) 63–67. See also I Navas Mondaca, 'COVID-19 e imputación objetiva de su contagio' (*Criminal Justice Network*, 9 June 2020), www.criminaljusticenetwork.eu/es/post/covid-19-e-imputacion-objetiva-de-su-contagio.

on the other hand, in accordance with the state of the science and in the absence of experience, no other behaviour or more reasonable behaviour than the decisions adopted by the authorities could be recommended according to the medical *lex artis* to reduce the risk. Having applied all these guarantees and decreased the risk in so far as possible, a risk still persisted that went beyond the control of present-day medical *lex artis*, for which reason the other dangers were inevitable. As Feijoó-Sánchez pointed out, 'the norms of care in no way seek to avoid all the results that can arise from behaviour that infringes duty, but only concrete results: plannable results',[42] foreseeable ex ante.

C. Offences Related to Actions that Cause Serious Bodily Harm (Assault; Grievous Assault; Assault with Intent to Cause Serious Bodily Harm)

The crime of bodily harm is foreseen in article 147.1:

> Whoever, by any means or procedure, causes another an injury that detracts from his bodily integrity or his physical or mental health, shall be convicted of the criminal offence of grievous bodily harm, ... whenever the injury objectively requires medical or surgical treatment for healing purposes, in addition to qualified first aid.

The protected legal good in this case is health, understood as the subjective state of complete physical, mental and social wellbeing, and not only the absence of complaints and illnesses.

Subjects of the crime: it is a crime that can be perpetrated by any physical person (but not for legal persons), on any class of victim.

Degrees of bodily harm:

> serious bodily harm can be subject to stiffer sentences when employing methods or instruments that are especially reproachable (*e.g.*, according to article 148, 'with weapons, instruments, objects, means, methods or ways that are specifically dangerous') or in case of injuries that have been aggravated by the result (article 149: 'forfeit or lose the use of a major organ or limb, or a sense, or sexual impotence, sterility, serious deformity or serious physical or mental illness'); and

> there are two modalities of bodily harm punished with lower penalties: firstly, article 147. 2. 'whoever, by any means or procedure, causes another an injury not included in the preceding Section [that is to say, article 147.1, injuries that require medical or surgical treatment for healing purposes], shall be punished with a fine of one to three months'; and, secondly, article 147.3: 'whoever hits or causes minor bodily harm to another without causing injury, shall be punished with a fine of one to two months'.

Constitutive elements:

> bodily harm can be perpetrated by any means; and

---

[42] Feijoó-Sánchez, *Homicidio y lesiones imprudentes* (n 15) 180.

bodily harm can be negligently caused: article 152.1 lists different punishments according to whether they are negligent injuries at a medium or an ordinary severity (those that need surgical treatment) or negligent injuries aggravated by the result. Of course, all the reflections relating to the sub-section on culpable homicide, about the concept of negligence and its (gross and less gross) modalities, the duty of care, the foreseeability of the harm,[43] are also applicable in the context of negligent bodily harm.

D. Offences Regarding Unborn Foetuses; Interrupting the Course of a (Viable) Pregnancy

The crime of intentional abortion is punished in article 144: 'Whoever perpetrates an abortion on a woman without her consent shall be punished with ... The same penalties shall be applied to whoever perpetrates an abortion having obtained the consent by the woman through violence, intimidation or deceit'. However, we should not go deeper on this issue as these elements are not applicable to the study.

E. Failure to Render Assistance

The crime of failure to render assistance is foreseen in article 195:

1. Whoever does not assist a person who is unprotected or in serious, manifest danger when able to do so without risk to himself or third parties, shall be punished with the penalty of a fine of three to twelve months 2. The same penalties shall be incurred by whoever, being unable to provide assistance, does not urgently call for outside help.

These are its elements:

the legally protected good in this crime is controversial. It is argued in some case-law that the 'social demand for solidarity' is protected.[44] There are authors, such as Gómez Tomillo, who understand that the protected goods are the endangered rights if assistance is not provided: life, physical integrity, sexual freedom.[45] Finally, the majority opinion in the doctrine (Muñoz Conde,[46] among others) and current case law[47] understand that specific human solidarity is protected or applied to individual and personal legal goods such as life;

subjects of crime: it is a crime that can be perpetrated by any physical person (with the exception of legal persons), on any class of unprotected victim who is in danger.

Constitutive elements:

this offence punishes mere inaction in the face of a situation that requires assistance to be provided to other people. The elements that must be present are: the defencelessness of the

---

[43] See s IV.B above.
[44] Supreme Court Judgment 860/2002 of 16 May 2002.
[45] M Gómez Tomillo, *El deber de Socorro. Artículo 195.1 del Código Penal* (Madrid, Tirant Lo Blanch, 2003) 44.
[46] F Muñoz Conde, *Derecho penal. Parte especial* (Valencia, Tirant lo Blanch, 2019) 303.
[47] Supreme Court Judgments 56/2008 of 28 January 2008; 648/2015 of 22 October 2015.

victim, a situation of manifest and serious danger, the objective and subjective capability to lend assistance to the individual without risk to oneself or to third parties, the necessity to provide assistance and failure to provide the required assistance; and

the commission of this offense has to be with intention; and

degrees of failure to render assitance. There is a higher penalty whenever the offender who fails to provide assistance is a health professional: a medical practitioner who, while under an obligation to do so, were to refuse to lend health assistance or abandon the provision of health services, if refusal or abandonment were to cause serious risk to personal health, shall be punished with the penalties of the preceding article, in the upper half and with that of special incapacitation from public employment and office, profession or trade, for a term of six months to three years (article 196).

V. DEFENCES, JUSTIFICATIONS AND EXCUSES

In Spanish criminal law, once it is affirmed that a behaviour is prohibited, there are principally two possibilities to minimise or to absolve criminal responsibility: to seek relief for having acted on lawful or on exculpatory grounds (that is to say, justification and exculpation grounds). Such circumstances are jointly foreseen under article 20 of the Criminal Code (*causes of exclusion from criminal accountability*):

the justification grounds are contemplated under sections 4 (acting in defence of his person or his own rights or those of others; generally known as legitimite defence) and 7 (acting in carrying out a duty or in the lawful exercise of a right, authority or office). The law authorises overriding a legal good to protect another of greater importance, hence the conduct is exceptionally justified. There is neither criminal liability nor civil liability ex delicto when acting for lawful reasons;

the exculpatory grounds are provided for under sections 1 (acting due to any mental anomaly or alteration), 2 (acting in a state of absolute intoxication due to consumption of alcoholic beverages, toxic and narcotic drugs or other substances), 3 (acting without awareness of reality due to alterations in perception from the time of birth, or from childhood) and 6 (acting driven by insurmountable fear). When acting in such states the law in no way justifies the behaviour, because it is at all times prohibited and in the specific case likewise (unlike the justification reasons), but the individual subject is exonerated because: (1) at the time of committing a criminal offence, he was unable to understand what he was doing because of his mental health ('declared exempt of criminal accountability'); (2) because no other alternative behaviour might be expected from him under the law. In these cases, there is a crime for which reason there is obligatory civil liability, but no criminal liability (or any such liability can be imposed in a limited way),[48] because the subject was not guilty; and

---

[48] C Jiménez Segado reminds us in, 'Excepción normalizada en derecho penal y covid-19' (2020) 99 *Juezas y Jueces por la Democracia* 83–84, that the circumstance of a state of necessity could be incompletely appreciated (if one of the requirements of art 20.5 were missing), but even so an attenuated sentence could fit, in accordance with art 66.1.1°: 'When only one mitigating circumstance concurs, the lower half of the punishment the Law sets for the criminal offence shall be applied'.

finally, there is a mixed circumstance foreseen under article 20.6: 'Whoever, in a state of necessity, in order to avoid damage to himself or others, causes damage to another's legally protected interest or fails to perpetrate a duty'. The state of necesity can constitute a justification ground when an interest is harmed that is of lesser importance than the one that the person wished to protect through the criminal behaviour; and it can be exculpation ground when harming an interest of equal importance as the one that the person wished to protect (*e.g.*, life versus life, which are precisely the cases of Covid-19 that we will analyse in what follows).

In the context of the Covid-19 context, one way or another, the doctrine seeks to relieve the authorities and doctors, who had to take complex decisions at that time, from any criminal responsibility. As Hilgendorf stated, jurists must accept each medical decision that appears defendable and must only classify those decisions that are quite evidently not defendable as unlawful.[49]

The debate among Spanish scholars regarding Covid-19 cases has focused on the liability of doctors and health workers who had to employ ventilators for certain patients and not for other patients (who therefore never received the necessary health care), complying with the protocols of either their hospital or the public authorities with responsibility for health matters. We think these workers could allege the justification of acting in carrying out of a duty, foreseen in article 20.7 Criminal Code. In accordance with article 4.7.b) of Law 44/2003, of 21 November 2003, on the Organization of Health Professionals, the protocols of clinical conduct will be based on scientific evidence and on the available means and should be used as a decision-making guide for the whole team of professional health workers. As Javato Martín affirmed, if they followed the protocol, a barometer that defines their professional obligations to establish prioritisation criteria among patients, they therefore acted in line with their duty in accordance with their odontological code (medical lex *artis*).[50]

A. Necessity

As pointed out above, one possibility for the exoneration of criminal liability of doctors and public health authorities is to invoke the state of necessity, as these professionals had to choose between the protection of legal goods of the same value (life versus life).[51]

[49] E Hilgendorf, 'Recomendaciones de triaje en la crisis del coronavirus: no importunar a los médicos con cuestiones jurídicas' (2020) 10 *En Letra: Derecho Penal* 26.

[50] AM Javato Martín, 'Protección penal de personas mayores' (2021) 25 *Anuario de la facultad de Derecho de Madrid* 344. The same author reasonably warns that the causes of justification might not even have to be reached, but it could be affirmed that there is not even imprudent behaviour that results in death. If the doctors applied the protocols, then they would be in compliance with the medical *lex artis*, which constitutes the reference norm for measuring the health care obligations of health workers (that is, *the technical rule that defines the objective duty of care*), following the terminology that we have used. And if there is no infringement of the duty of care, there is no imprudent behaviour. See also, MI Trespaderne Beracierto, 'La responsabilidad del profesional por defectuosa asistencia sanitaria a la luz de las condiciones organizacionales' (2012) 22 *Derecho y Salud* 30.

[51] See A Nieto Martín, 'El Derecho penal ante el coronavirus: entre el estado de emergencia y la gobernanza global' (*Almacén de Derecho*, 15 April 2020), https://almacendederecho.org/el-derecho-penal-ante-el-coronovirus-entre-el-estado-de-emergencia-y-la-gobernanza-global/; Javato Martín, 'Protección penal' (n 50) 340.

In these cases, the authorities were confronted with equivalent legal duties, for which reason they found themselves under the obligation to decide which to protect. If the doctors, when distributing the limited medical equipment had, ex ante, chosen one patient who had a greater likelihood of surviving – even if that patient were to have arrived after another – then the damage they would have caused, in the delicate and tragic situation in which they were working, could not have been any greater than the damage they wished to prevent (article 20.5.1° Penal Code: 'The damage caused is not greater than the damage sought to be prevented').[52] The above is always so except if the medical treatment had been assigned to a patient and was withdrawn to give it to another patient arriving later on but with a greater likelihood of surviving, because in this case the first patient, as Coca Vila argued, had a consolidated right to receive the treatment and to try to prolong his life, for which reason to withdraw that treatment ex post would imply unlawful homicide on the part of the doctor.[53]

VI. CORPORATE CRIMINAL LIABILITY

A. Overview of Corporate Criminal Liability

In 2010, there was a profound reform of the Spanish Criminal Code and, for the first time in history, the criminal liability of corporations was accepted in article 31*bis*. Corporate criminal liability is a relatively new concept to Spanish law. It is not, however, applicable to the crimes under consideration.

It could be of interest to value the behaviour of the communications media when covering and reporting on the health crisis and government measures to contain it. In Spain, no special conflict has affected criminal law, beyond legitimate criticism against the reporting standards of one or another media channel, something habitual and acceptable in all democratic and pluralist societies (all the more so in a situation of social tension such as the one during Covid-19). In any case, none of the crimes that could be imputed against them (slander or crimes relating to the protection of intimacy) form part of the catalogue of crimes that legal persons can commit, in accordance with the Criminal Code and its rules on imputation. It would solely imply the imputation of such crimes to individuals.

---

[52] The three requisites for state of necessity, according to art 20.5, are: 'One. The damage caused is not greater than the damage sought to be prevented; Two. That the situation of necessity has not been intentionally provoked by the subject; Three. That the person is need is not bound, due to his office or occupation, the obligation to sacrifice himself'. Regarding invoking state of necessity for doctors and other health workers, see especially M Pantaleón Díez, 'De kantianos y triajes' (*Almacén de Derecho*, 10 March 2021), https://almacendederecho.org/de-kantianos-y-triajes. See also Javato Martín, 'Protección penal' (n 50) 344; M Cancio Meliá and M Pantaleón Díaz, 'Derecho penal y coronavirus: algunos problemas de imputación' (2021) *Extraordinario Anuario de la facultad de Derecho de Madrid* 253. Against, I Coca Vila, 'Triaje y colisión de deberes jurídico-penal. Una crítica al giro utilitarista' (2021) 1 *InDret* 184–87, because human lives are imponderable, their quality cannot be compared and, therefore, no ex ante selection can be made so as to favour the second patient who arrived later.

[53] Coca Vila, 'Triaje y colisión' (n 52) 189.

VII. FORMS OF PARTICIPATION

The different forms of participation are foreseen in articles 27 and following of the Spanish Criminal Code. According to the first of them, we can distinguish between offenders (or prepetrators) and accessories:

offenders are those who perpetrate the deed themselves, alone, jointly, or by means of another used to aid and abet. The following shall also be deemed to be offenders: 'a) Whoever directly induces another or others to commit a criminal offence; b) Whoever co-operates in the commission thereof by a deed without which a criminal offence could not have been committed' (article 28); and

accessories are those who, not being included in article 28, co-operate in the perpetration of the criminal offence with prior or simultaneous deeds (article 29).

As a form of participation we should also refer to conspiracy and proposition. A conspiracy exists when one or more persons collude to commit a criminal offence and decide to carry it out (article 17.1). A proposition exists when he who has resolved to commit a criminal offence invites another or other persons to commit it (article 17.2). However, both forms of participation shall only be punishable in the cases specifically foreseen in the law (article 17.3) and this is the case of homicide and bodily harm. For such crimes, conspiracy and proposition are specifically punished with lower penalties than for homicide (article 141) or bodily harm (article 151), depending on if it was a consummated or attempted criminal offence or if the person was an offender or an accessory to the crime.

In cases arising from Covid-19, we might theoretically accept the basic forms of authorship (offender and inductor) and the different forms of vicarious liability (accessory) in cases of reckless homicide and injury. It is somewhat more difficult to accept, however, the existence of accessories in negligent crimes of homicide or injuries arising from Covid-19.[54]

VIII. ATTEMPT

We should distinguish between consummated criminal offence and attempted criminal offence. The difference appears in article 16 of Criminal Code:

An attempted criminal offence takes place when a person begins to perpetrate a criminal offence by direct deed, perpetrating all or part of the deeds that objectively should produce the intended result, and notwithstanding this, such is not attained due to causes beyond the control of the offender.

The attempted crime is only possible with intentional offences in which the individual wishes and seeks the prohibited outcome, but it is not possible in negligent crimes in which the individual is not seeking a particular outcome: if the negligent infraction of

---

[54] On the debate in Spanish criminal law doctrine regarding participation in negligent crimes, see especially R Robles Planas, 'Participación en el delito e imprudencia' (2000) 6 *Revista de Derecho Penal y Criminología* 223.

the duty of care does not cause a prohibited outcome (death or bodily harm), there is no crime of negligence. It means that, in cases arising from Covid-19, consummation is possible in every situation (intentional and culpable homicide, as well as intentional and culpable injuries); but we can only admit attempt for intentional crimes (homicide or injury derived from the virus), and not for negligent crimes.

IX. SANCTIONS, SENTENCING, PUNISHMENT, REPARATIONS AND/OR RESTORATIVE JUSTICE

A. General Sentencing Framework for the Crimes under Discussion

From the viewpoint of criminal liability:

whoever kills another shall be convicted of manslaughter, punishable with a prison sentence of 10 to 15 years (article 138). In case of murder, the penalty is a prison sentence of 15 to 25 years (article 139), and in the case of gross murder the punishment is permanent, reviewable imprisonment (article 140);

the offences of negligent manslaughter and negligent bodily harm have prison sentences attached to them: manslaughter due to gross negligence shall be punished 'with a prison sentence of one to four years' (article 142.1); if due to less serious negligence, the punishment is lighter: 'with a [daily] fine of three to eighteen months' (article 142.2);[55]

intentional bodily harm is punishable with a prison sentence of between three months and three years, or a fine of six to 12 months, whenever the injury objectively requires medical or surgical treatment for healing purposes (article 147) and with a prison sentence from six to 12 years in the case of intentional bodily harm with aggravated results (sterility, loss of senses, etc). Serious bodily harm is punishable with a prision sentence of three to six months or a [daily] fine of six to 18 months, in the case of medium level injuries, and with a prison sentence of one to three years, in the case of negligent injuries aggravated by the result (Article 152); and

intentional abortion is punishable with a prison sentence of four to eight years and incapacitation from practicing any health profession or from providing services of any kind at public or private gynaecological clinics for a term of three to 10 years (article 144); abortion without the waiting period established in the legislation having elapsed is punishable with a daily fine of six to 12 months and individual incapacitation from providing services of any kind at public or private gynaecological clinics for a term of six months to two years; gross negligent abortion is punishable with a sentence of imprisonment of three to five months, or a daily fine of between six to 10 months (article 146).

---

[55] According to Article 50 of Penal Code, 'Punishment by fine shall consist in sentencing the convict to pay a pecuniary punishment. Punishment by fine shall be imposed, except if the Law states otherwise, by the day-fine system. The minimum length shall be ten days and the maximum two years. The daily quota shall be a minimum of two and a maximum of four hundred euros'.

B. Sanctions Specifically for Senior Government/Public Officials

The Constitution establishes no specific sanctions for senior government officials or public authorities. As a maximum, article 70 refers to the Organic Law of the General Electoral Regime that establishes fines involving the deprivation of the right to passive suffrage. This norm establishes under article 6.2 that once convicted in a firm judgment to a term of imprisonment, the offender cannot be eligible for public office throughout the duration of the sentence. It must be added that some offences foreseen in the Penal Code also contemplate the fine of deprivation of the right to passive suffrage.[56]

C. Corporations and Sentencing

According to article 33.7 of the Criminal Code, penalties applicable to legal persons are:

a) Fine; b) Dissolution of the legal person; c) Suspension of its activities; d) Closure of its premises and establishments; e) Prohibition on performing the activities through which it has committed, favoured or concealed the criminal offence; f) Loss of the right to apply for public subsidies and aid, to enter into contracts with the public sector and to enjoy tax or Social Security benefits and incentives; g) Judicial intervention to safeguard the rights of the workers or creditors for the time deemed necessary.

Nevertheless, as we have pointed out, legal persons cannot be prosecuted for the crimes that are of interest to us in this study (homicide, injuries, abortion, failure to render assistance).

---

[56] eg perverting the course of justice by civil servants and other injustices in the conduct thereof (art 404), corruption (art 419), influence peddling (art 428), embezzlement (art 432), fraud and unlawful taxation (art 436) and prohibited negotiations and activities for civil servants (art 439).

13

Sweden

DENNIS MARTINSSON*

I. BACKGROUND AND CONTEXTUAL INTRODUCTION

IN SWEDEN THE possibilities to hold a member of government criminally liable for the policy on and legal response (or lack thereof) to the Covid-19 pandemic are extremely limited, almost zero. To understand why this is so, a contextual understanding of some basic features of the Swedish judicial, constitutional and administrative system is necessary. This section therefore begins by reviewing these features. There follows an overview of the most important legal and regulatory mechanisms introduced during the Covid-19 pandemic. This should provide insight into how Sweden is governed, which presumably is a key factor in explaining and grasping how the pandemic has been dealt with legally and constitutionally.[1]

To grasp the Swedish government's response to the Covid-19 pandemic, one should stress that Sweden is considered a welfare State.[2] Hence, traditionally the State has been viewed as 'good' in the sense that it strives to allocate welfare resources etc to those who need it. The Swedish welfare policies have resulted in the general public having a high

---

* The author would like to thank Mauro Zamboni for reading and commenting on selected parts of a previous version of the present text, Annika Suominen and Julia Dahlqvist for discussions and advice on various topics reviewed in the present text. Note that the present text was completed on 4 April 2022 and that developments in the statutory law etc after that date could therefore not be considered.

[1] Research on various responses from different States to the Covid-19 pandemic confirms that the constitutional and administrative tradition and culture offer an important explanation as to why States have adopted different strategies, see, eg S Kuhlmann et al, 'Tracing Divergence in Crisis Governance: Responses to the COVID-19 Pandemic in France, Germany and Sweden Compared' (2021) 87 *International Review of Administrative Sciences* 556; B Yan et al, 'Why Do Countries Respond Differently to COVID-19? A Comparative Study of Sweden, China, France and Japan' (2020) 50 *American Review of Public Administration* 762. See also S Andersson and N Aylott, 'Sweden and Coronavirus: Unexceptional Exceptionalism' (2020) 9 *Social Sciences* 232; E Petridou, 'Politics and Administration in Times of Crisis: Explaining the Swedish Response to the COVID-19 Crisis' (2020) *European Policy Analysis* 147; J Dahlqvist and J Reichel, 'Swedish Constitutional Response to the Coronavirus Crisis The Odd One Out?' in MC Kettemann and K Lachmayer (eds), *Pandemocracy in Europe: Power, Parliaments and People in Times of COVID-19* (Oxford, Hart Publishing, 2021) 150–51.

[2] See, eg G Esping-Andersen, *The Three Worlds of Welfare Capitalism* (Cambridge, Polity, 1990) 27–28; A Bergh, 'The Universal Welfare State: Theory and the Case of Sweden' (2004) 54 *Political Studies* 745; E Ferragina and M Seeleib-Kaiser, 'Welfare Regime Debate: Past, Present, Futures?' (2011) 39 *Policy & Politics* 583; N Edling, 'The Primacy of Welfare Politics: Notes on the Language of the Swedish Social Democrats and Their Adversaries in the 1930s', in H Haggrén et al (eds), *Multi-layered Historicity of the Present: Approaches to Social Science History* (Helsinki, University of Helsinki, 2013) 125–50.

degree of trust in relation to, for instance, government agencies. The high degree of trust can also be noted between government agencies and the government.[3] More importantly, the welfare State has a great bearing on the legal culture in Sweden,[4] illustrated by, for instance, consensus-based political decision-making, a separation of functions (rather than separation of powers), rather independent government agencies with a mandate to adopt non-binding guidance aimed at the general public which – due to the high degree of trust – often regard them as rules that should be adhered to. Thus, in a welfare State like Sweden, 'soft' legal instruments are commonly used as a mean of implementing social norms.[5]

Before turning to the constitutional context, some characteristic features of the Swedish judicial system need to be outlined. Sweden is a civil law jurisdiction, belonging to a Scandinavian legal tradition, in which, realism, pragmatism and practical considerations in legal reasoning are preferred to theoretical thinking.[6] Further, statutory law is emphasised and given great importance. The legislative procedure in Sweden is a rather slow and complex process which, for instance, includes the government's appointment of a commission of inquiry responsible for creating a legislative proposal. The procedure also includes mandatory consultations with external parties, such as government agencies and universities.[7] The result of the legislative procedure is the *travaux préparatoires*; a set of documents providing the judicial and political reasoning behind a certain piece of legislation and its provisions. Although the *travaux préparatoires* are not a binding legal source, the courts often refer to them, since they often provide support for legal argumentation.[8]

Concerning the constitutional context, Sweden is a parliamentary democracy characterised by consensus, including in matters pertaining to political decision-making. The governance of Sweden is based upon a separation of functions rather than a division of power, which follows from the principle of popular sovereignty, that is, 'all power proceeds from the people'.[9] Hence political power is transferred from the people to the Parliament, which, in turn, delegates the (main) executive functions to the government.[10]

---

[3] See generally B Jacobsson et al, *Governing the Embedded State: The Organizational Dimension of Governance* (Oxford, Oxford University Press, 2015) 77–105.

[4] See, eg P Letto-Vanamo and D Tamm, 'Nordic Legal Mind' in P Letto-Vanamo and D Tamm (eds), *Nordic Law in European Context* (Switzerland, Springer, 2019) 8–9.

[5] See, eg M Zamboni, '(Absence of) Omnibus Legislation in Sweden: When Legislative Drafting Affects the Political Discourse' in I Bar-Siman-Tov (ed), *Comparative Multidisciplinary Perspectives on Omnibus Legislation* (Cham, Springer, 2021) 319–20.

[6] See, eg U Bernitz, 'What is Scandinavian Law? Concept, Characteristics, Future' (2007) 50 *Scandinavian Studies in Law* 14; Letto-Vanamo and Tamm, 'Nordic Legal Mind' (n 4) 1–19.

[7] See generally O Petersson, 'Rational Politics: Commissions of Inquiry and the Referral System in Sweden' in J Pierre (ed), *The Oxford Handbook of Swedish Politics* (Oxford, Oxford University Press, 2016) 650–62; M Zamboni, 'Methods of Ex-Ante Evaluation in Legislation: The Swedish Model' in K Kye-Hong (ed), *Goals and Methods of Ex-Ante Evaluation of Legislation* (Seuol, KLRI, 2019) 3–31.

[8] See, eg HH Vogel, 'Sources of Swedish Law' in M Bogdan and C Wong (eds), *Swedish Legal System* 2nd edn (Stockholm, Norstedts Juridik, 2022) 28–31; Zamboni, '(Absence of) Omnibus Legislation' (n 5) 321–24.

[9] Instrument of Government (1974:152), c 1, s 1.

[10] Note that Sweden is governed by negative parliamentarism, ie the Prime Minister must not have a Parliament majority against him or her, see Instrument of Government (1974:152), c 6, s 3. See, eg T Möller, 'The Parliamentary System' in J Pierre (ed), *The Oxford Handbook of Swedish Politics* (Oxford, Oxford University Press, 2016) 115–18.

This transfer of power from the Parliament to the government is constitutionally important since it accentuates that the government is accountable to the Parliament.[11] Another core feature in the Swedish Constitution[12] is that government decisions are made collectively.[13] This is highly relevant during decisions made (or not made) during the Covid-19 pandemic, since the collective decision-making by the government clearly limits the possibility to hold a Swedish member of government liable for actions (or lack of action) taken during the pandemic. Since the government must adopt decisions as a whole, no Swedish member of government can single-handedly make decisions.

In line with the government's collective decision-making, the Swedish Constitution further limits the mandate of a member of government by strictly forbidding him or her from interfering with decisions of, for instance, a government agency or a court.[14] The rationale here is found in one of the cornerstones in the governance of Sweden: the 'dualism' between the government and government agencies. This concept of 'dualism' is characterised mainly by a high degree of autonomy for government agencies (in relation both to the government and to other agencies), since agencies in Sweden are responsible for matters that in other jurisdictions fall within the realm of the government. Additionally, the 'dualism' is manifested by the existence of small government departments, quite large government agencies which generally have the expertise, and quite weak individual ministers.[15] Thus, the government's political influence over government agencies is rather limited.[16] This is particularly so in the event of a crisis or an emergency. In that case, the function of the government is limited to a coordinating role and – if needed – to regulate through general provisions.[17]

The coordinating role is important, since Sweden's 21 regions and 290 municipalities have a strong level of local self-governance.[18] Generally, regions and municipalities are the main actors responsible for allocating various welfare resources, for example health care. Consequently, from a constitutional perspective, since the government is not primarily responsible for health care issues, it cannot be held responsible for regulations, policies and decisions made (or not made) within this policy area. Instead, the 21 regions and 290 municipalities have the (legal) competence to introduce policies in relation to health care.

---

[11] Instrument of Government (1974:152), c 1, s 6. For an overview of governmental accountability in relation to the Parliament, see, eg J Nergelius, *Constitutional Law in Sweden* 2nd edn (Alphen aan den Rijn, Wolters Kluwer, 2015) 78–84.

[12] The Swedish Constitution consists of four acts: the Act of Succession (1810:0926), the Freedom of The Press Act (1949:105), the Fundamental Law on Freedom of Expression (1991:1469) and the Instrument of Government (1974:152). For the purposes of the present text, only the latter is of relevance.

[13] Instrument of Government (1974:152), c 7, s 3.

[14] Instrument of Government (1974:152), c 12, s 2.

[15] See, eg P Hall, 'The Swedish Administrative Model' in J Pierre (ed), *The Oxford Handbook of Swedish Politics* (Oxford, Oxford University Press, 2016) 300–04; B Jacobsson et al, *Governing the Embedded State* (n 3) 29–31.

[16] See, eg M Zamboni, 'The Positioning of the Supreme Courts in Sweden – A Democratic Oddity?' (2019) 15 *European Constitutional Law Review* 668, 682.

[17] A Jonsson Cornell and J Salminen, 'Emergency Laws in Comparative Constitutional Law – The Case of Sweden and Finland' (2018) 19 *German Law Journal* 219, 226–27.

[18] Instrument of Government (1974:152), c 14, ss 2 and 3. On the matter of local self-governance, see, eg S Montin, 'Municipalities, Regions, and County Councils: Actors and Institutions' in J Pierre (ed), *The Oxford Handbook of Swedish Politics* (Oxford, Oxford University Press, 2016) 367–80.

In order to understand the constitutional context, a brief overview of the various legal norm-making powers is necessary. The statutory law consists of various legal norms of different value.[19] The Parliament has the authority to introduce statutes and may delegate to the government the power to enact an ordinance.[20] When doing this, the Parliament may allow the government to sub-delegate to a government agency, a region or a municipality, which can introduce statutory instruments.[21] Legislation created by this delegation is legally binding. Additionally, Swedish constitutional law allows for the creation of non-binding norms through the introduction of general recommendations and guidance. These non-binding norms are created by government agencies.

All of these constitutional characteristics are of great importance when examining the legal measures introduced in Sweden during the Covid-19 pandemic. First, note that the Swedish Constitution does not provide for the government – in peacetime – to declare a state of emergency.[22] Second, the question of whether the government, according to constitutional practice, has a mandate within a supra-legal state of emergency has been discussed in relation to executive, but not legislative measures.[23] The concept of a supra-legal state of emergency is not considered a constitutional principle in Sweden.[24] Third, this means that in the event of a crisis or an emergency, the principle of anticipatory 'statutorification' applies. Ordinary statutory law must accordingly be prepared for emergencies and applied also in such an event.[25] Hence, the principle of anticipatory 'statutorification' ensures that the rule of law should not be disregarded during a crisis.[26] Fourth, the party normally responsible for certain activities is also responsible in the event of a crisis or an emergency.[27] Thus, the government, government agencies, regions and municipalities all have the same responsibility in a crisis or emergency as under ordinary circumstances.

A selection of the most important legal instruments implemented during the Covid-19 pandemic is presented here.[28] Since the Swedish Constitution provides no procedure

---

[19] The matter of norm-making and the possibilities for delegation are rather complex. For a detailed overview, particularly in relation to legal measures introduced in Sweden during the Covid-19 pandemic, see H Wenander, 'Sweden: Non-binding Rules against the Pandemic – Formalism, Pragmatism and Some Legal Realism' (2021) 12 *European Journal of Risk Regulation* 127.

[20] Instrument of Government (1974:152), c 1, s 4 and c 8, s 1.

[21] Instrument of Government (1974:152), c 8, s 1.

[22] See, eg Jonsson Cornell and Salminen, 'Emergency Laws' (n 17) 227–37; Dahlqvist and Reichel, 'Swedish Constitutional Response' (n 1) 147–49; Nergelius, *Constitutional Law* (n 11) 137–39.

[23] The discussion has centred around three events that occurred during 1970s: a hijacking of a plane (1972), a bank robbery where hostages were taken in the Stockholm city centre (1973) and a terrorist attack on the West German Embassy (1975). In each of these events, members of government (allegedly) overstepped their executive powers. However, no member of government was considered liable by the Committee on the Constitution, see KU 1973:20, 16–17; KU 1974:22, 17–20; KU 1975:12, 26–27; KU 1975/76:50, 32–34.

[24] See, eg Jonsson Cornell and Salminen, 'Emergency Laws' (n 17) 228–33. See also M Klamberg, 'International Human Rights Law and States of Emergency', in D Rogers (ed), *Human Rights in War* (Singapore, Springer, 2022) 125–28.

[25] See, eg the *travaux préparatoires* SOU 2005:104, 56, 314; SOU 2020:80, 128–30.

[26] See, eg the *travaux préparatoires* SOU 2005:104, 56, 314.

[27] See, eg the *travaux préparatoires* SOU 2020:80, 130.

[28] For a thorough overview, see, eg I Cameron and A Jonsson Cornell, 'COVID-19 in Sweden: A Soft Power Approach' (*VerfBlog*, 24 February 2021), www.verfassungsblog.de/covid-19-in-sweden-a-soft-power-approach/; Wenander, 'Sweden: Non-binding Rules' (n 19); Dahlqvist and Reichel, 'Swedish Constitutional Response' (n 1) 135–54; Klamberg, 'International Human Rights Law' (n 24) 148–50; OL Larsson, 'The Swedish Covid-19 Strategy and Voluntary Compliance: Failed Securitisation or Constitutional Security Management?' (2022) 7

for imposing a wide lockdown, other legal measures have been used, and the legal mechanisms used during the pandemic have mainly had a 'soft' approach. Hence, in line with the traditional Swedish welfare State and its constitutional and administrative culture, emphasis has been on non-binding recommendations and guidance, *i.e.*, voluntary measures, stressing that each individual bears a responsibility to prevent Covid-19 infections.[29] An illustrative example is the Public Health Agency, which is responsible for coordinating measures against communicable diseases. The Public Health Agency has therefore adopted regulations and general recommendations on how to prevent Covid-19 infections.[30] The enacted, non-binding, general recommendations have for example advised people to stay at home when having symptoms of Covid-19, to wash their hands regularly and thoroughly, to refrain from meeting other people and when doing so, to try and ensure that this occurs outdoors.[31]

However, legally binding legislation has also been enacted. In the beginning of the Covid-19 pandemic, ordinary legislation was amended. One example was an amendment to the Communicable Diseases Act, enacted by the Parliament in April 2020, allowing the government various measures, including the closing down of commercial locations and the redistribution of medical supplies.[32] The amendment was limited in time, from 18 April 2020 to 30 June 2020, and was never used by the government. Another example is the temporary 2021 Covid-19 Act, enacted by the Parliament, which entered into force on 10 January 2021. With this, the Parliament delegated further powers to the government, mandating it to, for instance, limit public gatherings, public events, market places and public transport. Further, the Act allowed the government to limit fundamental rights, such as the freedom of assembly and demonstration, protected in the Instrument of Government, Chapter 2. The Act was originally designed to expire on 30 September 2021,[33] but was prolonged twice[34] before it expired on 31 March 2022.[35] Additionally, the government enforced a temporary entry ban,[36] which repeatedly was prolonged.[37] However, on 1 April 2022, the ban was lifted.[38]

European Journal of International Security 226, 236–45; J Pierre, 'Nudges Against Pandemics: Sweden's COVID-19 Containment Strategy in Perspective' (2020) 39 *Policy and Society* 478.

[29] See, eg an article in English from the Swedish Prime Minister's Office, 6 April 2020, at www.government. se/articles/2020/04/strategy-in-response-to-the-covid-19-pandemic, stating that '[p]eople in Sweden have a high level of trust in government agencies. This means that a large proportion of people follow government agencies' advice. In the current situation, people in Sweden are on the whole acting responsibly to reduce the spread of infection by, for example, restricting their social contacts'.

[30] The Public Health Agency had – far prior to the Covid-19 pandemic – been delegated powers to enact regulations and general recommendations, see Ordinance (2021:248) with Instructions for the Public Health Agency and Rules, s 38.

[31] Regulations and General Recommendations by the Public Health Agency Relating to Everyone's Responsibility to Prevent Covid-19 Infections (HSLF-FS 2020:12).

[32] Act (2020:421) on Amendment to the Communicable Diseases Act, c 9, ss 6A–6C.

[33] The Covid-19 Act (2021:4).

[34] Act (2021:861) on Prolongation of the Covid-19 Act; Act (2022:30) on Prolongation of the Covid-19 Act.

[35] Act (2022:214) on Repeal of the Covid-19 Act.

[36] Ordinance (2020:127) on a Temporary Entry Ban to Sweden. Originally, it was planned to expire on 17 April 2020.

[37] It was last prolonged by Ordinance (2022:35) on Prolongation on a Temporary Entry Ban to Sweden.

[38] Ordinance (2022:53) on Continued Validity of Ordinance (2020:127) on a Temporary Entry Ban to Sweden and Changes in its Application.

Note that several restrictions were successively lifted during the beginning of 2022, for instance, a majority of the restrictions were lifted on 9 February 2022[39] and other statutory law introduced during the pandemic expired on 31 March 2022. In line with these changes, as of 1 April 2022, Covid-19 was no longer classified as a disease that is a danger to the general public.[40]

A particular feature introduced during the Covid-19 pandemic is the establishment of the Corona Commission (Commission), mandated to evaluate the measures taken by the government, government agencies, regions and municipalities and their crisis management.[41] The Commission produced three reports. The first focused on the elderly care and concluded that the Swedish strategy regarding the elderly care has failed. Yet, the Commission does not hold a particular actor responsible – rather it points out structural shortcomings long known to the current and previous governments.[42] The second report made several conclusions: for instance, Sweden's handling of the pandemic has been marked by a slowness of response and the initial measures were insufficient to stop or to limit the spread of the virus, and Sweden was inadequately prepared. The Commission stressed that the existing legislation was inadequate in relation to a pandemic, noting that the prevention and control of the virus was (and is) decentralised, making it unclear who bears the overall responsibility during a pandemic.[43] The third and final report concluded that although the Swedish response in certain regards was correct (*e.g.,* economic crisis management, focus on voluntary advice and recommendations), Sweden's crisis management was criticised. The Commission concludes, for instance, that the government should have assumed a clearer leadership, that the government depended too one-sidedly on the Public Health Agency and that Sweden, in the beginning of the pandemic, should have opted for more rigorous and intrusive disease prevention and control measures.[44]

II. CONSTITUTIONAL, LEGAL AND POLICY OVERVIEW

A. Overview of and Specific Constitutional and Legal Principles Regarding Criminal Liability of High-Ranking Government/Public Officials

No particular constitutional and legal principles are available for high-ranking officials in Swedish constitutional law. Instead, if a high-ranking official is a criminal suspect, the

---

[39] See Ministry of Health and Social Affairs, 'Majority of COVID-19 restrictions to be removed on 9 February 2022' (3 February 2022), www.government.se/articles/2022/02/majority-of-covid-19-restrictions-to-be-removed-on-9-february-2022/.

[40] Act (2022:217) on Amendment to the Communicable Diseases Act (2004:168); Ordinance (2022:221) on Amendment to the Ordinance on Communicable Diseases (2004:255).

[41] The Corona Commission was established by the government on 30 June 2020 through dir. 2020:74. The objective of the Corona Commission is available in English, see 'Committee terms of reference', www.coronakommissionen.com/wp-content/uploads/2020/12/dir-2020-74-evaluation-of-the-measures-to-tackle-the-outbreak-of-the-virus-that-causes-the-disease-covid-19.pdf.

[42] See the *travaux préparatoires* SOU 2020:80. An English summary is available at: www.coronakommissionen.com/wp-content/uploads/2020/12/summary.pdf.

[43] See the *travaux préparatoires* SOU 2021:89. An English summary is available at: www.coronakommissionen.com/wp-content/uploads/2021/10/summary-sweden-in-the-pandemic.pdf.

[44] See the *travaux préparatoires* SOU 2022:10. An English summary is available at: www.coronakommissionen.com/wp-content/uploads/2022/02/summary_20220225.pdf.

standard procedure in criminal cases applies. However, Swedish constitutional law does offer special constitutional and legal principles regarding the possibilities to prosecute a member of government in some cases. Although Swedish constitutional law lacks a procedure for impeachment,[45] the Swedish Constitution provides a specific procedure, regulating the possibility to prosecute a member of government. The procedure is stipulated in the Instrument of Government, but has not been put into practice since it was introduced into Swedish constitutional law in 1974.

It should be emphasised that the specific procedure sets a high standard for its imposition. The reason is mainly pragmatic since members of government normally act under unique circumstances, where decisions and policies are often made after balancing various interests. With decisions of a political and societal nature, criminal liability seldom sits well in relation to a government member's decisions.[46]

According to the Instrument of Government, chapter 13, section 3, a current or a former member of government *can* be held liable for an offence committed while conducting his or her ministerial duties, but only if he or she has grossly disregarded official duty in committing the offence. Further, this provision states that the Committee on the Constitution (a part of the Swedish Parliament) decides whether a member of government should be prosecuted,[47] and if such a decision is made, the trial should be held before the Swedish Supreme Court,[48] with the Parliamentary Ombudsmen as prosecutor.[49] Note that the provision lacks instructions regarding the possible sentence, and this, at least partly, could be explained by the fact that it is not a criminal law provision. However, it could be argued that the specific procedure is rather odd; it clearly clashes with the idea that the government makes decisions collectively.

The conditions stated in the Instrument of Government, chapter 13, section 3, deserve further explanation. First, the provision is strictly limited to measures taken (or not taken) when executing the powers associated with the role of being a member of government, where a cabinet minister's actions, generally, are politically motivated.[50] Normally, a member of government acts in that capacity, for instance, during cabinet meetings (in particular when presenting proposals), when negotiating with foreign States, and when meeting with representatives of a government agency.[51] Second, the provision only includes liability for severe offences, *e.g.*, sedition, high treason, breach of trust in negotiations with a foreign power and genocide.[52] Third, the provision is further

---

[45] Historically, impeachment of some type was provided in Swedish constitutional law between 1772 and 1974. Prior to the 1974 Instrument of Government, impeachment had not been used since 1854, see, eg the *travaux préparatoires* prop. 1973:90, 421.

[46] See the *travaux préparatoires* prop. 1973:90, 421; SOU 1972:15, 205.

[47] Note that the provision only states that the Committee on the Constitution allows a member of government to be prosecuted, which – somewhat simplified – means that a pre-trial investigation can be initiated (by the Parliamentary Ombudsmen). However, it is later the Parliamentary Ombudsmen who – if there is enough evidence etc – indict a member of government. To avoid confusion for a reader from a common law jurisdiction, note that 'indictment' in Sweden is only the very end of the pre-trial investigation. Once the pre-trial investigation is completed, the prosecutor needs to issue the institution of prosecution, ie, the indictment.

[48] See also the Swedish Code of Judicial Procedure (1942:710), c 3, s 3, para 1.

[49] Act on Instruction for the Parliamentary Ombudsmen (1986:765), s 10.

[50] See the *travaux préparatoires* prop. 1973:90, 423; SOU 1972:15, 205–06.

[51] See the *travaux préparatoires* SOU 1972:15, 205–06.

[52] See the *travaux préparatoires* SOU 1972:15, 206.

limited to cases of gross disregard in relation to official duties. Thus, cases that do not meet this requirement will be handled either by the standard procedure of a criminal case or by a parliamentary declaration of no confidence. However, the latter is merely a mechanism for political accountability, which can result only in the cabinet minister's resignation.[53]

B. Scope of Responsibility and Area of Tolerated Risk

Note that the provision on the specific procedure in the Instrument of Government, chapter 13, section 3, is rather limited in its scope, since it includes only liability in cases where a member of government has grossly disregarded his or her official duty.

C. Impact of Immunities

No immunities are available in Swedish law for members of government or senior government officials. However, some argue that the procedure stated in the Instrument of Government, chapter 13, section 3, is a type of – very limited – (procedural) immunity since it requires a decision by a political organ (the Committee on the Constitution) to prosecute and since the provision is limited in its scope.[54] The argument is not convincing, since the provision does not constitute a real immunity.

D. Prosecutorial Matters

See above in Section II.A, where prosecutorial matters are considered in relation to the constitutional and legal policy regarding the possibilities of holding members of government liable.

III. CAUSATION

A. Causation (General Principles)

All offences that require an effect, *e.g.*, that someone was physically hurt, also require a causal connection between the act and the effect. However, only acts that are adequate in

---

[53] The procedure of a declaration of no confidence is stated in the Instrument of Government (1974:152), c 13, s 4. See also Instrument of Government (1974:152), c 6, s 7, stating that a member of government should be discharged from his or her office if the Parliament has declared that the minister no longer has its confidence. See also Nergelius, *Constitutional Law* (n 11) 78–84. Note that the Parliament rarely has declared a lack of confidence; until 2022 the procedure has been used 13 times, and seven of them concerned a declaration directed at the Prime Minister – only of the declarations aimed at the Prime Minister were successful. Note also that eight of the 13 declarations has occurred since 2015, which indicates that the Parliament uses the possibility to declare a lack of confidence more frequently today than in the past.

[54] See O Lundin, 'Riksdagsledamöternas och statsrådens rättsliga ansvar' in E Smith and O Petersson (eds), *Konstitutionell demokrati* (Stockholm, SNS, 2004) 162–64.

relation to the effect can establish causation for which criminal liability can be imposed. There is no guidance from the Supreme Court on causation.[55] Instead, the matter has been discussed in the literature.[56] Although Swedish authors prefer somewhat different terminology when addressing the matter, it is clear that they have a common idea; to offer guidance on how to limit criminal responsibility to appropriate acts. The following overview is greatly simplified.

Causation always requires that the act preceded the effect. It is not necessary that the act was the only one preceding the effect; the act can be one of several. Further, a causal connection can also be established if – by negating the act – the effect does not occur. Moreover, the prevailing opinion is that it is not difficult to establish a causal connection between the act and the effect, the reason being that a causal link is often followed by common-sense-based reasoning.[57] Instead, the main question is how to limit criminal responsibility only to acts that are adequate in relation to the effect.

The evaluation of whether an act is adequate needs to be individualised by assessing the act as it was in relation to the effect that actually occurred. In this assessment, the circumstances surrounding the act and the context in which the effect occurred etc are of great relevance. Therefore, it is difficult to present a precise and generalised method for determining which acts are adequate. However, the literature suggests that the assessment should focus on conducting an inventory of the possible risks that a certain act could result in and whether any of these risks potentially could be realised as an effect of a certain act. Consequently, at the time of the offence, the act should have involved an objective risk that the effect would occur in the way that it in fact did. Generally, this means that the risk assessment centres around the question whether the act was a departure from careful behaviour. Since it is impossible to specify this further, the assessment should centre around relevant standards available or general assumptions of human behaviour, for example that a person acts rationally (*e.g.*, a driver can expect other drivers to follow traffic rules) and that a person involved in a risky activity should take necessary precaution. Thus, if the act involves high risk (and the person is aware of this) and the effect occurs, it is generally enough to establish a causal connection that is adequate.

B. Causation and 'Thin Skull' Scenarios

Neither the Supreme Court nor the literature has addressed 'thin skull' scenarios. However, if such a scenario would occur, a court would most likely argue that there exists a causal connection. The reason being that a court presumably would assess the

---

[55] But see Supreme Court case NJA 2020 s 397, where two defendants were convicted of causing the death of another (Swedish Criminal Code, c 3, s 7) by selling a substance that at the time was legal. Some of the byers died after using the substance. However, the reasoning by the Court is not clear since it does not always differ between causation as an actus reus requirement and negligence as a mens rea requirement.

[56] See, eg P Asp et al, *Kriminalrättens grunder* 2nd edn (Uppsala, Iustus, 2013) 78–89, 134–80; I Strahl, *Allmän straffrätt i vad mån angår brotten* (Stockholm, Norstedt, 1976) 51–74; I Agge, *Straffrättens allmänna del. Föreläsningar. Andra häftet* (Stockholm, Norstedt, 1961) 289–305; N Jareborg, 'The Two Faces of Culpa' in N Jareborg (ed), *Essays in Criminal Law* (Uppsala, Iustus, 1988) 28–52.

[57] See, eg Asp et al, *Kriminalrättens grunder* (n 56) 78.

matter of causation ex ante by considering all knowledge available at the time of the (alleged) crime, including the fact that the victim, for instance, had a pre-existing heart condition. Although this would result in establishing a causal connection, the defendant still needs to fulfil the relevant mens rea requirement, *i.e.*, either intent or negligence (see Section IV.A below). Thus, 'thin skull' scenarios would presumably be handled as a matter of whether the defendant fulfils the mens rea requirement and not a matter of causation.

C. Restricting Causality: Policy and Doctrinal Issues

As mentioned in Section III.A above, causation has mainly been discussed in the literature, providing some guidance on when a causal connection can be established between the act and the effect that occurred. The discussion in the literature stems from the idea of restricting criminal responsibility to relevant deeds. Apart from the above-mentioned guidance in the literature, it is difficult to provide detailed norms and policies with general validity. The reason is mainly pragmatic; the assessment of which risks are adequate for establishing a causal connection between the act and the effect depends on the activities in question.

IV. THE STRUCTURE OF HOMICIDE OFFENCES AND ASSAULT/AGGRAVATED ASSAULT/SERIOUS BODILY HARM OFFENCES

A. Murder/Intentional Homicide

Swedish criminal law recognises three offences of homicide: (1) murder, (2) manslaughter and (3) causing the death of another. While the elements of the actus reus are similar for these three offences, they differ in the mens rea requirement; murder and manslaughter require that the perpetrator acted with intent, and the offence of causing the death of another requires that the defendant acted by negligence. The criteria for distinguishing between murder and manslaughter have changed through time. Today, Swedish criminal law strongly emphasises that murder is the primary offence to be applied in cases of intentional killing.[58]

The murder offence centres on the fact that the perpetrator has killed another living person. In Swedish law, life is considered to begin at birth, *i.e.*, when labour starts or when an operative intervention begins. Thus, a foetus is not considered to be alive and cannot be considered a victim of murder. Another important question is to determine the time of death. According to Swedish law, death occurs when all the brain's functions have been completely and irretrievably lost (Act on Criteria for Determining Human Death, section 1), which normally means that both blood circulation and respiration have ceased (Act on Criteria for Determining Human Death, section 2).

The provision on murder stipulates the actus reus as when 'a person who takes the life of another person is guilty of murder'.[59] Since the wording of the provision does not limit

---

[58] See, eg the *travaux préparatoires* prop. 1962:10, part B, 75; Supreme Court case NJA 2013 s 376, para 28.
[59] Swedish Criminal Code (1962:700), c 3, s 1.

how a murder – either by an act or omission – is committed, a murder can be conducted in several ways: by stabbing, by shooting, by poisoning, etc. Theoretically and practically, the difficulty in murder cases seldom concerns whether the prerequisite is fulfilled. Instead, several other complex legal issues may arise when determining whether to hold someone responsible for murder. To illustrate 'other legal issues', two examples will be mentioned here. First, the provision does in fact limit the possibility to hold someone responsible for murder. For example, the prerequisite 'tak[ing] the life of another person' suggests that there needs to be a causal link between the alleged deed and the effect (*i.e.*, the death of the other person), which may raise complicated questions whether the effect was relevant to the specific risks involved.[60] Second, the *mens rea* requirement of intent might raise questions of whether the defendant acted with intent. Therefore, it is relevant to review how intent is understood in Swedish criminal law.[61]

Two types of mens rea exist in Swedish law: intent and negligence. Intent is the standard mens rea requirement while negligence can only be applied if a certain provision explicitly states that this form of mens rea suffices to establish liability.[62] When the court assesses whether the relevant mens rea requirement is fulfilled, the principle of correspondence needs to be considered. This means that the defendant's perception of the course of events should be reasonably consistent with what the prosecutor is able to prove.[63]

Although Sweden is a civil law jurisdiction emphasising statutory law, no provision in Swedish criminal law defines intent.[64] Instead, the different forms of intent have been developed mainly through Supreme Court precedents, which – at least partly – has been influenced by the literature. Both Supreme Court precedents and the literature have focused mostly on the lowest form of intent (*i.e.*, how to define this in relation to the highest form of negligence). Today, Swedish criminal law recognises three forms of intent: direct intent, indirect intent and reckless intent. Unless otherwise stated, reckless intent is sufficient to prove that the defendant acted with intent.

Direct intent is applied if the elements of the offence are expressed in such a way that they require a particular result or effect, which normally follows from the wording of the applicable provision. Simply, this means that the defendant committed the deed with a certain purpose, for example that the defendant kills someone out of jealousy. Indirect intent means that the defendant is practically aware that an effect will occur or that a condition exists.[65] In other words, he or she has no doubt that an effect will

---

[60] M Ulväng, 'Sweden' in A Reed et al (eds), *Homicide in Criminal Law: A Research Companion* (New York, Routledge, 2019) 501.

[61] For a fairly recent overview of intent in Swedish criminal law written in English, see E Lekvall and D Martinsson, 'The *Mens Rea* Element of Intent in the Context of International Criminal Trials in Sweden' (2020) 66 *Scandinavian Studies in Law* 99, 104–08.

[62] Swedish Criminal Code (1962:700), c 1, s 2, para 1.

[63] See, eg I Agge, *Straffrättens* (n 56) 255–64; Strahl, *Allmän straffrätt* (n 56) 119–27; Asp et al, *Kriminalrättens grunder* (n 56) 64, 270, 323–61; A Bäcklund et al, *Brottsbalken* (1 December 2021, JUNO), commentary to the Swedish Criminal Code, c 1, s 2, under the heading Vad ska uppsåtet täcka?.

[64] It has been suggested that a legal definition should be introduced in the statutory law, see the *travaux préparatoires* SOU 1996:185, 55, 108–27. However, the government turned this suggestion down, see the *travaux préparatoires* prop. 2000/01:85, 9–13.

[65] See, eg Supreme Court cases: NJA 2004 s 176, particularly at 194–95; NJA 1977 s. 630, particularly at 638.

occur as a consequence of his or her conduct, or that a condition exists. The lowest form of intent – reckless intent – was formally established in a Supreme Court precedent pronounced in 2004.[66] Here, the Court stated that reckless intent is fulfilled when the following two criteria are met. First, the defendant must be indifferent to the existence of a certain effect, result or circumstance, which is another way of stating that the defendant must be aware or have knowledge of the risks relating to the deed he or she performed. Second, the defendant must be indifferent to the realisation of the effect, result or circumstance in the sense that he or she accepts the effect, result or circumstance that occurs – or might occur – because of his or her conduct. Consequently, it is the second requirement of reckless intent that determines whether the defendant acted with intent or negligence.

Note that the construction of reckless intent in Swedish law is a form of *dolus eventualis*,[67] which is used as the lowest form of intent in some civil law jurisdictions.[68] However, from a common law perspective, reckless intent might seem rather peculiar, since its meaning – at least partly – resembles how recklessness as a mens rea requirement is perceived in some common law jurisdictions.[69]

If the defendant is convicted of murder, the potential sentence is imprisonment for 10 to 18 years of life imprisonment.[70] In 2020 the provision on murder was amended, motivated politically by the desire to impose life imprisonment in more cases.[71] While the Supreme Court in three cases acknowledged that the amendment would result in an increased use of life imprisonment, it also stated that the standard sentence for murder is imprisonment for 16 years.[72]

Further, if the unlikelihood of enacting the procedure stated in the Instruction of Government, explained above in Section II.A, would occur, it would first be hard to prove a causal link between decisions made by members of government and people dying. Second, it would be rather difficult to prove beyond reasonable doubt that a member of government acted with intent to murder when deciding on matters relating to the Covid-19 pandemic. It would, for example, be undoubtedly difficult (if not impossible) to prove that a government member acted even with reckless intent during decisions concerning the pandemic.[73] Potentially, it could of course be argued that a member of government was aware that certain decisions taken during the Covid-19 pandemic could

---

[66] The reckless intent was formulated in Supreme Court case NJA 2004 s 176. Note that the Court prior to the 2004 precedent, has reasoned in terms of reckless intent, see, eg NJA 1975 s 594; NJA 1985 s 757; NJA 1990 s 210; NJA 1996 s 509.

[67] See, eg N Jareborg and M Ulväng, *Tanke och uppsåt* (Uppsala, Iustus, 2016) 116.

[68] See, eg I Marchuk, *The Fundamental Concept of Crime in International Criminal Law: A Comparative Law Analysis* (Berlin, Springer, 2014) 39–67.

[69] See, eg J Horder, *Ashworth's Principles of Criminal Law* 10th edn (Oxford: Oxford University Press, 2022) 217–24; AP Simester and WJ Brookbanks, *Principles of Criminal Law* 5th edn (Wellington, Thomson Reuters, 2019) 141–54.

[70] Note that after serving at least 10 years, a convicted person can apply to convert the life imprisonment to a fixed term sentence.

[71] Act (2019:805) on Amendment to the (Swedish) Criminal Code. See also the *travaux préparatoires* prop. 2018/19:138.

[72] See the following cases: NJA 2021 s 32; NJA 2021 s 377; NJA 2021 s 583.

[73] It should – again – be stressed that a member of government cannot act individually, since government decisions are made by the government as a collective.

result in people dying. However, it would be difficult to argue – and to prove – that a member of government was indifferent to the realisation of the effect (*i.e.*, taking the life of another person). Thus, it is not very likely that a member of government, due to decisions made (or not made) during the Covid-19 pandemic, will be held liable for murder.

B. Culpable Homicide/Manslaughter

In Sweden, manslaughter is an offence of intentional homicide, which, according to the Swedish Criminal Code, Chapter 3, Section 2, is 'less serious' than murder. Whether an intentional killing is 'less serious' than murder is assessed by taking into account all the relevant circumstances of the individual case.[74] However, since murder is the predominant provision to be applied in cases of intentional homicide, the provision on manslaughter is to be applied only in exceptional cases.[75] The Supreme Court has stated that, for the provision on manslaughter to apply, the circumstances in the case must be 'clearly mitigating'.[76] This might be the case where the perpetrator kills the victim out of mercy and for saving him or her from suffering an incurable disease,[77] where the defendant's psychological characteristics affected his or her deed,[78] where the perpetrator killed the victim in self-defence or where the perpetrator had long been abused psychologically and decided to kill the abuser.[79] Since manslaughter is an intentional homicide and the provision does not state a specific intent, the lowest form of intent (*i.e.*, reckless intent) is sufficient to establish liability. The possible sentence for manslaughter is imprisonment for a minimum of six years and a maximum of 10 years.

Regarding the possibility of holding a member of government liable for manslaughter due to decisions made (or not made) during the Covid-19 pandemic, the above-mentioned difficulties regarding murder have the same bearing in relation to manslaughter.

In addition to the two offences on intentional homicide, Swedish law criminalises negligent homicide through the offence of causing the death of another.[80] Although its construction of the actus reus seems simple, the offence raises some legal problems. Since the objective elements of the offence do not limit the possible ways of committing it, problems could arise in relation to causation and other issues relating to general principles of criminal responsibility, for example minimum standards for what constitutes an act, judgments of what is an unlawful risk and how to limit the scope of responsibility in cases of remote harm.[81] Further, the mens rea requirement of negligence must be fulfilled.

---

[74] See the *travaux préparatoires* prop. 1962:10, part B, 75; SOU 1953:14, 122.
[75] See, eg the *travaux préparatoires* prop. 1962:10, part B, 75.
[76] See, eg Supreme Court cases NJA 2013 s 376, para 28; NJA 2016 s 809, para 9.
[77] See, eg Supreme Court cases NJA 1979 s 802; NJA 2013 s 376, para 24.
[78] See, eg Supreme Court cases NJA 1989 s 97; NJA 1985 s 510, NJA 2002 s 116. Note that the defendant in each of these cases was convicted for murder.
[79] See the *travaux préparatoires* prop. 1962:10, part B, 75.
[80] Swedish Criminal Code (1962:700), c 3, s 7.
[81] See, eg Ulväng, 'Sweden' (n 60) 497.

Although the statutory law does not define negligence, Swedish criminal law recognises two types of negligence: conscious and unconscious. While conscious negligence is where the defendant is aware or has knowledge of the risks relating to the deed performed (*i.e.*, the first, but not the second requirement of reckless intent is fulfilled), unconscious negligence is where the defendant is unaware or lacks knowledge of the risks relating to the deed performed, but should have been aware of these risks.[82] Unless otherwise provided, unconscious negligence is sufficient to prove that the defendant acted with negligence.[83] Regarding the mens rea requirement of negligence for the offence of causing the death of another, Swedish criminal law does not provide a standard for when the defendant in general terms fulfils the subjective element. This is because the level and the nature of negligence must relate to the context in which the deed was committed. Yet, the literature mentions that this assessment aims at deciding whether the defendant at the time of the deed, had reason to regard the risk for a deadly outcome.[84]

The offence of causing the death of another is divided into three sub-categories: the minor degree, the standard degree and the gross degree. The statutory law indicates when the offence is gross. The provision states that the court should give particular consideration to 'whether the act involved deliberate risk-taking of a serious kind' and 'whether when particular attention or skill was required, the perpetrator was under the influence of alcohol or some other substance or was otherwise guilty of neglect of a serious kind'. Note that an offence might be considered gross in other situations than those mentioned in the provision.[85] The three sub-categories of the offence of causing the death of another differ in the sentencing. While the possible sentence for the minor degree is a fine, the sentence for the standard degree is imprisonment for a maximum of two years, and the sentence for the gross offence is imprisonment for a minimum of one year and a maximum of six years.

C. Offences Related to Actions that Cause Serious Bodily Harm (Assault; Grievous Assault; Assault with Intent to Cause Serious Bodily Harm)

Swedish criminal law recognises four degrees of assault: minor degree, standard degree, gross assault and exceptionally gross assault.[86] The design of the different degrees of assault centres around the fact that the defendant inflicts some form of bodily harm on the victim. Thus, the assault offence does not have a complex legal structure. Like the above-mentioned homicide offences, complicated questions may arise instead in relation

---

[82] See generally Bäcklund et al, *Brottsbalken* (n 63) commentary to the Swedish Criminal Code, c 1, s 2, under the heading Begreppet oaktsamhet; Asp et al, *Kriminalrättens grunder* (n 56) 314–19.

[83] When a provision states that 'gross negligence' is required, it generally means that conscious negligence is required for the mens rea requirement to be fulfilled. However, that does not exclude the possibility that an unconscious negligent defendant acted with gross negligence.

[84] See eg A Bäcklund et al, *Brottsbalken* (n 63) commentary to the Swedish Criminal Code, c 3, s 7, under the heading Den brottsliga gärningen.

[85] See, eg Supreme Court case NJA 1992 s 85, where the defendant was held responsible for a gross offence of causing the death of another; the reason being that the victim was a month-old child.

[86] The minor and standard degree of assault is regulated in the Swedish Criminal Code (1962:700), c 3, s 5, the gross and exceptionally gross degree of assault is regulated in the Swedish Criminal Code (1962:700), c 3, s 6.

to elements like causality, the relevant risk-taking, the mens rea requirement etc. The provision on assault of the standard degree stipulates the actus reus as when the defendant inflicts 'bodily injury, illness or pain' on the victim, or 'renders the [victim] helpless or in some other similar state'.[87] While 'bodily injury' includes for instance wounds, swelling, fracture and impaired vision, 'illness' includes for instance venereal disease, psychological disease and psychological trauma. 'Pain' is where the bodily harm caused is not too mild or momentarily short.[88] The offence of assault requires – regardless of the degree – that the defendant acted with intent and reckless intent is sufficient to establish liability. The various degrees of assault can, briefly, be explained as follows; the minor degree is applied when the defendant slaps the victim with an open hand, and the standard degree is applied when the defendant hits the victim with a closed fist. While the gross degree applies when for instance the assault was life-threatening, caused severe bodily harm or was particularly brutal, the exceptionally gross degree applies when, *e.g.*, the assault caused permanent bodily harm or exceptional suffering or the defendant displayed exceptional ruthlessness.[89]

The four sub-categories of the assault offence differ in the sentencing. While the possible sentence for the minor degree is a fine or imprisonment for a maximum of six months, the sentence for the standard degree is imprisonment for a maximum of two years, the sentence for gross assault is imprisonment for a minimum of one and a half years and a maximum of six years and the possible sentence for exceptionally gross assault is imprisonment for a minimum of five years and a maximum of imprisonment for 10 years.

D. Offences Regarding Unborn Foetuses; Interrupting the Course of a (Viable) Pregnancy

As mentioned above in Section IV.A, in Swedish law a foetus is not considered to be a living person, and thus cannot be a victim of crimes like murder, manslaughter or assault.[90] The fact that the defendant, for example, kills a pregnant woman might however be of relevance as an aggravating circumstance when determining the sentence.[91] However, Swedish law does criminalise some cases of interrupting the course of a viable pregnancy.

In Sweden, abortion is legal and freely available for a woman who wants to terminate her pregnancy. The procedure can only be performed by an authorised medical doctor and should take place in a hospital or other health care facility approved by the Swedish National Board of Health and Welfare.[92] A legal abortion can be performed through

---

[87] Swedish Criminal Code (1962:700), c 3, s 5.

[88] See the *travaux préparatoires* SOU 1953:14, 134–35.

[89] For Supreme Court precedents on these two degrees of assault, see, eg NJA 2011 s 89; NJA 2012 s 45; NJA 2013 s 1155; NJA 2020 s 564.

[90] Note that after 28 weeks, the foetal development is generally at a stage where the foetus – after being born – can be considered viable. Thus, if birth occurs after this period and regardless of viability, the born child could be considered a victim of eg murder, manslaughter or assault, see, eg Ulväng, 'Sweden' (n 60) 508.

[91] See, eg Court of Appeal for Western Sweden, judgment, 25 January 2016, reference number B 5154-15, where the Court sentenced the defendant to life imprisonment, arguing that the defendant (also) 'extinguished a life in creation'.

[92] Abortion Act (1974:595), s 5.

the eighteenth week of pregnancy *if* it is not assumed to present a serious danger to the woman's life or health.[93] After the end of the eighteenth week, an abortion is legal only if the Swedish National Board of Health and Welfare grants permission.[94] Further, if someone performs an abortion in breach of these rules, he or she may be held liable; for example, a doctor who intentionally does so can be sentenced to a fine or imprisonment for a maximum of six months.[95] An abortion performed by a person who is not an authorised medical doctor is deemed illegal.[96] If the performer acted with intent, he or she should be held responsible for the offence of conducting an illegal abortion, not for murder or manslaughter. The possible sentence is a fine or imprisonment for a maximum of one year and, if the deed is deemed to be an aggravated offence, the possible sentence is imprisonment for a minimum of six months and a maximum of four years.[97]

E. Failure to Render Assistance

Although criminalisation of failure to render assistance has been proposed on several occasions, an offence of this kind has not yet been introduced into Swedish law.[98]

V. DEFENCES, JUSTIFICATIONS AND EXCUSES

A. Necessity

In Swedish criminal law, necessity is considered a justificatory defence, meaning that the defendant's deed is not wrongful because it was legally acceptable to act the way he or she did.[99] Necessity is regulated in the Swedish Criminal Code, chapter 24, section 4, stating two conditions that must be met for an acquittal: (1) a necessity situation must be established, and (2) the deed must not be unjustifiable.

A necessity situation is defined as arising when a 'danger threatens life, health, property or some other, important interest that is protected by the legal order'.[100] The latter includes, for example, situations where a person prevents a spy from handling information over to a foreign State or where a person prevents and interrupts ongoing animal abuse.[101] Further, the condition of a necessity situation could be described as a filter

---

[93] Abortion Act (1974:595), s 1.

[94] Abortion Act (1974:595), s 3. Permission for conducting an abortion after the eighteenth week of pregnancy is granted rarely.

[95] Abortion Act (1974:595), s 10.

[96] Abortion Act (1974:595), s 9.

[97] Abortion Act (1974:595), s 9.

[98] For the most recent government committee investigating the possibility to introduce a general criminalisation of failure to render assistance, see the *travaux préparatoires* SOU 2011:16.

[99] For a theoretical discussion on the distinction between justifications and excuses in Sweden, see, eg N Jareborg, 'Justification and excuse in Swedish criminal law' in N Jareborg (ed), *Essays in Criminal Law* (Uppsala, Iustus, 1988) 11–27.

[100] Swedish Criminal Code (1962:700), c 24, s 4, para 2.

[101] See the *travaux préparatoires* SOU 1923:9, 172; SOU 1953:14, 41.

that restricts the potential to object successfully to criminal liability on this justifica-tory ground. The reason is that both the *travaux préparatoires* and the Supreme Court precedents state that the requirement of a 'necessity situation' should be applied rather restrictively.[102] However, if the court deems it as a necessity situation, the question arises of whether the defendant's action was justifiable.

When the court assesses whether the actions taken in a situation of necessity was justi-fiable, the provision on necessity states that regard should be given to 'the nature of the danger, the damaged caused to another, and the other circumstances'.[103] Thus, the provi-sion clearly signals that the question of justifiability is an assessment of whether the deed performed by the defendant was proportionate in relation to the relevant threat. This is, for example, shown by the fact that the court should consider 'the nature of the danger'; meaning that particular weight should be given to the threatened interest, *i.e.*, whether the danger was aimed at life, health or property. Additionally, when assessing the damage caused to another, the court should consider the degree of intrusion of the damage caused.[104] Together, these two factors indicate that an act of necessity can be justified if the interest protected by the legal system is clearly more important than what is being sacrificed. Consequently, it is generally considered justified to sacrifice others' property to save someone's life.[105] Concerning the question of whether the necessity provision can be applied in situations where the defendant has killed another person, Swedish law is clear: it cannot be applied in order to justify the killing of another person.[106] Further, note that the assessment of whether actions taken in a situation of necessity were justifiable in Swedish law is designed very restrictively: only in extremely rare cases will the defendant be acquitted on the ground of necessity.[107]

If the court considers that it was a necessity situation, but not deemed justifiable, Swedish criminal law offers the defence of excessive necessity, which is an excuse from criminal liability. According to the Swedish Criminal Code, chapter 24, section 6, the defendant should be excused if he or she 'had difficulty controlling [his or her] actions'. Although this signals that assessment should primarily be subjective, the *travaux prépara-toires* emphasise that consideration should be given to the character of the danger, the time available for the person to consider his or her actions and for the defendant to react adequately, and the defendant's individual characteristics.[108] From Supreme Court prec-edents it follows that the provision has been applied rather strictly.[109]

---

[102] See the *travaux préparatoires* SOU 1953:14, 412, 416; prop. 1962:10, part B, 337, prop. 1993/94:130, 34 and the following Supreme Court cases: NJA 1979 s 335; NJA 1982 s 621; NJA 1993 s 128; NJA 1996 s 443; NJA 1998 s 512; NJA 2000 s 302. But see NJA 2017 s 812, where the Supreme Court seems to have widened the concept of a necessity situation.

[103] Swedish Criminal Code (1962:700), c 24, s 4, para 1.

[104] See the *travaux préparatoires* SOU 1953:14, 412, 416; SOU 1923:9, 173–74.

[105] See the *travaux préparatoires* SOU 1953:14, 414–15.

[106] See, eg the *travaux préparatoires* prop. 1962:10, part B, 482. See also P Asp and M Ulväng, 'Sweden' in A Reed, M Bohlander, N Wake and E Smith (eds), *General Defences in Criminal Law: Domestic and Comparative Perspectives* (New York, Routledge, 2014) 309.

[107] See the *travaux préparatoires* SOU 1953:14, 416; SOU 1988:7, 81. Additionally, if the defendant is not excused on the ground of excessive necessity, the sentence could be reduced, Swedish Criminal Code (1962:700), c 29, s 3, para 1, point 5.

[108] See the *travaux préparatoires* prop. 1993/94:130, 45; SOU 1988:7, 141.

[109] See, eg the following Supreme Court cases: NJA 1977 s 655; NJA 1988 s 495; NJA 1994 s 48; NJA 1995 s 661. But see Supreme Court case NJA 2009 s 234, where the defendant had caused the surviving victim severe bodily harm and was excused due to excessive self-defence.

In the context of the Covid-19 pandemic a member of government can, in the unlikely event that the procedure stated in the Instruction of Government is enacted, invoke the Swedish provision on necessity.[110] Presumably, the court would most likely deem that the Covid-19 pandemic threatened both the lives and the health of people in Sweden. The court would thus regard it as a necessity situation. However, when assessing whether the action taken (or not taken) during the pandemic was justifiable, it is highly unlikely that a court would regard it as justifiable on the ground of necessity. This is because the Swedish provision on necessity cannot justify actions where the interest of someone's life stands against another human life.[111] Further, considering that the time available to the defendant is one important factor in this assessment, it is not very likely that a court would excuse a member of government on the ground of excessive necessity.

VI. CORPORATE CRIMINAL LIABILITY

A. Overview of Corporate Criminal Liability

In Sweden, only natural persons can commit an offence and only natural persons can be sentenced.[112] However, if an offence is committed within a business corporation, criminal liability may be awarded to the person(s) who committed the deed. To determine who, within a corporation, could potentially be held responsible for an offence, the case law and the literature have created guidelines.[113] First, liability can primarily be awarded to persons in leadership positions, meaning the CEO, board members etc. Second, it is not uncommon that certain areas of responsibility are delegated to those in lower positions. Delegation of this type could affect who is considered responsible for acts and omissions occurring within the corporation. Note that only tasks, not criminal liability, can be delegated. However, correct delegation points out the natural person(s) who could be held liable. For delegation to have this effect, four requirements must be fulfilled: (1) there is a clear need for the delegation, (2) the delegatee must have an independent position in relation to the leadership, (3) the delegatee must have sufficient competence or education for the delegated tasks and (4) it is sufficiently clear who gives the delegation and what its contents are. If any of these criteria are not met, the delegation cannot affect the criminal liability and liability will return to the delegator.

---

[110] See, eg N Jareborg, *Allmän kriminalrätt* (Uppsala, Iustus, 2001) 265.

[111] It is assumed here that a member of government would be held responsible for decisions made (or not made), resulting in some human lives being sacrificed/jeopardised to save as many other lives as possible, or – at least – that the health of some people had been jeopardised to maintain better health for a larger group of people.

[112] See, eg the *travaux préparatoires* SOU 1997:127, part A, 31.

[113] See generally *the travaux préparatoires* SOU 1997:127, part A, 95–118; H Thornstedt, *Om företagaransvar. Studier i specialstraffrätt* (Stockholm, Nordiska bokhandeln, 1948).

B. Accessory or Perpetrator

Since Swedish criminal law recognises that only natural persons can commit an offence and that the persons responsible can be liable for crimes committed within a business corporation, there are no particular regulations regarding matters concerning identification of the perpetrator and accessory to a crime. As mentioned above in Section VI.A, in some cases the identification of the perpetrator of or accessory to a crime depends on whether certain requirements are met. Aside from these requirements, there are no particular rules or norms that apply in a case of corporate criminal liability. Thus, the standard rules and norms regarding for example participation also apply in such a case.

VII. FORMS OF PARTICIPATION

The concept of participation in Swedish criminal law is highly complex. Therefore, the following description is greatly simplified.[114] Swedish criminal law recognises two types of participation: acting as a perpetrator and promoting an offence through complicity. The latter differentiates, in turn, between instigating an offence and abiding an offence. To understand participation in a Swedish context, a brief overview of the concept of who can be considered a perpetrator is necessary. To put it simply, only a person who fulfils both the actus reus and mens rea elements can be held liable as a perpetrator (in a strict sense). Note that when two (or more) persons commit a crime together, it is possible for both to be held liable as a perpetrator – either in a strict sense or as co-perpetrators. If two persons commit an offence by doing the same task (*e.g.*, two people hit the victim), they can both be viewed as perpetrators in a strict sense. When two persons commit an offence by performing different tasks (*e.g.*, when committing a robbery, while one person threatens the victim, the other person takes the victim's wallet) they can be considered co-perpetrators. The main difference is that while a perpetrator (in a strict sense) fulfils the actus reus requirements on his or her own, co-perpetrators do not fulfil the actus reus requirements individually but jointly. The following (minimum) requirements apply in relation to a co-perpetrator: he or she must fulfil at least some part of the actus reus that contributes to the common result and must fulfil the mens rea element, both in relation to the individual deed and the common result. Further, a co-perpetrator must be present at the crime scene at the time of the offence.[115]

---

[114] See generally P Asp and M Ulväng, 'Sweden' in A Reed and M Bohlander (eds), *Participation in Crime: Domestic and Comparative Perspectives* (London, Routledge, 2013) 433–50; T Bennet, 'Criminal Law' in A Bogdan and C Wong (eds), *Swedish Legal System* 2nd edn (Stockholm, Norstedts Juridik, 2022) 167–69. For a thorough analysis, see E Svensson, *Gärningsmannaskap vid fleras deltagande i brott* (Uppsala, Iustus, 2016). See also CE Herlitz, *Parties to a Crime and the Notion of a Complicity Object: A Comparative Study of the Alternatives Provided by the Model Penal Code, Swedish Law and Claus Roxin* (Uppsala, Iustus, 1992).

[115] See, eg Supreme Court case NJA 2006 s 535. Note that someone could be held responsible as a co-perpetrator even if he or she does not fulfil any of the actus reus requirements. However, it presupposes that the person has

If a person cannot be held liable as a perpetrator or co-perpetrator, the provision on complicity might apply. Complicity can only occur before or at the time of the offence.[116] According to the Swedish Criminal Code, chapter 23, section 4, paragraph 1, responsibility for complicity is generally criminalised for offences regulated in the Code and for offences in other statutes stating than an offence could result in imprisonment. Responsibility for complicity applies when someone has promoted an offence by advice or deed, and generally Swedish law distinguishes between instigating and aiding the offence.[117] While instigation includes psychological support to the perpetrator, aiding includes other means of support to the perpetrator. Further, the mens rea requirement of intent or negligence must be fulfilled,[118] meaning that the subjective elements of the instigator or the aider must include both his or her own deed and the deed performed by the perpetrator.

VIII. ATTEMPT

In Swedish criminal law, attempt is not generally criminalised.[119] Instead, criminal liability for attempt presupposes the existence of a provision stating which offences are criminalised as attempt. Additionally, the provision on attempt[120] states that criminal liability for attempt requires that an offence has not been completed, that the defendant has begun to commit a particular offence,[121] that there was a danger that the action would lead to the completion of the offence or that such a danger was only precluded because of chance circumstances.[122] Although the provision on attempt mentions no mens rea requirement, attempt requires that the defendant acted with intent. Unless the particular offence states otherwise, reckless intent is sufficient to prove intent. Note however, that attempt in

---

a very strong influence over the offence being conducted (by having a strong intent to the common result of the offence) and being present at the crime scene when the offence was committed.

[116] See, eg the *travaux préparatoires* SOU 1944:69, 101 and the following Supreme Court cases: NJA 2009 s 3; NJA 2000 s 372; NJA 1949 s 529.

[117] Swedish Criminal Code (1962:700), c 23, s 4, para 2.

[118] Swedish Criminal Code (1962:700), c 23, s 4, para 3. Note that responsibility for instigation or abiding is rarely applied in relation to negligence offences, see however Supreme Court cases NJA 1996 s 27 and NJA 1988 s 383.

[119] See generally Bäcklund et al, *Brottsbalken* (n 63), commentary to the Swedish Criminal Code, c 23, s 1; Asp et al *Kriminalrättens grunder* (n 56) 397–410. For a thorough review, see S Wennberg, *Försök till brott* 2nd edn (Stockholm, Norstedts Juridik, 2010).

[120] Swedish Criminal Code (1962:700), c 23, s 1.

[121] There are often difficulties in determining when the defendant has 'begun to commit a particular crime', since it is a matter of interpreting the particular offence regulating the (intended) crime that the defendant sought to commit. Therefore, when an offence has commenced can only be determined by interpreting the particular provision applicable in the case. The Supreme Court has stated some typical situations when someone has 'begun to commit a particular crime', see NJA 2017 s 531, paras 19–26.

[122] See, eg Supreme Court case NJA 1985 s 544, where two men were convicted of attempt to gross theft (Swedish Criminal Code, c 8, s 4) for attempting to steal suitcases containing jewels from a jewellery store. However, during the planning of their crime, they come to the attention of the police, who in turn contacted the store owner. The owner – with police help – employed fake copies of the jewellery. Thus, when the two men carried through their plan, they got the cases containing fake copies. The Supreme Court concluded that it was a case of 'chance circumstances' since it was a mere coincidence that the cases did not contain jewels.

Swedish law is constructed to include the mens rea requirement as a part of the actus reus. Thus, within the actus reus element, the court should assess whether the defendant acted with intent. Moreover, liability for attempt requires that the defendant acted with intent in relation both to the action(s) taken to conduct the attempt (*e.g.*, in relation to murder, pointing the weapon at the intended victim) and to the non-existing effect (*e.g.*, in relation to murder: that the defendant planned to pull the trigger and the bullet would have hit the victim, causing the victim's death).[123]

IX. SANCTIONS, SENTENCING, PUNISHMENT, REPARATIONS AND/OR RESTORATIVE JUSTICE

A. General Sentencing Framework for the Crimes under Discussion

Since matters concerning sentencing are intertwined with, yet separate from, the assessment of determining the degree of an offence,[124] the sentencing framework is presented in relation to each offence mentioned above in Section IV.

B. Sanctions Specifically for Senior Government/Public Officials

No particular sanctions are available in Swedish constitutional or criminal law for senior government officials. As mentioned above in Section II.A, the Swedish Constitution lacks a procedure for impeachment. Further, although it is not viewed as a sanction, a declaration from the Parliament of no confidence can be announced against a member of government. Note that this is a procedure of political accountability which a can only result in the minister's resignation. However, if the Parliament announces its intention to declare a vote of no confidence against a member of government, it is often assumed that he or she resigns before the Parliament declares a vote of no confidence.

C. Corporations and Sentencing

As mentioned above in Section VI.A, only natural persons can commit an offence and be sentenced under Swedish criminal law. However, this does not hinder corporations (and other legal persons) from being subject to other sanctions.[125] In Swedish criminal law there exists a special sanction – the corporate fine – which can be imposed on corporations and other legal persons for crimes committed within their operation. A corporate

---

[123] See, eg Supreme Court case NJA 2017 s 531, paras 15–18.

[124] Note, for example, that what constitutes a gross offence often is similar to the general aggravating circumstances (regulated in the Swedish Criminal Code, c 29, s 2) to which the court should give regard when sentencing someone. However, the court cannot regard the same aggravating circumstance twice: it is either relevant when determining the degree of the offence or for the sentencing.

[125] See, eg the *travaux préparatoires* SOU 1997:127, part A, 31.

fine is not considered a criminal sanction in Sweden.[126] Instead, it is considered a 'special legal consequence' that might apply in relation to a conviction.[127] A corporate fine might be imposed if the following conditions are fulfilled: (1) if the penalty for the offence is more severe than a fixed fine, (2) if the offence was committed when exercising (2a) business activities, or (2b) public activities equated with business activities, or (2c) other activities conducted by a corporation, if the offence was liable to lead to financial advantage for the corporation, (3) that the offence was committed by a leading person in the corporation or by a person with particular responsibility supervising or controlling the activities of the corporation.[128] The size of the corporate fine is a minimum of 5,000 Swedish crowns and a maximum of 10 million Swedish crowns.[129]

---

[126] In Sweden, the following punishments are considered criminal sanctions: fine, imprisonment, conditional sentence, probation and special care order, Swedish Criminal Code (1962:700), c 1, s 3.

[127] See, eg the *travaux préparatoires* prop. 1985/86:23, 18–23. The concept of 'special legal consequence' includes various legal sanctions that can be imposed when an offence has been committed.

[128] Swedish Criminal Code (1962:700), c 36, s 7.

[129] Swedish Criminal Code (1962:700), c 36, s 8, para 2. Note than one Swedish crown is approximately equal to 0.11 USD (4 April 2022). When determining the corporate fine, the sanction value is of great importance; meaning that the court should give regard to the damage or danger involved and the relationship of the offence to the business (Swedish Criminal Code, c 36, s 8, para 2). If the sanction value is at least 500,000 Swedish crowns, an increased corporate fine should be imposed. The increased corporate fine should be assessed with regard to the financial situation of the corporation and could, as a maximum, be set no higher than an amount corresponding to 50 times the sanction value (Swedish Criminal Code, c 36, s 9, para 1). Thus, theoretically, the largest amount of the increased corporate fine can be set to 500 million Swedish crowns.

14

Turkey

MURAT ÖNOK

I. BACKGROUND AND CONTEXTUAL INTRODUCTION

ACCORDING TO THE data provided in the Covid-19-related website run by the Ministry of Health[1] (MoH), 14,775,634 cases have been registered in Turkey with a death toll standing at 97,666, as of 6 May 2022.

For a long time, starting from the first statistical table published on 27 March 2020 (the first detected case being on 11 March), the MoH informed the public on a daily basis on the number for that day of 'incidences' (*vaka*). On 29 July 2020 the wording changed and the Ministry started informing the public of that day's number of *hasta*, which translates into English as both sick/ill person and patient. However, there was no significant change, in terms of numbers, between incidences and patients. The public, including medical experts, thought that those numbers indicated the number of positive test results. The numbers were rather low compared to European States. On 25 November 2020 the Ministry explained, for the first time, that until that date the daily number of patients/ill persons did not indicate all those who returned a positive test result, but only those who had actually manifested symptoms. The precise meaning of this criterion was never explained. On that day, the number of patients/ill persons was recorded as 6,814, and the number of 'today's incidence/case number' (*günlük vaka sayısı*) as 28,351. Hence it became clear that the actual number of Covid-19 infected people was much higher than the number provided to the public. Within a couple of days, all positive test results were added to the total number of *vaka* (incidence/case). Since 5 July 2021, the distinction between 'patients/ill persons' and 'number of incidences/cases' has been eliminated since only the latter number is given.

It was only starting from 28 June 2020 that the MoH started publishing daily reports which indicated the geographic spread per region. While Turkey is divided into seven geographical regions, these numbers showed the spread according to 11 divisions. In addition, the number of 'sick persons/patients' (but not the number of incidences/cases) was provided for Istanbul alone. Finally, starting from February 2021, the MoH has provided the number of incidences/cases for each of the 81 cities in Turkey, by showing the *weekly* number of incidences/cases for every 100,000 people.[2]

The number of losses has generated debate. It has been argued by physicians that the official cause of death of many Covid-related deaths has not been registered as such.

---

[1] TC Sağlık Bakanlığı, 'Günlük Covid-19 Aşı Tablosu', https://covid19.saglik.gov.tr/.

[2] Before that, starting from 2 April 2020, the daily numbers for each city were announced on a few isolated occasions.

For example, the Turkish Union of Physicians has argued that in 2020 the real number of Covid-19-related casualties was at least three and a half times higher than that announced officially.[3]

As regards the vaccination of the population, Turkey initially used the Sinovac vaccine, and later, added the Pfizer/BioNTech manufactured vaccine, leaving the choice to the person to be vaccinated. The statistics on the issue are also not very clear. The MoH has been giving the following numbers: nationwide *percentage* of persons that have been administered the first dose, the *percentage* of persons that have been administered the second dose, the *number* of total doses administered, the number of administered first, second and third doses. What this methodology does not show is the exact number of persons who have been fully vaccinated. In addition, the statistical breakdown with regard to the vaccine used is also not known. Finally, there is also no statistical information about the statistical spread of deaths (*e.g.*, age spread, whether they were vaccinated or not, geographical spread).

In sum, there was initially an almost total lack of transparency concerning statistical data on the effect of Covid-19 in Turkey. Gradually, more information and data have been provided to the public. However, some crucial data is still unknown, and, in addition, some of the statistics are unclear and/or difficult to interpret. This makes it more difficult for the citizen to make a personal risk assessment. It may be argued that a failure to provide proper information amounts by itself to the offence defined in Article 257 of the Turkish Penal Code (TPC), namely dereliction of duty.[4]

II. CONSTITUTIONAL, LEGAL AND POLICY OVERVIEW

Turkey is ruled through a Presidential system. Within the administration there are specialised ministries, such as the MoH, led by ministers.

A 'Coronavirus Scientific Advisory Board' was established within the MoH in January 2020. It consists of expert academics and its views are of an advisory nature. On various occasions individual members of this Commission have declared that they do not know about the precise statistical details of the pandemic any more than the public or that they are unaware of certain things declared by the Minister of Health, that they are only competent to make suggestions but not to take decisions, that some measures are futile, that some of the implemented measures were not within their knowledge, and that some of the objectives stated by the Minister were not attainable.[5] It is impossible

---

[3] Türk Tabipleri Birliği, 'TUİK 2020 ölüm verileri açıklanmadı. Pandeminin boyutları ve sonuçlarının şeffaf bir şekilde raporlanmadığını defalarca dile getirdik. COVID-19'a bağlı ölüm sayısı, 2020 yılında Bakanlığın açıkladığının en az 3,5 katı!' (*Twitter*, 23 June 2021), https://twitter.com/ttborgtr/status/1407788581926674440.

[4] Turkish Penal Code numbered 5237 dated 26 September 2004. Official Journal Date-No: 12 October 2004-25611. However, the legal definition of this crime requires that the omission causes one of three alternative results (or, according to a part of the doctrine, three alternative 'objective conditions for punishability'): the acts must have caused (1) victimisation to persons, or (2) public harm (which is interpreted in judicial decisions as an economic loss) or (3) illegal advantage to persons.

[5] See eg 'Bilim Kurulu Üyesi Prof. Dr. Pınar Okyay'dan çarpıcı açıklama: Açılmadan haberimiz yoktu' *BirGün* (online, 18 May 2021), www.birgun.net/haber/bilim-kurulu-uyesi-prof-dr-pinar-okyay-dan-carpici-aciklama-acilmadan-haberimiz-yoktu-345083; 'Bilim Kurulu üyesi: Koca'nın 'her vaka hasta değildir' açıklamasından haberimiz yok!' (*IZGAZETE*, 2 October 2020), www.izgazete.net/covid-19/bilim-kurulu-

to assess the level of governmental compliance with the Commission's advice because the latter has worked *in camera*, its findings and recommendations have not been made public, and nothing has been published concerning its work.

The 'Public Health Directorate-General' established within the MoH through a presidential decree is also entrusted with the task to protect public health, and to, inter alia, assess the risk emanating from contagious diseases and to take the necessary preventive measures.

A rather outdated law, the *Umumi Hıfzısıhha Kanunu* (which can be roughly translated as 'Law on General Health Protection')[6] which was adopted in 1930 regulates the measures which can be taken in response to health threats, including epidemics. This Law does not mention Covid-19, and has not been amended as to include any reference to it. This is problematic because certain measures, which have in practice been applied during the Covid-19 crisis, can only be implemented in response to diseases that are exhaustively listed in the relevant provision. Even so, no amendment has been made to this Law after 2018.

Some of the measures implemented in the fight against the pandemic have been brought before administrative courts for their annulment, but no decision seems to have been taken so far by higher courts. If the local (first instance) administrative courts reject such requests, it is possible to apply by way of appeal (*istinaf*) to the 'Regional Administrative Court'.[7] As a third step, it is possible to resort by way of cassation (*temyiz*) to the Council of State (*Danıştay*) which is the highest court judging on administrative court, and sitting in the capital *Ankara*. It is also possible to make an individual application before the Constitutional Court where the applicant can argue that his/her rights have been infringed by persons or institutions exercising public authority. However, the fundamental right and freedom in question must have been secured under the Turkish Constitution and must also fall within the scope of the European Convention on Human Rights (ECHR). Finally, Turkey has been a party to the ECHR since 1954, and recognised the right to individual application to the European Court of Human Rights in 1987 and the compulsory jurisdiction of this Court in 1990. Therefore, it is possible, as a last resort, to apply to the Strasbourg Court.

As regards the constitutional and legal context, the following provisions of the Constitution of 1982 (Constitution)[8] are of particular relevance. According to article 13 (*Restriction of fundamental rights and freedoms*):

> Fundamental rights and freedoms may be restricted only by law and in conformity with the reasons mentioned in the relevant articles of the Constitution without infringing upon their

---

uyesi-koca-nin-her-vaka-hasta-degildir-h53784.html; 'Bilim kurulu üyesi: 5 bin vaka ay sonu bile mümkün değil' *Diken* (online, 14 MaY 2021), www.diken.com.tr/bilim-kurulu-uyesi-bes-bin-vaka-ay-sonu-bile-mumkun-degil/; 'Bilim Kurulu Üyesi Prof. Dr. Kara: O sayıların artık neden verilmediğini bilmiyorum' *Sözcü* (online, 31 July 2020), www.sozcu.com.tr/2020/saglik/bilim-kurulu-uyesi-prof-dr-kara-o-sayilarin-artik-neden-verilmedigini-bilmiyorum-5963233/.

[6] Law on General Health Protection numbered 1593 dated 24 April 1930. Official Journal Date-No: 06 May 1930-1489.

[7] There are seven such Courts, one for each geographical region in Turkey.

[8] Turkish Constitution numbered 2709 dated 18 October 1982. Official Journal Date-No: 9 November 1982-17863 bis.

essence. These restrictions shall not be contrary to the letter and spirit of the Constitution and the requirements of the democratic order of the society and the secular republic and the principle of proportionality.

According to article 15, paragraph 1:

In times of war, mobilisation, a state of emergency, the exercise of fundamental rights and freedoms may be partially or entirely suspended, or measures derogating the guarantees embodied in the Constitution may be taken to the extent required by the exigencies of the situation, as long as obligations under international law are not violated.

According to article 17, paragraph 1:

Everyone has the right to life and the right to protect and improve his/her corporeal and spiritual existence', and according to para. 2 'The corporeal integrity of the individual shall not be violated except under medical necessity and in cases prescribed by law; and shall not be subjected to scientific or medical experiments without his/her consent.

According to article 119 (1):

In the event of ... occurrence of natural disasters, outbreak of dangerous epidemic diseases ... the President of the Republic may declare state of emergency in one region or nationwide for a period not exceeding six months.[9]

For the purpose of articles 13 and 17 the word 'law' is the counterpart of the Turkish legal term 'kanun', which refers to statutes, in other words, statutory laws enacted by the Parliament ('Turkish Grand National Assembly') (GNA). According to the Constitution's article 7: 'Legislative power is vested in the Grand National Assembly of Turkey on behalf of Turkish Nation. This power shall not be delegated'. Article 104 (17), meanwhile, provides that the President

may issue presidential decrees on the matters regarding executive power. The fundamental rights, individual rights and duties included in the first and second chapters and the political rights and duties listed in the fourth chapter of the second part of the Constitution shall not be regulated by a presidential decree. No presidential decree shall be issued on the matters which are stipulated in the Constitution to be regulated exclusively by law. No presidential decree shall be issued on the matters explicitly regulated by law. In the case of a discrepancy between provisions of the presidential decrees and the laws, the provisions of the laws shall prevail. A presidential decree shall become null and void if the Grand National Assembly of Turkey enacts a law on the same matter.

Throughout the pandemic the government, usually through administrative acts (but sometimes in the lack of any written and/or specific basis, even if of an administrative nature) has implemented many measures. The details of most measures have been spelt out in circulars issued by the Ministry of Interior.[10] Turkey has pursued a

---

[9] Unless a state of emergency is declared, under the Turkish constitutional system it is only possible to 'limit/restrict' fundamental rights and freedoms, but not to suspend their application. In addition, it is not possible under the ordinary regime to take any measure that is in contravention of the Constitution. See T Şirin, 'Tehlikeli Salgın Hastalıklarla Anayasal Mücadeleye Giriş' (2020) 17 *Journal of Constitutional Law* 43.

[10] The failure to publish these circulars in the Official Journal (or, sometimes, anywhere) has attracted criticism from the viewpoint of the transparency of the administration. See M Kasapoğlu Turhan, 'Covid-19

test-and-trace policy coupled with a variety of preventive and protective measures, including lockdown(s).

Some of the most notable measures that have been implemented since March 2020 are the following:[11]

Full or partial curfews. The first curfew, starting on 21 March, covered those aged over 65 and those with certain health conditions – certain 'free hours' were then declared starting from 31 May. On 3 April, the curfew extended to those born on or after 1 January 2000; between 10–12 April the first curfew covering everyone, and only in force for the weekend, was implemented in 30 metropolitan cities plus the city of Zonguldak – this measure was repeated many times but starting from the first half of May it now covered 23 cities. Between 22–26 May, on Ramadan Holiday, a full curfew was implemented in all 81 cities (however there was a rather long list of exceptions). In summer these restrictions were eased but stricter curfews were occasionally implemented. For example, on 20 November 2020 a new weekend curfew, only covering 10:00 AM–10:00 PM was implemented. On 30 November the curfew was extended to the whole weekend (Friday 9:00 PM to Monday 05:00 AM). On 14 April the weekday curfew was extended to 7:00 PM–05:00 AM. Between 29 April and 17 May a full curfew was applied. From 17 May to 1 June, a weekday curfew (9:00 PM to 5:00 AM) and a full weekend curfew was applied to everyone. For the next month, a weekday curfew (10:00 PM to 5:00 AM) and a full Sunday curfew was applied to everyone. Since 1 July 2021 there have been no more curfews.

Restricting international travel. On 13 March, entry to Turkey from nine states was suspended. Starting from 14 March, flight to certain states were suspended, the list was extended on 17 March. As of 21 March, flights to and from 68 states were suspended, the entry into Turkey of those who had been present in the last 14 days in one of these 68 states was prohibited. On 27 March all international flights were suspended. Any entry into Turkey was also, in principle, prohibited with the exception of Turkish nationals, holders of Blue Cards, and foreigners who held a residence registry in Turkey (some further exceptions also applied). Starting from 10 June 2020 flight restrictions were gradually lifted. Starting from 22 January 2021, flights from and to some states in which mutations of Covid-19 were discovered were suspended again.

After 18 March 2020, those entering Turkey have been subjected to 14-day quarantine. Apart from the above rules (which apply to certain states), incomers had to submit a negative PCR test result obtained within the last 72 hours or a negative rapid antigen test result obtained in the last 48 hours. However, those who have been vaccinated at least 14 days before their entry and those who have contracted the virus in the last six months were exempt from these requirements. In addition, those not fulfilling any of these requirements could enter Turkey after undertaking a PCR test (at the airport).

Pandemisinde İlan Edilen Sokağa Çıkma Yasaklarının İdare Hukuku Yönüyle Değerlendirilmesi' (2020) 11(2) *Inonu University Law Review* 550, 565.
[11] See generally MB Tahtalı, 'COVID-19 Çerçevesinde Alınan Tedbirlerin Temel Hak ve Özgürlükler, Hukuka Uygunluk ve İdarenin Sorumluluğu Bakımından Değerlendirilmesi' (2021) 79(3) *Ankara Barosu Dergisi* 147, 163 ff.

Ending face-to-face education in all educational institutions (starting from 9 March, with face-to-face education restarting in August 2021).[12]

Suspending or limiting the operation of many commercial activities (on 15 March 2020 the operation of discos, bars, night clubs, on the next day that of many public social places (such as theatres, cinemas, cafes, internet saloons, shopping malls, lunaparks, hamams, SPAs, sport centres) and on 21 March that of barber shops, hairdressers and beauty centres has been suspended, starting from 21 March restaurants and similar food and beverage providers were only permitted to serve takeaway food or to work in the form of home delivery). Starting from 1 July 2021 there have been no such restrictions.

Prohibiting or restricting intercity travels and/or entering or leaving certain cities.

Prohibiting the use by persons under or over a certain age of public transportation vehicles and imposing capacity restrictions.

Postponing all meetings (including general assembly ones) to be held by associations (starting from 16 March 2020), prohibiting or restricting the organisation of certain social events (like marriage ceremonies and celebrations), prohibiting or restricting the organisation of assemblies and meetings, prohibiting or restricting the organisation of, or the participation in, certain religious services and ceremonies,

The obligation to wear sanitary masks in *specific* places (later, a *general* and nationwide obligation to wear masks in *all* public spaces – including open ones – was declared on 8 September 2020).

On the other hand, the failure to take certain measures has sparked criticism and led to allegations that such omission led to the spread of the pandemic in Turkey, with the most notable example being an initial failure to take appropriate steps concerning returnees from the *umra* pilgrimage in Saudi Arabia.[13]

Some administrative organs have also introduced important restrictions echoing those announced in Ministry circulars. According to article 23 of the Law on General Health Protection, a 'general health protection assembly' shall meet in every city. This assembly consists of some health services-related civil servants, but also includes the elected mayor of that city. Article 27 of the Law empowers, in very general and abstract terms, these organs to 'take measures which serve to improve the sanitary situation and eliminate current problems' and to 'assist in' the implementation of measures that have been taken in order to eliminate infectious diseases. Article 72 then lists some specific measures that can be taken in case of manifestation (or the doubt thereof) 'of one of the illnesses mentioned in article 57'. This article 57, which provides for a closed list,[14] does not mention Covid-19. In addition, the organ competent to take each measure, their duration and the necessary safeguards are far from being clear[15] thus not providing for an accessible and foreseeable legal basis. Yet, general health protection assemblies nationwide

---

[12] In primary and intermediate education institutions there were a number of short-lived attempts to resume partial face-to-face education.

[13] Şirin (n 9) 82.

[14] The Turkish Constitutional Court has also decided that this list is restrictive (see eg the individual application decision of 23 March 2016, Appl No 2013/7246). See also Şirin (n 9) 79–80.

[15] Şirin (n 9) 85.

have often taken decisions announcing the implementation of measures restricting fundamental rights and freedoms, basing their competence on articles 27 and 72.[16] According to article 282 of this Law, those acting in violation of the prohibitions, or not complying with the obligations laid down in this law shall be subject, unless the act constitutes a criminal offence, to an administrative fine (250–1000 Turkish Liras). On the other hand, in some cases administrative fines were based on article 32 of the Law on Misdemeanours (*Kabahatler Kanunu*), which applies to those who act in contravention of lawful orders issues for the purpose of protecting, inter alia, public health.[17]

The 'Provincial Administration Law' (*İl İdaresi Kanunu*)[18] also fails to provide the clarity that is required from an accessible and foreseeable statutory basis,[19] although many administrative organs have sometimes referred, either in general terms or to article 11/C,[20] to this statutory law in order to (try to) legitimise certain administrative measures.

All of the above restrictions – to be lawful under the constitutional regime – should have been imposed pursuant to a statutory law. This required the existence of a clear (accessible and foreseeable) permissive rule embodied in a law adopted by the Parliament. This was not the case in Turkey.[21] The failure to either declare a state of emergency[22] or adopt, as required by article 13 of the Constitution, the necessary statutory laws in the Parliament means that under the constitutional system many of the restrictive measures implemented were unlawful.[23] This may mean that citizens who were subject to such measures may argue that their liberties were unlawfully restricted. In this case, depending on the restriction in question, article 109 of the Turkish Penal Code on 'depriving a

---

[16] For a critical view on the legality of grounding curfews on this provision see Kasapoğlu Turhan (n 10) 557. For the view that the prohibition to wear masks could not have been based on this law see V Maviş, 'Covid-19 Salgınının Ceza Hukuku Bakımından Değerlendirilmesi' in K Şenocak (ed), *COVID-19 Küresel Salgınının Hukuktaki Yansımaları* (Ankara, Yetkin Yayıncılık, 2021) 1008. See also MM Hekimoğlu, 'Covid-19 Pandemisi Kapsamında Alınan Tedbirlere Anayasa ve İdare Hukuku Açısından Bir Bakış' in M Batı and S Çağlayan (eds), *Bir Küresel Salgın ve Hukuku: Covid-19* (Ankara, Seçkin Yayıncılık, 2021) 218 ff; ZÖ İnci and I Karakuş, 'Yargıtay 19. Ceza Dairesinin Güncel Kararları Çerçevesinde Covid-19 Salgınıyla Mücadele Kapsamındaki Tedbirlerden Maske Takma Yükümlülüğünün Yasal Zemini Hakkında Düşünceler' in M Batı and S Çağlayan (eds), *Bir Küresel Salgın ve Hukuku: Covid-19* (Ankara, Seçkin Yayıncılık, 2021) 767, for the view that the legal ground of some measures was unlawfully based on these provisions.

[17] Law on Misdemeanours numbered 5326 dated 30 March 2005. Official Journal Date-No: 31 March 2005-25772 bis.

[18] Provincial Administration Law numbered 5442 dated 10 June 1949. Official Journal Date-No: 18 June 1949-7236.

[19] V Aslan, 'COVID-19 Salgını Sebebiyle Uygulanan Sokağa Çıkma Kısıtlamalarının 1982 Anayasası'na Uygunluğu' (2020) 78(2) *İstanbul Hukuk Mecmuası* 809, 819 ff.

[20] For the view that many measures based on this provision were in fact ultra vires see SR Doru, 'COVID-19 (Koronavirüs) Salgını Sürecinde Yapılan İdari Muamelelerin Hukuka Uygunluğu ve İdarenin Sorumluluğu Meselesi' (2020) 78(2) *İstanbul Hukuk Mecmuası* 769, 779; A Ulusoy and I Özkaya Özlüer, 'Covid-19 Pandemisi Kapsamında İdari Kolluk Önlemlerinin İdare Hukuku Açısından Değerlendirilmesi' in M Batı and S Çağlayan (eds), *Bir Küresel Salgın ve Hukuku: Covid-19* (Ankara, Seçkin Yayıncılık, 2021) 27; Maviş (n 16) 1010.

[21] See Aslan (n 21) 825.

[22] The current version of the Provincial Administration Law does not permit the implementation of curfews due to the spread of contagious diseases (see Aslan, (n 21) 831; Şirin (n 9) 127). More generally, some of the measures taken could only have been lawful if a state of emergency had been declared (Kasapoğlu Turhan (n 10) 559; Doru (n 20) 802; Hekimoğlu (n 16) 222).

[23] Hekimoğlu (n 16) 212 ff. The author argues that introducing restrictions affecting fundamental rights through the use of circulars is generally unconstitutional (at 178). See further Ulusoy and Özkaya Özlüer (n 20) 23, 29.

person of liberty' may apply to government officials who have unlawfully prevented the freedom of movement of citizens. Further, compelling citizens to undergo certain tests may fall under TPC article 108 entitled 'coercion' which penalises the use of (material/physical) coercion in order to force the victim to do or not to do something or to allow the perpetrator to do something. It may also be argued that forcing people to undergo certain invasive medical tests may fall under TPC article 86, penalising 'intentional wounding'. Article 257 on abuse of duty may also apply with regard to measures that were taken unlawfully, including administrative fines applied for the failure to comply with certain measures.

Vaccination has not been compulsory but serious restrictions have been put in place for persons that are not fully vaccinated. On 20 August 2021, the Ministry of Interior adopted a circular which indirectly imposed on certain persons an obligation to undertake PCR tests.[24] As of 6 September 2021, unvaccinated persons could only participate in public activities such as concerts, or be present at movies or theatres if they have recently recovered from Covid-19 or if they obtained a negative PCR test result within the last 48 hours. The same rule applied to the use of planes, busses, trains or other public transportation vehicles. In addition, the above-mentioned general health protection assemblies have been empowered, through the same circular, to impose the same rule with regard to the participation in any public event or activity.

Finally, there is TPC article 195 which concerns the crime of 'acting in violation of measures regarding contagious diseases'. However this provision only criminalises a failure to comply with measures concerning the quarantine of a specific place where someone who has contracted, or died of, a contagious disease is present. Thus, the provision will not apply to government officials who fail to take adequate measures, but only to those citizens who violate existing preventive measures.

A. Overview of and Specific Constitutional and Legal Principles Regarding Criminal Liability of High-Ranking Government/Public Officials

According to article 105 of the Constitution the President shall be responsible for all crimes. However, a special procedural regime shall apply to the investigation and/or prosecution of any crime, be it one committed in private or in official capacity.

All other high-ranking government officials are fully responsible for their criminal acts, but again, different special procedural safeguards apply.

B. Scope of Responsibility and Area of Tolerated Risk

The concept of 'permitted risk' (*izin verilen risk*) has never been utilised as the ratio decidendi in judicial decisions. However, academic writings refer to this concept. The general understanding is that certain activities which take place within the daily life of a

---

[24] Published on the Ministry's website, 'Bazı Faaliyetler İçin PCR Testi Zorunluluğu Genelgesi Gönderildi' (20 August 2021), www.icisleri.gov.tr/bazi-faaliyetler-icin-pcr-testi-zorunlulugu-genelgesi-gonderildi.

society, by their nature, entail certain risks, or even cause harm, to legal values belonging to individuals (and/or the society). Even so, such activities are deemed as generally useful and beneficial for the individual and/or the society, and it is not possible to pursue such activities without tolerating the risk or damage they inevitably generate, and this is why they are tolerated and met with permission by the state.[25] This is done in order to allow societal life to retain its vitality and to allow for technological development.[26] Today it is generally accepted that the doctrine applies to both intentional and negligent crimes.[27]

Since the doctrine of 'permitted risk' is not unanimously accepted in academic writings and has never been utilised in judicial decisions it is very unlikely to play any role in a potential judicial assessment of the criminal liability of members of government for the failure to take certain measures against the spread or the adverse results of Covid-19. This prediction is made even more likely by the fact that the criteria concerning how to balance the need to protect the legal values endangered by the risky activities and the freedom of movement are doctrinally unclear. If the permitted risk doctrine were to be applied, all necessary efforts to minimise foreseeable risks must have been made, and the necessary precautionary measures must have been taken in this regard. In addition, it may be argued that if it is not possible to bring an inherently risky/dangerous activity within the boundaries of permissible/tolerable risk, in other words, if no precautionary measure or preventive rule makes it possible to contain the risk, such activity shall not be permitted.

To make an assessment, the first point is that Covid-19 brings about a serious risk of death or grave health issues. Thus, government officials cannot rely on 'permitted risk' in case of a failure to take all necessary protective measures against the disease, or in case of allowing certain activities that create a risk of spread of the disease where no feasible measures can possibly prevent in an adequate manner the potential materialisation of such risk.

As an exception, it may be argued that where certain behaviour is deemed as tolerable or permissible by the society, this type of conduct is considered to be 'socially adequate'. As a result, harmful consequences arising from such conduct cannot be attributed to the perpetrator. An example may be the re-opening of educational institutions despite the continuing serious effects of the pandemic because the society deems that education is absolutely indispensable and that a certain level of risk has to be taken to make the continuation of educational activities possible. Of course, in this case too, feasible and adequate protective measures must be in place. The added value of the 'social adequacy' defence is thus that it may justify the fact that the government allowed for certain social activities, even if they would inevitably increase the number of cases. However, the precise meaning – and even doctrinal acceptance – of this doctrine is controversial.

What is much more likely is that the judiciary will consider the failure to take measures from the viewpoint of criminal negligence and assess what level of caution is required by the (objective) 'duty of care and attention' which forms the basis of criminal liability

---

[25] Y Ünver, *Ceza Hukukunda İzin Verilen Risk*, (İstanbul, Seçkin, 1998) 7; M Koca and İ Üzülmez, *Türk Ceza Hukuku Genel Hükümler* 13th edn (Ankara, Adalet, 2020) 208.

[26] H Zafer, *Ceza Hukuku Genel Hükümler* TCK m. 1-75, 8th edn (İstanbul, Beta, 2021) 378.

[27] Ünver (n 25) 271, 273; B Akbulut, *Ceza Hukuku Genel Hükümler* 8th edn (Ankara, Adalet, 2021) 386.

for negligent acts. Though Turkish courts have not dealt with this point so far, it may be argued that a higher level of care and attention is required in case of allowing inherently dangerous activities since the possibility of harm is easily foreseeable.

C. Impact of Immunities

Article 105 of the Constitution lays down a special procedure with regard to the investigation and/or prosecution of the President. An absolute majority of the Grand National Assembly has to table a motion requesting that the President be investigated on allegations of a crime. The GNA may decide to launch an investigation with three-fifths of the total number of its members by secret ballot. A specifically elected parliamentary committee of fifteen members shall conduct this investigation. Eventually, the GNA may decide, with a two-thirds majority of the total number of members (by secret ballot) to refer the matter to the 'Supreme Criminal Tribunal' (the Constitutional Court will act in this capacity). The last paragraph of article 105 further states that this procedure shall also apply after the termination of the term of office of the President as regards crimes alleged to have been committed during the term of his/her office.

The deputy Presidents and ministers also enjoy special protection by virtue of Constitution article 106. Different regimes apply to crimes committed in an official capacity and those committed in a private capacity. Here I shall only deal with the first category. According to article 106 (5), an absolute majority of the GNA may table a motion requesting that the Deputies or ministers be investigated. The rest of the procedure is the same as the one applied for the President. Again, the last paragraph states that this procedure shall also apply after the termination of their duties 'with respect to the crimes alleged to have been committed regarding their duties during their term of office'.

D. Prosecutorial Matters

In the case of a crime committed by a public official, the first determination relates to whether or not the crime has been committed in relation to his/her official duty. If this is not the case (and the crime is 'personal', *i.e.*, one committed in a private capacity) the general rules regarding criminal procedure set out in the Turkish Criminal Procedure Code (*Ceza Muhakemesi Kanunu*) (CPC)[28] shall apply. For the purpose of our study the alleged crimes will have been committed in relation to an official duty. In this case, additional procedural conditions under the 'Law Regarding the Adjudication of Civil Servants and Other Public Officials' (*Memurlar ve Diğer Kamu Görevlilerinin Yargılanması Hakkında Kanun*) (Law no 4483)[29] apply. However, even in case of crimes

---

[28] Criminal Procedure Code numbered 5271 dated 4 December 2004. Official Journal Date-No: 17 December 2004-25673.

[29] Law Regarding the Adjudication of Civil Servants and Other Public Officials numbered 4483 dated 2 December 1999. Official Journal Date-No: 4 December 1999-23896.

committed in relation to an official duty, the special procedural conditions laid down in Law no 4483 do not apply if (1) the alleged act constitutes a crime *in flagrante* requiring a heavy penalty (*i.e.*, more than 10 years of imprisonment), (2) constitutes the crime of torture or (3) concerns the misuse of a judicial duty. For the purpose of our study none of these apply.

The special conditions set out in Law no 4483 include the investigation and trial being carried out by specific prosecutors and courts, the requirement of a special 'authorisation of investigation' and some cases being tried with expediency.

For regular public officials, deputy governors and mayors, the investigation and trial are conducted by the prosecutor and court authorised under general rules. However, if the alleged perpetrator is a governor or deputy minister, the investigation is conducted by the prosecutor of the Court of Cassation and the case is tried by the relevant chamber of the Court of Cassation.

According to Law no 4483, in order to carry out an investigation concerning an alleged crime committed by a public official, the public prosecutor, without conducting any investigatory action other than the collection of evidence that may otherwise be lost, is required to submit a request for 'authorisation of investigation' from the prescribed authority. This authority is determined by Article 3 of the Law and is determined through the duty carried out by the official at the moment of the alleged commission of the crime.

The authority, directly or through an investigator, conducts a preliminary investigation in which he/she holds the powers granted to a prosecutor under the CPC, including the collection of evidence and taking the statement of the relevant official. The duration of the pre-investigation is 30 days, subject to a one-time renewal of up to 15 days. The decision on the request is open to appeal by the official or the prosecutor.

After the authorisation of investigation, the authorised prosecutor conducts the investigation, and the adjudication procedure is carried out according to the general rules under the CPC.

As for the matter of prosecutorial discretion, the general rule is that the prosecutor has to draw up an indictment and commit the case for trial if there is sufficient evidence showing that the alleged crime has been committed by the suspect. However, exceptionally, with regard to crimes which require less than a maximum sentence of three years, the prosecutor may decide to postpone committing the case for trial (CPC article 171). However there is no such discretionary power with regard to crimes committed by a public official on account of his/her duty. Hence, for the purpose of the crimes within the scope of our study, there will be no prosecutorial discretion where there is sufficient evidence and the prosecutor will have to commit the case for trial.

III. CAUSATION

A. Causation (General Principles)

The Penal Code does not provide any general rule on the requirement of causality, and the Court of Cassation does not openly rely on any given theory, but rather prefers to act on a case-by-case basis.[30] Academic writings adopt the '*conditio sine qua non*' theory which argues that any and all conditions which have an effect on the outcome (even if the consequence is a 'remote' one) are causal since the absence of any of these conditions would have prevented the result from occurring.[31] Unless a new condition which would have caused the same result by itself has intervened, the causal link exists.

Once causality is ascertained, one must assess whether the result is 'objectively attributable' to the perpetrator.[32] This is a theory that is used to complement and restrict the *conditio sine qua non* theory, especially for the purpose of eliminating liability for remote and coincidental consequences: after establishing the existence of the causal link, a second *normative* assessment should be made with a view to determining whether the result that has occurred can be attributed to the perpetrator as his or her own creation by assessing whether or not he/she had control over the risk created and the ensuing result.[33]

As regards commission and omission, the term 'act' (*fiil*) includes behaviour both by way of action (*icrai suç*) or omission (*ihmali suç*). Crimes of omission are further divided into two: (1) genuine criminal offences by omission where the crime may only be committed by omitting to act and (2) non-genuine criminal offences by omission where a prohibition which can normally be violated through an action is violated by omitting to act, in other words, a result that may be obtained by way of active action is achieved through refraining from acting (omission). In the latter case, the perpetrator is held responsible if he or she is under a legal duty to intervene/to act, in other words, if he/she is in a 'position of guarantorship'. There is no *general* provision in the penal code providing for the punishment of crimes committed by way of omission. However, in the special part of the Code there are certain specific references to omission (*e.g.*, article 83 regarding intentional killing by way of omission). Turkish judicial practice considers that all crimes, where structurally possible, may be committed by way of omission.

In case of omission it must be proved beyond reasonable doubt that 'it is almost certain' or 'it is very highly probable' that the same result would not have materialised had the perpetrator acted in accordance with his/her duty.[34] This determination is the main problem when it comes to holding governmental officials responsible for deaths (or injuries) caused by Covid-19. It must be proved that had all the necessary preventive and protective measures been employed, it would have been almost certain that the victim/patient would not have lost his or her life (or suffered the same health problems). Looking from the inverse angle, if there is a credible probability that the victim/patient could still have contracted Covid-19 despite the taking of all necessary measures, the failure to do so is no longer causal to the death (or injury) of the victim.

---

[30] N Centel, H Zafer, and Ö Çakmut, *Türk Ceza Hukukuna Giriş* 11th edn (İstanbul, Beta, 2020) 291–93.

[31] T Demirbaş, *Ceza Hukuku Genel Hükümler* 16th edn (Ankara, Seçkin, 2021) 264.

[32] Koca and Üzülmez (n 25) 137–39; Akbulut (n 27) 380–418; B Öztürk and MR Erdem, *Uygulamalı Ceza Hukuku ve Güvenlik Tedbirleri Hukuku* 20th edn (Ankara, Seçkin, 2020) 387–93; VÖ Özbek, K Doğan and P Bacaksız, *Türk Ceza Hukuku Genel Hükümler* 12th edn (Ankara, Seçkin, 2021) 243–53.

[33] Grand Criminal Chamber judgments of 21 April 2015 (no 704/121) and 16 May 2017 (no 271/278).

[34] D Tezcan, MR Erdem and RM Önok, *Teorik ve Pratik Ceza Özel Hukuku* 19th edn (Ankara, Seçkin, 2021) 149.

Considering how quickly and easily Covid-19 spreads, and that it is only possible for any state to only slow down and minimise its spread – but not to fully prevent it – the proof of causality becomes a difficult issue. Indeed, in a large country like Turkey which is at the crossroads of different continents, it is impossible to eliminate all contact with the 'outside world'. As a result, inevitably, at one rate or another, Covid-19 was going to affect Turkey. Maybe its spread throughout the country could have been better prevented, but again, it is impossible to prove that it could have been stopped altogether from affecting a specific location. That being the case, it is difficult to prove (beyond reasonable doubt) that had the government officials taken this and that measure, citizen (X) or (Y) would not have fallen ill with (or died of) Covid-19. In that case, the provisions on homicide and wounding would not be applicable. As a fall-back solution, one could resort to the above-mentioned TPC article 257 provision on dereliction of duty. However, this provision also requires the proof of causing 'victimisation to persons'. Maybe this requirement could be interpreted broadly, and the increased risk of contracting Covid-19, or the increase of the effects of the pandemic leading to hardship for citizens, could be taken as satisfying this requirement. On the other hand, if the harm requirement is not qualified as an 'objective condition for punishment' but a 'result' (as one of the material elements) of the offence, the government officials could be tried for attempted dereliction of duty even in the failure of proof of damage. The problem here, though, is that in case of qualifying harm as a result, the perpetrator's intent to cause such harm must be proved – in this regard only *dolus eventualis* could possibly be proved.

There is an additional problem here: in a criminal trial the relevant governmental official would be tried for the death (or injury) of a specific person or a specific set of persons. In this trial the prosecution would have to prove that the omissions of the defendant(s) are causal with the health issue experienced by this particular victim. Here the job for the prosecutor would become even harder, if not impossible. Resort to TPC article 257 could eliminate this problem.

B. Causation and 'Thin Skull' Scenarios

According to the '*conditio sine qua non*' theory, conditions existing before the act by the perpetrator which contribute, together with the perpetrator's act, to causing a certain result do not eliminate causality.[35] Similarly, conditions which emerge after the act of the perpetrator and contribute, together with the perpetrator's act, to causing a certain result do not eliminate causality.[36] Therefore, where an existing health condition (such as an existing heart illness or general weakness on account of advanced age) is aggravated by Covid-19 and the latter triggers a series of health issues, which together with the pre-existing condition, ultimately cause the death of the patient, Covid-19 (and the series of events leading to the patient's contraction of said virus) are still causal

---

[35] Öztürk and Erdem (n 32) 374–76.
[36] ME Artuk, A Gökcen, ME Alşahin and K Çakır, *Ceza Hukuku Genel Hükümler* 13th edn (Ankara, Adalet, 2019) 339.

to the resulting death. An intervening act only eliminates causality if it is such that it would have anyway caused the very same result in the absence of the contribution by the perpetrator.[37]

C. Restricting Causality: Policy and Doctrinal Issues

One of the main criticisms directed at the way the *conditio sine qua non* theory approaches causality is that it very much broadens the scope of responsibility.[38] This is why the above-mentioned 'objective attributability' theory has been introduced to limit its results. There is no academic agreement on which criteria shall be employed to determine whether the result (such as death due to Covid-19) is attributable to the perpetrator (*e.g.* the high-level government official who failed to slow down the spread of the virus). Here I shall discuss some of the criteria that may be relied upon. It should be borne in mind that the different criteria are not mutually exclusive but can, instead, be used in a mutually complementary fashion.

One criterion is whether the perpetrator's act or omission has raised the risk to a legally significant degree.[39] If this is not the case and the probability of the result occurring has not been increased significantly by the perpetrator, the result is not attributable to him/her.[40] Some of the decisions taken by the government, or the failure to implement certain measures may not have had a serious effect on the spread of Covid-19, in which case the relevant officials could escape responsibility.

A second 'tandem' of criteria serving a similar purpose is (1) where the 'victim has consciously assumed the risk' by wilfully participating in the risk-creating or harmful activity or (2) the 'principle of responsibility' whereby the victim acts completely freely and under his or her own responsibility.[41] In both cases, other actors' contribution to the risk or harm cannot lead to the attribution of the result to them. An example may be where the citizen has failed to apply for vaccination and/or has not used sanitary masks, or where the citizen has attended a crowded indoor party, as a result of which he/she has contracted the illness. However, for these criteria to enter into play, the person in question must be capable (in terms of mental capacity and level of information) to properly assess the risks involved in, and the potential consequences of, his/her conduct. Here, the initial failure to provide proper information to the public (and the allegations about the veracity of the information later provided) should be carefully assessed.

According to another criterion, where the perpetrator acts in contravention of a duty, thus contributing to a certain result, this result cannot be attributed to him/her if the same result would have occurred even if he/she had acted in accordance with his/her duty.[42] This criterion applies only to non-genuine criminal offences by omission and

---

[37] 16th Criminal Chamber of the Court of Cassation, judgment of 31 January 2017, no 6118/361.
[38] Artuk, Gökcen, Alşahin and Çakır (n 36) 340.
[39] Artuk, Gökcen, Alşahin and Çakır (n 36) 360; Özbek, Doğan and Bacaksız, (n 32) 253.
[40] K Doğan, *Neticesi Sebebiyle Ağırlaşmış Suçlar* (Ankara, Seçkin, 2011) 126.
[41] MV Dülger, *Ceza Hukuku Genel Hükümler* (İstanbul, Seçkin, 2021) 442 ff.
[42] Akbulut (n 27) 387.

to negligent crimes.[43] According to this criterion, a governmental official may escape liability by proving that the victim would have contracted the virus even if adequate and necessary preventive measures had been undertaken. With regard to the application of this criterion Turkish academic writings have put forward different ideas. According to the 'increased risk theory', it is possible to impute the result to the perpetrator if it can be shown that his/her act increased in an adducible/provable manner the probability of the result occurring.[44] According to this understanding it would suffice to show that the failure to implement a certain protective measure has heightened – compared to the alternative behaviour that was in compliance with the duty – the risk of a person contracting the virus. Where this theory is applied, it is no longer necessary to prove – in crimes by omission – that the probability of the same result occurring was still very high or almost certain even if the perpetrator had acted in proper performance of his/her duty. On the other hand, some of those who defend this strict understanding accept that there is no imputability where it is only *probable* that the risk was increased but there is no conclusive proof on this issue, while others argue that the perpetrator should be held responsible in these cases too. The theory of avoidability/inevitability is more favourable to the defendant: if it is seriously within probability that the same result would have materialised even if the perpetrator had acted in accordance with the duty, this result is no longer attributable to him/her.[45] In this case, it would suffice for the governmental official to escape liability to show that even if some additional feasible preventive and protective measures had been undertaken there are sufficient supporting points to believe that the result would not have changed. In Turkish doctrine this approach has been criticised for overly restricting responsibility.[46]

IV. THE STRUCTURE OF HOMICIDE OFFENCES AND ASSAULT/AGGRAVATED ASSAULT/SERIOUS BODILY HARM OFFENCES

A. Murder/Intentional Homicide

Intentional killing (*kasten öldürme*), as it is named in Turkish law, committed through a positive action is criminalised under TPC article 81 and entails a life-time sentence. Article 83 criminalises intentional killing through omission and attracts a mitigated minimum sentence of 15 years (or 20 years where aggravating circumstances exist) although the reduction is discretionary. These two articles provide for the 'basic' version of the crime. Article 82 provides for 'qualified circumstances' which require an increased punishment, *i.e.*, aggravating circumstances. Though not a unanimous view, article 82 applies to both articles 81 and 83.[47] In case of aggravated murder through commission, the punishment is an 'aggravated' life-time sentence.[48]

---

[43] Akbulut (n 27) 387; B Heinrich (Y Ünver ed), *Ceza Hukuku Genel Kısım I* 2nd edn (Ankara, Seçkin, 2014) 251.

[44] Özbek, Doğan and Bacaksız (n 32) 252.

[45] Koca and Üzülmez (n 25) 217.

[46] ibid 218.

[47] Tezcan, Erdem and Önok (n 34) 153.

[48] The major difference from a lifetime sentence is that the minimum time to be spent in prison prior to being eligible for conditional release is 30 years instead of 24.

Only those in 'a position of guarantorship', *i.e.*, under a legal duty to act, may be held responsible under article 83. According to this provision, the omission of an obligation which is the cause of the result must be 'equivalent' to an active conduct (*i.e.*, to commission). This is the case where: (1) there is an obligation to act in a certain active way arising from legislation or contract or (2) a previous conduct realised by the perpetrator has created a dangerous situation with respect to other people's lives. In our case, the source of the obligation for governmental officials would be the legislation, as they are duty bound to protect the life, health and well-being of their citizens.

The material object of the crime is a living human being. According to the Court of Cassation[49] and the majority academic view, life begins with 'full and alive birth',[50] and ends, according to the unanimous view, with cerebral death. At the same time, the material object of the crime is also the victim.

The act/conduct which leads to the satisfaction of article 81 is any act which brings about/causes the death of the victim. As regards article 83, it is any omission which brings about/causes the death of the victim. The act must be causal to the resulting death, and the death of the victim must be objectively imputable to the perpetrator, as explained above.

Both article 81 and 83 require proof of intent. Intent is defined in TPC article 21 (1) as:'knowingly and willingly conducting the elements in the legal definition of an offence'. Intent should include all the objective elements in the legal definition of the crime. Therefore, intent consists of an intellectual or knowledge (*bilme*) component and a component of will (*isteme*).

Intent is divided into two types: direct intent and probable (conditional)[51] intent (*dolus eventualis*). Direct intent may be then divided into two: direct intent first degree corresponds to the purpose of the perpetrator. Direct intent second degree exists when the perpetrator foresees with certainty (or close to certainty) that a given result will occur as a consequence of his or her conduct.

'Probable intent' exists when 'the individual commits an act while foreseeing that the elements in the legal definition of an offence may occur', as per TPC article 21 (2). In this case, the perpetrator is *aware* of the fact that the elements in the legal definition of the offence *may* materialise as a result of his or her conduct. According to academic writings, probable intent exists where the perpetrator 'consents to', 'accepts' or 'runs the risk of' that possibility.[52] The Court of Cassation often speaks of 'remaining indifferent' to such possibility.[53] In case of probable intent, the sentence has to be reduced as per article 21 (2). Both homicide through commission (TPC article 81) and through omission (TPC article 83) may be committed through direct or probable intent.

---

[49] 9th Criminal Chamber of the Court of Cassation, judgment of 24 December 2008, no 16443/14064.
[50] Against, see Tezcan, Erdem and Önok (n 34) 138–39.
[51] The Turkish lawmaker has opted for calling this type of intent 'probable'.
[52] Koca and Üzülmez (n 25) 177–79; Centel, Zafer and Çakmut (n 30) 377, 379; H Hakeri, *Ceza Hukuku Genel Hükümler* 25th edn (Ankara, Adalet, 2021) 217.
[53] For example see the Grand Criminal Chamber of the Court of Cassation, judgment of 2 July 2019, no 121/518.

With regard to the failure to take certain measures, at most, it could be argued that there is 'probable intent' with regard to the deaths caused by this omission, however it would be very hard to prove that the decision-makers knew of this eventuality, and yet, that they remained indifferent to its occurrence by knowingly and willingly failing to take the necessary measures.

As a further note, homicide can also be an underlying act of crimes against humanity, laid down in TPC article 77. However, the definition embodied in article 77 requires as an additional mental element that the perpetrator acts with special intent in the form of an *animus discriminandi*: crimes against humanity under TPC can only be committed with 'political, philosophical, racial or religious motives'. This additional element means that article 77 will be inapplicable to our case study.

B. Culpable Homicide/Manslaughter

Negligent homicide (*taksirle öldürme*) as it is named in Turkish law, is criminalised under TPC article 85. It encompasses both causing death through an active action and causing death through omission. It requires two to six years of imprisonment, but the upper limit of the sentence is 15 years where there are multiple victims (*i.e.*, multiple deaths or one or multiple injured victims in addition to a death).

The material elements are the same as the ones explained for intentional killing. What distinguishes article 85 from murder is the mental element: in case of article 85 the perpe-trator acts with negligence. Negligence is defined in TPC as conducting an act without foreseeing the results as stated in the legal definition of the offence, due to a failure to discharge a duty of care and attention (article 22 (2)). This, in reality, is the definition of inadvertent negligence. Negligence may be inadvertent (*bilinçsiz taksir*) or advertent/conscious (*bilinçli taksir*). An act is conducted with advertent/conscious negligence when the result is foreseen but is not wanted; in this case the punishment for the offence shall be increased by one-third to one-half (article 22 (3)). In this case, the perpetrator is aware of the fact that his action may cause a certain result, but – for various reasons – he or she thinks or believes or trusts that it will not. Compared to probable intent, it may be said that the materialisation of the material elements of the crime (especially, the result) is absolutely unwanted by the perpetrator.

It would be easier, in terms of the mental element, to charge those decision-makers failing to take the appropriate preventive measures with negligent homicide. However, causality and objective imputability problems would be the same.

C. Offences Related to Actions that Cause Serious Bodily Harm (Assault; Grievous Assault; Assault with Intent to Cause Serious Bodily Harm)

The crime of 'intentional wounding' (*kasten yaralama*), as it is named in Turkish law, is regulated under TPC article 86 and subsequent provisions. Article 86 (1) provides for the basic version of the crime: any person who intentionally inflicts pain on the body of another person, or causes a disruption in his/her health or capacity to perceive shall be punished by a term of imprisonment of one to three years. This crime requires the proof of intent, be it direct or indirect. The infection of a person with a virus certainly falls, in terms of actus reus, within this provision.[54] Proving intent, even if indirect, would be more difficult.

Article 86 (2) provides for a mitigating circumstance: if it possible to eliminate the effect of the crime on the victim with a 'simple medical intervention' (*basit tıbbi müdahale*) the punishment shall be decreased, and the crime becomes prosecutable upon complaint of the victim. This might be the case for non-serious cases of Covid-19.

Article 86 (3) provides for a set of 'qualified circumstances requiring an increase in the punishment' (*i.e.*, aggravating circumstances). The application of this provision is only possible if the perpetrator's intent covers the aggravating circumstance.

Article 87 regulates the result-qualified forms of the offence. For example, if an act of battery results in the permanent impairment of the functioning of any one of the senses or organs of the victim (article 87 (1) (a)), the punishment to be imposed shall be doubled. TPC article 23 provides that 'where an act causes a more serious result, or a result other than that intended, a person will only be held responsible if he has acted, at least, with negligence in regard to such result'. The basic condition for the existence of negligence is that the result be foreseeable. According to the majority view, this is the only thing that needs to be ascertained with regard to the aggravated result, *i.e.*, there is no need to determine whether the remaining requirements for criminal negligence are satisfied.[55] As a result, it is only if the more serious result (or the result other than the one intended, *e.g.*, the death of the victim) was foreseeable that the perpetrator will be held responsible.

The most important provision here will be that of article 87 (4), which lays down the punishment for causing death as an unintended result of the crime of wounding. In this case, depending on the basic act, the minimum punishment is eight years, and the upper limit may be as high as 18 years. Article 23, explained above, is of particular relevance here. Since the death of the victim as a result of Covid-19 is – be it objectively or subjectively – foreseeable, there is no problem in this regard.[56] However, the objective imputability of the result to the governmental officials will be more difficult to prove. Here I shall remind of one criterion explained before: has the perpetrator's omission raised the risk of death to a legally significant degree? It is not easy to immediately answer this in the positive. Even for the unvaccinated citizen the odds of dying of Covid-19 are relatively low. However, considering that the death ratio is not insignificant or negligible, this test may be satisfied.

There is a second imputability test which is specifically sought for result-qualified offences: the unintended (heavier or different) result must be a direct result of the typical danger inherent in the basic and intentional act, there must be a link or relationship between the unintended result and the danger encapsulated in the basic act.[57] For the

---

[54] Maviş (n 16) 1011. However, one view argues that where the person infected with Covid-19 displays no symptoms we can only speak of 'attempted' wounding, see MR Erdem, 'Covid-19'la Bağlantılı Ceza Hukuku Sorunları' (2020) 2(2) *Yaşar Hukuk Dergisi* 1, 3.

[55] Doğan (n 40) 49.

[56] On the applicability of TPC art 87 (4) to Covid-19 cases see Erdem (n 54) 7; Maviş (n 16) 1016.

[57] Akbulut (n 27) 412–18.

purpose of our study, this second test will be satisfied. An action or omission which caused the victim to contract Covid-19 creates a danger/risk of a nature and level that is capable of leading to death; in other words, the typical danger inherent in the basic act is the direct cause of the unintended result of death, or, to put it differently, death is the result of a typical danger inherent in the basic act.[58] To summarise, it will be more difficult to objectively impute the contraction of Covid-19 by the citizen to the government officials, but once that is done, interestingly, it would be easier under article 87(4) to impute the deaths caused by the virus.

Negligent wounding (TPC article 89) requires a term of imprisonment of three months to a year or a judicial fine. In case of a result-based qualified version of the crime, depending on the result, the punishment is increased by one-half (*e.g.*, in case of causing vital danger) or doubled (*e.g.*, functional loss of senses or organs). If there are multiple victims (through the same act), the punishment is a term of imprisonment of six months to three years. Again, it would be easy, in terms of the mental element, to charge those decision-makers failing to take the appropriate preventive measures with this crime but the causality and objective imputability problems would remain.

D. Offences Regarding Unborn Foetuses; Interrupting the Course of a (Viable) Pregnancy

Homicide offences may only be committed against a living person. Where the material object of the crime is an embryo or foetus, TPC article 99 concerning 'abortion' may apply. According to the basic version of this crime a person who terminates the pregnancy of a woman in the absence of her consent shall be sentenced to a term of imprisonment of five to 10 years. While there are variations of this offence, for the purpose of this study only the basic version of the crime may be relevant.

Under Turkish law this crime may only be committed intentionally. The crime may be committed through direct as well as indirect intent. Because of this intent requirement it is unlikely that the judiciary will ever envisage pregnancies ended due to Covid-19-related problems within the scope of this crime.[59]

E. Failure to Render Assistance

According to TPC article 98 it is a crime not to lend assistance to a person, or, in the alternative, immediately inform competent authorities of the situation, when such person is not in a condition to 'administer' himself/herself on account of age, illness or injury.

---

[58] Doğan (n 40) 144, 161, 166.

[59] On the other hand, according to TPC art 87 (1) regarding result-qualified forms of intentional wounding, where the act causes premature birth, the sentence is doubled (and the minimum sentence cannot fall below three years in case of the basic act falling under art 86 (1) and five years in case of it falling under art 86 (3)). Where the act causes termination of pregnancy (art 87 (2)), the sentence is trebled (and the minimum sentence cannot fall below five years in case of the basic act falling under art 86 (1) and eight years in case of it falling under art 86 (3)).

This basic version of the crime requires a sentence of imprisonment of one month to a year, or a judicial fine. According to article 98 (2), the sentence is increased if the victim dies as a result of the failure to fulfil the obligation to assist or notify, in this case the applicable punishment is an imprisonment term of one to three years.

This 'subsidiary' provision will not apply to governmental officials who are responsible for taking the necessary preventive and protective measures against Covid-19 and its effects. Indeed, where the perpetrator is in a position of guarantorship and a failure to fulfil his/her duty results in illness or death, this perpetrator will be held directly responsible for this result (*i.e.*, for intentional or negligent homicide or wounding), and not merely for the failure to assist or notify.[60] If there is no illness, then article 98 is also inapplicable because there is no victim who is unable to administer himself/herself due to illness.

V. DEFENCES, JUSTIFICATIONS AND EXCUSES

A. Necessity

Necessity is regulated under TPC article 25 (2). According to the official explanation of the article, the related provision of the CPC (article 223 (3) (b)) and the case law of the Court of Cassation[61] necessity does not constitute a justification but – in the words of the CPC – a ground lifting culpability. This means that the act is not 'justified' (it is not lawful) but as a result of a normative assessment made in the field of culpability it is deemed inappropriate to impose any punishment on the offender.

Article 25 (2) applies under the following conditions:[62]

There must be a serious and imminent danger.

The danger must be directed at a right to which the perpetrator, or a third person, is entitled.

The danger must not have been knowingly caused by the perpetrator himself.

The perpetrator should not be under a legal obligation to confront the danger.

There should be no other means of protection (in other words, it should be impossible to escape the danger without having to harm a third person).

The means used must be proportionate to the gravity and subject of the danger.

Under Turkish law it is accepted that necessity may excuse killing, even if intentional.[63]

According to the majority, the legal value sought to be protected must be of an equal or superior value to the one that is harmed through the protective act.[64] So, to many, a

---

[60] RM Önok, 'TCK'da Koruma, Gözetim, Yardım veya Bildirim Yükümlülüğünün İhlâli Suretiyle İşlenen Suçlar' (2012) 11(1) *İstanbul Kültür Üniversitesi Hukuk Fakültesi Dergisi* 31, 48–49.

[61] Grand Criminal Chamber of the Court of Cassation, judgment of 26 February 2008, no 1-281/37.

[62] RM Önok, 'Turkey' in Alan Reed and Michael Bohlander (eds), *General Defences in Criminal Law – Domestic, Comparative and International Perspectives* (London, Ashgate, 2014) 315–28, 324.

[63] Cf Hakeri (n 52) 390.

[64] Demirbaş (n 31) 327; Hakeri (n 52) 390; Artuk, Gökcen, Alşahin and Çakır (n 36) 586.

'reasonable level' of proportionality is not considered sufficient.[65] I do not agree with this view if necessity is to be considered an excuse and not a justification: in the former case a reasonable level should suffice. However, if we follow the majority view, the right to life cannot be sacrificed for economic prerogatives since the former will outweigh the latter, no matter how serious the economic adverse consequences of taking certain additional measures may be. In my opinion, the correct approach would be to do the balancing not by merely comparing the hierarchical value of the respective legal values. Exceptionally, it should be excusable to sacrifice a more important legal value.[66] This is because the balancing should be done pursuant to a general analysis which takes into account all the specific circumstances of the case.[67] Further, the balancing act should be done in light of the whole positive legal order and of all the applicable legal principles. However, this latter requirement poses a new problem: the protective act against the danger should be compatible with the legal order and its cardinal principles.[68] Sacrificing lives for economic reasons does not seem to live up to this standard. In support of this position is the following argument too: because an innocent third person is being harmed the requirement that 'there should be no other means of protection' has to be interpreted strictly.[69] The perpetrator may not rely on necessity where it is possible to escape the danger without committing a crime (or by committing a lesser crime).

On a more theoretical basis, although this is no place to enter into the details of the legal basis and rationale of recognising necessity as an excuse, two popular theories may be analysed. According to a widely adopted understanding in Turkey, the reason for not punishing the perpetrator must be explained with the psychological situation faced by him/her: the psychological pressure (moral coercion theory) that the perpetrator is faced with due to the danger confronted affects his/her freedom of will, and prevents the law from blaming and reprobating him/her.[70] It is very hard to argue that this type and level of moral coercion exists for government officials that decide to sacrifice lives.

According to normative theories,[71] the perpetrator must be deemed as excused because it cannot be expected and demanded from him/her to renounce certain legal values that are in danger.[72] These theories also cannot excuse the conduct of governmental officials who sacrifice lives in order to salvage the economy. Leaving aside the question of motive (does the government intend to protect the welfare of the citizens or is the concern not to lose electoral votes due to a degrading economy?), in a state ruled by law my opinion is that the protection of the lives of those within its jurisdiction is the main duty incumbent

---

[65] Cf Centel, Zafer and Çakmut (n 30) 332.

[66] Heinrich (n 43) 571.

[67] Z Kangal, *Ceza Hukukunda Zorunluluk Durumu* (Ankara, Seçkin, 2010) 306; E Bekar, *Türk ve Amerikan Ceza Hukukunda Zorunluluk Hali* (Ankara, Seçkin, 2013) 118–19.

[68] Hakeri (n 52) 391.

[69] Öztürk and Erdem (n 32) 483.

[70] F Erem, A Danışman and ME Artuk, *Ceza Hukuku Genel Hükümler* (Ankara, Seçkin, 1997) 581; A Nuhoğlu, 'Tıp Ceza Hukukunda Zaruret Halinin Sınırları' in *Tıp Ceza Hukukunun Güncel Sorunları: V. Türk Alman Tıp Hukuku Sempozyumu* (Ankara, TBB, 2008) 36.

[71] For different variations of these theories see Kangal (n 67) 437 ff.

[72] VÖ Özbek and K Doğan, 'Zorunluluk Halinin (TCK m.25/2) Hukuki Niteliği' (2007) 9(2) *Dokuz Eylül Üniversitesi Hukuk Fakültesi Dergisi* 195, 212.

on the state, and this primary obligation trumps any economic consideration. On the other hand, economic disaster is not a greater evil compared to the death of thousands. As for a possible assertion that a degrading economy *may* eventually lead to the loss of lives as well (for example, through famine or suicides based on despair), this potential future scenario would be speculative. This is different from the prospect of death due to Covid-19: if the number of patients increases, the number of deaths will certainly increase – this is not speculation but fact.

On the other hand, it may be argued that because the perpetrator is defending a protected legal value the 'content of wrongfulness' of the act is diminished, and this, along with the decrease in culpability, may serve to justify saving the perpetrator from punishment.[73] This dual approach could put the defendant in a better legal position. However, even in this case, the formal conditions that need to be satisfied for a necessity defence might be missing.

In addition to what has been said before, the danger must not have been knowingly caused by the perpetrator. According to the majority view, where the danger has been caused through inadvertent negligence, the perpetrator shall still benefit from the provision, the important thing is that the danger has not been caused intentionally or with advertent negligence.[74] If the government officials have knowingly ignored (or failed to adequately assess) the dangers arising from the pandemic, and the disease has spread (or spread further, or more easily) as a result of such shortcoming, the economic crisis brought about by this situation could be qualified as a 'self-induced' one due to advertent negligence. Thus, governmental officials may only escape responsibility by arguing that they did not foresee an economic crisis as a result of the adverse consequences of the pandemic deteriorating because of their failure to take certain measures.

Another problematic condition is that there should be no other means of protection. If there are other means to avoid the danger, or if it is possible to avert the danger by committing a lesser crime, or by violating the relevant legal interest to a lesser extent and degree, again necessity will not apply. Here it may be argued that the government could have found better ways of averting the danger than 'giving up' lives.

VI. CORPORATE CRIMINAL LIABILITY

Only natural persons can commit a criminal offence under Turkish law, as specifically stated in TPC article 20 which is entitled 'individuality of criminal liability'. According to article 20 (2) no 'criminal sanction' may be applied to legal persons. Only 'security measures' in the shape of annulling the licence to operate and confiscation may be applied under certain circumstances.

---

[73] Kangal (n 67) 439–40; C Canpolat, *Kusur İlkesi Işığında Mazeret Nedeni Olarak Zorlayıcı Cebir* (İstanbul, Adalet, 2016) 179.
[74] Öztürk and Erdem (n 32) 480.

VII. FORMS OF PARTICIPATION

Turkish penal law does not provide for a common purpose or joint criminal enterprise liability. The concept of conspiracy is also not recognised by the law or case law.

Participation may be technically divided into two types: perpetration (*faillik*) and complicity (*şeriklik*). 'Complicity' includes instigation (*azmettirme*) and assistance (*yardım etme*). In the TPC, assistance refers to providing both material assistance and moral assistance.[75]

Whereas perpetrators and instigators are subjected to the full punishment for the relevant crime, those lending assistance benefit from a mandatory mitigation. Perpetration is based on the German-based understanding of 'control over the act' or 'act domination' (or hegemony over the act). The official explanation of TPC article 37 on perpetration mentions this criterion. Those who establish control over the commission of the act, those who are a 'main actor' or the 'central figure' in the commission of the crime are regarded as perpetrators. Different definitions are used in academic writings to explain the meaning of control over the act: to be in a position to rein in the development of the typical event, the person who holds in his or her hands the process which leads to the materialisation of the result, the person who can prevent or direct the course of events according to his or her own will, the person who determines whether the crime will be committed or not, and how, etc.[76] At the end of the day, perpetration is an 'elastic' concept and whether control has been established over the crime can only be determined on a case-by-case basis.

The first category of 'perpetration' is 'direct/individual perpetration', where a perpetrator fulfils all the required objective and subjective legal elements of the crime with his or her own conduct. This type of perpetration is based on control over the conduct.

A second category of perpetration is co-perpetration (article 37 (1)), where a plurality of persons join their efforts in committing the crime. These persons must (1) act under a common plan to commit the crime and (2) must commit the act together. This is different from joint criminal enterprise or common purpose liability in that all participants must offer a functionally important contribution to the commission of the offence. Co-perpetration is based on 'functional' control over the act. Therefore, each contribution must be important. The absence of the contribution must be able to frustrate the commission of the offence, the contribution must be sufficiently important for the successful realisation of the criminal plan. What is not required is for the contribution to be indispensable. In addition, all participants must act with intent concerning the common crime. The participants offer a co-ordinated contribution, which may be of different natures, to the commission of the crime in pursuance of a common decision. It is by virtue of the common decision that the contribution provided by each participant is commonly attributable to all the others (principle of equivalent liability).

---

[75] For detailed discussion see RM Önok, 'Turkey' in Alan Reed and Michael Bohlander (eds), *Participation in Crime – Domestic, Comparative and International Perspectives* (London, Ashgate, 2013) 451–68.

[76] RM Önok, *Yapısal Suçlarda Failin Tespiti: Müşterek Suç Girişimi (Joint Criminal Enterprise) ve Örgütsel Hakimiyete Dayalı Dolaylı Faillik Doktrinleri* (Ankara, Seçkin, 2019) 56–57.

A third category is indirect perpetration where any person who uses another as an instrument in the commission of an offence shall be held responsible as a perpetrator (article 37 (2)). Indirect perpetration is based on control over the will.

For all accomplices to the crime, the basic condition for responsibility is that the act perpetrated by the principal be unlawful and committed intentionally (article 40). The physical perpetrator does not need to be culpable for the rules on participation to apply. Each person participating in the commission of the crime shall be sentenced according to his or her own culpable act, irrespective of the personal circumstances which exclude the punishment of the others. Therefore, TPC article 40 adopts the system which is known as 'limited' or 'partially derivative' accessorial liability. By virtue of the principle of dependence, for accomplices to be punished, the perpetrator must have commenced the execution of the crime in question.

VIII. ATTEMPT

According to TPC article 35 (1):

> A person who directly begins through suitable conduct the execution of a crime he intends to commit, but who is unable to complete such offence due to circumstances beyond his control, shall be responsible for attempt.

Thus, attempted crimes may be punished in the existence of the following conditions:[77]

(1) Intention to commit a crime: the perpetrator must act with intent. According to the prevailing academic view and the established case law of the Court of Cassation (save very rare exceptions), the provisions on attempt cannot apply in case of indirect intent. This is why the provisions on attempt will be very hardly applicable in our case.

(2) Commencing the execution of the crime: unless 'criminal thought' has been manifested through conduct, it cannot be punished. In principle, the execution of the crime must have commenced. A variety of different legal formula are advanced to distinguish mere preparatory acts from 'executory' acts. It may be said that article 35 (2) is based on the 'material objective' theory, as confirmed by the official explanation of the provision. According to this theory, acts which correspond to those defined in the definition of the crime, as well as acts naturally and inevitably connected with those, constitute executory acts.[78] A survey of the case-law reveals, though, that the Court of Cassation does not rely on one particular theory, and takes a very much case-by-case approach, although objective theories are applied the most often.

(3) Execution must have begun *through suitable conduct*: both the instruments used in the commission of the offence, and the conduct as a whole, must be adequate to realise all the definitional elements of the intended crime.

---

[77] RM Önok, 'Penal Law' in T Ansay, D Wallace, Jr and I Önay (eds), *Introduction to Turkish Law* 7th edn (Ankara, Kluwer International, 2020) 235–36.
[78] Centel, Zafer and Çakmut (n 30) 462.

(4) The crime shall not be completed due to reasons beyond the control of the perpetrator: this may be because the acts directed at the execution of the crime were interrupted, or because the result could not be obtained.

In cases of attempt, the sentence is determined according to the scale laid down in article 35 (2), and by taking into account the seriousness of the damage or danger that was caused by the conduct.

IX. SANCTIONS, SENTENCING, PUNISHMENT, REPARATIONS AND/OR RESTORATIVE JUSTICE

A. General Sentencing Framework for the Crimes under Discussion

The applicable sanctions have already been mentioned under the discussion for each crime.

B. Sanctions Specifically for Senior Government/Public Officials

According to TPC article 53, it is possible to deprive convicts from the exercise of certain rights. Examples are disqualification from holding public office, disqualification from acting as a guardian or being appointed in the role of guardian and trustee. Deprivation of certain rights is only temporary: in principle, it only lasts until the prison term is served. In principle, article 53 only applies to intentional crimes.

According to the Constitution's article 76 (2), a person who has been sentenced to an imprisonment term of at least one year for an intentional crime cannot be elected to the Parliament, even if he/she benefits of an amnesty.

According to article 48/A-5 of the Law on Civil Servants (Law no 657),[79] those who have been sentenced to an imprisonment term of at least one year for an intentional crime, or those who – even if they benefit from an amnesty – have been convicted for one of the exhaustively listed crimes cannot be civil servants.

According to article 105 (5) of the Constitution, if the President of the Republic is convicted by the Supreme Criminal Tribunal of a crime that prevents him/her from being elected (those listed in article 76 (2)), his/her mandate shall end. The same rule applies to his/her deputies and to ministers under Constitution article 106 (9).

C. Corporations and Sentencing

As explained above, there is no corporate criminal liability.

---

[79] Law on Civil Servants numbered 657 dated 14 July 1965. Official Journal Date-No: 23 July 1965-12056.

15

United States of America

PHILLIP WEINER AND DANA CURHAN

I. BACKGROUND AND CONTEXTUAL INTRODUCTION

A S THIS CHAPTER is being drafted, over one million people have died in the United States from the Covid-19 virus,[1] exceeding the number of Americans who died during the 1918 N1H1 influenza pandemic.[2] There have been over 80 million reported cases of the virus in the United States.[3] While 66 per cent of the American public has been fully vaccinated,[4] a significant portion of the population has refused the vaccines, either because they belong to a large and vocal anti-vaccine movement or because they are simply vaccine hesitant.[5] Further, a number of individuals and organisations have filed lawsuits challenging government efforts to mitigate the spread of Covid-19, including but not limited to vaccine and mask mandates.[6]

During the Covid-19 health crisis, State and local governments undertook various measures pursuant to their authority. While some of the actions and restrictions are no longer being used, other measures remain in force. For example, governments mandated the wearing of masks for indoor public settings,[7] in schools in grades K through 12,[8] in certain private businesses (such as gyms, grocery stores, restaurants, hospitals or

---

[1] Johns Hopkins University, 'Corona Virus Resource Center', http://coronavirus.jhu.edu.

[2] United States Centers for Disease Control and Prevention, '1918 Pandemic (H1N1 virus)', www.cdc.gov>flu>pandemic-resources>1918.

[3] Corona Virus Resource Center (n 1).

[4] ibid.

[5] See T Haelle, 'This Is the Moment the Anti-Vaccine Movement Has Been Waiting For' *New York Times* (online, 31 August 2021), www.nytimes.com/2021/08/31/opinion/anti-vaccine-movement.html.

[6] See *South Bay United Pentecostal Church v Newsom*, 592 US ___, 141 SCt 716 (2021).

[7] See, eg City of Boston Public Health Commission, 'Order Requiring Face Coverings In The City of Boston' (20 August 2021), www.boston.gov/sites/default/files/file/2021/08/BPHC%20COVID-19%20Face%20Coverings%20Order%208%2020%202021.pdf; King County, Washington State, 'Face Covering Directive' (18 May 2020), www.kingcounty.gov/depts/health/news/2020/May/18-covid.aspx; Secretary of Public Health, Washington State, 'Ordering a Face Covering Mandate' (24 June 2020), www.Secretary_of_Health_Order_20-03_Statewide_Face_Coverings.pdf.

[8] See Pennsylvania Department of Public Health, 'Directing Face Coverings in Schools' (31 August 2021), www.health.pa.gov/topics/Documents/Diseases%20and%20Conditions/Order%20of%20the%20Acting%20Secretary%20Directing%20Face%20Coverings%20in%20Schools.pdf; California Governor's Office, 'Governor Gavin Newsom Lays Out Pandemic Plan for Learning and Safe Schools' (17 July 2020), www.gov.ca.gov/2020/07/17/governor-gavin-newsom-lays-out-pandemic-plan-for-learning-and-safe-schools/.

entertainment facilities)[9] and even outdoor public facilities.[10] Some states excuse the mask requirement in public buildings if social distancing is possible[11] or if the person is already vaccinated.[12] Persons using public transportation are required to wear masks.[13]

Many state and local governments mandated the use of vaccines for all or certain public employees or for workers who regularly come in contact with the public.[14] Some states limit the mandate to certain professions such as health workers, educators or school staff.[15] In many of those jurisdictions, employees who decline to be vaccinated face dismissal or suspension without pay, and other jurisdictions require unvaccinated

[9] See, eg City of Berkeley, California, 'Order Of The Health Officer Of The City Of Berkeley Generally Requiring Members Of The Public And Workers To Wear Face Coverings' (17 April 2020), www. berke-leyca.gov/sites/default/files/2022-01/COB-health-order-2020-04-17-masks.pdf; S Collins, 'Mask Up, King County' (*Helsell Fetterman Blog*, 18 May 2020), www.helsell.com/2020/05/18/mask-up-king-county/; State of Illinois, 'Executive Order 2020-38' (29 May 2020), www.illinois.gov/government/executive-orders/executive-order.executive-order-number-38.2020.html; and City of Boston Public Health Commission, 'Face Coverings' (n 7).

[10] See King County, Washington State, 'Local Health Officer Outdoor and Indoor Masking Orders' (2 September 2021), www.kingcounty.gov/~/media/depts/health/communicable-diseases/documents/C19/LHO-masking-order.ashx (outdoor events over 500 people); City of Philadelphia, Pennsylvania, 'City of Philadelphia Implements New COVID-19 Vaccine and Mask Requirements' (11 August 2021), www.phila.gov/2021-08-12-city-of-philadelphia-implements-new-covid-19-vaccine-and-mask-requirements/ (non-seated outdoor events over 1,000 people); 'The latest COVID-19 vaccination and masking requirements for Bay Area entertainment venues' *San Francisco Chronicle* (online, 6 August 2021), www.datebook.sfchronicle.com/entertainment/the-latest-covid-19-vaccination-and-masking-requirements-for-bay-area-entertainment-venues.

[11] See L Dake, 'Oregon to expand COVID-19 restrictions, starting Friday' (*Oregon Public Broadcasting*, 7 July 2020), www.opb.org/news/article/oregon-covid-19-restrictions-expand-again/; King County, Washington State, 'Face Covering Directive' (n 7); Mayor of Kansas City, Missouri, 'Eleventh Amended Order 20-01' (16 November 2020), www.kcmo.gov/home/showdocument?id=6088.

[12] See State of Connecticut, 'Executive Order No. 12' (18 May 2021), www.portal.ct.gov/-/media/Office-of-the-Governor/Executive-Orders/Lamont-Executive-Orders/Executive-Order-No-12.pdf; State of Nevada, 'Declaration of Emergency Directive 050' (2 September 2021), www.nvhealthresponse.nv.gov/wp-content/uploads/2021/09/Directive-050.pdf; *cf* City of Saint Louis, Missouri, 'Health Commissioner's Order No. 1 and Proclamation – COVID-19 (2021)' (23 July 2021), www.stlouis-mo.gov/government/departments/health/communicable-disease/covid-19/orders/health-commissioner-order-1-july-2021.cfm.

[13] See United States Centers for Disease Control and Prevention, 'Requirement For Persons To Wear Masks While On Conveyances And At Transportation Hubs' (29 January 2021), www.cdc.gov/quarantine/pdf/Mask-Order-CDC_GMTF_01-29-21-p.pdf; City of Saint Louis, Missouri, 'Health Commissioner's Order No. 3' (1 October 2021), www.stlouis-mo.gov/government/departments/health/communicable-disease/covid-19/orders/upload/Health-Commissioner-Order-No-3-Mask-Mandate.pdf (public transportation on vessels).

[14] California Governor's Office, 'California Becomes First State in Nation to Announce COVID-19 Vaccine Requirements for Schools' (1 October 2021), www.gov.ca.gov/2021/10/01/california-becomes-first-state-in-nation-to-announce-covid-19-vaccine-requirements-for-schools/; City of Denver Department of Public Health and Environment, 'Order' (2 August 2021), www.denvergov.org/files/assets/public/covid19/documents/public-orders/ddphe-pho-8.2.21.pdf; Massachusetts Governor's Office, 'Executive Order No. 595 Implementing A Requirement For COVID-19 Vaccination For The Commonwealth's Executive Department Employees' (19 August 2021), www.mass.gov/doc/august-19-2021-executive-department-employee-vaccination-order/download.

[15] See, eg State of Washington Governor's Office, 'COVID-19 Vaccination Requirement' (20 August 2021), www.governor.wa.gov/sites/default/files/proclamations/21-14.1%20-%20COVID-19%20Vax%20Washington%20Amendment.pdf (workers at state agencies as well as education and health care settings must be vaccinated); State of Maine Governor's Office, 'Mills Administration Requires Health Care Workers To Be Fully Vaccinated Against COVID-19 By October 1' (12 August 2021), www.maine.gov/governor/mills/news/mills-administration-requires-health-care-workers-be-fully-vaccinated-against-covid-19-october; Oregon Secretary of State's Office, 'COVID-19 Vaccination Requirement for Healthcare Providers and Healthcare staff in Healthcare Settings' (5 August 2021), secure.sos.state.or.us/oard/viewSingleRule.action?ruleVrsnRsn=289353.

workers to submit to regular Covid-19 testing.[16] In some cities, unvaccinated persons may not enter a gym, restaurant or entertainment facility.[17] In Philadelphia, for example, persons entering private businesses were required to be masked unless the indoor business requires all employees and patrons to be vaccinated.[18] As another example, until recently, Hawaii required all persons arriving without proof of vaccination to quarantine for 10 days.[19]

To address the spread of the Covid-19 virus, some jurisdictions declared states of emergency,[20] ordered that schools close,[21] and directed that non-essential workers in both the public and private sectors stay at home.[22] Gathering and capacity restrictions have been used to limit crowds and the spread of disease at public events.[23]

---

[16] Pennsylvania Governor's Office, 'Governor Wolf Announces 'Vaccine or Test' Requirement for Commonwealth Employees in Health Care and High-Risk Congregate Facilities' (10 August 2021), www.governor.pa.gov/newsroom/governor-wolf-announces-vaccine-or-test-requirement-for-%E2%80%8Bcommonwealth-employees-in-health-care-and-high-risk-congregate-facilities/; Trial Court of Massachusetts, 'Policy to Require Vaccine Reporting & Weekly Testing for Unvaccinated Staff' (30 August 2021), www.mass.gov/doc/trial-court-policy-to-require-vaccine-reporting-weekly-testing-for-unvaccinated-staff/download; Vermont Governor's Office, 'Transcript: Governor Phil Scott and Dr. Mark Levine Discuss Delta, Vaccine Effectiveness And Pandemic Divisiveness At Weekly Covid-19 Briefing' (8 September 2021), www.governor.vermont.gov/press-release/transcript-governor-phil-scott-and-dr-mark-levine-discuss-delta-vaccine-effectiveness (weekly testing and masks required if unvaccinated).

[17] Mayor of San Francisco, California, 'San Francisco to Require Proof of Vaccination for Entry to Certain Indoor Businesses and All Large Indoor Events' (12 August 2021), www.sfmayor.org/article/san-francisco-require-proof-vaccination-entry-certain-indoor-businesses-and-all-large-indoor (ie, bars, restaurants, clubs and indoor gyms); J Diaz, 'Los Angeles will require proof of a COVID-19 vaccine for indoor establishments' (*National Public Radio*, 7 October 2021), www.npr.org/sections/coronavirsus-live-updates/2021/10/07/1043910547/los-angeles-mandates-covid-19-vaccines.

[18] City of Philadelphia Department of Public Health, 'Protect yourself and others from Delta: masks required indoors and at large outdoor gatherings in Philadelphia' (11 August 2021), www.phila.gov/2021-08-11-protect-yourself-and-others-from-delta-masks-required-indoorM220s-and-at-large-outdoor-gatherings-in-philadelphia/.

[19] See D Nakaso, 'Arriving air passengers in Hawaii without COVID-19 test to face 10-day quarantine' *Honolulu Star Advertiser* (online, 9 December 2020), www.staradvertiser.com/2020/12/09/hawaii-news/arriving-air-passengers-in-hawaii-without-covid-19-test-to-face-10-day-quarantine-2/. See also Kansas Department of Health and Environment, 'Travel list and travel-related quarantine guidelines (PDF)' (17 February 2022), www.coronavirus.kdheks.gov/175/Travel-Exposure-Related-Isolation-Quaran (the State of Kansas recommends quarantine for unvaccinated persons who have visited specified countries, have travelled on cruise ships or attended gatherings of over 500 people without masking and social distancing).

[20] See, eg Massachusetts Governor's Office, 'Governor Baker Declares State of Emergency to Support Commonwealth's Response to Coronavirus' (10 March 2020), www.mass.gov/news/governor-baker-declares-state-of-emergency-to-support-commonwealths-response-to-coronavirus; State of Washington Governor's Office, 'Proclamation by the Governor 20-05' (29 February 2020), www.governor.wa.gov/sites/default/files/proclamations/20-05%20Coronavirus%20%28final%29.pdf. See also Trump White House Archives, 'Proclamation on Declaring a National Emergency Concerning the Novel Coronavirus Disease (Covid-19) Outbreak' (13 March 2020), www.trumpwhitehouse.archives.gov/presidential-actions/proclamation-declaring-national-emergency-concerning-novel-coronavirus-disease-covid-19-outbreak/.

[21] See, eg 'The Coronavirus Spring: The Historic Closing of U.S. Schools (A Timeline)' *Education Week* (online, 1 July 2020), www.edweek.org/leadership/the-coronavirus-spring-the-historic-closing-of-u-s-schools-a-timeline/2020/07; J Cowin and S Patel, 'Schools Close Over Coronavirus Concerns' *New York Times* (online, 14 March 2020, updated 24 July 2020), https://www.nytimes.com/2020/03/14/us/california-coronavirus-cases.html (over 1 million students affected state-wide).

[22] See California Governor's Office, 'Executive Order N-33-20' (19 March 2020), www.gov.ca.gov/wp-content/uploads/2020/03/3.19.20-attested-EO-N-33-20-COVID-19-HEALTH-ORDER.pdf; J Bosman and J McKinley, 'One in Five Americans Ordered to Stay Home in Coronavirus Crackdown' *New York Times* (online, 20 March 2020, updated 26 March 2020), www.nytimes.com/2020/03/20/us/ny-ca-stay-home-order.html.

[23] See, eg Z Dym, 'Hawaiʻi Island loosens COVID-19 restrictions, increases outdoor gathering capacity' (*Hawaii Public Radio*, 15 October 2021), www.hawaiipublicradio.org/local-news/2021-10-15/hawaii-island-

As noted above, many of the restrictions ordered due to the Covid-19 pandemic have been challenged by private citizens,[24] schools,[25] churches[26] and even state and local governments. With regard to the latter, officials in some states enacted legislation to prevent local schools, governments or even private businesses from issuing mask or vaccine mandates. These acts have resulted in litigation in the federal and state courts.[27] In fact, the State of Florida has even filed a lawsuit in opposition to the federal government's vaccine mandate for federal workers,[28] and the United States Justice Department has filed suit against Florida for defunding schools that mandate face masks.[29]

At the federal level, the then President initially characterised the virus as a 'hoax',[30] but the administration eventually took action pursuant to each of the federal statutes described below. The government provided funding,[31] equipment, medication, supplies,[32]

loosens-covid-19-restrictions; S Solis, 'Massachusetts COVID reopening: Larger gathering sizes, fewer capacity restrictions in time for wedding season' (*Mass Live*, 28 April 2021), www.masslive.com/business/2021/04/massachusetts-covid-reopening-larger-gathering-sizes-fewer-capacity-restrictions-in-time-for-wedding-season.html; 'Colorado Lifting Capacity Restrictions On Indoor Gatherings And Changing Mask Requirements For Kids' (*CBS News Colorado*, 31 May 2021), www.cbsnews.com/colorado/news/colorado-lifting-capacity-restrictions-on-large-indoor-gatherings-changing-mask-requirements-kids/.

[24] See, eg *Ryan Klaassen, et al v Trustees of Indiana University*, 7 F. 4th 592 (7th Cir. 2021); *Travis Wise et al, v Governor Inslee et al*, __F. Supp 3d__, ORDER DENYING PLAINTIFFS' MOTION FOR TEMPORARY RESTRAINING ORDER/PRELIMINARY INJUNCTION, 2:21-cv-0288-TOR (E.D. Wash. 2021). See also K Reilly, 'School Masking Mandates Are Going to Court. Here's Why the Issue Is So Complicated' *Time* (online, 1 October 2021), https://time.com/6103134/parents-fight-school-mask-mandates/.

[25] *Resurrection School, et al v Hertel, et al*, 11 F.4th 437 (6th Cir.), vacated and remanded for rehearing en banc, 16 F.4th 1215 (6th Cir. 2021).

[26] *South Bay United Pentecostal Church v Newsom* (n 6).

[27] See, eg *Arizona School Boards Association Inc. et al, v State of Arizona et al*, __Ariz. Sup. Ct.__, WL4487632 (Maricopa Cty. 2021) aff'd 501 P.3d 731 (Ariz. 2022) (provisions banning masks in public schools are unconstitutional); *The Arc of Iowa et al, v Kim Reynolds et al*, 566 F. Supp 3d 921, (case no.: 4:21-cv-00264, 2021 WL 4166728)(S.D. Iowa 2021) aff'd in part, reversed in part, 33 F.4th 1042 (8th Cir. 2022) (Court bans enforcement of Iowa law banning masks in public schools since it violates federal law); *Disability Rights South Carolina et al, v McMaster et al*, 564 F. Supp. 3d 413, (civil action No.: 3:21- 02728-MGL) (D. S.C. 2021) vacated and remanded 24 F.4th 893 (4th Cir. 2022) (District Court enjoins state law banning face masks in schools, finding that it violates federal law); *G.S. v Lee*, (case no.: 21-cv-02552-SHL-atc, 2021 WL 4057812) 560 F. Supp 3d 1113 (W.D. Tenn. 2021) stay of District Court's preliminary injunction denied, ___ F.4th ___ (6th Cir. 2021) (Court enjoins Executive Order banning face masks in schools).

[28] Ron DeSantis's website, 'Governor Ron DeSantis Announces Lawsuit Against Biden Administration's Unconstitutional Vaccine Mandates' (28 October 2021), www.flgov.com/2021/10/28/governor-ron-desantis-announces-lawsuit-against-biden-administrations-unconstitutional-vaccine-mandates/.

[29] 'U.S. files court action against Florida over school funding' *Miami Herald* (online, 29 October 2021), www.miamiherald.com/news/local/education/article255364751.html.

[30] L Egan, 'Trump calls coronavirus Democrats' "new hoax"' (*NBC News*, 29 February 2020), www.nbcnews.com/politics/donald-trump/trump-calls-coronavirus-democrats-new-hoax-n1145721.

[31] See FEMA, 'COVID-19 Disaster Declarations', www.fema.gov/disaster/coronavirus/disaster-declarations (Stafford Act funds); United States Centers for Disease Control and Prevention 'COVID-19 Funding', www.cdc.gov/cpr/readiness/funding-covid.htm (Funding awarded by the Centers for Disease Control and Prevention).

[32] See US Department of Health & Human Services, 'Response to the COVID-19 Pandemic', www.phe.gov/about/sns/COVID/Pages/default.aspx (Strategic National Stockpile provided 'supplies, medicines and devices for lifesaving care'); 'Defense Production Act Speeds Up Vaccine Production' (*National Public Radio*, 13 March 2021), www.npr.org/sections/health-shots/2021/03/13/976531488/defense-production-act-speeds-up-vaccine-production (medicine, supplies and devices produced pursuant to the Defense Production Act).

services[33] and aid for research,[34] and ultimately prioritised the production of medication and supplies.[35] The current administration subsequently ordered that federal employees be vaccinated[36] and that masks be worn at certain locations, including transportation hubs – train, bus and subway stations and airports – as well as airplanes, trains, buses and other modes of mass transportation.[37]

The different responses by public officials at various levels – ranging from actions viewed as helpful in attempting to control the pandemic, to inaction, and to distinctly unhelpful actions – raise the question of whether any such officials can be held criminally liable if their conduct or their failure to act results in the deaths of members of the public. To answer this question, it is necessary to examine the various types of crimes for which they theoretically could be prosecuted, the showing required to successfully prosecute a public official, and the doctrines that may shield them from liability.

II. CONSTITUTIONAL, LEGAL AND POLICY OVERVIEW

In the United States, government agencies responsible for preventing and controlling disease are found at the federal, state and local levels. At the local level, cities and towns have health boards responsible for implementing health laws and even enacting local regulations for areas not covered by federal and state laws. For example, in the state of Massachusetts, each of the 351 cities and towns has a board of health. Those local health boards are required to immediately report cases of dangerous disease to the State and then work with State officials to investigate and control any outbreak,[38] which may include the isolation or quarantining of persons or animals.[39]

While the laws in each state may vary, states have extensive authority to address issues of public health.[40] Each state has an agency responsible for collecting information on dangerous diseases, investigating and monitoring their presence, and preventing and controlling such diseases.[41] Their authority includes isolating and quarantining infected

---

[33] See FEMA, 'Bringing Resources to State, Local, Tribal & Territorial Governments', www.fema.gov/disaster/coronavirus/governments (FEMA was coordinating the work of state and local governments to respond to the pandemic); see also United States Centers for Disease Control and Prevention, 'Operational Guidance for K-12 Schools and Early Care and Education Programs to Support Safe In-Person Learning', www.cdc.gov/coronavirus/2019-ncov/community/schools-childcare/k-12-guidance.html (CDC provides all types of advice to government agencies and the public).

[34] NPR, 'Defense Production Act' (n 32) (pursuant to the Defense Production Act).

[35] ibid.

[36] The White House, 'Executive Order on Requiring Coronavirus Disease 2019 Vaccination for Federal Employees' (9 September 2021), www.whitehouse.gov/briefing-room/presidential-actions/2021/09/09/executive-order-on-requiring-coronavirus-disease-2019-vaccination-for-federal-employees/.

[37] United States Centers for Disease Control and Prevention, 'Order: Wearing of face masks while on conveyances and at transportation hubs' (29 January 2021), www.cdc.gov/quarantine/masks/mask-travel-guidance.html.

[38] Massachusetts General Laws, c 111, s 6; see also 105 Code of Massachusetts Regulations, ss 100, 110, 134, 135 and 150.

[39] 105 Code of Massachusetts Regulations, ss 300.020 ('Isolation' and 'Quarantine'), 300.190, 300.200 and 300.210.

[40] *Bond v United States*, 572 U.S. 844, 854 (2014); *Medtronic, Inc. v Lohr*, 518 U.S. 470, 475 (1996); *Jacobson v Massachusetts*, 197 U.S. 11, 25 (1905).

[41] See nn 7 and 8.

persons,[42] as well as taking other steps to mitigate any outbreak, including mandating the wearing of face masks and compulsory vaccination programs.[43] Where the presence of a disease constitutes a health emergency, every state gives the governor or the health administrator broad powers to deal with the crisis.[44]

At the national level, the federal government possesses wide-ranging powers and extensive funding to address serious health crises emanating from dangerous diseases. For example, the Public Health Service Act provides that during a health emergency, the Secretary of Health and Human Services (Secretary):

> [M]ay take such action as may be appropriate to respond to the public health emergency, including making grants, providing awards for expenses, and entering into contracts and conducting and supporting investigations into the cause, treatment, or prevention of a disease.[45]

The Secretary also has access to a 'Public Health Emergency Fund',[46] which can be used for various projects ranging from the acceleration of research and development[47] to implementing any 'applicable and appropriate' measures.[48]

The Secretary is also required to maintain a national stockpile of pharmaceuticals, vaccines, medical devices and supplies 'for the emergency health security' of the country.[49] The Secretary may deploy this stockpile to respond to 'an actual or potential public health emergency'.[50]

In addition, the Surgeon General, with the approval of the Secretary, may develop and enforce regulations to prevent the spread of dangerous diseases from foreign countries or from one state to another.[51]

The Defense Production Act of 1950[52] provides the President with extensive powers for compelling private industry to assist the government during emergency situations. Specifically, the President can prioritise any order or contract,[53] can ensure that certain components or materials are available for production,[54] and can take action to prevent hoarding of scarce materials.[55]

---

[42] See n 8.

[43] *Jacobson v Massachusetts* (vaccination mandate); *Resurrection School et. al v Hertel et al*, 11 F.4th 437 (6th Cir.), vacated and remanded for rehearing en banc, 16 F.4th 1215 (6th Cir. 2021) (school mask mandate).

[44] See, eg Massachusetts General Laws, c 17, s 2A which states: 'Upon declaration by the governor that an emergency exists which is detrimental to the public health, the commissioner [of public health] may, with the approval of the governor and the public health council, during such period of emergency, take such action and incur such liabilities as he may deem necessary to assure the maintenance of public health and the prevention of disease. ... The commissioner [of public health], with the approval of the public health council, may establish procedures to be followed during such emergency to insure the continuation of essential public health services and the enforcement of the same'.
See also Arizona Rev. Statutes, 26-303; 20 Delaware Code ss 3115 and 3116; Ohio Rev. Code s 107.43; Missouri Rev. Statutes Ann. s 107.43; Texas Government Code s 418.014.

[45] 42 U.S. Code (USC) 247d(a)(2).

[46] 42 USC 247d(b)(1).

[47] 42 USC 247d(b)(2)(C).

[48] 42 USC 247d(b)(2)(F).

[49] 42 USC 247d-6b(a)(1).

[50] 42 USC 247d-6b(a)(3)(G).

[51] 42 USC 264(a).

[52] 50 USC 4501 ff.

[53] 50 USC 4511(a).

[54] 50 USC 4517.

[55] 50 USC 4512et.

Under the Stafford Act, the federal government can provide assistance to state and local governments responding to emergency situations.[56] Under this act, a state's governor can declare an emergency and request federal assistance,[57] or the President unilaterally can declare a national emergency.[58] The federal government may then provide assistance to the state(s), including 'personnel, equipment, supplies, facilities, and managerial, technical and advisory services'.[59] The federal government may also reimburse the states for medical services and related expenses.[60]

A. Overview of and Specific Constitutional and Legal Principles Regarding Criminal Liability of High-Ranking Government/Public Officials

The issue relating to the First Amendment to the United States Constitution will be addressed in Section VI below.

B. Scope of Responsibility and Area of Tolerated Risk

Not applicable.

C. Impact of Immunities

Pursuant to either statutory or common law, both elected and appointed public officials enjoy a form of qualified immunity that shields them from liability from all but the most egregious misconduct. While the particulars of qualified immunity differ among jurisdictions, their effect is substantially the same.

To be entitled to qualified immunity, a public official needs to show only that he or she was 'acting in his [or her] official capacity and within the scope of his [or her] discretionary authority'.[61] Discretionary authority exists when the law does not specify the precise action that the official must take.[62]

The central purpose of the qualified immunity doctrine is to protect public officials 'from undue interference with their duties and from potentially disabling threats of liability'.[63] Such qualified immunity does not simply act as a defence to liability but precludes the action from the outset.[64]

---

[56] See the Robert T Stafford Disaster Relief and Emergency Assistance Act, ff at 42 USC 5121 and 5143.
[57] 42 USC 5170 and 42 USC 5191(a).
[58] 42 USC 5191(b).
[59] 42 USC 5170a.
[60] 42 USC 5170b.
[61] *Barker v Norman*, 651 F.2d 1107, 1120 (5th Cir. 1981).
[62] *Davis v Scherer*, 468 U.S. 183, 196 n.14 (1984). See also *Jolly v Klein*, 923 F. Supp. 931, 948 (S.D. Tex. 1996) (an act is discretionary if it requires personal deliberation, decision and judgment).
[63] *Harlow v Fitzgerald*, 457 U.S. 800, 806 (1982).
[64] See *Mitchell v Forsyth*, 472 U.S. 511, 513 (1985).

The majority of cases addressing liability of public officials, whether state or federal, involve civil liability. Civil actions brought by individuals who may been harmed are far more common than criminal prosecutions of public officials. At the federal level, courts generally hold that public officials 'are shielded from liability for civil damages insofar as their conduct does not violate clearly established statutory or constitutional rights of which a reasonable person would have known'.[65] Notably, and of particular relevance to the present discussion, the United States Supreme Court has applied the civil standards to efforts to prosecute public officials for criminal misconduct.[66]

The laws of the various states can vary, but generally they either follow federal law or adopt a comparable scheme.[67]

Such immunity, while not unlimited, would make it difficult to prosecute a public official for a discretionary decision. Such decisions generally must be more than negligent. At a minimum, courts require a showing of at least gross negligence or recklessness approaching intentional conduct to support a finding of liability, and even then, courts are mixed as to whether a public official may be held liable.[68]

Therefore, allegations of negligent homicide and, in some jurisdictions even involuntary manslaughter would be barred as a matter of law based on the doctrine of qualified immunity.

D. Prosecutorial Matters

In the United States, prosecutors work at the federal, state and local levels. At the federal level, the Department of Justice has one or more offices in each state that enforces the federal laws. Each state has a chief legal officer known as the Attorney General, and District Attorneys at the county or municipal level to enforce the state and local laws.

---

[65] *Harlow v Fitzgerald*, 457 U.S. at 818. See 42 USC § 1983.

[66] See *United States v Lanier*, 520 U.S. 259, 271–72 (1997) (public official may be held criminally liable only if he/she meets the standards for civil liability).

[67] See, eg *Schlossberg v Goins*, 141 N.C. App. 436, 540 S.E.2d 49, 56 (N.C. Ct. App. 2000) (the doctrine of public official immunity protects public officials from individual liability for negligence in the performance of their discretionary acts executing a governmental function if done without corruption or malice); *Dallas Indep. Sch. Dist. v Finlan*, 27 S.W.3d 220, 242 (2000) (same); *People v Doyle*, 286 A.D. 276, 277–78 (1955) (public officials enjoy qualified civil and criminal immunity).

[68] See *Teague v Consolidated Bathurst, Ltd.*, 408 F. Supp. 980, 982 (E.D. Pa. 1976) (public officials are entitled to conditional immunity if they were acting within the scope of their authority and if their alleged action or failure to act was not intentionally malicious, wanton or reckless; they cannot be held liable for merely negligent conduct); *Kara B. by Albert v Dane County*, 198 Wis. 2d 24, 67 (1995) (to overcome this qualified immunity, a showing must be made that the public official's conduct is at least reckless); *Wilcox v City of Asheville*, 222 N.C. App. 285, 289 (2012) (in the context of public official immunity, where an actor's conduct is so reckless or so manifestly indifferent to the consequences and where the safety of life or limb is involved, such conduct may be deemed to be equivalent in spirit to an actual intent); *Cooper v Rodriguez*, 443 Md. 680, 686 (2015) (correctional officer was not entitled to common law public official immunity where his behaviour was grossly negligent, constituting an intentional failure to perform a manifest duty in reckless disregard of the consequences as affecting the life of another and with a thoughtless disregard of the consequences without the exertion of any effort to avoid them); *Bailey v City of Annapolis*, 258 A3d 894 (Md. App. 2021) (Public official loses qualified immunity only if his conduct is grossly negligent, amounting to wanton and wilful conduct – when he or she inflicts injury intentionally or is so utterly indifferent to the rights of others that he or she acts as if such rights did not exist – and where the consequences were foreseeable).

While each of these prosecution offices has its own area of prosecution, there is occasional overlap; for example, certain complex fraud or drug cases, or bank robberies could be prosecuted by officials at any level.

At all three levels, prosecutors possess broad discretion in determining 'when, whom, how and even whether' to prosecute an individual for criminal charges.[69] Moreover, no individual including a judge, can force a prosecutor to charge an individual or to recommend sentencing in a certain manner, as these decisions are within the prosecutor's sole discretion.[70]

III. CAUSATION

Negligent, reckless or intentional homicide, or indeed, any act that may result in harm to a person, requires a showing of causation.[71]

A. Causation (General Principles)

Causation is a determination that the defendant is responsible for the crime being charged. In a criminal case, the prosecution must prove this element beyond a reasonable doubt. In a case where different people have committed acts, a determination must be made as to who is responsible for any harm caused and for what crime. In cases of homicide, the prosecution must prove that the defendant caused the death.

There are generally two types of tests used to determine causation. First, is the two-part test where the defendant must be the (1) 'but for' or 'actual' cause of the harm, and that he or she is the (2) 'proximate cause' of such harm.[72] To satisfy the 'but for'/'actual cause' test, the prosecutor must prove 'that the harm would not have occurred in the absence of – that is, but for – the defendant's conduct' (citation omitted).[73]

The 'concept of "proximate cause" is obscure'[74] and 'serves, *inter alia*, to preclude liability in situations where the causal link between conduct and result is so attenuated that the consequence is more aptly described as mere fortuity'.[75]

---

[69] Justice Manual of the United States Department of Justice, Comments to s 9–27.110. See also *United States v Shaw*, 226 A. 2d 366, 368 (DC Ct. App. 1967); *State v Winne*, 91 A. 2d 65, 77 (N.J. Super Law Div. 1952).

[70] See *United States v Newman*, 382 F. 2d 479, 480 (D.C. Cir. 1967) ('very broad discretion'). *Shepard v Attorney General*, 409 Mass. 398, 401 (1991) ('wide discretion'); *Pace v State*, 566 S.W. 2d 861, 867 (Tenn. 1978).

[71] See *People v Tims*, 449 Mich. 83, 95 (1995) (courts in most jurisdictions require a showing of causation to convict for homicide, defined as either a 'but for' cause of the victim's death or a showing that the defendant's conduct was a 'substantial factor' in the death); *State v Bauer*, 471 N.W.2d 363, 366 (Minn. 1991) (manslaughter conviction requires a showing that the defendant's act was the 'proximate cause' of the victim's death without the intervention of an efficient independent force in which defendant did not participate); *State v Kalathakis*, 563 So. 2d 228, 231 (1990) (in homicide prosecution, element of the defendant's act or conduct in causing criminal consequences must be proved); *Commonwealth v Root*, 403 Pa. 571, 574 (1961) ('[U]nlawful or reckless conduct is only one ingredient of the crime of involuntary manslaughter. Another essential and distinctly separate element of the crime is that the unlawful or reckless conduct charged to the defendant was the *direct* cause of the death in issue.') (emphasis in original).

[72] See *State v Bauer*, 329 P. 3d 67, 70–71 (Wash. 2014).

[73] *University of Texas Southwestern Medical Center v Nassar*, 570 U.S. 338, 346–47 (2013).

[74] J Dressler, *Understanding Criminal Law* 8th edn (Durham, Carolina Academic Press, 2018) 189.

[75] *Paroline v United States*, 572 U.S. 434, 445 (2014).

B. Causation and 'Thin Skull' Scenarios

See Section III.A above.

C. Restricting Causality: Policy and Doctrinal Issues

The Model Penal Code (MPC) has adopted a different test for causation, rejecting 'proximate cause' and relying solely on the 'but for' test to determine if the defendant's conduct was the cause of the result.[76] It is the cause when 'it is an antecedent but for which the result in question would not have occurred'.[77]

The MPC establishes rules for criminal causation when recklessness and negligence are being charged. It states:

(1) Conduct is the cause of a result ...

(3) [w]hen recklessly or negligently causing a particular result is an element of an offense, the element is not established if the actual result is not within the risk of which the actor is aware or, in the case of negligence, of which he should be aware unless:

(a)   the actual result differs from the probable result only in the respect that a different person or different property is injured or affected or that the probable injury or harm would have been more serious or more extensive than that caused; or

(b)   the actual result involves the same kind of injury or harm as the probable result and is not too remote or accidental in its occurrence to have a [just] bearing on the actor's liability or on the gravity of his offense.[78]

During the pandemic, government officials took certain actions which it could be argued were harmful to the public and even led to deaths. These actions include (1) the failure to prepare for the virus, (2) the failure to respond more quickly to the problem, (3) the failure to issue 'stay at home orders' or mandate mask requirements, (4) the failure to close businesses open to the public (*i.e.*, restaurants, clubs and bars) and (5) the issuance of orders prohibiting schools from issuing forced mask mandates or private companies from issuing vaccine mandates.

However, courts addressing the pandemic have accurately described the Covid-19 outbreak as 'A pandemic which continues to cause widespread disease and death'.[79] Clearly, the virus itself is the efficient cause of the victims' deaths. In those jurisdictions requiring a showing of 'but for' causation, the conduct of a public official – regardless of how incompetent – simply would not meet that standard. Even in jurisdictions permitting conviction on a 'substantial factor' theory, given the nature of the virus, it is difficult to imagine that a decision by a public official would ever constitute a substantial factor in the death of any individual. In addition to the virus itself, other factors might contribute to a person becoming infected or succumbing to the virus, such as his or her behaviour, age, underlying health and other risk factors.[80] A prosecutor would have an onerous burden

[76] Dressler, *Understanding Criminal Law* (n 74) 196–97.
[77] Model Penal Code (MPC) 2.03 (1)(a).
[78] MPC 203(1) and (3)(a)(b).
[79] *Slidewaters LLC v Wash. State Dep't of Labor & Indus.*, 4 F.4th 747, 755 (9th Cir. 2021).
[80] See *United States v Mueller*, 471 F. Supp. 3d 625, 628–32 (E.D. Pa. 2020) (describing common risk factors).

of showing that the conduct in question directly caused or was a substantial factor in the death or harm to a specific person.[81]

IV. THE STRUCTURE OF HOMICIDE OFFENCES AND ASSAULT/AGGRAVATED ASSAULT/SERIOUS BODILY HARM OFFENCES

There is no uniform law of homicide in the United States, as each of the 50 states and the federal government has its own criminal laws and statutes. While the laws vary, there are some generalities which are helpful for this discussion.

The American law of murder originates from fourteenth-century English Common Law.[82] In the late eighteenth century, the American states divided the crime of murder into degrees in order to provide for penalties other than capital punishment for homicides where the defendant may be guilty of something less than an intentional homicide committed with malice.[83] Generally, 'The more heinous kinds of murder are identified in the first degree portion of the statute[s], and all other murders are deemed murder in the second degree'.[84] Degrees are still used to quantify different categories of murder, and it is not unusual to find state codes listing the crime of murder into two or more degrees.[85]

With the advent of the MPC, a number of States have adopted a new definition of homicide which does not include degrees of murder. It also provides for the crime of negligent homicide.[86]

A. Murder/Intentional Homicide

The common law of most jurisdictions generally defines murder as 'the unlawful killing of a human being by another with malice aforethought'.[87] The phrase malice aforethought refers to the various mental states needed to establish the crime of murder.[88] However, as to public officials, the traditional definition of an intentional killing with malice aforethought simply does not apply regardless of how negligent or

---

[81] See *Dorety v Princess Cruise Lines*, 2021 U.S. Dist. LEXIS 206358, *19 (California Central District Court October 1, 2021) (Plaintiff has not offered any specific, admissible evidence to support a finding that cruise operator caused decedent's death 10 days after he was removed from cruise ship); *Commonwealth v Walsh*, Superior Court No 2079CR00178 (Massachusetts November 21, 2021) (dismissing counts of elder neglect and permitting serious bodily injury to an elder by director superintendent and medical director of long-term care facility based on merger of two dementia units where, although their conduct increased the risk of harm to the residents, the evidence failed to support that the named resident contracted the virus or suffered harm as a result of such conduct).

[82] JM Kaye, 'The Early History of Murder and Manslaughter' (1967) 83 *Law Quarterly Review* 365.

[83] See Dressler, *Understanding Criminal Law* (n 74) 478.

[84] *Wharton's Criminal Law*, Vol 2, 16th edn (London, Thomson Reuters, 2021) 148.

[85] ibid 148–50, 175.

[86] Dressler, *Understanding Criminal Law* (n 74) 513–15.

[87] J Miller, *Handbook of Criminal Law* (St Paul, West Publishing Company, 1934) 262.

[88] Dressler, *Understanding Criminal Law* (n 74) 477.

reckless their conduct may be. Poor decision-making by a public official simply would not qualify as intentional conduct.

One of these forms of malice aforethought titled 'depraved and malignant heart' is relevant to the present analysis. It occurs when a person acts 'Under circumstances evincing depraved indifference to human life … recklessly engages in conduct which creates a grave risk of death to another person, and thereby causes the death of another person'.[89]

The MPC also established a form of murder based on recklessness that may be found where the act causing the death 'is committed recklessly under circumstances manifesting extreme indifference to the value of human life'.[90] Basically, 'The reckless defendant is aware of the risk and disregards it'.[91]

In *King v State* the court expounded on this mental state:

> Its gravamen is the act of reckless by engaging in conduct which creates a grave or very great risk of death under circumstances "manifesting extreme indifference to human life." What amounts to "extreme indifference" depends on the circumstances of each case, but some shocking, outrageous, or special heinousness must be shown … A person acts recklessly when he is aware of and consciously disregards a substantial and unjustifiable risk … The risk must be of such nature and degree that disregard thereof constitutes a gross deviation from the standard of conduct that a reasonable person would observe in the situation (citations omitted).[92]

It should further be noted that under this form of murder, 'The defendant does not intend to kill. He or she is indifferent as to whether death results or may even hope that it will not result'.[93]

B. Culpable Homicide/Manslaughter

Manslaughter has been defined as 'the unlawful killing of one human being by another without malice aforethought'.[94] The crime of involuntary manslaughter is a lesser included offence of reckless murder[95] and has been defined as 'an unlawful homicide unintentionally caused by an act which constitutes such a disregard of the probable consequences to another so as to amount to wanton or reckless conduct'.[96] 'Wanton or reckless conduct generally involves a wilful act that is undertaken in disregard of the probable harm to others that may result' and that there 'is a high likelihood that such harm will result'.[97]

---

[89] NY Penal Law s 125.25.4.
[90] MPC 210.2 (1) (b).
[91] *Wharton's Criminal Law*, Vol 2 (n 84) 250.
[92] *King v State*, 505 So 2d 403 (Ala Crim App 1987) 407; W LaFave, *Substantive Criminal Law*, Vol 2, 3rd edn (London, Thomson Reuters, 2017) 593 and 596.
[93] *Wharton's Criminal Law*, Vol 2 (n 84) 176.
[94] Miller, *Handbook* (n 87) 278.
[95] *United States v Arnt*, 473 F. 3d 1159, 1163 (9th Cir. 2007).
[96] *Commonwealth v Life Care Centers of America, Inc.*, 456 Mass. 826, 832 (2010).
[97] ibid.

While Massachusetts rejects the reliance on 'negligence or gross negligence' to establish the crime of involuntary manslaughter,[98] other states have determined that gross negligence would be sufficient for a conviction.[99]

It should also be noted that the failure to act can support a prosecution of involuntary manslaughter. This will occur

> [i]f an individual's actions create a life-threatening condition, there is a duty to take reasonable steps to alleviate the risk created, and the failure to do so may rise to the level of recklessness necessary for involuntary manslaughter.[100]

The MPC has added another form of homicide which relies on a lower degree of culpability and is called negligent homicide. Specifically, the Code states 'Criminal homicide constitutes negligent homicide when it is committed negligently'.[101] Stated differently, 'the negligent actor is not aware of the risk but should have been aware of it'.[102]

A number of states have adopted the crime of negligent homicide,[103] while others have limited the offence to deaths involving the operation of motor vehicles.[104]

C. Offences Related to Actions that Cause Serious Bodily Harm (Assault; Grievous Assault; Assault with Intent to Cause Serious Bodily Harm)

Since criminal liability for this type of offence in the United States generally requires a showing of intentional conduct, and the conduct addressed in this chapter primarily involves negligent or reckless acts, we will not be addressing this issue.

D. Offences Regarding Unborn Foetuses; Interrupting the Course of a (Viable) Pregnancy

Since criminal liability of an unborn foetus would be derivative of the mother's rights, this topic will not be addressed.

E. Failure to Render Assistance

See Section IV.B above concerning failure to act.

---

[98] ibid.

[99] See, eg *State v Hintz*, 61 Idaho 411, 102 P. 2d 639, 643 (1940); *People v Sealy*, 136 Mich. App. 168, 356 N.W. 2d 614, 616 (1984); *State v Albrecht*, 336 Maryland 475 (1994), 649 A 2d. 336, 347–48 (1994).

[100] *Commonwealth v Life Care Centers of America, Inc.* (n 96) 832.

[101] MPC 210.4 (1).

[102] *Wharton's Criminal Law*, Vol 2 (n 84) 250.

[103] See, eg New York Penal Code s 125.10; Arizona Criminal Code, s 13-1102(A); Louisiana Revised Statutes, Title 14 s 32A (1 and 2); Utah Criminal Code, Title 76, c 5, s 206(1).

[104] See, eg Hawaii Penal Code, 707-704(1); West Virginia Code, s 17C-5-1(a); Connecticut General Statutes, s 14-222a; Massachusetts General Laws, c 90 s 24G(c).

V. DEFENCES, JUSTIFICATIONS AND EXCUSES

Notwithstanding the steps that the United States ultimately took to mitigate the harm from the virus, in the beginning of the Covid-19 pandemic, the federal government essentially abdicated its traditional role of protecting its citizens from threats to their safety and well-being. In many instances, government officials minimised and at times concealed the dangers of the virus from the public. Aside from funding the development of vaccines, the federal government passed the responsibility for protecting the public to state and local governments, leaving them to fend for themselves and to compete against each other for scarce supplies and equipment. Many state and local governments did the best they could with limited resources; many did not, mirroring the inaction of the federal government. In fact, governors in some states actually outlawed mask mandates and other protective measures by local officials. The conduct of government officials at all levels no doubt resulted in hundreds of thousands of unnecessary deaths and immeasurable suffering.

Yet, as described above, the laws in the United States simply do not permit the prosecution of neglectful behaviour by government officials. Most politicians who failed to act or who acted in a manner that in retrospect turned out to be harmful arguably acted in good faith, balancing the benefits and harms from various courses of action. For example, governors in many states resisted shutdowns on the grounds that the damage to the economy and the increase in the prevalence of mental health issues and the suicide rate would be more harmful than any potential increase in the spread of the virus. While many experts decried their policy decisions, for the most part, the governors acted on the advice of their own experts.

As noted above, realistically, no public official in the United States at any level of government can or will be prosecuted for intentional homicide committed with malice aforethought for a poor decision that results in death. In such circumstances, the question is whether a public official could be prosecuted for reckless or negligent homicide. The answer is that such a prosecution might be theoretically possible but would be practically improbable or impossible. Any effort to prosecute a public official for negligent or reckless conduct would depend on the actor's mental state, would require a showing of causation and after all that, would likely be prohibited by qualified immunity.

In those states where involuntary manslaughter or 'malignant heart' murder could be charged, prosecutors must review the information known to the officials at the time that their decisions were made to determine whether the actions were reckless, and the extent or level of it. For example, in cases where malignant murder, has been found, the facts usually involve a person who fires one or more bullets into a room, bus or vehicle with people inside, drives at high-speed onto a main street, or plays 'Russian Roulette'.[105] Each of these actions involves an extreme level of recklessness that is a risk to human life.[106] The facts under present consideration are far different, as they involve a public official who is balancing conflicting opinions (some of which will be wrong) and

---

[105] See *King v State* (n 92) 406–07; LaFave, *Substantive Criminal Law*, Vol 2 (n 92) 596–99.
[106] See *King v State* (n 92) 405; Dressler, *Understanding Criminal Law* (n 74) 486.

interests to establish a public health policy. Even the United States Supreme Court will accord 'especially broad' latitude 'when state and local officials '"undertake ... to act in areas fraught with medical and scientific uncertainties"'.[107] The Court has similarly found that government officials who make policy decisions in very difficult situations – in that case, federal prison officials – must be 'accorded wide-ranging deference'.[108]

For example, a study concluded that if proper actions were taken nationally in the spring of 2020, the deaths of tens of thousands of Americans would have been prevented.[109] At that time, however, the officials had to balance[110] public health restrictions against economic adversity,[111] mental health issues[112] and its social impact to adults and children.[113] At the time, there was also a lack of scientific information supporting extensive restrictions[114] or agreement as to the danger of the virus.[115] As a result, officials received conflicting advice from scientists that they needed to make critical public health decisions.[116] Thus, public officials had to take various discretionary actions with initially limited and often conflicting information about this disease and how it is transmitted.

As a practical matter, the failure to take certain actions simply will not support a finding of recklessness and likely would not establish negligence when advisors presented the officials with conflicting opinions, when the knowledge of the disease was and is still limited, and when other competing interests such as the potential harm to the economy, to the mental health of the public and to the personal liberty of citizens must also be considered.

Similarly, based on the conflicting nature of expert information, the level of recklessness necessary for manslaughter would not exist. In *Duckworth v Franzen*,[117] a civil lawsuit was filed against prison officials when a transport bus caught fire while carrying prisoners. Due to the restraints used on the bus, it was difficult to remove the prisoners

---

[107] *Democratic National Committee et al v Wisconsin State Legislature, et al*, 590 U.S. ___, 141 S. Ct. 28, 32 (2020) (Justice Kavanaugh's concurring opinion in denial of an application to vacate stay).

[108] *Bell v Wolfish*, 441 U.S. 520, 547 (1979).

[109] S Pei et al, 'Differential Effects of Intervention Timing on COVID-19 Spread in the United States' (2020) 6 *Science Advances*, www.science.org/doi/10.1126/sciadv.abd6370#tab-citations.

[110] See *United States v Carroll Towing*, 159 F 2d. 169, 173–74 (2d Cir. 1947) (Justice Learned Hand establishes a mathematical balancing test to determine ordinary negligence); *Moisan v Loftus*, 178 F 2d 148, 149–50 (2d Cir. 1949) (the balancing test is extended to gross negligence).

[111] S Sah, 'Conflicts of Interest and COVID' (*Scientific American*, 3 December 2020), www.scientificamerican.com/article/conflicts-of-interest-and-covid/.

[112] V Saladino et al, 'The Psychological and Social Impacts of Covid-19: New Perspectives of Well-Being' (*Frontiers in Psychology*, 2 October 2020), www.frontiersin.org/articles/10.3389/fpsyg.2020.577684/full.

[113] ibid.

[114] See A Larsen, 'Where the CDC went wrong on COVID-19 spread, masks and vaccination benefits' *Salt Lake City Tribune* (online, 13 May 2021), www.sltrib.com/news/2021/05/13/andy-larsen-biggest/.

[115] V Prasad and J Flier, 'Scientists who express different views on Covid-19 should be heard, not demonized' (*statnews.com*, 27 April 2020), www.statnews.com/2020/04/27/hear-scientists-different-views-covid-19-dont-attack-them/.

[116] ibid (noting that in the Spring of 2020, there was 'massive uncertainty, with data and analyses shifting daily'). See also E Schumaker, 'CDC and WHO offer conflicting advice on masks. An expert tells us why' (*ABC News*, 29 May 2020), https://abcnews.go.com/Health/cdc-offer-conflicting-advice-masks-expert-tells-us/story?id=70958380.

[117] *Duckworth v Franzen*, 780 F 2d. 645 (7th Cir. 1985).

during the fire resulting in the death of one prisoner and injuries to several others. The Court noted:

> People often fail to foresee disasters of a kind that have not yet occurred and to take effective precautions against them, and ordinarily such lack of foresight is at worst negligence; it certainly is not recklessness in anything like the criminal law sense of the word.[118]

Alternatively, there may be situations where the knowledge possessed by the public officials cannot be established at the time that public health decisions were made. These situations may exist at the state and local levels of government, and it would be difficult to prosecute these officials for actions taken based on the limited information that was available.

There is also a long tradition of personal freedom and autonomy in the United States, and many decisions by public officials simply affirmed the right of citizens to make personal choices concerning their own personal safety. Although decisions such as whether to wear a mask and whether to take a vaccine will certainly impact the safety of others, public officials often cite these liberty interests as paramount in formulating policy. Especially where the vaccines were initially given only emergency use authorisation rather than full approval, there is at least some basis for arguments against vaccine mandates.

The behaviour of some public officials may well have been negligent, and to the extent that it resulted in deaths, such conduct may theoretically meet the definition of negligent homicide or manslaughter. But again, public officials are protected by qualified immunity and simply cannot be prosecuted for such behaviour. And even if their behaviour rises to the level of recklessness, it would be exceedingly difficult to prosecute a public official for such conduct.

Further, as a recent Massachusetts case illustrates, proof that the negligent or reckless behaviour of a public official resulted in the deaths of citizens generally requires a showing of causation – that is, that the conduct in question resulted in the deaths of specific persons. The fact that policies pursued by public officials resulted in an increased number of deaths simply would not support a finding of manslaughter or negligent homicide absent a showing that specific decisions resulted in specific deaths.[119]

So, as a practical matter, it is exceedingly unlikely that a public official anywhere in the United States would or could be prosecuted for a policy decision, regardless of how misguided that decision may have been.

A. Necessity

There are situations where the defence of necessity could arise in a criminal prosecution. For example, a high-ranking government official concerned that an economic disaster was imminent, might decide to keep businesses open and functioning at capacity. While this option protects the economy and may have beneficial effects, it allows the virus to

---

[118] ibid 654.
[119] *See Commonwealth v. Walsh, supra* at FN 81.

spread rapidly, potentially resulting in many deaths. Could the necessity ('choice of evils') defence be relied upon by an official charged with murder or manslaughter? While raising such a defence may be theoretically possible, as a practical matter, it would likely not apply to this circumstance.

As a matter of background, American common law has long recognised the necessity defence.[120] The defence has been codified in the MPC[121] and in many states under the title of necessity or choice of evils.[122] While the criteria for availing oneself of this defence may vary from state to state, there are certain general parameters. Specifically, it 'allows an actor to escape criminal responsibility for most offenses when the actor faces an imminent or immediate emergency not of his own making, and violating the law is necessary to avoid a greater evil'.

Turning first to the MPC, it characterises the defence as a 'choice of evils' defence, stating that:

(1) Conduct which the actor believes to be necessary to avoid a harm or evil to himself or to another is justifiable, provided that:

   (a) the harm or evil sought to be avoided by such conduct is greater than that sought to be prevented by the law defining the offense charged; and

   (b) neither the Code nor other law defining the offense provides exceptions or defenses dealing with the specific situation involved; and

   (c) a legislative purpose to exclude the justification claimed does not otherwise plainly appear.

(2) When the actor was reckless or negligent in bringing about the situation requiring a choice of harms or evils or in appraising the necessity for his conduct, the justification afforded by this Section is unavailable in a prosecution for any offense for which recklessness or negligence, as the case may be, suffices to establish culpability.[123]

Thus, the MPC is broader than its common law counterpart, as there is (1) no requirement of imminence, and (2) creating the situation may limit the defence but does not preclude an actor from relying on the defence. And it appears to be available for many crimes, including murder.[124] Significantly, though, criminal charges in the present circumstances would generally involve killings based on 'recklessness or negligence',[125] and the MPC eliminates necessity as a defence to reckless or negligent homicide.[126]

As for the common and statutory law, in most jurisdictions, the necessity defence would either be unavailable or severely limited. In the majority of jurisdictions, this defence is not available for the charge of murder.[127] Further, while the killing of an innocent person to save a greater number of people may be legally, morally and philosophically

---

[120] See *United States v Holmes*, 26 Fed. Cas. 360 (C.C. Pa. 1842).

[121] MPC 3.02(1) and (2).

[122] See, eg Hawaii Revised Statute, s 703–302; Kentucky Revised Statute, s 503.030; Title 17A of the Maine Criminal Code, c 5, s 103; Missouri Revised Statutes, s 563.026; New Jersey Revised Statutes, s 2C:3-2; New York Penal Law Article 35.05; Texas Penal Code, s 9.22; Wisconsin Statutes, s 939.47.

[123] MPC 3.02(1) and (2).

[124] American Law Institute, Comment to MPC s 3.02, 14–15.

[125] MPC 3.02(2).

[126] See s IV above.

[127] *Wharton's Criminal Law*, Vol 1 (n 84) 462.

debatable,[128] committing a homicide for economic reasons, whether intentional, reckless or negligent, would not be sanctioned.[129] Further, it would be difficult to argue that the deaths of a large number of people is greater than the economic harm that the official seeks to avoid.[130]

Finally, in some states, the necessity law requires that 'there is no legal alternative which will be effective in abating the danger'.[131] With the options of limited quarantine or closures or limiting the number of persons allowed entry a business establishment, financial support by the government or requiring certain personal protections at the location, it would be difficult if not impossible to argue that no other alternatives were available.[132]

Therefore, while the necessity defence is theoretically possible, it is highly unlikely to be a viable defence.

VI. CORPORATE CRIMINAL LIABILITY

It has long been held that a corporation can be subjected to criminal charges.[133] In *United States v Cincotta*,[134] the Court explained:

> A corporation may be convicted for the criminal acts of its agents, under a theory of respondent superior. But criminal liability may be imposed on the corporation only where the agent is acting within the scope of employment.

However, the issue is whether a television news broadcasting corporation or other media outlet could be prosecuted for presenting opinions that misinform the public resulting in harm to people who follow this advice. Further, could the anchor, host or guest be subject to criminal prosecution for arguing against vaccinations or spreading misinformation? While such a prosecution could be possible, as with the case of government officials, it is highly unlikely that it would occur.

---

[128] See J Cohan, 'Homicide by Necessity' (2006) 10 *Chapman Law Review* 119.

[129] See, *United States v Ashton*, 24 F. Cas. 873, 874, 2 Sumn. 13 (1834) ('The law deems the lives of all persons far more valuable than any property'); *People v Coffman*, 96 P.3d 30, 106 (Cal. 2004) ('The law must encourage, even require, everyone to seek an alternative to killing'). See also *People v Fontes*, 89 P.3d 484, 486. Colo. App. 2003) (economic necessity by itself cannot support a necessity defence); *State v Moe*, 24 P.2d 638, 640 (Me. 1933) ('Economic necessity has never been accepted as a defense to a criminal charge').

[130] See *Nelson v State*, 597 P.2d 977, 980 (Alaska 1979) (necessity defence was not viable since the expected harm was not greater than the harm caused by defendant's illegal actions). See also Cohan, 'Homicide' (n 127) 184.

[131] *Commonwealth v Leno*, 415 Mass 835, 839 (1993); See also *People v Fontes*, 486 ('A defendant who has a reasonable legal alternative as a means to avoid the threatened injury is foreclosed from asserting a choice of evils defense').

[132] *United States v Al-Rakabi*, 454 F.3d 1113, 1123–24 (10th Cir. 2006) (the necessity defence was not applicable since the defendant had legal alternatives available); *Nelson v State*, 980 (same).

[133] See, eg *United States v Socony-Vacuum Oil Company*, 310 U.S. 150, 165 n. 1 (1940) (27 corporations were charged with price-fixing in the oil industry); *United States v Automated Medical Laboratories*, 770 F.2d 399 (4th Cir 1985).

[134] *United States v Cincotta*, 689 F.2d 238, 241(1st Cir.) *cert denied*, 459 U.S. 991 (1982).

Aside from the onerous problem of establishing causation – that is, that information broadcast or disseminated resulted in the death of a particular person – members of the press or journalists possess certain constitutional protections. Specifically, the First Amendment to the United States Constitution states in relevant part that 'Congress shall make no law ... abridging the freedom of speech, or of the press'.

While some areas of false communication are not protected (such as perjury, fraud, defamation or claiming to be a federal agent),[135] opinions offered in books or broadcasts relating to the arts, philosophy, religion, science or history are highly protected by the First Amendment.[136] In fact, the United States Supreme Court has stated that

> Under the First Amendment there is no such thing as a false idea. However pernicious an opinion may seem, we depend for its correction not on the conscience of judges and juries but on the competition of other ideas.[137]

Similarly, the Court has recognised that in applying First Amendment protections 'some false statements are inevitable if there is to be an open and vigorous expression of views in public and private conversation'.[138]

As a result, the First Amendment has been relied upon to bar the prosecution of civil and criminal cases.[139] For example, courts have shielded publishers from liability when the books they published resulted in harm including death.[140] As one court noted, 'even if liability could be imposed consistently with the Constitution, we believe that the adverse effect of such liability upon the public's free access to ideas would be too high a price to pay'.[141]

This same protection has barred liability where the information was broadcast on television and injury resulted.[142] Therefore, based on the federal and state precedent, the First Amendment would almost certainly serve as a bar to any prosecution of broadcast companies or their employees.[143] And again, the defences or issues previously mentioned – such as causation[144] – would hamper any prosecution.

---

[135] *United States v Alvarez*, 567 U.S. 709, 719–20 (2012).

[136] ibid 751–52 (Dissenting, Alito, J.).

[137] *Gertz v Robert Welch, Inc.*, 418 U.S. 323, 339–40 (1974). See also, *United States v Alvarez* (n 134) 727 ('The remedy for speech that is false is speech that is true. This is the ordinary course in a free society. The response to the unreasoned is the rational; to the uninformed, the enlightened; to the straight-out lie, the simple truth').

[138] ibid 718. See also *New York Times Co. v Sullivan*, 376 U.S. 254, 271–72 (1964) ('That erroneous statement is inevitable in free debate, and that it must be protected if the freedoms of expression are to have the "breathing space" that they "need ... to survive."' [citation omitted]).

[139] See, eg *Smith v Linn*, 563 A.2d 123 (Pa Super Ct. 1989) aff'd. 587 A.2d 309 (Pa. 1991); *State v Vote No! Committee*, 957 P.2d 691 (Wash. 1998).

[140] See, eg *Alm v Nostrand Reinhold Co.*, 480 N.E. 2d 1263 (Ill. App. Ct. 1985); *Smith v Linn* (n 138).

[141] *Alm v Nostrand Reinhold Co.* (n 139) 1267.

[142] *DeFilippo v National Broadcasting Co*, 446 A 2d 1036 (1982).

[143] *State v Vote No! Committee* (n 138) 697 ('the First Amendment precludes punishment for generalized "public" frauds, deceptions and defamation', citing C Fried, 'The New First Amendment Jurisprudence: A Threat to Liberty' (1992) 59 *University of Chicago Law Review* 225, 238.

[144] See N Strossen, 'Disinfo v. Democracy' (*Tablet Magazine*, 19 September 2021), www.tabletmag.com/sections/news/articles/disinformation-nadine-strossen ('The impact of speech on a single human mind, let alone an entire community or society, results from the complex interplay of multiple factors, and hence cannot be confidently predicted, or even clearly assessed after the fact').

VII. FORMS OF PARTICIPATION

In the United States, allegations of misconduct based on the failure to address a pandemic generally focus on the individual politician, not groups.

VIII. ATTEMPT

Attempts in the United States generally require a showing of intentional acts, and are not applicable to negligent or reckless conduct.

IX. SANCTIONS, SENTENCING, PUNISHMENT, REPARATIONS AND/OR RESTORATIVE JUSTICE

Since we have found it to be exceedingly unlikely that any public official would or could be prosecuted, the issue of sanctions will not be addressed.

16

COVID-19 and Crimes against Humanity

GERHARD KEMP

I. PROBLEM STATEMENT

MILLIONS OF DEATHS have been reported worldwide from the start of the COVID-19 pandemic.[1] This grim reality forms the factual context of the question concerning criminal liability addressed in this book. Death and serious harm to physical and mental health affect not only the protected interests underlying various crimes under domestic law (notably murder, other homicide offences and assault), but can also be analysed in the context of the interests protected by international criminal law.[2] While the analyses in the comparative (national) chapters focus on criminal liability of government officials and corporations for crimes under domestic law, the focus in this chapter falls on criminal liability in the context of crimes that affect interests beyond those of the individual victims. The definitions and structures of the various crimes under domestic criminal law and international criminal law are different, of course, but there are, at the most fundamental level, also different interests at stake.[3] For instance, the crime of murder under domestic criminal law protects the individual right to life,[4] whereas the crime of genocide protects not only the right to life but also the existence and survival of specifically defined groups,[5] and crimes against humanity concerns the violation of fundamental human rights committed as part of a widespread or systematic attack on a civilian population.[6]

---

[1] As at September 2022, the number of deaths reported to the WHO stood at more than six million worldwide (see World Health Organization's tracking webpage, https://covid19.who.int/).

[2] See, eg 'The Role of Non-State Armed Groups in Addressing the COVID-19 Pandemic' (*Armed Groups and International Law*, 28 February 2022), www.armedgroups-internationallaw.org/2022/02/28/blog-symposium-the-role-of-non-state-armed-groups-in-addressing-the-covid-19-pandemic/.

[3] For a pronouncement on the distinction between 'ordinary crimes' and crimes under international law (such as war crimes, crimes against humanity and genocide) see *Prosecutor v Bagaragaza*, Decision on Rule 11*bis* Appeal, 30 August 2006, ICTR-05-86-AR11*bis*, paras 16–18.

[4] See, eg C McDiarmid, 'Killings Short of Murder: Examining Culpable Homicide in Scots Law' in A Reed and M Bohlander (eds), *Homicide in Criminal Law* (London, Routledge, 2019) 21.

[5] G Werle and F Jessberger, *Principles of International Criminal Law* 3rd edn (Oxford, Oxford University Press, 2014) 294.

[6] ibid 333.

The various national case studies in this book indicate that genocide, with its specific intent requirement, seems very unlikely[7] (despite what some commentators assert[8]) because there is insufficient to no evidence that anyone had the intent to destroy a protected group as a whole or in part.[9] The focus in this chapter thus is on crimes against humanity, not only as a hypothetical proposition in the context of the COVID-19 pandemic, but also with reference to some of the case studies in the comparative chapters.[10]

Article 7 of the Rome Statute of the International Criminal Court (Rome Statute, ICC) and the Elements of Crimes constitute the framework for the discussion of crimes against humanity. This choice is informed first by the fact that several (although not all) of the national case studies in this volume are countries that are states party to the Rome Statute.[11] Second, although the Rome Statute is not a universal instrument,

---

[7] For a critical assessment of the 'COVID-19 response as genocide' proposition (and with specific reference to the situation in the United States under former President Trump), see J Heieck, 'Trump's Coronavirus Response: Genocide by Default?' (*OpinioJuris*, 15 May 2020), http://opiniojuris.org/2020/05/15/trumps-coronavirus-response-genocide-by-default/. The author rejects the proposition that Trump and/or his subordinates are responsible for genocide. The main conclusions are as follows: (i) the crime of genocide (under both the Genocide Convention and the Rome Statute) prohibits the man-made physical destruction of a protected group, in whole or in part. (ii) The prohibited *actus rei* does not include natural phenomena (such as pandemics) unless there is proof that, for instance, a virus was intentionally created and released with 'the specific intent to destroy a protected group'. (iii) There is no proof that former President Trump or his subordinates created Covid-19 or released it on the American population. (iv) What about genocide by omission, or, 'failure to act' as basis for genocide? The specific intent element of genocide requires 'the highest level of intent'. Thus, although the US Centers for Disease Control and Prevention data indicated that certain racial and ethnic groups (in particular African-Americans) have been disproportionately affected by the Trump administration's ineffective COVID-19 response, there is no evidence that the US federal government specifically intended for these groups to get sick and die. There is no evidence of intent to physically destroy, in whole or in part, these disproportionately affected groups.

[8] L Moran, 'Epidemiologist Slams U.S. Coronavirus Response: "Close to Genocide by Default"' *Huffington Post* (online, 5 June 2020), www.huffingtonpost.co.uk/entry/epidemiologist-coronavirus-genocide-by-default_n_5eb2a5ebc5b63e6bd96f5d81.

[9] For the crime of genocide, intent to destroy, in whole or in part, a protected group as such, is required. This requirement is complex and difficult to interpret. The terms 'destroy' and 'part' are key markers of the scope of the crime of genocide. The predominant view is that there must be intent to *physically destroy* a national, racial, ethic, or religious group, in whole or in part. There is some (national) case law that suggests that the social (as opposed to physical) destruction of a group might also be enough, but this view seems to be an outlier. The second marker – 'in part' – means that the intent needs not to be the complete annihilation of a group, but a substantial part. 'Substantial' is not interpreted in absolute quantitative terms. Rather, a qualitative meaning is attached to the term 'substantial'. For more analysis, see C Kreß, 'The Crime of Genocide Under International Law' (2006) 6 *International Criminal Law Review* 461, 485–99.

[10] This chapter is about the *potential* applicability of elements of a crime under international law to national case studies pertaining to the COVID-19 pandemic and governmental and corporate reactions to it. Having said that, the warning of the ICC Pre-Trial Chamber (PTC) in *Gbagbo* that expressed serious concern that the Prosecutor relied heavily on NGO reports and press articles to build a criminal case, is well noted. The PTC stated that 'this kind of evidence is neither the product of a full and proper investigation, nor does it usually constitute a valid substitute for forensic and other material evidence and first-hand testimonial evidence'. *The Prosecutor v Laurent Gbagbo*, Decision adjourning the hearing on the confirmation of charges pursuant to art 61(7)(c)(i) of the Rome Statute, 3 June 2013, ICC-02/11-01/11, paras 35–36.

[11] The countries that are discussed in the comparative chapters, with their relative status as parties to the Rome Statute of the International Criminal Court, as at September 2022: Brazil (state party), England (the United Kingdom is a state party), France (state party), Germany (state party), India (non-state party), Indonesia (non-state party), Iran (non-state party), People's Republic of China (non-state party), South Africa (state party), Spain (state party), Sweden (state party), Turkey (non-state party), United States of America (non-state party). See Assembly of States Parties to the Rome Statute, 'The States Parties to the Rome Statute', https://asp.icc-cpi.int/states-parties.

it is widely ratified in all the major regions of the world.[12] Third, unlike genocide[13] and war crimes,[14] crimes against humanity is the only atrocity crime without a specialist international treaty.[15] There has been some progress towards the adoption of a Crimes Against Humanity Convention, but some legal and political obstacles remain.[16] Therefore, article 7 of the Rome Statute is employed here as a good (albeit imperfect) substitute for an international legal instrument on crimes against humanity. Reference will also be made (where appropriate) to the statutes and case law of the *ad hoc* UN criminal tribunals for the Former Yugoslavia (ICTY),[17] and Rwanda (ICTR),[18] both of which influenced the drafting and interpretation of article 7 of the Rome Statute.[19]

II. THE NORMATIVE CONTEXT

Crimes against humanity fundamentally affect human rights, in particular the rights to life, health, freedom and dignity. Widespread or systematic violations of the fundamental rights of a civilian population can, under the appropriate conditions, be regarded as crimes against humanity.[20] It is therefore necessary to briefly outline the applicable international human rights law framework. It should be noted, however, that not all violations of international human rights law would amount to crimes against humanity. Different protective interests are at stake. But the universal importance of certain human rights, including the rights to life, and physical and bodily integrity, informs the normative core of relevant crimes against humanity at stake here. Indeed, both serious human

---

[12] There are at present 123 states parties to the Rome Statute of the ICC. The states parties are from all the regions of the world. The Assembly of States Parties has the following composition: 33 African states, 19 Asia-Pacific states, 18 Eastern European states, 28 Latin-American and Caribbean states and 25 Western European and other states. See Assembly of States Parties to the Rome Statute, ibid.

[13] Convention on the Prevention and Suppression of the Crime of Genocide (1948).

[14] Convention for the Amelioration of the Condition of the Wounded and Sick in Armed Forces in the Field (1949), Convention for the Amelioration of the Condition of Wounded, Sick and Shipwrecked Armed Forces at Sea (1949), Convention relative to the Treatment of Prisoners of War (1949), Convention relative to the Protection of Civilian Persons in Time of War (1949), Protocol Additional to the Geneva Conventions of 12 August 1949, and relating to the Protection of Victims of International Armed Conflict (1977), and Protocol Additional to the Geneva Conventions of 12 August 1949, and relating to the Protection of Victims of Non-International Armed Conflicts (1977).

[15] There are instruments dealing with crimes that are forms of crimes against humanity, such as torture (Convention against Torture and Other Cruel, Inhuman or Degrading Treatment or Punishment (1984)), apartheid (International Convention on the Suppression and Punishment of the Crime of Apartheid (1973)), and forced disappearances (International Convention for the Protection of all Persons from Enforced Disappearance (2006)). But there is currently no comprehensive instrument that consolidates crimes against humanity.

[16] For the text of the draft articles on the Prevention and Punishment of Crimes Against Humanity, adopted by the International Law Commission, see UN A/CN.4/L.935, 15 May 2019, https://legal.un.org/docs/?symbol= A/CN.4/L.935. For background on the crimes against humanity initiative, see: L Nadya Sadat (ed), *Forging a Convention for Crimes Against Humanity* (Cambridge, Cambridge University Press, 2011).

[17] Statute of the International Criminal Tribunal for the Former Yugoslavia (1993).

[18] Statute of the International Criminal Tribunal for Rwanda (1994).

[19] H Fujita, 'Establishment of the International Criminal Court' (1999) *The Japanese Annual of International Law* 32, 50–52.

[20] Werle and Jessberger, *Principles* (n 5) 333.

rights violations of these core rights and crimes against humanity constitute violations of *ius cogens* norms.[21]

Several international instruments (not all of which are binding international law) contain expressions of the foundational right to life. For instance, the Universal Declaration of Human Rights states that 'everyone has the right to life, liberty, and security of person'.[22] The International Covenant on Civil and Political Rights (ICCPR) provides that 'every human being has the inherent right to life' and this right is to be 'protected by law'.[23] Also, 'no one shall be arbitrarily deprived of his life'.[24] Regional instruments, including the American Convention on Human Rights,[25] the European Convention on Human Rights[26] and the African Charter on Human and Peoples' Rights[27] provide for the right to life. There is support in various international instruments[28] and in the decisions of human rights bodies[29] for the proposition that the right to life is not only a foundational right, but also non-derogable, for instance in the context of states of emergency. This is not to say that the right to life is absolute. Thus, for instance, the European Convention on Human Rights provides that 'deprivation of life shall not be regarded as inflicted in contravention of [the right to life] when it results from the use of force which is no more than absolutely necessary'.[30] The right to life can be seen as more than a protection against extrajudicial or unjustified use of deadly force; in some contexts the right to life is linked to broader socio-economic notions of survival and development as positive duties on the state. However, this broader socio-economic and developmental view of the right to life is still limited to the protection of certain vulnerable groups, notably children.[31] Despite the relatively limited scope of a state's duty regarding the right to life, it seems that there is a core positive duty to take all reasonable actions necessary for the survival of individuals falling within a state's jurisdiction. This duty refers to both general conditions of life and environmental degradation.[32]

While the right to life under international human rights law is not yet fully linked to socio-economic and developmental obligations, there is one other right, the right to

---

[21] JP Pérez-León Acevedo, 'The Close Relationship Between Serious Human Rights Violations and Crimes Against Humanity: International Criminalization of Serious Abuses' (2017) *Anuario Mexicano de Derecho Internacional* 153.

[22] Universal Declaration of Human Rights, GA Res 217 (III) A (Paris, 10 December 1948), art 3.

[23] International Covenant on Civil and Political Rights (New York, 16 December 1966) (ICCPR), art 6(1).

[24] ICCPR, art 6(1).

[25] American Convention on Human Rights (San José, 22 November 1969), art 4(1).

[26] Convention for the Protection of Human Rights and Fundamental Freedoms (Rome, 4 November 1950) (ECHR), art 2(1).

[27] African Charter on Human and Peoples' Rights (Nairobi, 27 June 1981), art 4.

[28] ICCPR, art 4(2).

[29] 'General Comment No 3 on the African Charter on Human and Peoples' Rights: The Right to Life (Article 4)', *African Commission on Human and Peoples' Rights* (12 December 2015).

[30] ECHR, art 2(2).

[31] Notably, art 6(2) of the United Nations Convention on the Rights of the Child: 'States Parties shall ensure to the maximum extent possible the survival and development of the child'.

[32] I Bantekas and L Oette, *International Human Rights Law and Practice* 3rd edn (Cambridge, Cambridge University Press, 2020) 364.

health, which must also be considered when we look at the normative context informing the protected interests of crimes against humanity. The International Covenant on Economic, Social and Cultural Rights (ICESCR)[33] provides that everyone has the right 'to the highest attainable standard of physical and mental health'.[34] The ICESCR recognises certain state obligations to *realise* the right to health. These obligations are twofold in nature, namely the provision of adequate health care services, and the obligation to address conditions relevant to good health, which include basic shelter, food, water, sanitation, safe working environment, freedom from pollution and disease prevention.[35] Article 12(2) of the ICESCR provides for certain minimum government actions pertaining to the full realisation of the right to health. These include the prevention, treatment and control of epidemic, endemic, occupational and other diseases,[36] and the creation of conditions which would assure to all medical service and medical attention in the event of sickness.[37]

III. THE STRUCTURE OF CRIMES AGAINST HUMANITY

Article 7(1) of the Rome Statute provides that 'crime against humanity' means any of the specific acts listed in paragraph 1 when committed as part of a widespread or systematic attack directed against any civilian population, with knowledge of the attack.[38] For present purposes we will focus on the specific acts of murder, extermination and other inhumane acts of a similar character as those listed in article 7(1) that are committed with the intent to cause great suffering, or serious injury to body or to mental or physical health.[39] The structure of crimes against humanity will be analysed with reference to the various components mentioned in article 7(1): first, the contextual element, which includes the notion of a 'civilian population' as the object of the crime, the characterisation of the attack (widespread *or* systematic) and the 'policy element'. Second, the mental element, and third, a discussion of the specific acts (murder, extermination and other inhumane acts).

---

[33] International Covenant on Economic, Social and Cultural Rights (New York, 16 December 1966) (ICESCR).

[34] ICESCR, art 12(1). Regional human rights instruments follow the same formulation, see, eg African Charter on Human and Peoples' Rights, art 16; European Social Charter (Turin, 18 October 1962), art 11.

[35] Bantekas and Oette, *International Human Rights* (n 32) 443.

[36] ICESCR, art 12(2)(c).

[37] ibid, art 12(2)(d).

[38] For an overview of the structure of crimes against humanity under the Rome Statute, see K Ambos (ed), *Rome Statute of the International Criminal Court, Article-by-Article Commentary* 4th edn (Oxford, Hart Publishing, 2021) 145–70.

[39] The other acts are: enslavement; deportation or forcible transfer of population; imprisonment or other severe deprivation of physical liberty in violation of fundamental rules of international law; torture; rape, sexual slavery, enforced prostitution, forced pregnancy, enforced sterilisation, or any other form of sexual violence of comparable gravity; persecution against any identifiable group or collectivity on political, racial, national, ethnic, cultural, religious, gender, or other grounds that are universally recognised as impermissible under international law; enforced disappearance of persons; the crime of apartheid.

A. Contextual Element

i. Civilian Population

Crimes against humanity are by their nature directed against a civilian population *as such*; not against any individual specifically. The emphasis is thus on the collective. Individual victims are targeted not because of their individual attributes but rather because of their 'membership of a targeted civilian population'.[40] Some factors to consider when determining whether the attack was 'directed against' any civilian population, include: the means and method used in the course of the attack, the status of the victims, the number of victims, the discriminatory nature of the attack, and the nature of the acts committed in the course of the attack.[41] Membership in a certain group is not required. For evidentiary reasons and to establish the collective nature of the crimes,[42] it may be necessary to prove the existence of multiple victims, but, with the exception of the crime of extermination, 'a crime need not be carried out against a multiplicity of victims in order to constitute a crime against humanity'.[43] Indeed, 'an act directed against a limited number of victims, or even against a single victim, can constitute a crime against humanity, provided it forms part of a widespread or systematic attack against a civilian population'.[44] 'Civilian' has a broad meaning and includes every person in a population and in times of peace this includes even soldiers or members of the police.[45] This aspect of crimes against humanity is a reminder that its criminalisation is linked to international human rights law as protected interest.[46]

ii. The Attack Must Be 'Widespread' or 'Systematic'

'Attack directed against any civilian population' means conduct involving the 'multiple commission of acts' referred to in article 7(1), 'pursuant to or in furtherance of a State or organizational policy to commit such attack'.[47] 'Attack' in this context is a course of conduct, a campaign or operation conducted against the civilian population. Neither military force, nor violence, is required. 'Attack' is thus any widespread or systematic conduct aimed at a civilian population and involving the acts referred to in article 7(1).[48]

It is generally accepted that a 'widespread' attack refers to the scale of the attack in the quantitative sense, or indeed to the number of victims. There is no geographic meaning attached to 'widespread', and a large number of victims within a relatively small

---

[40] *Prosecutor v Tadić*, Trial Judgment, 7 May 1997, IT-94-1-T, para 664; *Prosecutor v Bemba*, Decision Pursuant to Article 61(7)(a) and (b) of the Rome Statute on the Charges of the Prosecutor Against Jean-Pierre Bemba Gombo, 15 June 2009, ICC-01/05-01/08-424, para 77.

[41] *Prosecutor v Kunarac et al*, Appeals Judgement, 12 June 2002, IT-96-23/1-A, para 91.

[42] Ambos, *Rome Statute* (n 38) 164.

[43] *Prosecutor v Nahimana et al* (Media case), Appeals Judgment, 28 November 2007, ICTR-99-52-A, para 924.

[44] ibid, para 924.

[45] Ambos, *Rome Statute* (n 38) 165.

[46] See also section II, above.

[47] Rome Statute of the ICC, art 7(2)(a).

[48] Ambos, *Rome Statute* (n 38) 155–56.

geographical area will also qualify as a widespread attack.[49] The alternative requirement is that the attack on the civilian population must be systematic. The case law of
the *ad hoc* tribunals and the ICC suggest that the attack must be carried out as part of
a pattern, *i.e.*, by way of the 'non-accidental repetition of similar criminal conduct on
a regular basis'.[50] Under customary international law, the existence of a preconceived
policy or plan informing the attack will be a clear indication that the attack was carried
out in a systematic way.[51] The policy element is now required for purposes of crimes
against humanity as defined in the Rome Statute of the ICC (see the discussion under
section III.A.iii below).

iii. The 'Policy' Element

Article 7(2)(a) of the Rome Statute provides that the attack on a civilian population
must be carried out 'pursuant to or in furtherance of a State or organizational policy
to commit such attack'. This 'policy' element applies to both widespread and systematic attacks.[52] While the 'policy' concept might at face value suggest a formalised and
well-articulated set of decisions and actions, commentators take the view that in the
absence of an unambiguously formulated policy, one should also be able to look at the
totality of the circumstances to determine the existence of a de facto policy. Indicators
of a 'policy' include 'actual events, political platforms or writings, public statements or
propaganda programmes, and the creation of political or administrative structures'.[53] An
important qualification to add is that the policy must be the responsibility of a specific
entity, namely a state or organisation.[54] The 'policy' element is better understood, and
arguably easier to detect, if it is expressed in terms of the commission of government
plans, administrative actions and the execution of decisions. But can an omission, or the
toleration of calamitous events affecting a civilian population, constitute the basis for
the required policy element? The Elements of Crimes, a document that assists the ICC in
the interpretation and application of the crimes, seems to suggest a narrow understanding of the policy element in crimes against humanity. The Introduction to the Elements
of Crimes pertaining to article 7[55] states the following: 'It is understood that "policy
to commit such attack" requires that the State or organization actively promote or
encourage such an attack against a civilian population'. This formulation could be read
to exclude omissions or toleration of events as constituting a 'policy' for purposes of
crimes against humanity. However, such a restrictive view regarding omissions and toleration as bases for the policy element, is not supported by the text of the Rome Statute,[56]

---

[49] ibid 160.
[50] See, eg the formulation in *Prosecutor v Ntaganda*, Decision Pursuant to Article 61(7)(a) and (b) of the
Rome Statute on the Charges of the Prosecutor Against Bosco Ntaganda, 14 June 2014, ICC-01/04-02/06-309,
para 24.
[51] Ambos, *Rome Statute* (n 38) 161.
[52] Werle and Jessberger, *Principles* (n 5) 340.
[53] Werle and Jessberger, *Principles* (n 5) 342.
[54] Rome Statute of the ICC, art 7(2(a).
[55] ICC Elements of Crimes, Art 7, Introduction, para 3.
[56] Rome Statute of the ICC, art 7(2)(a).

case law[57] or academic commentary.[58] The omission, toleration or failure to act must be a 'purposeful looking away' to be construed as a policy.[59]

B. The Mental Element

Crimes against humanity are crimes of intent. Article 7(1) of the Rome Statute provides that the perpetrator must act 'with knowledge' of the attack on the civilian population. It would not be unreasonable to assume that leaders of a state or organisation have more detailed knowledge of a policy or plan to attack a civilian population, compared to subordinates or lower-level functionaries. Article 7, read with article 30, does not require the perpetrator to be aware of the details of the policy or plan. This reading is also supported by the Elements of Crimes, which states that the mental element 'should not be interpreted as requiring proof that the perpetrator had knowledge of all characteristics of the attack or the precise details of the plan or policy of the State or organization'. The Elements further state that in the case of an emerging widespread or systematic attack against a civilian population, the mental element 'is satisfied if the perpetrator intended to further such an attack'.[60] It is clear that there must exist knowledge of the nexus between a perpetrator's individual acts and the overall attack on the civilian population. The standard of knowledge required corresponds to a risk-based approach, which in turn corresponds to recklessness and constructive knowledge forms of intent.[61] The relevance of risk in interpreting the mental element of the specific acts constituting crimes against humanity is further explored below.

C. Specific Acts

i. Murder

For murder as a crime against humanity, death must result from the act of murder. Murder may be committed by 'action or omission'.[62] Premeditation in the sense of planning is not necessary.[63] Direct intent is clearly covered by article 30 of the Rome Statute.[64] Where the perpetrator acted with a general or even specific awareness of circumstances that existed that included the likelihood (as opposed to the certainty) that death would occur, it becomes necessary to determine the applicability of risk and foreseeability

---

[57] *Situation in the Republic of Côte d'Ivoire*, Corrigendum to 'Decision Pursuant to Article 15 of the Rome Statute on the Authorisation of an Investigation into the Situation in the Republic of Côte d'Ivoire', 15 November 2011, ICC-02/11-14-Corr, para 42; *Prosecutor v Ruto et al*, Decision on the Confirmation of Charges Pursuant to Article 61(7)(a) and (b) of the Rome Statute, 23 January 2012, ICC-01/09-01/11-373, para 210.

[58] Werle and Jessberger, *Principles* (n 5) 345–46.

[59] ibid 346.

[60] ICC Elements of Crimes, Art 7, Introduction, para 2.

[61] Ambos, *Rome Statute* (n 38) 167–68.

[62] *Bemba*, Decision Pursuant to Article 61(7)(a) and (b) of the Rome Statute, para 132.

[63] Ambos, *Rome Statute* (n 38) 173.

[64] Art 30(2)(b), 'means to cause that consequence …'.

in the construction of the mental element of murder in the context of crimes against humanity. It was noted (in section III.B above), that the general standard of knowledge required for crimes against humanity[65] could potentially allow for recklessness as the mental element. However, ICC case law seems to favour a rather strict approach, with very little if any relevance of 'risk' in the construction of the mental element required for murder. The way the ICC interpreted the mental element of murder in a risk scenario is that the 'standard for the foreseeability of events is *virtual certainty*'.[66] The literal and strict interpretation of article 30(2)(b)[67] leaves very little if any room for risk and recklessness as factors in the interpretation of the mental element of murder as an act constituting crimes against humanity. On this reading, bad policy choices, unwise or even irresponsible conduct by senior government officials in the face of an unfolding pandemic, may come in for strong criticism but will be difficult to serve as the basis for a charge of murder as a crime against humanity. Indeed, even in some countries which eventually had high numbers of COVID-19 related excess deaths, governments acted early and with seriousness of purpose to delay the spread of the virus and to give the healthcare providers a window to prepare for the increase in cases which was all along expected.[68] The comparative national case studies in this book show that some government officials were more than just unwise, careless or ill-informed in their handling of the pandemic. A report on the President of Brazil's handling of the COVID-19 pandemic noted that the President acted with 'indirect intent', insofar as he 'assumed the risk of the deaths of thousands of Brazilians by refusing or delaying the purchase of vaccines that were insistently offered'.[69] The report concluded that the President acted intentionally in relation to the resulting deaths. It was further concluded that the President and some of his subordinates behaved in such a way that the course of the pandemic in Brazil was altered for the worse.[70] In the United Kingdom, the initial reaction of the Prime Minister and his government essentially boiled down to a 'mitigation strategy' which anticipated that the majority of people displaying COVID-19 symptoms would have mild-to-moderate symptoms, akin to the seasonal flu.[71] There were also early references to the misguided idea that 'herd immunity' could be achieved for COVID-19.[72]

---

[65] Rome Statute of the ICC, art 30.

[66] *Bemba*, Decision Pursuant to Article 61(7)(a) and (b) of the Rome Statute, para 362; *Prosecutor v Lubanga*, Public Redacted Judgment on the appeal of Thomas Lubanga Dyilo against his conviction, 1 December 2014, ICC-01/04-01/06-3121-Red, para 447 (emphasis added).

[67] The section provides: 'In relation to a consequence, that person means to cause that consequence or is aware that it *will* occur in the ordinary course of events'. The modal verb 'will', rather than 'may' or 'could', is a strong form and indicates that an occurrence is fairly certain (https://dictionary.cambridge.org/grammar/british-grammar/future-will-and-shall). See also Ambos, *Rome Statute* (n 38) 176.

[68] For an example of this approach, see ch 11, 'South Africa'.

[69] OAB Nacional, 'Comissão Especial Para Análise E Sugestões De Medidas Ao Enfrentamento Da Pandemia Do Coronavírus', https://s.oab.org.br/arquivos/2021/04/38a7e5c2-a16f-4aa6-8965-570b8d26efd9.pdf, 7.

[70] See discussion of the report (drafted as a legal opinion), at the behest of the Brazilian Bar, discussed in ch 3, 'Brazil'.

[71] The problem is that COVID-19 is not the flu. It is much worse. D Mackenzie, *COVID-19 – The Pandemic that Never Should Have Happened and How to Stop the Next One* (Paris, Hachette Books, 2020) 129.

[72] For a comprehensive critique of the UK government's 'herd immunity' strategy in the early days of the COVID-19 pandemic, see J Calvert and G Arbuthnott, *Failures of State* (London, Mudlark, 2021) 167–93. The authors concluded that the delay in taking decisive action (aka the 'herd immunity' strategy) would eventually cause large numbers of avoidable deaths.

The UK government's initial COVID-19 strategy prompted Imperial College to warn of the likelihood of 'hundreds of thousands of deaths' and of overwhelmed health systems (including intensive care units). There was a subsequent change of course towards the end of March 2020, and the UK government's COVID-19 policies became increasingly stricter, but not before a much-criticised delay of nine days between the Prime Minister's acceptance in principle of the necessity of a national lockdown and the actual announcement of it.[73]

It is not unreasonable to conclude that the governments of Brazil and the United Kingdom may not have had the direct intent to kill their civilian populations, but one can see clear scope for gross recklessness in both these case studies. Indeed, the Brazilian Bar in their legal opinion stated that the President of Brazil acted with intent (but it is not very clear if the form of intent is closer to *dolus eventualis* and recklessness than direct intent). For a finding of murder as a crime against humanity and following the narrow approach of the ICC regarding the standard for foreseeability of events, one will have to focus on evidence of gross recklessness in the sense of foreseeability of events that amounted to virtual certainty. In both the Brazil and UK examples there seem to be some, but perhaps not conclusive, indications of that.

ii. Extermination

Extermination as a crime against humanity 'includes the intentional infliction of conditions of life, inter alia the deprivation of access to food and medicine calculated to bring about the destruction of part of a population'.[74] Commentators noted that this form of crimes against humanity may require 'a substantial degree of preparation and organisation'.[75] The crime of extermination can come in many forms, but the intent is always to kill a large number of victims either directly (for instance with armed force), or indirectly (for instance by creating conditions of life causing the death of the victims).[76] While the wording of article 7 of the Rome Statute and the Elements of Crimes are elastic enough to cover different forms of conduct as basis for the crime of extermination, some commentators warn that one should not inflate the meaning of 'extermination'.[77] This is to say, one should be careful not to equate multiple murders under article 7(1)(a) of the Rome Statute with the crime of extermination under article 7(1)(b). Extermination should also be distinguished from the crime of genocide. Superficially, the crimes of genocide and 'mass killing', or extermination as a crime against humanity, share significant similarities. However, for genocide a special intent to destroy a group (in whole or in part) must be established;[78] no such special intent is required for the crime of extermination.

---

[73] For more detail, see ch 4, 'England'.
[74] The Rome Statute of the ICC, art 7(2)(b).
[75] Ambos, *Rome Statute* (n 38) 178.
[76] ibid 179.
[77] ibid 271–72.
[78] Rome Statute of the ICC, art 6. See also K Goldsmith, 'The Issue of Intent in the Genocide Convention and Its Effect on the Prevention and Punishment of the Crime of Genocide: Toward a Knowledge-Based Approach' (2010) 3 *Genocide Studies and Prevention*, 238; K Ambos, 'What Does "Intent to Destroy" in Genocide Mean?' (2009) *International Review of the Red Cross* 833; D Aydin, 'The Interpretation of Genocidal Intent under the Genocide Convention and the Jurisprudence of International Courts' (2014) *Journal of Criminal Law* 423–41.

The mental element of the crime of extermination is governed by the general provisions of article 30 of the Rome Statute.

A report on the President of Brazil's handling of the COVID-19 pandemic noted that the President assumed the risk of the deaths of thousands of Brazilians by refusing or delaying the purchase of vaccines that were insistently offered. This allegation is further contextualised with reference to the impact of the COVID-19 pandemic on indigenous peoples.[79] Along the same lines, one can note the disproportionate impact of COVID-19 on Black and other people of colour in countries such as the United Kingdom[80] and the United States.[81]

A case can be made that knowledge of the structural, biomedical and socio-economic conditions that caused the death of large numbers of people and, more pertinently, knowledge of the disproportionate impact of COVID-19 among vulnerable populations and minorities, can constitute the basis for extermination as a crime against humanity. However, if a substantial degree of preparation and organisation (as opposed to a more passive but reckless acceptance of a socio-economic and structural status quo) is indeed required as an element of this crime, an extermination finding may be unlikely.

iii. Other Inhumane Acts

The ICC Pre-Trial Chamber in *Katanga* stated that, for purposes of crimes against humanity under article 7 of the Rome Statute, 'inhumane acts'[82] 'are to be considered as serious violations of international customary law and the basic rights pertaining to human beings, drawn from the norms of international human rights law, which are of a similar nature and gravity to the acts referred to in article 7(1) of the Statute'.[83] This does not mean that any human rights violation, even if it can be characterised as a serious human rights violation, will fall under the rubric of 'inhumane acts'. Serious human rights violations may serve as a starting point for the analysis, but it is still necessary to determine if the required threshold was met.[84] Thus, the acts must be of a similar character to any other act referred to in article 7(1) of the Rome Statute. 'Character' in this context refers to the nature and gravity of the act.[85] The act concerned must be *another* inhumane act; thus, none of the acts constituting crimes against humanity according to article 7(1)(a) to (j) can be simultaneously considered as an 'other inhumane act' in terms of article 7(1)(k).[86] Conduct causing injury to body or mental or physical

---

[79] Ch 3, 'Brazil'.

[80] D Cowan and A Mumford (eds), *Pandemic Legalities* (Bristol, Bristol University Press, 2021) 65–71.

[81] Systemic, socio-economic and biomedical factors contribute to the disproportionate impact of COVID-19 on African American, Native American and LatinX communities. For an analysis, see D Bambino Geno Tai et al, 'Disproportionate Impact of COVID-19 on Racial and Ethnic Minority Groups in the United States: A 2021 Update' (2021) *Journal of Racial and Ethnic Health Disparities*, https://link.springer.com/content/pdf/10.1007/s40615-021-01170-w.pdf.

[82] Rome Statute of the ICC, art 7(1)(k).

[83] *Prosecutor v Katanga and Ngudjolo Chui*, Decision on the Confirmation of Charges, 30 September 2008, ICC-01/04-01/07, para 448.

[84] Ambos, *Rome Statute* (n 38) 247.

[85] ICC Elements of Crimes, fn 30; *Katanga and Ngudjolo Chui*, Decision on the Confirmation of Charges, para 451.

[86] *Katanga and Ngudjolo Chui*, Decision on the Confirmation of Charges, para 452.

health are not inhumane acts per se; there are qualitative and causational elements in the sense that there must be 'great suffering',[87] or 'serious injury to body or to mental or physical health' which must occur *by means of* an inhumane act.[88]

With reference to COVID-19, then, if the submission is that government officials caused the death of civilians by means of acts or omissions, and if the other contextual elements are present, such conduct could potentially be constructed as murder under article 7(1)(a), or extermination under article 7(1)(b). It will not be necessary to evaluate the situation under article 7(1)(k). However, one must go beyond the fatal consequences of COVID-19 and also look at some of the other serious and debilitating effects of this virus. While the impact of COVID-19 is most seriously felt in terms of fatalities, death is not the only adverse consequence of the virus. A phenomenon known as 'long Covid' is of great concern. Is this phenomenon so serious that it can be described as 'great suffering', or as causing 'serious injury to body or to mental or physical health'? There are still many uncertainties about the precise nature and effects of 'long Covid'. Nevertheless, some common symptoms have been identified and include persistent fatigue, breathlessness, 'brain fog' and depression. These symptoms may continue or develop in some people after acute COVID-19. It was noted by scientists that, at present, there are no proven treatments or rehabilitation guidance, with the result that 'long Covid' often affects a person's ability to lead a normal, healthy life. This results in a significant burden on society in general and the healthcare system in particular.[89] More research is needed to determine the qualitative and quantitative impact of 'long Covid'. Suffice to note that the most serious forms of this phenomenon could potentially be viewed as the types of injury to body or mental or physical health that can cause great suffering, thus justifying an analysis under article 7(1)(k).

---

[87] There is some guidance in war crimes law as to what 'causing great suffering' means. Deprivation of medical care can be a fact constituting severe physical and psychological suffering. See, eg *Prosecutor v Mucic et al* (Celibici), Trial Judgment, 16 November 1998, IT-96-21-T, paras 10, 16.

[88] *Katanga and Ngudjolo Chui*, Decision on the Confirmation of Charges, para 453.

[89] For more background on the phenomenon known as 'long Covid', see 'Understanding Long COVID: A Modern Medical Challenge' (Editorial) (2021) 398 *The Lancet* 725, www.thelancet.com/journals/lancet/article/PIIS0140-6736(21)01900-0/fulltext; United Kingdom National Health Service, 'Long-term Effects of Coronavirus (Long COVID)', www.nhs.uk/conditions/coronavirus-covid-19/long-term-effects-of-coronavirus-long-covid/.

Index

Milton Keynes UK
Ingram Content Group UK Ltd.
UKHW030624160224
437875UK00005B/142